Communications in Computer and Information Science 111

Miltiadis D. Lytras Patricia Ordonez De Pablos
Adrian Ziderman Alan Roulstone Hermann Maurer
Jonathan B. Imber (Eds.)

Knowledge Management, Information Systems, E-Learning, and Sustainability Research

Third World Summit on the Knowledge Society
WSKS 2010
Corfu, Greece, September 22-24, 2010
Proceedings, Part I

Volume Editors

Miltiadis D. Lytras
The American College of Greece
Aghia Paraskevi, Athens, Greece
E-mail: mlytras@acg.edu

Patricia Ordonez De Pablos
University of Oviedo, Spain
E-mail: patriop@uniovi.es

Adrian Ziderman
Bar-Ilan University, Ramat Gan, Israel
E-mail: zidera37@bezeqint.net

Alan Roulstone
De Montfort University, Leicester, UK
E-mail: aroulstone@dmu.ac.uk

Hermann Maurer
Graz University of Technology, Austria
E-mail: hmaurer@iicm.tu-graz.ac.at

Jonathan B. Imber
Wellesley College, Wellesley, MA, USA
E-mail: jimber@wellesley.edu

Library of Congress Control Number: Applied for

CR Subject Classification (1998): J.1, K.5.2, H.4, H.3, H.5, K.4

ISSN 1865-0929
ISBN-10 3-642-16317-3 Springer Berlin Heidelberg New York
ISBN-13 978-3-642-16317-3 Springer Berlin Heidelberg New York

springer.com

Printed in Germany

Typesetting: Camera-ready by author, data conversion by Scientific Publishing Services, Chennai, India
Printed on acid-free paper 06/3180

Preface

It is a great pleasure to share with you the Springer *CCIS* 111 proceedings of the Third World Summit on the Knowledge Society—WSKS 2010—that was organized by the International Scientific Council for the Knowledge Society, and supported by the Open Research Society, NGO, (http://www.open-knowledge-society.org) and the *International Journal of the Knowledge Society Research*, (http://www.igi-global.com/ijksr), and took place in Aquis Corfu Holiday Palace Hotel, on Corfu island, Greece, September 22–24, 2010.

The Third World Summit on the Knowledge Society (WSKS 2010) was an international scientific event devoted to promoting the dialogue on the main aspects of the knowledge society towards a better world for all. The multidimensional economic and social crisis of the last couple years brings to the fore the need to discuss in depth new policies and strategies for a human-centric developmental process in the global context.

This annual summit brings together key stakeholders of knowledge society development worldwide, from academia, industry, government, policy makers, and active citizens to look at the impact and prospects of it information technology, and the knowledge-based era it is creating, on key facets of living, working, learning, innovating, and collaborating in today's hyper-complex world.

The summit provides a distinct, unique forum for cross-disciplinary fertilization of research, favoring the dissemination of research into new scientific ideas relevant to international research agendas as the EU (FP7), OECD or UNESCO. We put in the center of our focus the key aspects of a new sustainable deal for a bold response to the multidimensional crisis of our times.

Eleven general pillars provide the constitutional elements of the summit:

Pillar 1. Information Technologies—Knowledge Management Systems—E-business and Business, Organizational and Inter-organizational Information Systems for the Knowledge Society

Pillar 2. Knowledge, Learning, Education, Learning Technologies and E-learning for the Knowledge Society

Pillar 3. Social and Humanistic Computing for the Knowledge Society—Emerging Technologies for Society and Humanity

Pillar 4. Culture and Cultural Heritage—Technology for Culture Management—Management of Tourism and Entertainment—Tourism Networks in the Knowledge Society

Pillar 5. E-Government and e-Democracy in the Knowledge Society

Pillar 6. Innovation, Sustainable Development, and Strategic Management for the Knowledge Society

Pillar 7. Service Science, Management, Engineering, and Technology

Pillar 8. Intellectual and Human Capital Development in the Knowledge Society

Pillar 9. Advanced Applications for Environmental Protection and Green Economy Management

Pillar 10. Future Prospects for the Knowledge Society: From Foresight Studies to Projects and Public Policies

Pillar 11. Technologies and Business Models for the Creative Industries

In the Third World Summit on the Knowledge Society, six main tracks and three workshops were organized. This *CCIS* volume summarizes excellent, full research articles that were selected after a double-blind review process from 245 submissions, contributed by 412 co-authors.

We are very happy because in this volume you will find high-quality research that summarizes sound propositions for advanced systems towards the knowledge society.

I would like to thank the more than 400 co-authors from 45 countries for their submissions the Program Committee members and their subreviewers for the thoroughness of their reviews, and the colleagues in the Open Research Society for the great support they offered in the organization of the event in corfu.

We are honored with the support and encouragement of the editors-in-chief of the six-ISI SCI/SSCI-listed journals that agreed to publish special issues from extended versions of papers presented in the summit:

International Journal of Manpower
http://info.emeraldinsight.com/products/journals/journals.htm?PHPSESSID=tefp40i8epkijs6fgk752rnlt4&id=ijm

Special issue: Human Resources Management and Emerging Technologies: Manpower Primer for the Knowledge Society

International Journal of Engineering Education
http://www.ijee.dit.ie/
Special issue: New Learning and Teaching Approaches for Computer Engineering Education in the Knowledge Society

Society Journal
http://www.springer.com/social+sciences/journal/12115
Special issue: Knowledge Society

Service Industries Journal
http://www.tandf.co.uk/journals/titles/02642069.asp
Special issue: Services Management and Services Science for the Knowledge Society

Disability and Society
http://www.tandf.co.uk/journals/carfax/09687599.html

A great thank you also to Alfred Hofmann and Leonie Kunz at Springer DE for the excellent support in all the phases of *CCIS* 111 and 112, proceedings development.

Last but not least my Thank you to the staff and members of the Open Research Society, for their through efforts in all the phases of the summit's organization and in realizing the joint vision to promote a better world for all—based on knowledge and learning.

We need a better therefore world and we contribute with our sound voices to the agenda, policies and actions. We can invite you to join your voice with ours and all together shape a new deal for our world: education, sustainable development, health, opportunities for well being, culture, collaboration, peace, democracy, technology for all.

Looking forward to see you in the fourth event of the series, for which you can find more information at: http://know-summit.org.

With 25 special issues already agreed for WSKS 2011, and six main tracks, we want to ask for your involvement and we would be happy to see you joining us.

Thank—Efharisto Poli—on behalf of the Program and Organizing Committee.

July 2010 Miltiadis D. Lytras

Organization

WSKS 2010 was organized by the International Scientific Council for the Knowledge Society, and supported by the Open Research Society, NGO, (http://www.open-knowledge-society.org) and the International Journal of the Knowledge Society Research, (http://www.igi-global.com/ijksr).

Executive Committee

General Chair of WSKS 2010

Miltiadis D. Lytras

Research Professor, The American College of Greece, Deree College, Greece

President, Open Research Society, NGO

Miltiadis D. Lytras is the President and Founder of the Open Research Society, NGO. His research focuses on the semantic Web, knowledge management and e-learning, with more than 100 publications in these areas. He has co-edited/co-edits, 25 special issues in international journals (e.g., *IEEE Transaction on Knowledge and Data Engineering, IEEE Internet Computing, IEEE Transactions on Education, Computers in Human Behavior, Interactive Learning Environments, Journal of Knowledge Management, Journal of Computer Assisted Learning*, etc.,) and has authored/[co-]edited 25 books (e.g., *Open Source for Knowledge and Learning Management, Ubiquitous and Pervasive Knowledge Management, Intelligent Learning Infrastructures for Knowledge Intensive Organizations, Semantic Web Based Information Systems, China Information Technology Handbook, Real World Applications of Semantic Web and Ontologies, Web 2.0: The Business Model,* etc.,). He is the founder and officer of the Semantic Web and Information Systems Special Interest Group in the Association for Information Systems (http://www.sigsemis.org). He serves as the (Co) Editor-in-Chief of 12 international journals (e.g., *International Journal of Knowledge and Learning, International Journal of Technology Enhanced Learning, International Journal on Social and Humanistic Computing, International Journal on Semantic Web and Information Systems, International Journal on Digital Culture and Electronic Tourism, International Journal of Electronic Democracy, International Journal of Electronic Banking, International Journal of Electronic Trade* etc.,) while he is associate editor or editorial board member with seven more.

WSKS 2010 Co-chairs

Patricia Ordonez De Pablos
University of Oviedo, Spain
patriop@uniovi.es

Adrian Ziderman
Editor, *International Journal of Manpower*
Wolfson Professor Emeritus
Economics Department
Bar-Ilan University
Ramat Gan 52900, Israel
Homepage:
http: www.biu.ac.il/soc/ec/ziderman/ziderman.htm
zidera37@bezeqint.net

Alan Roulstone
Professor of Applied Social Sciences
Executive Editor-Disability and Society
Faculty of Health and Life Sciences
De Montfort University
Portland Building 0.12
Gateway
Leicester
LE1 9BH
Office 0116 207 8632
Home Office 0191 516 9744
aroulstone@dmu.ac.uk

Hermann MAURER
Professor of Informatics, Graz University of Technology,
Inffeldgasse 16c,
A- 8010 Graz/ Austria, Chair of the IS of the Academia Europaea,
www.ae-info.org
Ph. +43-316- 873 5612 Personal Website: www.iicm.edu/maurer
hmaurer@iicm.tu-graz.ac.at

Jonathan B. Imber
Jean Glasscock Professor of Sociology
Department of Sociology
Wellesley College
Wellesley, MA 02481
Director, Program in American Studies
Editor-in-Chief, Society Magazine
Office: 781-283-2139
FAX: 781-283-3662
www.societymagazine.org
jimber@wellesley.edu

Program Chairs

Miltiadis D. Lytras	American College of Greece, Greece
Ambjorn Naeve	Royal Institute of Technology, Sweden
Patricia Ordonez De Pablos	University of Oviedo Spain

Knowledge Management and E-Learning Symposium Chair

Miguel Angel Sicilia	University of Alcala, Spain

Publicity Chair

Ekaterini Pitsa	Open Research Society, Greece

Exhibition Chair

Efstathia Pitsa	University of Cambridge, UK

Program and Scientific Committee Members

Senior Advisors –

World Summit on the Knowledge Society / IJ of Knowledge Society Research Council

Horatiu Dragomirescu	Bucharest University of Economics, Romania
Michel Grundstein	Paris Dauphine University, France
Ott Michela	National Research Council, Italy
Matthew K. O. Lee	University of Hong Kong , Hong Kong
Ravi S. Sharma	Nanyang Technological University, Singapore
Toyohide Watanabe	Nagoya University, Japan
Carel S. De Beer	University of Pretoria, South Africa
Sean Siqueira	Federal University of the State of Rio de Janeiro, Brazil
Saad Haj Bakry	King Saud University, Saudi Arabia
Nitham Hindi	Qatar University, Qatar
Maria Braz	Technical University of Lisbon, Portugal
Przemysław Kazienko	Wrocław University of Technology, Poland
José María Moreno-Jiménez	University of Zaragoza, Spain
Marco Temperini	Sapienza University of Rome, Italy
Michal Žemlička	Charles University, Czech Republic

International Review Board

Roberto García	University of Lleida, Spain
Francisco José García-Peñalvo	University of Salamanca, Spain
Blanca García Riaza	University of Salamanca, Spain
Gretchen Geng	Charles Darwin University, Australia
Mark Glynn	Institutes of Technology of Ireland, Ireland
Ana Belén González Rogado	University of Salamanca, Spain
Eloy Irigoyen Gordo	University of the Basque Country, Spain
Francesca Grippa	University of Salento, Italy
Rugayah Hashim	Universiti Teknologi Mara (UITM), Malaysia
Ángel Hernández García	Polytechnic University of Madrid, Spain
Saad Ines	Amiens Business School, France
Luis Iribarne	University of Almeria, Spain
Peiquan Jin	University of Science and Technology of China, China
Min Jou	National Taiwan Normal University, China
Jowati Juhary	National Defense University of Malaysia, Malaysia
Przemyslaw Kazienko	Wroclaw University of Technology, Poland
Gerassimos Kekkeris	Democtius University of Thrace, Greece
Georgiadou Keratso	DUTH, Greece
Kathy Kikis-Papadakis	FORTH/IACM, Greece
George M. Korres	University of the Aegean, Greece
Kornelia Kozovska	Joint Research Center, Italy
Panagiotis Kyriazopoulos	Graduate Technological Education Institute of Piraeus, Greece
Habin Lee	Brunel University, UK
Jean-Marc Lezcano	Sogeti, France
Carla Limongelli	Università degli Studi Roma Tre, Italy
Alessandro Longheu	University of Catania, Italy
Margarida Lucas	University of Aveiro, Portugal
Aristomenis Macris	University of Piraeus, Greece
Giuseppe Mangioni	University of Catania, Italy
Davide Mazza	Politecnico di Milano, Italy
Miroslav Minovic	University of Belgrade, Serbia
El-Mekawy Mohamed	Royal Institute of Technology (KTH), Sweden
Olmo Moreno	Modelo University, Mexico
Beniamino Murgante	University of Basilicata, Italy
Rita C. Nienaber	University of South Africa, South Africa
Nicolae Nistor	Ludwig-Maximilians University Munich, Germany
Angela Paleologou	University of Ioannina, Greece
Plácido Pinheiro	University of Fortaleza, Brazil
Yossi Raanan	College of Management, Israel
Liana Razmerita	Copenhagen Business School, Denmark
Eva Rimbau-Gilabert	Open University of Catalonia, Spain
Lorayne Robertson	University of Ontario Institute of Technology, Canada

Marco Ronchetti	Università Di Trento, Italy
Elisabet Ruiz-Dotras	Open University of Catalonia, Spain
Lazar Rusu	Stockholm University, Sweden
Luis Alvarez Sabucedo	University of Vigo, Spain
Saqib Saeed	University of Siegem, Germany
Irene Samanta	Graduate Technological Education Institute of Piraeus, Greece
Jesús David Sánchez De Pablo González Del Campo	University of Castilla-La Mancha, Spain
Juan M. Santos	University of Vigo, Spain
Akila Sarirete	Effat University, Saudi Arabia
Fabio Sartori	University of Milan-Bicocca, Italy
Chaudhary Imran Sarwar	Creative Researcher, Pakistan
Filippo Sciarrone	Università degli Studi Roma Tre, Italy
Giustina Secundo	University of Salento, Italy
Enric Serradell-Lopez	Open University of Catalonia, Spain
Khurram Shahzad	Royal Institute of Technology (KTH), Sweden
Ravi S. Sharma	Nanyang Technological University, Singapore
Elizabeth Sherly	Indian Institute of Information Technology and Management-Kerala, India
Sean Siqueira	Federal University of the State of Rio de Janeiro, Brazil
Pedro Soto-Acosta	University of Murcia, Spain
Vladimir Stantchev	Berlin Institute of Technology, Germany
Dušan Starčević	University of Belgrade, Serbia
Nouha Taifi	University of Salento, Italy
Antonio Trigo	ISCAC, Portugal
Giuseppe Vadalà	University of Bergamo, Italy
Kin Choong Yow	Nanyang Technological University, Singapore

Table of Contents – Part I

Erratum

Erratum

Table of Contents – Part II

Generic Competences for the IT Knowledge Workers: A Study from the Field

Ricardo Colomo-Palacios[1], Fernando Cabezas-Isla[1], Ángel García-Crespo[1], and Pedro Soto-Acosta[2]

[1] Universidad Carlos III de Madrid, Computer Science Department
Av. Universidad 30, Leganés, 28911, Madrid, Spain
{ricardo.colomo,fernando.cabezas,angel.garcia}@uc3m.es
[2] University of Murcia, Department of Management & Finance,
Campus de Espinardo, 30100 Murcia, Spain
psoto@um.es

Abstract. This paper aims to identify generic competency levels relevant to a particular kind of knowledge workers: software engineers. Based on previous works, and in particular in the description of a professional career, authors review of the literature related to the characterization of the labor force in the Software Engineering (SE) domain. Subsequently, using a quantitative analysis based on investigative surveys administered to a number of representative professionals, authors provide with a generic competency ladder adapted to the given career description.

Keywords: Competences, Competency Levels, Software Engineering, Career.

1 Introduction

The development of intellectual capital of corporations represents one of the most significant challenges for today's managers, and one of the most fertile fields for business innovation, human resource management and education research [1]. In Information Technology (IT), a knowledge intensive activity in which organizations support their activities [2], the importance of people is unquestionable. Within IT, software development is an intense human capital activity, more based in intellectual capital [3]. But, in spite of its importance, some authors (e.g. [4]) have indicated that the influence of competencies on the success of projects has not been successfully explored. Such competencies, key factor for project success, in the case of IT workers must be continually revised and improved in order to adapt workers competences' to technical innovations and soft skills to evolving markets [5].

Based on the professional career stated in [6], in which it was established from seven consecutive profiles (a pyramidal model), in this paper, via an empirical research, is established the generic competency levels for every role in that professional ladder.

The remainder of the paper is organized as follows. Section 2 outlines relevant literature in the area about the field of study. In Section 3, the study conducted is

M.D. Lytras et al. (Eds.): WSKS 2010, Part I, CCIS 111, pp. 1–7, 2010.

presented along with the description of the sample and the methods used. Conclusions and future work are discussed in Section 4.

2 Competency: The Technical and the Generic

Competences can be defined as an individual's core skills that are causally related to a specific, effective criterion and/or a superior performance at work [7]. Early 20th century scientific management used the concept of competence [8], and is well established in the field of human resources management since the middle of the seventies, due to the works by McClelland [9]. The concept of competence is associated with the analysis of professional activities and the inventory of what is necessary in order to accomplish the missions involved in these activities [10]. In [10] a taxonomy of competence is set. In this taxonomy particular or technical competences are established as those that are necessary to carry out a very specific task of a particular job position and include knowledge, abilities, and skills. On the other hand, universal or generic competences are those that, though not linked to a specific activity or function, do make possible the competent performance of the tasks related to the work position, inasmuch as they refer to characteristics or abilities of the individual's general behaviour. These competences permit individuals to adapt to changes in a more efficient and rapid way [10]. Generic competences and may be crucial for IT project success [11] but also for a wider range of organizational contexts, including all knowledge workers [12].

Due to its importance many studies have been devoted to work out which competences are crucial for IT people, some of them devoted to specific profiles (e.g. [13], [14), while others are more general (e.g. [15], [16]). A few studies are devoted specifically to set generic competences (e.g. [1], [17]), while others take advantage of ongoing education normalization processes (e.g. [18], [19]) and set both technical and generic competences. In this study, taking advantages of the career ladder defined in [6] and using the generic competences defined in [19], for each professional profile defined it is set a level of generic competency by means of the application of a questionnaire to a selected group of IT professionals.

3 The Study: Putting Generic Competencies into a Software Engineering Career Structure

Competency studies for software engineers do not show competency levels, and focus only on the possession of competencies evident in professionals which are relevant for successful job fulfillment. Given this current status, it was regarded fundamental to perform a study which analyses the opinions of professionals active in the IT field today [6].

To do so, in the first term, there's a need to describe software engineering career ladder described in [6] in which 7 consecutive steps from G (lower & entry level) to A (higher level) is defined. It is also needed to specify the set of generic competences used for the study. Table 1 displays a list of generic competence for computer science according to Casanovas et al. [19].

Table 1. Set of generic competences for computer science according to [19]

Competence	#
Capacity for analysis and synthesis	1
Organization and planning	2
Oral and written communication in mother tongue	3
Problem solving	4
Decision-making	5
Critical thinking	6
Team work	7
Interpersonal skills	8
Ability to work on an interdisciplinary team	9
Information management	10
Ability to work in an international context	11
Ethical commitment	12
Environmental sensibility	13
Adaptation/flexibility	14
Creativity	15
Leadership	16
Understanding of other cultures and customs	17
Ability to work in an autonomous way	18
Initiative and enterprise	19
Quality concern	20

3.1 Research Design

The study consists of the application of a questionnaire in order to define competencies for the SE professional profiles. A Likert scale with an even number of values was used, ranging from 1 to 4 points. The description of the scale will be generic for all competencies, showing the following order of values and descriptions:

1= Low Level; 2= Medium Level; 3= High Level; 4= Very High Level

Once final formats were edited, subjects received their questionnaires through email and sent their responses using this mean in a given period of time.

3.2 Sample Description

The sample consists of 47 professionals working in software development jobs within large enterprises (over 500 employees) during a period of, at least, five years. The distribution of the subjects within the categories identified previously was subsequently established, based on the interviews: 21 "D" (42%), 20 "C" (40%), 5 "D" (10%) and 4 "A" (8%). The distribution of experimental subjects shows that it was comprised of 6 women (13 %) and 41 men (87 %). The average age was 36.2, with an average experience in the business of 10.52 years.

3.3 Results and Discussion

With the objective of determining the scores obtained for each element, an average and standard deviation was calculated for the results obtained in relation to the

Table 2. Results of the study (Average and Standard Deviation)

Com#	G		F		E		D		C		B		A	
	A	St	A	St	A	St	A	St	A	St	A	St	A	St
1	1.66	0.90	2.34	0.80	3.26	0.63	3.84	0.37	3.74	0.43	3.34	0.75	3.12	1.00
2	1.58	0.76	2.08	0.83	2.78	0.76	3.30	0.61	4.00	0.00	3.90	0.36	3.76	0.52
3	2.02	1.02	2.28	0.93	2.88	0.77	3.22	0.71	3.64	0.60	3.86	0.54	3.78	0.71
4	2.06	0.91	2.64	0.90	3.18	0.83	3.58	0.61	3.62	0.53	3.46	0.76	3.42	0.86
5	1.26	0.60	1.68	0.74	2.48	0.68	2.98	0.69	3.74	0.44	3.90	0.30	3.94	0.31
6	2.10	0.95	2.48	0.89	3.04	0.81	3.48	0.71	3.62	0.64	3.50	0.68	3.44	0.86
7	3.18	0.90	3.46	0.71	3.72	0.54	3.80	0.45	3.78	0.47	3.12	0.77	2.76	1.10
8	1.84	0.87	2.08	0.83	2.46	0.71	2.98	0.77	3.68	0.47	3.76	0.48	3.78	0.51
9	2.32	1.02	2.64	0.96	3.14	0.81	3.48	0.68	3.70	0.58	3.40	0.73	3.14	0.97
10	1.64	0.66	2.12	0.77	2.94	0.77	3.48	0.58	3.74	0.49	3.70	0.54	3.60	0.73
11	1.48	0.73	1.80	0.76	2.18	0.75	2.64	0.75	3.18	0.72	3.56	0.71	3.70	0.68
12	2.62	1.09	2.78	0.95	3.04	0.83	3.30	0.79	3.60	0.67	3.66	0.59	3.58	0.76
13	1.88	0.96	1.96	0.95	2.06	0.94	2.16	0.98	2.34	1.00	2.34	1.03	2.86	1.13
14	2.54	1.07	2.78	1.00	3.18	0.75	3.44	0.58	2.64	0.56	3.46	0.79	3.40	0.81
15	2.38	0.99	2.72	0.93	3.28	0.76	3.58	0.61	3.32	0.77	3.00	0.93	2.88	1.06
16	1.18	0.44	1.62	0.67	2.32	0.65	3.02	0.69	3.70	0.46	3.78	0.42	3.90	0.36
17	1.56	0.81	1.76	0.87	1.92	0.85	2.18	0.77	2.64	0.90	2.96	0.94	2.82	0.90
18	3.08	0.94	3.30	0.79	3.46	0.68	3.36	0.72	3.16	0.87	2.98	0.94	2.82	1.08
19	2.08	0.99	2.46	0.89	2.72	0.81	3.04	0.73	3.38	0.60	3.40	0.65	3.60	0.68
20	2.90	1.00	3.30	0.79	3.54	0.61	3.82	0.39	3.86	0.41	3.58	0.54	3.46	0.76

relative importance of the scores. The results are demonstrated in Table 2 (A= Average; St= Standard Deviation).

Standard deviations are, in general, less than unity. The cases of significant variability, for a total of thirteen, are presented on five occasions to the figures of "A" and "G", demonstrating once to the figures of "B", "C" and "F". With regards to competences, two roles present standard deviations greater than unity for "Environmental sensibility".

The most important competence for all professional figures, according to the sum of their averages is "Quality concern" followed by "Team Work". The competence less valuable is "Environmental sensibility" followed by "Understanding of other cultures and customs". With respect to professional figures, the one that requires more generic competency, according to respondents is "C" followed by "B" and "A".

3.4 Competency Level Proposal

Table 3 shows the competency level required for generic competence and SE professional profile. Competency values have been attributed according to the scores given by the experimental subjects, reflecting competency requirements for different professional profiles. Scores, expressed in a Likert scale ranging from 1 to 4, have initially been assigned by rounding the average scores for different professional profiles. Subsequently, they have been refined according to the competency scales which had been defined previously, in order to finally establish the evolution of competencies of employees in the business environment defined. This proposal however is different in a sense from sample opinions. According to them, the top level of generic competency levels is reached in "C". Our proposal is to reach this rank #1 in A. This is due the conviction that, opposite from technical competence as stated in [6], generic competence improves with the time.

Table 3. Generic competence level per profile

Competence	A	B	C	D	E	F	G
Capacity for analysis and synthesis	4	4	4	4	3	2	2
Organization and planning	4	4	4	3	3	2	2
Oral and written communication in mother tongue	4	4	4	3	3	2	2
Problem solving	4	4	4	4	3	3	2
Decision-making	4	4	4	3	2	2	1
Critical thinking	4	4	4	4	3	3	2
Team work	4	4	4	4	4	3	3
Interpersonal skills	4	4	4	3	2	2	2
Ability to work on an interdisciplinary team	4	4	4	3	3	3	2
Information management	4	4	4	4	3	2	2
Ability to work in an international context	4	4	3	3	2	2	1
Ethical commitment	4	4	4	3	3	3	3
Environmental sensibility	4	3	2	2	2	2	2
Adaptation/flexibility	4	4	4	4	3	3	2
Creativity	4	4	3	4	3	3	2
Leadership	4	4	4	3	2	2	1
Understanding of other cultures and customs	4	4	3	2	2	2	1
Ability to work in an autonomous way	3	3	3	3	3	3	3
Initiative and enterprise	4	4	3	3	3	2	2
Quality concern	4	4	4	4	4	3	3

4 Conclusions and Future Work

People are a critical information technology (IT) issue [20]. Competences and competence structures for IT professionals can be seen as enablers for the Knowledge Society, needed also of intellectual capital and competent IT workers [21], moreover. Individual differences have been identified as one of the paradigms for the research of human factors in software development [22]. Those differences can be measured using the competence paradigm. However, in order to know the performance of a given worker, competency levels for each of the roles must be defined.

This paper aims at the identification of those levels using two known tools. On the one hand, the pyramidal model for professional careers, identifying one single professional track going from Junior Programmer to IT Director, identified in [6]. On the other hand, generic competences list provided by [19]. The result of the study conducted states generic competence levels for the ladder. According to its results, generic competence excellence is reached in a determined professional profile, in this case "C", followed by "B" and "A". The reason why "C" and not "A" is the top of the competence ranking can be found in that generic competences list provided by [19] is designed to be applied in a computer science academic context, without including management related competences. About most valued generic competences, "Quality concern" and "Team Work" can be seen as the most valued competences for software engineering professionals.

As future research, we propose to investigate the inclusion of more manager-like competences that can draw in a more accurate way higher roles. Moreover, authors suggest the creation of an evaluation model allowing the identification of strengths and weaknesses of the competencies of their employees using state of the art tools and technologies.

Referentes

1. Casado-Lumbreras, C., García-Crespo, Á., Colomo-Palacios, R., Gómez-Berbís, J.M.: Emotions and Interpersonal Skills for IT Professionals: an Exploratory Study. International Journal of Technology Enhanced Learning (2010) (in press)
2. Trigo, A., Varajao, J., Barroso, J.: A practitioner's roadmap to learning the available tools for Information System Function management. International Journal of Teaching and Case Studies 2(1), 29–40 (2009)
3. Sommerville, I., Rodden, T.: Human social and organizational influences on the software process. In: Fuggetta, A., Wolf, A. (eds.) Software Process (Trends in Software, 4), pp. 89–110. John Wiley & Sons, New York (1996)
4. Turner, J.R., Müller, R.: The Project Manager's Leadership Style as a Success Factor on Projects: A Literature Review. Project Management Journal 36(2), 49–61 (2005)
5. Casado-Lumbreras, C., Colomo-Palacios, R., Gómez-Berbís, J.M., García-Crespo, Á.: Mentoring programmes: a study of the Spanish software industry. International Journal of Learning and Intellectual Capital 6(3), 293–302 (2009)
6. Colomo-Palacios, R., Tovar-Caro, E., García-Crespo, A., Gómez-Berbis, M.J.: Identifying Technical Competences of IT Professionals. The Case of Software Engineers. International Journal of Human Capital and Information Technology Professionals 1(1), 31–43 (2010)
7. Spencer, L.M., Spencer, S.M.: Competence at Work. Models for Superior Performance. Willey and sons, New York (1993)
8. Taylor, F.W.: The Principles of Scientific Management. Harper & Brothers, New York (1911)
9. McClelland, D.C.: Testing for competence rather than for 'intelligence'. American Psychologist 28, 1–14 (1973)
10. Levy-Leboyer, C.: La gestion des compétences [Competence management]. Les Editions d'Organisation, Paris (1996)
11. Sukhoo, A., Barnard, A., Eloff, M.M., Van der Poll, J.A., Motah, M.: Accommodating Soft Skills in Software Project Management. Issues in Informing Science and Information Technology 2, 691–704 (2005)
12. Rimbau-Gilabert, E., Miyar-Cruz, D., López-de Pedro, J.M.: Breaking the boundary between personal- and work-life skills: parenting as a valuable experience for knowledge workers. International Journal of Knowledge and Learning 5(1), 1–13 (2009)

13. McMurtrey, M.E., Downey, J.P., Zeltmann, S.M., Friedman, W.H.: Critical skill sets of entry level IT professionals: An empirical examination of perceptions from field personnel. Journal of Information Technology Education 7, 101–120 (2008)
14. Ruano-Mayoral, M., Colomo-Palacios, R., García-Crespo, A., Gómez-Berbís, J.M.: Software Project Managers under the Team Software Process. A Study of Competences Based on Literature. International Journal of Information Technology Project Management 1(1), 42–53 (2010)
15. Trigo, A., Varajão, J., Soto-Acosta, P., Barroso, J., Molina-Castillo, F.J., Gonzalvez-Gallego, N.: IT Professionals: An Iberian Snapshot. International Journal of Human Capital and Information Technology Professionals 1(1), 61–75 (2010)
16. Kovacs, P.J., Caputo, D., Turchek, J., Davis, G.A.: A survey to define the skill sets of selected information technology professionals. Issues in Information Systems Journal 7(1), 242–246 (2006)
17. García-Crespo, A., Colomo-Palacios, R., Gómez-Berbís, J.M., Tovar-Caro, E.: IT Professionals' Competences: High School Students' Views. Journal of Information Technology Education 8(1), 45–57 (2009)
18. González, J., Wagenaar, R.: Tuning educational structures in Europe. Final report – Pilot project phase. University of Groningen and University of Deusto, Groningen and Bilbao (2003)
19. Casanovas, J., Colom, J.M., Morlán, I., Pont, A., Ribera, M.: Libro Blanco sobre las titulaciones universitarias en Informática en España [White Book: University degrees in computer engineering]. ANECA (2004)
20. Casado-Lumbreras, C., García-Crespo, A., Colomo-Palacios, R., Gómez-Berbís, J.M.: Emotions and interpersonal skills for IT professionals: an exploratory study. International Journal of Technology Enhanced Learning 2(3), 215–226 (2010)
21. Hernández-López, A., Colomo-Palacios, R., García-Crespo, A., Soto-Acosta, P.: Trust Building Process for Global Software Development Teams. A review from the Literature. International Journal of Knowledge Society Research 1(1), 66–83 (2010)
22. Curtis, B., Hefley, W.E., Miller, S.A.: People Capability Maturity Model (P-CMM®) Version 2.0. CMU/SEI-2001-MM-01 (2001)

Ontology-Based Modelling of Ocean Satellite Images*

Jesús M. Almendros-Jiménez, José A. Piedra, and Manuel Cantón

Dpto. de Lenguajes y Computación
Universidad de Almería Spain
{jalmen,jpiedra,mcanton}@ual.es

Abstract. In this paper we will define an ontology about the semantic content of ocean satellite images in which we are able to represent types of *ocean structures*, *spatial* and *morphological* concepts, and knowledge about *measures* of temperature, chrolophyll concentration, among others. Such ontology will provide the basis of a classification system based on the low-level features of images. We have tested our approach using the *Protegé* semantic web tool.

1 Introduction

The need to access information in large volumes of image data, e.g. big images, large image archives, distributed image repositories, etc, has motivated the research in the field of *Image Retrieval (IR)* [DJLW08, LZLM07]. Images can be described by means of the name, date, author, color, resolution, etc. However, images can be also described by means of the so-called *"semantic content"*. In this context, the so-called *Content-based Image Retrieval (CBIR)* technology [Han08, DJLW08, WL08] is focused on the definition of mechanisms for analysing, detecting and extracting the *high-level* semantic content of images from *low-level* features, the representation of the semantic content, and the retrieval of images. Some tools of CBIR: VisualSEEK [SC97], SIMPLIcity [WLW01] and ALIPR [LW08], among others, have been already developed.

On the other hand, the CBIR community is interested in the combination of IR with the *Semantic Web (SW)* [BLHL+01] in order to have a framework for semantic content modelling. The SW aims to provide mechanisms for representation and exchange of knowledge through the net. Two formalisms, named *RDF (Resource Description Format)* [LS04] and *OWL (Web Ontology Language)* [GHM+08] have been proposed for the SW. This later is an extension of the former, and they provide languages for describing semantic information about a *domain* of interest. Semantic information is considered as an *ontology* (and *meta-data*) about the domain. An ontology expresses the elements of the domain: *classes*, *properties* and *individuals*, and the intended meaning of the elements: *hierarchical relationships*, *restrictions*, combinations of concepts, etc.

* This work has been partially supported by the Spanish MICINN under grant TIN2008-06622-C03-03.

M.D. Lytras et al. (Eds.): WSKS 2010, Part I, CCIS 111, pp. 8–12, 2010.

In this context, some authors have proposed the introduction of ontologies in images (and multimedia) annotation and retrieval. This is the case, for instance, of the proposed [TPC04, IT04, NST+06, ATSH09] ontology based modelling of *MPEG-7* [CSP01]. Basically, the proposed ontology based models aim to adapt the *XML*-based *MPEG-7* specification to a more general framework based on *RDF* and *OWL*, looking for a semantic framework for multimedia features. Such ontology-based semantic framework is more suitable for combination of *multiple resources* of multimedia elements in which low and high level features can be semantically described, allowing to use the *reasoning* capabilities of ontology based models. An interested line of research in this context is the study on how ontologies can be used for modelling *concrete domains*. This is the case of [GC05] for music meta-data, the *M-OntoMat-Annotizer* domain specific tool [BPS+05], and the *Rules-By-Example* [LH10] approach used in the fuel cell domain.

On the other hand, the research field of *Computer Vision (CV)* has studied how to analyse and detect the content of images by applying *pattern recognition* techniques (see [May99, EM09, MME05, MEM07]) based on *decision trees*, *expert rules* and *neural networks*, among others (see [PGMC05, PCG07] for some examples). One of the domains in which such techniques have been successfully applied is *satellite images* of the land and the ocean. Basically, such techniques are based on the *pre-processing* of images and *segmentation*, and in applying *machine learning* methods in which an *expert* participates. Such *training* methods are able to obtain *image classifiers* that can detect, for instance in the case of ocean images, *ocean structures* like *upwellings*, *eddies* and *wakes* from low-level features of images. Such low-level features of images are related to the *spatial* and *morphological* relationships: *shape*, *size*, *land distance*, among others, and *measures* about *temperature* and *chlorophyll temperature*, among others.

In this paper we will define an ontology about the semantic content of ocean satellite images in which we are able to represent types of *ocean structures*, *spatial* and *morphological* concepts, and knowledge about *measures* of temperature, chrolophyll concentration, among others. Such ontology will provide the basis of a classification system based on the low-level features of images. We have tested our approach using the *Protegé* [GMF+03] semantic web tool.

2 Ontology Based Modelling of Ocean Satellite Images

Our work can be summarized as follows:

- We have a repository of *images* about a certain area of the ocean. For each image we have the date, the latitude and the longitude.
- We can have several types of images: images about *temperature* and about *chlorophyll concentration*, among others, usually of the same area and date. The type of image depends of the type of band used.
- Each image is *pre-processed* and *segmented* for obtaining a set of *regions* for each image. Each region is described by means of a set of low-level features including: *perimeter*, *area*, *volume*, *grey scale*, *barycenter*, *inertia moments*,

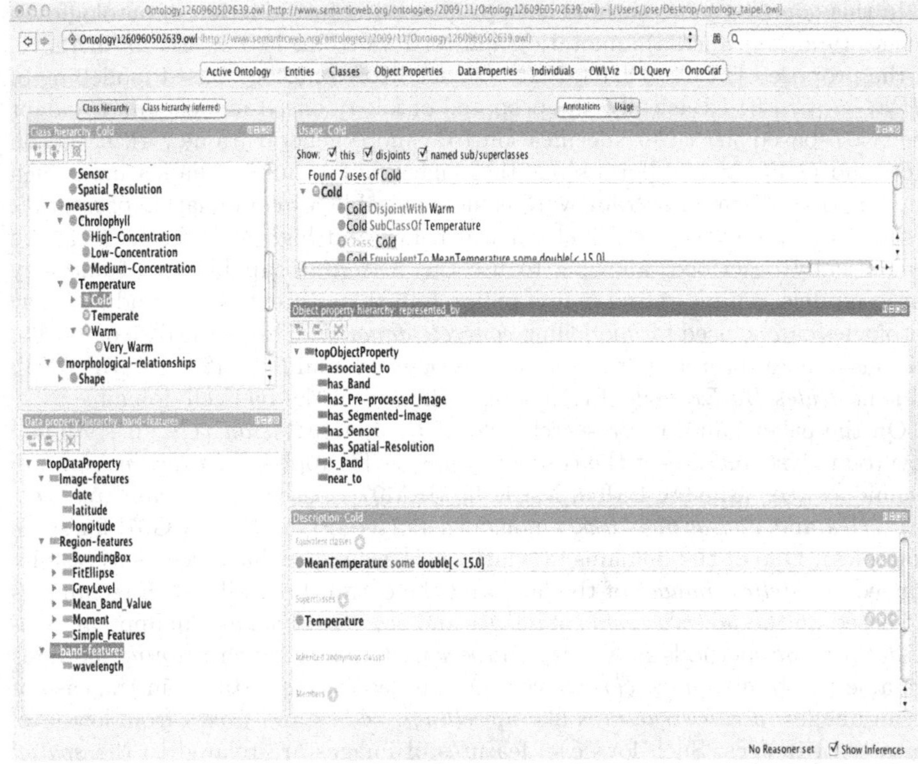

Fig. 1. Snapshot of the Tool

among others. Depending of the type of the image, we can have data about temperature, chlorophyll, etc.

– The processing of images depends on the *type of satellite*, the *type of sensor*, the *band* and the *spatial resolution*. In particular, a given satellite (for instance, *NOAA*, *AQUA*) can be equipped with sensors (for instance, *AVHRR*, *MODIS*) and each sensor can cover several bands (for instance, *thermic infrared*, *visible*), each one with an spatial resolution (for instance, *1 km*, *250 m*).
– Now, we would like to model the parameters for classifying satellite images by means of an ontology. With this aim, we have used the *Protegé* tool in which data about images, processed images and regions associated to processed images, and the type of images (temperature, chlorophyll concentration, etc) are introduced. The classifiers have to be organised in terms of the type of image for which is suitable, including satellite, band, sensor, etc.
– In summary, the ontology should be able to represent:
    • The types of images we handle and the information about images: satellites, sensors, bands and spatial resolutions.
    • Processed images, regions detected from processed images and low-level features.

- Kinds of ocean structures and their relationships.
- Parameters required for classifying images.

3 Using the Protegé Tool

In summary, the *Protegé* tool provides support (Figure 1 shows an snapshot of the tool) for the following tasks:

- Definition of a suitable ontology of semantic concepts and relationships between them, about the content of images. Such concepts can be hierarchically defined.
- Detection of inconsistences about the semantic concepts.
- Definition of a suitable ontology for spatial and morphological concepts and measures. Such concepts and measures can be hierarchically defined.
- Detection of inconsistences about spatial and morphological concepts and measures.
- Defining parameters and elements of a classifying system for ocean satellite images.

References

[ATSH09] Arndt, R., Troncy, R., Staab, S., Hardman, L.: COMM: A Core Ontology for Multimedia Annotation. Handbook on Ontologies, 403–421 (2009)

[BLHL+01] Berners-Lee, T., Hendler, J., Lassila, O., et al.: The semantic web. Scientific American 284(5), 28–37 (2001)

[BPS+05] Bloehdorn, S., Petridis, K., Saathoff, C., Simou, N., Tzouvaras, V., Avrithis, Y., Handschuh, S., Kompatsiaris, Y., Staab, S., Strintzis, M.G.: Semantic annotation of images and videos for multimedia analysis. In: Gómez-Pérez, A., Euzenat, J. (eds.) ESWC 2005. LNCS, vol. 3532, pp. 592–607. Springer, Heidelberg (2005)

[CSP01] Chang, S.F., Sikora, T., Purl, A.: Overview of the MPEG-7 standard. IEEE Transactions on Circuits and Systems for Video Technology 11(6), 688–695 (2001)

[DJLW08] Datta, R., Joshi, D., Li, J., Wang, J.Z.: Image retrieval: Ideas, influences, and trends of the new age. ACM Computing Surveys 40(2), 1–60 (2008)

[EM09] Eugenio, F., Marcello, J.: Featured-based algorithm for the automated registration of multisensorial / multitemporal oceanographic satellite imagery. Algorithms 2(3), 1087–1104 (2009)

[GC05] Garcia, R., Celma, O.: Semantic integration and retrieval of multimedia metadata. In: 5th International Workshop on Knowledge Markup and Semantic Annotation, pp. 69–80 (2005)

[GHM+08] Grau, B.C., Horrocks, I., Motik, B., Parsia, B., Patel-Schneider, P., Sattler, U.: OWL 2: The next step for OWL. Web Semantics: Science, Services and Agents on the World Wide Web 6(4), 309–322 (2008)

[GMF+03] Gennari, J.H., Musen, M.A., Fergerson, R.W., Grosso, W.E., Crubézy, M., Eriksson, H., Noy, N.F., Tu, S.W.: The evolution of Protégé: an environment for knowledge-based systems development. International Journal of Human-Computer Studies 58(1), 89–123 (2003)

[Han08] Hanbury, A.: A survey of methods for image annotation. Journal of Visual Languages & Computing 19(5), 617–627 (2008)

[IT04] Isaac, A., Troncy, R.: Designing and Using an Audio-Visual Description Core Ontology. In: Workshop on Core Ontologies in Ontology Engineering (2004)

[LH10] Little, S., Hunter, J.: Rules-By-Example: A Novel Approach to Semantic Indexing and Querying of Images. In: McIlraith, S.A., Plexousakis, D., van Harmelen, F. (eds.) ISWC 2004. LNCS, vol. 3298, pp. 534–548. Springer, Heidelberg (2004)

[LS04] Lassila, O., Swick, R.R.: Resource description framework (RDF) model and syntax. World Wide Web Consortium (2004), `http://www.w3.org/TR/WD-rdf-syntax`

[LW08] Li, J., Wang, J.Z.: Real-Time Computerized Annotation of Pictures. IEEE Transactions on Pattern Analysis and Machine Intelligence 30(6), 985 (2008)

[LZLM07] Liu, Y., Zhang, D., Lu, G., Ma, W.Y.: A survey of content-based image retrieval with high-level semantics. Pattern Recognition 40(1), 262–282 (2007)

[May99] Mayer, H.: Automatic object extraction from aerial imagery–a survey focusing on buildings. Computer Vision and Image Understanding 74(2), 138–149 (1999)

[MEM07] Marcello, J., Eugenio, F., Marques, F.: Methodology for the estimation of ocean surface currents using region matching and differential algorithms. In: IEEE International Geoscience and Remote Sensing Symposium, IGARSS 2007, pp. 882–885 (2007)

[MME05] Marcello, J., Marques, F., Eugenio, F.: Automatic tool for the precise detection of upwelling and filaments in remote sensing imagery. IEEE Transactions on Geoscience and Remote Sensing 43, 1605–1616 (2005)

[NST+06] Naphade, M., Smith, J.R., Tesic, J., Chang, S.F., Hsu, W., Kennedy, L., Hauptmann, A., Curtis, J.: Large-scale concept ontology for multimedia. IEEE Multimedia, pp. 86–91 (2006)

[PCG07] Piedra, J., Cantón, M., Guindos, F.: Application of fuzzy lattice neurocomputing (FLN) in ocean satellite images for pattern recognition. In: Computational Intelligence Based on Lattice Theory, pp. 215–232 (2007)

[PGMC05] Piedra, J., Guindos, F., Molina, A., Cantón, M.: Pattern Recognition in AVHRR Images by Means of Hibryd and Neuro-fuzzy Systems. In: Moreno Díaz, R., Pichler, F., Quesada Arencibia, A. (eds.) EUROCAST 2005. LNCS, vol. 3643, pp. 373–378. Springer, Heidelberg (2005)

[SC97] Smith, J.R., Chang, S.F.: VisualSEEk: a fully automated content-based image query system. In: Proceedings of the Fourth ACM International Conference on Multimedia, pp. 87–98. ACM, New York (1997)

[TPC04] Tsinaraki, C., Polydoros, P., Christodoulakis, S.: Integration of OWL ontologies in MPEG-7 and TV-Anytime compliant Semantic Indexing. In: Persson, A., Stirna, J. (eds.) CAiSE 2004. LNCS, vol. 3084, pp. 143–161. Springer, Heidelberg (2004)

[WL08] Wan, G., Liu, Z.: Content-based information retrieval and digital libraries. Information Technology and Libraries 27(1), 41 (2008)

[WLW01] Wang, J.Z., Li, J., Wiederhold, G.: SIMPLIcity: Semantics-Sensitive Integrated Matching for Picture LIbraries. IEEE Transactions on Pattern Analysis and Machine Intelligence 23, 947–963 (2001)

Use of the Question and Test Specification to Define Adaptive Test

Hector Barbosa[1], Francisco Jose García-Peñalvo[2], and Maria Jose Rodríguez-Conde[3]

[1] Computer Science Department / GRIAL Research Group
[2] Computer Science Department / Science Education Research Institute / GRIAL Research Group
[3] Science Education Research Institute / GRIAL Research Group
University of Salamanca
{barbosah,fgarcia,mjrconde}@usal.es

Abstract. This article presents how we used an open specification innovatively to define and construct adaptive test considering the user´s presentation needs and also using the traditional adaptation process involving the level of complexity of each item.

Keywords: On-Line Assessments, Open Source Standards and Specifications, Adaptability.

1 Introduction

In general students and educative institutions has been adopted the Internet technologies as their first source of information. The Web and its intrinsic characteristics allow the content to evolve from a static to a dynamic organization by including adaptive processes, making the user's experience to be improved and enhanced [1]. This content, developed in form of Units of Learning (UoL) include one or several learning objects and their related multimedia material.

To ensure that material have some desirable characteristics like to be standardized, open, compatible and interchangeable be must use standards and specifications to define and construct the UoL. One way to achieve that is to see those units in a semantic way instead of been seen in a syntactical way and the conceptualization used is the Semantic Web in which the meaning (semantics) of information and services on the web is defined, making it possible for the web to "understand" and satisfy the request of people and machines to use the web content [2].

2 Applicable Standards and Specifications

The proliferation of web platforms focused to support educative environments forced the creation of new conceptions about how the learning and teaching processes must be performed and innovative ideas to set new interactions between the involved

M.D. Lytras et al. (Eds.): WSKS 2010, Part I, CCIS 111, pp. 13–21, 2010.

agents, and also to define new requisites to define the educative elements to be interoperable, reusable and interchangeable between several systems and platforms.

Before the bloom of the Web, the educative environments were developed considering closed communities, closed context and proprietary technologies. As the Web evolves, it is palpable the possibility to interchange and share elements and resources, lessons, courses or even data about students. To achieve that is necessary to use a common language to identify the characteristic of those elements independently of its origins.

In consequence several organizations, universities and research centers across the world are working to define specifications and standards to define how the instructional elements must be annotated to ensure their compatibility and reusability. In this way the possibilities of the learning processes supported in technologies are broaden to support personal formation and task automation [3].

The technologies of educative metadata identify and annotate in a homogeneous way the techniques, methods and elements involved in the formative processes with the aim to ease their interchange, distribution and reuse in several systems and resources. Through those technologies we can identify learning resources, student profiles, test and evaluations, digital repositories, competences or vocabularies, among others [4].

So some initiatives become into proposals know as standards, specifications and application profiles that help us to annotate educative elements by defining their attributes or characteristics named as educative metadata. Between the organizations involved in the development of those standards we must to mention the IMS consortium and inside those, the IMS QTI[1] (Question and Test) specifically.

Two main concepts inside the educative standards and specifications are the Learning Objects (LO) and metadata. A LO is any digital or not digital entity that can be used to educate as it is described in the IEEE LOM (Learning Object Metadata) [5], also is a digital entity that can be used, reused and being referenced in an educative lesson. A metadata is a data about data that can be used to identify information about a LO to know their characteristics. The use of metadata in an educative context is useful because we can manipulate easily the educative resources. The educative metadata can be seen as descriptors but also contain information for management and structure purposes.

The internal structure of each standard or specification can vary but most of them define a data model indicating the necessary and optional elements also their labels, attributes. Most of them ensure the interdependency and interoperability using the XML Language (eXtensible MarkUp Language) [6].

3 Standardized Description of Educative Test

From the computational way of view, the challenge is to design tools that not only be directed to the content and resource development but also that support the instructive design modeling without prescribing any specific approach, also it must be ensured that the resources and elements can be reused so the time and effort to define can be

[1] http://www.imsglobal.org

reduced. This is the goal of educative modeling languages (EML). One example of this technology is the IMS QTI.

The kind of test we considered to develop in our research was an objective test to ease the categorization of items and the automatic evaluation. The IMS QTI specification describes a core structure to show questions and test and the corresponding results. This specification uses the XML language to describe an item, containing the question, associated data, score and feedback. The basic element is an item covering the definition of the question, variables and response(s) (Fig. 1).

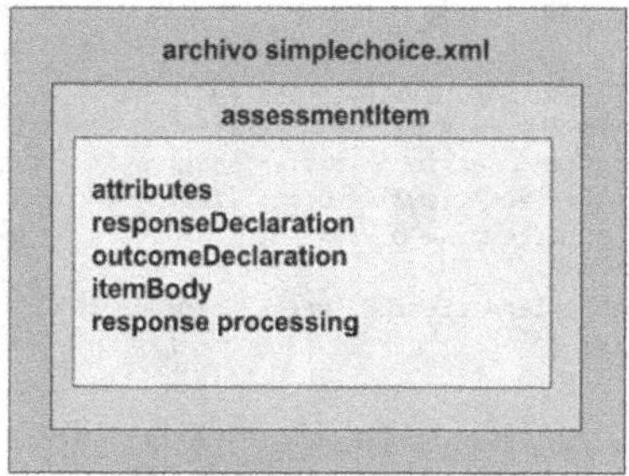

Fig. 1. QTI-XML file containing a simple item

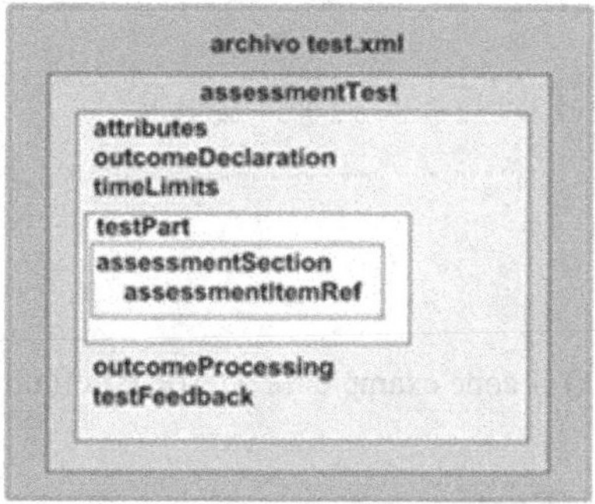

Fig. 2. QTI-XML file containing a Test

To define a test, the QTI specification group many items or *assessmentItem* whiting a group of associated rules to show only selected items with a specific order. Those rules describe specific routes inside the test structure, when the responses will be send to processing and when (if exist) the feedback will be showed to the student.

A test structure covers the definition of an *assessmentTest* element, including the *attributes, outcomeDeclaration, timeLimits, testPart, outcomeProcessing and test-Feedback* (Fig. 2).

As you can notice, in a Test element, we can define one or more *testPart* sections, those sections could help us to define special characteristics like specific navigation modes (linear or random), session controls, maximum number of attempts, and special configuration to show the possible solutions to the students after they answer a question.

Inside a *testPart* section (that we can identify for our purposes as a second level inside the definition of a test element) we can set another special section: the *assessmentSection*. This sub-section could group one item definitions that, in this case share some considerations or characteristics. One characteristic we like to mention in special are the branch and precondition labels that we can define and use in this sub-section. Those instructions were the ones that allow us to define the adaptation characteristics in the test we defined. In Fig. 3 we show a QTI with the definition of a testPart with the basic inner-labels to define sections, branch and bifurcations.

```
<?xml version="1.0" encoding="UTF-8"?>

<testPart navigationMode="linear" submissionMode="individual">
  <itemSessionControl showFeedback="true" maxAttempts="1" showSolution="false" />
  <assessmentSection identifier="sectionA" title="Section A" visible="true">
    <assessmentItemRef identifier="item034" href="item034.xml">
      <itemSessionControl maxAttempts="0" />
    </assessmentItemRef>
    <assessmentItemRef identifier="item160" href="item160.xml">
      <!-- Despliega el item solo si la respuesta previa tiene valor de Y -->
      <preCondition>
        <match>
          <variable identifier="item034.RESPONSE" />
          <baseValue baseType="identifier">Y</baseValue>
        </match>
      </preCondition>
      <!-- Salta el item653 si la respuesta es "N" -->
      <branchRule target="item656">
        <match>
          <variable identifier="item347.RESPONSE" />
          <baseValue baseType="identifier">N</baseValue>
        </match>
      </branchRule>
    </assessmentItemRef>
  </assessmentSection>
</testPart>
```

Fig. 3. QTI code example for a testPart definition

4 Double Adaptation Test

Our proposal is the definition of items and complete test incorporating multimedia material to adapt the final presentation to the needs or preferences of the students so we can reduce the stress that in general used to be present when a student answers a test (First form of adaptation). Also we categorized and organized each item inside structures to split those according their level of complexity defined in the authoring phase (Second form of adaptation).

We take in consideration the fact that in QTI you can design elements with high granularity by defining an item in which you can refer to external files (such as multimedia files) and in consequence those items being referenced from more complex objects (like complete test) or being packaged in an auto contented file that could be used by LMS (Learning Management Systems).

The test structure include several items with specific use characteristics such as bifurcation and branch labels allowing an adaptive navigation, that will be executed depending the result of the evaluation of the labels defined before (precondition) or after (branch). We used those structures to organize and define adaptive test in an innovative way.

The adaptive presentation methods use prerequisites, comparative, additional or alternative explications (for example, to show the same information in different ways) or enhanced information to adapt the final presentation according to the user's needs or preferences. From those methods we focused in the alternative explication because with this, we can store several versions of the same information to show to the users following pre-stored conditions in user profiles in the LMS.

In such way we split one single item (the one that fulfill one instructional objective) into several ones, each one with different external multimedia file reference (audio, video or text). We then grouped those items with the same type of multimedia references into a *testPart*, so we defined at least three *testPart* in complete test: *Auditive testPart*, *video testPart* and *text testPart*.

From the view point of the adaptation techniques, we categorized our adaptive test object into the adaptive hidden of links, which hides, disable or eliminates links that are not relevant to the user. When the student is answering a test the system take into account the response to the last item to show the next item, in this way we "hide" or ignore all those items whose level of complexity are not relevant to the student.

4.1 QTI Elements to Perform the Adaptation

An item is the basic element of a test. In this we consider the QTI label ***<img src>*** which allow the item designer to define the physical route to a multimedia file. In this way the teacher, in the authoring phase could define a general item to fulfill a single instructional objective and set up to three different routes (each for audio, text or video file). Those item objects are the core elements in which we define the first adaptation process taking in consideration the user's presentation preferences.

The next level in the test definition is the QTI label ***<assessmentSection>***, which allows us to group one or more items according to the type of external multimedia file referenced. We then use the ***<testPart>*** label to group at last three assessment sections.

Also we use the ***<precondition>*** and ***<branchRule>*** labels to control the flow in which each item element is showed to the student. The precondition structure allows us to evaluate a condition before the execution of an item. The result of that condition determines if an item is showed or not. The *branchRule* structure allows us to evaluate a condition after the execution of an item. The result of that condition determines which item will be displayed to the student.

In Figure 4 we show the basic notation with the definition of a *testPart* including only items with external references to video files.

```
<xml version="1.0" encoding="UTF-8"?>
<! - Previous testPart definition for auditive and text items… -- >
...
<testPart identifier="visualTest" navigationMode="linear" submissionMode="individual">
   <!-special section to display the first normal item to start the adaptation in the complexity level -->
   <itemSessionControl showFeedBack="false" maxAttempts=1 showSolution="false"
   <assessmentSection identifier="firstNormalItem" title="first Normal Item to start the
                 adaptation in the complexity level" visible="true">
      <assessmentItemRef identifier="firstNormalItem" href="firstNormalItem.xml">
         <!-If student answer correctly then the process make a bifurcation to the high complexity level -- >
         <branchRule target="highSection">
            <match>
               <variable identifier="firstNormalItem.unifiedResult" / >
               <baseValue baseType="identifier">Y</baseValue>
            </ match>
         </branchRule>
         <!-If student answer incorrectly then the process make a bifurcation to the low complexity level -- >
         <branchRule target="lowSection">
            <match>
               <variable identifier="firstNormalItem.unifiedResult" / >
               <baseValue baseType="identifier">N<7baseValue>
            </match>
         </branchRule>
      </assessmentItemRef>
   </assessmentSection>

   <assessmentSection identifier="highSection" title=" Section with high level items" visible="true">
      <assessmentItemRef identifier="highLevelItem1" href="highLevelItem1.xml">
         <precondition>
            <match>
               <variable identifier="firstNormalItem.unifiedResult" />
               <baseValue baseType="identifier">Y</baseValue>
            </match>
         </precondition>
         <branchRule target="highLevelItem2" href="highLevelItem2.xml">
            <match>
               <variable identifier="highLevelItem1.Response" />
               <baseValue baseType="identifier">Y</baseValue>
            </match>
         <branchRule target="NormalSection">
            <match>
               <variable identifier=highLevelItem1.Response" />
               <baseValue baseType="identifier">N</baseValue>
            </match>
         </branchRule>
      </assessmentItemRef>
   </assessmentSection>

   <assessmentSection identifier="lowSection" title=" Section with low level items" visible="true">
      <assessmentItemRef identifier="lowLevelItem1" href="lowLevelItem1.xml">
         <precondition>
            <match>
               <variable identifier="firstNormalItem.unifiedResult" />
               <baseValue baseType="identifier">N</baseValue>
            </match>
         </precondition>
         <branchRule target="NormalSection">
            <match>
               <variable identifier="lowLevelItem1.Response" />
               <baseValue baseType="identifier">Y</baseValue>
            </match>
         <branchRule target="lowLevelItem2" href="lowLevelItem2.xml">
            <match>
               <variable identifier=lowLevelItem1.Response" />
               <baseValue baseType="identifier">N</baseValue>
            </match>
         </branchRule>
      </assessmentItemRef>
   </assessmentSection>

   <assessmentSection identifier="normalSection" title=" Section with Normal level items" visible="true">
      <assessmentItemRef identifier="normalLevelItem1" href="normalLevelItem1.xml">
         <branchRule target="normalItem2" href="normalItem2.xml">
            <match>
               <variable identifier="normalLevelItem1.Response" />
               <baseValue baseType="identifier">Y</baseValue>
            </match>
         <branchRule target="lowLevelItem2" href="lowLevelItem2.xml">
            <match>
               <variable identifier=normalLevelItem1.Response" />
               <baseValue baseType="identifier">N</baseValue>
            </match>
         </branchRule>
      </assessmentItemRef>
   </assessmentSection>
</testPart>
```

Fig. 4. Basic QTI notation for an Adaptive Test [7]

Please note the first item definition: *firstNormalItem*. This item is always displayed in first time to determine the level of complexity of the next items. This first normal item is, obviously a normal level complexity and does not score to the final result of the test.

After this first normal item has been displayed and answered by the student, the response is evaluated and the systems branch (in blue in the QTI code) to the correct next question: to a higher level question if she/he responded correctly or to a lower level question if the response is wrong. Let's assume that the student responded correctly to this first normal item, then the process branch to the high level assessment section and display the first high level item but before that a precondition instruction is evaluated. The process continues by evaluating the responses every time an item is displayed, performing branching processes, going from high, normal or lower assessment sections. Please note that the processing of a test in real time allow to show only the items never displayed before to avoiding the display of a same question several times.

5 Implementation and Results Obtained

We develop an authoring tool to construct items and test with adaptation characteristics, following open standards and specifications like the IMS QTI, CP (Content Packaging) and LD (Learning Design) and the XML language. The aim is to allow to the author to define items and test using a graphical interface starting from the definition of single questions to the construction of complete test packaged using IMS CP and delivered in a .zip package [8], [9].

The application covers the following activities: (1) Question Construction management, (2) Test Construction management, (3) User management, (4) Test management.

To verify that an adapted test is better for the students in terms to ease their answer and understanding, we apply an exam to evaluate the level of knowledge in English language to a group of students in the University of Salamanca. We split this group into two: for the first group we applied the test with questions and accompanying multimedia material that matches their preferences of presentation (audio, text or video); for the second group we applied a test that did not match these preferences. Also, we applied a test a test to determine the learning style of each student, prior to the adaptive test.

Please, recall that this test also perform an adaptation in the level of complexity of each item, for this we organize the items grouping them according this characteristic and, in a higher level, we set a classification according to the multimedia material they are refereeing to.

The aim of this activity is to evaluate our thesis hypothesis that, if a student is presented with an adaptive test that matches its preferences of presentation of the accompanying multimedia material he/she could average better results in a test.

The evaluation included the following statistical test [7],[10]:

- Final note: To check if the final note of the test is higher for the students with adapted test.
- Time to response: To check if the total time to answer the test is lower when an adapted test is presented to the student.
- Level of satisfaction: To check if the level of satisfaction reported by the student is higher when the test is adapted to his/her preferences.

For the final note test the results were: the average final note obtained by the students with an adapted test was 6.6 points, whilst for students without adapted test, the final note was of 5.9 points (t test = 0,836).

In the time of response the results were: the average time for an adapted test was 17 minutes whilst for an not adapted test was 20 minutes (t test=0.964).

The level of satisfaction was obtained from the students themselves from a poll after they answer the test. It cover level of satisfaction from 1 (lower satisfaction) to 5 (highest satisfaction). The results were: for an adapted test 3.9 and for not adapted test 3.6 (t test=0.821).

Bring to mind that, the statistical test was applied only to verify the results for the adaptation process in the presentation of the multimedia material, but this test also performs the adaptation in the complexity level for all participants.

Also, we think that these results must be taken with some considerations at the time to make generalizations. In other words the results obtained in this work may change in other learning environment and stated that this is an internal work. Upon this, we consider that our conclusions are a science contribution for future works in this area.

6 Conclusions

Online assessment is an important step inside the e-learning process, helping to improve the learning and teaching experience. New developments in this area look to be compliant with accepted standards like the IMS QTI. This gives the convenience to those works to be interoperable and adaptable to several learning platforms. In concordance, referring to the assessment activity, we can think that it must be interoperable as well, because it is one element of the e-learning process and play an important role inside this task.

Adaptability is another key factor in assessment. Given the fact that assessment is an important element of the e-learning process and the fact that this process look to be interoperable, then we can think that the assessment tool could be used with different educative content administrators with different conceptualizations and ways to design an ways of purposes to the students. To face this situation it is necessary to develop a test with different types of resources, different kind of assessments, groups of students, kind of questions, etc.

Under this conceptualization, we created and applied an adaptive test to a group of students to evaluate the hypothesis that, if an assessment tool is adapted to the user`s needs or preferences we can reduce the time to answer the test while we increase the level of satisfaction of the user at the same time.

Acknowledgment

This work is partially supported by the Regional Ministry of Education of Junta de Castilla y León through the project GR47.

Héctor Barbosa thanks the National System of Technological Institutes (SNIT–Mexico) for its financial support.

References

1. Barbosa, H., Garcia, F.: Importance of the online assessment in the e-learning process. In: 6th International Conference on Information Technology-based Higher Education and Training ITHET & IEEE, Santo Domingo (2005)
2. Barbosa León, H.G., García Peñalvo, F.J., Rodríguez-Conde, M.J.: Construction of Assessments with Double Adaptation Process. In: Iskander, M. (ed.) Innovative Techniques in Instruction Technology, E-learning,E-assesment, and Education, pp. 156–160. Springer Science + Business Media B. V., Heidelberg (2008) ISBN 978-1-4020-8738-7, e-ISBN 978-1-4020-8739-4
3. Barbosa, H., García, F.: Adaptive Assessment Tool for the Hypertext Composer, ICTE 2005. In: Proceedings of the 3th, Internatonal Conference on Multimedia and Information and Communication Technologies in Education: m-ICTE 2005, Cáceres, Spain, vol. 11, pp. 16–20 (2005)
4. Berlanga, A., García, F.: Diseños Instructivos Adaptativos: Formación Personalizada y Reutilizable en Entornos Educativos. Tesis Doctoral. Departamento de Informática y Automática. Universidad de Salamanca, España (2006)
5. IEEE LOM. IEEE 1484.12.1-2002 Standard for Learning Object Metadata `http://ltsc.ieee.org/wg12` (retrieved January 2006)
6. Bray, T., Paoli, J., Sperberg-MacQueen, C.M., Maler, E., Yergeau, F. (eds.): Externsible Markup Language (XML), 3rd edn. v 1.0. World Wide Web Consortium Recommendation, `http://www.w3.org/TR/2004/REC-xml-20040204` (retrieved January 2006)
7. Barbosa, H., García, F., Rodríguez-Conde, M.: Generador de Pruebas Objetivas Adaptadas a las Preferencias de Presentación de los Usuarios. Doctoral Thesis (In revision). Departamento de Informática y Automática. Universidad de Salamanca, España (2007)
8. Barbosa, H., Garcia, F., Rodriguez, M.: A Tool for Online Assessment in Adaptive e-Learning Platform. In: Proceedings of the eUniverSAL Conference, Virtual, Salamanca, Spain (2008)
9. Barbosa, H., Garcia, F., Rodriguez, M.: Construction of Assessments with Double Adaptation Processes. In: Elleithy, K. (ed.) Advanced Techniques in Computing Sciences and Software Engineering (2010) ISBN: 978-90-481-3659-9
10. Barbosa, H., Garcia, F., Rodriguez, M.: Adaptive Assessments Using Open Standards. In: Proceedings of the CISSE 2009 Congress, University of BridgePort, USA (2009)

A Survey on Ontology Metrics

Juan García, Francisco Jose' García-Peñalvo, and Roberto Therón

Computer Science Department. Science Education Research Institute (IUCE). GRIAL Research Group. University of Salamanca
University of Salamanca, Spain
{ganajuan,fgarcia,theron}@usal.es

Abstract. Ontologies have been widely used in almost any field of application. The use of ontologies should involve the possibility of evaluation of the quality and correctness of them. Some tools and metrics have been proposed to reach this goal. ONTOMETRIC, OntoQA and Protégé represent the most important tools to evaluate ontologies. On the other hand, diverse cohesion, coupling and ranking metrics have also been proposed, as well as methodologies such as OntoClean. This paper analyses these tools and metrics, compare them and finally reviews the current state-of-the-art concerning to ontology metrics.

Keywords: Ontology metrics, OWL, ontology cohesion, ontology coupling and ontology ranking.

1 Introduction

In general, an ontology describes formally a domain of discourse. Typically, an ontology consists of a finite list of terms and the relationships among these terms. Ontologies play an important role to provide shared knowledge models to semantic-driven applications targeted by Semantic Web. Ontology metrics represent an important approach due to they can help to assess and qualify an ontology. From the viewpoint of ontology developers, by assessing quality of ontology, they can automatically recognize areas that might need more work and specify some parts of the ontology that might cause problems. Furthermore metrics are useful in the process of reuse because before using a previously defined ontology would be desirable to evaluate it in order to determine the worthiness of using it. Metrics should always be taken into account to evaluate ontologies both during engineering and application processes. This paper starts with a brief introduction of ontologies and metrics, and then the second section includes some metric definitions. The third section includes an overview of the tools that implement some metrics. The fourth section makes a comparative over the different metrics and finally the conclusions are discussed.

2 Metric Definitions

Diverse ontology metric proposals have been done in the past years; such as [6] that describes some metrics to normalize ontologies and [7][12] that represent a way to

M.D. Lytras et al. (Eds.): WSKS 2010, Part I, CCIS 111, pp. 22–27, 2010.

rank them. The paper [6] reviews the current state-of-the-art and basically proposes normalization as a pre-process to apply structural metrics. This normalization process consists of five steps: name anonymous classes, name anonymous individuals, classify hierarchically and unify the names, propagate the individuals to the deepest possible classes and finally normalize the object properties. This proposal is focused on content metrics based on OntoMetric framework and basically they have been proposed to improve ontology behavior or to fix some mistakes. Papers [7][12] propose some metrics to rank ontologies. Basically this proposal consists of a Java Servlet to process as inputs some keywords introduced by the user. Then the framework searches using Swoogle[1] engine and retrieves all the URI's representing the ontologies related with these keywords. Then the framework searches on its internal database if these ontologies have been previously analyzed and retrieves their information. Finally the framework ranks retrieved ontologies.

Orme et al. [10] proposed a set of coupling metrics for ontology-based systems represented in OWL, these metrics are: the number of external classes (NEC), reference to external classes (REC), and referenced includes (RI). This proposal defines a new type of coupling measurement for system development that defines coupling metrics based on ontology data and its structure. The first proposed metric is NEC, representing the number of distinct external classes defined outside the ontology but used to define new classes and properties in the ontology. The external classes can include standard classes defined as ontology language primitives and user-defined classes from other ontologies. The second metric REC is the number of references to external classes in the ontology. As we described above, NEC is a direct measure of the number of classes in the ontology. REC is a direct measure of the number of fanouts (in this case fanouts are different class hierarchies with external roots) within the ontology resulting from external classes. RI is a direct measure of the number of referenced includes in the ontology. Authors have also proposed some cohesion metrics for ontologies [13]. They proposed a set of ontology cohesion metrics to measure the modular relatedness of OWL ontologies. These metrics are Number of Root Classes (NoR), Number of Leaf Classes (NoL) and Average Depth of Inheritance Tree of all Leaf Nodes (ADIT-LN). Authors define NoR metric as the total number of root classes explicitly defined in the ontology. A root class in an ontology means the class has no semantic super class explicitly defined in the ontology. NoL metric is defined as the number of leaf classes explicitly defined in the ontology. A leaf class in an ontology means the class has no semantic subclass explicitly defined in the ontology. Finally ADIT-LN is defined as the sum of depths of all paths divided by the total number of paths. A depth is the total number of nodes starting from the root node to the leaf node in a path. The total number of paths in an ontology is all distinct paths from each root node to each leaf node if there exists an inheritance path from the root node to the leaf node. And root node is the first level in each path.

Yinglong et al. [14] proposed another set of ontology cohesion metrics to measure the modular relatedness of ontologies in the context of dynamic and changing Web. These metrics have been defined taking into account the cohesion principle from Object Oriented Approach adapted to ontologies. Authors concentrate on measuring inconsistencies in ontologies and fully consider the ontological semantics rather than

[1] http://swoogle.umbc.edu

structure. The metrics they propose are Number of Ontology Partitions (NOP), Number of Minimally Inconsistent Subsets (NMIS) and the Average Value of Axiom Inconsistencies (AVAI). This work also describes the algorithms to compute these metrics and validate the metrics by using validation frameworks. These metrics are focused on assessing the quality of ontologies. Authors define NOP metric as the number of semantical partitions of a knowledge base. NMIS is defined as the number of all minimally inconsistent subsets in a knowledge base. This metric is useful to measure the scope of inconsistency impacts of a knowledge base. The third metric AVAI is defined as: the ratio of the sum of inconsistency impact values of all axioms and assertions to the cardinality of the knowledge base. Moreover, the article analyses and validates the proposed metrics. Generally speaking, the advantages of these metrics include the possibility of assessing the quality of a consistent ontology.

OntoClean methodology [4], [5] proposes the use of some defined metaproperties. These metaproperties are rigidity, unity, identity and dependency. Authors have borrowed these concepts from their ancient philosophical counterparts. The methodology consists of assigning these metaproperties to the entities in order to provide with a logical and semantic meaning. Applying these metaproperties results on imposing several constraints on the taxonomic structure of an ontology and let to develop a conceptual analysis of the concepts and their validity. Moreover this methodology let to analyze and detect not logically consistent relationships.

YANG et al. [15] proposed metrics from a different point of view taking into account the evolution of the ontologies. Authors suggest a metrics suite of complexity, which mainly examine the quantity, ratio and correlativity of concepts and relationships, to evaluate ontologies from the viewpoint of complexity and its evolution. These metrics are divided into two groups: Primitive Metrics and Complexity Metrics. The Primitive metrics include TNOC (Total Numbers of Concepts or Classes), TNOR (Total Number of Relations), TNOP (Total Number of Paths), where a path is defined as a trace that can be taken from a specific particular concept to the most general concept in the ontology. The first Complexity Metric defined is the average relations per concept that is calculated by dividing TNOR by TNOC. The second metric is the average paths per concept, and is calculated by dividing TNOP by TNOC.

3 Tools That Implement Metrics

There are some developed tools that implement diverse metrics. ONTOMETRIC, OntoQA and Protégé represent the main available proposals. We consider that OntoQA [8][9] represents the main proposal about metrics on ontologies. It proposes some Schema Metrics to measure the richness of schema relationships, attributes and schema inheritance. These metrics are focused on evaluating the ontology in general. Other proposed categories are class richness, average population, cohesion, importance of a class, fullness of a class, class inheritance and class relationship richness, connectivity and readability. Class Relationship Richness is defined as the number of relationships that are being used by instances that belong to the class. On the other hand, the Connectivity of a class is defined as the number of instances of other classes that are connected to instances of the selected class. All these metrics are focused on the structure of the ontology.

Currently Protègè[2] is the most widely used tool to create or modificate an ontology. The metrics are classified into 6 categories. The first one is related with general metrics such as counters for classes, object properties, datatype properties and individuals. The second category is related with class axioms and includes counters for subclass axioms, equivalent class axioms, disjoint classes axioms, GCI and hidden GCI. The third category includes counters for object properties axioms. These counters are total of sub object properties, equivalent, inverse, disjoint, functional, inverse functional, transitive, symmetric, anti symmetric, reflexive and irreflexive object properties. Furthermore object property domain and range counters are also included. The fourth category is dedicated for datatype properties counters. This category includes total values for sub datatype properties, equivalent, disjoint and functional datatype properties, as well as counters for data properties domain and range. The fifth category is focused on individuals. It defines counters for class assertions, object and datatype property assertions, negative object and negative datatype assertions and same or different individual axioms. Finally, the last category involves annotation axioms and defines just two metrics, the entity annotation axioms count and the axiom annotation axioms count. All these metrics represent simple counters for the items in the ontology and do not provide any kind of semantic metric.

ONTOMETRIC [11] is a framework proposed to measure the suitability of existing ontologies. This tool was defined to quantify the suitability of ontologies. Authors propose a taxonomy of 160 characteristics, also called *multilevel framework of characteristics* that provides the outline to be able to choose and to compare existing ontologies. This framework is used as a representation template of the information and starts by defining an analytic hierarchy process. This process involves building a hierarchy tree with the root node being the objective of the problem. The intermediate are the criteria and finally the lowest levels contain the alternatives. Then as the second step, the methodology applies the analytic hierarchy process to decide whether or not to reuse ontologies.

Ontology Metrics [3] is a web-based tool that validates and displays statistics about an OWL ontology, including the expressivity of the language it is written in. This tool calculates the same metrics than Protégé. These metrics include counters for classes, properties, individuals, logical axioms, as well as specific counters described above in the Protégé section.

4 Comparing Metrics

Comparing the diverse analyzed metrics, we consider that OntoQA offers the best set of metrics for analyzing the structure and ranks of the ontologies according to these metrics. Just Yinglong proposal and OntoClean are clearly focused on the semantics. On the other hand Orme, Yinglong and OntoQA have proposed different metrics to calculate the cohesion. It is important to highlight that they represent three completely

[2] Protégé Ontology Editor `http://protege.stanford.edu/`

[3] `http://owl.cs.manchester.ac.uk/metrics/`

different ways to define cohesion. OntoQa defines cohesion as the number of separate connected components of the graph representing the Knowledge Base. In contrast Orme's proposal metrics measure the modular relatedness of OWL ontologies while Yinglong focuses on measuring ontologies in the context of dynamic and changing web. The metrics proposed by Orme et al. [10] represent the coupling among entities from diverse ontologies. There is another coupling that has not been taken into account: the coupling among entities in the same ontology that provides useful information about the connection among the classes in the same ontology. Sometimes systems use no more than one ontology then the coupling metrics proposed by Orme become completely useless. The metrics proposed by Yang et al. [15] are intended to reflect the complexity of an ontology during its lifecycle and evolution.

Table 1. Summary of the analyzed metrics and comparison of some interesting properties

Metric	Semantic / Structure	Ranking	Cohesion	Coupling
Vrandecic	Structure	No	No	No
Alani	Structure	Yes	No	No
Orme	Structure	No	Yes	Yes
Yinglong	Semantic	No	Yes	No
OntoClean	Semantic	No	No	No
Ontometric	Structure	No	No	No
Protégé	Structure	No	No	No
OntoQA	Structure	Yes	Yes	No
Ontology Metrics	Structure	No	No	No
Yang	Structure	No	No	No

5 Conclusions and Future Work

Most of the current metrics and tools are focused on the evaluation of structure of the ontologies such as Protégé, Ontology Metrics tool or OntoQA. Other metrics are focused on cohesion such as NoR, NoL, ADIT-LN, NOP, NMIS and AVAI. There are a few of them focused on coupling such as NEC, REC and RI. OntoClean represents an interesting approach based on ontologies semantics. Moreover some metrics are defined to rank ontologies, normalize them or to qualify them as ONTOMETRIC. A completely different approach is proposed by Yang, which is based on measuring the complexity of an ontology taking into account the evolution. We have analyzed diverse metrics for ontologies. Furthermore we have also provided with a classification based on different aspects such as semantics or structure. Finally we can conclude that diverse metrics have been proposed to cover diverse aspects to evaluate, being most of them focused on the structure instead of semantics. Our future work includes the definition of some metrics focused on coupling among entities within the same ontology, based on the semantics.

Acknowledgements

This work was supported by the Spanish Industry Ministry (project TSI-020302-2009-35) and by the Castile and Lion Regional Government through GR47 excellence project.

References

1. Makris, K., Bikakis, N., Gioldasis, N., Tsinaraki, C., Christodoulakis, S.: Towards a Mediator Based on OWL and SPARQL. In: Lytras, M.D., Damiani, E., Carroll, J.M., Tennyson, R.D., Avison, D., Naeve, A., Dale, A., Lefrere, P., Tan, F., Sipior, J., Vossen, G. (eds.) WSKS 2009. LNCS, vol. 5736, pp. 326–335. Springer, Heidelberg (2009)
2. Salguero, A., Delgado, C., Araque, F.: STOWL: An OWL Extension for Facilitating the Definition of Taxonomies in Spatio-temporal Ontologies. In: Lytras, M.D., Damiani, E., Carroll, J.M., Tennyson, R.D., Avison, D., Naeve, A., Dale, A., Lefrere, P., Tan, F., Sipior, J., Vossen, G. (eds.) WSKS 2009. LNCS, vol. 5736, pp. 326–335. Springer, Heidelberg (2009)
3. Antoniou, G., van Harmelen, F.: A Semantic Web Primer, 2nd edn. The MIT Press, Cambridge (2008)
4. Guarino, N., Welty, C.: An Overview of OntoClean. In: The Handbook on Ontologies, pp. 151–172. Springer, Berlin (2004)
5. Guarino, N., Welty, C.: Evaluating Ontological Decisions with OntoClean. Communications of the ACM, 61–65 (2002)
6. Vrandecic, D., Sure, Y.: How to Design Better Ontology Metrics. In: Franconi, E., Kifer, M., May, W. (eds.) ESWC 2007. LNCS, vol. 4519, pp. 311–325. Springer, Heidelberg (2007)
7. Alani, H., Brewster, C., Shadbolt, N.: Ranking Ontologies with AKTiveRank. In: Cruz, I., Decker, S., Allemang, D., Preist, C., Schwabe, D., Mika, P., Uschold, M., Aroyo, L.M. (eds.) ISWC 2006. LNCS, vol. 4273, pp. 1–15. Springer, Heidelberg (2006)
8. Tartir, S., Arpinar, B., Moore, M., Sheth, A., Aleman-meza, B.: OntoQA: Metric-based ontology quality analysis. In: CiteSeerX - Scientific Literature Digital Library and Search Engine (2005)
9. Tartir, S., Arpinar, B.: Ontology Evaluation and Ranking using OntoQA. In: Proceedings of the International Conference on Semantic Computing (2007)
10. Orme, A., Yao, H., Etzkorn, L.: Coupling Metrics for Ontology-Based Systems. IEEE Software, 102–108 (2006)
11. Lozano-Tello, A., Gómez-Pérez, A.: ONTOMETRIC: A Method to Choose the Appropiate Ontology. Journal of Database Management (2004)
12. Alani, H., Brewster, C.: Metrics for Ranking Ontologies. In: 4th Int. EON Workshop, 15th Int. World Wide Web Conference (2006)
13. Yao, H., Orme, A., Etzkorn, L.: Cohesion Metrics for Ontology Design and Application. Journal of Computer Science 1(1), 107–113 (2005)
14. Ma, Y., Jin, B., Feng, Y.: Semantic oriented ontology cohesion metrics for ontology-based systems. The Journal of Systems and Software (2009)
15. Yang, Z., Zhang, D., Chuan, Y.E.: Evaluation Metrics for Ontology Complexity and Evolution Analysis. In: IEEE International Conference on e-Business Engineering, ICEBE 2006 (2006)

The Impact of Team Project on Students' Learning: An Analysis of a Global IT Management Course

Lazar Rusu

Department of Computer and Systems Sciences
Stockholm University, Sweden
lrusu@dsv.su.se

Abstract. The research paper is analyzing the contribution of the team project (project based learning) as a group assignment in Global IT Management course offered at the master level in international programs at Royal Institute of Technology (KTH) Stockholm and Stockholm University towards the enhancement of students' learning. The research methodology is a qualitative one and has been conducted through formal structured interviews with a group of students who have been acting as group leaders in Global IT Management course. Based upon the results coming from interviewing 7 out of 15 group leaders plus two additional interviews with students that were not group leaders we have found that the team project is enhancing their knowledge, is an assessment method better than a classic written exam and the students' perception about the impact of the team project upon their learning is positive. Moreover the analysis of the data collected from these interviews has also provided usefully information about if the team project objectives are relevant in contributing to the enhancement of students learning, and what it can be done further for increasing students' motivation in their team project work.

1 Introduction

Today, we are seeing an increased level of business globalization, international trade and competitiveness on the global market. In such a global business environment the firms are facing many challenges like for example political, economic, legal, technological and cultural [9]. In fact in [27] the authors have examined the key issues that Information Systems (IS) executives are facing in IS management in ten nations and regions around the world and they have noticed that are substantial differences between these key issues. Their explanation was that the national cultural and economic development could explain these differences. On the other hand according to [16] "the ability to manage and control the business processes involved in maintaining global business is enhanced by the success of IT infrastructure and technologies support it". Furthermore in [15] the author noticed that the "global business creates greater uncertainty and complexity" and to handle these challenges firms will have "to rely more on IT to manage organization". In the last twenty years many researchers like for example [19][23][4][21] have mentioned the importance of the role of information systems and information technology in support of multinational corporations.

M.D. Lytras et al. (Eds.): WSKS 2010, Part I, CCIS 111, pp. 28–40, 2010.

In this context a new course like the Global Information Technology Management was obvious a necessity to be introduced in the curricula of the master programs in Information Technology (IT) from Royal Institute of Technology (KTH) and Stockholm University. But what is Global Information Technology Management? Global Information Technology Management or shortly named Global IT Management is in fact a discipline that is covering referent disciplines like: Political Science, Economics, Law, Management, International Business, Human-computer interface, Cross-cultural studies, Sociology, Psychology, Telecommunications, and Computer Science [18]. According to [2] Global Information Systems Management (another name for Global IT Management) is as a multidisciplinary field covering information management, international business and information technology (Figure 1). The authors from [2] have mentioned that in their view Global Information Systems Management represents on one hand a subset of Management Information Systems "that is concerned with multinational firms, cross cultural exchanges and national and regional polices". On the other hand Global Information Systems Management "represents a subset of International Business that is concerned with the role of information systems". In opinion of [2] which are citing [17] they argues that Global Information Systems Management is overlapping management and technology in which there is both a "an International Business component and an Information Systems aspect, and the intersection requires management".

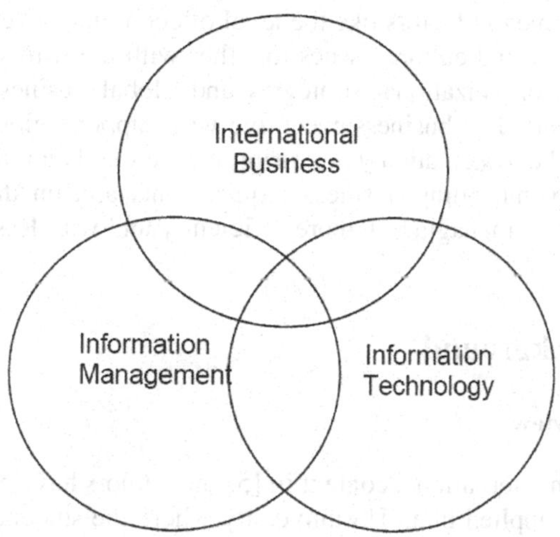

Fig. 1. Global Information Systems Management as a Multidisciplinary Field [2]

But at the base of developing the Global IT Management course at KTH has stayed the model proposed by [20] and shown in Figure 2, "that captures the most important factors influencing IT management in firms in different parts of the world" and in which the key variable is *"key IT Management issues* of firms in a country or in a homogeneous region of the world".

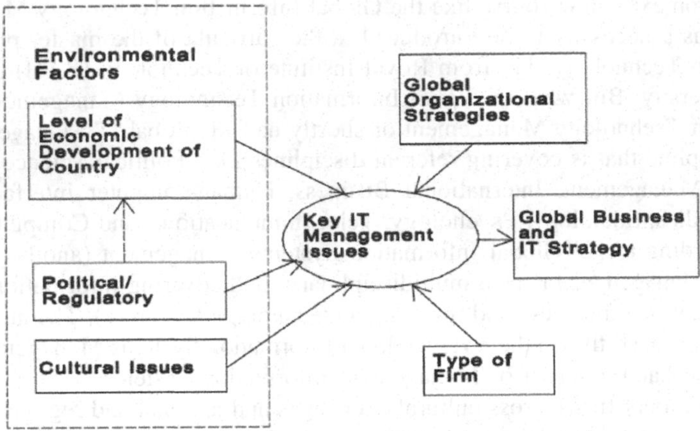

Fig. 2. Determinants of key global IT issues [20]

From the model proposed by [20] and shown in Figure 2, we can see that the environmental factors are influencing the key IT management issues of a firm from a country which consequently are influencing the global business and IT strategy from a firm. Therefore in the study of Global IT Management we should consider and analyze both the environmental factors like the level of economic development of a country, political/regulatory and cultural issues together with the firm specific factors like type of firm, global organizational strategies and global business and IT strategy. Moreover according to [1] a business executive who supports global IT management is very important to be systematic by "ensuring on the one hand, that IT can respond on a global scale to impending business requirements and on the other hand, that viable opportunities for managing IT more efficiently and with less risk are identified and explored".

2 Research Background

2.1 Literature Review

For teaching IT in an international context in [5] the authors have presented a successful teaching method applied in an US university where the students are doing project assignments and create a repository named "IT landscape" that can be usefully for them and for those who use this repository. The impact of global information technology in universities from Australia is also examined by [26] that has proposed some strategies for solving some issues that the international education are facing and also for the development of global information technology and global information systems courses.

According to [8] the case studies (like for example project based learning) are usefully pedagogical tools and the assessment through the team project (project based learning) is one that is increasing the students' motivation and interest in the subject [8]. Moreover according to [14] the team projects "allow for learning behaviors that cannot be realized in an individual learning environment". On the other hand in [7] the authors believe that overall the team project are "a good idea in theory but can be challenging to implement in practice" so in their opinion "the assessment process holds the key to a successful learning experience in team project work".

Therefore this research paper has focused in analyzing the impact of the team project and sees the contribution towards enhancement of students' learning in Global IT Management course. In this direction one step was already done two years ago when in this course was introduced a peer-review system part of team project assessment process that according to [3] has as effect the enhancement of students' learning. Furthermore because in Global IT Management course we have larger classes the group assessment method like is team project it seems to be a suitable one in such cases [3]. According to [12] in case of group projects the assessment of the contribution of each member from a group is in fact not an easy task. For example in [10] the authors suggests a management strategy (one that replicates those in industry) that provides a "framework for a supported learning environment – one in which students can be confident that the many benefits of working on a group assignment can be enjoyed". Moreover in [11] the authors are suggesting some ideas that a teacher "can use to facilitate the learning experience of students projects" together with strategies in "forming groups, managing teams, assigning the project, and evaluating the team and project". In opinion of [14] some of issues that are motivating the students in doing the team projects are according to them the followings: "a. the assessment that takes into account the individual contribution; b. projects that can be practically implemented in real life; c. major company clients –where students can get a placement or a job; and d. projects that have high expectations of students". But in spite of the difficulties regarding the assessment process the team project as assessment method could be an intrinsic motivation to students for deep learning approach and for this purpose it's also needed a positive climate together with a planned reflected upon and processed learning activity. Therefore we expect that the interaction during the team project work through an in time usefully feedback gave it by the teaching team through tutoring [14] or mentorship[1] like the author in [13] is mentioning (mentors who have knowledge about the subject and personality of mentor[2]) will have a positive climate for students to enhance their motivation in the team project work.

2.2 The Assessment through a Team Project in a Global IT Management Course

The Global IT Management course (7.5 ECTS) has been introduced for the first time in 2004 in the master programs in Internetworking and Engineering and Management of Information Systems at KTH in order to enhance students knowledge in information and communications technologies (ICT) support in globalization and companies that operates in a global business environment. From the experience of former students in Global IT Management course we have found that for most of them this

[1] Mentorship is according to [13] who is citing [24] defined "as when people see more in other people than they do in themselves".

[2] In opinion of [13] "the best criterion for a mentor would be the willingness of the mentor to duplicate himself and to have a passion for helping others to also succeed in the project, almost to get them on higher level than they were".

course was an opportunity and challenge to enhance their knowledge in the IT Management area and develop new skills about how to deal with different cultures, and work in multicultural teams. Moreover the course is preparing students to be able to:

- Explain the environment factors that are affecting international business, the cultural context of global management and global organization structure.
- Explain why ICT is a catalyst in globalization and international business.
- Analyze the role and responsibilities of a Chief Information Officer in a multinational company.
- Analyze and compare the IT organization, IT architecture and IT strategies implemented in different multinational companies.
- Explain why companies are outsourcing and offshoring IT and Information Systems.

The assessment through a team project in Global IT Management course is including the following parts: the work in doing a team project report, the presentation of the report including the opposition for another report in the final seminar and the evaluation of the other reports done by each group. The activities before mentioned are planned by the teaching team to be run over a period of 7 weeks. For doing the work on their team project the students are forming groups of up to 5-6 students and each group is having a group leader (selected by his group members) that has the role to establish the tasks that has to be done by his group members and also to inform and communicate during the project work period with the teaching team. The main objective of team project work is to analyze the management of IT resources in a multinational company through an interview with a Chief Information Officer (CIO) or an IT manager from that company. The main sections that every group will have to include in their team project reports will be an *analysis of the CIO or IT manager role and responsibilities in managing the IT resources successfully; the analysis of IT organization structure; IT architecture in place*; and *the IT strategy implemented in the studied multinational company*. Regarding the report structure this must be according to the guidelines that are posted on the course web page in the team project description and with a length of up to 30 pages where all sources must be cited where they are used in the report including a written list of the complete references. The team project report and the presentation have to be uploaded on the course web page with one day before the final seminar. In case that a group is not sending in time their team project report or is not doing the team project presentation that group will receive a grade of fail. Concerning the presentation of the team projects this activity is compulsory to be attended by all the groups and each group will have a maximum of 30 minutes allocated for his presentation and other 10 minutes for questions and discussions. Before the presentations each group will be appointed by the course leader to discuss another team's report and a written feedback with comments on the report has to be sent to the presenters and the course leader after the presentation. Moreover there are two important tasks that I would like to mention here one is regarding is the tutorial activities and the second one is regarding the progress on project work. In fact regarding the second activity previously mentioned this is part of the assessment process and therefore during the course period all the group leaders will have to submit to the teaching team a weekly short note informing about the progress on their project work. In these weekly notes every group leader will have to write and describe on what they have worked, the problems they have encountered and the planned work for the next week in order that the teaching team to asses in time their project work and be prepared to offer support and guidance. Concerning the grade for the team project part this is the same for all the students from a group but the grade it could be different for some students from a group based upon the self-assessment of the work load (in percentages) done by the group leaders for each of his group members.

2.3 Research Methodology

The research methodology used in my research is a qualitative one and has been done through interviews with the students that they have attended the Global IT Management course in 2007. The interviews has been conducted with the group leaders who are according to [6] 'knowledgeable people' about the activities and work done in the team projects. The collection of the data in this research was done in Spring 2008 and is consisting in seven formal structured-interviews with the group leaders (team project leaders) from Global IT Management course in 2007. In support of these data collected from the interviews with the group leaders two additional interviews were performed with students that were not group leaders for having another angle about the impact of the team project upon their learning in this course.

Regarding the validity of the interviews according to [6] a practical way to achieve a greater validity is to minimize the bias as much as possible (because bias is one cause of invalidity). In fact in [6] the authors are mentioning that the main sources of having a bias are related to the characteristics of the interviewer and respondent and also are concerning the content of the questions. Therefore the interviews with the group leaders and the other two students in Global IT Management course 2007 were conducted in order to follow the recommendations of controlling the reliability in the way that [25] has suggested by having "structured interviews with the same format and sequence of words and questions" so each interviewee "understand the question in the same way". According to [25] interviews have also "to satisfy the need for low-inference descriptors by: a. tape–recording all interviews; b. carefully transcribing these tapes according to the needs of a reliable analysis"; c. presenting long extracts of data in your research report- including the question that provoked any answer".

For investigating how the team project has contributed towards the enhancement of the students' learning the following questions (as analytical framework) has been considered in the interviews:

- What are the students' perceptions regarding the team project?
- Are the team project objectives relevant in contributing to the enhancement of students learning?
- Are the tutorial activities relevant in increase of team projects quality?
- Are team project presentations and the team project peer review system contributing to the enhancement of students learning?
- Has the team project enhanced your knowledge? (please detailed)
- How much time has your group spent each week in working on the team project?
- How you appreciate the contribution of every group members in doing the team project?
- In what way do you see a possibility to increase the students' motivation in their work on the team project?

In this study the research questions that we have mainly looked to analyze are the followings: "Are the team project objectives relevant in contributing to the enhancement of students learning?", "Is the team project a suitable assessment method in this course?" and finally "How could I increase the students' motivation in doing the team project?". Through the research questions addressed before we have looked in fact to find concrete answers about the impact of the team project on students' learning and also to find new ways for the improvement of the team project as assessment method in Global IT management course.

3 Data Analysis and Results

Based upon the data collected from the interviews done with the group leaders an analysis will be drawn in this section in order to see in which way the team project is contributing in enhancement of students' learning. Moreover this analysis will look also to see if there is a relation between the tutorial activities during the team project work and the increase of the projects quality, and if the team projects presentations and peer-review system is contributing to enhancement of the students' learning. As in [22] the author has noticed it is an obvious thing to explore how the students' "have experienced learning in order to judge to extent to which development takes place", the perception about the course and the way they react and perceive in particular here about team project as an important part of Global IT Management course. The data collected from the interviews with the students that were acting as group leaders and the results of this analysis will be detailed on the main questions used in the interviewees by including the students (identified with student 1 to 7) comments to each question addressed to them.

To the 1st question (*What are the students' perceptions regarding the team project?)* the students answers have pointed different comments which are reflecting the idea that the team project has been a useful learning experience for them. For example student 1 comments were: "*From a student's perspective, really good for me, quite excellent. You have to interview a CIO, and to understand, and write it, it is not the same like you just read it, you have to analyze it and then put it into paper*". Furthermore student 4 has noticed: "*The course as a whole is an exciting subject to dig into, and the team project is a very good way of starting thinking by your self, starting to make your own conclusion, and to see your own investigation to really sum up, the whole group was really excited to do it actually, but it was a little bit confusing at the beginning, when we selected a company. I think team project is always a good way of making everyone to think by themselves, to think about what we gonna do, and how each chapter could contribute to the project, so you have to list all the books, you have to really look into what does this mean and how could we use it into our team project*". While student 7 comments are considering the team project to be a very good type of examination: "*I believe the team project is a very good type of examination. Because you chose the theory from the university and you have to put it into the practical life, because you need to contact a company, and use your knowledge when you talk to the CIO. That is a good structure instead of having exams. You have to show everything you have learned, in a few hours. Also it is good to mix different people from different countries. We have different knowledge to put into the team project work*".

To the 2nd question (*Are the team project objectives relevant in contributing to the enhancement of students learning?*) the students' answers are converging to the idea that the team project objectives are relevant to the enhancement of students learning. For example student 2 has mentioned that: "*Yeah, to large extent. Because all these are based on decision-making and business processing. So the chapters that you specified in the course are equivalent to making the project successful*". While student 3 has described the objectives as a good idea: "*Good idea to put such those objectives, it is a good way; these four things are the main things of the whole project. We can learn a lot through it*". Furthermore student 4 has noticed that: "*Yes. It is really good, because most students just come from studying, so it is a good framework for building the team project, and also for you as a teacher to teach in the subject. It is good to understand and limit the area of IT, because some people at the beginning wanted to discuss some more subjects. So we have to really list the discussion on a certain level. We don't have time to dig into whatever the students are interested in. We have to find a good balance between all of these subjects. I have this advantage, because I have working experience before, so I know what we are going to do, otherwise it will take time to decide what we are going to do ,and in which level*".

To the 3nd question (*Are the tutorial activities relevant in increase of team projects quality?*) the students answers were not given a clear indication if this activity is contributing to the increase of the team projects quality instead the students were emphasis about the need of tutorial mainly for guidance. For example student 5 comments were the followings: "*Because every team project is different from others, there are different templates, different goals so it is good to have a guidance, to have opportunity to get the help, get some details and key words from the teachers. Because when you have a template, you only need to fill in the words, it is easier*". On the other hand student 4 has pointed that: "*Our group had such a problem, and I believe other groups had the same. We started really slow at the beginning, so I think the tutorial activity is most valuable at the beginning. But the group didn't really start to discuss all the things at that time, everything was a bit. I think perhaps the tutorial activity is not only the quality, but the direction of the work. If you go deeper into different aspects, the tutorial activity could be a way to guild the group into different directions, I am not sure the quality, but I am sure it will get better*".

To the 4th question (*Are team project presentations and the team project peer review system contributing to the enhancement of students learning?*) the students answers were more pro team project presentations and peer–review system contribution but some of them have seen some problems in working well in practice the peer-review system. For example student 4 has stated that: "*In theory, I think it is a very good way. But the quality has become getting inconsistent. If the people have bad presentation technique, you will lose your attention to listen to what he/she is saying. If they have good presentation technique, it is easier to focus attention to it. It is good way to attend all the presentations and have your own review, but the students have many going-on at the same time, so after their own presentation, everything is done for them. So maybe it is good way to let them listen to all the presentations and think about their own reviews*". On the other hand student 3 has noticed that: "*The rule is good to have a peer review system, but the application is not so good. Most people they even did not see the report, they just gave the grades. It is not fitable. And also it is hard for the teacher to justify which is a good peer review or not*". While student 5 is very convinced about the peer-review system utility as it could be seen from his comments: "*I like the idea of peer review system. Because when I read the reports of other groups, I learn more about the topics. The thing is I don't know if every student feels that way. Maybe they wouldn't really read it, they just gave a grade. For me, it is a good way to enlarge my knowledge. When I was grading others, I was not sure if they were really carefully grading on me. So I would really read their reports carefully, which I would like to see others do the same*".

To the 5th question (*Has the team project enhanced your knowledge? - please detailed*) the students answers were positive and most of them they have pointed the role of this team project through a case study approach in enhancing their knowledge.

For example the student 1 has stated that: "*Very much, now I got a lot of knowledge, and now I understand what we should do in a company with IT*". Moreover the student 4 has noticed that: "*I think so, for sure. A good way to interview someone to get into the real world, not only in theory, you can really know what and how the work done by the CIO. However, it is hard for the team project to keep going with what you have learned from the lectures hand in hand all the time*". While student 5 comments were: "*I think so. It was fun, in this course we could work with people from different countries. I would like to work with people even I had not met before; we have different cultures, which are really good*".

To the 6th question (How much time has your group spent each week in working on the team project?) the students' answers varied from each group to another. For example student 1 has said the followings: "*We met twice a week, around 4 hours. Because we had to read the book, go though the materials on Internet before the interview, and we had to write the report together*". Furthermore student 4 has noticed that: "I *can not say the exact time, maybe 8-10 hours per week. We four people spent much time on it, and made the whole project*". While student 7 comments were: "*First week, not so much time, it was just some conversation but in the end 2 days per week, 6 hours per day*".

To the 7th question (*How you appreciate the contribution of every group members in doing the team project?*) the students' answers are as I have perceived not so precisely and most of the group leaders have seen the group members' contribution to be equally in doing their team project. For example student 2 has said that: "*30% each member. I gave every member an average grade*". Furthermore student 5 has noticed "*I would say equally in our group. Everyone contributed in their own way, did different parts*". Student 7 has noticed that: "*Very equally in our group. They all had very good perspectives of the team project. The outcome was really good*" while student 3 comments were that: "*Some people worked really hard while some did not*".

Finally to the 8th question (*In what way do you see a possibility to increase the students' motivation in their work on the team project?*) the students' comments varied but have brought me some relevant answers concerning in which way I could act in the near future to increase the students' motivation in their work on the team project. For example student 4 has suggested me that: "*To increase the motivation, I think you can use some kind of success stories and examples of the previous team projects, to show to the students. And also it is about networking, because people will start to contact the companies which they are interested in, maybe they want to work there afterwards, so they want to have the connection of the company, maybe it will motivate people a lot*" which it could be in a way an interesting approach. Student 5 has noticed that: "*This course was quite different from others. Other courses we just focus on getting the grade, but in this course we have really got the chance to interview the organization, or maybe your future employer. I know they want the copy of the report, which will be a big motivation for me. And for other people also, because people will think that this is a good chance for them to go out, and to show themselves, which will be a big motivation for the team members*". While student 7 comments were: "*It is a good way to get into the company. And also students have the opportunity to put the knowledge into the real life, that will be a motivation*" which have brought me a new perspective about how could be increased the students' motivation in doing the team project in this course.

In support of the analysis of the data presented below and also for having another perspective that is different from that of the 7 group leaders that I have interviewed, additional interviewees I have done with two students (that were not group leaders in Global IT Management course 2007; identified as students 8 and 9) by asking them the same questions in order to have more information about team project contribution on students' learning. For example the students' answers to one of the main questions concerning if the team project has enhanced their knowledge were the followings: student 8 - "*Actually yes, in way of understanding how they work in really life, because knowledge to the real world is important, for me at least*" while student 9 comments were: "*Yes. Because we don't have a final exam in this course, so if we don't have this team project, maybe I won't pay much attention to it. And during the team project, everyone is working and sharing their knowledge, so that I have to do the same, it will enhance our knowledge in this way. If I have to choose one from exam and team project, I will choose team project. Because it is more fun and if I just have exam, maybe I will prepare it 3-4 days in advance, and after that, I will forget it. But if it is a team project, I will remember it more specifically, and force me to study from the beginning*".

In summary the students 8 and 9 answers' were at most of the questions addressed in our interviews following my comments given at each question and presented before in the interviews done with the group leaders. Moreover the results of these two interviews were added in account to the lessons learned that are drawn in the next section.

4 Lessons Learned

Apart from the results presented previously the following lessons learned have been drawn from the analysis of the impact of team project on students learning in the Global IT Management course:

- The students' perception about the team project is in general a very good one and is focusing on the advantages that are bringing the work in a group and the challenging of doing an analysis in the topics of the course in a multinational company.
- The students' answers concerning if the team project has enhanced their knowledge is reflecting the idea that the team project (through a case study approach that is done in a multinational company) have provided to students' knowledge that are corresponding to an in deep learning approach.

- The tutorial activities in support of the team project were found to be very relevant especially at the start of the course but also lately too but their impact was not reflected in an increase of the team project reports quality. This issue in students' opinion is mainly because most of the work in doing the team project is let to be done in the last week before the deadline of report submission which definitely affects its quality.
- The students' contribution in doing their team project work has been reported by the group leaders as being equally and in a few cases unequally. The reason for doing this issue it could be related to the fact that some groups have been agreed from the beginning of the project about everyone workload or it could be a mutual agreement between the students from a group (mainly of those which they worked more that the rest of the students) to not affect the grades of the others team mates which they work less than them.
- The formation of the groups has been suggested by some students to be done differently and instead of letting the students to do that they thing that is better that the teachers should form the groups. The reason for why some students have claimed this issue is that in most of the groups there are students who are friends and in case that one of them is becoming the group leader his friend will not perform very properly his tasks in the team project.

5 Conclusions and Recommendations

Following the analysis done in the previous section a summarize of the results will be presented here regarding how the team project is contributing in support of students' learning in Global IT Management course together with further recommendations in this direction.

As we have noticed from the analysis done in the previous section the team project objectives are considered by the students as being relevant because they have to investigate and find how they work in the real world. Moreover performing a case study in a company is a very good approach to evaluate in practice the theoretical knowledge and concepts presented in the course for a better understanding of them. Furthermore regarding if the team project is enhancing the students knowledge the students comments have emphasis on the important role of performing the project through a case study in a company as being challenging and a usefully experience too.

Concerning the second research question if the team project is a suitable assessment method in this course we have seen that the students perception is that the team project is an assessment method better than a classic exam and in their opinion is having a long term positive impact upon their learning.

Finally regarding the last research question addressed in this paper about how could we increase the students' motivation in doing the team project? The study has found that a good approach could be the presentation of successful stories about the positive experience of the students that have worked in doing a team project in a company and which they have continue after the course was ended to cooperate with that company either in doing their master thesis work there or as employees of that company. In this way such an example could be a very important reason for the students' in developing a really motivation for doing a team project of a very good quality apart from that one of getting of a very good grade. Last but not the least as a further recommendation in this study I see in my opinion as very important too a research investigation in finding a better way of the assessment of students' work in doing their team project which could add new results to this research towards a holistic approach regarding the impact of team project on students' learning.

Acknowledgments

To students from Royal Institute of Technology (KTH) Stockholm and Stockholm University participants in Global IT Management course 2007 which they have provided usefully information for completing this research paper.

References

1. Barton, R.: Global IT Management: A Practical Approach, p. 3. John Wiley & Sons, Chichester (2003)
2. Beise, C., Collins, R.W., Niederman, F., Quan, J.J., Moody, J.: Revisiting Global Information Systems Management Education. Communications of the Association for Information Systems 16, Article 30, 625–641 (2005)
3. Biggs, J.: Teaching for Quality Learning at University, 2nd edn., pp. 191–197. The Society for Research into Higher Education & Open University Press (2005)
4. Boudreau, M., Loch, K.D., Robey, D., Straub, D.W.: Going global: Using IT to advance the competitiveness of the virtual transnational organization. Academy of Management Executive 4(12), 120–128 (1998)
5. Carmel, E., Mann, J.: Teaching about IT in Nations: Building and Using the "Landscape of IT Repository". Journal of Information Technology Education 3, 91–104 (2003)
6. Cohen, L., Manion, L., Morrison, K.: Research Methods in Education, 6th edn., pp. 97, 150–151. Routledge, London (2007)
7. Cooper, G., Heinze, A.: Centralisation of Assessment: Meeting the Challenges of Multi-year Team Projects in Information Systems Education. Journal of Information Systems Education 18(3), 345–356 (2007)
8. Davis, C., Wilcock, E.: Case Studies in Engineering. In: Baillie, C., Moore, I. (eds.) Effective Learning and Teaching in Engineering, pp. 52–53. RoutledgeFalmer, London (2004)
9. Deresky, H.: International Management: Managing Across Borders and Cultures, 6th edn., p. 15. Prentice-Hall, Englewood Cliffs (2008)
10. Ford, M., Morice, J.: How Fair are Group Assignments? A Survey of Students and Faculty and a Modest Proposal. Journal of Information Technology Education 2, 367–378 (2003)
11. Lane, P.L., Alshare, K.A., Nickels, D.W., Armstrong, D.J., Rodriguez-Abitia, G.: AMCIS 2008 Panel Summary: Managing Student Projects - Learning from the Past. Communications of the Association for Information Systems 24, Article 1, 1–6 (2009)
12. Lejk, M., Wyvill, M.: Peer assessment of contributions to a group project: a comparison of holistic and category based approaches. Assessment and Evaluation in Higher Education 26, 61–72 (2001)
13. le Roux, G.: Improving the Development of Students in IS Projects - The Role of Mentorship. In: Proceedings of the AIS SIG-ED IAIM 2007 Conference, Montreal, Canada, December 7-9, pp. 1–13 (2007)

14. Lynch, K., Heinze, A., Scott, E.: Information technology team projects in higher education: An international viewpoint. Journal of Information Technology Education 6, 181–198 (2007)
15. Lucas, H.C.: Information Technology: Strategic Decision Making for Managers, p. 94. John Wiley & Sons, Chichester (2005)
16. Luftman, J.N.: Managing the Information Technology Resource: Leadership in the Information Age, p. 13. Prentice-Hall, Englewood Cliffs (2004)
17. Niederman, F., Boggs, D., Kundu, S.: International Business and Global Information Management Research Toward a cumulative tradition. Journal of Global Information Management 10(1), 33–47 (2002)
18. ISWorld Net, What is Global Information Technology? (2008), `http://www.fb.cityu.edu.hk/is/research/ISWorld/GIT/define.htm` (accessed on 2008-03-22)
19. Ives, B., Jarvenpaa, S.L.: Applications of Global Information Technology: Key Issues for Management. MIS Quarterly 15(1), 33–49 (1991)
20. Palvia, P.C., Palvia, S.C.J., Whitworth, J.E.: Global information technology: a meta analysis of key issues. Information & Management 39, 403–414 (2002)
21. Palvia, P., Pinjani, P.: Challenges of the Global Information Technology Management Environment: Representative World Issues. In: Palvia, P., Palvia, S., Harris, A.L. (eds.) Managing Global Information Technology: Strategies and Challenges, pp. 3–28. Ivy League Publishing (2007)
22. Ramsden, P.: Learning to Teach in Higher Education, p. 26. Routledge-Falmer, London (2003)
23. Roche, E.M.: Managing Information Technology in Multinational Corporations, pp. 2–12. Macmillan, New York (1992)
24. Schrubbe, K.F.: Mentorship: A critical Component for Professional Growth and Academic Success. Journal of Dental Education 3(68), 324–328 (2004)
25. Silverman, D.: Interpreting Qualitative Data, 3rd edn., pp. 121, 286-287. Sage Publications Ltd., London (2006)
26. Sun, Z.: Teaching Information Systems to International Students in Australia: A Global Information Technology Perspective. In: Raisinghani, M.S. (ed.) Handbook of Research on Global Information Technology Management in the Digital Economy, Information Science Reference, pp. 432–451 (2008)
27. Watson, R.T., Kelly, G., Galliers, R.D., Brancheau, J.C.: Key issues in IS management: An international perspective. Journal of Management Information Systems 13(4), 91–115 (1997)

LONS: Learning Object Negotiation System

Antonio García, Eva García, Luis de-Marcos, José-Javier Martínez
José-María Gutiérrez, José-Antonio Gutiérrez,
Roberto Barchino, Salvador Otón, and José-Ramón Hilera

Computer Science Department, University of Alcalá
Ctra Barcelona km 33.6, 28871, Alcalá de Henares, Madrid, Spain
{a.garciac,eva.garcial,luis.demarcos,josej.martinez,
josem.gutierrez,jantonio.gutierrez,roberto.barchino,
salvador.oton,jose.hilera}@uah.es

Abstract. This system comes up as a result of the increase of e-learning systems. It manages all relevant modules in this context, such as the association of digital rights with the contents (courses), management and payment processing on rights. There are three blocks:

- A normalized application following the worldwide accepted standards or recommendations (SCORM, IMS, IEEE, etc.) containing the courses and implementing the organization of users and their subscriptions in the courses.
- Another application will be in charge of managing the digital rights of the courses following ODRL [1]. It considers the creation of these courses, its offers with different costs and its requirements.
- In order to negotiate the digital rights it is necessary another application implementing a device to manage and make payments using the secure payment methods currently used in the network.

Keywords: ODRL, e-Learning, web services, LMS, digital rights, payment.

1 Introduction

The project introduces a new idea about the current e-learning systems. Due to the expansion of the education in this area it is necessary to create and administer the digital rights [2] on the digital learning contents non-existent so far. This project aims to develop a prototype called "Learning Object Negotiation System" which will allow the management of economic/financial aspects [3] related to the e-learning process and the learning objects (figure 1).

This new education using e-learning systems is becoming a learning method increasingly used. This phenomenon can be observed in universities and higher education institutions, but also in companies where continuing training of employees is taken into account. Within this so wide topic, our aim is focused on the location, acquisition and secure payment of learning units by the members taking part in the electronic learning system.

M.D. Lytras et al. (Eds.): WSKS 2010, Part I, CCIS 111, pp. 41–50, 2010.

The contents are stored in repositories and designed so that it is not necessary a previous knowledge of the structure. This way, it is possible to contain the resources as the metadata. The reference model for access to the repositories has been determined by the specification DRI (Digital Repositories Interoperability).

Therefore it is aimed the reuse of educational resources and the access to the stored resources from:

- Learning management platforms (LMS: Learning Management System), where EDVI will be used.
- Learning content management systems (LCMS: Learning Content Management System)
- Content search portals (for example search systems of digital libraries, Web searchers, etc.).
- Any application or software agent developed to access to this kind of information.

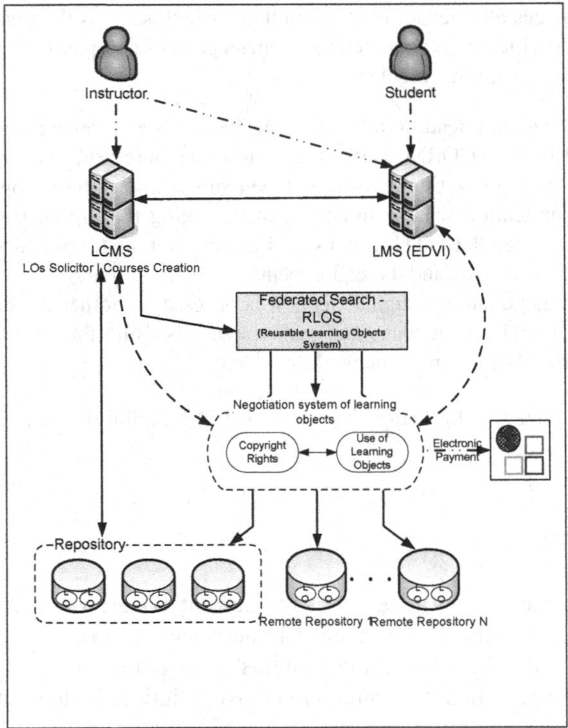

Fig. 1. Architecture of LONS

The means of payment give way to the commerce in the Internet and transactions, although its development is slow, mainly due to user's lack of confidence to the existing means of doing it. So, it is necessary to provide mechanisms that help to alleviate these security deficiencies.

In addition to the user's distrust, there are organizations that want to create digital learning contents in a market where the pertinent standards are not defined. There is a difficult and unprofitable situation:

- Each client has his/her own platform in which it is difficult to integrate his/her contents (courses) without a previous adaptation, which requires an investment of time and money.
- There is no control on the use and access to the contents, so rights from the copyright can be broken copying or distributing materials without permission.
- The use monitoring and access to the contents must be manually done, together with the control and pay associated to the use of those digital resources.

It will be necessary the creation of the following items for the execution of the system able to solve this needs of the user and the organization:

- A new way of specifying the copyright rights in the learning objects.
- The specification of the way of carrying out the monitoring of courses and learning objects.
- The mechanisms needed to integrate the system with the existing electronic means of payment in the Internet.

This enables us to determine the restrictions to be satisfied for the developers and distributors of contents, from the use of those carried out by the platform users.

Therefore, the basic idea lies in the distribution, reuse, management of rights and pay per use of Learning Objects, understanding as Learning Objects the minimum units in which virtual courses can be organized. For an effective search, location and reference of Learning Objects it is necessary that those objects are built using worldwide accepted standards of recommendations, such as the ones developed by SCORM, IMS [4], IEEE, etc. Likewise, for the effective management of digital rights it must be adjusted its definition to the existing rules and standards, such as the ones developed by ODRL as a language for expressing rights. Finally, to make the system valuable to the different interested organizations, it must be integrated with the existing commercial payment methods in the Internet to carry out the economic transactions (VeriSign, Western Union, ClickBank, Pay-Pal, CyberPack, 2CheckOut, E-Gold o Telepago 4B).

2 Main AIMS

The aim of this project is to correct all problems and deficiencies in the e-learning education systems. As a main aim it must be a system to manage the learning objects, so they can register its digital right. To meet this aim we have EDVI. To manage the digital rights of each learning object we will focus on the outline provided by LOM (Learning Object Metadata).

This schema defines a category that allows describe intellectual property rights and conditions of use of the learning objects. LOM [5] will be completed using the Open Digital Rights Language specification (ODRL), because the base outline provided by LOM can be extended in the way that best suits (figure 2).

The proposed idea tries to take advantage of the description of Digital Rights and the possibility of extending LOM to include a reference in a XML [6] file describing the Digital Rights of the Learning Object. This reference will be done including a small XML structure (with the file imsmanifest.xml) in the description, including all the courses that follow the standards ADL SCORM [7] and IMS-Content Packaging. The specification identifier of Digital Rights (ODRL) assigned to the Learning object will be there. It can be seen in the following picture:

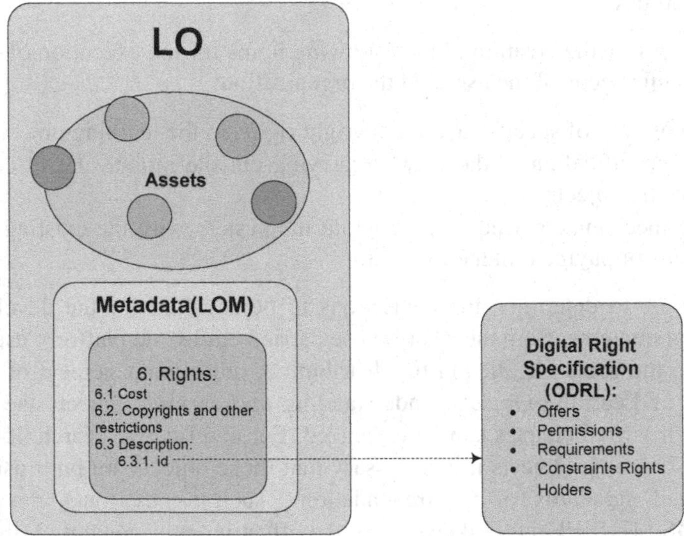

Fig. 2. LOM with Digital Rights

This allows the inclusion of Digital Rights [8] within the Learning Object, making it possible to control the payments. Moreover, this proposal allows the reuse both of Learning Objects and Digital Rights.

There are two systems; EDVI, with its own database to manage learning objects and the students using such objects, and the Digital Rights solicitor.

Digital Rights management aims to implement an application to manage all issues related to digital rights of the learning objects.

Some of the aims of this module are:

- Creation of digital rights: it will allow us to create, display and modify them. It must be an offer associated with the rights.
- Creation, modification and display of offers associated with digital rights.
- Participants can be created with the different information fields. After creating them, they must have the possibility of being associated with the diverse created offers.

- Assignment of permissions or what is allowed to do with the learning object. There are several types of permissions such as use (print, execute…), transfer (sell, rent…) and management (delete, duplicate…)
- Requirements can be created to associate both offers and permissions. The characteristics include defining the possible cost of the learning object use and the kind of payment to be done (prepay or postpay).
- The possibility of add constraints to the permissions, such as temporary constraints (time of use) or user constraints (use by the user or a group).
- The IMSManifest must be updated with all defined and finished characteristics in order to include the digital right in the learning object.
- Together with the provided web server it allows the formation of the document according to the specification ODRL required to make the payments. It implies all previous aims must meet the ODRL specifications.

Once we have the digital rights with the learning object, we have to manage the means of payment for the economic/financial data of the clients and information related to the associated students and the receipts and invoices for the courses of each client. The aim of this module is to make the prepayment and post-payment of the followed courses.

Therefore they can be separated in two independent modules for a better management.

- Means of payment: One of them is responsible for managing the information of the clients, that is, data related to the company and each one of the students belonging to that company. All this information must include the company VAT number, address and phone number. Students must include in the information his/her identificator, name, surname and the company VAT number. Also there is a part in charge of add and modify the means of payment of each company. That is, the means of payment shall be added for a company with all information related to the collection. If we want to add a payment by paypal, it will be necessary the company VAT number and the associated e-mail address to the paypal account. While a transfer will require the current account number and VAT number, and by credit card it is necessary besides the just mentioned, the card number and expiration date.
- Payments: The second module within the payments management is in charge of making the collection, and it is divided in two types. Independently, the student must be registered in the course. To make the payment with any method the specific type of the digital right must be defined. There are two types of payment: prepayment and post-payment. Prepayment is done before the student starts the course; s/he is required to make the whole payment before the beginning and post-payment is done when the student has a whole course; all outstanding courses shall be automatically paid for each client.

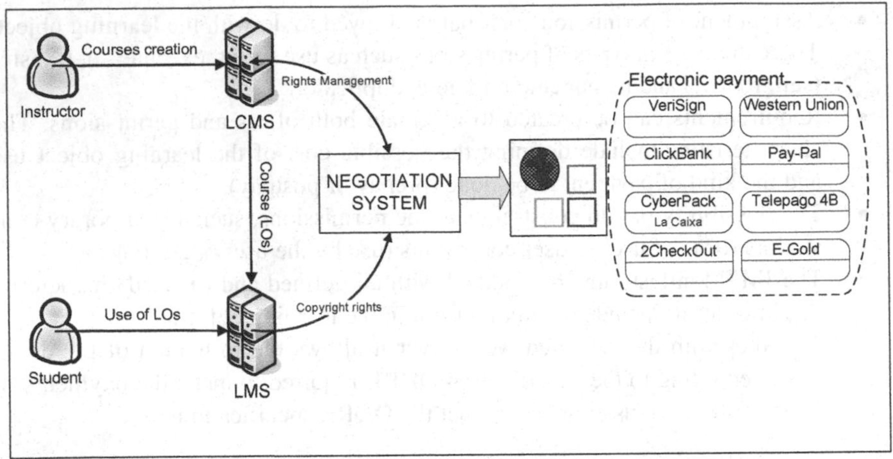

Fig. 3. Payments with LONS

This could not be carried out if there is not a database managing all information related to the client, such as the means of payment available for each client, storing information about the type of transaction (transfer, credit cards, paypal…).

Also, it takes into account the students belonging to a specific client, the identificator within the EDVI system, this way it can be obtained the amount and information for each student (and the courses s/he is registered in) and hence the client's transactions. The modules Payments and Means of payment use a common database which allows them to communicate with the different modules in order to make the payments.

It must be taken into account that the application will have different profiles in each module, and each one will perform a series of functions, whilst other task won't be allowed. This is logical, since a system administrator (for example) will have access to information related to the system users that the rest does not have. Basic profiles are required; such as the administrator, mainly in charge of the administration of users accessing to the system; an advanced user able to perform all functions related to the module without including the administration of the system users; and a limited user capable of accessing to some information.

3 Description of the Developed Project

Here is described the LONS system specifying its scope, technological environment and main users.

3.1 Determining the Scope of the System

This project is set out because of the absence of an element regulating the digital rights associated to learning objects. It is a system able to locate, obtain and manage learning objects so that they may become commercialized through digital rights.

The system is made up of the following elements:

- A learning management platform (LMS) such as EDVI. It will work with its own database and will have the IMSManifest file.
- A web application called Digital Rights Management with its own database in charge of modifying the IMSManifest file containing all the characteristics related to the digital right of the learning object.
- The system in charge of managing the clients' data and their means of payment to make the payments. It uses the bd_mp database.
- The other system involved in the collections' management. It is responsible for making the outstanding payments to the different clients. As "means of payment" it uses the bd_mp database.
- Web Services in charge of integrating the different applications making up a single system.

This makes it possible to make the commercialization of the different learning objects, depending on the needs and requirements. Ie, it is possible to sell a whole course, allowing its use to a group of students or any other type of uses depending on the purpose that those learning objects have. Thus the use is regulated depending on the characteristics:

- First there is a learning object with specific characteristics.
- The digital right is included through a IMSManifest file depending on the defined characteristics, among the associated parameters they are the offers, participants, permissions, requirements and constraints.
- These characteristics will indicate us the use of the learning object and how we can make the collections to the different clients.

This project provides a range of opportunities for the commercialization in the e-learning field, respecting the copyright rights and having a greater control on the use of learning elements.

3.2 Identification of the Technological Environment

Here it is given a high level definition of the technological environment required to complete the system use requirements, specifying its possible conditions and constraints. To do that it is taken into account the technology for the correct system functioning.

It must be taken into consideration that object-oriented programming tools have been used; in this case java has been used together with JSP. and XML to integrate the data with the application. It is necessary to have this system as web applications integrated with databases.

3.2.1 Area of Action

They are web applications, so they shall be used from anywhere with an Internet connection, while the system shall be set in one equipment or separated ones communicated with a network.

3.2.2 Databases

Since the use of databases is something crucial for this system, they can be taken into account different approaches about the distribution of databases. In the database context they have been used:

- Hibernate: it has been used to facilitate the integration of the database with the system.
- PostgreSQL: it is a database management system which holds the three databases belonging to the system: the EDVI database, the database of digital rights and the database for the means of payment (used by the applications Payments and Means of Payment).

3.2.3 Web Applications

As the databases the applications will be included in a server. Regarding to the location of each one of these applications, the most logical thing would be to include all of them in the same server, this way the integration would be easier and quicker, since it would be unnecessary to request certain data to other equipments.

These web applications have to be set up on a web server; the Tomcat application has been chosen for this task. As mentioned, all applications would be included in this server, making its management easier.

The four web applications making up the system are:

- EDVI: as a learning management platform which has learning objects (courses).
- Digital Rights Management: application for the creation, modification and display of digital rights associated to learning objects.
- Means of payment: it manages the clients' information and the means of payment available for each of them.
- Payments: it makes the collections with the clients with outstanding payments.

3.2.4 Web Services

For the integration of all applications web services integrating them are required. These web services are implemented on the Axis 2 application. At the same time Axis2 is implemented on Tomcat as another web application. Hence the most logical thing is to include the same server where all web services are placed. Although it is possible to have separated applications and the integration web services in the different servers making all applications connect with each other. All these possibilities give a greater portability to the project.

3.2.5 SSL

The application has been developed thinking on security improvements, so web applications are accessible from a secure channel. SSL (Secure Sockets Layer) produces a Server authentication, and the creation of a certificate is needed. In this case an unsigned certificate has been created, although it allows a secure connection, it does not appear very secure to the final user.

3.3 Identification of Participants and End Users

It is important to define the users who will use the different applications, since it is a project where the user profiles play a great role.

3.3.1 Administrator

This user is mainly responsible for managing the users. This user provides to the different systems the possibility of creating, consulting, modifying or deleting the users and assigning them the profiles. This profile is included in the three groups of applications: EDVI, Digital Rights Management and Payments-Means of Payment.

3.3.2 Student

This user will just use EDVI application; s/he will take the courses and will belong to a company which will pay for the courses that s/he takes. In this way s/he will not have to use any other application.

3.3.3 Client (company)

This user is responsible for making the outstanding payments of the students belonging to a company. The user must have an advanced user profile in the system in order to access as "client". This user can just access to the Payments application, where s/he can make the outstanding payments of the students in the different courses.

3.3.4 Advanced User

This user can perform the administrative tasks of each application, that is, s/he will be the real user of the application. EDVI will allow s/he to manage the information about courses and statistics. In the case of Digital Rights Managament s/he will be the user in charge of all tasks related to the creation of digital rights, offers, permissions and their management and modification. Finally s/he will manage information about clients and students; whilst add the means of payment in the clients application so that they can make the payments with the Payments application.

3.3.5 Limited User

This user will have the possibility of obtaining some limited information in the different applications, but s/he can neither modify nor add new data under any circumstance.

4 Conclusions

The carried study on the e-learning issue shows that there are several standards to facilitate the interoperability among the different applications and educational materials nowadays. In this way, the e-learning technology acquires a great power and it is increasingly used by the educational organizations.

It is important to reflect on several issues after the finalization of the project, such as:

- **Scope:** this project has been developed with the main idea of creating a prototype to determine the bases of the e-learning process and the learning object from an economic point of view. Therefore it could have repercussions on future developments of systems that manage the whole environment, including education.
- **Possible improvements:** Indeed, the application would have a more secure appearance if it would have a digital signed certificate from a certifying entity.
  In addition it should be considered an improvement for the integration of the applications for a greater system optimization. It could be developed an application integrating all the others, or unify Digital Rights Management, Payments and Means of Payment in the same application.
- **Acquired knowledge:** Once finalized the project there are technologies on which we have acquired new knowledge: XML, JSP, SSL, Hibernate and Servers.

References

1. Open Digital Rights Language, `http://www.odrl.net/`
2. Liu, Q., Safavi-Naini, R., Sheppard, N.P.: Digital Rights Management for Content Distribution, UOW, Wollongong (2003)
3. Binemann-Zdanowicz, A., Schulz-Brünken, B., Tschiedel, B., Thalheim, B.: Flexible e-Payment for Adaptive Content in the e-Learning System DaMiT, BTU Cottbus, Cottbus (2003)
4. IMS Global Learning Consortium Inc., `http://www.imsglobal.org/`
5. IEEE, Draft Stadard for Learning Object Metadata(February 16, 2005), `http://ltsc.ieee.org/doc/wg12/LOM_1484_12_1_v1_Final_Draft.pdf` (retrieved)
6. Bourda, Y., Hilier, M.: What Metadata and XML can do for Learning Objects. WebNet Journal: Internet Technologies, Applications & Issues (2000)
7. SCORM, SCORM Concepts (2005), `http://www.eduworks.com/LOTT/tutorial/index.html`
8. Downes, S., Mourad, M., Piccariello, H., Robson, R.: Digital Rights Management in E-learning Problem Statement and Terms of Reference. National Research Council, Canada (2003)

Knowledge Services for Knowledge Workers

Dehua Ju[1] and Beijun Shen[2]

[1] Application Solutions & Technologies, Inc. (ASTI), Shanghai 200233, China
asti-gm@online.sh.cn
[2] Shanghai Jiaotong University, Shanghai 200240, China
bjshen@sjtu.edu.cn

Abstract. Knowledge services have been proposed in this paper as a main component and measure in the knowledge society to promote the professional development of knowledge workers and improve their productivity. The basic design principles of knowledge services are discussed to integrate advantages of modern learning systems. A 5 layer design framework is proposed for developing the knowledge service platform to maximize the value of knowledge services. The prototype project has being started to build the Public Knowledge Service Platform (PKSP) to meet the urgent needs of talents development in China and progress is reported. The novel features of the proposed solution are given in the conclusion.

Keywords: Knowledge Service, Knowledge Workers, BOK-based, On-the-Job Learning, Learning On-Demand, Community of Practice.

1 Introduction

Peter F. Drucker said: "The primary resource in post-capitalist society will be knowledge, and the leading special groups will be "knowledge workers." [1] "The most important contribution management needs to make in the 21st Century is similarly to increase the productivity of KNOWLEDGE WORK and the KNOWLEDGE WORKER."[2] and "The performance of an individual, an organization, an industry or a country in acquiring and applying knowledge will increasingly become the key competitive factor."

How to improve the productivity of the knowledge worker and maximize their value creation? A vital issue is how to build an effective infrastructure for promoting professional development and work of knowledge workers. Knowledge workers "are characterized by a high degree of professional knowledge, the foundations of which have normally been acquired through sound formal education processes. However, due to the ever increasing rate of development in applied knowledge most of their individual 'knowledge capital' needs to be developed and accumulated during their professional lives, through a constant, ongoing process of learning new knowledge and applying it as part of daily work.

Continuous innovation in all aspects is characteristic of the knowledge society. This puts three demands to citizens and workers: lifelong learning, knowledge development and knowledge sharing. In the knowledge society learning is a continuous process:

M.D. Lytras et al. (Eds.): WSKS 2010, Part I, CCIS 111, pp. 51–59, 2010.

learning is lifelong learning. Knowledge work requires continuous learning still further while seeing exponential growth of knowledge in a knowledge society. The knowledge worker should be a lifelong learner with high autonomy and capability in learning to learn (L2L). Learning all the knowledge available to us will not take place in the confines of the classrooms alone. Much of the learning that shall happen in the knowledge society shall happen outside of the formal classrooms. The infrastructure concerned refers to technology infrastructure in support of the learning and knowledge services that we must provide. It would be an ICT-enabled Lifelong Learning (LLL) system.

Class teaching is a prevailed traditional school education and training model. However, it is not the best model for lifelong learning because class teaching is essentially an one-direction pouring and 'teacher-centered' ('think as I do and do as I say') model for which all of learning contents are pre-defined by the teacher, not well meeting personalized needs of varied learners. For the knowledge worker, a shift is required from a teacher-centered to a learner-centered learning environment to provide learning on-demand (LOD) in the working context.

From traditional teaching/learning to knowledge services and active learning is a solution proposed in this paper.

2 Design Principles of Knowledge Services

'Knowledge Service' is proposed to provide an ideal ICT-enabled lifelong learning support environment for professional development of knowledge workers. Knowledge service is not a new concept which has many applications already in practice, for example, the NHS/UK's National Knowledge Service (NKS), ISI/UK Web of Knowledge, and World Bank's Knowledge Services for Developing Countries etc. However, here we regard it as a basic infrastructure of the knowledge society and a valuable component of modern service economy to turn knowledge into exploitable resource, asset or capital.

More important, knowledge is not only a resource/asset waiting for mining, but also an active service. Knowledge as a Service (KaaS) has being emerged as an interesting view in which we envision to construct a service platform that can send knowledge directly into brains of knowledge workers and they can utilize this stage to serve their knowledge for others or the society.

What are differences between the knowledge service system and traditional education/learning system? We will declare its basic design principles as follows:

2.1 Open Knowledge Model

Peter Senge said: "The world's knowledge belongs to the world." The open knowledge model targets at serving a much larger community and means:

- Open Access: free and equitable access with no or minimal cost. The more open and free access to knowledge and information in education and science is, the higher the chances for innovation in industry and commerce;

- Expandable Contents and Services: Knowledge is generated through a collective and can and should be dynamically changed and expanded over time. New domain knowledge is easily added in via a design of module-based structure;
- Open Ideas: no specific bias or favor in content selection to keep different viewpoints for user own comparison and judgment;
- Open Innovation through crowdsourcing.

2.2 Learner-Centered

- Domain-specific knowledge services devotes to professional development of knowledge workers;
- Comprehensive knowledge resources can meet personalized needs of varied knowledge workers to support learning on-demand (LOD);
- Application-oriented & Context-based Knowledge Acquisition: Adapting knowledge to the local context to provide Just-in-Case/ Just-in-Time/ Just-for-Me services for higher value creation.

2.3 Collaborative and Participatory

- Support knowledge share and transfer;
- Promote building of Community of Practice (CoP) for collaborative learning and working to achieve the shared vision;
- A participatory and high interactive platform for which knowledge workers act as both knowledge consumers and contributors for co-creation with best utilizing existing resources;
- A collaborative environment and Climate are beneficial to knowledge flow.

2.4 ICT-Enabled

- Enact e-Knowledge, based on digitalize and networked technologies;
- Single point of access for one-stop service via virtual connection of knowledge network;
- Provide 5A Services: Anytime, Anywhere, Anything, Anyway and Any pace;
- Intelligent Support;
- Imitate Learning 2.0 supported by Web 2.0 technologies;
- Computer-Supported Collaborative Learning and Work (CSCL/CSCW).

Bill Gates said: "The single most important use of information technology is to improve education."Based on these principle and ideas, we will put forward a design framework for Knowledge Service Platform in the next section.

3 Design Framework of Knowledge Services Platform

We have proposed a design framework for the knowledge service platform, as shown in Fig. 1:

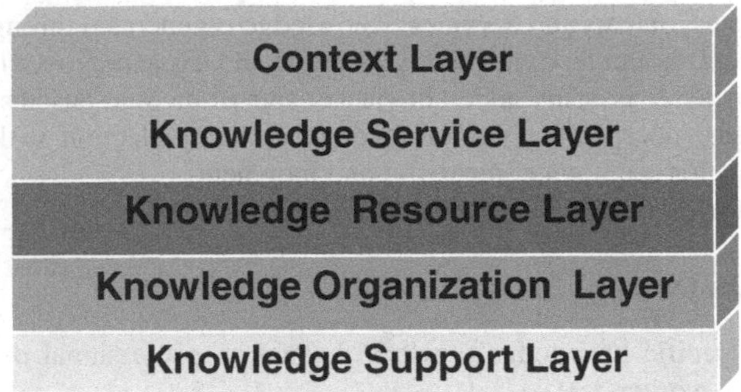

Fig. 1. 5-Layer Framework

3.1 Knowledge Support Layer

The focal point in knowledge services is its contents design. As an authoritative knowledge source, its development must have robust backup expertise to cover enough broad spectrum and degree of depth in its knowledge resources. Therefore, in the knowledge support layer, it must have the participation of domain experts, either direct or indirect. One solution suggested for that purpose is to fully apply available Body of Knowledge of related domains (BOKs) and standards (international and industry) as a scientific guide in collecting knowledge resources.

In addition, a dedicated professional team, called 'Professional Knowledge Service Workers' (PKSW), for knowledge services is a must. The PKSW is also a kind of knowledge workers whose responsibilities are to discover, collect, organize, disseminate, and update knowledge resources and provide best knowledge services for other knowledge workers.

In this layer, it adheres to the open and collaborative principle as well, including participation of third-party knowledge service providers (KSP) and active knowledge workers. Besides the 'Pull' efforts of the own PKSW team, a 'Push-in' strategy from KSPs is more welcome.

3.2 Knowledge Organization Layer

Professional knowledge is systematic and high interrelated, forming an organic collection. Unorganized and scattered information cannot embody the value of knowledge. In view that, we adopt a BOK-based strategy, in the knowledge organization layer, to organize the knowledge resources into a higher order with value-added as the BOK is defined by the domain experts, that specify what knowledge and skills should be mastered by professionals in the specific domain. This approach is also helpful for professional development of knowledge workers who are domain-specific, a promotion towards HR professionalism, internationalization and standardization.

It's PKSW's job to search, collect and compile the domain specific BOKs and standards. Domain Experts can add emerging BOKs or new versions, a 'Push' model. The layer is open for dynamic update of BOKs, including incorporation of new technologies, applications and recommended best practices etc. as time going on.

3.3 Knowledge Resource Layer

It is a centralized knowledge resources repository collected by PKSWs based on related BOKs. It's mainly a virtual repository, rather than physical, in which the resources are located by associated URLs. Therefore, it is easily to be expanded without demanding large storage, a distributed solution. Recommend resources can be 'Push' in by KSP, knowledge workers, CoPs, related organizations etc. The value of resources can be assessed by their calling rate and feedback from learners.

BOK-based resources deployment brings about a domain-oriented and module-based structure as well as an ontology-based one which is readily expandable and useful for supporting professional development of knowledge workers.

3.4 Knowledge Service Layer

Five main service functions identified so far in this layer, also called as 'five centers' they are:

(1) Technology Transfer Center;
(2) e-Learning Center;
(3) Knowledge Resources Center;
(4) Consulting Center;
(5) Community Center.

The technology transfer center is used to inform latest technical progress and reflect the leading-edge technology to knowledge workers. It can be an active 'Push' model based on the observation on the interesting areas of knowledge workers. Domain-specific PKSW is assigned for information tracking and search. A participatory information network is also useful here.

The e-Learning center collects and reuses existing knowledge assets developed to be shared over a more wide scope. Although they still are in old learning model, it's useful as a quick entry or area roadmap for most new comers.

The knowledge resources center is very similar to the web of knowledge, a centralized knowledge resources repository based on BOKs-based collections. Guided by the interested BOK, learners can clearly know what knowledge gap they have and easily access what knowledge points/areas he/she wants to know. The resources repository provides one-stop services just simply via a browser. Its user likes entering a specialized reading room with very rich collections and can learn anything what he/she wants. We refer this function as "A Learning Paradise" for knowledge workers. All these resources will help users to fulfill a 'self-paced' learning with on-demand knowledge acquisition.

The consulting center has capability to provide so-called 'On-The-Job Learning' or 'Contextual Learning', a more interesting and valuable learning platform – a new direction of next-generation learning environment. Learn while working / learn by doing, learn for better job will be very attractive to all enterprises as it can provide performance support either. Learning for Use and Use after Learning will bring about high-motivation learning and help much deeper grasp. For veterans, it can review what has been learned and learn something new. For new comers, it would be a new model and tool for internship. It looks like that a teacher, expert, master or knowledge base always accompanying you, providing online and real-time assistance.

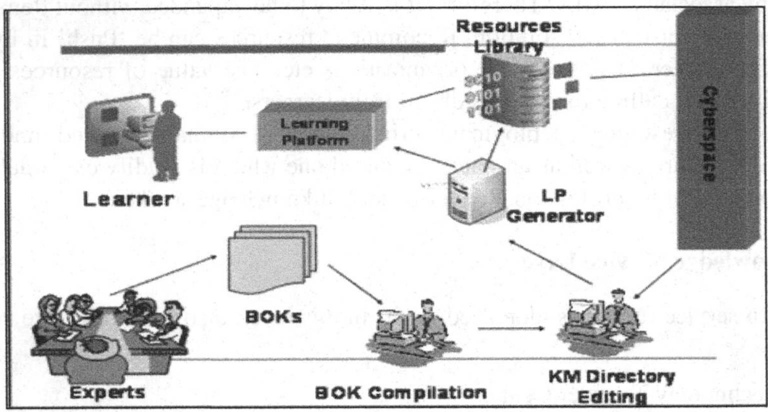

Fig. 2. OJL Platform Development Process

The Figure 2 shows a development process of the new learning platform in which you can find the related BOK will also act an important role that ensure the knowledge collected can fully cover all key points in the domain workflow and the keywords presented in all knowledge points will help for an ontology -based search.

This OJL platform has all advantages of contextual learning systems. More important is that it can promote the construction of Community of Inquiry, especially the Community of Practice (CoP) – to formulate a community center.

It is really an open system and community. After wide trail by thousands users, the drawbacks and problems of applied systems can be fully exposed and new solutions and improvements can continued. Even in the case of no satisfied answer from the system, the requester still can call for a 'SOS' help via internet from other CoP members, including e-mentors/e-coaches as well as peer practitioners. In fact, the platform has accomplished three virtual links within same CoP: A link to leading experts in CoP through the domain BOK development; a link to worldwide experienced CoP members during collecting knowledge resources written by them; and a physical link to active CoP members for peer cooperation while involving in an idea and experience exchange.

This platform will be a participatory web supported by web 2.0 technology, facilitating knowledge and experiences sharing and promoting collaborative learning and working (CSCL/CSCW). Each member is not only a learner, but also a contributor which will recommend new knowledge contents and experiences as well as the feedback for system improvement. The emerging new technologies and applications will dynamically expand the related BOKs. All these will enhance and perfect the collective knowledge repository at the end.

In the user's viewpoint, the platform is a web of knowledge to meet the needs of their knowledge work (Fig. 3).

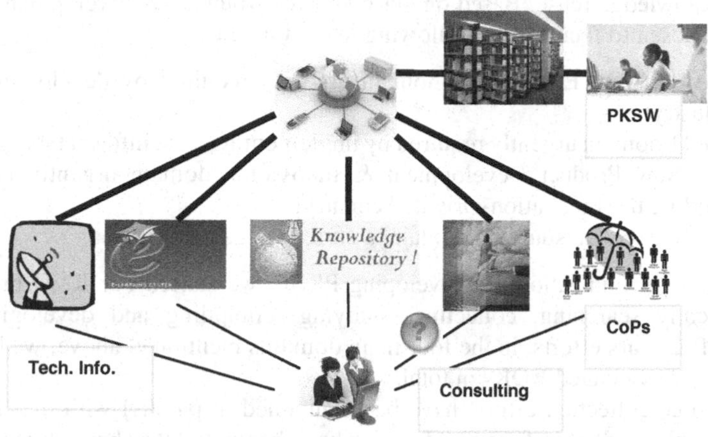

Fig. 3. Knowledge Service Platform

3.5 Context Layer

The domain-based knowledge services can be used at many levels, including

- Individual knowledge workers for their professional role & career development and workplace support with application context, also useful for development of interdisciplinary talents;
- CoP/CoI level for collaborative learning and work with common vision;
- Organization/Enterprise level for building learning organization and organizational learning. To do so, a specific sub-KS platform can be constructed based on their business objectives and competence gap analysis;
- Industry level for providing knowledge services in a specific domain based on same design framework;
- National or regional level, for which a 'public knowledge service platform' (PKSP) will be established to be shared a much large scope. Even knowledge service platforms for different domains can be distributed over many places for convenience. It can still look like a centralized platform via virtual links among knowledge service networks if they are based on same design framework.

4 Prototype Systems Being Developed

The development of knowledge service platforms is massive system engineering. Facing with high pressing of professional talents shortage in China, we tried to find an alternative solution beyond formal schooling education only. A prototype project was initialed to develop prototype knowledge service systems as our conceptual experiment and validation.

The key for KaaS is having knowledge at the time of maximum opportunity. Thus, the priority in our development is put on what demanded most from society development. The target is to build the public knowledge service platform (PKSP) for higher value of knowledge reuse. Based on our own background, our development in PKSPs has been chosen to focus on the following main domains:

- The Software Engineering domain urgently required by developing software industry;
- The IT domain urgently required by implementing state informatization strategy;
- The New Product Development & Innovation domain urgently required by building the Innovation-Oriented country;
- The Service Outsourcing domain, a current hot spot in China.

To gain a solid foundation for developing PKSP, we started our R&D project from systematically searching, collecting, studying, compiling and developing related BOKs. After years efforts, in the four main domains mentioned above, we have so far gathered 132 associated BOKs in total.

A resource collection efforts have been launched in parallel with the 'first things first' principle. A dozen of special domains have begun to take sharp already, such as:

- SE domain: Software Architecture, Requirements Engineering, Project Management, Quality Management, Software Testing, SWEBOK and SSMED;
- IT domain: ITSM/ITIL, Information Security;
- Innovation domain: New Product Development, Innovation Methods, Knowledge Management;
- Service Outsourcing domain: OPBOK, SSMED, ISTQB, SQuBOK.

Besides these resources, we have also developed abundant training materials in our e-Learning center for three domains mentioned above, including 226 e-learning modules with 59904 .ppt pages – a valuable knowledge asset for learners as an entry shortcut.

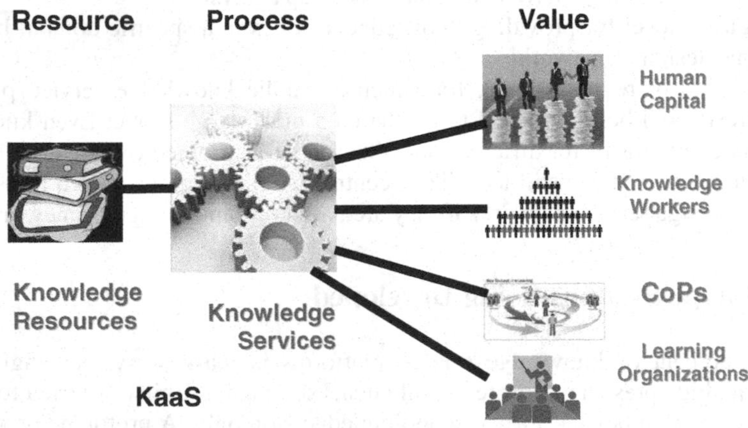

Fig. 4. Knowledge Services in Knowledge Society

5 Conclusions

Knowledge service is looked as a key component and essential infrastructure of knowledge society, which can be used as an effective measure to promote professional development of knowledge workers and improve their productivity.

By applying the RPV Innovation Theory [3] to the knowledge society (Fig.4), the knowledge services can be looked as an IT enabled process which transforms knowledge resources into real value in knowledge society, including human capital, knowledge worker productivity, bridging knowledge divides [5], building of CoPs and learning organizations, causing continuous innovation and sustainable economic growth in the knowledge society.

In this paper, we described the design principles of knowledge services to integrate the advantages of emerging modern learning new concepts and technologies. A 5 -layers design framework for knowledge service platform is proposed to embody a '5C' combination of e-Knowledge, i.e. Content, Context, Community, Connection and Computer-supported Collaboration, which greatly enhances the value of knowledge services.

The main philosophy behind our knowledge services is very simple, that is: Send knowledge into everybody's hands; as a knowledge charger; your knowledge is mine! It provides an open, low cost, ubiquitous, easily accessible lifelong learning support environment for HRD urgently needed, to enable personalized learning on-demand.

Some prototype systems have being developed, aiming at building the Public Knowledge Service Platform for knowledge workers in SE, IT, Outsourcing and Innovation domains. Significant progress has been accomplished in collecting knowledge resources and related BOKs developed. This work would be more meaningful while digital competence is a general key for future knowledge workers as declared by the European Commission [6]. The PKSPs proposed with comprehensive resources will like a stretch of fertile land with rich knowledge nourishment to speed up the growth and mature of knowledge workers.

References

1. Drucker, P.: Post-capitalist Society. Harper Business, New York (1993)
2. Drucker, P.: Management Challenges for the 21st Century, p. 135. Butterworth-Heinemann, Oxford (2009)
3. Christensen, C.: The Innovator's Dilemma. Harvard Business School Press, Boston (1997)
4. Christensen, C.M., Anthony, A.D., Roth, E.A.: Seeing What's Next. Harvard Business School Press, Boston (2004)
5. Pant, L.P.: Learning networks for bridging knowledge divides in international development: aligning approaches and initiatives (2009), http://wiki.ikmemergent.net/files/090817-ikm-working-paper-4-learning-networks-for-bridging-knowledge-divides.pdf
6. Punie, Y., Cabrera, M.: The Future of ICT and Learning in the Knowledge Society (2005), http://ftp.jrc.es/EURdoc/eur22218en.pdf

Towards an Ontology for the Description of Learning Resources on Disaster Risk Reduction

Thomas Zschocke[1] and Juan Carlos Villagrán de León[2]

[1] United Nations University (UNU-EHS), UN Campus, Hermann-Ehlers-Str. 10, 53113 Bonn, Germany
zschocke@ehs.unu.edu

[2] United Nations Office for Outer Space Affairs (UNOOSA), Vienna International Centre, E-09 72, P.O. Box 500, 1400 Vienna, Austria
juan-carlos.villagran@unoosa.org

Abstract. One of the priority areas of the Hyogo Framework for Action 2005-2015 for disaster risk reduction is the use of knowledge, innovation and education to build a culture of safety and resilience at all levels. The collection, compilation and dissemination of relevant information and knowledge on disaster risks and to cope with such risks are critical to inform and educate individuals as a basis on which to establish a culture of disaster prevention and resilience. However, in many cases these resources are scattered over multiple repositories in different places and lack a common, shared framework for their description to improve the search and retrieval process. This research intends to contribute to the Hyogo Framework of Action by building a domain ontology on disaster risk reduction for education. The goal is to provide semantically enriched descriptions of learning resources for the use in training curricula and learning programs. The ontology builds on the terminology of disaster risk reduction, published by the United Nations International Strategy for Disaster Reduction (UN/ISDR) in 2009. It extends the terminology by reusing other relevant ontology sources and incorporating the knowledge of subject matter experts.

Keywords: Disaster risk reduction, ontology, semantic web, education, learning repositories.

1 Introduction

The international community has continuously emphasized that improved management of natural hazards and the integration of disaster risk reduction (DRR) are critical elements of policies for sustainable development. The United Nations General Assembly had designated the 1990s as the International Decade for Natural Disaster Reduction (IDNDR) [1] in order to establish international actions to reduce the loss of life, property damage and social and economic disruption caused by natural hazards. The supporting Yokohama Strategy for a Safer World [2] highlights the importance to exchange information on natural disaster reduction, strengthen capacities as well as provide education and training in disaster

M.D. Lytras et al. (Eds.): WSKS 2010, Part I, CCIS 111, pp. 60–74, 2010.

prevention, preparedness and mitigation. In 2000, the International Strategy for Disaster Reduction (ISDR) [3] was adopted as a successor arrangement to the IDNDR. The corresponding Hyogo Framework for Action 2005-2015 (HFA) [4] reiterates the need for informing and motivating people towards a culture of disaster prevention and resilience through the use of knowledge, innovation and education in order to reduce disasters as the goal of one of the five priorities for action. This particular priority includes two groups of key activities that are of special importance in the context of this paper, that is, (1) information management and exchange, and (2) education and training. Among others, the HFA suggests to develop directories, inventories and information-sharing systems and services for the exchange of information on good practices, DRR technologies, and lessons learned on policies, plans and measures for DRR. This not only implies the collection, compilation and dissemination of relevant knowledge and information on hazards, vulnerabilities and capacities, but also the capturing and sharing of relevant learning resources in digital repositories to enhance the education and training in DRR at all levels.

An accompanying guide to the HFA by the United Nations Secretariat of the International Strategy for Disaster Reduction (UN/ISDR) [5] suggests that the identification, compilation and dissemination of information and knowledge about natural hazards, disaster management and risk reduction needs to be improved. One of the steps is to create a detailed inventory of existing information that can and should be made public. In a corresponding website, PreventionWeb [6], UN/ISDR makes available reports, policy and technical guidance to support the implementation of the HFA. UN/ISDR also launched the Field Library for Disaster Reduction initiative [7], which contains about one hundred books and journals on disaster-related subjects, which have been distributed to many developing countries affected by natural disasters. The Regional Disaster Information Center (CRID) [8] in Latin America and the Caribbean is a good example of a virtual library in this context that also provides free access to many electronic documents on DRR that are relevant to a particular region.

On a global level, the NatCatSERVICE [9] of the Munich Re Group is one of the world's leading databases for natural catastrophes. The Centre for Research on the Epidemiology of Disasters (CRED) maintains similar information in its international disaster database EM-DAT [10]. The Global Risk Identification Programme (GRIP) [11] is an example of a multi-stakeholder initiative that provides data and information on risk identification, assessment and monitoring. Together, CRED and GRIP maintain DisDat [12], a Web portal to collect information on disaster data collection initiatives worldwide. More hazard-specific information is provided on specialized websites, for instance, the International Tsunami Information Centre [13], the Jakarta Tsunami Information Centre [14], both administered by the United Nations Educational, Scientific and Cultural Organization (UNESCO), or the ASEAN Earthquake Information Center [15].

In the area of capacity development, the Capacity for Disaster Reduction Initiative (CADRI) [16] was launched in 2007 as a joint programme of the United Nations Development Programme (UNDP), the United Nations Office for the

Coordination of Humanitarian Affairs (UNOCHA), and the UN/ISDR Secretariat. CADRI succeeded the United Nations Disaster Management Training Programme (DMTP), a global learning platform that addressed crises, emergencies and disasters for the UN Member States, the UN system, donors and international and non-governmental organizations, and trained United Nations, government and civil society professionals between 1991-2006. Noticing that capacity development is a cross-cutting activity for DRR, CADRI relates to all of the five priorities of the HFA. It serves the UN/ISDR system and engages with the wider professional communities working in capacity development.

Another example is the multi-stakeholder project on Emergency Capacity Building (ECB) [17], which maintains a Web portal with relevant documentation in an effort to improve the speed, quality and effectiveness of the humanitarian community in saving the lives, safeguarding the livelihoods and protecting the rights of people affected by emergencies. Similar to this, UNOCHA maintains a website on a disaster response preparedness toolkit [18]. The site is dedicated to essential and practical information, checklists, guides, presentations and other tools to assist UNOCHA staff and its partners to prepare for disaster situations.

While critical data and information on natural disasters and hazards are provided on various specialized websites on international, regional and national levels, such a comprehensive service does not exist for learning resources on DRR. Although many of the specialized natural disaster websites also include sections dedicated to education and training in DRR, they are not easy to navigate or even to locate. Often these sites do not provide an appropriate mechanism to enhance the search and retrieval of learning resources, which makes it difficult to find them. For instance, CADRI makes available on its website the extensive set of training manuals that were produced as part of DMTP, but does not provide any functionality to search through the material. Generally, what is also lacking are semantically enhanced educational metadata, which would allow end users to more easily retrieve the materials and incorporate them into the teaching and learning process. For example, PreventionWeb makes accessible a large set of educational materials on DRR, but only provides very limited browse functionalities with just a small set of generic metadata.

Still lacking is a central repository where comprehensive information about DRR learning resources is captured and semantically enriched through educational metadata. The joint activity between UNU-EHS and UNOOSA/UN-SPIDER as presented in this paper tries to address this issue by working towards establishing a clearinghouse for learning resources on DRR. This initiative contributes to one of the measures of the strategic plan of the United Nations University (UNU) to serve as a key international clearinghouse for e-learning on sustainability [19]. In the context of UN-SPIDER, this initiative will be an essential pillar in facilitating efforts along the lines of capacity development as documented in its Capacity Building Strategy [20]. In this context, this paper examines the development of an ontology that captures domain-specific knowledge for the description of learning resources on DRR. For the purpose of this research, an upper ontology on DRR is being defined along with associated lower ontology concepts and relations to enrich the description of learning resources on DRR.

The paper is structured as follows. In Section 2 we discuss some of the issues of using semantic-aware applications to enhance knowledge sharing in the area of disaster risk and education. Section 3 describes the preliminary steps taken to create a domain ontology for describing learning resources on DRR. In Section 4, we draw some preliminary conclusions and present an outlook of future work.

2 Enhanced Knowledge Sharing with Ontologies

When the seminal article about the Semantic Web was published in 2001 [21] the authors envisioned an extension of the current Web that would facilitate the closer cooperation of computers and users by providing well-defined meaning to actionable information. The main enabling technologies for developing the Semantic Web are the eXtensible Markup Language (XML), the Resource Description Framework (RDF), and ontologies. The latter furnish the semantics of the Semantic Web and should be developed, managed, and endorsed by communities of practice. However, the meaning of terms and their relations are not fixed, and change over time. Although these communities of practice alter norms, conceptualizations, and terminologies, they also advance necessary new concept definitions that can be used in a changing context [22].

An ontology is a shared understanding in a given subject area [23]. It entails some sort of a world view of a community of practice with respect to a given domain as a unifying framework to solve a particular problem. In general, a body of formally represented knowledge is based on a conceptualization, that is, a set of concepts, their definitions and inter-relationships. Ontologies, thus, are the explicit specification of a conceptualization [24]. An ontology is basically an artifact or model of (some aspect of) the world. It introduces vocabulary capturing the various aspects of the domain and provides explicit specification of the intended meaning of that vocabulary [25]. Basically, ontologies constitute content theories in that they identify a taxonomy of specific classes of objects, the relations among them, and a set of inference rules. As such they form the core of any system of knowledge representation for a particular domain [26].

2.1 Ontologies on Disaster and Risk

Although experts on disaster mitigation and planning and risk management constitute a community of practice, there appears to be no common conceptualization of their domain because of the interdisciplinary approach to the multifaceted nature of disaster mitigation, disaster planning, and DRR. For instance, a glossary about the core terminology of disaster preparedness and reduction developed by UNU-EHS [27] revealed that a shared language and shared concepts on disaster and risk do not exist. On the contrary, what eventually is needed are a common terminology and definitions, which are a prerequisite for integrated approaches for improved disaster reduction by experts from different disciplines and competencies.

Research on natural hazards was initially conducted by geographers who viewed natural disasters as the result of interacting natural and underlying social processes as illustrated in the Pressure and Release (PAR) model on the progression of vulnerability [28], or the framework for the expanded vulnerability analysis in coupled human-environment systems [29]. While the use of ontologies in the geosciences is well advanced and documented [30], ontologies for disaster and risk are only slowly devloping. NASA's Semantic Web for Earth and Environmental Terminology (SWEET) [31] is an example of an extended set of ontologies in the geosciences. The hydrogeology ontology, for instance, has been developed as an extension of the SWEET upper-level ontologies [32].

An example of an ontology at the cross-section of geosciences and disaster management is a system for ontology-based searches for information sources on disturbances and the susceptibility in an ecosystem, e.g., storm hazards [33]. Another example for the management of natural disasters is the description logic model developed for a municipal flood protection plan [34]. The data model includes an event library and predefined disaster situations, which can be mapped to the corresponding situation concept in the situation taxonomy through inference. Similar to this model, the approach to support incident management based on disaster plans [35] allows for the specification and analysis of different scenarios of organizational behavior based on the formal structural description from a disaster plan. The conceptual model of disasters affecting critical infrastructure [36] extends the incident management approach [35] by adding the elements of the physical infrastructure that can be affected by a disaster. Similar to [36] the proposed Disaster Management Data Model [37] incorporates information about the physical environment as a foundation for a spatial reasoning process that considers topology, neighborhood relations, orientation as well as distance aspects.

The scalable semantic framework for disaster mitigation and planning using ontologies is another example of an integrated approach to provide ubiquitous, standard, and reusable domain descriptions that can be processed by different hazard analysis and disaster preparedness tools [38]. Recently, a factual ontology of risk and disaster has been proposed, which consists of four sub-systems, that is, structure, dynamics, characterization, and actor, where the latter helps to specify how different actors can characterize the system's structure and dynamics [39], [40].

Related to this work is the Simple Emergency Alerts for All (SEMA4A) ontology for emergency notification systems accessibility [41]. SEMA4A has been designed to enhance the communication of emergencies and corresponding critical information to various groups of users within different emergency situations using multiple communication media. Another approach to emergency response is an ontology-driven knowledge sharing and application of the tasks involved in the area of production network management to decision-making in disaster response operations [41]. Connected to these applications is the Common Alerting Protocol (CAP) from the Organization for the Advancement of Structured Information Standards (OASIS) [42]. This protocol provides an interchange format for collecting and distributing "all-hazard" safety notifications and emergency warnings over information networks and public alerting systems. Finally, the ontology-based risk management framework for the construction industry is an example of using an ontology as a means for enhancing the risk management workflow of identifying, analyzing and responding to possible risks in the life cycle of a construction project [43].

2.2 Ontologies for Educational Purposes

It is generally agreed that semantic-aware applications have great potentials in education in the medium future [45]. They provide mechanisms to enhance the process of searching and finding learning resources. And, they have the capability to organize and display information that make it easier for learners to draw connections, for instance, by visualizing relationships among concepts and ideas.

Ontologies as indicated earlier represent consensual knowledge representations of communities of practice in a particular domain or discipline. They allow to manage the growing volume of data and information by annotating these resources and providing automated mechanisms to support the acquisition, maintenance, and access of usually weakly structured information sources [46]. Consequently, this notion of ontologies equally applies to semantically enriched learning resources in terms of ontology-based annotations of learning objects [47]. This integration of the design and description of learning objects through specialized ontologies for describing the corresponding educational metadata would actually require separate ontologies, addressing the needs of the authors in the knowledge creation process on the one hand and the learners in the actual learning process on the other [48].

The principle of making formal annotations of learning resources based on ontologies has been applied in the Organic.Edunet Web portal [49]. This website provides access to a federation of several learning repositories that have resources related to the general topic areas of organic agriculture and agroecology. Organic.Edunet uses the electronic portfolio system Confolio [50], which provides a folder-based portfolio view for managing and annotating learning objects [51], [52]. The annotation of learning resources with an ontology derived from a set of existing controlled vocabulary for agriculture has been applied in the context of Organic.Edunet based on the AGROVOC thesaurus [53] of the United Nations Food and Agriculture Organization (FAO) [54], [55]. Because of the high degree of consensus in the agricultural community regarding its terminology, the formal representation of knowledge in the AGROVOC thesaurus was transformed into an ontology language for describing the learning resources contained in the Organic.Edunet Web portal.

The AquaRing (Accessible and Qualified Use of Available digital Resources about the aquatic world in National Gatherings) Web portal [56] is another example about the use of an ontology for the annotation and improved retrieval of learning resources, in this case on marine and aquatic topics [57]. Its terminology also contains terms from AGROVOC. An ontology-based approach has also been applied to enhance the design and development of training materials on sustainable development [58]. Here, this approach has been used to record domain concepts and their interrelationship from experts in the ontology, which in turn is linked by the learning content authors with the corresponding multimedia materials in the system to create educational scenarios within ontology-based knowledge networks for training.

As the examples show, Semantic Web technology can help to greatly enhance the semantic querying and the conceptual navigation of learning materials by linking learning resources to commonly agreed ontologies, providing flexible access to the knowledge base, and offering a uniform platform to integrate learning activities into the business processes of organizations [59]. In an educational context, learning ontologies do not only consist of descriptions of the basic concepts of a domain in which learning takes place, but can also be distinguished further in ontologies that address educational issues such as classifying the type of material into lecture, tutorial, exercise, etc., as well as those that describe the structure of the learning resources in terms of hierarchical and navigational relations. To conclude, the Semantic Web assists not only learners in locating, accessing, querying, processing, and assessing learning materials across a distributed network, but also instructors in generating, locating, using, reusing, sharing and exchanging learning resources [60].

Despite the encouraging prospects of using Semantic Web technologies in education, we are not aware of any reports on similar developments in using semantically enriched annotations of learning resources for education on DRR. The next section describes the first steps towards creating a solution to resolve this issue.

3 Constructing a Domain Ontology for DRR Learning Resources

It is generally accepted that domain ontologies can help to improve knowledge management practices within organizations. Ontology can significantly enhance these practices when a specific knowledge perspective, or "knowledge lens" is applied [61]. Based on this perspective controlled vocabulary is extracted and, through a top-down and bottom-up perspective, the conceptual model is developed by applying relationships, attributes, and axioms. These two perspectives in semantic collaboration involve the design of a common ontology from shared core concepts by reaching a consensus among all participating stakeholders (top-down), and a conceptual calibration of similarities and differences between existing conceptual models of the participating stakeholders (bottom-up). The goal is to create semantic mappings or ontological bridges between the different perspectives by coming to an agreement on (1) shared views, (2) opposite views, and (3) documenting the first two points in a way that a consensus can be reached [62].

The issue of reaching a consensus when developing an ontology is even more important in the field of DRR not only because of the need for an interdisciplinary approach when dealing with natural disasters, but also because of the international context of the authors' work in developing countries. This is also illustrated in the comparative glossary on the components of risk [27], which shows that there are various conceptualizations of the key terms in this field.

As has been commented, there is a vast amount of information on DRR hosted in a variety of websites and portals. However, searching for such information is not yet an efficient process. The lack of a consensus on definitions for terms, and the use of different terms by different agencies to target the same concept are critical issues that make it difficult to search efficiently through standard search engines. The next critical issue to recognize is the fact that different institutions and experts may disagree on how some terms are related. For example, some experts define risk as the combination of hazard and vulnerability, while others may also include coping capacities or exposure in the definition. As a consequence, the learning process in this field is best conducted through a case-based learning approach, where learners view specific examples which make use of one set of terms and their meanings in real world scenarios [63], [64].

Various websites exist independently to share learning resources and other related technical documentation on reducing the risk of natural disasters. Each system uses its own approach to describe and make available these resources. It is desirable to integrate these systems in such a way that users can more easily locate and retrieve the required information. However, the different ways of describing and presenting the resources are a barrier not only for learners and instructors, but also in terms of the interoperability of the different systems. The solution is to build a semantic Infrastructure that supports a federation of learning repositories on DRR. This requires the capturing of key underlying concepts, define them, assign terms to them and note their important interrelationships. A unifying framework of this kind would help to facilitate increased knowledge sharing between users and improved interoperability between separate repositories.

The purpose of the proposed DRR learning resources ontology is to describe the components of DRR in terms of the feature classes of natural disasters and the types of processes involved in the risk management cycle with the intention of facilitating increased sharing and reuse of learning resources through semantically enriched descriptions and improved interoperability between different repositories by enabling the exchange of federated search queries and the harvesting of metadata. Technological or human-induced disasters will not be included.

The intended users are learners and instructors in the fields of work of our organizations, that is, higher education and technical training on disaster risk management. The goal is to use the ontology about DRR when semantically enriched information is needed in teaching and learning about managing the risk of natural disasters. Although the focus is on higher education and technical training of mid-career professionals, we assume that the ontology could also be reused in other contexts in the educational system, for instance, K-12 schools, or in more specialized application areas, for example, remote sensing for disaster management and emergency response, which is the mandate of UNOOSA/UN-SPIDER.

The scope of the proposed DRR learning resources ontology is to describe the conceptual framework of and the main processes and activities involved in DRR to reduce the overall risk of natural disasters to a level of detail that identifies all such components and which are considered stable, being recognizable from one event to another. For instance, key concepts in the domain of DRR are `risk`, `hazard`, `disaster`, `vulnerability`, `resilience`. Concepts in the ontology are usually organized in taxonomies through which inheritance mechanisms can be applied. For example, we can represent a taxonomy of natural disasters, which distinguishes between different types of disasters (geophysical, meteorological, hydrological, climatological, biological, and extra-terrestrial), where an earthquake is a sub-class of geophysical disasters, a tsunami a sub-class of earthquake. Relations represent a type of association between concepts of the domain. For instance, the word `triggers` in "an earthquake triggers a tsunami" constitutes a binary relation. The ontology will also provide information about the elements and properties of the disaster risk management cycle, incorporating concepts, such as prevention, mitigation, preparedness, early warning, response, evacuation, relief, recovery, rehabilitation, reconstruction, among others.

The proposed DRR ontology will address the different classes of objects, relationships among them, including hierarchical relationships, and inference rules. Through this ontology, links can be established so that learners are able to identify the different meanings for particular terms, the typical connections among such terms, and visualize their connections in a simpler fashion. Furthermore, the ontology should allow learners and practitioners to navigate through the difficulty that has risen due to the lack of consensus. From the point of view of learning resources, it is expected that the semantically enhanced educational metadata contained in the ontology will facilitate the discovery of examples regarding how these terms are applied. This flexibility in the discovery of content would be essential in the context of a case-based learning approach targeting DRR as mentioned earlier.

In developing our ontology for the description of DRR learning resources we have adapted the steps in the method of Mizen et al. [65] in correspondence with Uschold's approach [23] and METHONTOLOGY [66], [67], [68]. We also consulted the summary overviews by Fernández-Lopez [69], [70], [71] and Antoniou and van Harmelen [59]. The level of formality of the ontology is semi-informal in that it is expressed in a restricted and structured form of natural language. In constructing the ontology we have consulted subject matter experts in the organizations of the authors and conducted informal text analysis of books, conceptual models, other controlled vocabularies and ontologies, etc. In building a complete glossary of terms we have captured concepts, instances, verbs, properties, for instance, through capturing and analyzing statements such like the following [28]:

"Risk of disaster is a compound function of the natural hazard and the number of people, characterised by their varying degrees of vulnerability to that specific hazard, who occupy the space and time of exposure to the hazard event." (p. 49)

"A disaster occurs when a significant number of vulnerable people experience a hazard and suffer severe damage and/or disruption of their livelihood system in such a way that recovery is unlikely without external aid." (p. 50)

During this knowledge elicitation process we also heavily relied on general and specialized glossaries and thesauri, such as the one from the UNU on risk components [27], the international glossaries on disaster risk of the United Nations [72] [73], the Australian emergency management terms thesaurus [74], but also the General Multilingual Environmental Thesaurus (GEMET) [75] or more hazard-specific glossaries, such as on tsunamis [76] or wildland fires [77]. We also consulted risk management terms from international [78], [79] and national standards [80]. And, we incorporated terms from the common accord on disaster category classification from CRED and Munich RE [81] and corresponding terms from the EM-DAT glossary [82].

We anticipate to break the ontology down into discrete modules in order to manage its complexity by reviewing and observing the relations and attributes of the conceptual aspects involved in the ontology. Each module of the ontology will be functionally an ontology in itself, describing a logical aspect of the entire domain for DRR. For instance, as indicated above it seems helpful to separate the conceptual frameworks of DRR into a domain knowledge class and the risk management processes with the corresponding analysis procedures into a task and method class.

In building the ontology we are using the Protégé system [83]. The ontology will be formally documented and expressed in RDF/OWL. In designing the ontology we follow the criteria from Gruber [24], that is, clarity, coherence, extendibility, minimal encoding bias, and minimal ontological commitment. The final ontology will be verified in terms of its correctness and validated by examples using existing materials in typical use scenarios of search and retrieval.

4 Conclusions and Future Work

Introducing ontology-based descriptions of DRR learning resources would certainly not come without a cost. Although ontology engineering research has developed mechanisms to translate and use learning object metadata into formal semantic descriptions, further tools for annotations and the integration of e-learning specifications with Semantic Web languages are needed. These measures should also be flanked by supporting organizational practices to facilitate the effective and consistent adoption of ontologies for educational purposes [48].

Ontologies for education not only provide an innovative way of browsing, navigating and searching for learning resources in a repository. They are also well suited to enhance the teaching and learning process itself by involving learners in a collaborative process of reviewing and constructing threshold concepts of a particular domain as it is especially the case in DRR [84]. We view the use of ontology-based descriptions of DRR learning resources within the novel concept of the "semantic learning organization" [85] "in which learning activities are mediated and enhanced through a kind of technology that provides a shared knowledge representation about the domain and context of the organization" (p. 406). Organizations responsible for disaster risk management would benefit from such an enhanced infrastructure where the corresponding educational metadata and specialized domain ontologies would not only describe relevant learning resources, but would also provide contextual information for linking to the organizational mission and goals as well as the required competencies in dealing with natural disasters.

Expanding on the notion of semantic (e-) learning "to build collaborations that exploit local contributions within a global vision" (p. 484) [86] we intend to extend the process of developing the ontology by involving more experts and possible users. We are currently setting up a Semantic MediaWiki installation [87], [87], a free extension of MediaWiki [89], to collect and review DRR terms by a wider group and encourage online distributed collaboration on capturing learning resources. Eventually, we hope to benefit from projects like Ogranic.Edunet [49] and establish a repository based on an environment such as Confolio [50] to provide semantically enriched learning about DRR globally.

References

1. UN: International Decade for Natural Disaster Reduction (A/44/236). United Nations, New York, NY (1989)
2. UN: Report of the Word Conference on Disaster Reduction, Yokohama, Japan, 23-27 May 1994 (A/CONF.172/9). United Nations, New York, NY (1994)
3. UN: International Decade for Natural Disaster Reduction: successor arrangements (A/RES/54/219). United Nations, New York, NY (2000)
4. UN: Report of the Word Conference on Disaster Reduction, Kobe, Hyogo, Japan, 18-22 January 2005 (A/CONF.206/6). United Nations, New York, NY (2005)
5. UN/ISDR: Words into action: A guide for implementing the Hyogo Framework. United Nations secretariat of the International Strategy for Disaster Reduction (UN/ISDR), Geneva, Switzerland (2007)
6. PreventionWeb, `http://www.preventionweb.net/`
7. UN/ISDR Field Library for Disaster Reduction, `http://www.unisdr.org/eng/library/field-lib/fl-introduction.htm`
8. Regional Disaster Information Center (CRID), `http://www.crid.or.cr/`
9. Munich RE NatCatSERVICE, `http://www.munichre.com/en/ts/geo_risks/natcatservice/default.aspx`
10. EM-DAT, The International Disaster Database, Centre for Research on the Epidemiology of Disasters (CRED), `http://www.emdat.be/`
11. Global Risk Identification Programme (GRIP), `http://www.gripweb.org/`
12. Disaster Data Portal (DisDat), `http://www.gripweb.org/grip.php?ido=18635122&lang=eng`
13. International Tsunami Information Centre, `http://ioc3.unesco.org/itic/`
14. Jakarta Tsunami Information Centre, `http://www.jtic.org/`
15. ASEAN Earthquake Information Center, `http://aeic.bmg.go.id/`
16. Capacity for Disaster Reduction Initiative (CADRI), `http://www.unisdr.org/cadri/`
17. Emergency Capacity Building (ECB) Project, `http://www.ecbproject.org/`

18. OCHA Disaster Response Preparedness Toolkit,
`http://ocha.unog.ch/drptoolkit/`
19. UNU: Strategic plan 2009–2012. Towards sustainable solutions for global problems. United Nations University (UNU), Tokyo, Japan (n.d. [2008]), `http://www.unu.edu/about/files/UNU_Strategic_Plan_2009-2012_en.pdf`
20. Committee on the Peaceful Uses of Outer Space of the United Nations (COPUOS): Capacity-building strategy of the United Nations Platform for Space-based Information for Disaster Management and Emergency Response (A/AC.105/947), United Nations, New York, NY (2009)
21. Berners-Lee, T., Hendler, J., Lassila, O.: The Semantic Web. Scientific American 284(5), 34–43 (2001)
22. Shadbolt, N., Hall, W., Berners-Lee, T.: The Semantic Web revisited. IEEE Intelligent Systems 21(3), 96–101 (2006)
23. Uschold, M., Gruninger, M.: Ontologies: Principles, methods and applications Knowledge Engineering Review 11 (2), pp. 93–136 (1996)
24. Gruber, T.R.: Toward principles for the design of ontologies used for knowledge sharing. International Journal of Human-Computer Studies 43(5-6), 907–928 (1995)
25. Horrocks, I.: Ontologies and the Semantic Web. Communications of the ACM 51(12), 58–67 (2008)
26. Chandrasekaran, B., Josephson, J.R., Benjamins, V.R.: What are ontologies, and why do we need them? IEEE Intelligent Systems 14(1), 20–26 (1999)
27. Thywissen, K.: Components of risk. A comparative glossary (SOURCE No. 2/2006). United Nations University (UNU-EHS), Bonn, Germany (2006), `http://www.ehs.unu.edu/file.php?id=118`
28. Wisner, B., Blaikie, P., Cannon, T., Davis, I.: At risk: Natural hazards, people's vulnerability and disasters, 2nd edn. Routledge, London (2004), `http://www.unisdr.org/eng/library/Literature/7235.pdf`
29. Turner II, B.L., et al.: A framework for vulnerability analysis in sustainability science. Proceedings of the National Academy of Sciences of the United States of America (PNAS) 100(4), 8074–8079 (2003), `http://www.pnas.org/content/100/14/8074.full`
30. Deliiska, B.: Thesaurus and domain ontology of geoinformatics. Transactions in GIS 11(4), 637–651 (2007)
31. NASA Semantic Web for Earth and Environmental Terminology (SWEET), `http://sweet.jpl.nasa.gov/`
32. Tripathi, A., Babaie, H.A.: Developing a modular hydrogeology ontology by extending the SWEET upper-level ontologies. Computers & Geosciences 34(9), 1022–1033 (2008)
33. Klien, E., Lutz, M., Kuhn, W.: Ontology-based discovery of geographic information services – An application in disaster management. Computers, Environment and Urban Systems 30(1), 102–123 (2006)
34. Grathwohl, M., de Bertrand de Beuvron, F., Rousselot, F.: A new application for description logics: Disaster management. In: International Workshop on Description Logics (1999)
35. Hoogendoorn, M., Jonker, C.M., Popova, V., Sharpanskykh, A.: Automated verification of disaster plans in incident management. Disaster Prevention and Management 17(1), 16–3 (2008)
36. Kruchten, P., Woo, C., Monu, K., Sotoodeh, M.: A human-centered conceptual model of disasters affecting critical infrastructures. In: 4th International Conference on Intelligent Human-Computer Systems for Crisis Response and Management, pp. 327–344 (2007)

37. Lucas, C., Werder, S.: Modeling spatial scenes in disaster domain ontologies. In: The International Archives of the International Society for Photogrammetry and Remote Sensing and Spatial Information Sciences, ISPRS Congress Beijing 2008. Part B4, Commission IV, vol. XXXVII, pp. 1091–1096 (2008)
38. Joshi, H., Seker, R., Bayrak, C., Ramaswamy, S., Connelly, J.B.: Ontology for disaster mitigation and planning. In: Proceeding of the 2007 Summer Computer Simulation Conference (SCSC), Article No. 26 (2006)
39. Provitolo, D., Müller, J.P., Dubos-Paillard, E.: Validation of an ontology of risk and disaster through a case study of the 1923 Great Kanto Earthquake. In: 3rd International Conference on Complex Systems and Applications (ICCSA 2009a), p. 11(2009), `http://litis.univ-lehavre.fr/ pigne/media-iccsa2009/data/ProvitoloMullerDubos.pdf`
40. Provitolo, D., Müller, J.P., Dubos-Paillard, E.: Vers une ontologie des risques et des catastrophe: le modèle conceptuel. In: XVI ème rencontres interdisciplinaires sur les systèmes complexes naturels et artificiels de Rochebrune (2009b), `http://gemas.msh-paris.fr/dphan/rochebrune09/papier/ProvitoloDamnienne.pdf`
41. Malizia, A., Onorati, T., Diaz, P., Aedo, I., Asorga-Paliza, F.: SEMA4A: An ontology for emergency notification systems accessibility. Expert Systems with Applications 37(4), 3380–3391 (2010)
42. Smirnov, A., Levashova, T., Pashkin, M., Shilov, N., Komarova, A.: Disaster response based on production network management tasks. Management Research News 30(11), 829–842 (2007)
43. Organization for the Advancement of Structured Information Standards (OASIS), Common Alerting Protocol (CAP), `http://www.oasis-emergency.org/cap`
44. Tserng, T.P., Yin, S.Y.L., Dzeng, R.J., Wou, B., Tsai, M.D., Chen, W.Y.: A study of ontology-based risk management framework of construction projects through project life cycle. Automation in Construction 18(7), 994–1008 (2009)
45. Johnson, L., Levine, A., Smith, R.: The 2009 Horizon report. The New Media Consortium, Austin, TX (2009)
46. Fensel, D.: Ontology-based knowledge management. IEEE Computer 35(11), 56–59 (2002)
47. García, E., Sicilia, M.-Á.: User interface tactics in ontology-based information seeking. PsychNology Journal 1(3), 242–255 (2003)
48. Sicilia, M.-Á., García-Barriocanal, E.: On the convergence of formal ontologies and standardized e-learning. International Journal of Distance Education Technologies 3(2), 13–29 (2005)
49. Organic.Edunet Web portal, `http://www.organicedunet.eu/`
50. Confolio, `http://www.confolio.org`
51. Ebner, H., Manouselis, N., Palmér, M., Enoksson, F., Palavitsinis, N., Kastrantas, K., Naeve, A.: Learning object annotation for agricultural learning repositories. In: 9th IEEE International Conference on Advanced Learning Technologies, pp. 438–442 (2009)
52. Manouselis, N., Carrión, J.S., Ebner, H., Palmér, M., Naeve, A.: A semantic infrastructure to support a federation of agricultural learning repositories. In: 8th IEEE International Conference on Advanced Learning Technologies, pp.117–119 (2008), `http://kmr.nada.kth.se/papers/SemanticWeb/OrganicEdunet_ICALT08.pdf`
53. FAO AGROVOC thesaurus, `http://aims.fao.org/agrovoc`
54. Sánchez-Alonso, S., Sicilia, M.-Á.: Using an AGROVOC-based ontology for the description of learning resources on organic agriculture. In: Sicilia, M.-Á., Lytras, M.D. (eds.) Metadata and Semantics, pp. 481–492. Springer, Heidelberg (2009)

55. Sánchez-Alonso, S.: Enhancing availability of learning resources on organic agriculture and agroecology. The Electronic Library 27(5), 792–813 (2009)
56. AquaRing (Accessible and Qualified Use of Available digital Resources about the aquatic world in National Gatherings) Web portal, http://www.aquaringweb.eu/
57. Bianchi, S., Mastrodonato, C., Vercelli, G., Vivanet, G.: Use of ontologies to annotate and retrieve educational contents: The AquaRing approach. Journal of e-Learning and Knowledge Society 5(1), 211–220 (2009), http://www.je-lks.it/en/09_01/9Ap_bianchi_ing09.pdf
58. Macris, A.M., Georgakellos, D.A.: A new teaching tool in education for sustainable development: ontology-based knowledge networks for environmental training. Journal of Cleaner Production 14, 855–867 (2006)
59. Antoniou, G., Van Harmelen, F.: A Semantic Web primer, 2nd edn. MIT Press, Cambridge (2008)
60. Dicheva, D.: Ontologies and Semantic Web for e-learning. In: Adelsberger, H.H., Kinshuk, Pawlowski, J.M., Sampson, D. (eds.) Handbook on Information Technologies for Education and Training, 2nd edn., pp. 47–65. Springer, Heidelberg (2008)
61. Edgington, T., Choi, B., Henson, K., Raghu, T.S., Vinze, A.: Adopting ontology to facilitate knowledge sharing. Communications of the ACM 47(11), 85–90 (2004)
62. Naeve, A.: The human Semantic Web: Shifting from knowledge push to knowledge pull. International Journal on Semantic Web and Information Systems 1(3), 1–30 (2005), http://kmr.nada.kth.se/papers/SemanticWeb/HSW.pdf
63. Kolodner, J.L., Cox, M.T., González-Calero, P.A.: Case-based reasoning-inspired approaches to education. The Knowledge Engineering Review 20(3), 299–303 (2006)
64. Kolodner, J.L., Owensby, J.N., Guzdial, M.: Case-based learning aids. In: Jonassen, D.H. (ed.) Handbook of Research on Educational Communications and Technology, 2nd edn., pp. 829–861. Lawrence Erlbaum, Mahwah (2004)
65. Mizen, H., Dolbear, C., Hart, G.: Ontology ontogeny: Understanding how an ontology is created and developed. In: Rodríguez, M.A., Cruz, I., Levashkin, S., Egenhofer, M.J. (eds.) GeoS 2005. LNCS, vol. 3799, pp. 15–29. Springer, Heidelberg (2005)
66. Fernández-López, M., Gómez-Pérez, A., Juristo, N.: METHONTOLOGY: From ontological art towards ontological engineering. In: Association for the Advancement of Artificial Intelligence (AAAI) Spring Symposium (Technical Report SS-97-06), pp. 33–40 (1997)
67. Fernández-López, M., Gómez-Pérez, A., Sierra, J.P.: Building a chemical ontology using METHONTOLOGY and the ontology design environment. IEEE Intelligent Systems and their Applications 14(1), 37–46 (1999)
68. Corcho, O., Fernández-López, M., Gómez-Pérez, A., López-Cima, A.: Building legal ontologies with METHONTOLOGY and WebODE. In: Benjamins, V.R., Casanovas, P., Breuker, J., Gangemi, A. (eds.) Law and the Semantic Web. LNCS (LNAI), vol. 3369, pp. 142–157. Springer, Heidelberg (2005)
69. Fernández-López, M.: Overview of methodologies for building ontologies. In: IJCAI 1999 workshop on Ontologies and Problem-Solving Methods (KRR5), pp. 4-1–4-13 (1999)
70. Fernández-López, M., Gómez-Pérez, A.: Overview and analysis of methodologies for building ontologies. The Knowledge Engineering Review 17(2), 129–156 (2002)
71. Corcho, O., Fernández-López, M., Gómez-Pérez, A.: Methodologies, tools and languages for building ontologies. Where is their meeting point? Data & Knowledge Engineering 46, 41–64 (2003)

72. Terminology on disaster risk reduction. UN/ISDR, Geneva, Switzerland (2009), http://www.unisdr.org/eng/terminology/terminology-2009-eng.html
73. UNDHA: Internationally agreed glossary of basic terms related to disaster management (DHA/93/36). United Nations Department of Humanitarian Affairs (UNDHA), Geneva, Switzerland (1992), http://www.reliefweb.int/rw/lib.nsf/db900sid/LGEL-5EQNZV/file/dha-glossary-1992.pdf?openelement
74. Australian emergency management terms thesaurus, http://library.ema.gov.au/emathesaurus/
75. General Multilingual Environmental Thesaurus (GEMET), http://www.eionet.europa.eu/gemet
76. Intergovernmental Oceanographic Commission: Tsunami glossary (IOC/2008/TS/85). UNESCO, Paris (2008), http://ioc3.unesco.org/itic/contents.php?id=328
77. National Wildfire Coordinating Group (NWCG): Glossary of wildland fire terminology, http://www.nwcg.gov/pms/pubs/glossary/index.htm
78. ISO 31000:2009(E), Risk management – Principles and guidelines. Geneva, Switzerland, International Organization for Standardization (2009)
79. ISO Guide 73:2009, Risk management – Vocabulary. Geneva, Switzerland, International Organization for Standardization (2009)
80. AS/NZS ISO 31000:2009: Risk management – Principles and guidelines. Standards Australia, Sydney; Standards New Zealand, Wellington (2009)
81. Below, R., Wirtz, A., Guah-Sapir, D.: Disaster category classification and peril terminology for operational purposes. CRED, Brussels; Munich RE, Munich (2009), http://www.cred.be/publication/disaster-category-classification-and-peril-terminology-operational-purposes
82. EM-DAT glossary, http://www.emdat.be/glossary/9
83. Gennari, J.H., et al.: The evolution of Protégé: An environment for knowledge-based systems development. International Journal of Human-Computer Studies 58(1), 89–123 (2003)
84. Meyer, J.H.F., Land, R.: Concepts and troublesome knowledge (2): Epistemological considerations and a conceptual framework for teaching and learning. Higher Education 49(3), 373–388 (2005)
85. Sicilia, M.-Á., Lytras, M.D.: The semantic learning organization. The Learning Organization 12(5), 402–410 (2005)
86. Lytras, M., Naeve, A.: Semantic e-learning: Synthesising fantasies. British Journal of Educational Technology 37(3), 479–491 (2006), http://www.qou.edu/homePage/arabic/researchProgram/eLearningResearchs/semantic.pdf
87. Vrandečić, D., Krötzsch, M.: Semantic MediaWiki. In: Davies, J., Grobelnik, M., Mladenicpp, D. (eds.) Semantic Knowledge Management Integrating Ontology Management, Knowledge Discovery, and Human Language Technologies, pp. 171–179. Springer, Heidelberg (2009)
88. Krötzsch, M., Vrandečić, D., Völkel, M., Haller, H., Studer, R.: Semantic Wikipedia. Web Semantics: Science, Services and Agents on the World Wide Web 5(4), 251–261 (2007)
89. Semantic MediaWiki (SMW), http://semantic-mediawiki.org/

Designing an Instrument to Measure the QoS of a Spanish Virtual Store

Beatriz Sainz de Abajo[1], Isabel de la Torre Díez[1], Enrique García Salcines[2], Javier Burón Fernández[2], Francisco Díaz Pernas[1], Miguel López Coronado[1], and Carlos de Castro Lozano[2]

[1] Department of Communications and Signal Theory and Telematics Engineering, Higher Technical School of Telecommunications Engineering, University of Valladolid, Campus Miguel Delibes, Paseo de Belén nº 15, 47011 Valladolid, Spain
{beasai,isator,pacper,miglop}@tel.uva.es
[2] Department of Computer Science, University of Córdoba, Campus of Rabanales Madrid-Cádiz Road, km.396-A, Albert Einstein Building, 14071 Córdoba, Spain
{egsalcines,jburon,ma1caloc}@uco.es

Abstract. This article describes the development of an instrument, in the form of a survey, which is distributed to users of a B2C website selling electronic books in order to ascertain their satisfaction. The opinions compiled from a pilot sample and the exploratory factor analysis carried out point to factors that best summarise the quality of the application analysed here. Analysis of the initial survey, with a total of 40 items, shaped the final instrument, encompassing 18 items divided into 6 dimensions, which measure the perceptions of users of the application in order to improve the contents of the website. Subsequently, a confirmatory factorial analysis is performed, ensuring the reliability of the study and which confirms that the structure of the instrument developed truly measures service quality in accordance with the requirements of the website in terms of offering a space that fulfils consumer expectations in the Information Society.

Keywords: Service quality; Web application; goodness of fit indices; factor analysis; Business to Consumers (B2C).

1 Introduction

Of all the different kinds of electronic commerce, the highest volume of commercial transactions is registered by Business to Consumer (B2C) type enterprises. At times it tends to be considered a kind of generic electronic commerce, in which implementation, hosting and maintenance is not costly, and is therefore attractive to both small and large companies, and many models can be encompassed by this classification [1]. The eMarketer report, point out how the impact of young consumers on electronic commerce is particularly visible since they share recommendations about products through the Internet, which encourage others to buy from sites that have proven to be reliable [2].

M.D. Lytras et al. (Eds.): WSKS 2010, Part I, CCIS 111, pp. 75–82, 2010.

We must take advantage of this trend among users to share information and criticise or praise a store from which they have ordered in order to improve the website for future users. Just by taking into account the opinion of buyers we can resolve the conflicts and requests that arise. The use of indicators will be fundamental to prevent this from happening. Although there are indicators that have been tested, their measurement is still somewhat vague and, therefore, they must be improved in order to predict the success or failure of the application.

Quality of Service (QoS) and, therefore, customer satisfaction must be at all times the ultimate goal when developing an application. The aim of this study is precisely to quantify service quality to give the developer a scientific basis when making design decisions.

Since 1988, the measurement of service quality has been a concern for researchers [3], and owing to the different nature of services, instruments used for quantification cannot be the same in all cases.

The examination of different studies and in-depth analysis of methodology have led to the development of an instrument in the form of a survey, distributed among users with a view to providing clear measurements of their satisfaction.

The different concepts that are inseparably associated with QoS offer a global vision of the service provided by an application. The different nature of the services offered on the Web and their specific characteristics require an analysis of the factors that have the greatest influence on user opinions. It will be necessary therefore to develop a specific instrument to quantify the QoS delivered by each application.

2 Background

Parasuraman, with his SERVQUAL model, identified QoS using the discrepancy between the perceptions and expectations of users in relation to different aspects that he termed dimensions. These dimensions were made up of sets of questions or items that aimed to describe characteristics such as reliability, response capacity and the security of the service. This set of dimensions was referred to as a construct [3].

Subsequent models advocated that the measurement of perceptions made for a more reliable model; hence SERVPERF, with a similar structure to SERVQUAL [4], would guide the steps of models to come. This was followed by several varied instruments to measure each of the possible services.

3 Development of the Instrument

Initially, a battery of 50 questions was developed referring to different aspects of the service provided by the publishing firm Creaciones Copyright S.L, founded in 2003 and dedicated to creating, editing and producing technical scientific documentation (books, manuals, etc., in any format) and which sells its contents in bookshops and through a website. The prior revision of the initial survey, taking into account the different aspects in which the management was interested in order to improve the website, resulted in a questionnaire with 40 items that users had to rate using a 7-point Likert scale [5].

3.1 Pilot Survey - Exploratory Factor Analysis

To confirm the validity of the results of this study, the survey was distributed by e-mail to users who had previously made a purchase through the webpage. Of the 357 surveys sent out, a positive result was received for a total of 243, of which only 180 were valid. The other surveys were disregarded due to incoherence or incongruence in the responses given to the questions.

To refine the tool, an exploratory factor analysis (EFA) was conducted to identify the underlying factors or dimensions that model service quality. The instrument was examined using Varimax rotation to facilitate the interpretation of the factors generated using principal components analysis with Kaiser's criterion.

The initial analysis pointed to the existence of 15 factors that explained QoS in the application. Similarly, it revealed factor loadings of certain items on multiple factors or factors explained by a single item. For this reason [6], it was necessary to eliminate 11 items in two rounds.

The next step was to characterise the dimensions on the basis of the remaining items. The impossibility of characterising three of the factors gave rise to the elimination of 7 additional items. Therefore, the initial instrument was pared down to 7 perfectly characterisable dimensions with eigenvalues greater than unity and a total of 22 items.

The Kaiser-Meyer-Olkin (KMO) measure was 0.671, above the recommended threshold of 0.5, which ensures the suitability of the sample. Furthermore, Bartlett's test of sphericity revealed significant values, thereby supporting the validity of the instrument [8].

To complete the analysis, Cronbach's α coefficient [7] was measured for each dimension, giving a minimum value of 0.704, above the recommended threshold of 0.7. The lowest item-total correlation [8] was 0.461, above the recommended value of 0.4. Hence, the reliability of the factors is assured and, as indicated in Table 1, it is not advisable to eliminate any of the items to improve the respective Cronbach's α coefficients. The refined instrument explained 69.777% of the accumulated variance.

Following this initial study, the QoS provided by the Copyright S. L. B2C website was represented by 7 dimensions: quality, browsability, usefulness, interactivity, style, security and availability.

3.2 Reliability Survey - Confirmatory Factor Analysis

For the second study, the refined survey was distributed in October 2009 following the same methodology as with the first study. Of the total of 220 responses collected,

Table 1. Results of the EFA of the refined instrument

		Item-Total Correlation	Cronbach's α coefficient if item is eliminated	Cronbach's α coefficient
Benefits of the information	Q1	.597	.564	.720
	Q2	.546	.624	
	Q6	.494	.686	
Customer Service	Q8	.573	.649	.741
	Q9	.608	.608	
	Q11	.526	.702	
Browsability	Q14	.709	.773	.836
	Q15	.714	.777	
	Q19	.617	.815	
	Q20	.641	.805	
Interactivity	Q22	.659	.[a]	.791
	Q23	.659	.[a]	
Style/ Look	Q29	.580	.771	.802
	Q30	.697	.719	
	Q31	.687	.719	
	Q32	.525	.801	
Security	Q34	.487	.653	.704
	Q35	.622	.476	
	Q36	.461	.687	
Availability	Q38	.670	.725	.809
	Q39	.685	.718	
	Q40	.629	.776	

206 (93.6%) were valid, which represents a significant improvement on the 74% of the pilot survey, explained by the elimination of items relating to the technical characteristics of the system, about which the users could not know. The fewer questions included in a survey, the greater the chances of receiving a response.

The next step was to carry out a Confirmatory Factor Analysis (CFA) in order to confirm the validity of the instrument [8]. Using the software package AMOS 17.0 a structure was obtained for the instrument, shown in Fig. 1.

This model displayed a Chi Square goodness of fit index of 290 with 188 degrees of freedom. The Goodness of Fit Index (GFI) was 0.877 and the Adjusted Goodness of Fit Index (AGFI) was 0.835. The Comparative Fit Index (CFI) was 0.917 and Tukey's test gave a value of 0.898. Finally, a value of 0.054 was obtained for the error of approximation (RMSEA).

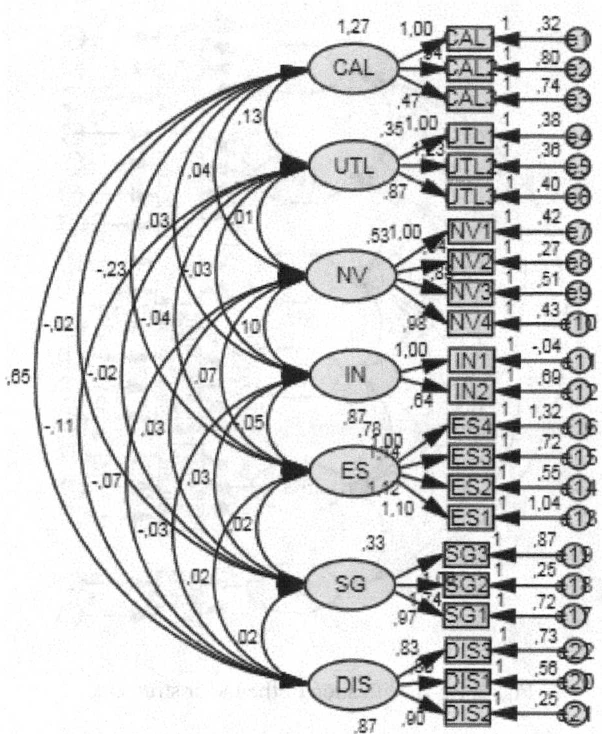

Fig. 1. First order factor structure

Lai and Li [7] suggested that for a model to be considered appropriate, the values obtained for TLI, GFI and CFI should be over 0.9 and the AGFI higher than 0.8. The RMSEA, on the other hand, should not exceed 0.08. Hence, using these criteria, the fit of the model was not good and, therefore, it needed to be re-estimated in order to measure QoS in the application being studied.

Analysis of the normalised residuals matrix identified values in excess of 2.58, revealing prediction errors [9] which, when combined with the high modification index between DIS3 and CAL2, indicated a high correlation between the dimensions of information quality and availability. The results supported the elimination of the first of these two items, which yielded a significant improvement in the goodness of fit indices, with a CFI of 0.944, a GFI equal to 0.898, AGFI of 0.860 and a value of 0.931 for Tukey's test (TLI). These values indicated that the model required further re-specification. The analysis of co-variance of the error terms in the items of the dimension information quality was particularly high, which is a clear indication of scant differentiation between dimensions in the perceptions of those surveyed [10]. The decision was made to eliminate the dimension discussed previously. The new analysis of the model presented the factor structure shown in Fig. 2.

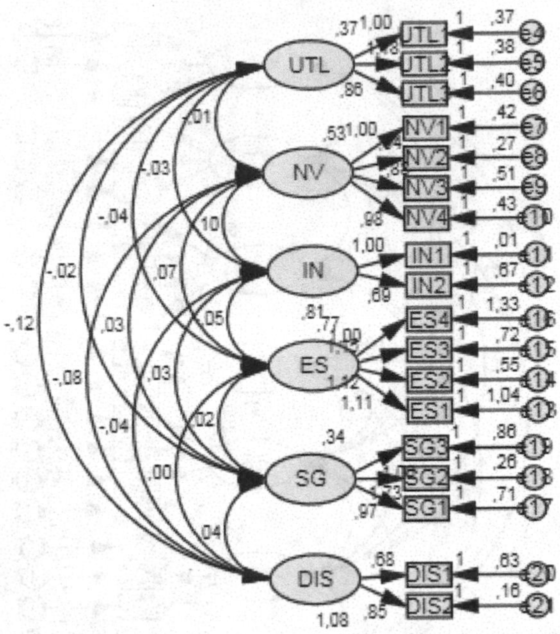

Fig. 2. Re-specification of the factor structure

On this occasion, the results were more encouraging, giving values that supported a high goodness of fit, as shown in Table 2.

Table 2. Goodness of fit indices of the instrument developed

	Instrument developed	Recommended threshold [3]
GFI	0.921	0.9
AGFI	0.887	0.8
TLI	0.958	0.9
CFI	0.967	0.9
RMSEA	0.037	0.08

It should not be forgotten that the ultimate aim of the study design was to develop an instrument to measure QoS; hence the existence of a second order factor is assumed that explains the first order factors or dimensions proved above [11]. Therefore, to complete the analysis, the second order model shown in Fig. 3 was examined.

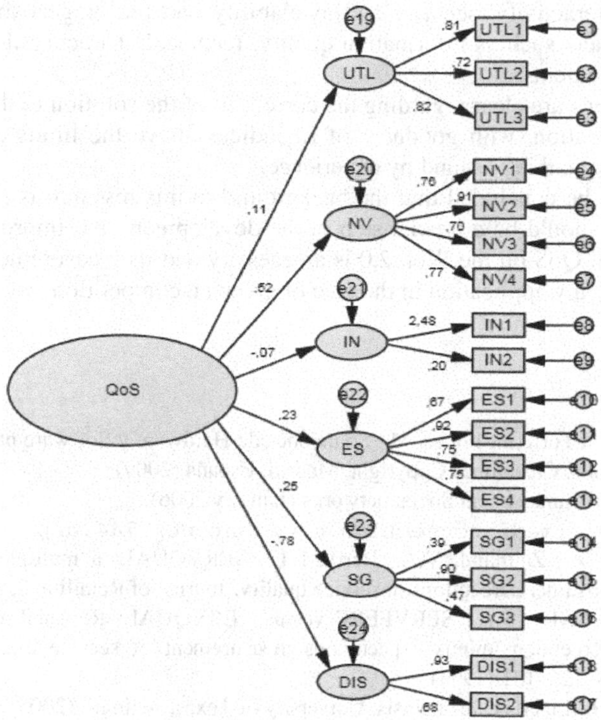

Fig. 3. Second order factor model

The data obtained corroborated the observations made in the previous study, displaying an outstanding goodness of fit in the model. On this occasion, a Chi Square goodness of fit index of 417.297 was found with 129 degrees of freedom. Goodness of Fit (GFI) was 0.992 and the Adjusted Goodness of Fit (AGFI) was 0.990. The Comparative Fit Index (CFI) was 0.956 and Tukey's Test gave a value of 0.948. Finally, a value of 0.079 was obtained for the error of approximation (RMSEA). Hence, in the absence of future invariability tests between demographic groups with real users of the application, it can be concluded that the instrument developed presents an outstanding fit to the requirements of the application.

4 Conclusions

Examination of previous studies and an in-depth analysis of methodology have led to the development of an instrument that takes the form of a survey that, when distributed among users, can give clear measurements of their satisfaction.

The final instrument, which has 18 items divided into 6 dimensions, will provide completely reliable measurements of the perceptions of users of the application in order to improve the contents of the website, given that the company is particularly concerned to satisfy its customers and to develop and enhance its B2C platform. It was concluded that characteristics regarding the usefulness of the application, browsability, interactivity, security and availability had the biggest impact on user opinion over others such as information quality, technical characteristics, or the personalisation of contents.

The conclusions are clear regarding the correct fit of the solution to the characteristics of the application, with goodness of fit indices above the limits established by numerous studies in this area and by experience.

Hence, it can be concluded that the background to this research is perfectly justified, and that it should be a crucial step in the development and improvement of future applications. QoS on the Web 2.0 is a necessity and its measurement is essential to the success of any application in the face of growing competition.

References

1. Sainz, B., de la Torre, I., López, M.: Soluciones de Hardware y Software para el desarrollo de Teleservicios. Creaciones Copyright. Madrid, España (2009)
2. Emarketer. Ecommerce and Social networks (January 2006), `http://www.imediaconnection.com/content/7744.asp`
3. Parasuraman, A., Zeithaml, V.A., Berry, L.L.: SERVQUAL: a multiple-item scale for measuring consumer perceptions of service quality. Journal of Retailing 2, 12–40 (1988)
4. Cronin, J.J., Taylor, S.A.: SERVPERF versus SERVQUAL: Reconciling performance-based and perceptions-minus expectations measurement of service quality. Journal of Marketing 58, 125–131 (1994)
5. Bernstein, I.H.: Likert scale analysis. University of Texas, Arlingto (2005)
6. Hair, J.F., Anderson, R.E., Tatham, R.L., Black, W.C.: Análisis Multivariante. Prentice Hall Iberia, Madrid (1999)
7. Cronbach, L.J.: Coefficient alpha and the internal structure of tests. Psychometrika 16(3), 297–334 (1951)
8. Reilly, T.: A necessary and Sufficient Condition for Identification of Confirmatory Factor Analysis Models of Complexity One. Sociological Methods and Research 23(4), 421–441 (1995)
9. Armstrong, J.S., Overton, T.S.: Estimating non-response bias in mail surveys. Journal of Marketing Research 14, 396–402 (1977)
10. Satorra, A., Bentler, P.M.: Scaling corrections for chi-square statistics in covariance structure analysis. In: Proceedings Annual Statistics Association, pp. 308–313 (1988)
11. Byrne, B.M.: Structural equation modeling with AMOS: basis concepts, applications and programming Multivariate application series. Taylor and Francis Group, USA (2001)

The Applications of Mindfulness with Students of Secondary School: Results on the Academic Performance, Self-concept and Anxiety

Clemente Franco, Israel Mañas, Adolfo J. Cangas, and José Gallego

University of Almería, Spain
cfranco@ual.es

Abstract. The aim of the present research is to verify the impact of a mindfulness programme on the levels academic performance, self-concept and anxiety, of a group of students in Year 1 at secondary school. The statistical analyses carried out on the variables studied showed significant differences in favour of the experimental group with regard to the control group in all the variables analysed. In the experimental group we can observe a significant increase of academic performance as well as an improvement in all the self-concept dimensions, and a significant decrease in anxiety states and traits. The importance and usefulness of mindfulness techniques in the educative system is discussed.

Keywords: Mindfulness, students, academic performance, self-concept, anxiety.

1 Introduction

Many studies have established a causal relationship between a student's academic self concept and academic performance, to the point where academic self-concept is considered the basis of a student's future success or failure [39], [48]. A high self-concept contributes to scholastic success, which in turn favors development of a positive self-concept [34], [46]. It has also been demonstrated that high levels of stress in the academic environment cause attention and concentration deficits, difficulties in memorizing and problem solving, deficits in study skills, low productivity and academic performance [42]. In fact, high stress levels usually cause alterations diminishing the triple response (cognitive, motor and physiological) involved in academic performance [36].

Anxiety is also one of the main factors negatively affecting academic performance. Carbonero [10] says that anxiety can lead to deterioration of academic performance because the student focuses on negative thoughts about his abilities more than on the task itself. Rivas [45] notes that students with high anxiety levels tend to focus their attention on how hard the task is, on their academic failures and on their lack of personal skills. High levels of anxiety therefore tend to alter the student's psychological functioning to the extent that memory, attention and concentration are affected and diminished, disturbing academic performance, as this requires attention, concentration and sustained effort to be maintained at an optimum, effective level [43]. Research, such as the studies by Del Barrio [10] and Mestre [40] has demonstrated both an

M.D. Lytras et al. (Eds.): WSKS 2010, Part I, CCIS 111, pp. 83–97, 2010.

increase in emotional disorders (anxiety and depression) in teenagers, as well as the relationship between these disorders and the student's academic performance. Therefore, promoting and training the affective strategies based on self-control, techniques increasing attention and improving self-knowledge, can exert a positive effect on the student's academic performance [8].

Psychology is currently employing meditation under the label *mindfulness* as an intervention technique or clinical method. Mindfulness has been demonstrated to be effective in a number of medical, psychological and educational problems, so it has captured the attention of psychology and has been included in a wide variety of psychological interventions and therapies, whether explicit or implicit, exclusive or integrated as one more component in a treatment program composed of a multitude of clinical elements or techniques [2], [24], [26]. Mindfulness in contemporary psychology has been adopted as an approach for increasing awareness and responding skilfully to mental processes that contribute to emotional distress and maladaptive behaviours [7]. The practice of mindfulness teaches one to approach internal experiences with curiosity and acceptance, which allows for intensive self-observation without judgement, elaboration, or attempts to fix or change the experience. Mindfulness has been described as a process of bringing a certain quality of attention to moment-by-moment experience [29].

Meditation or mindfulness techniques, have shown their effectiveness in improving psychological discomfort in its various forms of anxiety [4], [15], [30]. Other effects of meditation related to stress and anxiety are reduced nervousness, worry and emotional discomfort, and increased muscular relaxation and emotional calm [37], [38]. It also diminishes cortisol levels [35], [52], and blood lactate [50] which, among others, are markers of stress and anxiety.

One of the characteristics of meditation is the ability to project a single set of signals at the same time, such as breathing or thoughts. This produces changes in the physiological structure of the organism, which at the same time results in a tendency towards normalizing reactions and to more healthy, relaxed physiological behavior. In this way, tension and anxiety are reduced, the heart beat and metabolism are slowed and there is an increase in attention and ability to concentrate [33]. Some studies have found that with practice, meditation is able to train mental activity and processes, strengthening all the cognitive abilities upon acquiring the skill of methodically exercising mental attention and concentration [28], [55]. Meditation increases the ability to focus attention and ignore distractions, and improves cognitive performance in demanding situations, tension and concentration [49], [53], as for example, during an exam. Furthermore, meditation has also been related to improvements in self-concept [54], [56].

In the sphere of education, mindfulness has also been demonstrated effective in different ways. Barnes, Bauza, and Treiber [3] used a meditation program with students with classroom behavior problems, and found that their class attendance and school behavior improved. Barragán, Lewis, and Palacio [5] found that mindfulness intervention in a sample of university students improved their ability to focus and sustain attention, to follow a stimulus closely and to manage distraction. More specifically, meditation has been directly related to increasing and improving academic performance. Chang and Hierbert [11] showed how primary students significantly improved their schoolwork after mindfulness intervention. Cranson, Orme-Johnson,

Gackenbach, Dillbeck, Jones, and Alexander [12] demonstrated that university students that practiced mindfulness twice a day increased their academic performance. León [32] found a significant relationship between the levels of mindfulness and academic performance in secondary education students. Finally, Beaucheim, Hutchins, and Patterson [6] carried out a study in which they applied meditation to a group of 34 students with learning problems and low academic performance, and found that after training, this group significantly improved its academic performance, its social skills and diminished trait anxiety.

Recently, a mindfulness program called 'Meditación Fluir' [16], [18] has also been effective in the field of education in different ways. For example, by reducing stress perception in students of teacher education [19], increasing the verbal creativity levels in a group of high school [20], reducing levels of educational stress and of the days taken off work on sick leave, in teachers of obligatory secondary education [21], as well as psychological distress [22], or by improving the values in a sample of university students [23]. However, the efficacy of Meditación Fluir has still not been examined on the variables academic performance, self-concept and anxiety.

To summarize, the literature available seems to indicate that stress and anxiety, as well as self-concept, play a decisive role in academic performance. Furthermore, meditation has been demonstrated to reduce stress and anxiety, at the same time it leads to improved cognitive skills, such as attention, memory and concentration, as well as academic performance. Therefore, the main goal of this study is to examine whether the application of the meditation program Meditación Fluir, which has demonstrated to be effective in the field of education in different ways, could also be effective in improving academic performance and self-concept, and in reducing the levels of anxiety in secondary school students.

2 Method

2.1 Participants

A total of 61 1st-year high school students, 31 male and 29 female, between the ages of 16 and18 (M = 16.75; SD = 0.83), in the first year of *Enseñanza Secundaria Obligatoria* (Compulsory Secondary Education) at three public schools in the province of Almería, Spain, participated in this study.

2.2 Materials

2.2.1 Academic Performance

To evaluate their academic performance, their grades in the subjects studied by all of the students in the first year of high school (i.e., Spanish language and literature, foreign language and philosophy) were added up, and this score was then divided among the number of subjects. This provided academic performance rates for each of the subjects as well as a total academic performance rate.

2.2.2 Cuestionario de Autoconcepto (Self-concept Questionnaire, Form A) [41]

This 36-item self-administered questionnaire measures four dimensions of self-concept (academic, social, emotional and family) and gives a total score. This questionnaire's high internal consistency has an alpha of 0.82.

2.2.3 Cuestionario de Ansiedad Estado-Rasgo (Spanish Version of the State-Trait Anxiety Inventory (STAI) [51]

This questionnaire is composed of two scales that measure two independent concepts of anxiety, state and trait. It is made up of 40 items (20 for each scale) in which the subjects must evaluate how they feel generally (trait anxiety), and at the moment (state anxiety) on a 0-3-point Likert scale. The coefficient of internal consistency is 0.91 and 0.94 for the trait-anxiety and state-anxiety scales, respectively, and test-retest reliability is 0.81 for trait anxiety and 0.40 for state anxiety.

2.3 Design and Procedure

To analyze the effects of the mindfulness program (independent variable) on academic performance, students' self-concept and anxiety (dependent variables), a group comparison design (randomized controlled trial) with pretest-posttest measurement was used on an experimental and a control group.

First place, three schools in the province of Almería were chosen at random. Then the principals of those schools were contacted to offer them an extracurricular workshop on meditation and relaxation techniques for their first year high school students free of charge. A total of 67 students signed up for the course, of which only 61 were used for the study, since the results from students who said they had had some experience with a relaxation technique, such as yoga, tai-chi, etc., were disqualified. Prior to their participation, informed consent was received from all parents or tutors.

Sixty-one subjects were allocated at random into to groups, 30 were in the control group and the remaining 31 were in the experimental group. The students did not receive any kind of compensation for participating. Once the two groups had been formed, we proceeded to pretest evaluation of anxiety and self-concept levels in each group using the *Cuestionario de Ansiedad Estado-Rasgo* (State-Trait Anxiety Inventory) and the *Cuestionario de Autoconcepto* (Self-Concept Questionnaire), respectively. For the academic performance score, we contacted the students' tutors, who provided us with their first-quarter grades in the academic year in progress.

Once this first measurement was found, the subjects in the control group were told that the workshop would begin in three months and the intervention program was begun with the participants in the experimental group.

The meditation program was given in 1 hr 30 min session per week for 10 weeks. The intervention program consisted of learning the mindfulness technique called Meditación Fluir [16], [18], and practicing daily for 30 minutes. The main goal of this technique is not to try and control thoughts or change them or replace them with others, but on the contrary, just let them alone, and accept any idea that might appear or emerge spontaneously, developing a state of full attention to this mental activity, while being aware that they are transitory and nonpermanent.

The practice of Meditación Fluir consists of repeating a word, or mantra, with a free, open mentality, while directing attention toward the abdomen and noticing how air goes in and out while breathing, but not trying to change or alter respiration itself, since only awareness of how it happens naturally and without effort is necessary. Therefore, what is essential when Meditación Fluir is practiced is not the thoughts in themselves, but the awareness of them without evaluating, judging or analyzing them, and just watching how they appear and disappear, and letting them go by.

In each of the 10 sessions, in addition to learning and practicing the Meditación Fluir technique, a variety of Acceptance and Commitment Therapy [26] metaphors and exercise are used along with tales from the Zen Tradition [14] and from the *Vipassana* meditation [25] in order to stress and reinforce the assumption of how the attempt to control annoying and unpleasant private events only makes them chronic and aggravates the psychological discomfort they cause, and therefore, the best thing to do is let them flow freely.

Finally, body-scan exercises [29], [31], were another part of the meditation program learned and practiced during all 10 sessions. The body-scan is a meditation technique where attention is brought in systematic fashion to different regions of the body –from head to foot and from foot to head– and then, in an expansive awareness of the entire body; without judgement, or attempts to fix or change anything (e.g., body sensations, mental reactions, etc.), being present, moment to moment.

At the end of the mindfulness training, the subjects' academic performance, self-concept and anxiety were evaluated again in both the control and experimental groups, under the same conditions and with the same instruments as those used before intervention.

When the study was completed, the meditation course was given to the control group. All the subjects participating in the study were informed of its purpose at the end of it, and written consent was requested from their parents for the use of the data acquired, guaranteeing to maintain all data confidential and anonymous.

3 Results

All of the statistical analyses were done using the SPSS ver. 15.0 statistics package. Table 1 shows the pretest and post test measurements and standard deviations in academic performance, self-concept and anxiety for the experimental and the control groups. To find out whether there were any statistically significant differences between the pretest and posttest measurements, the Student's t-test for related samples was used on both the experimental and control group. The control and experimental groups were also analyzed for differences before and after intervention in both groups with the Student's t-test for independent samples. The Student's *t* was employed because it is the statistical technique recommended in quasi-experimental pre-test/post-test studies when the group to compare are only two (control and experimental) due to its sensibility and capacity of discrimination to little samples [44].

The statistical analysis of the differences in pretest scores between the experimental and control group showed that there were no significant starting differences between the groups for the variables studied (see Table 2). Differences in experimental and control group posttest measurements were analyzed to find whether there had been significant improvement in the experimental group over the control group after intervention. Statistically significant differences appeared between the groups in all the variables analyzed: total academic performance (t=3.62; p=.001), and each subject (philosophy [t=2.71; p=.01], Spanish language and literature [t=2.51; p<.05], and foreign language [t=3.02; p<.005]); total self-concept (t=10.1; p<.001), and in all of the self-concept dimensions (academic [t=3.62; p=.001], social [t=3.97; p=.001], emotional [t=8.73; p<.001], and family [t=2.72; p=.001]); and, finally, state anxiety (t=3.22; p<.005) and trait anxiety (t=3.14; p<.005) (see Table 2).

Table 1. Pretest and posttest means and standard deviations in the experimental and control groups for academic performance, self-concept and anxiety

	PRE-TEST				POST-TEST			
	Control		Experim.		Control		Experim.	
Variable	*M*	*SD*	*M*	*SD*	*M*	*SD*	*M*	*SD*
Philosophy	5.45	2.35	5.32	1.82	5.15	2.58	6.95	1.31
Spanish Language	5.80	1.98	4.58	1.57	5.75	2.22	7.21	1.27
Foreign Language	5.10	1.74	5.21	2.09	4.75	2.14	6.74	1.93
Acade. Performance	5.44	1.67	5.03	1.35	5.21	1.80	6.95	1.09
Self- Con. Academic	22.5	2.39	23.3	3.14	22.9	3.01	26.9	2.98
Self-Concept Social	12.6	1.98	13.5	1.46	12.4	2.13	14.4	2.81
Self-Con. Emotional	17.6	2.83	18.4	2.89	16.8	2.43	22.9	1.87
Self-Concept Family	14.6	2.51	15.3	1.63	14.8	1.76	16.5	2.09
Self-Concept Total	67.4	4.87	70.5	5.52	66.7	4.64	80.3	6.46
State Anxiety	20.3	9.81	16.0	8.55	21.2	9.61	12.8	6.17
Trait Anxiety	23.5	8.83	21.5	8.10	15.6	9.67	15.6	5.77

Table 2. Student's t-test for independent samples of the pretest and posttest differences between the experimental and control groups for academic performance, self-concept and anxiety

	PRE-TEST		POST-TEST	
Variable	*t*	*p*	*t*	*p*
Philosophy	.198	.844	2.71	.010***
Spanish Language	2.06	.166	2.51	.017****
Foreign Language	.179	.859	3.02	.004**
Acade. Performance	.846	.403	3.62	.001*
Self- Con. Academic	.858	.396	4.86	.001*
Self-Concept Social	1.56	.127	3.97	.001*
Self-Con. Emotional	.895	.337	8.73	.001*
Self-Concept Family	.973	.227	2.72	.010***
Self-Concept Total	1.87	.098	10.1	.001*
State Anxiety	1.45	.154	3.22	.003**
Trait Anxiety	.725	.473	3.14	.003**

Note: *p=.001; **p<.005; ***p=.01; ****p<.05.

The Student's t-test for related samples was applied to find out whether there were significant differences between the pretest and posttest scores in the control group, and no significant differences appeared between pretest and posttest scores on any of the variables analyzed in this group (see Table 3). The Student's t-test for related samples was also applied to find whether there were any significant pretest-posttest differences in the experimental group scores, and statistically significant differences were again found in all of variables analyzed: academic performance (t=12.5; p<.001), and all of the subjects (philosophy [t=7.03; p<.001], Spanish language and literature [t=9.12; p<.001], and foreign language [t=4.78; p=.001]); total self-concept (t=8.63; p<.001) and in its different dimensions (academic [t=5.33; p<.001], social [t=3.39; p<.005], emotional [t=8.10; p<.001], and family [t=2.11; p<.05]); and finally, state anxiety (t=3.89; p=.001) and trait anxiety (t=6.86; p<.001) (see Table 3).

The Cohen's *d* (1988) was used for evaluating the effect-size of the change in the control group and in the experimental group after intervention. Over 1.5 indicated

Table 3. Student's t-test for pretest-posttest differences in the experimental and control groups, and Cohen's d in the experimental group for academic performance, self-concept and anxiety

	CONTROL			EXPERIMENTAL		
Variable	*t*	*p*	*d*	*t*	*p*	*d*
Philosophy	.922	.368	.121	7.03	.001*	1.03
Spanish Language	.127	.900	.023	9.12	.001*	1.85
Foreign Language	.907	.376	.180	4.78	.001*	.760
Acade. Performance	1.13	.271	.132	12.5	.001*	1.57
Self- Con. Academic	.857	.402	.147	5.33	.001*	1.17
Self-Concept Social	1.15	.262	.097	3.39	.003**	.400
Self-Con. Emotional	1.54	.190	.304	8.10	.001*	1.85
Self-Concept Family	.448	.659	.092	2.11	.049***	.640
Self-Concept Total	.892	.384	.147	8.63	.001*	1.63
State Anxiety	1.72	.100	.092	3.89	.001*	.430
Trait Anxiety	.254	.802	.227	6.86	.001*	.840

Note: *p=.001; **p<.005; ***p<.05.

very large changes, from 1 to 1.5 large and from .5 to 1 medium. In Table 3, Cohen's *d* scores demonstrate that there were not any important changes in the control group, all Cohen's *d* scores were between .0 and .3. However, in the experimental group there were very large changes in Spanish language (d=1.85), emotional self-concept (d=1.85), total self-concept (d=1.63), and academic performance (d=1.57). Large changes appear in academic self-concept (d=1.17), and philosophy (d=1.03). There were medium effect changes in trait anxiety (d=.84), foreign language (d=.76), and family self-concept (d=.64). And finally, there were small changes in state anxiety (d=.43) and social self-concept (d=.40) (see Table 3).

The experimental group was also divided into three subgroups by pretest score (high, medium and low scores) on each of the variables (total academic performance, total self-concept, state anxiety and trait anxiety) to analyze the effects of the intervention program in more detail. Tables 4 and 5 show the pretest and posttest mean scores and standard deviations for each variable for the high, intermediate and low-score subgroups.

Table 4. Pretest means and standard deviations for the experimental group with high, medium and low academic performance, self-concept, and trait and state anxiety

	High		Medium		Low	
Variable	*M*	*SD*	*M*	*SD*	*M*	*SD*
Academic Performance	6.52	.597	5.38	.271	3.83	1.07
Self-Concept Total	77.5	2.66	69.5	.548	65.5	2.63
State Anxiety	25.1	3.65	17.0	1.82	5.67	3.98
Trait Anxiety	29.2	4.23	21.6	2.25	12.5	5.28

Table 5. Posttest means, standard deviations and Cohen's d for the experimental group with high, medium and low academic performance, self-concept, and trait and state anxiety

	High			Medium			Low		
Variable	*M*	*SD*	*d*	*M*	*SD*	*d*	*M*	*SD*	*d*
Acade. Performance	8.12	.725	2.49	7.00	.715	3.05	6.18	.874	1.67
Self-Concept Total	82.8	2.56	2.04	79.5	5.05	2.78	79.0	2.64	5.12
State Anxiety	19.0	2.60	1.95	13.7	3.77	1.11	5.67	2.25	0.00
Trait Anxiety	20.0	3.16	.406	17.0	4.00	1.44	9.17	3.60	.730

Then the Cohen's *d* was calculated to analyze the effect size of the change caused by the intervention program in each of these subgroups. As observed in Table 5, all three subgroups underwent very large changes in academic performance after the meditation program, with the largest effects in the subgroup with medium academic performance (*d*=3.05), followed by the subgroup with a high score (*d*=2.49) and finally, the subgroup with a low score (*d*=1.67). There were also very large changes in total self-concept in all three groups, where this time the largest effects are found in the subgroup with the originally low self-concept (*d*=5.12), followed by the medium-score group (*d*=2.78) and, finally, by the high-score group (*d*=2.04). Subjects who started out with a high score in state-anxiety on the pretest benefited most after the meditation intervention, and the effect-size of the intervention program in this group is very large (*d*=1.95). In the subgroup with an originally low state anxiety, the change undergone between pretest and posttest is large (*d*=1.11), with no change in the subgroup with an originally low score in this variable (d=0.00). Finally, there were large changes in trait anxiety in the subgroup with medium pretest scores, (d=1.44), medium changes in the subgroup with originally low scores (d=.730), and small changes in the subgroup with an originally high score on this variable.

4 Discussion

The results show that, in the first place, the academic performance of the participants in the experimental group improved significantly more than the control group, and furthermore, this improvement affected all three subjects (philosophy, Spanish language and literature and foreign language). We can further state that the intervention program also caused important changes in total self-concept, the second variable analyzed, as well as in its various dimensions (academic, social, emotional and family). Finally, the meditation program significantly reduced state and trait-anxiety levels. Therefore, it is possible to conclude that Meditación Fluir can also be effective in improving academic performance and self-concept, at the same time as reducing the levels of anxiety in a sample of adolescent students. These results are in agreement with those found by other studies that show the beneficial effects of practicing meditation on academic performance [6], [11], [12], [32], [53], and relate them to improvement in self-concept [54], [56], and lowered anxiety levels [4], [6], [15], [30].

The results obtained were quite similar to those reported by Beaucheim et al. [6]: both studies demonstrated improved academic performance and diminished levels of state and trait anxiety in a group of adolescents in a natural environment. However, there are some important differences between both studies. Firstly, apart from academic performance and self-concept, a third variable was analyzed in each: self-concept in the present study *versus* social skills in the Beaucheim study. Secondly, the sample in Beaucheim's study was smaller (i.e., 34) and was composed of adolescents diagnosed with learning disabilities and low academic performance, whereas in this study the sample was bigger (i.e., 61) and the participants were adolescents without learning disabilities or low academic performance. Thirdly, 53% of the 34 students from the Beaucheim study had had some previous experience with meditation and/or relaxation training and they participated. However, in this study only 9% of the 67 students had had any previous experience with meditation and/or relaxation techniques and so were disqualified, that is, they did not participate. Next, the Beaucheim study used a pre-post no control-design, whereas this study employed a randomized controlled trial, with pre-post measurements for two groups, an experimental and a control.

Considering the previous three differences, the external and internal validity of the current study could have been higher. That is, the outcomes obtained could be generalized to a greater number of people (not only to those with learning disabilities and/or low academic performance) and attributed in a stronger way to the training program or intervention (i.e., the cause or the independent variable) and not to other possible causes or variables (e.g., effects of the previous experience). Finally, the mindfulness techniques employed in the mindfulness training program by Beaucheim were exclusively those from the meditation-based stress reduction (MBSR) program [31]. However, the mindfulness training program used in this study included, in addition to usual mindfulness techniques (i.e., Meditación Fluir and body-scan), another of Acceptance and Commitment Therapy (ACT). That is, the components of both programs were different. Consequently, the most important original contributions of this study were, on the one hand, to examine the effectiveness of mindfulness, specifically the program Meditación Fluir, on the variables academic performance, self-concept and anxiety at the same time, and the other hand, to employ traditional mindfulness techniques simultaneously with others from ACT. Nevertheless, in order to isolate the relative effect of ACT techniques, it would be necessary to carry out controlled studies comparing trainings in mindfulness with and without ACT components. Further investigations are clearly necessary to clarify this issue.

Campagne [9] believes that training both attention and distraction through the practice of meditation leads to greater control over the constant interference that makes the mind a "noisy place" and does not allow one to think clearly, or distinguish what is essential from what is irrelevant. Meditation may be considered an effective technique for controlling chaotic and repetitive thought which may limit cognitive abilities and also personal balance. Therefore, one of the main benefits of continually practicing meditation is the cessation of the frenetic, chaotic rhythm of thoughts that surge automatically, without any control, as that constant flow of uncontrolled thoughts distracts and impedes one's capacity for attention and concentration [1].

It is also evident that becoming aware of our emotions causes increased and improved attention and memory, since this emotional awareness keeps uncontrolled emotions from interfering and impeding cognitive functioning, at the same time that appropriate emotions facilitate it [27]. Mindfulness may incorporate other elements or components which might explain the change in academic performance, such as training in certain cognitive skills (such as attention, concentration and memory), a feeling of wellness and emotional balance –not just relaxation–, an improvement in self-control, which could favor optimal execution in tense and demanding situations, such as those typical during an exam, improvements in own self-concept, etc.

Between-group differences found for the various dimensions of school performance analyzed were, in order of importance, the following: in subjects, foreign language (p=<.005), philosophy (p=.01) and, last, Spanish language and literature (p<.05). In the self-concept dimensions, the differences were most significant in the emotional component (p<.001), followed by academic and social (p=.001), and somewhat less in the family dimension (p=.01). The differential effect of the intervention on variables may also be observed in a comparison of the experimental group's pretest and posttest scores using the Cohen's d. There were very large effects on the total academic performance (d=1.57) and total self-concept (d=1.63) variables, large effects on trait (d=.84) and less on state anxiety (d=.43).

We may therefore suggest a certain differential effect of the meditation program on the variables analyzed in this study and we propose the need for future research that can isolate the differential effects of meditation more clearly, not only between variables (e.g., academic performance and self-concept), but also on the dimensions within a same variable (e.g., in the various subjects). It is reasonable to assume that, for example, in the case of academic performance, practicing meditation could produce differential effects on the subjects depending on the type of cognitive skills they demand. It would also be interesting to compare the efficacy of different meditation techniques, and to find out which technique or program is best for a type of variable or cognitive skill. This way, meditation programs could be adapted to the educational environment with precise goals, such as academic performance. Another matter of capital importance which also requires future research, is finding out the differential effects that the various components of a meditation program like this one have, isolating those responsible for change and discarding those that are not.

Finally, we consider that although the results of this study were positive, precaution should be used in their generalization, since the study sample can be considered relatively small. The long-term permanence of the results must also be confirmed with follow-up studies that verify whether the academic performance, self-concept and anxiety levels are maintained over time.

References

1. Austin, J.H.: Zen and the Brain. MIT Press, Cambridge (1998)
2. Baer, R.: Mindfulness training as a clinical intervention: A conceptual and empirical review. Clinical Psychology: Science and Practice 10(2), 125–142 (2003)
3. Barnes, V.A., Bauza, L.B., Treiber, F.A.: Impact of stress reduction on negative school behavior in adolescents. Health Qual Life Outcomes 1(10), 5–30 (2003)
4. Barnes, V.A., Treiber, F.A., Davis, H.: Impact of transcendental meditation in cardiovascular function at rest and during acute stress in adolescents with high normal blood pressure. Journal Psychosomatic Research 51(4), 597–605 (2001)
5. Barragán, R., Lewis, H., Palacio, J.E.: Autopercepción de cambios en los déficit atencionales intermedios de estudiantes universitarios de Barranquilla sometidos al método de autocontrol de la atención (mindfulness) [Auto-perception of the changes in the intermediary attention deficits of university students in Barranquilla submitted to the attention self-control mindfulness method]. Salud Uninorte 23, 184–192 (2007)
6. Beaucheim, J., Hutchins, T., Patterson, F.: Mindfulness meditation lessen anxiety, promote social skills, and improve academic performance among adolescents with learning disabilities. Complementary Health Practice Review 13(1), 34–45 (2008)
7. Bishop, S.R., Lau, M., Shapiro, S., Carlson, L., Anderson, N., Cardomy, J., et al.: Mindfulness: A proposed operational definition. Clinical Psychology: Science and Practice 10, 230–241 (2004)
8. Camero, F., Martín, F., Herrero, J.: Estilos y estrategias de aprendizaje en estudiantes universitarios [Styles and learning strategies in university students]. Psicothema 12(4), 615–622 (2000)
9. Campagne, D.M.: Teoría y fisiología de la meditación [Theory and physiology of meditation]. Cuadernos de Medicina Psicosomática y Psiquiatría de Enlace 69/70, 15–30 (2004)
10. Carbonero, I.: Ansiedad y rendimiento académico [Anxiety and academic performance]. Punto y Aparte 7, 123–136 (1999)
11. Chang, J., Hierbert, B.: Relaxation procedures with children: A review. Medical Psycotherapy: An International Journal 22, 163–173 (1989)
12. Cranson, R.W., Orme-Johnson, D.W., Gackenbach, J., Dillbeck, M.C., Jones, C.H., Alexander, C.N.: Transcendental meditation and improved performance on intelligence-related measures: A longitudinal study. Personality & Individual Differences 10, 1105–1116 (1991)
13. Del Barrio, V.: Depresión infantil: Concepto, evaluación y tratamiento [Infant depression: Concept, evaluation and treatment]. Ariel, Barcelona (1997)
14. Deshimaru, T.: La práctica del Zen [The practice of Zen]. RBA, Barcelona (2006)

15. Epply, K.R., Abraham, A.I., Shear, J.: Differential effects of relaxation techniques on trait anxiety: A meta-analysis. Journal of Clinical Psychology 45, 957–974 (1989)
16. Franco, C.: Técnicas de relajación y desarrollo personal [Relaxation and personal development techniques]. Cepa, Granada (2007)
17. Franco, C.: Programa de relajación y de mejora de autoestima en docentes de educación infantil y su relación con la creatividad de sus alumnos [Relaxation and self-esteem program for preschool teachers and their relationship to the creativity of their students]. Revista Iberoamericana de Educación 45(1) (2008)
18. Franco, C.: Meditación Fluir para serenar el cuerpo y la mente [Meditación Fluir for tranquilizing body and mind]. Bubok, Madrid (2009a)
19. Franco, C.: Reducción de la percepción del estrés en estudiantes de Magisterio meditante la práctica de la Meditación Fluir [Reducing stress perception in students of teacher education through the practice of Meditación Fluir]. Apuntes de Psicología 27(1), 99–109 (2009b)
20. Franco, C.: Efectos de un programa de meditación sobre los niveles de creatividad verbal de un grupo de alumnos de Bachillerato [Effects of a meditation program on verbal creativity levels in a group of high school students]. Suma Psicológica (in press)
21. Franco, C., Mañas, I.: Reducción de los niveles de estrés docente y de los días de baja laboral por enfermedad en profesores de educación secundaria obligatoria a través de un programa de entrenamiento en meditación [Reducing levels of educational stress and of the days taken off work on sick leave, in teachers of obligatory secondary education by means of a meditation training programme]. Manuscript submitted for publication (2009)
22. Franco, C., Mañas, I., Cangas, A., Moreno, E., Gallego, J.: Reducing of psychological distress in teachers by a mindfulness training programme. The Spanish Journal of Psychology (in press)
23. Franco, C., Navas, M.: Efectos de un programa de meditación sobre los valores de una muestra de estudiantes universitarios [Effects of a meditation program on values in a sample of university students]. Electronic Journal of Research in Educational Psychology (in press)
24. Germer, C.K., Siegel, R.D., Fulton, P.R.: Mindfulness and psychotherapy. Guilford Press, Nueva York (2005)
25. Hart, W.: La Vippasana. El arte de la meditación [Vippasana. The art of meditation]. Luz de Oriente, Madrid (1994)
26. Hayes, S.C., Stroshal, K.D., Wilson, K.G.: Acceptance and commitment therapy. The Guilford Press, New York (1999)
27. Iriarte, C., Alonso-Gancedo, N., Sobrino, A.: Relaciones entre el desarrollo emocional moral a tener en cuenta en el ámbito educativo: propuesta de un programa de intervención [Relationships between moral and emotional development to be taken into account in the educational environment: proposal for an intervention program]. Electronical Journal of Research in Educational Psychology 4(1), 177–212 (2006)
28. Jha, A.P., Krompinger, J., Baime, M.J.: Mindfulness training modifies subsystems of attention. Cognitive, Affective & Behavioral Neuroscience 7, 109–119 (2007)
29. Kabat-Zinn, J.: Full Catastrophe Living: using the wisdom of your body and mind to face stress, pain, and illness. Dell Publishing, New York (1990)
30. Kabat-Zinn, J., Massion, A.O., Kristeller, J., Peterson, L.G., Fletcher, K.E., Pbert, L., et al.: Effectiveness of a meditation-based stress reduction program in the treatment of anxiety disorders. American Journal of Psychiatry 149, 936–943 (1992)
31. Kabat-Zinn, J.: Where you go there you are. Hyperion, New York (1994)

32. León, B.: Atención plena y rendimiento académico en estudiantes de educación secundaria [Mindfulness and academic performance in secondary education students]. European Journal of Education and Psychology 1(3), 17–26 (2008)
33. LeShan, L.: Cómo meditar [How to meditate]. Kairós, Barcelona (2005)
34. Liu, X., Kaplan, H.B., Risser, W.: Decomposing the reciprocal relationships between academia achievement and general self-stem. Youth and Society 24, 123–148 (1992)
35. MacLean, R.K., Walton, K.G., Wenneberg, S.R., Levitsky, D.K., Mandarino, J.P., Waziri, R., et al.: Altered responses of cortisol, GH, TSH and testosterone to acute stress after four months' practice of Transcendental Meditation (TM). Annals of the New York Academy of Sciences 746, 381–384 (1994)
36. Maldonado, M.D., Hidalgo, M.J., Otero, M.D.: Programa de intervención cognitivo-conductual y de técnicas de relajación como método para prevenir la ansiedad y el estrés en alumnos universitarios de enfermería y mejorar el rendimiento académico [Cognitive-behavioral intervention and relaxation techniques program as a method for preventing anxiety and stress and improving academic performance in university nursing students]. Cuadernos de Medicina Psicosomática y Psiquiatría de Enlace 53, 43–57 (2000)
37. Mañas, I., Sánchez, L.C., Luciano, M.C.: Efectos producidos por un ejercicio de mindfulness (body-scan): Un estudio piloto [Effects of a mindfulness exercise (body-scan): A pilot study]. In: Poster Session Presented at the VII Congress of the Spanish Society of Experimental Psychology, San Sebastián-Donostia, Spain (2008)
38. Mañas, I., Luciano, M.C., Sánchez, L.C.: Beginners practising a basic mindfulness technique: An experimental analysis. Paper Presented at the 4th Conference of the European Association for Behaviour Analysis, Madrid, Spain (2008)
39. Marsh, H.W.: A multidimensional, hierarchical self-concept: Theoretical and empirical justification. Educational Psychology Review 2, 77–172 (1990)
40. Mestre, V.: La depresión en población adolescente valenciana [Depression in a teenage population in Valencia]. Consejería de Sanidad y Consumo, Valencia (1992)
41. Musitu, G., García, F., Gutiérrez, M.: Cuestionario de Autoconcepto Forma A [Self-Concept Questionnaire: Form A]. TEA, Madrid (1994)
42. Pérez, M.A., Martín, A., Borda, M., Del Río, C.: Estrés y rendimiento académico en estudiantes universitarios [Stress and academic performance in university students]. Cuadernos de Medicina Psicosomática y Psiquiatría de Enlace 67/68, 26–33 (2003)
43. Rains, D.: Principios de neuropsicología humana [Principles of human neuropsychology]. McGraw-Hill, México (2004)
44. Rial, A., Valera, J.: Estadística práctica para la investigación en ciencias de la salud [Practical statistics for investigation in health sciences] A Coruña: Netbiblo (2008)
45. Rivas, F.: El proceso de enseñanza/aprendizaje [The teaching/learning process]. Ariel Planeta, Barcelona (1997)
46. Roberts, R.L., Sarigiani, P.A., Petersen, A.C., Newman, J.L.: Gender differences in the relationship between achievement and self-image during early adolescence. In: Pierce, R.A., Black, M.A. (eds.) Life Span Development, pp. 126–139. Kendall, Dubuque (1993)
47. Ruiz, F.J.: Aplicación de la terapia de aceptación y compromiso (ACT) para el incremento del rendimiento ajedrecístico. Un estudio de caso [Application of acceptance and commitment therapy (ACT) to improve chess-players performance. A case study]. International Journal of Psychology and Psychological Therapy 6(1), 77–97 (2006)
48. Skaalvik, E.M., Hagtvet, K.A.: Academic achievement and self-concept: An analysis of causal predominance in a developmental perspective. Journal of Personality and Social Psychology 58, 292–307 (1990)

49. Solberg, E.E., Berglund, K.A., Engen, O., Ekeberg, O., Loeb, M.: The effect of meditation on shooting performance. British Journal of Sports Medicine 30(4), 342–346 (1996)
50. Solberg, E.E., Halvorsen, R., Holen, A.: Effect of meditation on immune cells. Stress Medicine 16, 185–190 (2000)
51. Spielberger, C. D., Gorsuch, R. L., Lushene, R. E.: Cuestionario de Ansiedad Estado-Rasgo (STAI) [State-Trait Anxiety Inventory (STAI)]. TEA, Madrid (1988)
52. Sudsuang, R.: Effect of Buddhist meditation on serum cortisol and total protein levels, blood pressure, pulse rate, lung volume and reaction time. Physiology & Behavior 50(3), 543–548 (1991)
53. Sugiura, Y.: Detached mindfulness and worry: a meta-cognitive analysis. Personality & Individual Differences 37, 169–179 (2004)
54. Trumbulls, M.J., Norris, H.: Effects of Transcendental Meditation on self-identity indices and personality. British Journal of Psychology 73, 57–68 (1982)
55. Valentine, E.R., Sweet, P.L.: Meditation and attention: A comparison of the effects of concentrative and mindfulness meditation on sustained attention. Mental Health, Religion & Culture 2, 59–70 (1999)
56. Van der Berg, W.P., Mulder, B.: Psychological research on the effects of the transcendental meditation technique on a number of personality variables. Gedrag: Tijdschrift voor Psychologie 4, 206–218 (1976)

An Infrastructure Approach for the Evaluation of E-Learning

Bernhard Ertl[1], Katharina Ebner[1], and Kathy Kikis-Papadakis[2]

[1] Universität der Bundeswehr München, Werner-Heisenberg-Weg 39, 85579 Neubiberg, Germany
{bernhard.ertl,katharina.ebner}@unibw.de

[2] Foundation for Research and Technology - Hellas / Institute of Applied and Computational Mathematics, N. Plastira, Vassilika Vouton, 70013 Heraklion, Greece
katerina@iacm.forth.gr

Abstract. This paper presents an infrastructure approach for the evaluation of e-learning. It elaborates [12]'s concept of infrastructures for learning considering a cognitive, an epistemological, a social and a technical infrastructure. Within each infrastructure, the paper takes specific aspects that are important for evaluation. The paper concludes with stressing the importance of evaluation for building knowledge societies.

Keywords: E-Learning, infrastructures; cognitive, epistemological, social, technical.

1 Introduction

The concept of evaluation is rather broad and relates often to quality management. [25] defines four possible results of an evaluation: to get insights into the project and receive data necessary for decisions, to get control over a project and to be able to make refinements, to establish a dialogue between different stakeholders, e.g. financiers, providers and the target group, and to legitimize costs and sustainability of a program. In sum, evaluation means to exactly define and measure a product's or programme's usefulness and worth [17].

In the field of e-learning, evaluation focuses mainly on quality of the learning environment and on learners' negotiation within the learning environment. Thereby, evaluation has two main purposes: To improve and to adept the learning environment to learners' needs (which combines the functions of insights and control) and to prove the quality of the learning environment and the values and benefits of the courses to financiers and participants (legitimization). In this context, [13] emphasize the importance for evaluators to learn about the particular functions and effects of a learning environment for giving learners best benefits.

If we take a socio-cultural perspective on e-learning and its evaluation, we may have to deal with some peculiarities. According to this perspective, learning is more than the pure cognitive act of knowledge acquisition - it includes also the participation in cultural practices [22] and the enculturation in a community [11].

M.D. Lytras et al. (Eds.): WSKS 2010, Part I, CCIS 111, pp. 98–104, 2010.

2 Dimensions and Parameters for Evaluation

There are many different approaches about which dimensions to consider for an evaluation. They are dependent on the goal of an evaluation. [8] emphasized instructional, organisational and economical aspects, [3] focused on technical aspects and [1] on the ISO 9126. Of course, such dimensions are important for evaluation, because they evaluate the framework of a course and prerequisites for an economical and technical success.

In this paper, we will have a closer look to issues which may be important from a socio-cultural perspective. Therefore, it is necessary to consider different contexts of the course. [28] distinguish four different contexts, which are relevant for e-learning scenarios: an individual context for learning, which relates to the learner, a context of application, which relates to the content, an educational context, which comprises of the methods of instructional design, and a technological context, which comprises of learning technology and media. However, this model omits the collaborative aspect of e-learning. [12] suggests a framework of pedagogical infrastructures. She suggests to classify, design and evaluate the elements of technology-based collaborative learning according to a cognitive, an epistemological, a social and a technical infrastructure.

Using this framework for evaluation, each of the dimensions describes different parameters to evaluate. The cognitive dimension relates to learners' cognitive prerequisites and evaluates if learners have the knowledge, skills and strategies, which are necessary for working in the learning environment. The epistemological dimension relates to the content and evaluates the quality and structure of the content, its implementation and its effects on the learners. The social dimension is related with sociability which comprises of facilitation and tutoring, and learners' opportunities to have social interactions and finally the technical dimension deals with the usability of the learning environment and support for learners' technical problems. In the following, we will describe these dimensions in more detail.

3 Cognitive Dimension

The cognitive dimension relates to the issue how far learners have the ***learning prerequisites*** and appropriate ***learning strategies*** to work within the learning environment. In contrast to the epistemic dimension, which mainly focuses on aspects of the target group, this cognitive dimension focuses more on the individual learner.

The evaluation of *learners' prerequisites* is essential for running an e-learning course. [9] calls this input analysis. This helps to characterize and define a target group and particular learning goals. The most obvious prerequisite is a learner's individual prior knowledge (see e.g. [6], [23]). Knowledge about how learners with different levels of prior knowledge perform in a learning environment can be an important aspect for specific facilitation and the tailoring of the learning environment (see [24]).

One specific prerequisite are individual learning strategies (see [14], [16]). E-learning allows many different learning scenarios ranging from drill and practice exercises to case based learning scenarios and inquiry. These different learning scenarios also require different *learning strategies* to benefit of the learning environment.

Learners of different educational backgrounds may also differ with respect to their strategies and therefore, they may be important to evaluate.

4 Epistemological Dimension

The epistemological dimension relates to the structure and implementation of the content. This dimension should cover three parameters, the issue about the ***correctness and appropriateness*** of the content, the issue of the presentation of the content (***didactical design***) and the issue of learner perception of the content (***acceptance***).

The parameter of *correctness/appropriateness* is crucial for the development of learning material. It is obvious that designers should take care not to teach wrong facts. Different approaches to explain certain phenomena should be categorized as approach rather than as evidence. Furthermore, the appropriateness of content for the target group may be important to consider. Appropriateness of the content may relate on its level of difficulty as well as on learners' social and cultural context.

The parameter of the *didactical design* evaluates which instructional efforts are made to facilitate learners' knowledge construction [27]. Evaluating the didactical design, one can make conclusions about the appropriateness of the teaching methods. The evaluation of the didactical design may comprise of several aspects, e.g. the theoretical foundation of the learning environment, goals for the learners, curriculum integration and motivation.

The parameter of *acceptance* relates to the issue how learners perceive the contents and the teaching methods ([4], [5]). The acceptance of a learning environment is of particular importance for its success, because if learners don't accept a learning environment, they would hardly use it beneficially.

5 Social Dimension

With respect to the social dimension, the focus should be on ***facilitation/tutoring*** and ***sociability***.

Facilitation/tutoring is an important parameter, because it may cover several aspects. It may evaluate tutor support for learners' content specific problems, e.g. if learners have difficulties with comprehension, as well as the moderation and guidance through learners' collaborative work [21]. E-learning environments may be subject to particular group phenomena (e.g. lurking, flaming, illusions of consensus; [29]) and a tutor's intervention may be an important mean for the success of the collaborative work.

Sociability relates to the issue how far learners perceive the learning environment as a social medium [10]. This may be important for learning environments which requires learners' commitment over a longer period of time. Ensuring the learner's commitment is in the focus of social validity as well which is an important quality criteria in diagnostics. Social validity makes the diagnostic aspect of a situation to an "acceptable one" and is achieved through transparency (in terms of background information about the evaluation situation), the learner's participation, his information, and feedback [20]. In sum, it can be seen as fairness of the situation. Social aspects of evaluation are important and must not be neglected. The sociability of the learning environment may have effects on the drop off rates of a course and therefore it is important to evaluate.

6 Technical Dimension

Regarding the technical dimension, ***usability*** and technical ***support*** should be evaluated.

The parameter of *usability* is important for evaluation, because it reveals if the learning environment provides particular problems for learners when working within. Usability is defined as "the extent to which a product can be used by specified users to achieve specified goals effectively, efficiently and satisfactory in a specified context of use" [9]. Usability describes how easy a product or media can be used. It considers the satisfaction of the user who wants to fulfil a specified task with the aid of the product. It is a multidimensional property of a system or user interface [15]. Thus, Usability may cover several aspects. Considering e-learning in first line, it should particularly focus on the computer literacy of the target group.

The parameter of *support* receives importance because many e-learning environments use proprietary media format and rely on particular player software. Furthermore, streaming contents rely on high-performance streaming servers, which should be placed in an appropriate network structure. Learners may experience technical problems and need therefore technical support.

7 Summary

Evaluation is an important aspect of any e-learning project. Taking a socio-cultural perspective, evaluation should focus on participants' background and differences in attitudes, values and stereotypes. Even evaluation methods may be influenced by social-cultural issues, because different methods are accepted differently from country to country depending upon the culture's openness to evaluation in general and its familiarity with diagnostic methods.

The paper first gave a general definition of evaluation. Different parameters for evaluation then were in the centre: a thoroughly conducted evaluation from a social-cultural perspective must not ignore to consider a cognitive dimension (learner perspective), an epistemological dimension (structure and content of medium), a social dimension (interaction between learner and facilitator), and a technical dimension (usability and technical support).

[19] emphasizes that evaluations can be substantially better, if they take place already in an early stage of development to prevent inefficient developments, if they ask questions which are oriented on the goals of development, if they consider the particular context of a course and if they take different perspectives into account, e.g. deciders and developers, teachers and learners, and directly involved persons and external experts.

In the future, the knowledge about evaluation of e-learning must be sensitively transferred onto the socio-cultural perspective which may be a challenge for scientists, evaluators and practitioners.

8 Outlook

This paper focused on evaluation mainly on the level of course implementation and allows thereby continuous optimization and quality assurance. As we mentioned before, evaluation may also be decision-oriented. CIPP-models which analyze context, input process and product (see [26]) can furthermore provide insights on a macro level with respect to how far particular measures, e.g. e-learning courses have an impact on organizational development. Such analyses look beyond aspects of a particular course on the integration of e-learning and its penetration towards the development of a knowledge society. As knowledge societies aim at new forms of learning, e.g. by changing lecture models [18] or implementing educative networks [6], it is important to explore the values and benefits of such approaches. However, there is the need for high quality project management [2] and thorough evaluation of each single measure.

Acknowledgements. Parts of this contribution were funded by EU (LLP-Program, Projects EFELSE 147760-LLP-2008-GR-KA1-KA1NLLS and PREDIL 141967-2008-LLP-GR-COMENIUS-CMP), DAAD and IKY (Project D0813016 resp. Agreement number 136 IKYDA 2009: Comparative study on gender differences in technology enhanced and computer science learning: Promoting equity).

References

1. Abran, A., Khelefi, A., Suryn, W., Seffah, A.: Usability meanings and interpretations in ISO standards. Software Quarterly Journal 11, 325–338 (2003)
2. Bodea, C.-N., Dascalu, M., Coman, M.: Quality of project management education and training programmes. International Journal of Knowledge Society Research 1, 13–25 (2010)
3. Buendia Garcia, F., Hervas Jorge, A.: Evaluating e-learning platforms through SCORM specifications. In: Proceeding of the IADIS Virtual Multi Conference on Computer Science and Information Systems, MCCSIS 2006 (2006)
4. Bürg, O., Mandl, H.: Akzeptanz von E-Learning von Unternehmen. Zeitschrift für Personalpsychologie 4, 75–85 (2005)
5. Davies, F.: Perceived usefulness, perceived ease of use and user acceptance of information technology. MIS Quarterly 13, 319–339 (1989)
6. Diaz Gibson, J., Civis Zaragoza, M., Longas Mayayo, J., Murat, L.: The study of educative network organizations in the city of Barcelona: The Nou Barris district. International Journal of Knowledge Society Research 1, 26–37 (2010)
7. Ertl, B., Kopp, B., Mandl, H.: Effects of an individual's prior knowledge on collaborative knowledge construction and individual learning outcomes in videoconferencing. In: Computer Supported Collaborative Learning 2005: the Next 10 Years!, pp. 145–154. Lawrence Erlbaum Associates, Mahwah (2005)

8. Henninger, M., Balk, M.: Integrative Evaluation: Ein Ansatz zur Erhöhung der Akzeptanz von Lehrevaluation an Hochschulen. Ludwig-Maximilians-Universität, München (2001)
9. Information Society for All. Definitions & Glossary, `http://is4all-web@ics.forth.gr`
10. Kreijns, K., Kirschner, P., Jochems, W.: The sociability of computer supported collaborative learning environments. Educational Technology & Society 5, 8–22 (2002)
11. Lave, J., Wenger, E.: Situated learning: Legitimate peripheral participation. Cambridge University Press, New York (1991)
12. Lakkala, M.: The pedagogical design of technology enhanced collaborative learning, `http://www.elearningeuropa.info/files/media/media13028.pdf`
13. Mandl, H., Hense, J.: Lässt sich Unterricht durch Evaluation verbessern?. In: Spuren der Schulevaluation. Zur Bedeutung und Wirksamkeit von Evaluationskonzepten im Schulalltag, pp. 85–99. Klinkhardt, Bad Heilbrunn (2007)
14. Mandl, H., Friedrich F.: Handbuch Lernstrategien. Hogrefe, Göttingen (2005)
15. Nielsen, J.: Usability 101: Introduction to Usability, `http://www.useit.com/alertbox/20030825.html`
16. Pintrich, P., Smith, D., Garcia, T., Mckeachie, W.: Reliability and predictive validity of the motivated strategies for learning questionnaire (MSLQ). Educational and Psychological Measurement 53, 801–813 (1993)
17. Reinmann-Rothmeier, G., Mandl, H., Erlach, C., Neubauer, A.: Wissensmanagement lernen. In: Ein Leitfaden Zur Gestaltung Von Workshops und zum Selbstlernen. Beltz, Weinheim (2001)
18. Ronchetti, M.: A different perspective on lecture video-streaming: how to use technology to help change the traditional lecture model. International Journal of Knowledge Society Research 1, 50–60 (2010)
19. Schaumburg, H.: Die 5 Ws der Evaluation von E-learning, `http://www2.hu-berlin.de/didaktik/de/personal/schaumburg/Texte/Text_II_Schaumburg_75_83.pdf`
20. Schuler, H., Stehle, W.: Neuere Entwicklungen des Assessment-Center-Ansatzes – beurteilt unter dem Aspekte der sozialen Validität. Zeitschrift für Arbeits- und Organisationspsychologie 27, 33–44 (1983)
21. Schweizer, K., Pächter, M., Weidenmann, B.: A field study on distance education and communication: Experiences of a virtual tutor. Journal of Computer Mediated Communication 6 (2001)
22. Sfard, A.: On two metaphors for learning and the dangers of choosing just one. Educational Researcher 27, 4–13 (1998)
23. Shapiro, A.: Prior Knowledge Must Be Included as a Subject Variable in Learning Outcomes Research. American Educational Research Journal 41, 159–189 (2004)
24. Stark, R., Mandl, H.: "Unauffällige", "Vorwissensschwache", "Unmotivierte" und "Musterschüler": Homogene Untergruppen beim Lernen mit einem komplexen Lösungsbeispiel im Bereich empirischer Forschungsmethoden. Ludwig-Maximilians-Universität, München (2002)
25. Stockmann, R.: Evaluation in Deutschland. In: Evaluationsforschung. Grundlagen und ausgewählte Forschungsfelder, pp. 11–40. Leske + Budrich, Opladen (2000)
26. Stufflebeam, D.L.: An introduction to the PDK book. Educational evaluation and decision-making. In: Educational Evaluation: Theory and Practice, pp. 128–150. Charles A. Jones Publication, Wadsworth Publishing Company, Belmont, CA (1978)

27. Tennyson, R., Schott, F., Seel, N., Dijkstra, S.: Instructional Design: International Perspectives. Lawrence Erlbaum Associates, Mahwah (1997)
28. Tergan, S.-O., Schenkel, P.: Was macht Lernen erfolgreich? Evaluation des Lernpotentials von E-learning. In: Handbuch E-learning, ch. 4.20. Fachverlag Dt. Wirtschaftsdienst, Köln (2001)
29. Weinberger, A.: Scripts for computer-supported collaborative learning. Ludwig-Maximilians-Universität, München (2003)

Metadata and Ontologies in Learning Resources Design

Christian Vidal C.[1], Alejandra Segura Navarrete[1], Víctor Menéndez D.[2], Alfredo Zapata Gonzalez[2], and Manuel Prieto M.[3]

[1] Universidad del Bio-Bio, Avda. Collao 1202. Concepción, Chile
[2] Univ. Autónoma de Yucatán. FMAT Periférico Norte. 13615, 97110 Mérida, Yuc, Mexico
[3] Univ. de Castilla-La Mancha. ESI. Po. de la Universidad. 4, 13071 Ciudad Real, Spain
{cvidal,asegura}@ubiobio.cl, {mdoming,zgonzal}@uady.mx, manuel.prieto@uclm.es

Abstract. Resource design and development requires knowledge about educational goals, instructional context and information about learner's characteristics among other. An important information source about this knowledge are metadata. However, metadata by themselves do not foresee all necessary information related to resource design. Here we argue the need to use different data and knowledge models to improve understanding the complex processes related to e-learning resources and their management. This paper presents the use of semantic web technologies, as ontologies, supporting the search and selection of resources used in design. Classification is done, based on instructional criteria derived from a knowledge acquisition process, using information provided by IEEE-LOM metadata standard. The knowledge obtained is represented in an ontology using OWL and SWRL. In this work we give evidence of the implementation of a Learning Object Classifier based on ontology. We demonstrate that the use of ontologies can support the design activities in e-learning.

Keywords: Ontology, Instructional Design, knowledge acquisition, web semantic.

1 Introduction

In the words of Tim Berners-Lee [1] "The Semantic Web is an extension of the current web in which information has a well-defined meaning, more understandable by computers, and where people work cooperatively". In such sense, including technologies used in recent times, ontologies enable better define the meaning of things on the web. They are designed so that this meaning could be processed by machines and humans, due to its precise semantic [2]. Languages based on XML as OWL or RDF allows specifying ontological models. OWL is the ontology language recommended by the World Wide Web Consortium [3]. OWL exploits many of the capabilities of Description Logic, including a well-defined semantics and some techniques for practical reasoning. Another important language is SWRL (Semantic Web Rules Language) that allows as to define rules in ontologies. This language is used as a complement to the ontological structure described by OWL.

M.D. Lytras et al. (Eds.): WSKS 2010, Part I, CCIS 111, pp. 105–114, 2010.

Educational Ontologies are those that can be used in Web based teaching [4]. According to [5] in e-learning, ontologies have been largely used to systematically describe resources; to enable semantic search and to provide users with a benchmark for shared concepts and terminology.

WWW offers teacher-designers a huge amount of resources that can be used to support learning. Although many of these resources are stored in Repositories, Learning Objects do not always have enough information to use them correctly from an educational perspective. In e-learning environments, the design of learning resources becomes an essential activity. The ultimate goal of learning resources is to enable and enhance learning, but according to [6], a large amount of these resources lack a defined instructional strategy, which causes many of them to fail in their goals. The use of Instructional Design theories can guide the construction of learning resources and help to achieve learning objectives. According to Reigeluth, an Instructional Design theory is a theory that offers explicit guidance on how to help people to learn [7]. For this reason, it is believed to be useful for designers of e-learning resources the knowledge modelling of these theories in precise semantic structures. For example, ontologies can be used to develop processes that support design [8] [9].

In the terminology of Instructional Design, sequencing meant taking individual Learning Objects (LO) and combining them in a way that made instructional sense [10]. To achieve this, there must be enough information in LO from the educational perspective. Some of this information about LO instructional use, can be found in metadata. IEEE-LOM standard [11] in its educational category provides important information for this purpose. Other categories that help to describe some educational aspects of the LO's are: relation, annotation and classification. However, this information is insufficient for many purposes. For example, for sequencing, to it, would be desirable to classify LO's from a pedagogical perspective in order to meet those objects that encourage learning as active or passive, or with a high level of interaction. Thus, course designers might use LO's for their instructional requirements. But this requires more complex analysis of the instructional information provided by metadata individually and collectively.

Machine learning techniques can be used to automatically extract characterizations of LO collections. Indeed, the application of Data Mining (DM) techniques in the e-learning domain, have become more frequent in recent years [12],[13]. DM in e-learning has been mainly oriented to analyze student's behaviour, outcomes and interests in their interaction with learning technology and learning resources.

This article presents the process of obtaining useful knowledge for Instructional Design by applying DM techniques to LO metadata contained in a repository. The resulting knowledge is represented using semantic web technology, particularly with ontological languages, to support Learning Object Classification according to instructional needs.

The structure of the paper is as follows: Section 2 presents the general approach used to obtain knowledge. Section 3 describes the ontology model which represents the resulting knowledge. Section 4 presents the way to use the ontology in the practice. Finally conclusions are presented and the direction of future work of this research.

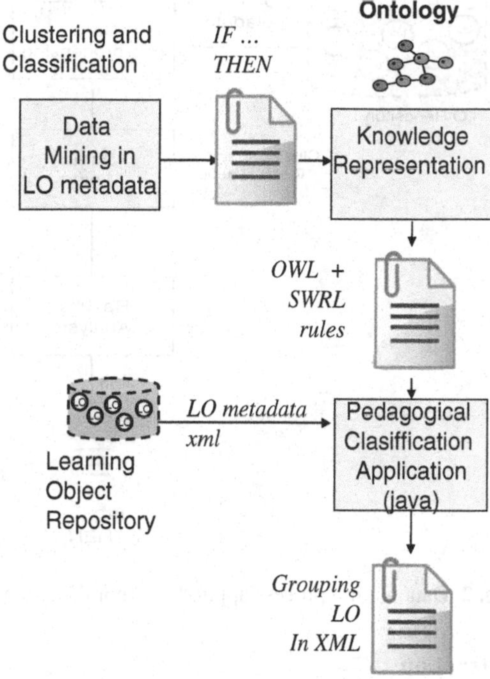

Fig. 1. Process of generation and representation of knowledge

2 Knowledge Acquisition

Here we focus on analyzing metadata stored in Agora[14]. This system has several modules that interact with each other to provide metadata assisted generation, LO management and resource recovery in its own repository as well as a management and knowledge representation generated by the user activity.

The knowledge gained through data mining techniques, is represented in the ontology. Figure 1 shows the process of generation and representation of knowledge. The following sections detail the relevant aspects of the approach used.

2.1 Knowledge Discovering

The process of knowledge discovery applied on data provided by the Agora Repository considered the information pre-processing, the application of DM algorithms and the post-processing. Metadata were extracted for 200 objects stored in Agora. The study used those objects that are of greater completeness in its metadata. Subsequently, clustering and classification techniques were applied to metadata. Results were interpreted and transformed into a rules set. This process is documented in [15] and is summarized in Figure 2.

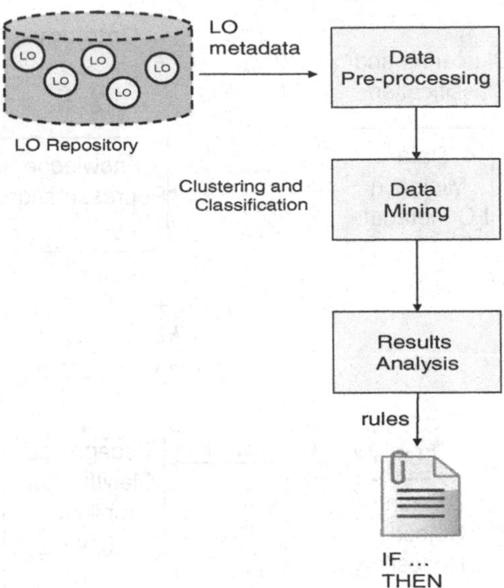

Fig. 2. Data mining process applied to Agora's metadata

2.2 Knowledge Extraction

Applying Simple K-means algorithm allows to establish 3 clusters as shown in Table 1.

Table 1. Clustering results obtained form LOs in Agora

		Cluster#		
Attribute	Full Data	0	1	2
	(200)	(99) 50%	(58) 29%	(43) 22%
aggregation_level	one	one	two	One
structure	atomic	atomic	atomic	Atomic
cat_format	flash	flash	ppt	Pdf
cat_context	high	high	high	High
difficulty	medium	medium	medium	Easy
interactivity_level	very_low	high	low	very_low
interactivity_type	expositive	active	expositive	Expositive
cat_learn_res_type	sld	exe	sld	Rea
semantic_density	medium	high	medium	Medium

Clusters can be described in terms of objects grouped as follows:

- Cluster 0 (actives): Objects more active and highly interactive for the learner. These are mainly resources of type exercise. They have a high semantic density and high complexity level also.
- Cluster 1 (pasives): Objects with low interactivity level and expositive. These resources are mainly slides with a medium level of both complexity and semantic density.

- Cluster 2 (very_pasives): Expositive objects with very low interactivity. They are mainly type resources reading that are easy to use with medium semantic density.

Clustering resulting provides important evidences for Instructional Design. A system for instructional design assistance may use information resulting from clustering for classify LO into the three discovered groups and thus to recommend these resources in different instructional contexts.

3 Knowledge Representation

The knowledge gained in DM process must be represented for later use. This section shows how the knowledge is represented in LOSO ontology.

3.1 LOSO Ontology Model

The rules obtained through the application of DM techniques provided rules that are stored in an ontology to support the sequencing of LOs [16]. This ontology, called LOSO (Learning Object Sequencing Ontology), was created with the intent to support the generation of sequencing strategies for LO. The generation of the Instructional Design Strategy (IDS) is performed according to an Instructional Requirement (IR), which indicates for example, if one require active or passive learning; or some specific student's cognitive style as well as the instructional context, among other information.

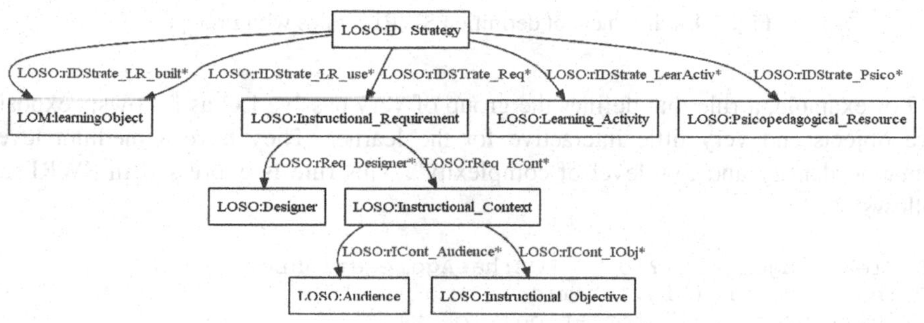

Fig. 3. Fragment of classes and relations of LOSO

All knowledge associated with a IR and other items, are stored in the ontology. A view of the classes and relations that make up the ontology, can be seen in Figure 3. A central concept of the model is ID_Strategy that represents the IDS responding to an IR, related to a specific Instructional_Context. The ID_Strategy relates Learning_Resource, Learning_Activity and Psicopedagogical_resource.

3.2 Representation of Rules in SWRL

OWL was used as representation language with Semantic Web Rules Language (SWRL). Code generation OWL-DL was performed using [17]. OWL allows building hierarchies of concepts and defining them through an axioms language for reasoning and interpretation. SWRL adds an additional layer of expressiveness allowing the definition of inference rules in these models [18].

Rules were implemented using the Protegé SWRLTab plugin, with the Jess rules machine [9]. A view of the execution environment of the rule is displayed in Figure 4.

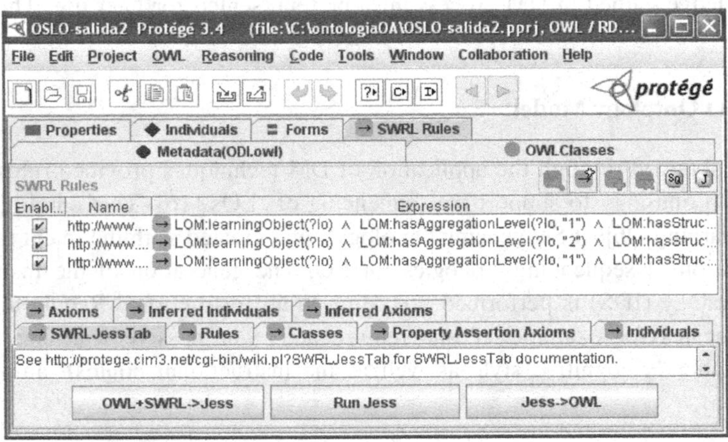

Fig. 4. Environment of definition SWRL's rules with Protégé

For example, a rule that defines the group of very passive LO as follows: "expositive objects and very little interactive for the learner. They have a medium level semantic density and low level of complexity". This rule is expressed in SWRL as follows:

```
LOM:learningObject(?lo) ^ LOM:hasAggregationLevel(?lo,"1") ^
LOM:hasStructure(?lo,"atomic") ^
LOM:hasEducationalInformation(?lo,?x) ^
LOM:isIntendedForContext(?x,"higher education") ^
LOM:hasDifficulty(?x,"easy") ^
LOM:hasInteractivityLevel(?x,"verylow") ^
LOM:hasInteractivityType(?x, "expositive") ^
LOM:hasSemanticDensity(?x, "medium")
→ LOSO:LOGroup(?lo,LOSO:very-pasive )
```

Table 2 shows other rules defined in the ontology. First and the second rules allow classifying LO as active and passive respectively. Rule 3 supports the creation of the IDS.

Table 2. Other rules defined in LOSO

No	Rule	Expression SWRL
1	Active objects	LOM:learningObject(?lo) ^ LOM:hasAggregationLevel(?lo, "1") ^ LOM:hasStructure(?lo, "atomic") ^ LOM:hasEducationalInformation(?lo, ?x) ^ LOM:isIntendedForContext(?x, "higher education") ^ LOM:hasDifficulty(?x, "medium") ^ LOM:hasInteractivityLevel(?x, "high") ^ LOM:hasInteractivityType(?x, "active") ^ LOM:hasSemanticDensity(?x, "high") → LOSO:LOGroup(?lo, LOSO:active)
2	Pasive objects	LOM:learningObject(?lo) ^ LOM:hasAggregationLevel(?lo, "2") ^ LOM:hasStructure(?lo, "atomic") ^ LOM:hasEducationalInformation(?lo, ?x) ^ LOM:isIntendedForContext(?x, "higher education") ^ LOM:hasDifficulty(?x, "medium") ^ LOM:hasInteractivityLevel(?x, "low") ^ LOM:hasInteractivityType(?x, "expositive") ^ LOM:hasSemanticDensity(?x, "medium") → LOSO:LOGroup (?lo,LOSO:pasive)
3	IDS Generation	LOSO:ID_Strategy (?i) ^ LOSO:Instructional_Requirement (?r) ^ LOSO:rIDSTrate_Req (?i,?r) ^ LOSO:Instructional_Context (?ic) ^ LOSO:rReq_ICont (?r,?ic) ^ LOSO:Audience (LOSO:high-education) ^ LOSO:rICont_Audience (?ic, LOSO:high-education) ^ LOSO:rICont_Audience (?ic, LOSO:programming) ^ LOSO:Instructional_Objective (?io) ^ LOSO:Learning_type (LOSO:cognitive-strategies) ^ LOSO:rIObj_LearnType (?io, LOSO:cognitive-strategies) ^ LOSO:Knowledge_type (LOSO:procedural) ^ LOM:learningObject (?lo) → LOSO:rIDStrate_LR_use (?i,?lo)

Rules presented in the ontology can mainly support the classification of LO used in sequencing activities. This provides some degree of automation in this process. Our group is now working in the representation of instructional design theories that may support the sequencing.

4 Knowledge Use: The Pedagogical Resource Classifier

In this section, we present an application that uses LOSO ontology. This application is designed to support the resource design task. It implements a Pedagogical Resources Classifier (PRC) in order to help designer to find the most appropriate resources according to the instructional context. Classifier has two main components: the Instantiation component and the Inference component. The first, performs the instantiation of XML documents into the ontology. This XML document contains metadata for LOs in the IEEE-LOM standard. The second process the inference based on SWRL rules. This application was built in Java and it use Jena Framework to manipulate the ontology, SWRLtab to make inference and JDOM for processing and generation of XML documents. Using PRC a teacher-designer, who works in a LO management environment, repository or LMS, can request items from any of the groups founded: active, passive or very passive. These groups are related to the instructional context where objects are used. As an example, we show the possible context of use for objects of cluster 0 (active): it can be used in constructivist learning environments and based on experience (interactivity_level= high, interactivity_type= active, resource_type= exe), for students with active and intuitive learning styles [19]. These objects can be used in courses with intermediate or advanced students (difficulty= medium, semantic_density= high).

Figure 5 show the interaction between PRC and the Agora repository. The use of XML as data exchange technology, allows communication with other systems that generate the metadata schema of the objects in this format.

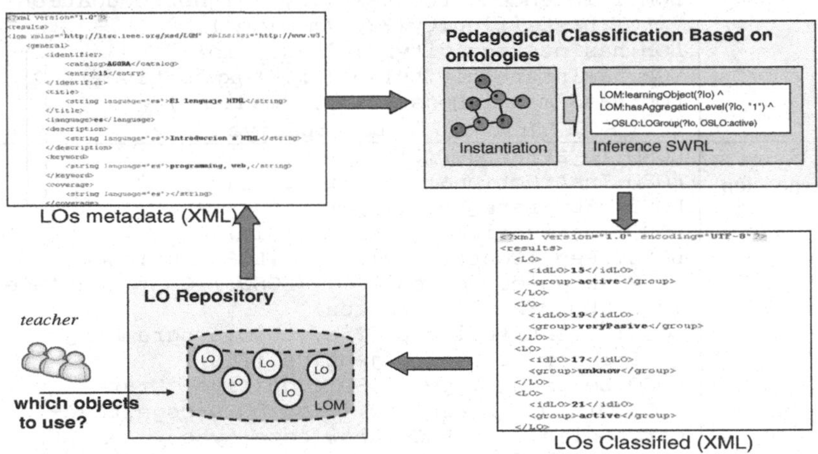

Fig. 5. Interaction between the Classifier and Agora Repository

5 Initial Testing

Some tests have been carried out in order to analyse the tool performance. First, a collection of 49 LO's from the Agora system has been obtained. Next, this collection has been processed by PCR. In this test we achieve: 7 LO's classified as active, 3 LO's as passive, 2 LO's as very_passive and 28 LO's as unknown or not classified.

Second, tests was made witch LO's obtained from Ariadne repository [20]. The classifier processed correctly 300 LO's, but its results were poor. This is because LO from Ariadne have not completed their educational metadata (category 5 IEEE-LOM).

Other test was executed using LO from Mace repository [21]. 115 LO's were processed by PCR with the following results: 13 LO's classified as active, 12 LO's as passive, 14 LO's as very_passive and 76 as unknown. This results show that PCR works correctly but rules for classification must be improved, because they depend on the completeness of metadata.

6 Conclusions and Future Works

This paper presented an approach to incorporate the generation and representation of knowledge as an important input for learning resource development. We demonstrate that the use of ontologies can support design activities in e-learning environments. Results also evidence the importance of using metadata in the Instructional Design process and the possibilities of supporting this process with Semantic Web technologies. We present also an application that supports the resources design task.

The use of ontologies enables that represented knowledge can be used by other applications that provide automated support to this process. We show evidences of use with Agora system and other LO Repository as Ariadne and Mace.

Currently we are also trying to use other models and techniques to improve the knowledge structure and the details provided by the ontology. Additionally, we are working in the use of the obtained results into Learning Object's searching and in metadata assisted generation.

Acknowledgments

This work is partially supported by MECESUP UBB 0305 project, Chile; the National Council of Science and Technology (CONACYT, México); the Council of Science and Technology of Yucatán State (CONCyTEY, México); the TIN2007-67494 project of the Science and Innovation Ministry; The PEIC09-0196-3018 project of the Autonomous Government of Castilla-La Mancha.

References

1. Berners-Lee, T., Hendler, J., Lassila, O.: The Semantic Web. Scientific American 284(5), 28–37 (2001)
2. Horrocks, I., Patel-Schneider, P., McGuinness, D., Welty, C.: OWL: a Description Logic Based Ontology Language for the Semantic Web. In: Baader, F., et al. (eds.) The Description Logic Handbook: Theory, Implementation, and Applications, 2nd edn., ch. 14. Cambridge University Press, Cambridge (2007)
3. OWL Web Ontology Language- Overview (2010), `http://www.w3.org/TR/owl-features/`
4. Hernández, H., Saiz, M.: Ontologías mixtas para la representación conceptual de objetos de aprendizaje. Procesamiento del Lenguaje Natural N. 38 (abr. 2007), pp. 99–106 (2007)
5. Marengo, A., Albanese, D., Convertini, N., Marengo, V., Scalera, M., Serra, A.: Ontological support for the creation of learning objects. In: 28th International Conference on Information Technology Interfaces IEEE, pp. 361–366 (2006)
6. Zouaq, A., Nkambou, R., Frasson, C.: An Integrated Approach for Automatic Aggregation of Learning Knowledge Objects. Interdisciplinary Journal of Knowledge and Learning Objects (IJKLO) (3), 135–162 (2007)
7. Reigeluth, C.M.: What Is Instructional-Design Theory and How Is It Changing? In: Reigeluth, C.M. (ed.) Instructional-Design Theories and Models. A New Paradigm of Instructional Theory, vol. II. Lawrence Erlbaum Associates, Mahwah (1999)

8. Sicilia, M.A.: On the general structure of ontologies of instructional models. In: SPDECE 2007: Proceedings of the IV Simposio Pluridisciplinar sobre Diseño, Evaluación y Desarrollo de Contenidos Educativos Reutilizables, Bilbao, Spain (2007)
9. Hayashi, Y., Bourdeau, J., Mizoguchi, R.: Ontological Support for a Theory-Eclectic Approach to Instructional and Learning Design. In: Nejdl, W., Tochtermann, K. (eds.) EC-TEL 2006. LNCS, vol. 4227, pp. 155–169. Springer, Heidelberg (2006)
10. Willey, D.: Connecting learning objects to instructional design theory: A definition, a metaphor, and a taxonomy. In: Wiley, D.A., et al, eds. (2007), `http://www.reusability.org/read/chapters/wiley.doc`
11. Draft Standard for Learning Object Metadata. IEEE P1484.12.1, IEEE Learning Technology Standards Committee (2002), `http://ltsc.ieee.org/wg12/files/LOM_1484_12_1_v1_Final_Draft.pdf`
12. Romero, C., Ventura, S.: Educational data mining: A survey from 1995 to 2005. Expert Systems with Applications 33(1), 135–146 (2007)
13. Romero, C., Ventura, S., Garcia, E.: Data mining in course management systems: Moodle case study and tutorial. Computers & Education 51(1), 368–384 (2008)
14. Prieto, M., Menéndez, V., Segura, A., Vidal, C.: A Recommender System Architecture for Instructional Engineering. In: Lytras, M.D., et al. (eds.) WSKS 2008. LNCS (LNAI), vol. 5288, pp. 314–321. Springer, Heidelberg (2008)
15. Segura, A., Vidal, C., Menéndez, V., Zapata, A., Prieto, M.: Exploring Characterizations of Learning Object Repositories Using Data Mining Techniques. In: MTSR 2009: Proceedings Metadata and Semantic Research Third International Conference, pp. 215–225. Springer, Heidelberg (2009)
16. Vidal, C., Prieto, M.: Una Ontología de apoyo a actividades de Diseño Instruccional. In: Prieto, M., Sanchez-Alonso, S., et al. (ed.) Recursos Digitales para el Aprendizaje, Editorial Universidad Autónoma de Yucatán (2009) ISBN 9876077573173
17. Protegé. Ontology Tool (2010), `http://protege.stanford.edu/`
18. O'Connor, M., Knublauch, H., Samson, T., Grosof, B., Dean, M., Grosso, W., Musen, M.: Supporting Rule System Interoperability on the Semantic Web with SWRL. In: Gil, Y., Motta, E., Benjamins, V.R., Musen, M.A. (eds.) ISWC 2005. LNCS, vol. 3729, pp. 974–986. Springer, Heidelberg (2005)
19. Felder, R., Silverman, L.: Learning and Teaching Styles in Engineering Education. Engineering Education 78(7), 674–681 (1988)
20. Duval, E., Forte, E., Cardinaels, K., Verhoeven, B., Van Durm, R., Hendrikx, K., Wentland Forte, M., Ebel, N., Macowicz, M., Warkentyne, K., Haenni, F.: The Ariadne knowledge pool system. Communications of the ACM 44(4), 72–78 (2001)
21. Stefaner, M., Vecchia, E.D., Condotta, M., Wolpers, M., Spech, M.T., Apelt, S., Duval, E.: MACE - Enriching architectural learning objects for experience multiplication. In: Duval, E., Klamma, R., Wolpers, M. (eds.) EC-TEL 2007. LNCS, vol. 4753, pp. 322–336. Springer, Heidelberg (2007)

Open Integrated Personal Learning Environment: Towards a New Conception of the ICT-Based Learning Processes*

Miguel Ángel Conde[1], Francisco José García-Peñalvo[1], Mariá José Casany[2], and Marc Alier Forment[2]

[1] Computer Science Department. Science Education Research Institute (IUCE), GRIAL Research Group. University of Salamanca
{mconde, fgarcia}@usal.es

[2] Services & Information Systems Engineering Department, UPC - Campus Nord, building Omega, office 1116, 08034 Barcelona, Spain
mjcasany@lsi.upc.edu, marc.alier@upc.edu

Abstract. Learning processes are changing related to technological and sociological evolution, taking this in to account, a new learning strategy must be considered. Specifically what is needed is to give an effective step towards the eLearning 2.0 environments consolidation. This must imply the fusion of the advantages of the traditional LMS (Learning Management System) – more formative program control and planning oriented – with the social learning and the flexibility of the web 2.0 educative applications.

For this goal, it is compulsory the evolution of the actual LMS to contexts where the new technological trends are integrated with them, introducing the social characteristics and putting the student in the centre of the educative process. These new systems are the Personal Learning Environments (PLE). Thus, we propose a learning personalization system construction that boosts student-centered educative actions. Two aspects are going to be considered, student learning personalization with information from the LMS and student learning personalization inside of an institution context.

Keywords: PLE, LMS, Moodle 2.0, eLearning, SOA.

1 Introduction

Learning processes are changeable elements and therefore they are changing continuously. The evolution of learning processes may be due to new sociological or technological trends, or simply due to pedagogical [1].

The eLearning is one of those evolutions, and eLearning is almost completely assimilated into the educational environments. This learning model has relied on technology without obtaining, in many cases, the expected benefit, as if it has occurred in other areas. One initiative that has gained general acceptance has been the

* This work was supported by the Spanish Industry Ministry (project TSI-020302-2009-35) and by the Castile and Lion Regional Government through GR47 excellence project.

M.D. Lytras et al. (Eds.): WSKS 2010, Part I, CCIS 111, pp. 115–124, 2010.

use of learning platforms (Learning Management System, LMS). These systems provide students and teachers a set of tools for improving learning processes and managing them. However, despite the acceptance they have, the LMS have not achieved the expected improvements due to: 1) The tools provided are not used properly and often are used as mere spaces to publish courses [2], 2) The LMS restrict opportunities to collaborate on student learning and promote social constructivism not limited to a period of time (i.e. academic year) [3], 3) They are focused on the course and the institution rather than the student and their needs [4].

Besides this should be noted that online learning does not end with the LMS, but there are plenty of online tools to supplement and improve it: sources of information (such as communication tools), exchange of experience, etc.

Therefore, new applications must be taken into account, such as the search applications, news applications, location-enabled applications, content repositories, forums, blogs, calendars, online games, virtual worlds, etc. That is, the new initiatives arising from Web 2.0 [5].

Given this situation will be necessary to evolve the LMS to its integration with contexts that include new technological trends, to provide social characteristics and be focused on the student, these contexts are personalized learning environments (Personal Learning Environments, PLE) [6].

The present project aims to define a personal learning system that enhances learning actions considering the student as the center of the processes. To do this two aspects are being considered:

- Personalization of learning by the student, where he will be able to obtain information and combine it with LMS 2.0 educational tools. To do this learning portable components, with information from the LMS, must be provided. They will be known as widgets.
- The personalization of learning by the student in the area of an institution. That is, to empower the student so that within the platform he could include a set of 2.0 tools established by the institution.

In order to extend the possibilities of the project must not be forgotten pedagogical issues or the potential possibilities for expansion to other contexts such as it use in mobile devices.

Throughout this article firstly PLE and its relationship with tools 2.0 will be described. Later we talk about a possible deployment by using service-oriented architectures. Then other possible future applications will be explained. Finally the proposed architecture will be exposed.

2 Personal Learning Environments

Every day becomes more essential developing learning to the trends related to Web 2.0. The education must be supplemented by new applications, tools and paradigms that lead to what is called eLearning 2.0 [7]. This new trend in learning requires tools that facilitate: 1) changes in the ways of interacting socializing the learning; 2) access to tools considering the new performers in learning, natives and digitals immigrants;

3) support to educational trends such as learning throughout life or informal learning, students mobility and so on, related to the Bolonia process; 4) the student-centered learning.

As a proposal to solve all these needs are the PLE, which according to Wilson[6], are defined as learning student-centered contexts that integrate any tool, service, content, evidence and person involved in eLearning process. This way the responsibility of the learning is given to the student, which benefits itself and its formative process[8]. However, some limits could be necessary (generally derived from an institution concerned about the formality of their teaching/learning process) in the means used by the student to define its learning. Hence it's necessary that PLE can be constructed by integrating tools 2.0 and LMS[9]. Define a system that enables both aspects will be the main object of this proposal.

Incorporating Web 2.0 applications into learning processes involves bringing in new styles of communication, new roles, new ways of intervention, new scenarios, a wide range of activities, generally, involves opening a series of educational challenges [10]. Through these trends, students are no longer passive subjects of learning to become active students in classes, with no restrictions, being able to use things like Google, Facebook, Twitter, etc. to support learning processes; they can use digital devices such as computers, mobile phones, mp3, recorders and so on to improve the learning.

The potential of these tools is enormous, as evidenced by experiences such as Jekins [11], Downes [4], and it's increasingly expanding in the different educational environments [12]. Despite all that power is necessary to take into account a number of problems which have arisen through the application of these tools: 1) The improvisation in the use of 2.0 tools and customization of student-centered learning can lead to the wrong idea that the use of this tools into learning should not be planned, this is not correct, they should be estimated, validated and evaluated according to different criteria [13]; 2) Among the problems hampering the full educational utilization of Web 2.0 should be mentioned some technological problems – insufficient bandwidth and lack of access to computers in schools and students' homes – and other pedagogical issues where the biggest challenge is that students don't create products and prefer to "copy and learn", students assessment procedures are not formatives and do not "mix" means. [14]; 3) Lack of support from LMS to the use of these kind of tools.

PLE can solve many of these problems and, after determining their use, you must think how to deal with the system definition. Maybe the first question should be whether starting a solution from scratch or based it on another LMS. Considering existing initiatives is convenient in this regard, as well as the benefits that would have either decision. In this sense there are some studies and experiences such as [15]:

- Analysis concerning the adequacy of integrating 2.0 applications in continuing training context, as well as in web application hybrid (*mash-ups*).
- Definition of PLE from a hybrid approach, describing a customizable web portal as a base of PLE in which would be aggregated different web tools interconnected from different contexts, and providing an interaction language among its users.

- Research of the limitations of the integration of applications derived from the exchange of information between them, the use of REST is proposed to solve them.
- Design and implementation of strategies for PLEs definition.
- Implementation of an institutional PLE for the University of the Basque Country, thus, a PLE where applications 2.0 which student can use are defined by the University.
- RWTH Aachen University was commissioned to develop the *Learning Environment Framework* (PLEF) (http://eiche.informatik.rwth-aachen.de:3333/PLEF/index.jsp), a PLE service that takes care of composing a set of subservices to support the students' activity when composing, manage, tag, annotate and share their favorite resources.

The discussed initiatives define in some cases PLE, but do not consider all areas of information. Most of them only integrate different tools 2.0 in a container, regardless of LMS information. One of them, the Basque Country University works to integrate tools in the LMS, but this integration will be through *widgets* and will not exist, therefore, interaction between tools and platform.

Hence, the system proposed here covers a broader spectrum of communication and do not forget in any case the LMS. Taking into account these experiences could be decided that it might be better to hold the system from scratch, taking the architecture referred to the *mash-ups* and the interaction languages, but should be necessary to consider the futility of reinventing the wheel again. To define a PLE should not assume to discard the functionalities of the LMS, these functionalities can enrich student learning, and 2.0 components integrated in the learning platform would enhance exponentially the possibilities of learning in institutions. Neither should be neglected the acceptance of certain LMS such as Moodle in Spain (and elsewhere in the world).

Once the base has been established, the conversion of LMS into a PLE begins. At this point, the two possibilities of PLE that this project offers should be considered. First, the need to export information from the LMS to a PLE, i.e., the export system of educational portable components, while on the other hand would be the integration of tools 2.0 in the LMS in order to redefine them as iPLE (integrated PLE or institutional PLE, depending on the approach).

Insomuch as the export of information of the platform, you must determine what to import, how to import it and how to display the information.

With regard to what to export, pedagogical criteria must be met considering what information is most critical, which activities are more representatives and enrich the personal student environment, in addition to what information is more appreciated by the students.

Regarding to how to export is considered the usage of a service-oriented architecture (SOA - *Service Oriented Architecture*). It allows, so, the integration of the system regardless of the technology that is implemented, the scalability is improved, more flexible systems are defined, easier to maintain and more resistant to change. It also facilitates the interconnection of heterogeneous contexts such as LMS and mobile devices, as discussed below.

3 Architectures Oriented to Services in Educational Web Environments

There is currently a trend towards modularization of computing systems. This modularization is due to the advantages that it entails, such as independence of development, increase in security, scalability, etc. Moreover, work is being carried out towards the production of software services independent of the underlying implementation. The result of merging both ideas is Service Oriented Architectures (SOA). Among the elements that favored the development of SOA are the developments of different types of applications, computer networks, client-server architectures, etc. [16]. SOA implies a step further in the development of information systems architecture. In its most basic form, SOA is a set of services that communicate with one another[17].

In educational contexts, the application of SOA will be useful in order to adapt the current LMS to emerging technologies, frameworks and specifications and, this way, to transform these legacy systems into service-based eLearning platforms[18]. It is clear, therefore, that the application of these architectures enables communication with learning platforms. Accordingly, there are some initiatives of application of SOA to learning platforms with different purposes, among which we could mention the following:

- Adaptation of part of an LMS services seeking mobility [19]
- Definition of SOA to information recovery and search based on semantic contents [20]
- Integration of learning tools in other systems [21].

Regarding the LMS we have selected (Moodle), the groups that propose this project (GESSI, from the Polytechnic University of Catalonia and GRIAL, from the University of Salamanca) are working together towards the integration of a SOA in this LMS. To adapt Moodle into SOA is not an easy task, as it requires a profound knowledge of the main libraries in Moodle, the functionalities available, the capabilities of each user, etc. In 2008, the GESSI group was entrusted by Martin Dougiamas, founder of Moodle, with the development of a new API to access the services of the Moodle kernel regardless of its implementation which would remain stable in future Moodle implementations. This API consists of a set of web services where most functionalities of an external application might need are encapsulated. In October, 2008, the web service layer was integrated in some Moodle distributions for testing purposes. This layer aims at being useful for all developers who wish to define applications for Moodle without the need to touch the LMS code. This API will become, in the present project, the base for the development of a Service Oriented Architecture consisting of: 1) a scalable layer of connectors that will keep separated the communication protocol applications from the web services and that will allow the addition of new protocols that might appear in the future; 2) an integration layer that serves as an access point for the initial functionalities of Moodle, such as authentication; 3) a web service layer that actually interacts with the Moodle kernel and its inner functionalities.

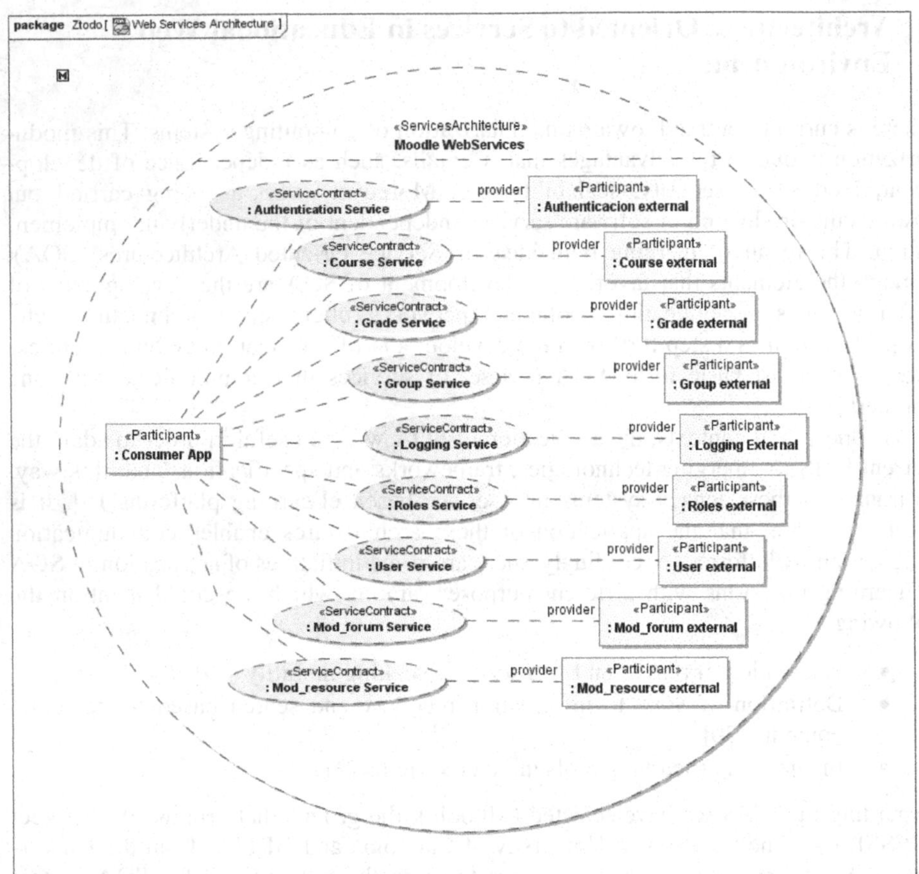

Fig. 1. Moodle Service Contracts

Some of the main services developed for Moodle are shown in the Figure 1, described using SOAml.

This architecture will be responsible for providing information, but it has to be considered how to visualize this information and how to integrate it as a portable educational element, in this case, as a widget. Widgets are small and portable elements that can be run in any HTML context [22], providing functionality "live", content or functionality from some other website. Therefore, information from different 2.0 applications could be shown, as well as information present in an LMS. As far as the application of the project is concerned, a system capable of generating widgets out of information from Moodle would have to be implemented. To make these widgets easy to integrate in different containers, different types of widgets must be considered.

Therefore, the widget generation model has to be defined following the information in Moodle as the source of portable educational components for their integration in PLEs external to the LMS.

Another possibility to take into account is the idea of integrating external tools into Moodle with the aim of providing students with a PLE within Moodle. For each of these tools, careful attention should be paid to how they should be implemented and how they should be presented to students and teachers so that they could find them useful. Also, there needs to be determined the type of feedback that would be useful both for the teacher and for the institution or, in other words, how the integrated tool would interact with Moodle.

4 Architecture Proposal

Given the above, it will pose an architecture that exploits the SOA layer component of Moodle. Specifically, the external layer will be a layer which access to internal Moodle information, also a set of web services will be defined, geared to the specific needs of the types of environments to define, and connectors will be the link to other systems. On that basis, the architecture will incorporate an educational component model that enables portable platform information and export it to contexts 2.0. This capability allows users to construct their knowledge, but also must be considered to control the process. That is why we consider the possibility of incorporating 2.0 tools within the LMS. To do this, an IMS LTI gateway will be used, allowing that external applications could be included transparently into Moodle.

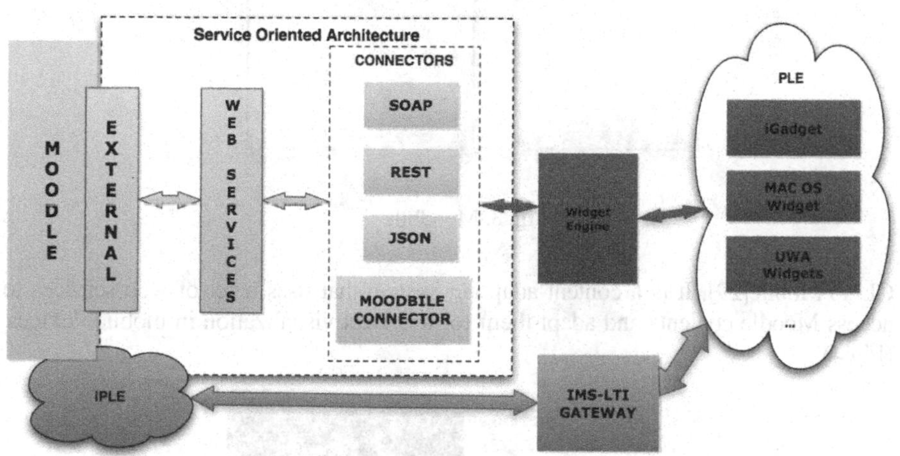

Fig. 2. Architecture Proposal

Figure 2 shows the distribution of the different architectural components. Gray color shows the SOA components as well as a set of connectors to facilitate access to it. An engine to define learning portable components will use those connectors, and those components will compose the PLE (red). And in order to the integration of 2.0 tools an IMS LTI gateway will be used (in blue).

5 Other Applications

In order to define a really innovative system with great potential for learning it has been considered the possibility of generating portable educational components so that these could be used not only in web containers, but also in mobile devices. Mobile phones are also employing 2.0 applications[23], and this fact, applied to learning, offers new alternatives as both traditional learning support and a fundamental element in informal learning [24]. There exist initiatives seeking integration of LMS in mobile phones [25-27], but our project does not intend to follow that path. The goal of this project is to integrate portable defined elements in a widget container of a mobile device. The experience of the members of both groups will prove very valuable in order to achieve this task, using previous work done, such as Moodbile and Claymobile:

- Moodbile[28]. It is a program implemented to test Moodle web services and their application in mobile clients. Forums, wiki contents, glossary entries, instant messages, calendar, etc. Can be viewed using this application. (Fig 3).

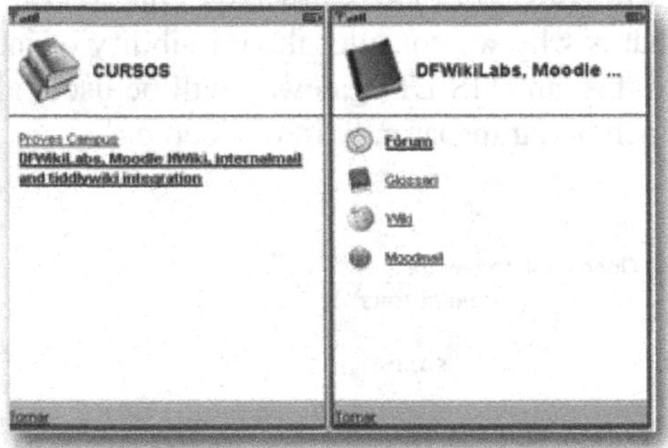

Fig. 3. Moodbile

- CLAYMobile[29]. It is a content-adapting system that uses a set of web services to access Moodle contents and adapt them for a correct visualization in mobile devices. (Fig 4).

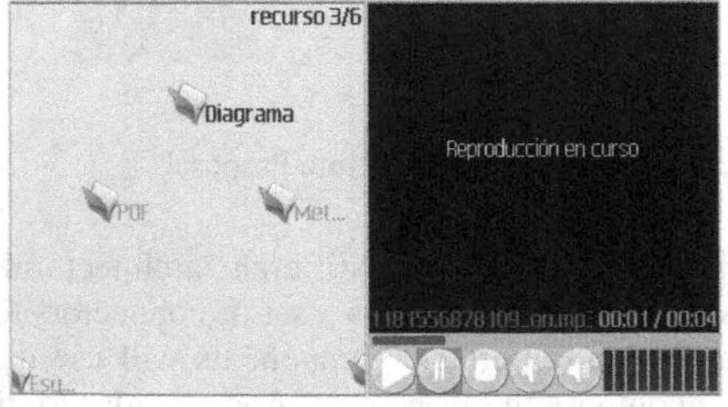

Fig. 4. ClayMobile

These two projects are being merged into a mobile client for Moodle called Moodbile (http://moodbile.org), which consists of a set of SOA components that package Moodle services with a HTML 5.0 + AJAX client. This client implements a mobile application designed to experience Moodle from a mobile browser (such as those provided by Android, iPhone, etc.). Once this is achieved, the SOA defined on Moodle and Moodbile adaptation and visualization systems will be used in order to integrate in a single device the portable educational components and a set of 2.0 applications.

6 Conclusions

eLearning needs evolve, and this evolution must consider the student. Usually, in online learning processes, the student is conditioned to temporal issues, LMS technical constraints or an inefficient use of learning platforms features. If we don't consider the students as the center of eLearning processes, if new technological and sociological trends are not considered, any eLearning activity will fail.

To avoid this situation will be necessary the personalization of LMS and its integration with 2.0 tools and applications. This is the main reason of the definition of PLE and our proposal considers the two possible ways of its application. Free personalization leaded by the student and the possibility of personal learning environments conducted by an organization. These two new learning practices must be supported by technologies, and must consider existent Learning Management Systems such as Moodle. This platform includes a web service layer that allows the connection with other application and establishes a medium of exchange of information, which could be used to define learning portable components that will compound new personalized learning contexts.

This proposal will be a core for different learning initiatives and could be used in different context such as mobile environments.

References

1. García Peñalvo, F.J.: Estado Actual de los Sistemas E-Learning. Teoría de la Educación. Educación y Cultura en la Sociedad de la Información 6 (2005)
2. Carolina, U.o.N.: Sakai Pilot Evaluation Final Report (2009)
3. Brown, J.S., Adler, R.P.: Minds on Fire: Open Education, the Long Tail, and Learning 2.0. Educause Quarterly 42, 16–32 (2008)
4. Downes, S.: E-learning 2.0. Elearn magazine (2006)
5. O'Reilly, T.: What is Web 2.0: Design Patterns and Business Models for the Next Generation of Software (2005)
6. Wilson, S., Liber, O., Johnson, M., Beauvoir, P., Sharples, P., Milligan, C.: Personal Learning Environments: Challenging the dominant design of educational systems. Journal of e-Learning and Knowledge Society 3, 27–38 (2007)
7. Ajjan, H., Hartshorne, R.: Investigating faculty decisions to adopt Web 2.0 technologies: Theory and Empirical Tests. The Internet and Higher Education 11, 71–80 (2008)
8. Lepper, M.R.: Microcomputers in education: Motivational and social issues. American Psychologist 40, 1–18 (1980)

9. Gogoulou, A., Gouli, E., Grigoriadou, M., Samarakou, M., Chinou, D.: A Web-based Educational Setting Supporting Individualized Learning, Collaborative Learning and Assessment. Educational Technology & Society 10, 242–256 (2007)
10. SCOPEO: Formación Web 2.0. Monográfico SCOPEO (2009)
11. Jenkins, H.: Convergence Culture: Where Old and New Media Collide. NYU Press, New York (2006)
12. De Pablos, J.: El cambio metodológico en el espacio europeo de educación superior y el papel de las tecnologías de la información y la comunicación. Revista Iberoamericana de Educación a Distancia 10, 15–44 (2007)
13. Suárez, C.: Educación y virtualidad. URP (2008)
14. BECTA: Web 2.0 technologies for learning at KS3 and KS4 Project overview (2008)
15. Casquero, O., Portillo, J., Ovelar, R., Benito, M., Romo, J.: PLE Network: an integrated eLearning 2.0 architecture from University's perspective. Interactive Learning Environments (in Press)
16. Ramaratnam, R.: An analysis of service oriented architectures. In: System Design and Management Program. Massachusetts Institute of Technology (2007)
17. Payne, B.R., Barrody, A.J.: Service oriented architecture. Rochester Institute of Technology (2006)
18. Dagger, D., O'Connor, A., Lawless, S., Walsh, E., Wade, V.P.: Service-Oriented E-Learning Platforms: From Monolithic Systems to Flexible Services. IEEE Internet Computing 11, 28–35 (2007)
19. Kurz, S., Podwyszynski, M., Schwab, A.: A Dynamically Extensible, Service-Based Infrastructure for Mobile Applications (2008)
20. LUISA: Learning Content Management System Using Innovative Semantic Web Services Architecture (2009)
21. Pätzold, S., Rathmayer, S., Graf, S.: Proposal for the Design and Implementation of a Modern System Architecture and integration infrastructure in context of e-learning and exchange of relevant data. In: E-Learning, E.I.F. (ed.) ILearning Forum 2008, pp. 82–90 (2008)
22. W3C: Widgets 1.0 Packaging and Configuration. In: Draft, W.C.W. (ed.) (2008)
23. Jaokar, A., Fish, T.: Mobile Web 2.0: The Innovator's Guide to Developing and Marketing Next Generation Wireless/Mobile Applications. Futuretext (2006)
24. Cobcroft, R., Towers, S., Smith, J., Bruns, A.: Mobile learning in review: Opportunities and challenges for learners, teachers, and institutions. In: Learning on the Move Brisbane, Australia (2006)
25. Cheung, B., Stewart, B., McGreal, R.: Going Mobile with MOODLE: First steps. IADIS Press (2006)
26. Podwyszynski, M., Schwab, A.: A dynamically extensible service-based infrastructure for mobile applications. In: Song, I.-Y., Piattini, M., Chen, Y.-P.P., Hartmann, S., Grandi, F., Trujillo, J., Opdahl, A.L., Ferri, F., Grifoni, P., Caschera, M.C., Rolland, C., Woo, C., Salinesi, C., Zimányi, E., Claramunt, C., Frasincar, F., Houben, G.-J., Thiran, P. (eds.) ER Workshops 2008. LNCS, vol. 5232, pp. 155–164. Springer, Heidelberg (2008)
27. Riad, A.M.: A service oriented architecture to integrate mobile assessment in Learning Management Systems. Turkish Online Journal of Distance Education 9 (2008)
28. Alier, M., Casado, P.: A Mobile extension to a web based Moodle virtual classroom. In: E-challenges International Conference, Netherlands, vol. 4 (2007)
29. Conde, M.Á., Muñoz, C., García, F.J.: Sistemas de Adaptación de contenidos para dispositivos móviles. In: Lozano, M., Gallud, J.A. (eds.) Actas del congreso de IX Congreso Internacional de Interacción Persona - Ordenador, Albacete, pp. 143–147 (2008)

An Assessment of Node Classification Accuracy in Social Networks Using Label-Dependent Feature Extraction

Tomasz Kajdanowicz, Przemysław Kazienko, Piotr Doskocz, and Krzysztof Litwin

Wrocław University of Technology, Wyb. Wyspiańskiego 27, 50-370 Wrocław, Poland
{tomasz.kajdanowicz,kazienko,piotr.doskocz, krzysztof.litwin}@pwr.wroc.pl

Abstract. Node classification in Social Network is currently receiving raising attention in the Social Network Analysis research. The main objective of node classification is to assign the correct label to the unlabeled nodes from a set of all possible class labels. This classification task is performed using features extracted from a Social Network dataset. The success of proper feature extraction significantly influences classification accuracy, providing more discriminative description of the data. This paper describes label-dependent features extraction and examines the classification accuracy based on features extracted with this approach. The experiments on real-world data have shown that usage of label-dependent features can lead to significant improvement of classification accuracy.

Keywords: Label-dependent features, collective classification, feature extraction, classification, social network analysis.

1 Introduction

One of the most important concepts in Machine Learning is classification. It is usually based on the data that represents relationships between a fixed set of attributes and one target class. These relations describe each object independently. However, there are many classification tasks where dataset's instances are implicitly or explicitly related. Knowledge about those relations brings additional input information that may be utilized in classification.

There are some applications and research methods, especially related to social networks, which are able to produce data with dependencies between labels of interconnected objects, referred as relational autocorrelation [9]. Based on these connections additional input information should be added to the classification process that has been observed in a wide variety of data autocorrelation situations [4].

According to [11], all network objects may be described by three distinct types of information that can be easily used in label classification: correlation between the object's label (class) and its attributes, correlation between the object's label and the

M.D. Lytras et al. (Eds.): WSKS 2010, Part I, CCIS 111, pp. 125–130, 2010.

observed labels of other objects in its neighborhood and, consequently, correlation between the object's label and unobserved labels of other objects in its neighborhood.

In collective classification, cases that can be interrelated are being simultaneously classified. When autocorrelation is utilized, accuracy of a classification process can be highly improved [7, 10, 12].

Basic task of within-network classification [1, 8] is to assign the correct labels to the unlabeled nodes from a set of the possible class labels. Main difficulty here is to extract the set of most discriminative features from the network nodes and their connections to achieve the best classification model.

In further sections the paper briefly covers related work (Section 2) and node classification using label-dependent features (Section 3). Section 4 contains description of the experimental setup and the obtained results. The paper is concluded in Section 6.

2 Related Work

In recent years, there has appeared a great number of works describing models and techniques for classification in network data. Analogously to classical machine learning problems, classification in network data requires specialized solutions for feature extraction, high performance supervised and unsupervised learning algorithms, sparse data handling, etc.

In general, network classification problems, may be solved using two main approaches: by within-network and across-network inference. Overall, the networked data have several unique characteristics that simultaneously complicate and provide leverage to learning and classification. More generally, network data allow the use of the features of the node's neighbors to label them, although it must be performed with care to avoid increase of variance estimation [5].

There have been developed many algorithms and models for classification in the network. Two distinct types of classification in networks may be distinguished: based on collection of local conditional classifiers and based on the classification stated as one global objective function. The most known implementations of the first approach are iterative classification (ICA) and Gibbs sampling algorithm (GS) [11].

One of the most crucial problems in the network classification is feature extraction. According to [2] the derived features are divided into two categories: label-dependent (LD) and label-independent (LI). Features LD use both structure of the network as well as information about labels of the neighboring nodes labels. Features LI, in turn, are calculated using the network structure only. What is worth mentioning, most of the proposed network classification methods were usually applied to the data sets with very limited access to labels. Their authors assumed that their applications need to deal even with only 1% labeled nodes. This problem is known as classification in sparsely labeled networks [2, 3].

3 Node Classification Using Label-Dependent Features

A social network may be defined as a graph $G = (V, E, X, L, Y, A)$, where V is a set of nodes; E is a set of edges e_{ij} between two nodes v_i and v_j, $E=\{e_{ij}: v_i,v_j \in V, i \neq j\}$; X is a set of attribute vectors x_i, a separate one for each node v_i (a profile of v_i), $X=\{x_i: v_i\in V\Leftrightarrow x_i\in X\}$; L is the set of distinct labels possible to be assigned to nodes; Y is a list of actual labels assignments to nodes, $Y=\{<v_i,y_i>: v_i\in V \wedge y_i\in L\}$; A is a set of edge weights, $\forall a_{ij}\in A\ a_{ij}\geq 0$ and a_{ij} indicates the strength of edge e_{ij}.

Classification in social network may be described as the process of inferring the values of y_i for the remaining set of nodes V^U, $V^U = V\setminus V^K$ where the values of y_i for a given subset of nodes $V^K\subset V$ is known.

The first step in the process of node classification is a translation of network data into a set of unified vectors, one for each node. A single vector corresponding to node v_i contains all information from x_i as well as some additional information (new attributes) derived by feature extraction methods based on the network profile. Next, the obtained set of vectors is used in classical, supervised classification.

Among all possible other features extracted from social network, the label-dependent features are composed based on the idea of selective definition of sub-networks based on the labels assigned to each node. It means that a sub-network for a given label l consists of only those nodes that share label (class) l together with all edges connecting these selected nodes.

In the domain of social network analysis, a number of measures characterizing network nodes have been introduced in the literature. Majority of them is label-independent and it is possible to define many methods that will extract label-dependent features based on them. A general concept of creation of any label-dependent feature $M_l(G,l,v_i)$ for label l and node v_i in the social network G applies label-independent feature M to the appropriate labeled sub-network $G_l=O(G,l)$, as follows:

$$M_l(G,l,v_i)=M(G_l,v_i), \tag{1}$$

where:

$M_l(G_l,v_i)$ - denotes any structural network measure for node v_i applied to sub-network; $G_l=O(G,l)$, e.g degree, betweennes or clustering coefficient derived from sub-network returned by selection operator $O(G,l)$ that returns a sub-network G_l labeled with l: $G_l=(V_l,\ E_l,\ X_l,\ \{l\},\ Y_l,\ A_l)$ such that $V_l=\{v_i: <v_i,l>\in Y_l\}$, $Y_l=\{<v_i,y_i>: v_i\in V\wedge y_i=l\}$, $E_l=\{e_{ij}: v_i,v_j\in V_l\wedge e_{ij}\in E\}$, $X_l=\{x_l: v_l\in V_l\Leftrightarrow x_l\in X\}$.

4 Experiments

4.1 Data Sets

Three, data sets were chosen for classification accuracy assessment experimentation. First one is the "Attendee Meta-Data" (AMD), downloaded from UCI Network Data Repository (http://networkdata.ics.uci.edu/ data.php?d=amdhope). This data set is an output from a project, which used RFID (Radio Frequency Identification) technology to help connect conference participants at "The Last HOPE" Conference held in July 18-20, 2008, New York City, USA. In general, the data set contains information about conference participants, conference talks and presence on talks. Imported and cleansed contained 334 persons with 99 lectures and 3,141 presences. For the purpose of experiments the social network was build, where ties were constructed based on the fact that participants were present on the same talks and strengths of the connections between each pair of contributors were calculated as the proportion of number of talks attended by both participants by the total number of talk presences of the first participant. The raw data contained 4 attributes describing nodes: 3 nominal (sex, cell phone provider, country) and 1 numerical (age). Additionally, each participant was described by his interest that in our experiments was chosen as the classification target.

The second is the CORA research papers database, where papers are classified into one of 73 topics. The data set is relational as the citations provide relations among papers. The social network is constructed using ties constructed based on the citation facts between papers. As a classification target paper's topic assignment was chosen.

Table 1. Social Networks derived from data sets used in experiments

Dataset	Number of node attributes	Number of nodes	Number of connections	Directed connections	Weighted connections
AMD	4	334	68,770	☑	☑
CORA	4	6527	10394	☑	☒

4.2 Classification

Experiments were conducted for described above data sets using 3 classification algorithms, AdaBoost, Multilayered Perceptron, SVM. Classification was performed in 10% - 90% proportion of labeled and unlabeled nodes, respectively, using 10-cross fold validation. According to Eq. 1 degree and betweeness features were computed based on appropriate sub-networks to formulate label-dependent features. The mean absolute error obtained in label-dependent features based classification was compared to results returned in classification based on standard features.

4.3 Results

The obtained results have revealed that the mean absolute error using label-dependent features is significantly smaller than in classification based only on standard data set's features.

As presented in Fig. 1 and Fig. 2, the mean absolute error in AMD and CORA data sets is smaller by about 94% and 83%, respectively, for classification based on label-dependet features.

Irrespectively of the used feature data set, all utilized classification algorithms: AdaBoost, Multilayered Perceptron, SVM, provide similar results (see Fig. 1 and Fig. 2).standard.

Owing to the carried out experiments, it is visible that the proposed label-dependent features used in classification undoubtedly provide the better results.

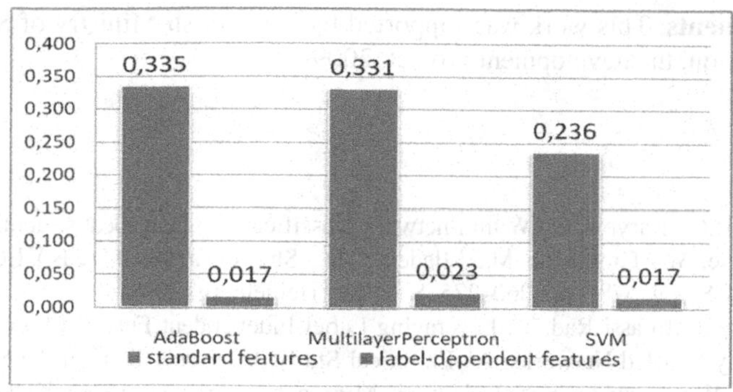

Fig. 1. Mean absolute classification error for AMD data set

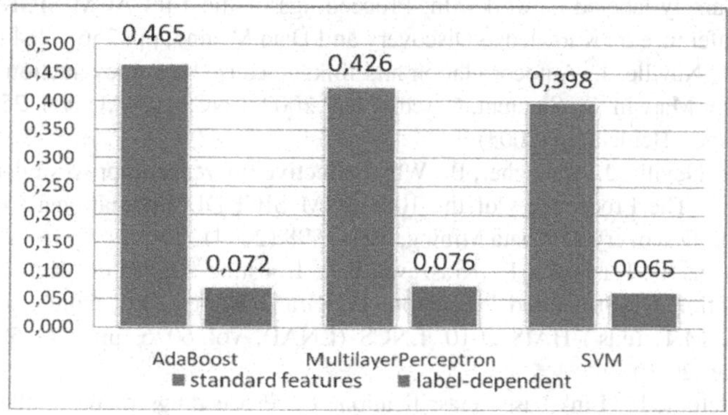

Fig. 2. Mean absolute classification error for CORA data set

5 Conclusions and Future Work

A new method for label-dependent feature extraction from the social network was proposed in the paper. The main principle behind the method is based the selective definitions of sub-graphs for which new features are defined and computed. These new features provide additional quantitative information about the network context of the case being classified.

According to collected experimental evidences, the proposed label-dependent feature extraction appears to be significantly more effective and improves classification performance in high extent. These results have shown that the new approach to classification extended with features derived from the social network may return very satisfactory and promising outcomes.

Feature work will focus on further experimentations on the method, especially in terms of its validity for variety of local network measures. Additionally, the proposed feature extraction method will also be examined against the usage of global objective functions for classification.

Acknowledgments. This work was supported by The Polish Ministry of Science and Higher Education, the development project, 2009-11.

References

[1] Desrosiers, C., Karypis, G.: Within-network classification using local structure similarity. In: Buntine, W., Grobelnik, M., Mladenić, D., Shawe-Taylor, J. (eds.) ECML PKDD 2009. LNCS, vol. 5781, pp. 260–275. Springer, Heidelberg (2009)

[2] Gallagher, B., Eliassi-Rad, T.: Leveraging Label-Independent Features for Classification in Sparsely Labeled Networks: An Empirical Study. In: Proceedings of the Second ACM SIGKDD Workshop on Social Network Mining and Analysis (SNA-KDD 2008), Las Vegas, NV (2008)

[3] Gallagher, B., Tong, H., Eliassi-Rad, T., Faloutsos, C.: Using ghost edges for classification in sparsely labeled networks. In: Proceedings of the 14th ACM SIGKDD International Conference on Knowledge Discovery and Data Mining, pp. 256 – 264 (2008)

[4] Jensen, D., Neville, J.: Autocorrelation and linkage cause bias in evaluation of relational learners. In: Matwin, S., Sammut, C. (eds.) ILP 2002. LNCS (LNAI), vol. 2583, pp. 101–116. Springer, Heidelberg (2003)

[5] Jensen, D., Neville, J., Gallagher, B.: Why collective inference improves relational classification. In: The Proceedings of the 10th ACM SIGKDD International Conference on Knowledge Discovery and Data Mining, 593 – 598 (2004)

[6] Kajdanowicz, T., Kazienko, P., Kraszewski, J.: Boosting Algorithm with Sequence-loss Cost Function for Structured Prediction. In: Graña Romay, M., Corchado, E., Garcia Sebastian, M.T. (eds.) HAIS 2010. LNCS (LNAI), vol. 6076, pp. 573–580. Springer, Heidelberg (2010)

[7] Lu, Q., Getoor, L.: Link-based classification. In: Proceedings of the 20th International Conference on Machine Learning ICML 2003, pp. 496 – 503 (2003)

[8] Macskassy, S., Provost, F.: A brief survey of machine learning methods for classification in networked data and an application to suspicion scoring. In: Airoldi, E.M., Blei, D.M., Fienberg, S.E., Goldenberg, A., Xing, E.P., Zheng, A.X. (eds.) ICML 2006. LNCS, vol. 4503, pp. 172–175. Springer, Heidelberg (2007)

[9] McPherson, M., Smith-Lovin, L., Cook, J.: Birds of a feather: Homophily in social networks. Annual Review of Sociology 27, 415–444 (2007)

[10] Neville, J., Jensen, D.: Collective Classification with Relational Dependency Networks. In: Proceedings of the Second International Workshop on Multi-Relational Data Mining, Washington, DC, pp. 77–91 (2003)

[11] Sen, P., Namata, G., Bilgic, M., Getoor, L., Gallagher, B., Eliassi-Rad, T.: Collective classification in network data. Artificial Intelligence Magazine 29(3), 93–106 (2008)

[12] Taskar, B., Abbeel, P., Koller, D.: Discriminative probabilistic models for relational data. In: Proceedings of UAI 2002, Edmonton, Canada (2002)

Improving Web Search and Navigation Using Summarization Process

Antonella Carbonaro

Department of Computer Science, University of Bologna,
Mura Anteo Zamboni, 7, Bologna, Italy
antonella.carbonaro@unibo.it

Abstract. The paper presents a summarization process for enabling personalized searching framework facilitating the user access and navigation through desired contents. The system will express key concepts and relationships describing resources in a formal machine-processable representation. A WordNet-based knowledge representation could be used for content analysis and concept recognition, for reasoning processes and for enabling user-friendly and intelligent content exploration.

Keywords: Summarization, WordNet, Semantic Web Search, personalized navigation framework.

1 Introduction

The Semantic Web offers a generic infrastructure for interchange, integration and creative reuse of structured data, which can help to cross some of the boundaries that Web 2.0 is facing. Currently, Web 2.0 offers poor query possibilities apart from searching by keywords or tags. There has been a great deal of interest in the development of semantic-based systems to facilitate knowledge representation and extraction and content integration [1], [2]. Semantic-based approach to retrieving relevant material can be useful to address issues like trying to determine the type or the quality of the information suggested from a personalized environment. In this context, standard keyword search has a very limited effectiveness. For example, it cannot filter for the type of information, the level of information or the quality of information.

Potentially, one of the biggest application areas of content-based exploration might be personalized searching framework (e.g., [3],[4]). Whereas today's search engines provide largely anonymous information, new framework might highlight or recommend web pages related to key concepts. We can consider semantic information representation as an important step towards a wide efficient manipulation and retrieval of information [5], [6], [7]. In the digital library community a flat list of attribute/value pairs is often assumed to be available. In the Semantic Web community, annotations are often assumed to be an instance of an ontology. Through the ontologies the system will express key entities and relationships describing resources in a formal machine-processable representation. An ontology-based knowledge representation

M.D. Lytras et al. (Eds.): WSKS 2010, Part I, CCIS 111, pp. 131–138, 2010.

could be used for content analysis and object recognition, for reasoning processes and for enabling user-friendly and intelligent multimedia content search and retrieval.

Text summarization has been an interesting and active research area since the 60's. The definition and assumption is that a small portion or several keywords of the original long document can represent the whole informatively and/or indicatively. Reading or processing this shorter version of the document would save time and other resources [8]. This property is especially true and urgently needed at present due to the vast availability of information. Concept-based approach to represent dynamic and unstructured information can be useful to address issues like trying to determine the key concepts and to summarize the information exchanged within a personalized environment.

2 Personalized Searching Framework

Traditional approaches to personalization include both content-based and user-based techniques. If, on one hand, a content-based approach allows to define and maintain an accurate user profile (for example, the user may provides the system with a list of keywords reflecting him/her initial interests and the profiles could be stored in form of weighted keyword vectors and updated on the basis of explicit relevance feedback), which is particularly valuable whenever a user encounters new content, on the other hand it has the limitation of concerning only the significant features describing the content of an item. Differently, in a user-based approach, resources are processed according to the rating of other users of the system with similar interests. Since there is no analysis of the item content, these information management techniques can deal with any kind of item, being not just limited to textual content. In such a way, users can receive items with content that is different from that one received in the past. On the other hand, since a user-based technique works well if several users evaluate each one of them, new items cannot be handled until some users have taken the time to evaluate them and new users cannot receive references until the system has acquired some information about the new user in order to make personalized predictions. These limitations often refer to as the sparsity and start-up problems. By adopting a hybrid approach, a personalization system is able to effectively filter relevant resources from a wide heterogeneous environment like the Web, taking advantage of common interests of the users and also maintaining the benefits provided by content analysis. A hybrid approach maintains another drawback: the difficulty to capture semantic knowledge of the application domain, i.e. concepts, relationships among different concepts, inherent properties associated with the concepts, axioms or other rules, etc [9].

In this context, standard keyword search is of very limited effectiveness. For example, it does not allow users and the system to search, handle or read concepts of interest, and it doesn't consider synonymy and hyponymy that could reveal hidden similarities potentially leading to better retrieval. The advantages of a concept-based document and user representations can be summarized as follows: (i) ambiguous terms inside a resource are disambiguated, allowing their correct interpretation and, consequently, a better precision in the user model construction (e.g., if a user is interested in computer science resources, a document containing the word 'bank' as it is meant in the financial context could not be relevant); (ii) synonymous words belonging to the same meaning can contribute to the resource model definition (for example, both 'mouse' and 'display' brings evidences for computer science documents, improving the coverage of the document retrieval); (iii) synonymous words belonging to the same meaning can contribute to the user model matching, which is required in recommendation process (for example, if two users have the same interests, but these are expressed using different terms, they will considered overlapping); (iv) finally, classification, recommendation and sharing phases take advantage of the word senses in order to classify, retrieve and suggest documents with high semantic relevance with respect to the user and resource models.

For example, the system could support Computer Science last-year students during their activities in courseware like Bio Computing, Internet Programming or Machine Learning. In fact, for these kinds of courses it is necessary an active involvement of the student in the acquisition of the didactical material that should integrate the lecture notes specified and released by the teacher. Basically, the level of integration depends both on the student's prior knowledge in that particular subject and on the comprehension level he wants to acquire. Furthermore, for the mentioned courses, it is necessary to continuously update the acquired knowledge by integrating recent information available from any remote digital library.

The home page of the web search and navigation framework is showed in the following Figures.

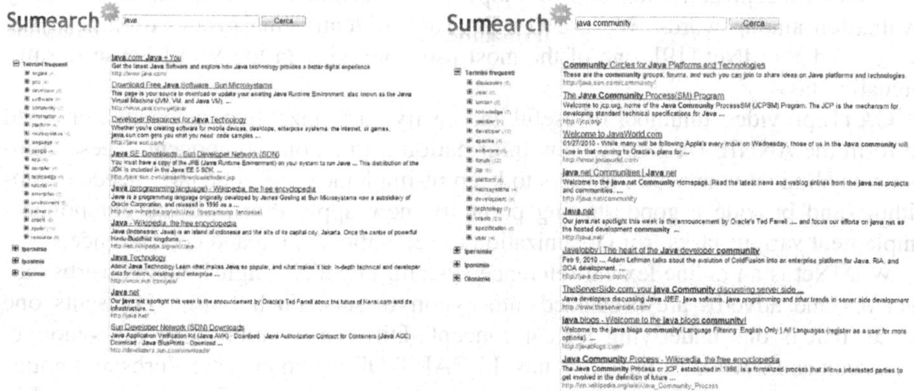

3 Inside Summarization

Summarization is a widely researched problem. As a result, researchers have reported a rich collection of approaches for automatic document summarization to enhance those provided manually by readers or authors as a result of intellectual interpretation. One approach is to provide summary creation based on a natural language generation (as investigated for instance in the DUC and TREC conferences); a different one is based on a sentence selection from the text to be summarized, but the most simple process is to select a reasonable short list of words among the most frequent and/or the most characteristic words from those found in the text to be summarized. So, rather than a coherent text the summary is a simple set of items.

From a technical point of view, the different approaches available in the literature can be considered as follows. The first is a class of approaches that deals with the problem of document classification from a theoretical point of view, making no assumption on the application of these approaches. These include statistical [10], analytical [11], information retrieval [12] and information fusion [13] approaches. The second class deals with techniques that are focused on specific applications, such as baseball program summaries [14], clinical data visualization [15] and web browsing on handheld devices [16]. [17] reports a comprehensive review.

The approach presented in this paper produce a sets of items, but involves improvements over the simple set of words process in two means. Actually, we go beyond the level of keywords providing conceptual descriptions from concepts identified and extracted from the text. We propose a practical approach for extracting the most relevant keywords from the forum threads to form a summary without assumption on the application domain and to subsequently find out concepts from the keyword extraction based on statistics and synsets extraction. Then semantic similarity analysis is conducted between keywords to produce a set of semantic relevant concepts summarizing actual forum significance.

In order to substitute keywords with univocal concepts we have to build a process called Word Sense Disambiguation (WSD). Given a sentence, a WSD process identifies the syntactical categories of words and interacts with an ontology both to retrieve the exact concept definition and to adopts some techniques for semantic similarity evaluation among words. We use GATE [18] to identify the syntactic class of the words and WordNet [19], one of the most used ontology in the Word Sense Disambiguation task.

GATE provides a number of useful and easily customizable components, grouped to form the ANNIE (A Nearly-New Information Extraction) component. These components eliminate the need for users to keep re-implementing frequently needed algorithms and provide a good starting point for new applications. These components implement various tasks from tokenization to semantic tagging and co-reference.

WordNet is an online lexical reference system, in which English nouns, verbs, adjectives and adverbs are organized into synonym sets. Each synset represents one sense, that is one underlying lexical concept. Different relations link the synonym sets, such as IS-A for verbs and nouns, IS-PART-OF for nouns, etc. Verbs and nouns senses are organized in hierarchies forming a "forest" of trees. For each keyword in WordNet, we can have a set of senses and, in the case of nouns and verbs, a generalization path from each sense to the root sense of the hierarchy. WordNet could be used as a useful resource with respect to the semantic tagging process and has so far been used in various applications including Information Retrieval, Word Sense Disambiguation, Text and Document Classification and many others.

Noun synsets are related to each other through hypernymy (generalization), hyponymy (speciali-zation), holonymy (whole of) and meronymy (part of) relations. Of these, (hypernymy, hyponymy) and (meronymy, holonymy) are complementary pairs. The verb and adjective synsets are very sparsely connected with each other. No relation is available between noun and verb synsets. However, 4500 adjective synsets are related to noun synsets with pertainyms (pertaining to) and attra (attributed with) relations.

The subset of keywords related to each thread forum helps to discriminate between concepts. In such a way, two texts characterized using different keywords may result similar considering underling concept and not the exact terms. We use the following feature extraction pre-process. Firstly, we label occurrences of each word as a part of speech (POS) in grammar. This POS tagger discriminates the POS in grammar of each word in a sentence. After labelling all the words, we select those ones labelled as noun and verbs as our candidates. We then use the stemmer to reduce variants of the same root word to a common concept and filter the stop words.

A vocabulary problem exists when a term is present in several concepts; determining the correct concept for an ambiguous word is difficult, as is deciding the concept of a document containing several ambiguous terms. To handle the word sense disambiguation problem we use similarity measures based on WordNet. Budanitsky and Hirst [20] give an overview of five measures based on both semantic relatedness and semantic distance considerations, and evaluate their performance using a word association task.

4 Summarization System Architecture

After several transformations and reductions of the input text, the result is a semantics map representing the terms and the relative frequency. Depending on their frequency, we can consider the term more or less important within the context. Each term is reduced to common root using a stemming process.

The next step is to reduce the list according to term frequency: we calculate the average value of frequencies and we discard the terms corresponding to the frequency below the average. In fact, we do not want to completely delete the results obtained up until now, but we would like to offer to the end-user different semantic maps relating to the different stages of reduction and refinement of the text.

Last process step is more complex but very effective. For each remaining term we evaluate its synset, that is names, verbs, adjectives and adverbs grouped into sets of cognitive synonyms. Each of these is compared with the others 'parent terms' so verifying the existence of a conceptual link between analyzed words. If this succeeds, we delete an entire branch of the tree, otherwise, the process continues with subsequent comparisons.

This last stage is recursive so to prune more possible branches and to obtain a reduced and significant set of terms. The project is structured so that any user, while not having read the text of the post, understand the concept underlying the message.

Figure 1 shows the whole process information flow. The first computation is a php-based reading of the web content. Next, we transfer XML document to the python compiler that, through the use of WordNet and Natural Language Toolkit libraries, returns the reduced tree in a text-based format (ALS_tree, Lexical and Semantic Analisys tree). Successively, we extract, using WordNet and python language, the main concept representing analyzed text. The main concept contains one or more meaningful phrases.

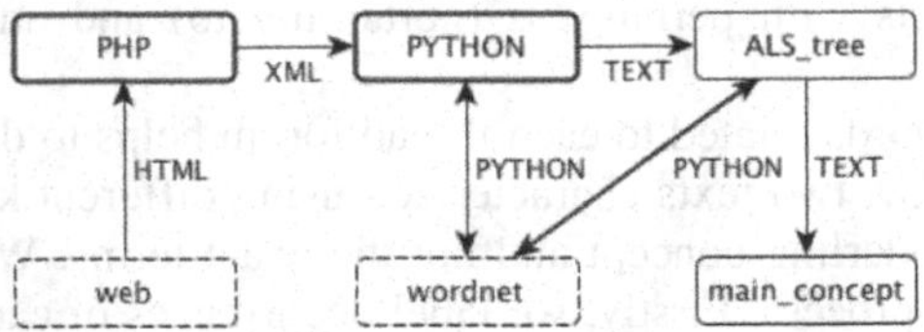

As final result, we obtain a key term list who, through the semantics of its terms can summarize the concept expressed in the analyzed post. Less detail, i.e. a greater granularity of the information (more posts, whole discussion or whole forum) is easily available by recursively applying described reduction process.

The interface of web search procedure using hypernymy, hyponymy and holonymy is proposed in following Figures.

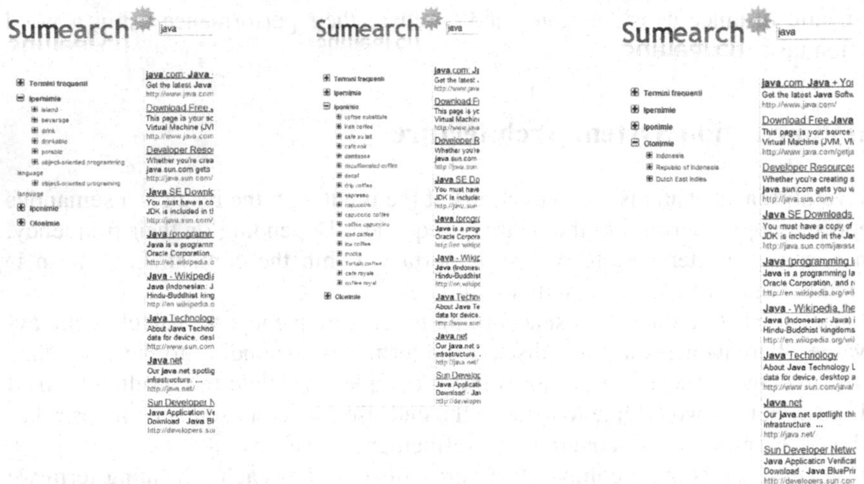

5 Considerations

Summarization can be evaluated using intrinsic or extrinsic measures; while the first one methods attempt to measure summary quality using human evaluation, extrinsic methods measure the same through a task-based performance measure such the information retrieval-oriented task. In our experiments we utilized intrinsic approach analyzing W3Schools forums, official forum of the W3C (http: //www.w3cforum.com/).

We have performed a lot of intrinsic experimental tests obtaining and elaborating a corpus of about 100 threads. This experiment is to evaluate the usefulness of concept extraction in summarization process, by manually reading whole thread content and comparing with automatic extracted concepts. The results show that automatic concept-based summarization greatly improves the performance and produces useful information extraction supporting tutors and making learning communities effective. The extracted concepts represent a good summarization of thread contents.

Advanced in concept-based representation appears as a promising technology for implementing distance learning environment, enabling the organization and delivery of learning materials around small pieces of semantically enriched resources [21, 22]. Items can be easily organized into customized learning courses and delivered on demand to the user, according to her/his profile and business needs [23].

An important step in the searching process is the examination of the results retrieved. In order to test developed framework we have collected over 50 different documents concerning actual domain. We have extracted several concepts used during the annotation phase and performed tests to verify searching functionalities. It is currently difficult to replicate or make objective comparisons in personalized retrieval researches, so to evaluate search results we have considered the order used by the framework to present retrieved results. During this step, the searcher browses through the results to make judgments about their relevance and to extract information from those found to be relevant. Because information is costly (in terms of time) to download, displays of result lists should be optimized to make the process of browsing more effective. Using implemented tools, searchers found relevant documents more efficiently and effectively and they found relevant documents that otherwise went undiscovered.

The work described in this paper represents some initial steps in exploring concept-based search retrieval within a focused team of searchers. It could be considered as one possible instance of a more general concept. While the initial results arc encouraging, much remains to be explored. For example, most of the current research on sensemaking has been at the individual level, with little understanding of how sensemaking occurs in collaborative search tools.

References

1. Henze, N., Dolog, P., Nejdl, W.: Reasoning and Ontologies for Personalized E-Learning in the Semantic Web. Educational Technology & Society 7(4), 82–97 (2004)
2. Bighini, C., Carbonaro, A.: InLinx: Intelligent Agents for Personalized Classification, Sharing and Recommendation. International Journal of Computational Intelligence. International Computational Intelligence Society 2(1) (2004)
3. Pickens, J., Golovchinsky, G., Shah, C., Qvarfordt, P., Back, M.: Algorithmic Mediation for Collaborative Exploratory Search. To appear in Proceedings of SIGIR
4. Freyne, J., Smyth, B.: Collaborative Search: Deployment Experiences. In: The 24th SGAI International Conference on Innovative Techniques and Applications of Artificial Intelligence, Cambridge, UK, pp. 121–134 (2004)
5. Calic, J., Campbell, N., Dasiopoulou, S., Kompatsiaris, Y.: A Survey on Multimodal Video Representation for Semantic Retrieval. In: The Third International Conference on Computer as a tool. IEEE, Los Alamitos (2005)
6. Carbonaro, A.: Defining Personalized Learning Views of Relevant Learning Objects in a Collaborative Bookmark Management System. In: Ma, Z. (ed.) Web-based Intelligent ELearning Systems: Technologies and Applications, pp. 139–155. Information Science Publishing, Hershey (2006)
7. Bloehdorn, S., Petridis, K., Simou, N., Tzouvaras, V., Avrithis, Y., Handschuh, S., Kompatsiaris, Y., Staab, S., Strintzis, M.G.: Knowledge Representation for Semantic Multimedia Content Analysis and Reasoning. In: Proceedings of the European Workshop on the Integration of Knowledge, Semantics and Digital Media Technology (2004)

8. Zhou, L., Hovy, E.: On the summarization of dynamically introduced information: Online discussions and blogs. In: AAAI Spring Symposium on Computational Approaches to Analysing Weblogs (2006)
9. Carbonaro, A., Ferrini, R.: Considering semantic abilities to improve a Web-Based Distance Learning System. In: ACM International Workshop on Combining Intelligent and Adaptive Hypermedia Methods/Techniques in Web-based Education Systems (2005)
10. McKeown, K., Barzilay, R., Evans, D., Hatzivassiloglou, V., Kan, M., Schiffman, B., Teufel, S.: Columbia Multi- Document Summarization: Approach and Evaluation. In: Workshop on Text Summarization (2001)
11. Brunn, M., Chali, Y., Pinchak, C.: Text Summarization Using Lexical Chains. In: Work on Text Summarization (2001)
12. Aho, A., Chang, S., McKeown, K., Radev, D., Smith, J., Zaman, K.: Columbia Digital News Project: An Environment for Briefing and Search over Multimedia. Information J. Int. J. on Digital Libraries 1(4), 377–385 (1997)
13. Barzilay, R., McKeown, K., Elhadad, M.: Information fusion in the context of multi-document summarization. In: Proc. of ACL 1999 (1999)
14. Yong Rui, Y., Gupta, A., Acero, A.: Automatically extracting highlights for TV Baseball programs. ACM Multimedia, 105–115 (2000)
15. Shahar, Y., Cheng, C.: Knowledge-based Visualization of Time Oriented Clinical Data. In: Proc. AMIA Annual Fall Symp., pp. 155–159 (1998)
16. Rahman, A., Alam, H., Hartono, R., Ariyoshi, K.: Automatic Summarization of Web Content to Smaller Display Devices. In: 6th Int. Conf. on Document Analysis and Recognition, ICDAR 2001, pp. 1064–1068 (2001)
17. NIST web site on summarization, Columbia University Summarization Resources, and Okumura-Lab Resources
`http://wwwnlpirnist.gov/projects/duc/pubs.html`,
`http://www.cs.columbia.edu/~hjing/summarization.html`,
`http://capella.kuee.kyoto-u.ac.jp/index_e.html`
18. Cunningham, H., Maynard, D., Bontcheva, K., Tablan, V.: GATE: A Framework and Graphical Development Environment for Robust NLP Tools and Applications. In: Proceedings 40th Anniversary Meeting of the Association for Computational Linguistics (ACL 2002), Budapest (2002)
19. Fellbaum, C. (ed.): WordNet: An Electronic Lexical Database. MIT Press, Cambridge (1998)
20. Budanitsky, A., Hirst, G.: Semantic distance in wordnet: An experimental, application-oriented evaluation of five measures. In: Workshop on WordNet and Other Lexical Resources. Second Meeting of the North American Chapter of the Association for Computational Linguistics, Pittsburgh (2001)
21. Carbonaro, A.: Defining Personalized Learning Views of Relevant Learning Objects in a Collaborative Bookmark Management System. In: Ma, Z. (ed.) Web-Based Intelligent ELearning Systems: Technologies and Applications, pp. 139–155. Information Science Publishing, Hershey (2006)
22. Bighini, C., Carbonaro, A., Casadei, G.: Inlinx for document classification, sharing and recommendation. In: Devedzic, V., Spector, J.M., Sampson, D.G., Kinshuk (eds.) Proc. of the 3rd Int'l. Conf. on Advanced Learning Technologies, pp. 91–95. IEEE CS, Los Alamitos (2003)
23. Andronico, A., Carbonaro, A., Colazzo, L., Molinari, A., Ronchetti, M.: Designing Models and Services for Learning Management Systems in Mobile Settings. In: Crestani, F., Dunlop, M.D., Mizzaro, S. (eds.) HCI 2003. LNCS, vol. 2954, pp. 90–106. Springer, Heidelberg (2004) ISBN 3-540-21003-2

PRIOR-WK&E: Social Software for Policy Making in the Knowledge Society

Alberto Turón[1], Juan Aguarón[1], María Teresa Escobar[1], Carolina Gallardo[2], José María Moreno-Jiménez[1], and José Luis Salazar[1]

[1] Grupo Decisión Multicriterio Zaragoza, Facultad de Economía y Empresa, Universidad de Zaragoza, Gran Vía nº 2, 50005 Zaragoza, Spain
{turon,aguaron,mescobar,moreno,jsalazar}@unizar.es

[2] Grupo de Validación y Aplicaciones Industriales, Escuela Universitaria de Informática, Universidad Politécnica de Madrid, Ctra. de Valencia, Km. 7, 28031 Madrid, Spain
carolina@opera.dia.fi.upm.es

Abstract. This paper presents a social software application denominated as PRIOR-WK&E. It has been developed by the Zaragoza Multicriteria Decision Making Group (GDMZ) with the aim of responding to the challenges of policy making in the Knowledge Society. Three specific modules have been added to PRIOR, the collaborative tool used by the research group (GDMZ) for considering the multicriteria selection of a discrete set of alternatives. The first module (W), that deals with multiactor decision making through the Web, and the second (K), that concerns the extraction and diffusion of knowledge related to the scientific resolution of the problem, were explained in [1]. The new application strengthens securitization and includes a third module (E) that evaluates the effectiveness of public administrations policy making.

Keywords: Knowledge Society, Policy Making, Multicriteria, Social Software, PRIOR.

1 Introduction

The Zaragoza Multicriteria Decision Making Group recently presented their collaborative tool (PRIOR-W&K) for decision making in the Knowledge Society [1]. PRIOR-W&K is based on the more primitive computer tool (PRIOR) developed by the group for the discrete selection of alternatives in complex situations [2] involving multiple scenarios, actors and tangible and intangible factors. The new tool includes two new modules: the first concerns decision making with spatially distributed multiple actors (Web module) and the second (Knowledge module) is associated with the discussion stage in which the arguments that support the decisions are given. The latter module encompasses a key aspect of decision making in the knowledge society: the continuous learning process of the actors implicated in the resolution of the problem.

M.D. Lytras et al. (Eds.): WSKS 2010, Part I, CCIS 111, pp. 139–149, 2010.

When the social software PRIOR-W&K is applied in the public decision making, that is to say, in the design of public policies, there are some problems associated with the practical application of the collaborative tool in the context of policy science. The implication of the citizenry in the construction of a better society by means of the incorporation of their preferences and arguments requires the methodological approach followed for modelling and solving the problem to be flexible, realistic and friendly enough to ensure collaboration.

In the context of public decision making it is necessary to sacrifice part of the accuracy usually required by the scientific studies, in favour of the greater implication of the citizen in the construction of the different public policies the most important thing is democratisation of knowledge, i.e. the extraction and dissemination of the arguments that support the decisions that are made.

An essential issue in the management of public goods which is not usually taken into account in the resolution of problems when analysed from the point of view of decision theory, is the evaluation of the behaviour of the system. In order to make up for this shortfall, a new module (Evaluation) has been incorporated into the PRIOR-W&K program, giving us the PRIOR-WK&E social software system.

From a philosophical perspective, the approach followed in the design of public policies corresponds to the steps of the methodology associated with the e-cognocracy [3-7]. In this case, is undertaken by means of structural equation models, as in [8].

The structure of this paper is as follows: Section 2 briefly describes the philosophy of public policy making in the Knowledge Society; Section 3 analyses the methodology for the study of the effectiveness of e-cognocracy; Section 4 outlines the components of the new social software (PRIOR-WK&E); Section 5 discusses the most important and relevant aspects of the work.

2 Background

2.1 Knowledge Society

In system theory literature, 'effectiveness' is generally understood as doing the right thing, that is to say, the appropriate identification of the relevant aspects when solving a problem. This leads to the question of how this concept is to be interpreted in the context of the Knowledge Society.

The Knowledge Society [9] can be understood as a space oriented to the talent, intelligence, ingenuity, imagination and creativity of the human being. The importance of human factor and the interconnection between the actors involved in the decision making processes are two of the main characteristics of this new society, which is oriented to the conjoint construction of a better world.

In order to define the effectiveness of public administration in the governance of society (democratic models), we follow a cognitive perspective based on the evolution of living systems: only species that learn –extract and spread knowledge– and which adapt to the context, are able to survive and progress.

As classical Greek (Plato) and medieval Arabic (Averroes and Ibn Jaldum) thinkers suggest [10], the evolution of democratic models is not an arbitrary process. It depends on needs derived from human nature and the functioning of society, which are interconnected. In this context (Knowledge Society), we must promote new governance models oriented towards improving social life by means of the citizen's education, as it is the case of e-cognocracy.

2.2 Policy Making

Policy Making refers to the process of making important organizational decisions, including the identification of different alternatives such as programs or spending priorities, and choosing among them on the basis of the impact they will have. With respect to the classical methodology employed in the design of public policies, this follows a cyclical scheme that includes the following steps [11], [12], [13], that basically are those of the scientific methodology followed in decision making:

(1) *Policy selection*: This considers five steps: (a) agenda setting; (b) problem definition; (c) forecast; (d) establishment of objectives and (e) selection of options.

(2) *Implementation*: This concept [14] is one of the steps considered in the scientific resolution of problems (policy formulation) and not and independent step in the process. Barret and Fudge [15] see implementation "as a continuous procedure of elaboration and action in which there is negotiating between those who want to put policy into practice and those on whom the action depends". The political system is responsible for the implementation of public policies.

(3) *Evaluation, continuity or change*: The evaluation of public policy making may be carried out with respect to the goals established for the relevant objectives for the resolution of the problem. These goals usually refer to the efficiency and efficacy, although more recently, the evaluation of the effectiveness of the administration and its public policy is seen as more important.

2.3 E-Cognocracy

E-cognocracy [3-7] is a new democratic model that tries to make more ambitious use of democracy than the mere election of political representatives. In this regard, based on the evolution of living systems (only species that learn and adapt to the context are able to survive), e-cognocracy focuses on the extraction and social diffusion of the knowledge derived from the scientific resolution of highly complex problems associated with public decision making related with the governance of society. It is oriented to the conjoint (political representatives and citizens) construction of a better and freer society. This is done by means of the continuous individual and societal education (aptitudes and attitudes) in decision making.

E-cognocracy uses Internet as the technological support, multicriteria decision making tools (AHP in this case) as the methodological support and the democracy as the catalyst for the democratisation of knowledge.

It combines the two most extended democratic models [16], representative democracy and participative (direct) democracy, in a cognitive democracy. Decisions are made by synthesising the results obtained from the political parties (representative democracy) and citizens (participative democracy). To aggregate these results, we use different weights (w_1 and w_2) depending of the context of the problem (local, regional, national or supranational) and the objectives of the system.

The combination of these two democratic models with appropriate weights allows us to overcome most of the limitations of both systems. With respect to representative or legal democracy, where elected "functionaries" assume the representation of the citizens' interests in a legal framework, these limitations are [6]: specific participation confined to the election of representatives; control of electoral list by the political parties; hiding of critical positions and interest, as well as a clumsy system with slow participation. As regards participative or direct democracy, where the citizens are directly implicated in the decision making process, the limitations are [5]: populism and the lack of a global perspective of problems.

Summarising, e-cognocracy tries to educate people (intelligence and learning), promote relationship with others (communication and coexistence), improve society (quality of life and cohesion) and construct the future (evolution) in a world of increasing complexity [4].

The e-cognocracy process follows these stages ([9], [16], [17]): (1) *Problem Establishment*; (2) *Problem Resolution*; (3) *Model Exploitation*; (4) *Discussion*; (5) *Second round in problem resolution*; (6) *Knowledge Extraction and Democratisation and* (7) *Evaluation.*

When public resources are employed to respond to citizens' needs or provide services, (transparency and accountability) the inclusion of a new stage in the e-participation processes -the evaluation of the system's behaviour- is highly recommended. Along with the traditional analysis of the efficiency (doing things correctly) and efficacy (achieving the goals) of public administrations, which reflects behaviour in the short and medium term (operational and tactical planning), we must also evaluate the most important aspect of a system's behaviour: the effectiveness (to doing what is correct) of the system in the long term (strategic planning). This is an important and difficult task which is being studied [8] as part of an ongoing research project.

3 The Effectiveness in Policy Making in Knowledge Society

As seen in Section 2, in the context of Knowledge Society we must promote new governance models oriented towards improving social life by means of the citizen's education, as it is the case of e-cognocracy. The specific objectives of e-cognocracy are: (i) to improve the transparency of the democratic system, (ii) to increase the control of citizens and (iii) to encourage the participation of citizens in the governance of society [4], [5], [8].

The creation and dissemination of knowledge is achieved through internet discussion in which political parties and citizens put forward arguments that support decisions and justify preferences. Transparency is increased because the political parties are forced to express their viewpoint before the resolution of the problem; the citizen's control is increased because the political parties must win the vote.

Citizens and opposition political parties may request that a specific problem be resolved by means of e-cognocracy and this could involve a vote of censure on a specific political measure. Public participation in the governance of society enables citizens to be directly implicated in the final decision on an issue, not just in the election of representatives (representative democracy).

In order the e-cognocracy to be effective when it comes to democratizing knowledge it is necessary to achieve the participation, or rather, the implication, of the citizenry in public decision making. To that end, social computing allows the citizens, in a synchronous or asynchronous way, to engage, interact and collaborate in learning and educational strategies and the conjoint (representatives and citizens) construction of a better world.

To evaluate the effectiveness of this new model of cognitive democracy and the efficacy in the achievement of the goals, a model of structural equations is proposed. Empirical research using these models requires the setting up of a conceptual framework of analysis in order to be able to develop a hypothetical model that leads to the suitable empirical tests. One of the main purposes of the project is to define the appropriate contexts that affect the effectiveness of the e-cognocracy. In order to define these contexts (which are necessary for building the hypothetical model of structural relationships and the announcement of the hypothesis to be tested), the users of the methodology must fill in a questionnaire.

An evaluation of the effectiveness of e-cognocracy was undertaken in [8] by means of an experimental study consisting of a questionnaire completed by students of Multicriteria Decision Making at the Zaragoza University Faculty of Economics. The questionnaire was based on the proposed "Gran Scala" leisure complex development - the construction of one of the world biggest entertainment centres with an estimated investment of 17,000 million euros, 25 million visitors per year and the creation of 65,000 jobs in the 70 hotels, 32 casinos and five theme parks.

The electronic survey provided the information necessary for the Structural Equation Model (SEM) empirical analysis. The following dimensions in the study of e-cognocracy behaviour were considered: "web service quality", "quality of available information" and "knowledge transfer".

To evaluate the effectiveness of e-cognocracy as a latent construct, multiple objectives (such as increasing the degree of trust, responsibility and commitment between government and citizens, legitimacy through participation and representation of the citizens in decision making), must be considered [8]. All these aspects are reflected in the items included in the electronic survey. The three hypotheses are reflected in the model structure [8], as shown in Figure 1.

The analysis revealed [8] that the latent construct items in "Web service quality" saturate in three factor loadings (or dimensions) called "Visual design", "Degree of personalization" and "Availability of information". The analysis also shows that there are two factors for the latent construct "Quality of information available", which are called "Information accessibility" and "Comprehensiveness of the information".

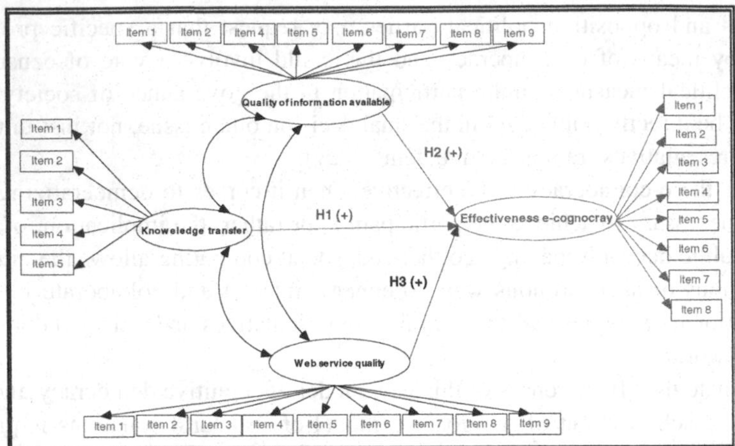

Fig. 1. Hypothetical Structural Model

Currently, our research group is continuing with the structural equations models and the study of the effectiveness of e-cognocracy reported in [8]; we are trying to establish a comprehensive view of the several aspects that influence on the effectiveness of the citizen participation systems, taking into consideration the three levels of systems planning: strategic, tactical and operational.

The methodology aims to extend the evaluation procedure traditionally used by Public Administrations in the study of efficacy and efficiency to explicitly consider the effectiveness of the administration. This approach seeks to avoid the well-known 'Type III error' (poor identification of the relevant aspects and poor specification of the model in question) and to offer a more realistic and appropriate response to the problem of evaluating and improving the systems.

The methodology simultaneously evaluates the behavior of these systems in the long (effectiveness), medium (efficacy) and short (efficiency) terms. The identification of the most outstanding attributes at each step and the setting of the measurement indicators and their interdependences, are some of the more relevant aspects of the study. The assessment methodology proposed will be applied in the municipality of Cadrete (Zaragoza, Spain), where an e-governance experiment related to the design of cultural and sports events is being implemented.

The assessment will be carried out in two different periods (ex-post and during). Rather than auditing what has been done in the past, the purpose is to test what is happening at present, with the aim of improving what will be done in the future by strengthening the learning process. This futuristic and cognitive approach (learning), based on the evolutionism of the living systems ([3], [4], [18]), is a means to improve the behavior, rather than an instrument for inspection and penalty.

With regards to the citizen participation processes, evaluating the behavior of the public administrations is an open matter, as highlighted in several research projects of the OECD in 2001 and 2009. It has also been proved (OECD 2009) that despite the existence of assessment standards, they have been not used (at least, this is the case in a high percentage of the countries concerned).

Traditionally, the assessment of the citizen participation has focused on quality and results, rather than on outputs. In the last few years, in the context of the Knowledge Society, assessment has been oriented towards institutional learning and continuous improvement, and this requires more dedication, time and investment.

4 PRIOR-WK&E: Social Software for Policy Making

The web module (W) is in charge of the elicitation process. It was developed with the aim of providing the spatially distributed actors involved in the problem resolution with a tool for the secure incorporation of their judgments by means of the Internet [19]. It is based on the World Wide Web, so the only requirement for the decision maker is to have a browser and an Internet Access.

The browser allows the users to insert the consistency stability intervals for judgments, alternatives and criteria and the secure elicitation process. A multiactor decision making module includes the consistency consensus matrix, the aggregation of individual preference structures and some graphical visualization tools, as well as web functionalities for the elicitation of judgments when the actors are spatially distributed.

The knowledge module (K) of PRIOR-WK&E includes functionalities oriented to knowledge extraction and diffusion. A forum supports the discussion stage of the e-cognocracy process; in it, the decision makers can express their opinions and debate their ideas with regard to the problem, as well as incorporate some quantitative information by means of numerical values assessing the other users' comments. The ultimate aim of this step is to identify the arguments emerged in the discussion that support the different patterns of behavior and the changes in the preferences of the decision makers from one round to the other.

The information collected in this stage is treated in two different ways:

A) A quantitative knowledge extraction process, in which the arguments that support each alternative are identified by exclusively taking into account the quantitative information relating to the resolution process, i.e., the priorities of the alternatives in both rounds and the information on comment importance. This information is synthesized by a procedure that determines the importance of each alternative in the thread. The valuation assigned to each alternative for each message in the thread is calculated by summing up the valuation given to each alternative for each message in the thread made by a given decision maker. To obtain this valuation, the weight assigned to the message made by the decision maker and the priority given to the alternative by this same decision maker using the multicriteria decision making technique AHP are multiplied. The weight assigned to a message made by a given decision maker is calculated taking into account the importance given to the message by its author, the number of assessments received by the message, the mean assessment of the message and the mean direction of the assessments of the message. Finally, the quantitative procedure assigns to each discussion thread the alternative with the greatest valuation. This process allows the identification of the comments and messages that support each alternative and the different patterns of behavior.

B) A qualitative knowledge extraction process, based on test mining tools, in which the arguments embedded in the messages that support the different positions of the actors are identified. This procedure is based on the analysis of the different patterns defined by an expert in order to clarify a message. Firstly, an expert performs a manual classification of the messages, taking into account the presence of specific assertions that allow the expert to reasonably infer the participant's position underlying in the message. Next, the set of identified assertions are analyzed and codified into linguistic patterns that are implemented in a text mining system.

The knowledge extraction process is based on the use of some graphical visualization tools [20], by means of which the knowledge extraction, the discussion through collaborative web tools, the negotiation processes between the actors involved in the problem resolution and, in general, the learning process either individual or collective, are favored.

In order the decision maker to relay on the e-voting and e-discussion stages of e-cognocracy the technological properties usually demanded for this kind of electronic participation must be guaranteed. A new feature comes on top of the usual properties such as unforgeability or anonymity: the linkability of the votes is necessary as a number of rounds are allowed (usually two) and this forces the linking of the ballots as both the options preferences and the distribution of intensities among them are incorporated. Moreover, the e-discussion carried out by means of a collaborative tool must keep all comments linked to their authors' votes without breaking those security issues. In this regard, PRIOR-WK&E incorporates a new voting protocol [16], [21] that ensures the technological security of the whole process. The protocol is based on the use of short linkable ring signatures, a cryptographic primitive that allows one person to sign as a member of a group without giving any information about his own identity. All the signatures from the same signer can be linked together whilst maintaining anonymity [22].

A survey of students of Multicriteria Decision Making at the Faculty of Economics of Zaragoza University was undertaken with the aim of assessing the effectiveness of e-cognocracy (Figure 2). In the week prior to the survey, using a forum as a collaborative tool, the students held discussions and votes, completing the stages described above for e-cognocracy, with regards to a decisional problem on the opening of a Las Vegas-style leisure complex in the area of Los Monegros (Aragon, Spain).

In the forum, the participants posted 77 messages, 257 comments to the messages and 186 valuations. To strengthen the citizens' participation in the problem resolution the Analytic Hierarchy Process (AHP) was used [23] as methodological support, Internet as communication tool and the forum as collaborative tool for public discussion.

The survey was in 6 parts with 36 questions (34 of them closed and 2 open-ended) distributed as follows: I. Identification (3 questions); II. Web Quality (9); III. Quality of Information (9); IV. Knowledge Transfer (5); V. Impact of Knowledge (1) y VI. Effectiveness of E-cognocracy (9).

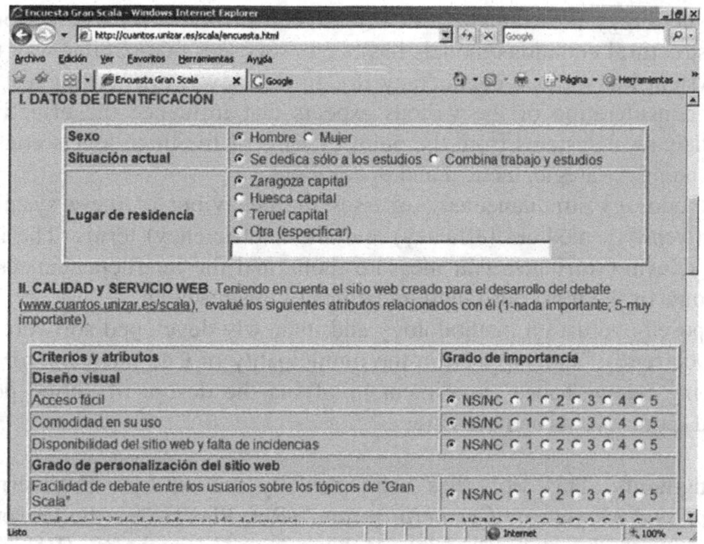

Fig. 2. Structure of the survey related to the Gran Scala problem

The empirical context is the opinion expressed by the students who participated in the forum at the end of the debate, obtained by means of an electronic survey. The design of the survey allows the participant to assess (using a scale ranging from 1 to 5 where 1 is 'not important at all' and 5 is 'very important/good'), the degree of importance of several items related with four of the multiple dimensions covered by e-cognocracy organization and development techniques: website quality, quality and openness of the available information, exchange of opinion/information and criteria related to the effectiveness of e-cognocracy.

The information obtained from the surveys allows the analysis of the constructs and the contrast of the hypothesis foreseen for the analysis of effectiveness. For each latent construct a number of items between 5 and 11 were used and aimed to take most of the criteria needed for an accurate interpretation into account. The selection of variables for the structural equations model was based on two criteria: the variables that the e-cognocracy model showed to be the most significant and the analytic techniques concerning the trustworthiness and validity of the measurement scale.

5 Conclusions

There is a real need for the evaluation of citizen participation systems and, in general, the evaluation of any system which includes the use of public resources. The evaluative process is not only necessary for informing the citizenry (transparency and accountability), it should be obligatory.

In accordance with the evolutionism of living beings, its true contribution is related with the system of effectiveness (doing the right thing), as it allows for learning and both individual and social training. This fosters the conjoint building of the future as the future events are more easily foreseen.

As a methodology for evaluating the effectiveness of citizen participation systems the use of structural equations models has been proposed, in a similar way to the democratic system known as e-cognocracy [8]. In this new work we suggest the comprehensive consideration of the various aspects that influence the effectiveness of citizen participation systems from the point of view of the three levels considered in systems planning: strategic, tactical and operational.

The methodology simultaneously assesses the behaviour of these systems in the long (effectiveness), medium (efficacy) and short (efficiency) terms. The identification of the relevant attributes that measure them, and the interdependences between them, are some of the most outstanding features of this research.

The proposed evaluation methodology and its newly developed software (PRIOR-WK&E) is currently being applied in the municipality of Cadrete (Zaragoza, Spain), in an ongoing e-governance experiment involving the design of public policies on cultural and sports events and activities.

Acknowledgments. This work has been partially funded by: "E-government, *E-participation and Knowledge Democratization*" (Ref. PI-127/09), the Government of Aragon and "*Collaborative Decision Making in e-Cognocracy*" (Ref. TNI2008-06796-C04-04), the Spanish Ministry of Science and Innovation. We would also like to thank David Jones for his help with the English edition of the paper.

References

1. Moreno-Jiménez, J.M., Aguarón, J., Cardeñosa, J., Escobar, M.T., Ruiz, J., Toncovich, A., Turón, A.: PRIOR-W&K: A Collaborative Tool for Decision Making in the Knowledge Society. In: Sent to E-GOV 2010 Conference, Lausanne, Switzerland (2010)
2. Aguarón, J., Escobar, M.T., Moreno-Jiménez, J.M., Turón, A.: A Module for Discrete Multicriteria Selection in Environmental Decisional Systems. In: Mendes, I. (ed.) Decision Support Systems: Viewpoints and Applications. European Commission. Joint Research Center. Ispra, Italia. EUR 17295 EN, pp. 9–20 (1996)
3. Moreno-Jiménez, J.M.: Las Nuevas Tecnologías y la Representación Democrática del Inmigrante. IV Jornadas Jurídicas de Albarracín. Consejo General del Poder Judicial (2003)
4. Moreno-Jiménez, J.M.: E-cognocracia y Representación Democrática del Inmigrante. Anales de Economía Aplicada (2004)
5. Moreno-Jiménez, J.M.: E-cognocracia: Nueva Sociedad, Nueva Democracia. Estudios de Economía Aplicada 24(1-2), 559–581 (2006)
6. Moreno-Jiménez, J.M., Polasek, W.: E-democracy and Knowledge. A Multicriteria Framework for the New Democratic Era. Journal Multicriteria Decision Analysis 12, 163–176 (2003)
7. Moreno-Jiménez, J.M., Polasek, W.: E-cognocracy and the participation of immigrants in e-governance. In: Böhlen, et al. (eds.) TED Conference on e-government 2005. Electronic democracy: The challenge ahead, Schriftenreihe Informatik, vol. 13, pp. 18–26. University Rudolf Trauner-Verlag (2005)
8. Mamaqi, X., Moreno-Jiménez, J.M.: The effectiveness of e-cognocracy. In: Lytras, M.D., et al. (eds.) WSKS 2009. LNCS (LNAI), vol. 5736, pp. 417–426. Springer, Heidelberg (2009)

9. Moreno-Jiménez, J.M., Piles, J., Ruiz, J., Salazar, J.L., Sanz, A.: Some Notes on e-voting and e-cognocracy. In: Proceedings E-Government Interoperability Conference 2007, Paris, France (2007)
10. García Lizana, A., Moreno-Jiménez, J.M.: Economía y Democracia en la Sociedad del Conocimiento. Estudios de Economía Aplicada 26(2), 181–212 (2008)
11. Lasswell, H.D.: The Political Science of Science: An Inquiry into the Possible Reconciliation of Mastery and Freedom. American Political Science Review 50(4), 961–979 (1956)
12. Lasswell, H.D.: A Pre-View of Policy Sciences. Elsevier, New York (1971)
13. Hogwood, B., Gunn, L.: Policy Analysis and the real world. Oxford University Press, Oxford (1984)
14. Presuman, J.L., Wildavsky, A.B.: Implementation. California University Press, New York (1973)
15. Barret, S., Fudge, C.: Policy and Action: Essays on Implementation of Public Policy, Methuen, New York (1981)
16. Moreno-Jiménez, J.M., Piles, J., Ruiz, J., Salazar, J.L.: E-cognising: the e-voting tool for e-cognocracy. Rio's Int. Jour. on Sciences of Industrial and Systems Engineering and Management 2(2), 25–40 (2008)
17. Moreno-Jiménez, J.M., Piles, J., Ruiz, J., Salazar, J.L., Turón, A.: Securization of Policy Making Social Computing. An application to e-cognocracy. Computers in Human Behaviour (2010) doi: 10.1016/j.chb.2010.07.039
18. Capra, F.: The Web of Life. Anchor Books, NY (1996)
19. Aguarón, J., Escobar, M.T., Moreno-Jiménez, J.M., Turón, A.: PRIOR-WEB: A discrete multicriteria prioritization tool for the global economy context. In: Respicio, A., et al. (eds.) Bridging the Socio- technical Gap in Decision Support Systems. IOS Press, Amsterdam (2010)
20. Turón, A., Moreno-Jiménez, J.M., Toncovich, A.: Group Decision Making and Graphical Visualization in e-Cognocracy. Computación y Sistemas 12(2), 183–191 (2008)
21. Salazar, J.L., Piles, J., Ruiz, J., Moreno-Jiménez, J.M.: E-cognocracy and its voting process. Computer Standards and Interfaces (30/3), 124–131 (2008)
22. Salazar, J.L., Piles, J., Ruiz, J., Moreno-Jiménez, J.M.: Security approaches in E-cognocracy. Computer Standards and Interfaces 32(5-6), 256–265 (2010)
23. Saaty, T.: The Analytic Hierarchy Process. McGraw-Hill, New York (1980)

Learning Assessment Using Wikis: Integrated or LMS Independent?

Marc Alier Forment[1], Xavier De Pedro[2], Maria Jose Casañ[1], Jordi Piguillem[1], and Nikolas Galanis[1]

[1] Technical University of Catalonia, c/Jordi Girona Salgado 1-3, 08034 Barcelona, Spain
[2] University of Barcelona, Pavelló Rosa. Travessera de les Corts 131-159, Barcelona 08028, Spain
{ludo,mjcasany,jpiguillem,ngalanis}@essi.upc.edu, {xavier.depedro}@ub.edu

Abstract. Wikis have a potentially huge educational value. This article outlines a feature set that wiki engines need in order to successfully host collaborative educational scenarios using wiki technology. One of the first issues to solve is the need for assessment methodologies supported by the software. And the second one is to choose between using an integrated wiki engine inside the Learning Management System (LMS), or an external standalone wiki engine. Advantages and disadvantages from both options of this second issue are discussed, with each choice presenting different implications as far as individual student assessment, feedback and grading are concerned. Among the expected results, the most notable are incentives to incorporate wikis in the teaching procedure, significant enhancements in usability, as well as allowing teachers to provide more timely written feedback on their students' individual contributions on wiki based activities, on top of the usual numerical grading.

This paper exposes the conclusions of 5 years of experience of work in the field of wikis in education, development of improvements on open source wiki engines and thus, building from scratch accordingly the new wiki engine for the LMS Moodle 2.0.

Keywords: Education, E-Learning, Social Learning, Wikis, LMS.

1 Introduction

The use of wikis in education is of a potentially huge value. Wikis can be applied to foster collaborative work, to promote project based learning experiences, to open the work conducted in classroom to the world, to facilitate information exchange between groups and educational institutions, etc. The possibilities are practically endless [1][2][3][4]. So, using wikis as environments for educational activities is definitively an appealing idea.

The question is what kind of wiki application we need in order to host the educational wiki experiences. We can choose from two basic software architectures: the

M.D. Lytras et al. (Eds.): WSKS 2010, Part I, CCIS 111, pp. 150–158, 2010.

first one is to use a wiki engine embedded and highly integrated inside the Learning Management System (LMS), host of the "virtual campus" of the educational institution, such as Moodle (http://moodle.org), Sakai (http://sakai.org) or Dokeos (http://dokeos.org). The second option is to use some vertical wiki application, such as MediaWiki (http://mediawiki.org) or Tiki Wiki CMS/Groupware (http://tiki.org), stand-alone web applications, to conduct a fairly free wiki experience outside of the boundaries of the educational institution.

In both cases, basic conclusions from previous works have to be taken into account as premises in order to ensure the effective use of wikis in Education. These include:

a) WYSIWYG (What You See Is What You Get) is not necessarily a "must" feature because basic wiki markup seems to be easy enough to understand and use even for primary education pupils [5].
b) The main handicaps that prevent users from having a successful activity seem to be the lack of motivation and usability [6].
c) Our experience indicates that students usually don't participate much (if any) in wikis if there is no grading "retribution" for that participation. This is similar to what has been reported for professional sites where potential contributors don't see its worth, provided the institution hosting the wiki does not offer any benefits to make up for the time spent contributing [7].
d) In order to enhance their learning, students need "on time" feedback for their individual contributions in the class or the workgroup [8]. Teachers, on the other hand, need tools that facilitate the task of quickly providing objective feedback, assessment, and grading of groups and individuals alike [9].

2 Integrated in LMS, or Standalone Wiki?

Some benefits and drawbacks arise from any of these two contrasted options. Some of them will affect the possibilities to establish certain teaching, assessment and grading strategies.

The managers of educational institutions will prefer the use of wiki integrated in the LMS, provided it complies with the basic features and selection criteria commonly requested [10]. The main reasons are pretty obvious: out of the box integration of user authentication and authorization, plus the fact that the wiki is integrated in the LMS structure (course, categories, permissions and roles, tags, search features, course information, access logs, etc). Moreover, the corporate image is preserved due to the use of the institution "theme/skin", color scheme, etc.

This way the wiki becomes part of the institution's portfolio of educational software tools, and educators can be instructed on how to use it in their courses. So everything is kept under control for the educational site managers. Some examples of this type of wiki would be the Wiki Module packages for Moodle (eWiki, the default wiki engine for installations up to branch 1.9, included), dfWiki, nWiki or ouWiki [11]; RWiki: Sakai Wiki Tool [12], or CoolWiki extension for Dokeos [13].

Usually the embedded Wikis are more limited in features compared to some full featured and mature Wikis. Under some pedagogic scenarios, or technical requirements in some specific areas, simple wikis seem to be lacking [14][15]. Some times there is the need to receive RSS feeds or email notification of changes on multiple pages from some student groups on long term collaborative work, in order to help to provide prompt feedback whenever needed [16]. Some other times, there is the need to allow multimedia rich content on the wiki pages of the students (artistic type of courses, animations for scientific lessons, mathematic formulae, etc.). And in some cases, the teacher needs some higher degree of permission handling for pages and categories of pages, in order to easily define whatever complex settings for pedagogic activities, visual editing of tables or linked spreadsheets and concept maps, so that those wiki-based activities simply work on their particular pedagogic strategy [17]. Therefore, some specific criteria beyond the basic ones used by other institutions must be taken into account, in order to successfully set the pursued pedagogic scenario and high level technical [15].

Thus, teachers who are more engaged in innovative activities or pedagogic scenarios might feel that the integrated wikis commonly available inside LMS platforms are less versatile than what they need for their teaching. Some of them have reported feeling handicapped, because they were unable to add on the fly new courses or workspaces beyond the initial course wiki, or they could not grant access to users outside the institution. For seminars, conferences, postgraduate and other special courses, this is a daily issue, and that's why many external wikis (or even full external LMS sites) can be commonly found on the Internet (pbwiki.com, wikilearning.com, wikispaces.com, to name a few), alongside their base institutional campus sites.

When working inside the institutional wiki, and once motivated to contribute, students tend to behave with more caution. They are more reluctant to rush into a wiki page and change content. Thus, the pedagogical experience of participation in an open wiki is contaminated by an excess of formalism and aspirations to excellence. Students usually do not dare to contribute to high quality content, but often do not mind doing so to an external wiki were non students can also contribute, such as in Wikibooks from the Wikipedia Foundation, where excellence can be achieved by peer reviewing and fearless collaboration [18]. However, student contributions on those environments increase the difficulty for teachers to easily review them, and to provide in-context feedback without dispersing comments on too many different environments, with all the inconveniences this may cause [14].

The use of external wiki engines requires an extra effort for integrating user authentication and synchronization systems. Sometimes the adopted solution consists of creating separate accounts for the students in a completely separated application administered by the teachers (like in the experiences behind [19][20][21][22][9]), sometimes hosted in a desktop computer in the teacher's office (Bernat Claramunt, personal communication).

As examples, we can cite the case of MediaWiki installations which are fully external to the main LMS (the most common case everywhere in the world), or partly integrated within installations of Moodle [23], or Dokeos [24], for instance, even if some integration issues are well known [25][15]. Elsewhere, Tikiwiki CMS/Groupware has been chosen as the wiki engine besides the main LMS installation: several departments at University of York, UK [26]; all faculties in Bages University Foundation, Spain, alongside their Dokeos based campus (http://wiki.fub.edu vs. http://virtual.fub.edu); several departments at University of Barcelona [21][22].

There are also some extreme cases where the institution adopted the external wiki site (such as Tikiwiki CMS/Groupware), with its companion's built-in features to act as Content Management System and Groupware site (including specific modules to act as an LMS). In fact, Tikiwiki was already highly ranked by international institutions when evaluating portal systems including wikis [27]. Some examples of this type of institution are Harbor City International School (Minnesota, USA; http://torch.harborcityschool.net), Trinity School Insite (Cheshire, UK; http://trinitysch.org.uk/insite), Colegio María Virgen (Madrid, Spain; http://www.cmariavirgen.org), and University of Strathclyde (UK) and Stanford University (USA) using a modified version of Tikiwiki called "LauLima" (http://www.didet.ac.uk).

The last and most recent case is a mixed approach: the Open University of Catalonia, Spain (http://www.uoc.edu) already started for their 2008/09 course, a dual approach were teachers are be able to use either the integrated wiki engine in their main LMS sites (based on Moodle, among others), as well as a separate and customized Tikiwiki 2 installation for cases were teacher need higher degree of features and more complex pedagogic scenarios (Begoña Gros, Personal Communication).

3 Learning in Wikis: Assessment, Feedback and Grading

Assessment and feedback of the student learning process in wikis are very delicate tasks, which can be used by students to enhance their teaching, and especially when they include enough oral or written individual feedback on their performance, beyond simply grading their activity. The quality of a wiki page or set of pages is usually the result of a combined work of several students. But not all them necessarily deserve the same grade, nor need the same feedback on their individual contributions for the common document. Some students fake edits, abuse copy and paste, or alter their participation in other ways. So, it is important to state the size and type of contributions that each student performs on wiki activities.

Most wiki engines, due to their general purpose design, do not consider tagging the type of student contributions, do not allow rating by teachers or student peers, do not facilitate the task of submitting written feedback on students' single edits, nor include a grading feature linked to the course grade book. A wiki engine aspiring to be useful for educational scenarios needs to provide a way to easily track and assess each student's individual contributions, to easily report prompt feedback on them, and should allow grading the participation in the wiki, while transferring this information to the course grade book. When the wiki engine is not integrated in the LMS, then it should provide an easy way of exporting the action log of all student contributions, tagged by student, group, category and time, in order to facilitate the assessment and provide objective information for written feedback or oral tutorship by the teachers.

Therefore, some balance has to be achieved between the need for more features in an educational wiki, and its usability for its users (students, but also teachers, some of whom are even more novice to new technologies than their pupils). Some educational institutions opt for an integrated wiki engine in their main LMS site. In some other cases, either the institution or the lecturers opt for setting their own external wiki sites for maximum control and a more complete feature set. In both cases, in order to have a successful engine that helps students and teachers on their daily life, the wiki should include some rating mechanism that takes into consideration several aspects:

- The quality of the pages.
- The participation of each student in each edition.
- The possibility of having a review being not only a number or a letter, but also some extended form of written feedback.
- The page or edition evaluation being just a part of the whole activity grade, which is what the teacher sends to the course's grade book.

4 Including the Findings on the Moodle 2.0 Wiki Engine

After 5 years of working with wikis in education, developing education specific features for wiki engines (TikiWiki, Moodle Nwiki module) the authors have applied all the lessons learned to the design and development of the Moodle 2.0 official Wiki module.

The new Wiki Module to be released in Moodle 2.0 and back ported to 1.9 branch, includes the following features:

- "Multiple markup wiki". NWiki allows the page creator to choose from several markups: Mediawiki plus Creole 1.0 markup [28], the native DFWiki markup (a subset of Mediawiki's with simplified tables), efurtWiki markup for backwards compatibility, and the Moodle internal HTML editor plus wikilinks.
- Import/Export features. Moodle courses can be saved and restored via backups, DFWiki allows to export the wiki contents to a single XML file, and import them in another wiki activity (to merge two wiki contents for example) or in another course in another Moodle server. Another feature is the possibility to export the content to HTML, PDF and some experimental export plug-ins such as Tiddlywiki export (http://moodle.tiddlyspot.com) and OpenOffice Writer import/export.

- Customizable Blocks inside the wiki activity (Figure 2). Moodle design includes Blocks: small micro web applications that the teacher can place in both sides of the Moodle screen. NWiki provides a number of blocks with useful information and functions such as:
    - Dynamic tree index (from the first or the current page). The teacher can choose which of these blocks to enable in their wiki.
    - Wanted pages.
    - Orphaned pages.
    - Alphabetical page list.
    - Search engine.
    - Page synonyms.
    - New page block: a small form to create a new page. The creation of this small form was a very requested feature in the Moodle.org forums.
    - Latest contributions list.
    - Page ranking. The teacher can enable votes in the wiki pages. The following block shows the ranking.

Moreover, similarly to Mediawiki and Tikiwiki, Moodle 2.0 Wiki implements discussion pages and allows two page comparison views: line by line and inline changes.

The activity (editions and page views) in Moodle 2.0 Wiki instances is logged in the Moodle reporting system, so the teacher can easily track the student's participation in the wiki. This is a common need when using Wikis in educational scenarios [14][9].

Moodle's course design is customizable. There are several available built in formats like a weekly schedule, topics, social (with a forum as main activity), Scorm, IMS, etc. Moodle 2.0 Wiki will include a wiki course format with a wiki as the main course activity.

Finally, Moodle 2.0 Wiki incorporates a redesigned assessment and grading feature. Each page can be assessed and graded. And grades are set according to a Moodle grading scale. Teachers or students (if they are allowed) can grade pages through a small combo box in the bottom of the page (Figure 3).

When grading a page, a user can give one line of feedback. This feedback is added into the discussion page (Figure 4).

Moreover, teachers and peers can rate single editions with a symbol (+, = or -), as well as giving the student a line of feedback (Figure 5). The feedback is sent to the students through Moodle internal messaging system (that pipes into the students email if they are not online).

Finally the teacher has access to a special page where he can see all the information about the pages where a student has participated in: page editions, views and received ratings. In this page, the teacher can give an overall grade for the student's contributions to the whole wiki activity and send it to the course's grade book (http://docs.moodle.org/en/gradebook).

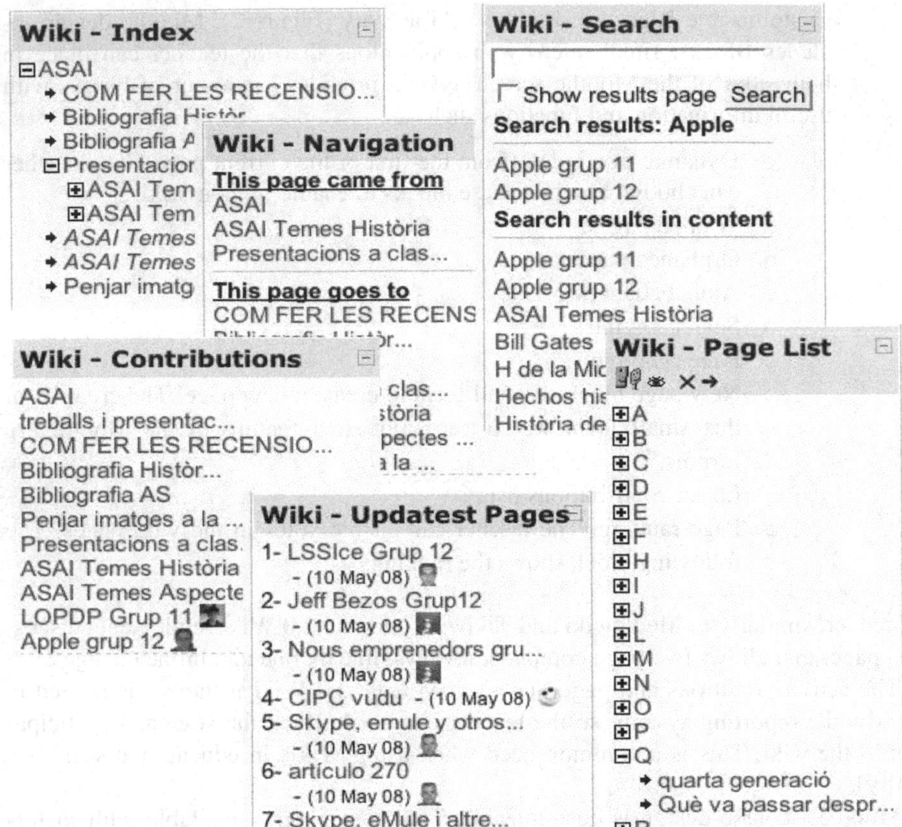

Fig. 1. Moodle 2.0 Wiki blocks. Depending on the purposes of the use of the wiki activity the teacher can choose from several useful blocks with key live information about what's going on in the wiki.

5 Future Work and Aknowledgements

The Moodle community is already providing feedback and requesting new features to extend this feature set, in a similar way as other wiki engines do as external applications to the institutional LMS infrastructures [29]. Future versions of Moodle shall address some of these new requests.

A special issue to address is the growing wish of the students to use rich web based document editors like Google Docs as their collaborative editors.

Our thanks to Begoña Gros, Lluïsa Núñez, Miquel Barceló, Ruth Raventós, Pablo Casado and Enric Mayol for providing feedback on the usage of the Institutional Learning Management Systems on their respective campuses (UOC, UB and UPC respectively).

This work has been funded by Google, and the Spanish Ministry of Science and Innovation with the project : TIN2010-21695-C02-02.

References

[1] Augar, N., Raitman, R., Zhou, W.: Teaching and learning online with wikis. In: Beyond the Comfort Zone: Proceedings of the 21st ASCILITE Conference, pp. 95–104 (2004)

[2] Educause Learning Initiative. 7 things you should know about... wikis (2005)

[3] Fountain, R.: Dossiers technopédagogiques: wiki pedagogy, http://www.profetic.org/dossiers/dossier_imprimer.php3?id_rubrique=110

[4] García Manzano, A.: Blogs y wikis en tareas educativas (2006), http://observatorio.cnice.mec.es/modules.php?op=modload&name=News&file=article&sid=378

[5] Désilets, A., Paquet, S., Vinson, N.G.: Are wikis usable? In: Proceedings of the 2005 International Symposium on Wikis, October 17-18, pp. 3–15 (2005)

[6] Kickmeier-Rust, M., Ebner, M., Holzinger, A.: Wikis: do they need usability engineering? In: M3 – Interdisciplinary Aspects of Digital Media & Education, pp. 137–144 (2006)

[7] Giordano, R.: An investigation of the use of a wiki to support knowledge exchange in public health. In: Proceedings of the 2007 International ACM Conference on Supporting Group Work (2007)

[8] Diamond, M.: The usefulness of structured mid-term feedback as a catalyst for change in higher education classes. Active Learning in Higher Education 5, 217–231 (2004)

[9] De Pedro, X.: New method using wikis and forums to evaluate individual contributions in cooperative work while promoting experiential learning: results from preliminary experience. In: Wikis at Work in the World: Open, Organic, Participatory Media for the 21st century, pp. 87–92 (2007)

[10] Schwartz, L., Clark, S., Cossarin, M., Rudolph, J.: Educational wikis: features and selection criteria. The International Review of Research in Open and Distance Learning 5 (2004)

[11] Moodle forums thread about NWiki, and OUWiki, http://moodle.org/mod/forum/discuss.php?d=89653

[12] Sakai wiki tool (rwiki), http://confluence.sakaiproject.org/confluence/display/RWIKI/Home

[13] Coolwiki extension for dokeos lms, http://www.dokeos.com/extensions/index.php?section=tools&id=33

[14] Choy, S.O., Ng, K.C.: Implementing wiki software for supplementing online learning. Australasian Journal of Educational Technology 23, 209–226 (2007)

[15] De Pedro, X.: Informe sobre wikis en educació per a la universitat oberta de catalunya (2008)

[16] Mutch, A.: Exploring the practice of feedback to students. Active Learning in Higher Education 14, 24–38 (2003)

[17] Wikis that work. Practical and pedagogical applications of wikis in the classroom, http://julielindsaylinks.pbwiki.com/Wikis-that-Work

[18] Sajjapanroj, S., Bonk, C., Lee, M.M., Lin, M.G.: A window on wikibookians: surveying their statuses, successes, satisfactions, and sociocultural experiences. Journal of Interactive Online Learning 7, 36–58 (2008)

[19] De Pedro, X., Rieradevall, M., López, P., Sant, D., Piñol, J., Núñez, L., Llobera, M.: Writing documents collaboratively in higher education using traditional vs. wiki methodology (i): qualitative results from a 2-year project study. In: Libro De Comunicaciones Del 4° Congreso Internacional De Docencia Universitaria e Innovación (2006), http://cidui.upc.edu

[20] De Pedro, X., Rieradevall, M., López, P., Sant, D., Piñol, J., Núñez, L., Llobera, M.: Writing documents collaboratively in higher education using traditional vs. wiki methodology (ii): quantitative results from a 2-year project study. In: Libro De Comunicaciones Del 4° Congreso Internacional De Docencia Universitaria e Innovación (2006), `http://cidui.upc.edu`

[21] De Pedro, X.: Cómo evitar el 'café para todos' al evaluar trabajos en grupo, y de paso, estimular el aprendizaje reflexivo: resultados preliminares en el marco del proyecto awikiforum. In: Entorns Col·Laboratius Per Aprendre: Comunitats Virtuals d'Aprenentatge (2006)

[22] De Pedro, X.: Estimulación y evaluación del aprendizaje 'experiencial-reflexivo' del alumnado mediante la formulación explícita del tipo de contribuciones, pp. 1–100 (2006)

[23] Moodle development: wiki, `http://docs.moodle.org/en/Development:Wiki`

[24] Integration of mediawiki in dokeos, `http://www.dokeos.com/wiki/index.php/Integration_of_mediawiki`

[25] Integrating moodle and mediawiki, `http://www.verso.co.nz/learning-technology/35/integrating-moodle-and-mediawiki/`

[26] Davies, J.: Wiki brainstorming and problems with wiki based collaboration (2004)

[27] Catalyst IT Limited. Technical evaluation of selected portal systems (2004)

[28] Sauer, C., Smith, C., Benz, T.: Wikicreole: a common wiki markup. In: In Proceedings of the 2007 International Symposium on Wikis, pp. 131–142. ACM Press, New York (2007)

[29] CosmoCode Wikimatrix, `http://www.wikimatrix.org`

How to Analyze Company Using Social Network?

Sebastian Palus, Piotr Bródka, and Przemysław Kazienko

Wroclaw University of Technology, Wyb. Wyspianskiego 27,
50-370 Wroclaw, Poland
{sebastian.palus,piotr.brodka,przemyslaw.kazienko}@pwr.wroc.pl

Abstract. Every single company or institution wants to utilize its resources in the most efficient way. In order to do so they have to be have good structure. The new way to analyze company structure by utilizing existing within company natural social network and example of its usage on Enron company are presented in this paper.

Keywords: Social network, social network analysis, company structure.

1 Introduction

The growing number of opportunities and ways people can communicate and exchange information within an organization provide us with a previously unknown way to evaluate company's structure [5]. The data extracted from email services, phone calls, other communication systems or common activities allow to create social networks which contain information about humans interaction and collaboration. On the other hand all companies have always sought to obtain the best and most effective structure. By utilizing, already existing within company, social network we can help to achieve this goal. In this paper it is presented how to do this using the Enron company as an example.

2 Enron

The Enron Hierarchy Structure is not publicly available. However, there are sources which can provide information about names of job positions of many employees and their department or division. In [8] there is an Excel file with a list of over 160 employees and their job title. Many of them do not exist in Enron Corpus, though. Using this list and charts available in [6], four groups from Enron North American West Power Traders were chosen where it was able to distinguish levels of hierarchy by assigning them to job titles. An assumption was made that the job ranking looks as presented in Fig. 1. where Analysts, Specialists and Staff are at the same level.

It is impossible to find direct relationships of superior-inferior from such limited data. The knowledge of hierarchy levels is however complete enough to perform some tests. The organization chart which was used for analysis is presented on Fig. .

M.D. Lytras et al. (Eds.): WSKS 2010, Part I, CCIS 111, pp. 159–164, 2010.

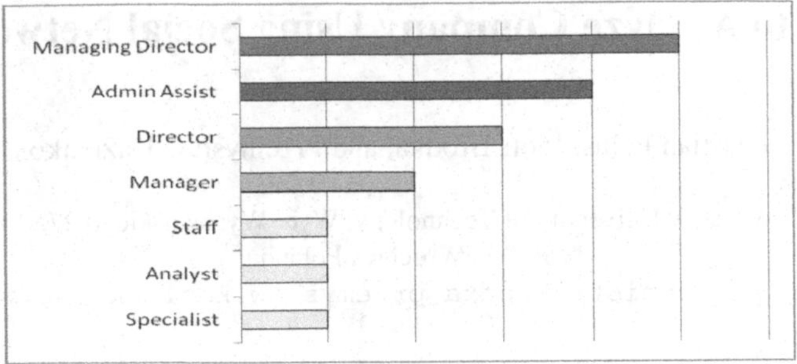

Fig. 1. Job titles hierarchy

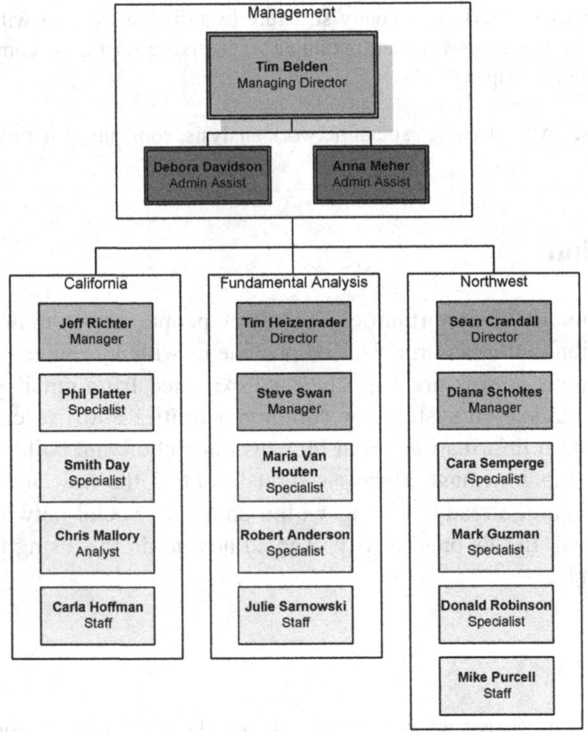

Fig. 2. Part of Enron hierarchy used for analysis

2.1 Enron Email Dataset Specification

Enron Corpus is a set of mail messages, each email in separate file [1]. The messages are grouped in *maildir* folders by their owner and organized into folders such as Inbox, Sent, Trash etc.

Every message is in a standard mail format [9] and contains elements such as: Message-id; Date; From; To (CC, BCC); Subject; X-Fields with user-friendly Active Directory names (X-To, X-CC etc.); Message body;

The whole email dataset was made public after the Federal Energy Regulatory Commission during its investigation on the Enron Scandal. The email dataset had a number of integrity problems which have been corrected by researchers at MIT and SRI International. The dataset does not include attachments, and some messages have been deleted as part of a redaction effort due to requests from affected employees. Invalid email addresses were converted to the form user@enron.com whenever possible (i.e., recipient is specified in some parse-able format like "Doe, John" or "Mary K. Smith") and to no_address@enron.com when no recipient was specified.

It contains data from 150 Enron employees, mostly Senior Management. There are total number of 517,430 messages.

2.2 Enron Communication Social Network

The social network of Enron is extracted from the email dataset. Using all emails in the dataset, one can construct an undirected graph, where vertices represent accounts and edges represent communication between two accounts. Then several measures for each node are applied [7,10]. The approach presented in [6] was used, where social score is computed from:

a) Emails count – number of email the user has sent and received.
b) Average response time - the time elapsed between a user sending an email and later receiving an email from that same user. An exchange of this nature is only considered a "response" if a received message succeeds a sent message within three business days.
c) Response score – a combination of the number of responses and average response time.
d) Number of cliques – the number of maximal complete subgraphs that the account is contained within.
e) Raw clique score – a score computed using a size of the given account's clique set. Bigger cliques are worth more than smaller ones, importance increases exponentially with size.
f) Weighted clique score – a score computed using the importance of the people in each clique, which is computed strictly from the number of emails and the average response time.
g) Centrality Degree - count of the number of ties to other actors in the network.
h) Clustering coefficient - likelihood that two associates of a node are associates with themselves.
i) Mean of shortest path length from a specific vertex to all vertices in the graph.
j) Betweenness centrality - reflects the number of people who a person is connecting indirectly through their direct links.
k) "ubs-and-Authorities" importance – refers to the algorithm proposed in [3].

Above metrics are then weighted and normalized to a [0, 100] scale.

3 Organizational Structure Evaluation

For each employee in the corporate hierarchy it is possible to find people who are higher or lower in the hierarchy. The Hierarchical Position (HP) is a measure that shows the importance of an employee within a company. For each user ui in a company C there is a sum of hierarchical differences D between ui and every user uj in the company divided by the number of other users.

$$HP(u_i) = \frac{\sum_{u_j \in C \wedge u_i \neq u_j} D(u_i, u_j)}{m-1} \tag{1}$$

The hierarchical difference *D(x,y)* is computed as follows:

$$D(x,y) = \begin{cases} 1, & \text{if } x \text{ is higher in the hierarchy than } y \\ 0, & \text{if } x \text{ and } y \text{ are at the same level of the hierarchy} \\ -1, & \text{if } x \text{ is lower in the hierarchy than } y \end{cases} \tag{2}$$

At first, the Kendall's rankings comparison method was used [2]. To compare two rankings we have to compare the positions in each pair in both rankings. If the position of node A is related to the position of node B in both rankings monotonicly in the same direction (lower or higher in the both hierarchies) then this pair is well correlated. It is assumed that when the level in hierarchy is the same within the pair, then it does not matter whether they are in different positions in the second ranking. Kendall's τ rank correlation coefficient is a value from a [-1,1] scale, where 1 means that rankings are perfectly correlated and -1 means that they are completely different. It is impossible to distinguish the importance of departments, e.g. whether the Director of Northwest is higher in the hierarchy than the Director of Fundamental Analysis. Thus, analyses were not performed globally, but locally at department level.

4 Evaluation for the Enron Company

The list of Enron employees sorted by their *Social Score* is presented on Table 1. The *HP* measure (see Section 6) and *Position* column indicates official hierarchy structure. It can be seen very clearly that Social Scores of the Management is far higher than the others.

Table 1. Social measures for Enron employees sorted by SocialScore

Name	Surname	Position	Level	HP	Degree	Betweenness	Hubs	Clustering	SocialScore
Tim	Beldon	Managing Director	1	1,00	83	370,35	0,04	0,40	75,68
Debora	Davidson	Admin Assist	2	0,83	66	278,35	0,04	0,41	63,51
Anna	Meher	Admin Assist	2	0,83	62	260,94	0,04	0,42	62,84
Carla	Hoffman	Staff	5	-0,44	55	143,98	0,04	0,49	61,67
Cara	Semperger	Specialist	5	-0,44	63	82,96	0,03	0,52	53,68
Diana	Scholtes	Manager	4	0,33	45	21,44	0,03	0,70	53,31
Sean	Crandall	Director	3	0,61	42	40,04	0,03	0,62	43,64
Tim	Heizenrader	Director	3	0,61	33	19,45	0,02	0,71	35,56
Donald	Robinson	Specialist	5	-0,44	27	6,67	0,02	0,81	33,03

Table 1. *(continued)*

Jeff	Richter	Manager	4	0,33	25	12,80	0,02	0,74	32,53
Julie	Sarnowski	Staff	5	-0,44	28	25,94	0,02	0,63	32,14
Mike	Purcell	Staff	5	-0,44	24	5,02	0,02	0,79	30,36
Chris	Mallory	Analyst	5	-0,44	27	9,92	0,02	0,76	30,19
Phil	Platter	Specialist	5	-0,44	33	34,34	0,02	0,63	27,90
Robert	Anderson	Specialist	5	-0,44	8	0,15	0,01	0,96	20,06
Smith	Day	Specialist	5	-0,44	6	0,00	0,01	1,00	20,00
Mark	Guzman	Specialist	5	-0,44	18	6,84	0,01	0,75	19,97
Steve	Swan	Manager	4	0,33	9	0,20	0,01	0,93	19,55
Maria	VanHouten	Specialist	5	-0,44	7	0,11	0,01	0,95	19,44

The diagram of *Hierarchical Position* should be descending, but there are deep structural holes in Fig. 3.

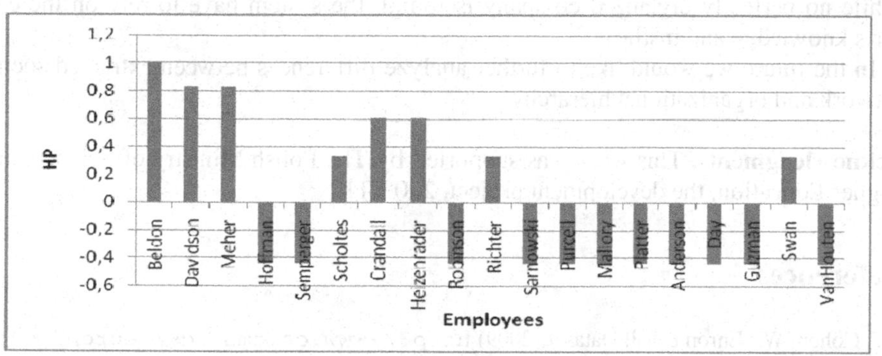

Fig. 3. Hierarchical Positions of Enron employees sorted by Social Score

On Table 2 there is a summary of Kendall correlation coefficient between the official hierarchy (ordered by *HP*) and one derived from social network (ordered by *Social Score*) for chosen departments.

Table 2. Kendall coefficient for each department between official hierarchy and social network

Department	Kendall's τ
Management (official vs SN)	1,0
California (official vs SN)	0,8
Fundamental Analysis (official vs SN)	0,6
Northwest (official vs SN)	0,6

The main problem with the Enron dataset is the lack of information about direct hierarchy structure. All analysis were performed with assumptions of the structure of levels and departments. However, the analysis shows the rankings are very similar with Kendall rank over 0.6 with Management department perfectly identical (Kendall rank of 1).

An interesting fact is that all employees who are lower in the hierarchy than it comes from social network are women. There are 7 women among 19 analyzed employees and there are 5 female workers in the top 6 of the social ranking (Table 1), while 4 have been classified as lowest level employees according to the hierarchy. There are three possible reasons of such case. First is that a wrong assumption has been made while ranking job titles. Secondly, there can be a simple but important reason that women are underestimated and should occupy higher company positions. Last, but not less probable, is that women are more likely than men to gossip [4] and this fact is disrupting the process of proper social network extraction. It is very likely that the real reason is combined of these three.

5 Conclusions and Future Work

Managing human resources in a company can be very well supported by the social network approach. However, for the results be more reliable, a perfect company to *calibrate* the system would be needed, where all social leaders are in fact directors. While no perfectly organized company is found, the system have to rely on the experts knowledge and instincts.

In the future we would like to further analyze differences between extracted social network and organizational hierarchy.

Acknowledgments. This work was supported by The Polish Ministry of Science and Higher Education, the development project, 2009-11.

References

1. Cohen, W.: Enron Email Dataset (2009) http://www.cs.cmu.edu/~enron/
2. Kendall, M.G.: Rank Correlation Methods. Oxford (1948)
3. Kleinberg, J.: Authoritative sources in a hyperlinked environment. Journal of the ACM 46 (1999)
4. Levin, J., Arluke, A.: An exploratory analysis of sex differences in gossip. Sex Roles 12(3-4), 281–286 (1985)
5. Palus, S., Kazienko, P.: Social Network Analysis in Corporate Management. In: Multimedia & Network Information Systems, MISSI 2010, Wrocław, Advances in Intelligent and Soft Computing. Springer, Heidelberg (2010) (accepted)
6. Rowe, R., Creamer, G., Hershkop, S., Stolfo, S.J.: Automated Social Hierarchy Detection through Email Network Analysis. In: Proceedings of the 9th WebKDD and 1st SNA-KDD 2007 Workshop on Web Mining and Social Network Analysis, pp. 109–117 (2007)
7. Scott, J.: Social network analysis: A handbook, 2nd edn. Sage, London (2000)
8. Shetty, J., Adibi, J.: Ex employee status report (2004) http://www.isi.edu/~adibi/Enron/Enron_Employee_Status.xls (retrieved)
9. The Internet Society. RFC 2822 - Internet Message Format (2001), http://www.faqs.org/rfcs/rfc2822.html (retrieved)
10. Wasserman, S., Faust, K.: Social network analysis: Methods and applications. Cambridge University Press, New York (1994)

Teacher, What Do You Mean by "Creativity"? An Italian Survey on the Use of ICT to Foster Student Creativity

Michela Ott, Francesca Pozzi, and Mauro Tavella

Istituto Tecnologie Didattiche – CNR
Via De Marini, 6, Genoa Italy
{ott,pozzi,tavella}@itd.cnr.it

Abstract. This paper illustrates how the issue of "creativity raising" is currently tackled by teachers in Italy and what is, in their view, the potential role of ICT to support creativity development. By referring to the results of a small–scale survey conducted among Italian teachers, and starting from the meaning and value they attribute to the concept of "creativity", the paper provides an overview of teachers' prevailing attitudes towards the issue and reports on the kinds of actions they usually carry out within their own classes.

Keywords: Creativity, education, ICT (Information and Communication Technology), creativity-oriented activity, school, TEL (Technology Enhanced Learning).

1 Introduction

Education to creativity is a hot issue mainly because it is widely acknowledged that creativity is a powerful catalyst for innovation, progress and growth. In addition, the debate about whether creativity can be triggered and fostered by means of educational intervention, is almost over and nowadays there is substantial agreement among researchers that creativity can be fostered and, to some extent, *taught* by means of appropriate educational interventions (Csikszentmihalyi, 1997; Nickerson, 1999; Treffinger et al., 2002, Hewett, 2005).

What needs further investigations is, instead, whether and how the issue of "creativity raising" is presently tackled in today's school. What does exactly mean creativity for contemporary teachers? What are their main attitudes towards this issue and the actual actions they usually carry out with this purpose (if any)?

According to an online survey launched by the European Commission in the context of the European Year of Creativity and Innovation 2009 and expressly aimed at shedding light on teachers' opinions concerning creativity in schools: "*An overwhelming majority of teachers believe that creativity can be applied to every domain of knowledge and every school subject. They do not see creativity as being only relevant for intrinsically creative subjects such as arts, music or drama. This is of paramount importance for the development of creative thinking as a transversal skill*" (Cachia et al., 2009).

M.D. Lytras et al. (Eds.): WSKS 2010, Part I, CCIS 111, pp. 165–171, 2010.

The above mentioned survey, which involved around 10.000 teachers from the 27 member States of the European Union, offers an overview of teachers' opinions, attitudes, feelings and specific actions in the field and thus should be regarded as a key contribution to the ongoing debate around the issue.

This paper aims at giving a further contribution to the research field by focusing on the Italian situation and by illustrating how the issue of "creativity raising" is currently tackled by Italian teachers. In particular, it also concentrates on the perceived potential and the actual use made by Italian teachers of ICT (Information and Communication Technologies) to support creativity development. As a matter of fact, nowadays, the potential of ICT to support educational interventions aimed at developing student creative attitudes, has been widely acknowledged (Lubart, 2005; Johnson and Carruthers, 2006) and a number of research projects have investigated ways to trigger creativity through ICT in formal educational settings and the features of ICT tools that better serve this scope (Greene, 2002).

Thus the present paper is based on the results of a small-scale survey, this time conducted by the authors of this paper among Italian teachers; the survey is different from the European one (Cachia et al., 2009), not only in figures, which are of course lower, but also in nature, as it looks at the matter by using a different, more qualitative lens. The paper investigates teachers' concept of creativity, basing on the idea that the approach they adopt largely depends on the "meaning" they give to the term "creativity". It then explores how Italian teachers tackle the issue of "creativity raising", what are their prevailing attitudes towards this issue, what are the actual types of educational actions they take in their daily practice and, finally, what is, in their opinion, the role of ICT in sustaining creativity and to what extent they adopt digital resources at this end.

2 The Survey: Aims and Methods

In order to investigate teachers' attitudes towards creativity, a questionnaire has been developed and delivered to a sample of Italian teachers of any discipline, school kind and level. In particular the questionnaire aimed to explore:

- teachers' concept of creativity (what it is)
- approaches/methods adopted by teachers to support creativity (whether and how creativity can be fostered through educational interventions)
- teachers' awareness of the potential role of digital tools to support creativity.

The questionnaire was composed of 12 questions, namely:

1. Respondent's profile (age, discipline, school level, etc.)
2. What do you mean by creativity?
3. Do you think at creativity as a natural gift/talent?
4. Do you think it is possible to foster students' creativity with ad hoc educational interventions?
5. Do you think it is part of the school mission to do it?
6. Does the national curriculum of your discipline make direct reference to creativity and its enhancement?

7. Do you usually propose learning activities explicitly oriented to foster creativity in your daily practice?
8. If yes, what kind of learning activities? If no, explain why you don't.
9. In order to develop students' creativity, do you think it is useful to propose specific activities equally in all the disciplines, or do you think this is more important in some disciplines and less in others?
10. Do you think ICT may play any role in developing students' creativity?
11. Have you ever used any ICT tools to foster students' creativity?
12. What kind of ICT tools?

The questionnaire was conceived in such a way to include both multi-choice questions, as well as open questions, so that respondents were let free to express themselves.

The total number of respondents is 160 subdivided as shown in Table 1 according school level- teaching subject- age.

Table 1. Sample of respondents to the survey

School	
Kindergarten	15%
Primary	34%
Low secondary	28%
Upper secondary	19%
Other	4%

Subject	
Humanities	45%
Science	17%
Special needs	10%
Arts	8%
Other	20%

Age	
20 - 30	9%
31 - 40	13%
41 - 50	34%
> 51	44%

3 Results

The results of the small-scale survey are presented here in terms of: 1) what is the actual meaning assigned by Italian teachers to the word "creativity" 2) what is the actual relationships between school and creativity (namely whether creativity is felt as an important issue in the Italian school, and whether its development is regarded as one of the target objectives to be met); 3) whether and to what extent specific actions are carried out within the Italian school to foster creativity development; 4) what is the role that, in teacher's opinions, ICT may play in creativity development; 5) are ICT actually used in the Italian school with the explicit aim of support creativity development and, eventually 6) which specific ICT tools are used to this end.

3.1 The Meaning of Creativity

Looking at the definitions given by teachers to the term "creativity" (question 2), one may note that they mostly think at creativity as a capacity (in Italian "capacità", see Fig. 1) to "see" ("vedere") / find out ("trovare") / use ("utilizzare") / or even invent ("inventare"), new ("nuovo") or diverse ("diversi") solutions ("soluzioni") / ways ("modo") to problems ("problemi").

Fig. 1. Wordle representing the terms used by teachers to define "creativity" (dimensions of words depend on the number of occurrences for each term)

Such a definition is interesting as it points out that teachers do not think at creativity only as a natural gift which leads a person to a sudden insight or creation, but also as a process of (ri-)elaboration, definition which is basically in line with what most researchers in this field have stated (Rhodes, 1961; Shneiderman, 2000; Plucker and Beghetto 2004; Selker, 2005; Sternberg, 2005; Burleson, 2005). Despite this, as it will be shown in the following, it is interesting to note that such a definition is not always coherent with what teachers do in practice to support creativity.

3.2 School – Creativity Relationships

In accordance with what teachers of the European survey declared, also the very majority of the Italian teachers who participated to the small-scale survey, agrees that in principle student creativity can be developed and fostered by means of suitable educational interventions (question 4) (95% of the teachers agrees with the statement that creativity can be developed by means of suitable educational interventions, while only the 5% declares they don't know), and on average (60%) they do not think at creativity as a natural gift (question 3).

Besides, the very majority of Italian teachers (again 95%), agrees that in principle it is a specific mission of school to foster and develop student creativity (question 5).

As to school policies, looking at national curricula of the Italian Ministry of Education, there is uncertainty among teachers about the curricula specifically addressing creativity as an objective to be pursued (question 6). Despite this, teachers (86%) think that creativity should be pursued in all the disciplines (question 9).

3.3 Actions towards Creativity Development

Not surprisingly, the enactment of *ad hoc* activities to enhance student creativity decreases as school level increases (question 7). In particular, 83% of pre-school teachers declare they often carry out activities oriented to creativity, while 63% of the primary school teachers do it; for lower secondary teachers, it is the 58%, while 53% of the upper secondary teachers often propose creativity-oriented activities.

When teachers "confess" they do not take specific actions to promote creativity (question 8), the main reason seems to be lack of time, together with organizational problems and lack of suitable resources; only 1-out of 9 individuals- affirmed he has no ideas about it, nor motivation to do it.

As to the kind of activities proposed to support creativity, it seems that group activities are more widely used with respect to individual activities (question 8, 56% against 27%).

3.4 Perceived Role/Potential of ICT to Foster Creativity

As to the role of ICT, most Italian teachers believe that ICT tools can be used to support creativity, but as to their effectiveness, they do not think ICT is in principle more effective than other tools (question 10): 30% of teachers think ICTs are extremely suitable tools to support creativity; 64% of them think ICTs are no more useful than other tools; 6% think they are not useful at all.

3.5 Actual ICT Based Actions to Support Creativity

Despite this, it seems that most teachers have used – at least once – ICT as a mean to foster creativity; only 28% of the teachers affirms they have never used ICT tools to develop student creativity (question 11). The situation is almost the same at all school levels, with the exception of pre-school, where there are an higher percentage of teachers (62%) that affirms they do not use ICT with creativity purposes. This may be explained also by the fact that in Italy ICT resources are very seldom available at this school level.

In practice, among those teachers who often propose creativity-oriented activities, the 34% of them uses ICT tools, against a 28% who does not use ICTs at all.

3.6 ICT Tools Used to Support Creativity

Finally, when looking at the kind of ICT tools are used by teachers to support creativity, it seems that images ("immagini"), graphics ("grafica") and videos ("video") are the most used terms, followed by games ("giochi"), writing ("scrittura") and LIM (see Fig.2).

Fig. 2. Wordle representing the terms used by teachers to describe the ICT tools they use to support creativity (dimensions of words depend on the number of occurrences for each term)

The answers provided to this question of the survey highlights that many teachers have to use what is available at their labs or – those who are more autonomous – are able to choose among open educational resources (OER). In any case, it seems that most of the tools cited by the Italian teachers, are much more oriented to the production of artifacts (a text, an hypertext, a video, an audio, a picture, etc.), rather than at fostering some kind of mental process; for example, it is surprising that only a couple of teachers cited Internet and search engines as tools to help students find out new information, new connections, new ideas. Similarly, only a few teachers mentioned the use of communication and collaborative tools, as a way to share data or write collaboratively (wikis, bogs, etc.). Even software for creating mental maps are mentioned very rarely (i.e. CMap).

Interestingly enough, these results are only partially coherent with the definitions provided by teachers to the term "creativity" (question 2, see Fig. 1); rather, they bring back to an older definition of creativity as something definitely related to some specific fields, such as arts, painting and literature and to the ability to create digital artifacts.

4 Discussion and Conclusions

When looking at the relationship between education and creativity, one should consider that there is a double bond: on the one side, education should foster students' attitudes towards creative thinking by proposing more open-ended, problem-based activities (Carrol & Borge, 2007); on the other side, education should contribute to create a solid "culture of innovation" that is a key aspect of all the productive sectors of modern societies (Kyriazopoulos & Samanta, 2009) and, in this perspective, it should be per se "creative", by adopting and proposing to students new, innovative and creative strategies to pursue the educational goals (both standard and non-standard).

Creativity can be regarded as an attribute of a mental process. Such mental process can be considered "creative" if it leads to either creative outputs, or if it allows the attainment of specific goals by following new, original paths/ways. So, as already mentioned, there is a basic distinction between "creativity of product" and "creativity of process". Aim of the teacher should be to foster both them (Craft, 2005) by also "*motivating people to apply their critical thinking and their imagination*" (Lytras, 2007).

On the contrary, the results of the mini-scale study presented here, demonstrate that – at least in Italy – despite what teachers declare about their way to conceive creativity, what they do in their daily practice is basically oriented to make students produce artifacts, instead of orienting their efforts towards organizing or structuring existing data, possibly by looking at them from a variety of perspectives, so to allow reflections, comparison, syntheses, connections.

The old idea that allowing students to play, draw or write freely is something that *per se* will help creativity emerge, is some way still persisting in the Italian school and it seems that, in practice, the way to go is still a long one.

References

Burleson, W.: Developing creativity, motivation, and self-actualization with learning systems. International Journal of Human-Computer Studies 63(4-5), 436–451 (2005)

Cachia, R., Ferrari, A.a., Kearney, C., Punie, Y., Van Den Berghe, W., Wastiau, P.: Creativity in Schools in Europe: A Survey of Teachers (2009), `http://ipts.jrc.ec.europa.eu/publications/pub.cfm?id=2940` (accessed March 2010)

Carroll, J.M., Borge, M.: Articulating case-based learning outcomes and assessment. International Journal of Teaching and Case Studies 1(1/2), 33–49 (2007)

Csikszentmihalyi, M.: Creativity: Flow and the Psychology of Discovery and Inven-tion. Harper Perennial (1997)

Craft, A.: Creativity in schools: tensions and dilemmas. Routledge, London (2005)

Edmonds, E.A., Weakley, A., Candy, L., Fell, M., Knott, R., Pauletto, S.: The studio as laboratory: combining creative practice and digital technology research. International Journal of Human–Computer Studies 63(4-5), 383–409 (2005)

Greene, S.L.: Characteristics of applications that support creativity. Communications of the ACM 45(10), 100–104 (2002)

Johnson, H., Carruthers, L.: Supporting creative and reflective processes. Interna-tional Journal of Human-Computer Studies 64(10), 998–1030 (2006)

Hewett, T.T.: Informing the design of computer-based environments to support creativity. International Journal of Human-Computer Studies 63(4-5), 383–409 (2005)

Kyriazopoulos, P., Samanta, I.: Creating an innovation culture through knowledge management: the Greek firms. International Journal of Knowledge and Learning 5(1), 81–95 (2009)

Lubart, T.: How can computers be partners in the creative process: Classification and commentary on the Special Issue. International Journal of Human-Computer Studies 63(4-5), 365–369 (2005)

Lytras, M.D.: Teaching in the knowledge society: an art of passion. International Journal of Teaching and Case Studies 1(1/2), 1–9 (2007)

Nickerson, R.S.: Enhancing creativity. In: Sternberg, R.J. (ed.) Handbook of Creativity. Cambridge University Press, Cambridge (1999)

Petrides, L., Nguyen, L., Jimes, C., Karaglani, A.: Open educational resources: inquiring into author use and reuse. International Journal of Technology Enhanced Learning 1(1-2), 98–117 (2008)

Plucker, J., Beghetto, R.: Why creativity is domain general, why it looks domain specific, and why the distinction does not matter. In: Sternberg, R.J., Grigorenko, E.L., Singer, J.L. (eds.) Creativity: From Potential to Realization, pp. 153–167. American Psychological Association, Washington (2004)

Rhodes, M.: An analysis of creativity. Phi Delta Kappa 42, 305–311 (1961)

Selker, T.: Fostering motivation and creativity for computer users. International Journal of Human–Computer Studies 63(4-5), 410–421 (2005)

Shneiderman, B.: Creating creativity: user interfaces for supporting Innovation. ACM Transactions on Computer-Human Interactions 7(1), 114–138 (2000)

Sternberg, R.J.: Creativity or creativities? International Journal of Human-Computer Studies 63(4-5), 370–382 (2005)

Treffinger, D.J., Young, G.C., Selby, E.C., Shepardson, C.: Assessing Creativity: A Guide for Educators (2002), `http://www.creativelearning.com/PDF/AssessCreatReport.pdf` (accessed March 2010)

Turisbook: Social Network of Tourism with Geographical Information

Eva García, Antonio García, Luis de-Marcos, and José-Ramón Hilera

Computer Science Department, University of Alcalá
Ctra Barcelona km 33.6, 28871, Alcalá de Henares, Madrid, Spain
{eva.garcial,a.garciac,luis.demarcos,jose.hilera}@uah.es

Abstract. This article presents the social network of tourism Turisbook. This social network allows sharing information and opinions about worldwide travel destinations. It incorporates a geo-location system of points on a map, so that user can search quickly and easily tourist points in a given area. The system allows users to upload their own tourist points with associated information and photos. In this manner, the system feeds with user contributions, allowing discovering places that usually do not appear in traditional guidebooks.

Keywords: E-Tourism, social network, Web 2.0, geographical information.

1 Introduction

Spain is one of the major tourist destinations in the world, providing a large amount of revenue to the country, year after year, with nearly 500 million visitors in the last five years [1]. The arrival of new technologies has greatly changed the habits of tourists [2], from the time of selection of destination to their behavior while they are enjoying their vacation.

It has been these thoughts and the need to promote tourism that have generated the idea for this project: a social network of tourism where tourists can view or add new tourist points to the system. In this manner, the system is fed with the contributions of tourists, thus having a rich tourist guide with all the points and prominent places which are advisable to visit when a tourist travels.

The system consists of a centralized server that contains information of all stored tourist points and their associated photos, videos and comments. In addition to the centralized server, the system is completed with a web platform for managing all information. Web 2.0 Technologies like Google Maps have been integrated to display geographical tourist points so that is easy for users to discover them, due to the large use of this technology today.

The social network user can perform many actions on the system. One of them will be to register new tourist points to deliver them to other users. This can add photos and videos, which will serve to get an idea of the place before visiting it. The system offers users the ability to add comments to the tourist points, so as to be available to

M.D. Lytras et al. (Eds.): WSKS 2010, Part I, CCIS 111, pp. 172–179, 2010.

all social network users, thus helping the future tourists to have an initial idea about the place who will be visiting, based on the experiences of users who visited the same location. This system can be used to recommend, for example, places to stay or where to eat, both key aspects when traveling, especially if a place is not known.

2 Objectives

The main objective of this project was to create a system to promote tourism to exploit the potential of countries recognized as being famous tourist destinations (as is the case of Spain [3]), and to promote tourism in those countries that fail to grow completely. For these countries will be crucial an aid such as this, because they will make available to the rest of the world little known places to attract more tourists. It is also important that, being a free platform that works with the collaboration of users, there are no extra costs.

Another pursued objective has been the use of new Web 2.0 technologies [4] by the population because they are becoming more widespread on the Internet. To meet the above objectives, there has developed a social network where you can share as much information as possible that exists in the tourism sector, including places that, although non-tourism, are vital when traveling (for example, establishments like hotels, restaurants, etc.). This has been possible by taking advantages of new technologies for provide the dissemination of contents, photo viewing and playback of audios and videos.

3 Description of the Developed System

The system consists mainly of a social network, which is the tool used by tourists for the insertion of new tourist points and comments about them. This module consists of a database, a web application and a web server that lets to manage, in a quick and easy way, the information stored in the system. In short, the system consists of the following modules:

- **Database:** is responsible for storing all the information about the system, i.e., tourist points, comments, users, etc.
- **Web Application:** contains all the application logic, allowing the user to perform the necessary operations on depending on the type that he is (administrator or tourist).
- **Web server:** enables the deployment of web application for execution and publication to all users.

The component parts of the system are illustrated as related in figure 1.

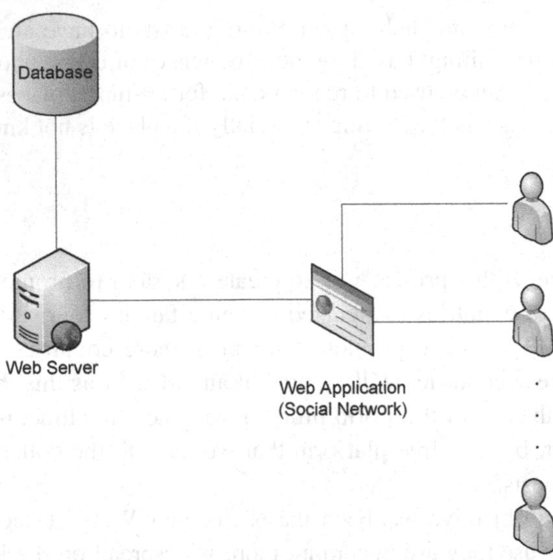

Fig. 1. Elements of which system is composed

3.1 Functionality

Turisbook currently offers social network users the following features:

- **View News:** displayed the most relevant news related to social network and the tourist points of the system.
- **Top 10:** shows the ten top tourist points displayed by users.
- **Last points:** it shows the last introduced tourist points, and the date and the time, so if a user takes a while without getting into the social network, can see recent activity.
- **View tourist points:** you may see small tourist information of a point simply by locating it on the map (figure 4) and clicking on its icon.
- **View details about a tourist spot:** you can get more information from a tourist point (extended description, photos, videos, comments, etc.) (Figure 7).
- **View a user profile:** it is possible to see the profile of a user of the system where, besides some of their personal data, are displayed all the tourist points he has uploaded to the system. Moreover, from the list of items uploaded by the user can expand the information of each point by simply clicking on the name of the tourist point.
- **Search points of interest:** in addition to find points of interest through the main map page, the system also allows searching for tourist points of the system using a simple form.

It is available a functionality of the system that is only accessible to registered users. Once a user is registered, he can perform the following functions:

- **View the profile data:** you can view data inserted by the user during registration.
- **Changing the profile data:** from this option, a user can edit data in his profile.
- **Register tourist points:** the system enables registered users, register tourist points (things to see, where to eat, accommodation and entertainment).
- **Enter comments in the points of interest:** a very interesting operation is to discuss the points of interest introduced, so that users can collaborate with their opinions about the places they have visited, so that other tourist network users have previous experiences on which to base before a trip.
- **Cancel request:** users can send a request to unsubscribe in the system, in case they do not wish to remain registered.

For users who are administrators of the system will also include the following operations:

- **Cancellations and modifications of points of interest:** it is necessary to have an option of cancellations and modifications to manage tourist points in the database.
- **Registrations, cancellations and modifications of users:** although users can self-register, it's interesting that administrators can also register users, for cases in which they themselves cannot. The cancellation and modification of user data is also important for quickly and easily management.
- **Insertion of news:** you may add a new to the system via a simple form.
- **Add, edit and delete links:** in order to make the management of the links, it has added a form that allows you to add new links, one to modify existing products and another for those who want to eliminate.

The social network now exists in two languages, but efforts are underway to port to other different and that it reaches more users worldwide. The way to add a new language to the system is very simple, since all the texts of the social network are in separate files of source code and it is enough to translate these files into the desired language for the system to appear in a new language.

3.2 Interface

By accessing Turisbook, it will automatically appear in the language given the user's browser, provided that the social network supports that language. If Turisbook is not yet available in that language, the page will be displayed in English. Such language can be changed at any time by clicking on the desired language flag shown on the left, under the main menu.

The navigability between screens of the social network is maximum: when viewing a tourist point, the user who introduced it is shown, so you can see directly the profile of this user simply by clicking on the username; and vice versa, when viewing the profile of a user, all items that the user has entered can be shown, and can expand the information of any of them by simply clicking on the name of the point. In addition, at all times are displayed in the main menu (home, news, search, register and links) and the specific menu of the registered user (new point, see my profile, log out, etc.),

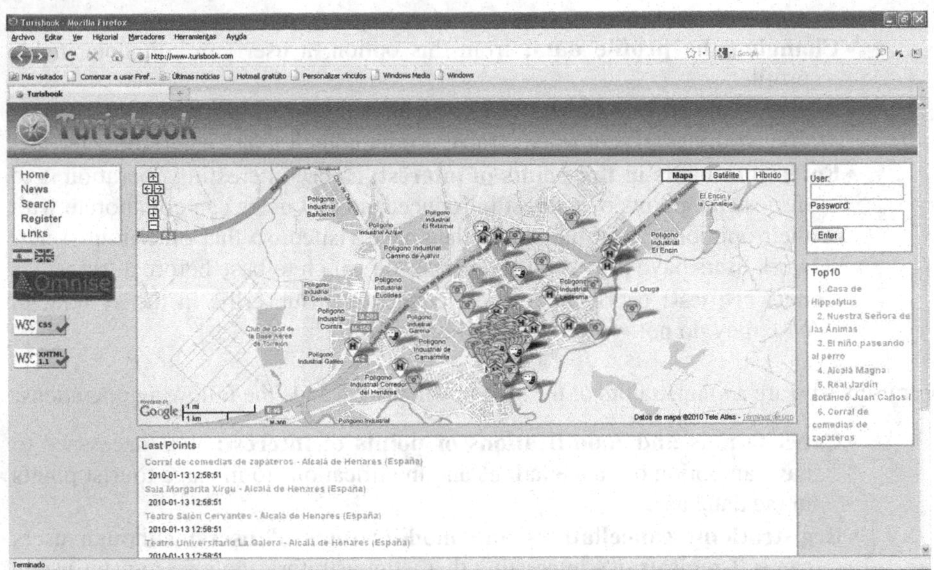

Fig. 2. Turisbook home page

if you are logged in, and the possibility of changing the language in which you are viewing the social network.

The main screen (figure 2) shows a map that users can scroll to see the introduced points. These points are easily located thanks to an icon indicating the type they belong to: things to view, where to eat, accommodation or entertainment (figure 3).

Fig. 3. Types of tourist points

Clicking on any of them a speech bubble will appear (figure 4) which includes a part of the description of the point, plus a small photo, in case this point has anything associated. From this speech bubble you can click on the "+ info" link to see the full information of the point.

The most important innovation has been introduced into this social network is the display of all the tourist points in Google Maps [5], so they can be easily located on the map. But in this project has gone beyond that, while you are viewing the map to zoom out, the points on the screen will group by proximity (figures 5, 6). In this way Google Maps is not locked when there are too many points on the screen, coming to stuck the browser.

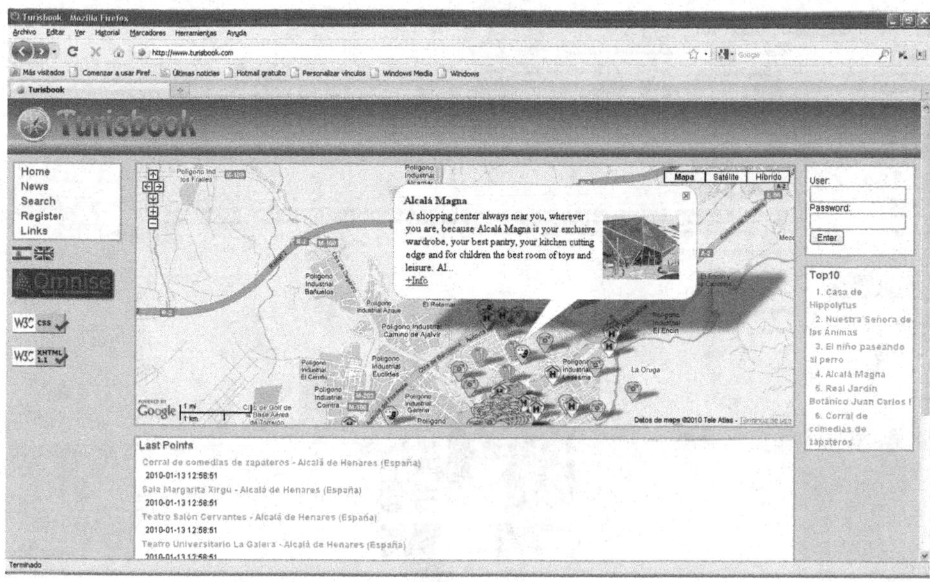

Fig. 4. Speech bubble with information of a tourist point

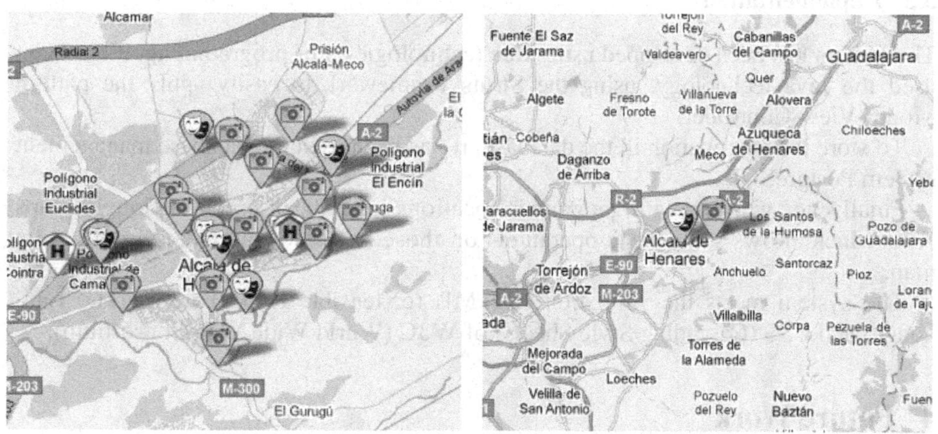

Fig. 5. Not grouped Tourist Points

Fig. 6. Grouped Tourist Points

When viewing the information of a point (figure 7), it appears in the language the user has selected, or in the language of the browser, if you have not selected language. If the item does not exist in any of these languages, it will appear in English (if it exists), or alternatively, in the language that was inserted. This allows us to have a system of tourist points in different languages and also to be displayed correctly to the user.

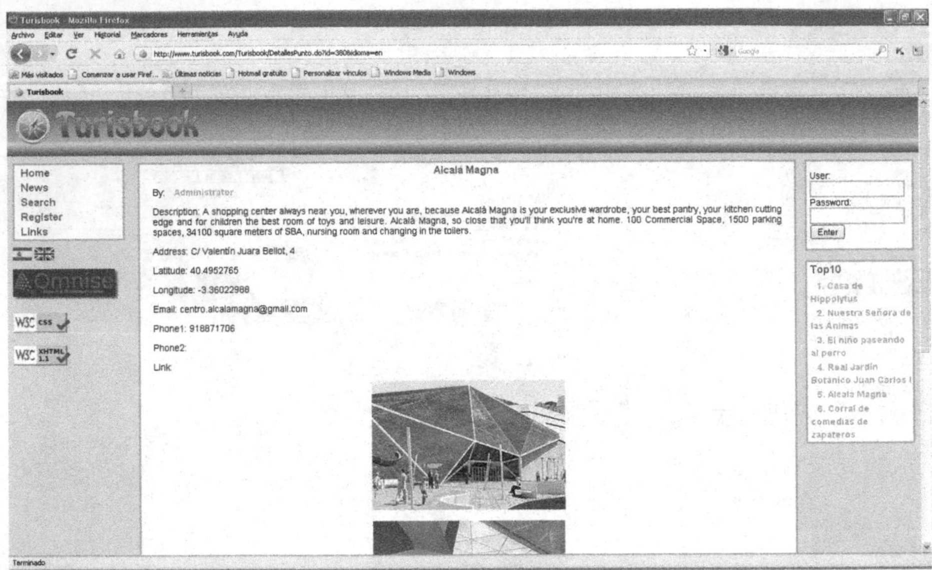

Fig. 7. Information of a tourist point

3.3 Implementation

The system has been developed using free technologies. For programming, it has been used the Java technology, using the Struts Framework to easily apply the pattern Model-View-Controller.

To store the information in the database, it has been used the database management system PostgreSQL.

Finally, for working with geographic locations it has been used the Google Maps API, which allows some basic operations on those items, to find them visually on a map.

The system meets the validation XHTML (eXtensible HyperText Markup Language) and CSS (Cascading Style Sheets) of W3C (World Wide Web Consortium).

4 Future Work

It has developed a first version of Turisbook that has been well accepted within the Internet, allowing tourism enthusiast users [6] to share this passion with others. The system allows users, in an easy and intuitive way, to have at their disposal information about all tourist destinations in the world. There are still improvements planned for this new system, so there are a number of features wanted to add to the application but have not yet been implemented:

- **Send messages to other users:** being a social network, communication between users through it is crucial. This will develop a module that allows users to send messages to them, so they can share opinions of different tourist destinations.

- **Establish a system of groups:** users can join their favorite destinations so they can receive information about the destination or to relate to people who also share these favorite destinations.
- **Mobile device system:** currently is developing a version of Turisbook accessible from different mobile devices and will allow nearly all of the functionality of the Web application. It is still under development (figure 8).

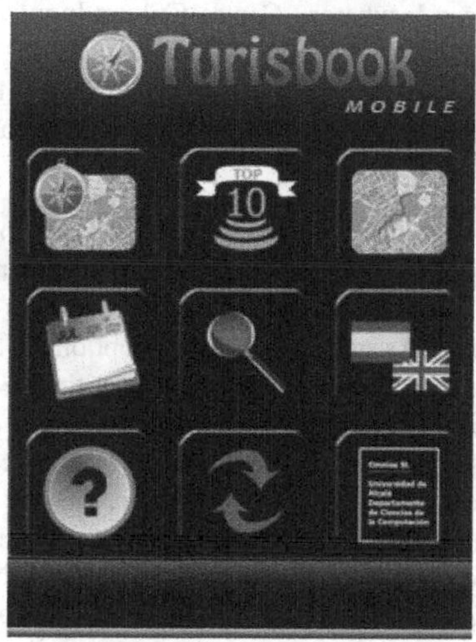

Fig. 8. Prototype of Turisbook Mobile

References

1. INE – Instituto Nacional de Estadística, http://www.ine.es
2. Buhalis, D., Law, R.: Progress in information technology and tourism management: 20 years on and 10 years after the Internet (2008)
3. UNWTO World Tourism Barometer, http://www.unwto.org/facts/eng/pdf/barometer/UNWTO_Barom09_update_sept_en.pdf
4. Schmallegger, D., Carson, D.: Blogs in tourism: Changing approaches to information exchange
5. Google Maps API, http://code.google.com/intl/en/apis/maps/
6. World Tourism Organization. WTO. Tourism Vision (2010), http://www.unwto.org/facts/eng/vision.htm

Sustaining Tunisian SMEs' Competitiveness in the Knowledge Society

Pasquale Del Vecchio, Gianluca Elia, and Giustina Secundo

Euro Mediterranean Incubator - Centro Cultura Innovativa d'Impresa
University of Salento
Campus Ecotekne - Via per Monteroni s.n. 73100 Lecce Italy
{pasquale.delvecchio,gianluca.elia,giusy.secundo}@unisalento.it

Abstract. The paper aims to contribute to the debate about knowledge and digital divide affecting countries' competitiveness in the knowledge society. A survey based on qualitative and quantitative data collection has been performed to analyze the level of ICTs and e-Business adoption of the Tunisian SMEs. The results shows that to increase the SMEs competitiveness is necessary to invest in all the components of Intellectual capital: *human capital* (knowledge, skills, and the abilities of people for using the ICTs), *structural capital* (supportive infrastructure such as buildings, software, processes, patents, and trademarks, proprietary databases) *and social capital* (relations and collaboration inside and outside the company). At this purpose, the LINCET *"Laboratoire d'Innovation Numerique pour la Competitivité de l'Entreprise Tunisienne"* project is finally proposed as a coherent proposition to foster the growth of all the components of the Intellectual Capital for the benefits of competitiveness of Tunisian SMEs.

Keywords: e-Business, ICTs, SMEs, Digital Divide, Knowledge divide, Competitiveness, Innovation, Intellectual Capital.

1 Introduction

In the beginning of the 21st century, we are assisting to a sort of convergence and mutual interaction between the paradigm of the Knowledge Society, that sees the society nurtured by its diversity and its capacities (UNESCO, 2005) and the phenomenon of the Digital Divide, interpreted in terms of presence or absence of technological infrastructures and devices enabling wired/wireless communications (Information Society Commission, 2002; UNESCO, 2005). These new paradigms have the power to reshape the global economy (Information Society Commission, 2002). At macro-economic level, this brought to a natural mechanism of "*casting out*" of some economic realities from the global competitive landscape. This bi-polarization trend differentiates the economies involved in the global market from those excluded from the new production systems based on the access to information, knowledge and technology (Bontis, 1998). Actually, today, it's necessary to evolve towards new scenarios in which it must to develop abilities to use effectively the digital infrastructures to exchange and apply knowledge, to share experiences, to participate and interact within the global knowledge flows. According to this vision,

M.D. Lytras et al. (Eds.): WSKS 2010, Part I, CCIS 111, pp. 180–189, 2010.

Knowledge Society and Digital Divide are becoming a multidimensional reality reshaping the map of the world (Cardoso, Bostrom & Sheth, 2004; Daniel, 2003; Norris, 2001). The wished leapfrog of countries in the age of digital networks, knowledge and globalization (Clark, Cronson & Schiano, 2001) can be achieved only if a competitive ascending spiral is activated starting from growing investments in technological infrastructures, human resources, and innovation, focusing on a productivity increase in traditional sectors and development in sectors knowledge and technology intensive. In the Mediterranean area, this phenomenon is largely evident and interests many countries. Tunisia is among them and presents interesting dynamics in terms of Digital / Knowledge Divide measurements and indexes. At the global level, Tunisian socio-economic context is called to face the challenges related to the new competitive dynamics emerging as a consequence of globalization of markets and industries and ICTs development and diffusion.

In order to understand under which conditions the drivers for competitiveness can support Tunisian national economy, a major focus on the main needs of the Tunisian SMEs, as well as the exploration of the opportunities for their growth, will be addressed by the following research questions: a) *How is the level of ICT and e-Business adoption in the Tunisian SMEs? b) Which are the main motivations, obstacles and competency needs of SMEs to initiate and maintain a process of "digitization"?*

To address these points, the paper is organized as follow: the next paragraph illustrates the background on Knowledge and Digital divides and the Tunisian social and economic context. Paragraph 3 describes the Research questions and methodology. Paragraph 4 describes the main results of the research about the rate of adoption of ICTs and e-business solutions among Tunisian SMEs. Finally, paragraph 5 concludes the paper highlighting the main evidences of the study and presenting the LINCET, *"Laboratoire d'Innovation Numerique pour la Competitivité de l'Entreprise Tunisienne")* a project framed for speeding up the diffusion and the adoption of the ICTs in the Tunisian SMEs.

2 Background on "Knowledge Divide" and "Digital Divide"

Under the forces of globalization, the world economy is entering into a new phase where knowledge becomes the fundamental competitive resource. The rising of the ICT use, and the Internet as an enabling technology are becoming more and more the expression of an asymmetry in the access to and application of knowledge. It is in this perspective that the discussion about the traditional phenomenon of Digital Divide is enriching of new elements related to Knowledge Divide (Information Society Commission, 2002; UNESCO, 2005). The concept of Knowledge Divide is used to describe the gap in living conditions between those who can find, manage and process information or knowledge, and those who are impaired in this.

The analysis of the current economic scenario requires the application of indicators able to express the consistency of the "*Digital and Knowledge Divide*", and to correlate it to the perspectives of the medium-long term development dynamics. Several institutions and international research centres have investigated the phenomenon of the divide elaborating interesting indicators and parameters for describing the socio-economic context of the countries. Among them, the "Networked Readiness

Index" (NRI) is a complex measure, able to weight the different components of the "*Digital and Knowledge Divide*". Developed in 2007 at INSEAD in collaboration with "World Bank" (www.worldbank.org/kam) and "World Economic Forum", NRI index allows for a better understanding of a nation's strength and weaknesses with reference to ICT (Lal, 2005), according to three main pillars represented by: *Readiness* (development and usage of ICT at individual, business, and governmental level); *Environment* (macroeconomic and regulatory environment for ICT); and *Usage* (rate and the impact of ICT on the three stakeholder's categories).

A nation's level of competitiveness reflects the extent to which it is able to provide rising prosperity to its citizens. Global Competitiveness Index (GCI) (INSEAD 2007) is significant in this direction. This index is based on 12 pillars grouped in three categories: "basic requirements" (about institutions, infrastructure, macro-economic stability, health and primary education); "efficiency enhancers" (about higher education and training, goods market efficiency, labour market efficiency, financial market sophistication, technological readiness, market size); and "innovation and sophistication factors", (about business sophistication, and innovation).

This index, that captures the stages of economic development of a country, seems to be positively correlated with the NRI (Mentzas, Apostolou, Kafentzis & Georgolios, 2006). This result suggests that if the actors of an economy are not "networked-ready", it will be hard for the economy to move fast toward the innovation driven stage of development.

Looking at the Mediterranean Area, the NRI 2006 – 2007 gives evidence of the cited divergence. The average value at the world level of 3.93 marks the approximate ridge of the "in" and "out" countries, and draws the separation of European side countries, with an average value of 4.50, and the African side, with an average value of 3.87.

A further evidences about readiness of a country or region towards the Knowledge Economy, is offered by the Knowledge Economy Index (KEI), an aggregate index, developed by the World Bank's Knowledge Assessment Methodology (KAM, available at *www.worldbank.org/kam*) (Molla & Licker, 2005). Based on the simple average of 4 sub-indexes (Economic Incentive and Institutional Regime (EIR), Education and Training, Innovation and Technological Adoption, Information and Communications Technologies (ICT) Infrastructure) the KEI average value at the world level of 6.33 shows again a different situation in the Mediterranean regions, between the two opposite sides: with the north side presents an average value of 8.16, while the south one has an average value of 4.07.

2.1 Assessing Tunisian Macro-economic Context in the Digital Economy

In this paragraph an overview of the Tunisia national context is presented as the results of an integrative desk analysis based on the adoption of several indexes. The integrative reading of the "Networked Readiness Index" as well as "Knowledge Economy Index" allowed understanding the characteristics of the Tunisian macro-economic context by offering the possibility to observe under which dimensions the phenomena of digital and knowledge divide, described in the previous sections of this work, can be perceived at national level. Characterized by a growing institutional attention for the policies of ICTs diffusion and adoption, Tunisia presents a good level of competition at national and international scale: it is ranked 30th in the Global Competitiveness Index and 35th out of the 125 countries (first between African Countries) according to the *Networked Readiness Index* as illustrated in the *Global Information Technology Report* (2006-2007) (INSEAD, 2007). However, a deepen analysis of the NRI components allows to identify some areas of improvements:

- the Environment Component (scored at 3.84) an area of improvement at level of the Infrastructure Environment (Tunisia is ranked 57th with a score of 2.63);
- the Usage Component (scored at 3.95), an area of improvement at level of the Individual Usage (Tunisia is ranked 69th with a score of 1.64).

On the contrary, the good rank registered for the Readiness Component (scored at 4.92) reveals a favorable general context for the ICT adoption and diffusion, and creates motivation to continue and enhance the efforts to afford previous drawbacks.

Referring to the same period, the Knowledge Assessment Methodology (KAM) developed by World Bank offers two other significant evidences about the main areas of intervention. Ranked 10th between the Countries of the Middle East and North Africa and 72nd out of 140 countries at global scale, the analysis of KAM's Knowledge Economic Index and Knowledge Index has showed as at Educational (score 4.04) and ICTs (score 4.89) levels, Tunisia presents the main gaps.

Event if the analysis of Tunisian context performed through the integration of the mentioned indexes has showed a quite rank, the identification of some areas of intervention allows bringing back the discussion about national development in terms of Knowledge and Digital Divide. Of consequence, this imposes to look at Country's competitiveness in the Knowledge Society in terms of SME's ICT and e-Business adoption to understand which are the main obstacles and competences needed to leapfrog into the Knowledge Society, and so, to narrow the Digital / Knowledge Divide.

3 Research Design

In order to understand under which conditions the drivers for competitiveness can support Tunisian national economy, a major focus on the main needs of the Tunisian SMEs, as well as the exploration of the opportunities for their growth, will be addressed by the following research questions:

- *How is the level of ICT and e-Business adoption of Tunisian SMEs?*
- *Which are the main motivations, obstacles and competency needs of SMEs to initiate and maintain a process of "digitization"?*

Aimed to offer an exhaustive answer at these questions, a quantitative and qualitative field analysis has been performed.

The "Field Analysis" has been structured to identify which are the conditions for enhancing the competitiveness at national level, to understand the state of the art about the ICT penetration and the e-Business adoption in Tunisian SMEs, to be aware of the needs and the opportunities for Tunisian enterprises. The study has been conducted according to the main steps illustrated in the fig.1. The implemented survey was aimed to:

- offer a representation of the level of diffusion of ICTs among Tunisian enterprises;
- identify the profile of the enterprises (in terms of size, structure and sector) that are more oriented at the transition toward an e-Business scenario;
- identify the main obstacles and limits at the adoption of ICTs;
- offer a significant evidence about the opportunities coming from the adoption of ICTs and e-Business in the several sectors of the Tunisian economy.

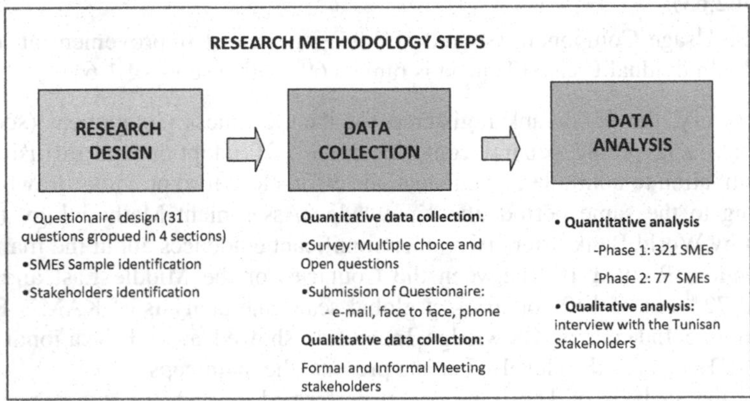

Fig. 1. Research Methodology

The questionnaire at the basis of the survey was composed by 31 questions, multiple choice and open questions, structured mainly according to 4 sections devoted to: the description of the organization; the characteristics of the ICT and e-Business infrastructure; the managerial competences and the attitude at the investments; the main reasons and limits at the adoption of ICTs and e-Business solutions.

The submission of the questionnaires, realized by e-mails, by phone or in a face to face meetings, and for a period of almost six months (January 2007 – June 2007), has allowed to collect a significant amount of data. The observed population was represented by 321 enterprises, on the basis of which 77 enterprises have been selected for a deepen analysis more focused on human capital development and competences needs. The identification of this last second sample was performed according to the following criteria of a major involvement of the top management; the level of representativeness of the industries; the presence of ICTs solutions.

The enterprises interviewed, in both the phases of the analysis, offered an exhaustive representation of the Tunisian economy under different perspectives: in terms of size (they were mainly SMEs), of industrial sector (almost 16 different industrial sectors on the basis of the classification offered by the Tunisian National Institute of Statistic, such as Agrifood, Textile, Transport, Hotel and Restaurant, Financial services) and area of localization (Grand Tunis, Bizerte, Sousse, Sfax, and Nabeul). Another relevant source of evidences in this part of the study was represented by several, formal and informal meetings, with authoritative stakeholders and representatives of Tunisian economy. Representing a further source of information, those meetings allowed to verify the goodness of the evidences obtained and to integrate the results with their on field experiences.

4 Research Findings: The Adoption of ICTs and e-Business in Tunisian SMEs

In this paragraph, the main results of analysis concerning the level of adoption of ICTs and e-Business solutions among Tunisian SMEs are presented in order to identify the motivations, obstacles and competency needs for initiating and maintaining a process of digitalization.

At macro-level, the study has allowed to register a trend of general growth for the adoption of ICTs by Tunisian enterprises in the period from 2002 to 2006, as showed in Fig. 2. In particular, among the 321 enterprises interviewed, in 2006, more than 90% have a network connection, against 53% of 2002; about the usage of IP and VOIP systems, the rate of their adoption has growth from the 6% of 2002 to the 30.5% of 2006; almost 75% of them have adopted a LAN (year 2006). The implemented survey was aimed to:

- offer a representation of the level of diffusion of ICTs among Tunisian enterprises;
- identify the profile of the enterprises (in terms of size, structure and sector) that are more oriented at the transition toward an e-Business scenario;
- identify the main obstacles and limits at the adoption of ICTs;
- offer a significant evidence about the opportunities coming from adoption of ICTs and e-Business in the several sectors of the Tunisian economy.

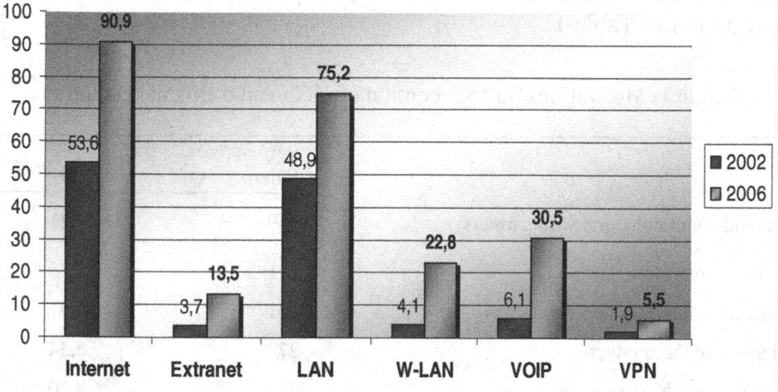

Fig. 2. Adoption rate of ICT in Tunisian enterprises

Another important result of the study is represented by the awareness about the needs in terms of ICT and e-Business solutions among the enterprises interviewed. In all the sectors a demand for solutions like Enterprise Resource Planning (ERP), Intranet, e-Learning, Knowledge Management Systems has registered a sensible growth, as illustrated in figure 3.

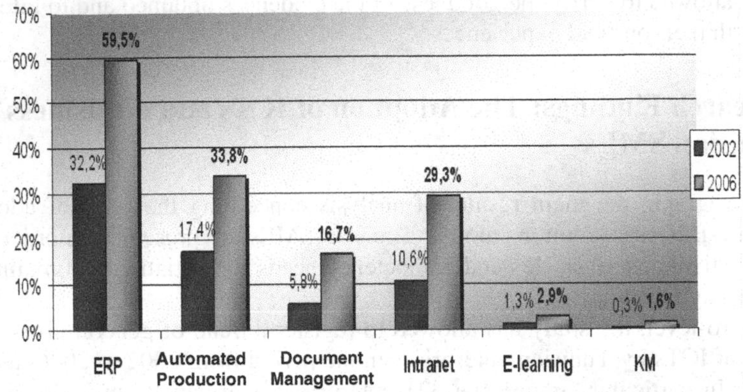

Fig. 3. Adoption rate of e-Business solutions in Tunisian enterprises

In particular, the survey allowed to register a growing demand about mainly for ERP systems, from 32.2% of 2002 to 69.5% of 2006, a similar growth has been registered also for solutions of Supply Chain Management (SCM) and Customer Relationship Management (CRM). The situation is not so developed yet for the knowledge management (KM) systems, adopted in 2006 by 1.6% of the enterprises interviewed, as well as for the e-learning programs, realized only by 3%.

Another important result of the analysis is represented by the reasons behind the demand for ICT and e-Business solutions. Listed from the most to the less relevant motivations, on a scale from 1 (not important) to 5 (very important), the 321 enterprises have expressed their motivations at the adoption of ICTs and e-Business solutions, as reported in Table 1.

Table 1. Motivations for the adoption of ICTs and e-Business solutions

	Responding Enterprises	*Average*
Promotion and communication with partners	269	4,21
Entrance in new market segments	271	4,05
Reinforcement of the image on the market	271	3,91
Personalization of the product	272	3,34
Creation of new products/services	273	3,20
Reduction exploitation costs	270	3.53
Reduction of production costs	208	3.41
Improvement of quality	273	3,77

Furthermore, another important result of the research on field is represented by the identification of the limits to the adoption of ICTs and e-Business solutions, as reported in Table 2.

Table 2. Limits to the adoption of ICTs and e-Business solutions from SMEs

	Responding Enterprises	*Average*
Absence of an appropriate offer	225	1,98
Electronic security	225	2,23
Complexity of technologies	228	2,51
Costs of the SW solutions	226	3,07
Costs of the HW solutions	227	2,81
Size of enterprises	226	2,47

In the second stage of the analysis, the questionnaire submitted for understanding the main needs in terms of human capital at 77 enterprises has showed the following needs: the lack of competencies and capabilities of the employees, the resistance to change and an insufficient level of education in the field.

In particular, this evidence results extremely pertinent in offering a comprehensive understanding about the limitation regarding cultural and managerial change necessary to reconfigure the organization in a different way from the traditional aspect.

The digital divide manifests itself both at the international and domestic levels and therefore needs to be addressed by national policy makers as well as the international community. In synthesis, the main results about the level of ICTs and e-Business adoption among the Tunisian SMEs, show:

- a high usage of Internet (more than 90% of the sample) but very limited to standard services (e-mails and search of information);
- a high interest toward the adoption of ICT and e-Business solutions, perceived as powerful tools for enhancing their competitiveness;
- a medium and high demand for competency development programs in ICT and e-Business capabilities;
- a lack of collaboration among SMEs.

Of consequence, the adoption of ICT and e-Business by Tunisian SMEs requires increasing investments in all the components of Intellectual capital (IC) [12], identified by many practitioners (Edvinsson & Malone, 1997; Kaplan & Norton, 2004; Seemann, De Long, Stucky & Guthrie, 2000): *human capital* (knowledge, skills, and the abilities of people for using the ICTs), *structural capital* (supportive infrastructure such as buildings, software, processes, patents, and trademarks, proprietary databases) *and social capital* (the strength and loyalty of relations, the connections and collaboration inside and outside the company). All the discussion about the strategic importance of IC for competitiveness have been concentrated at organizational level, and it is still an open question to what extent the organizational IC approaches can be extended to national levels. Some authors think that there is a clear opportunity to mobilize IC based resources for supporting an organization's/a nation's performance if the effective IC drivers are properly identified (Bounfour, 2003; Pulic, 2005; Stahle & Stahle, 2006).

5 Conclusions and Future Development

The rising of the Knowledge Society, enhanced by the fast diffusion of ICTs, drives a wider perspective on the divide among Countries, interpreting it more and more as the result of an asymmetry in the access to knowledge and in the readiness to apply it. At macro-economic level, this brought to a natural mechanism of "*casting out*" of some economic realities from the global competitive landscape.

The analysis of these processes brings to the interpretation of the "*Digital Divide*" as "*Knoweldge Divide*", a multidimensional phenomenon reshaping the map of the world [5]. Looking at the Mediterranean area, the phenomenon of divergence results evident also in Tunisia. As the study has showed, the main challenge for the competitiveness of Tunisia and its economic actors in the Knowledge society is represented by the capability to invest in the growth of all the components of the Intellectual Capital. It is in this perspective that LINCET "*Laboratoire d'Innovation Numerique pour la Competitivité de l'Entreprise Tunisienne*" can offer a significative contribution.

LINCET is project launched in 2007 by the "Euro Mediterranean Incubator of Business Innovation Leadership" of Scuola Superiore ISUFI – University of Salento (Italy; www.ebms.it) and Technopole Elgazala (Tunisia, http://www.elgazalacom.nat.tn). The project aims to speed up the diffusion and the adoption of the ICTs in the Tunisian SMEs. The LINCET represents the Tunisian node of a wider network of Competence Centers situated in Southern Mediterranean Countries and specialized in sensitize and diffuse Digital, Strategic and Organizational innovation in private industries and public administration. Currently, the network is composed of 4 nodes: beyond the headquarter represented by the Euro-Mediterranean Incubator of Scuola Superiore ISUFI (www.ebms.,it), there is the Moroccan node (situated in Casablanca Technopark and created in partnership with Al Akhawayn University), the Jordanian node (situated in Amman at the University of Jordan and created in partnership with the University of Jordan), and the Tunisian node, represented by the LINCET.

Focused on the evidences collected about the needs and opportunities in terms of usage and adoption of ICTs and e-Business solutions among Tunisian enterprises, the strategic and operational model of LINCET has to evolve for assuming the configuration of a *Knowledge Hub* for the creation of Intellectual Capital able to accelerate and drive the transition of the Tunisian economy towards the knowledge economy.

Assuming the role of a KIBS "knowledge intensive business service" [19], and contributing at the economic growth in terms of employment, productivity and innovation, LINCET will operate with its initiatives in different fields by promoting and realizing *innovation projects, entrepreneurship initiatives, competencies development programs, as well as researches and studies* focused on the most relevant industries of the Tunisian economy.

References

1. UNESCO World Report. Towards Knowledge Societies (2005), `http://unesdoc.unesco.org/images/0014/001418/141843e.pdf` (retrieved December 16, 2009)

2. Information Society Commission. Building the Knowledge Society - Report to Government (2002), http://www.isc.ie/downloads/know.pdf (retrieved December 16, 2009)
3. Bontis, N.: Intellectual capital: An explanatory study that develops measures and models. Management Decision 36(2), 63–76 (1998)
4. Cardoso, J., Bostrom, R.P., Sheth, A.: Workflow management systems and ERP systems: differences, commonalities, and applications. Information Technology and Management 5, 319–338 (2004)
5. Daniel, E.M.: The role of dynamic capabilities in e-Business transformation. European Journal of Information Systems 12(4), 282–296 (2003)
6. Norris, P.: Digital Divide: Civic Engagement, Information Poverty, and the Internet World Wide. Cambridge University Press, Cambridge (2001)
7. Clark, T.H., Croson, D.C., Schiano, W.T.: A hierarchical model of supply-chain integration: information sharing and operational interdependence in the US grocery channel. Information Technology and Management 2, 261–288 (2001)
8. Lal, K.: Determinants of the adoption of e-Business technologies. Telematics and Informatics 22(3), 181–199 (2005)
9. INSEAD. Global Technology Information Report 2006-2007 (2007), http://www.insead.edu/v1/gitr/wef/main/explore/framework.cfm (retrieved December 16, 2009)
10. Mentzas, G., Apostolou, D., Kafentzis, K., Georgolios, P.: Inter-organizational networks for knowledge sharing and trading. Information Technology and Management 7, 259–276 (2006)
11. Molla, A., Licker, P.S.: e-Commerce adoption in developing countries: a model and instrument. Information & Management 42(6), 877–899 (2005)
12. Bernerth, J.: Expanding our understanding of the change message. Human Resource Development Review 3(1), 36–52 (2004)
13. Edvinsson, L., Malone, M.S.: Intellectual capital: Realizing your company's true value by finding its hidden brainpower, New York, NY. Harper Business, Boston (1997)
14. Seemann, P., De Long, D., Stucky, S., Guthrie, E.: Building intangible assets: A strategic framework for investing in intellectual capital. In: Morey, D., Maybury, M., Thuraisingham, B. (eds.) Knowledge Management: Classic and Contemporary Works. MIT Press, London (2000)
15. Kaplan, R.S., Norton, D.P.: Measuring the strategic readiness of intangible assets. Harvard Business Review, 52–63 (February 2004)
16. Bounfour, A.: The IC-dVAL approach. Journal of Intellectual Capital 4(3), 393–413 (2003)
17. Pulic, A.: Value creation efficiency at national and regional levels: case study – Croatia and the European Union. In: Bounfour, A., Edvinsson, I. (eds.) Intellectual Capital for Communities, Nations, Regions and Cities. Elsevier Butterworth-Heinemann, Burlington (2005)
18. Stahle, P., Stahle, S.: Intellectual capital and national competitiveness: conceptual and methodological challenges. In: Bounfour, A. (ed.) Capital Immateriel, Connaisance et Performance. L'Harmattan, Paris (2006)
19. O'Mahony, M., van Ark, B.: EU Productivity and Competitiveness: An Industry Perspective. Can Europe Resume the Catching-up Process? (2004), Published on line at http://www.enterpriseeuropenetwork.sk/docs/NB5503035ENC_002.pdf

An Approach to Metadata Generation for Learning Objects

Victor Menendez D.[1], Alfredo Zapata G.[1],
Christian Vidal C.[2], Alejandra Segura N.[2], and Manuel Prieto M.[3]

[1] Univ. Autónoma de Yucatán. FMAT Periférico Norte. 13615, 97110 Mérida, México
[2] Universidad del Bio-Bio, Avda. Collao 1202. Concepción, Chile
[3] Univ. de Castilla-La Mancha. ESI. Po. de la Universidad. 4, 13071 Ciudad Real, Spain
{mdoming,zgonzal}@uady.mx, {cvidal,asegura}@ubiobio.cl,
manuel.prieto@uclm.es

Abstract. Metadata describe instructional resources and define their nature and use. Metadata are required to guarantee reusability and interchange of instructional resources into e-Learning systems. However, fulfilment of large metadata attributes is a hard and complex task for almost all LO developers. As a consequence many mistakes are made. This can cause the impoverishment of data quality in indexing, searching and recovering process. We propose a methodology to build Learning Objects from digital resources. The first phase includes automatic preprocessing of resources using techniques from information retrieval. Initial metadata obtained in this first phase are then used to search similar LO to propose missed metadata. The second phase considers assisted activities that merge computer advice with human decisions. Suggestions are based on metadata of similar Learning Object using fuzzy logic theory.

Keywords: Metadata Generation, Learning Object, Methodology.

1 Introduction

The development of instructional resources for e-Learning requires much work, effort, time and resources, and many times the result only works for some specific e-Learning System. The interchange and reuse between e-Learning platforms has been improved with a new concept: The Learning Object (LO).

In the approach presented in this article, teachers can build Learning Objects from digital resources in an assisted and simplified way. The LO building methodology is made up of sequenced and iterative stages. At each stage some process are defined. These processes can be carried out in an automatic or semi-automatic way using techniques from data mining, information retrieval, and soft-computing.

This document is structured in four sections. In the section 2, main topics about LO generation are explained. The conceptual framework of metadata assisted generation for Learning Object is presented in section 3. And finally, section 4 contains the conclusions and future works.

M.D. Lytras et al. (Eds.): WSKS 2010, Part I, CCIS 111, pp. 190–195, 2010.

2 Learning Object and Metadata Generation

Learning Object is a modern term in e-Learning [2]. A LO is a small piece of knowledge that can be used in different instructional contexts. Its objectives are to simplify the construction of instructional experiences, motivate reusability and interchange between e-Learning systems [10, 11].

All LO have two elements: instructional content (multimedia, text, simulation) and tags, called metadata [8]. Metadata describe Learning Objects in some relevant aspects as: what it is, who created it, which are its functions, objective, duration, etc. Metadata allow Learning Object classification, in order to be searched for reuse or to modify it.

These metadata must be conforming to e-Learning standard with the aim of get a useful reusable and interoperable LO. Any instructional resource can be transformed into a Learning Object if their metadata could be established and expressed correctly.

The fulfilment of a large metadata list (for standard IEEE-LOM [5] there are more than 60 metadata) is a hard task for the teacher. As consequence of this manual task, many mistakes are made when metadata are created: typing errors, wrong values, conceptual mistakes, among other [1]. All this errors and shortcomings can cause the impoverishment of data quality in indexing, searching and recovering process for Learning Objects.

An automatic approach for metadata generation could be a solution because many values of metadata can be inferred by analyzing the content of an instructional resource. These generated metadata are mainly related to technical aspects (like format, size, date, etc.) There are many researches about this option [2, 3, 6]. But the fact is that many other metadata values only can be obtained from the author's expertise. This includes instructional goal, didactical structure, interaction level or learning type among other.

An intermediate approach to metadata obtaining is an alternative option. Some tasks can be done in automatic way using, for instance, data mining, information retrieval techniques. Others can be done by the teacher in an assisted way. An assistant can improve the work, suggesting values for metadata, actions to do, etc. This allows employing the teacher's experience and knowledge together with the computer system advice.

2.1 Learning Object Similarity

Any teacher knows that different students have different learning styles and they must induce the use of instructional resources and strategies to help the learning process. In e-Learning, that means employ different Learning Objects to teach the same instructional goal in a different way for a particular student. For this work, the concept of similarity between LO is defined as the interchange level between Learning Objects to get the same instructional experience in equivalent instructional contexts.

If metadata describe to Learning Objects, then the LO similarity is present into their metadata's values. To compare metadata, it is necessary to define their value types for development specific similarity metrics.

Generally, metadata´s values could be controlled vocabularies, numeric (number, date, time, duration) and free typing text. In some cases, the similarity can be reduced to compare equality into values, also can define equal ranges. In other cases, imply to define the semantic significance of the text, the Jaccard index [4] or WordNet::Similarity [7] can be used to calculate the semantic distance between two paragraphs.

It is possible to define similarity metrics for Learning Objects based on their metadata but not all metadata have the same importance: in some situations certain metadata could be significant but in others there are deprecated. The context defines this relevance. We define an instructional context as a set of weight which affects Learning Object metadata.

For each Learning Object metadata, the similarity level between their values is calculated and weighed with the instructional context where they will be used. An additional vector considerers others requirements defined by external agent likes the user or computer assistant.

3 Metadata Assisted Generation for Learning Objects

The methodology is made up of four sequenced and iterative stages (Figure 1). Each stage is focused to perform specific function in the metadata generation process. These stages are grouped in two phases. In the first phase, called automatic generation, an initial metadata collection is generated from a digital resource. The second, called assisted generation, involves the user participation to establish metadata not solved in the first phase. Since both processes are iterative, results can be adjusted to obtain more consistent metadata.

3.1 Extracting

In this stage, the digital resource is examined in order to extract all useful information contained in it and to transform it in a textual representation.

To obtain all available text from the resource content, technical specifications can be used for the development of specific filters for particular formats. Some file formats allow extract all contained text in a relatively easy way. In other cases (for instance, images or videos), this task becomes harder.

Some technical characteristics like format, size, edition date, etc. can be obtained easily via operating system. Some file formats (Office documents, Acrobat and Flash files) can store additional information: keywords, subject, author name, document version, etc., which is very useful to describe the resource.

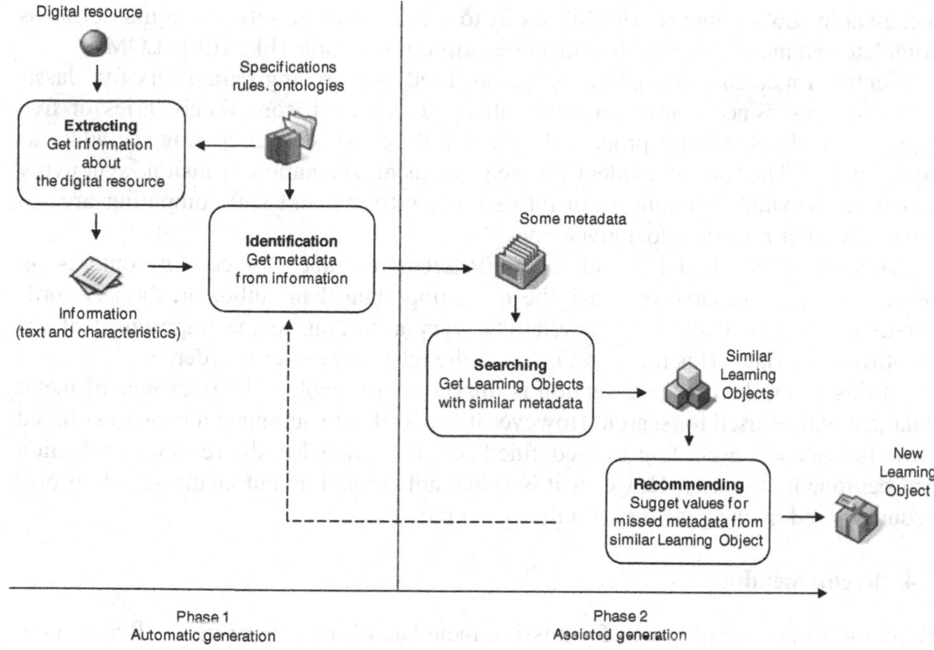

Fig. 1. Metadata generation methodology for Learning Object

The context where the resource is used can provide information for specific metadata. In the case of e-Learning, resources are usually located in online courses into e-Learning platforms. So, it is possible to know the thematic content, the average time of use, the end user role, etc., from the description and activity recording within the course. As result, we obtain a collection of technical features and a textual representation of the resource content.

3.2 Identification

The generated information is analyzed to identify an initial metadata set. Some metadata can be identified directly from technical characteristics. However, other metadata as keywords, title, description, language, subject, etc. could be inferred from the text content or from initial information. Techniques from data mining, text mining and information retrieval are useful for perform this task.

For this purpose, it is required to have a rule set which associates information chunks with standard-complaint metadata. By other hand, we need rules to generate new metadata from other metadata. Knowledge representation for these rules, for instance ontologies, can improve this identification process.

3.3 Searching and Selection

The goal of this stage is to obtain a resources set that could be classified as similar to a given resource. We consider that resource similarity is represented by metadata, so that metadata of the selected resources will be used as sources to fulfill missing metadata in new resources. This allows us to create metadata sets that could define as complete and match to some document description standards (like IEEE-LOM).

Identified metadata in previous stage are used as searching parameters for classified resources. Since many metadata values can proceed from vocabularies or free typing text, the searching process does not only consist of comparing metadata as equal or not. This makes evident the need of using semantic expansion, synonymy and other semantic relations from information retrieval and soft-computing area to retrieve similar resources to a given one.

Each one of the initial metadata has different relevance for certain contexts (in some situations, resource type may be more important than author or, the keywords versus subject) so that, search results can vary according to the importance of the identified metadata. This fact is reflected in the retrieved resource order.

At this point, the user intervention is important to establish the relevance of metadata that will be used for search. However it is possible to automate this process based on indicators sets according to predefined settings. Likewise, the resources selection can be done by the user. However it is achievable to call up automatic selection procedures based on the generated similarity degree.

3.4 Recommending

Here, the values are proposed for missing metadata of the new resource. Recommendations come from extracted metadata of the resources selected in the previous stage. The values are sorted with respect to the similarity degree of resources. In this way, the user can select a value from a menu or to provide a new (more appropriate) one.

This stage can be improved by means of an iterative process using the stage identification to restrict and identify new metadata from the already established. Then, new metadata could be generated to be conforming to a similar resources set.

The product of this activity is a complete metadata set for a digital resource. This metadata must be accordance to some metadata standard. Although the methodology has been developed initially for the metadata generation of instructional resources, we consider that accomplish the criteria to be used with other digital documents.

4 Conclusions and Future Works

Learning Objects are the basic structure in order to build learning experiences that can be reusable and adaptable. Building a quality LO consumes many resources and involves technological and instructional knowledge that not all users have.

In our approach, the metadata are generated from a sequence of automatic and assisted processes. We employ techniques from data mining, information retrieval and soft-computing to improve it. The similarity concept is basic to implements the metadata assisted generation for Learning Object. The similarity between LO is reflected in its metadata's values.

The methodology presented has been implemented into the Learning Object Management module of the AGORA project [9]. This module exposes services for storage, generation, edition, search and recovery of Learning Objects. A wizard based on proposed methodology facilitate the metadata generation for new LO.

We are working to improve the knowledge models and techniques used to define rules for metadata deducing. Additionally we are trying to incorporate new assistance models for metadata filling and generation, as example, the user profile have information related to learning object's topic and taxonomy.

A quality model must be implemented into searching and selection process for a best result. We are developed a completeness model for learning objects. This model is planned to be integrated in the AGORA project.

Acknowledgments

This work is partially supported by the National Council of Science and Technology (CONACYT, México); the Council of Science and Technology of Yucatán State (CONCyTEY, México); MECESUP UBB 0305 project, Chile; projects SCAIWEB2 (PEIC09-0196-3018) and PLINIO (POII10-0133-3516) of the Autonomous Government of Castilla-La Mancha, Spain.

References

1. Cechinel, C., Sanchez-Alonso, S., Sicilia, M.A.: Empirical Analysis of Errors on Human-Generated Learning Objects Metadata. In: Proceedings Metadata and Semantic Research Third International Conference (MTSR 2009), Milan, Italy, pp. 60–70 (2009)
2. Farrell, R.G., Liburd, S.D., Thomas, J.C.: Dynamic assembly of learning objects. In: Proceedings of the 13th International World Wide Web Conference on Alternate Track Papers & Posters, New York, NY, USA, pp. 162–169 (2004)
3. Greenberg, J.: Metadata extraction and harvesting: A comparison of two automatic metadata generation applications. Journal of Internet Cataloging: The International Quarterly of Digital Organization, Classification and Access 6(4), 58–82 (2004)
4. Hamers, L., Hemeryck, Y., Herweyers, G., Janssen, M., Keters, H., Rousseau, R., Vanhoutte, A.: Similarity measures in scientometric research. The Jaccard Index Versus Salton's Cosine Formula 25(3), 315–318 (1989)
5. IEEE Standard for Learning Object Metadata (2002), `http://ltsc.ieee.org/wg12/`
6. Ochoa, X., Cardinaels, K., Meire, M., Duval, E.: Frameworks for the Automatic Indexation of Learning Management Systems Content into Learning Object Repositories. In: Kommers, P., Richards, G. (eds.) Proceedings of World Conference on Educational Multimedia, Hypermedia and Telecommunications 2005, Montreal, Canada, pp. 1407–1414 (2005)
7. Pedersen, T., Patwardhan, S., Michelizzi, J.: WordNet: Similarity: measuring the relatedness of concepts. In: Demonstration Papers at HLT-NAACL 2004 on XX (HLT-NAACL 2004). Association for Computational Linguistics, Boston (2004)
8. Polsani, P.: Use and Abuse of Reusable Learning Objects. Journal of Digital Information 3(4), 1–10 (2003)
9. Prieto, M.E., Menendez, V., Segura, A., Vidal, C.: A Recommender System Architecture for Instructional Engineering. In: Lytras, M.D., et al. (eds.) WSKS 2008. LNCS (LNAI), vol. 5288, pp. 314–321. Springer, Heidelberg (2008)
10. SCORM: Sharable Course Object Reference Model (2004), `http://adlnet.org/`
11. Sicilia, M.A., Garcia, E.: On the Concepts of Usability and Reusability of Learning Objects. International Review of Open and Distance Learning 4(2) (2003)

Web-Based Learning Information System for Web 3.0

Hugo Rego[1], Tiago Moreira[1], and Francisco Jose García-Peñalvo[2]

[1] Computer Science Department / GRIAL Research Group
[2] Computer Science Department / Science Education Research Institute / GRIAL Research Group
University of Salamanca
hugo_rego05@yahoo.com, thm@mail.pt, fgarcia@usal.es

Abstract. With the emergence of Web/eLearning 3.0 we have been developing/adjusting AHKME in order to face this great challenge. One of our goals is to allow the instructional designer and teacher to access standardized resources and evaluate the possibility of integration and reuse in eLearning systems, not only content but also the learning strategy. We have also integrated some collaborative tools for the adaptation of resources, as well as the collection of feedback from users to provide feedback to the system. We also provide tools for the instructional designer to create/customize specifications/ontologies to give structure and meaning to resources, manual and automatic search with recommendation of resources and instructional design based on the context, as well as recommendation of adaptations in learning resources. We also consider the concept of mobility and mobile technology applied to eLearning, allowing access by teachers and students to learning resources, regardless of time and space.

Keywords: eLearning 3.0, Web 3.0, Standards and Specifications, Knowledge Management, Metadata.

1 Introduction

As the world naturally evolves, internet does too. Nowadays we live times of change on the web with web 2.0, social networking and mass collaboration [4], even showing already some signs of what Tim Berners-Lee and guru Nova Spivak predicted as semantic web, intelligent web or in broader terms Web 3.0 [10].

One of the fields that have expanded information technology lies in the implementation of systems for distance learning. Currently, there are many eLearning systems, but the main difficulty lies in structuring the in line content and information with the existing learning models in order to achieve greater integration and comprehensiveness of the learning environment and by this providing better quality education. At the same time, yet there aren't too many tools and e-Learning systems for web/e-Learning 3.0, enabling the practical point of view or preparing to implement the semantic web, mobility of resources, as well as the universality of learning design, allowing teachers to approach the design process in an intuitive and practical way.

M.D. Lytras et al. (Eds.): WSKS 2010, Part I, CCIS 111, pp. 196–201, 2010.

In these kinds of learning environments the access to standardized information is very important where it has to be perceived and processed into knowledge. One of the problems that have emerged from this process was how to represent knowledge. Standardization was indispensable, to provide semantic representation of knowledge through ontologies where concepts are clearly and unambiguously identified, providing a set of semantic relation types to represent meaning by linking concepts[7][2].

Trying to address these needs we have been developing AKHME [9] a system that uses the IMS specifications in order to reach goals like: learning object management and quality evaluation; standardization of all resources; and the interaction of all subsystems through the feedback between them allowing the platform to adapt to students/teachers characteristics and to new contexts.

Regarding Web/eLearning 3.0 we have been developing/adjusting this system to meet some requirements of this great concept, addressing issues like collaboration, machine learning, the need of global database, and integration between systems.

In this paper we will start to present the importance/impact of the called evolution to Web/eLearning 3.0, the structure of AHKME and the developments/evolutions made to the system. Finally we'll present some conclusions and future work.

2 Web/eLearning 3.0

While the concepts behind Web 2.0 are about social networking, where systems/platforms like myspace, twitter, facebook and orkut were introduced, and mass collaboration, where the boundaries between authors and the users are thin, the concept behind Web 3.0 is slightly different, is based on web applications that provide value to the user through the usage of intelligent applications giving them a more accurate and precise information [3]. The idea behind this concept is that information should be available anytime, anywhere, anyhow, by this meaning that it should not only be available on common desktops but also in all types of devices that can somehow display web contents. This kind of concept raises the issue of interoperability where different devices and applications must interact with each other, allowing a freer environment for the final user. The main idea is to use technologies like XML, EDF, OWL, SPARQL, to standardize the information so it can be readable by anyone, allowing this way the desired interoperability between systems.

Besides this, Web 3.0 aims a little further with the usage of 3D where virtual environments may become a common use like Second Life and personalized 3D avatars.

One of the main concepts behind Web 3.0 is the semantics, where using semantic technologies and tolls powered with semantic understanding we can provide valuable information to users. All these may be achievable through the usage of a common language (standards) and intelligent systems that may extract meaningful information.

As for the eLearning 3.0 concepts, they aren't too distant from the Web 3.0 concepts since the all idea is to use all these potentialities of Web 3.0 on eLearning.

According to Steve Wheeler eLearning 3.0 will have at least four key drivers: Distributed computing; Extended smart mobile technology; Collaborative intelligent filtering; 3D visualization and interaction [11]. All these key drives meet the concepts behind Web 3.0.

eLearning 3.0 aims to reach a wider range and variety of persons being available on different kinds of platforms/systems, through different tolls and devices, where users will have the possibility to personalize their learning and have an easier access to comprehensive information. The usage of mobile technologies will certainly have a great impact in eLearning 3.0, nonetheless the availability of tools, services, resources and support will play an important role, since a new perspective of usage is being created.

This situation may turn eLearning into a cross-social learning methodology since it will be possible to be applied in all contexts, making collaboration easier.

The 3D visualization devices will become more readily available, with interfaces like the ones provided by iPhone or Microsoft Surface, and the usage of 3D avatars.

3 Preparing for Web/eLearning 3.0

To address the issues mentioned before, we have been developing/adjusting/expanding AHKME in order to include tools and features to support them. AHKME is an eLearning system, that is mainly divided in four different subsystems (Learning Object (LO) Manager and Learning Design (LD), Knowledge Management, Adaptive, Visualization and Presentation subsystems), that were structured taking into account a line of reasoning, where first we have the process of LOs creation and management, which is followed by the course creation process through the learning design.

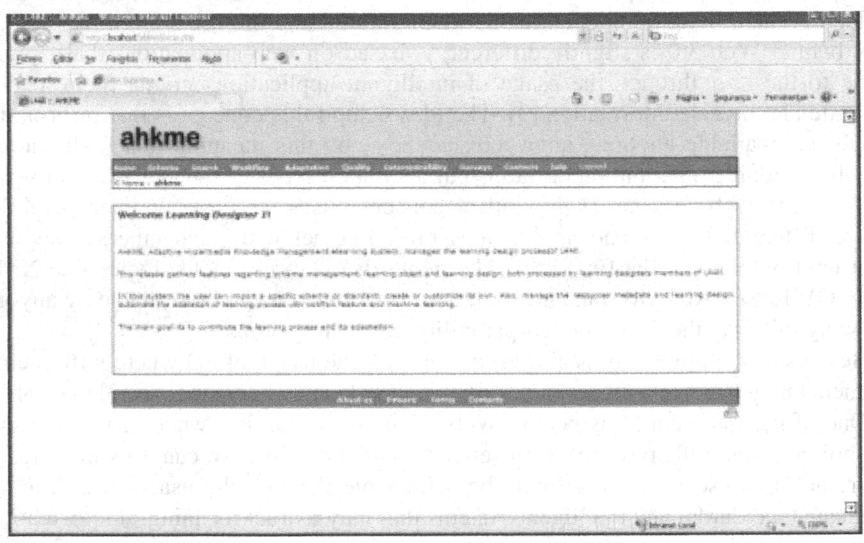

Fig. 1. AHKME's frontend

In parallel with these two processes the Knowledge Management subsystem evaluates the quality of the available LOs and courses. Then they pass through an adaptive process based on the students' characteristics to be presented to them a screenshot of the system is presented on Figure 1.

We will now focus on the components of the system that have been developed/adjusted/expanded to address the needs of Web/eLearning 3.0 and that provide the management and evaluation of resources.

3.1 Subsystems and Tools

The LO Manager and Learning Design subsystem is the subsystem that deals with the LOs and Course management. It allows teachers to define/create metadata to describe LOs using the IMS Learning Resource Metadata (IMSLRM) specification [1] and define the learning design components, create and structure courses using the IMS Learning Design specification [6].

All the information is stored in XML manifests that gather all the XML files with their metadata and all the resources used by it. It has an information packaging feature that gathers the LOs with their manifests enabling the management of the packages that will be used in the design of courses. The information packaging of LOs and courses with their metadata facilitates the transport and reuse of the resources in other systems going towards interoperability.

In the design of learning units the participants can assume different roles. These roles can be student or staff, what makes possible collaborative and group learning, which importance is recognized at the training and educational levels [6].

All files and packages are validated to check if they're in conformance with the specifications and are in constant evaluation made by the KM subsystem.

In order to facilitate the insertion of metadata we provide an automation of this process, advising the most commonly used values for the elements on the LO cataloguing in order to describe the LO's through the most adequate metadata elements.

To address the issue of collaboration we have been developing a workflow and feedback tool where teachers may collaborate in the creation of resources and get feedback from the courses and resources. In this tool teachers may create their own questionnaires/surveys and collect data taking into account the feedback they want to get. This tool allows the automation of procedures during which documents, information or tasks are passed from one participant to another in a way that is governed by rules or procedures allowing flexibility and collaboration increasing efficiency [5].

As for the issue of machine learning we've been using intelligent agents in the knowledge management and adaptive subsystem.

The main objective of the Knowledge Management subsystem is to avail the quality of the resources that are on the system. One of the tools we have been developing is an intelligent agent that automatically evaluates LOs that acts when some kind of interaction is made on the LOs in order to readjust its quality evaluation. The evaluation is made taking into account the criteria defined by Morales where several educational issues are address [8][9]. The agent starts to import the LO to evaluate and others already evaluated, then applies decision trees algorithms (ID3,CART,CHAID) to the educational characteristics defined in the IMSLRM specification to calculus its final evaluation.

Regarding adaptation we are using data mining techniques for recommendation of the attributes that are more relevant to facilitate de adaptation of the resources.

In order to reach the so called global database issue it is important to use standards, so that information can be readable by different systems and cross-platform. In the development of AHKME we have adopted the IMS specifications, since they allow most of the aspects we've analyzed and that we considered important to reach our goals like metadata support, learning design, content packaging, among others [9], allowing the desired interoperability. We have also developed a tool, which is a schema generator that allows the teacher to create his own structure/schema/ontology or personalize a schema that has already been imported to the system in a simple form approaching the teacher to the learning design process without having great knowledge/experience in educational technologies.

3.2 Integration with Other Systems and Mobility of Resources

We have been developing a subsystem, Visualization and Presentation subsystem, which main objective is to give a frontend to AHKME, presenting the educational contents to students taking into account the adaptive meta-model generated for each student, and to act as an integrator with other systems like LMSs and Social Networking Systems. The objective for this integration is to give an opportunity for LMSs/social networking systems to benefit from AHKMEs' functionalities, as well as to give a front-end to AHKME system.

This integration can be done in different ways depending on the type of LMS or Social network. We can develop specific or general plugins depending of the LMS or Social Network that we are trying to integrate. For example if we want to integrate with Moodle we may develop a plugin in PHP and MySQL database and to integrate with Blackboard it can be done, through a plug-in like a building block. It always gives the possibility of integrating the courses by importing it to the LMS that supports the IMS specifications.

This subsystem also gives a front-end to AHKME, allowing the combination from different platforms, collaborative, interactive, communication and community tools.

4 Conclusions

In this article we've presented how we are developing the platform AHKME in order to meet the needs of Web/eLearning 3.0.

We use the IMS specifications, that combine metadata and XML potentialities, to represent knowledge, dividing information in several meaningful chunks (LOs) providing their description through metadata and storage in XML files, therefore permitting their cataloguing, localization, indexation, reusability and interoperability, through the creation of information packages. These specifications grant the capacity to design learning units that simultaneously allow users with different roles promoting several types of both collaborative and group learning.

Through knowledge management we have a continuous evaluation of contents, granting quality to all the resources in the platform for teachers and students to use.

With the tools we are developing with are looking forward to meet some of the needs of Web/eLearning 3.0 regarding collaboration, machine learning, the need of global database, and integration between systems.

AHKME's main contributions are: management and quality evaluation of resources; usage of the specifications to standardize all the resources to reach interoperability and compatibility of learning components; interaction of all subsystems in order to adapt to students and teachers characteristics and to new contexts, and to grant success in teaching/learning process, being able to be applied to several kinds of matters, students, learning strategies training and educational environments.

In terms of future work, we will add the level B of the IMS LD specification to the learning design tool. In the adaptive subsystem we will add functionalities according to the IMS Question and Test Interoperability and Enterprise specification. In the KM subsystem we will add the feature of course quality evaluation through the development of some tools. We will also upgrade the system to store information using databases based on the RDF or OWL formats.

Acknowledgments

GRIAL Research Group and the Castile and Lion Government (Spain) through GR47 Excellence Project.

References

1. Barker, P., Campbell, L.M., Roberts, A., Smythe, C.: IMS Meta-data Best Practice Guide for IEEE 1484.12.1-2002 Standard for Learning Object Metadata - Version 1.3 Final Specification. IMS Global Learning Consortium, Inc. (2006)
2. Berners-Lee, T., Hendler, J., Lassila, O.: The Semantic Web. Scientific American 284(5), 34–43 (2001)
3. Cho, A.: What is Web 3.0? The Next Generation Web: Search Context for Online Information (2008), http://internet.suite101.com/article.cfm/what_is_web_30
4. Downes, S.: E-Learning 2.0, eLearn Magazine (2005), http://www.elearnmag.org/subpage.cfm?article=29-1§ion=articles
5. Future Strategies Inc: e-Worflow – the workflow standards portal (2009), http://www.e-workflow.org/
6. Koper, R., Olivier, B., Anderson, T.: IMS Learning Design Information Model - Version 1.0 Final Specification. IMS Global Learning Consortium, Inc. (2003)
7. Mendes, M.E.S., Sacks, L.: Dynamic Knowledge Representation for e-Learning Applications. In: Proceedings of the 2001 BISC International Workshop on Fuzzy Logic and the Internet, FLINT 2001, Memorandum No. UCB/ERL M01/28, University of California Berkeley, USA, pp. 176–181 (August 2001)
8. Morgado, E.M.M., Peñalvo, F.J.G., Riuz, A.B., Rego, H., Moreira, T.: Learning Objects for eLearning Systems. In: Lytras, M.D., et al. (eds.) The Open Knowledge Society – A Computer Science and Information Systems Manifesto. CCIS, vol. 19, pp. 153–162. Springer, Heidelberg (2008), ISBN-13: 978-3-540-87782-0, ISBN-10: 3-540-87782-7, ISSN: 1865-0929
9. Rego, H., Moreira, T., Morales, E., García, F.J.: Metadata and Knowledge Management Driven Web-Based Learning Information System. In: Lytras, M.D., et al. (eds.) The Open Knowledge Society – A Computer Science and Information Systems Manifesto. CCIS, vol. 19, pp. 308–313. Springer, Heidelberg (2008), ISBN-13: 978-3-540-87782-0, ISBN-10: 3-540-87782-7, ISSN: 1865-0929
10. W3CSW: Semantic Web Activity, W3 (2009), http://www.w3.org/2001/sw/
11. Wheeler, S.: Learning with 'e's - e-Learning 3.0 (2009), http://steve-wheeler.blogspot.com/2009/04/learning-30.html

Immersive Environments – A Connectivist Approach

Ana Loureiro and Teresa Bettencourt

CIDTFF (Research Center for Didactics and Technology in Teacher Education) / Department of Education / University of Aveiro
Aveiro / Portugal
Higher School of Education / Polytechnics Institute of Santarém
Santarém / Portugal
accloureiro@gmail.com
CIDTFF (Research Center for Didactics and Technology in Teacher Education) / Department of Education / University of Aveiro
Aveiro / Portugal
tbett@ua.pt

Abstract. We are conducting a research project with the aim of achieving better and more efficient ways to facilitate teaching and learning in Higher Level Education. We have chosen virtual environments, with particular emphasis to Second Life® platform augmented by web 2.0 tools, to develop the study. The Second Life® environment has some interesting characteristics that captured our attention, it is immersive; it is a real world simulator; it is a social network; it allows real time communication, cooperation, collaboration and interaction; it is a safe and controlled environment. We specifically chose tools from web 2.0 that enable sharing and collaborative way of learning. Through understanding the characteristics of this learning environment, we believe that immersive learning along with other virtual tools can be integrated in today's pedagogical practices.

However, before we can apply and suggest best practices we need to get to know the virtual environments we intend to use (2D and 3D). We must characterize and understand how interactions and relationships are established, in particularly, between the users of this Multi-User Virtual Environment. We have made preliminary observations of residents' behaviour at Second Life®, including some informal or natural learning contexts. Our analysis of those observations led strongly to theory of Connectivism approach, which is defined as a learning theory for the digital age.

This paper will present the outlined research and a literature review about the Connectivism theory and its application to the virtual environments.

Keywords: Connectivism, connective knowledge, e-learning 2.0, learning contexts, virtual environments, web 2.0.

1 Introduction

We are living in the era of the networked society; networks include and organize the essential of our richness, knowledge, power, communication, technology [23] and

M.D. Lytras et al. (Eds.): WSKS 2010, Part I, CCIS 111, pp. 202–214, 2010.

therefore the way we learn. Every day and pretty much along our whole day we have a close contact with various forms of technology. We all carry gadgets that allow us to keep in touch with this "world of fast context-switching" [1] where we live. No matter if we use them to communicate, cooperate, interact, work, share or learn. Whether 'digital natives' or 'digital immigrants' [4].

Technologies and networks are a reality and they are available for almost everyone. Education cannot ignore this evolution and must be aware of the new demands that arise with the connected society. As Brandão said "it is broadly recognised that the role of teacher is changing and the new teaching methodologies must be implemented in the classroom and in the school projects, creating favourable environments for pupils and teachers to fully benefit from information and communication technologies. Teachers will have to promote key skills such as collaborative working, creativity, multidisciplinarity, adaptiveness, intercultural communication and problem-solving among themselves and transfer to pupils" [25]. Although, and in many situations, what we see is not an evolution but a stagnation of the ways of delivering teaching. Old approaches remain, and more often than not "students are asked to sit in rows and listen to lectures, take notes or solve exercises given by teachers. It's a teaching strategy that doesn't prepare students to be critical citizens and professional workers on their specialty, nor give them the skills and competences needed to be autonomous and constructors of knowledge" [2]. In fact it seems students of this networked society "have limited patience with an educational system that has not changed substantially since the 19th century. They think and learn in environments that are fast-paced, multimedia, multimodal, interactive, and, of course, digital. These volatile, interconnected, and complex social milieus (Cohill, 2000) call for learning options that are critical, collaborative, creative, and futures oriented" [3].

Today's students are interconnected, living in a digital age, multiprocessing and multitasking. The Web is now not only an informational and social resource, but also a learning tool that enables new ways of creating and sharing knowledge. With today's networked society we can observe a new way of learning that is discovery based. Education cannot ignore those changes, cannot cling to the old habits and methods of teaching and learning from the last century. As Prensky said "our students have changed radically. Today's students are no longer the people our educational system was designed to teach" [4].

Some people tend to think that "kids who are multiprocessing can't be concentrating. (…) the attention span of the teens at PARC-often between 30 seconds and five minutes-parallels that of top managers, (…) the short attention spans of today's kids may turn out to be far from dysfunctional for future work worlds" [1]. Consequently teachers are becoming challenged to develop new strategies in order to fulfil the needs and enhance the skills of their digital age students; to achieve better ways of capturing and maintaining students' attention.

We believe that we can only engage our students' attention and motivation if we leverage the same tools. By getting to know their digital and immersive worlds; and becoming part of it. Teaching students in new ways is critical for creativity and innovation to evolve. Web 2.0 tools are a way to reach digital natives, a way to connect with them and to catch and maintain their attention and motivation, particularly through games and other virtual 3D environments.

Today's students have a close contact with a huge number of digital tools, creating, changing, rebuilding, and updating their profiles and their knowledge. They establish a network of connections that enables "Involve, Create, Discuss, Promote, Measure" [5] information and knowledge. It is now understood that information and knowledge are no longer for life nor in possession of a handful of eminent thinkers. It is public and it changes rapidly. It is now possible for everyone to build, share, acquire and innovate through the social Web, using the facilities and the potential of Web 2.0. These tools are available from any space and time, they are user friendly and with free access. New contents in different contexts grow, allowing a "connective knowledge" [6] between networked users. We have what we can call as a "learnovation" society. In fact, as Siemens refers, "the capacity to form connections between sources of information, and thereby create useful information patterns, is required to learn in our knowledge economy", and "connections that enable us to learn more are more important than our current state of knowing" [7].

In the follow section we will present and characterize our ongoing study. We will also present the learning theory that we find as being the best one for supporting the study.

2 The Study

We are conducting a research study that is being developed as part of a Doctoral Program in Multimedia in Education at the University of Aveiro, under the name *Knowledge Building in Virtual Environments – Influence of Interpersonal Relationships.* The study will be conducted in the tridimensional virtual environment called Second Life® (SL®) and with the support of Web 2.0 tools (like Diigo and Facebook).

Before we chose the 3D environment we explored others like Activeworlds, BlueMars, IMVU, MOOVE, There. We asked students for some cooperation in this task, asking them to select their favorite environment and why. The elected one was SL®. Second Life® itself as many of other "virtual worlds are not themselves games" [8]. Second Life® is a free to use 3D multi-user virtual environment, it is immersive, and it is imagined, designed, built and created by its residents (avatars). Second Life® is a playground for our imagination, a limitless platform - design, build, code, perform and collaborate, expanding the boundaries of creativity. It is a real life simulator, allowing all sorts of experiences and studies (from every field of science, humanities and art), all in a safe and controlled environment.

Multi-user virtual environments (MUVE), with special emphasis on SL® have been used in an education context. Actually some of the major universities all over the world have a virtual representation/campus at Second Life® (*cf.* http://secondlife.com/whatis/destinationguide/category.php?c=learning).

We perceived that we could learn in, with and from virtual environments. MUVE allows learning "through exploring environments, 'realia', lived and virtual experiences with tutorial and peer-based support" [9]. These environments make students feel more confident, more open, more participative, more creative, and more responsive. In fact, in the immersive virtual environments, students seem to attend training sessions because they want to learn. Students actually can interact with the simulated world "allowing them to engage with content (Bricken, 1991). Being able to learn subject matter in the first person, as opposed to the third person" which is "experiential, nonsymbolic, interactive, and multisensory" [3].

To contextualise this study we can refer that this research emerged from the need to "observe some of the variables that have been already identified by Bettencourt' (*aka* Bekkers) study (2009) and give it continuity" [10]. These variables are related with three major areas: the person and their motivations; the relationships that exist or are established between avatars or between avatars and persons; and finally the social integration in Second Life® (by which we mean sense of community). We define avatar as "a digital persona that we can create and customize, it is our virtual 3D representation" [22]. Although the three main areas are related and can't be observed independently since they all are interconnected and influence one another. Our research concerns are more focused on learning relationships that are established in real life and then flow into a virtual environment and then flow back into real life again, we are looking to establish whether this flow is complementary.

We are observing in world teachers and learners in a formal context of learning and in an informal – or natural - context of learning. These teachers and learners represent our research sample – picked up among the Portuguese universities and polytechnics population. This is an intentional sample, non probabilistic type.

The researcher (and teacher), is working with a target group of students (a regular class and an adult class, both Higher education students). Both sets of students are from an Education and Multimedia Communication Course. Each group of students was given a research challenge, their performance in this task was use to evaluate the effectiveness of Second Life®/Diigo in promoting collaboration, communication and interaction skills. Prior to work commencing, the students were asked to select a virtual environment that could host students/teacher meetings. After a class discussion about the advantages and disadvantages of some virtual environments (2D and 3D), one was selected - Second Life®. Most of the students had no prior experience of Second Life®. The main goal was to help students to understand the importance of sharing information and discuss contents in an open place. The teacher only meets each class (in a formal way) once a week. The teacher also has some hours of contact out of the classroom (support hours). These hours suit the regular students but don't meet the adult students' needs (since they are part time, and have full-time jobs). The only way we found to give an extra support to the adult class was through a virtual environment. We discovered there were further opportunities for enrichment to everyone by encouraging the regular students to join the virtual tutorials. The teaching methodology uses the physical classroom hours to develop and work through practical content. The virtual classroom is being used to work and discuss around the theoretical content of the subject (using both Diigo - http://groups.diigo.com/group/lah2010 - and Second Life®). None of these spaces is closed to the community. Anyone can join us and contribute to the discussion and content sharing. We are working under the missive "I store my knowledge in my friends" [18]. If one of us does not know something we just check it with a friend. The students are connected to the network through other Web 2.0 tools (Facebook, HI5, Digg, LinkedIn, Plaxo, Twitter, several blogs), using the connections they establish in there to enrich the contents and discussions around the class topics. The virtual meetings in Second Life® happen at the Academia Portucalis (*cf.* http://slurl.com/secondlife/Portucalis/218/167/22). The choice of this location was left for the students to decide, (the other option was the official Higher School Island - SLESES). We should mention, at this point, that this tutorial methodology is not an obligation for students. They are cooperating with this task and in the virtual meetings of their own free will. We show an example of a virtual meeting (*cf.* Fig. 1). We are applying a pedagogical philosophy of learning where the knowledge is built by students [24].

The teacher is no longer the center of the knowledge; the role has evolved to being a guide, a facilitator. Helping students to search, select, relate, analyze, synthesize and apply information and therefore build knowledge. Teacher's role changed from formal into informal and collaborative. Teacher is there available (sharing and using the same virtual environments), motivating, promoting team work, cooperative learning and dialogue, stimulating the intellectual accuracy and facilitating student's autonomy in their search for knowledge and understanding. The teacher becomes a mentor for students in a more reflective learning context.

Fig. 1. Virtual meeting in Second Life®

It is an exploratory and qualitative study. We intend to use surveys (with closed answers) to inquire about the reasons why people enter into Second Life® and also what kind of difficulties they experience in using the environment; if they felt curiosity about exploring the environment; what kind of activities are they doing, where and how long; what is the frequency of logging in and how many hours they stay logged in. We also intend to make some interviews when, and if, we feel need of an additional information, or a clarification / explanation about some of the collected data. Besides these two instruments we also will be working, and mostly, as observers, to identify key indicators (such as the avatar appearance and how the avatar behaves when in a group or community), that will help us to clarify the level of growth or socialization of the avatar / person in the virtual environment of Second Life®.

The main goals of our research are:

- understand in which way the interpersonal knowledge in real life can combine with the personal development/grow in virtual worlds – in particular Second Life®, and in this way achieve insights to a better understanding of the way knowledge is built in virtual worlds optimizing is use and then transfer it to real life contexts of learning – with an impact in the traditional classrooms;
- analyse the several contexts of users logging in and identify the reasons for them to stay, how they grow, what they experience in Second Life®.

We will try to understand the major differences of behavior between people who come to Second Life® by free will and the ones who were required to join the environment. We intended to provide some "insights for all educators and researchers interested in using those environments as a teaching medium in real life, and propose new approaches to better prepare the university students for the marketplace that will emerge" [2], as well as to achieve a better understanding of how people grow and build knowledge in Second Life® in both formal and informal or natural learning contexts. And like in everything we believe informal or natural context is the one that seems more valuable.

To achieve those goals we set our research questions along the following themes:

- what are the main reasons / motivations for people to join Second Life®
- what are the main factors for them to stay and play in Second Life®
- what are their personal paths of development/growth in Second Life®
- and in what way interpersonal knowledge cycling around real world and virtual world.

We expect this study to achieve improved understanding and better knowledge about immersive learning in order develop best practices for teaching and learning strategies in virtual environments. Subsequently, we will transfer that knowledge to real life learning contexts and in this way provide best approaches for teaching and learning in a higher level.

After a careful comparison with learning theories more often used to define and characterise learning contexts and learning environments we have concluded that Connectivism theory is the best one to support this particularly study.

In the next section we will drew some insights about Connectivism and connective knowledge, presenting a literature review about these two topics.

3 Connectivism and Connective Knowledge

Connectivism is described as being the learning theory for the digital age. As Siemens said the theories most often used to describe the learning process (Behaviorism, Cognitivism and Constructivism) do not preview in their outlines the way learning is impacted by technology, which is something that we cannot ignore in digital age. More often than not, technology "has reorganized how we live, how we communicate, and how we learn" [7], there so learning theories of the new age should be reflective and with a glance at social environments, since learning (especially in its informal and natural form) often is widely influence by it. Other ways of achieving and reaching learning have arisen, due to social networks and the types of connections that the World Wide Web allows. As Vaill said, referred by Siemens, "learning must be a way of being – an ongoing set of attitudes and actions by individuals and groups" [11]. It is important to refer that we perceive learning as a "lifelong process of transforming information and experience into knowledge, skills, behaviors, and attitudes" [12]. To learn is to "acquire certain patterns" [13]. It is also the result of interactions and connections that we establish with fellows of our community, peers, personal or social networks. In this way; "to know something is to be organised in a certain way, to exhibit patterns of connectivity" [13]. Connectivism learning theory states that "knowledge – and therefore the learning of knowledge – is distributive, that is, not located in any given place (and therefore not 'transferred' or 'transacted' per se) but rather consists of the network of connections formed from experience and interactions with knowing community" [13]. In a digital society, as the one we live, connections and networks are a reality, as the links that are established between users are. The Web's users are no longer simple information collectors (Web 1.0), they are active and reactive users, developing and sharing content and information, influencing the build of knowledge of the other users. Each one of us has an intrinsic need of being part of cyberspace, of being known by our partners, an unfulfilled eagerness for communication, and to share our thoughts, needs and knowledge. We are now swimming in the "real time, co-creative Web" [20]. We all are now content builders, information sharers, communicators. We all belong to a common space with no barriers, made of links, nodes and connections. Every day we establish new contacts, increasing our networks, sharing and collecting new information, rebuilding our knowledge, and learning.

At this point we can take a close look to the most considerable directions of learning in a digital interconnect society, according with Siemens [7]:

- More often than likely we move into a variety of different and probably unrelated areas of knowledge over our life time;
- We learn walking around through several chains of our life, such as communities of practice, social and personal networks, and while we develop "work-related tasks";
- We cannot separate learning and work activities anymore, since they are in many situations related. We are in continuously learning process, life-long learning;
- Our brains, somehow, are being shifting by technology since "the tools we use define and shape our thinking";
- A theory that explain the links that are established between "individual and organizational learning" is needed since they both are learning organisms;
- Technology can now support and deliver many of the learning processes (no matter if using the informal tools of Web 2.0 or a MUVE, if using a formal platform – LMS, PLE);
- More important than know-how and know-what, is to know "where to find knowledge needed".

Bessenyei supports this by stating that "the motivation for gaining and contextualising information becomes stronger if searching and evaluation becomes a cooperative, network activity. Students can significantly improve the efficiency of their learning if they take part in a network, or virtual community dealing with the given subject. Thus the collective knowledge once again becomes a source of individual knowledge ('cycle of knowledge development'). As the number of cooperative activities increases, personal social networks become the scene of informal exchange of expertise, and 'communities of practice' develop. Besides the questions of 'how' and 'what' to learn, we now have the question of 'where to learn'" [14].

Connectivism is "the integration of principles explored by chaos, network, and complexity and self-organization theories" [7]. It puts the emphasis of enable students with skills to search for, filter, analyze and synthesize information that they gather while exploring networks in order to achieve knowledge. This aspect gets importance every time information or knowledge "is needed, but not known, the ability to plug into sources to meet the requirements becomes a vital skill. As knowledge continues to grow and evolve, access to what is needed is more important than what the learner currently possesses" [7].

Knowledge has two dimensions, explicit and tacit ones. According with Brown, "explicit dimension deals with concepts - the 'know-what' - whereas the tacit deals with 'know-how', which is best manifested in work practices and skills. Since the tacit lives in action, it comes alive in and through doing things, in participation with each other in the world. As a consequence, tacit knowledge can be distributed among people as a shared understanding that emerges from working together" [1].

Connectivism is based in the assumption that decisions are made under conditions that change fast allowing new information to continually be acquired. For this reason the capacity to distinguish and select what is important becomes essential, and there so the capacity to recognise when the new information alters what we previously known, reshaping the knowledge, rebuilding the learning.

Connectivism main assumptions are [7]:

- "Learning and knowledge rests in diversity of opinions.
- Learning is a process of connecting specialized nodes or information sources.
- Learning may reside in non-human appliances.
- Capacity to know more is more critical than what is currently known
- Nurturing and maintaining connections is needed to facilitate continual learning.
- Ability to see connections between fields, ideas, and concepts is a core skill.
- Currency (accurate, up-to-date knowledge) is the intent of all connectivist learning activities.
- Decision-making is itself a learning process. Choosing what to learn and the meaning of incoming information is seen through the lens of a shifting reality. While there is a right answer now, it may be wrong tomorrow due to alterations in the information climate affecting the decision".

In the next section of the paper we will relate Connectivism and Second Life® and how this learning theory can be applied into learning contexts that are developed and build in this virtual environment.

4 Connectivism and Immersive Worlds

As Siemens observed, the major learning theories do not take into account the impact of technology. In fact, these major theories (Behaviorism, Cognitivism and Constructivism) do not relate, or explore, the concept of learning that occurs outside of a person. With technology much of the information, and therefore learning and knowledge, is stored and manipulated by technology. Connectivism intends to fulfil a gap in learning theory, delivering a one that is based in the "impact of technology and new sciences (chaos and networks) on learning" [7]. Nowadays people store pretty much everything in networks, depending of technology for their daily lives. We work, learn, socialize, and interact through technologies.

Second Life® is an online immersive 3D multi-user virtual environment, where each user (or resident, as they are called) is able to have a life that can simulate the real life in almost every aspects (adding some other features that humans can't do at real life) and it is represented in world by his/her avatar. In fact, and according to Linden Lab® itself, "Second Life is a virtual world that allows its residents to create completely original content using atomistic building tools in a shared and globally accessible space" [15].

As we previous stated we believe that Second Life®, having itself MUVE's (Multi-User Virtual Environment) characteristics, have great possibilities if used for education and learning purposes. This environment is like an "ever growing virtual playground that is limited only by the creativity of its users" [16]. According with Federation of American Scientists it will allow us "to build 3-D objects collaboratively and in real time with others in the same world" [17], with major applications at "building, design, and art principles". On the other hand, Second Life®, is a "rough simulation of the natural world, with meteorological and gravitational systems, the possibilities of experimenting with natural and physical sciences are endless"[17], and all this "in a safe and controlled environment" [17]. The twist is that in an immersive environment we are walking inside the material, not just viewing it from a distance. In fact, Second Life® and other MUVEs "have attracted a growing and increasingly sophisticated community of practice (Wenger, 1998) focused on the topic of teaching and learning in 3D immersive worlds" [3].

SL® is not designed primarily as an educative tool, however, as previously indicated, it can be used in several learning contexts. Second Life® seems to be a good option to emulate a virtual classroom. To facilitate a more effective learning environment SL® requires augmentation through adding tools that enable, for instance, students' and teachers' content sharing. The combination of the tools will connect students to the network and to the links of information. Each virtual environment has its role and importance in the knowledge building.

SL® as a learning platform reflects the assumptions of the Connectivism theory in many ways. We know nowadays that information and knowledge are transitory, chaotic and unstable, there is an inherent need of a continuous learning (life-long learning). SL® enables a contact and connection with a diversity of opinions, nodes, links and specialized information sources. Because it is digital, virtual and immersive it allows those information links to be more interactive, which enhances the learning and information sharing. It is an endless network of links allowing contacts to flow in between virtual platforms (2D, 3D) and real life.

On the other hand, the motivation, feelings and sense of community belonging that are generated among SL® users helps to create, develop and maintain connections, and facilitates a process of continuous and natural learning. The environment has available a huge number of communities and groups, according with likes, needs, interests. It is easy to find a group with who we feel affinity for one or other reason. Inside these groups or communities relationships are established and information flows. Members build and share, becoming content providers themselves.

Connections are made and the network of relationships grows and gets enforced progressively. The bonds that are created between the members in many situations jump the borders of the 3D environment. They are enforced outside through a 2D platform or even at real life. Connections are like a snowball effect. The individual network is made of, or complemented, with their friends' networks. As Stephenson said "I store my knowledge in my friends" [18]. In this digital age we have a network of connections that is made of links and nodes with people. It is a "collective knowledge through collecting people" [18]. Actually most people know an 'expert' who they can go to, and that is the power of a network, all contributing expertise. Once again we go into the premise of Connectivism "Know-how and know-what is being supplemented with know-where (the understanding of where to find knowledge needed)" [7]. Internet provides new ways of making those connections, provides an extra dimension of collaborative sharing. Knowledge is "distributed, because it is spread across more than one entity. A property of one entity must lead to or become a property of another entity in order for them to be considered connected; the knowledge that results from such connections is connective knowledge" [6].

Knowledge management is about maintaining the nodes (a node is a knowledge base plus human interpretation), adding fresh ideas, removing outdated knowledge, rebuilding perceptions and therefore learning. And again ability to "know more is more critical than what is currently known". Virtual environments, like SL®, can be an endless network of connections, or relationships, where knowledge can be distributed across a community of people.

The establishment of ties and bonds between people are required since "to learn is to immerse oneself in the network" [13]. In a virtual environment, in theory, there are no barriers or borders, and information flows, people build and share content, relationships are set up, the net of connections extends and we achieve knowledge. This acquisition is made in a natural way, by participating in a community, by sharing, discussing and launching ideas, contents and information, therefore a "learning activity is (...) a conversation undertaken between the learner and the other members of the community" [13]. It is a natural process of interaction and reflection with the guidance and correction of expertises or peers.

Second Life, as a natural and informal virtual environment, can be used for the set of e-learning 2.0 contexts. Downes defines e-learning 2.0 as being "an approach to learning that is based on conversation and interaction, on sharing, creation and participation, on learning not as a separate activity, but rather, as embedded in meaningful activities such as games or workflows" [13]. In the virtual 3D environments we can do everything we just described. Actually, these immersive environments "bridges the gap, so people live the experience, live the learning, and thereby learn better" [10]. For us these are alternative methods of presenting content, as an attempt to catch and maintain student's attention. In fact immersive worlds have a huge potential for education because they can facilitate "collaborations, community and experiential learning" [19].

5 Conclusion

In this paper we set out to share some of the literature review that we are outlining currently, related with the learning theory of Connectivism and its relation with immersive virtual environments.

As we have mentioned previously we expect, with this research, to achieve a better knowledge about immersive learning and therefore transfer that knowledge to real life learning contexts and in this way provide best approaches for teaching and learning in a Higher level. Immersive environments seem to facilitate the development of e-learning 2.0 situations specifically because it stimulates teachers' innovation of their practices and leads them into a collaborative approach with students. Teachers and students become partners and interact socially to a common goal. The process of teaching and learning tend to be more focused on the development of skills: critical thinking, making initiatives, entrepreneurship, responsibility, teamwork, respect for others and their differences, inter-culturality" [2]. We tend to agree with Wagner when he refers that MUVEs are "an ideal pedagogical resource" [17], special because, "acting in virtual communities is nothing new to homo zappiens and is part of normal life" [21], actually, in this digital age and for the most common users "both real and virtual life are components of their lives, without considering one less valuable or real than the other" [21].

The immersive virtual environments, based on its characteristics, favour the social interactions and the creation of links, connections and nodes. These are the basis for knowledge building, and therefore for learning. Fundamentally, this is what Connectivism is all about: establishing personal and social networks. In these networks a natural learning context emerges, a natural way of seeking knowledge. Digital students have a whole net of connections and relationships, real and virtual ones. Virtual environments tend to facilitate the contacts, tend to favour the person's emancipation. Everyone can access to information and therefore transform it into knowledge, through conversations and interactions with others. Since virtual immersive worlds, like Second Life® are by its nature informal environments, access to knowledge becomes also natural and an easiest process. If we add to it the other tools we can use at web 2.0 and the connections we establish there, then we can have a huge network of connections, links and nodes and knowledge building achieve a whole new dimension. In a networked society the knowledge is build by students (with teachers' guidance) and learning becomes a process of social nature.

References

[1] Brown, J.: Growing up digital (2002), http://www.usdla.org/html/journal/FEB02_Issue/article01.html (retrieved February 26, 2009)

[2] Bettencourt, T.: Teaching & Learning in SL: Figuring Out Some Variables (2009), http://cleobekkers.wordpress.com/2009/01/28/teaching-learning-in-sl-figuring-out-some-variables/ (retrieved January 30, 2009)

[3] Richter, J., Inman, L., Frisbee, M.: Critical engagement of teachers in Second Life®: progress in the SaLamander Project. In: Livingstone, D., Kemp, J. (org.) Pro-ceedings of the Second Life® Education Workshop 2007 - Part of the Second Life® Community Convention, pp. 19–26 (2007), http://www.simteach.com/slccedu07proceedings.pdf (retrieved January 20, 2009)
[4] Prensky, M.: Digital Natives, Digital Immigrants (2001), http://www.marcprensky.com/writing/Prensky%20-%20Digital%20Natives,%20Digital%20Immigrants%20-%20Part1.pdf (retrieved January 25, 2010)
[5] Hayes, G., Papworth, L.: The Future of Social Media Entertainment (2008), http://www.personalizemedia.com/the-future-of-social-media-entertainment-slides/ (retrieved January 25, 2010)
[6] Downes, S.: An Introduction to Connective Knowledge (2007), http://www.downes.ca/files/connective_knowledge.doc (retrieved January 25, 2010)
[7] Siemens, G.,, C.: A Learning Theory for the Digital Age (2004), http://www.elearnspace.org/Articles/connectivism.htm (retrieved February 26, 2009)
[8] Austin, T., Boulder, C.: The Horizon Report, 2007. New Media Consortium and EDUCAUSE Learning Initiative (2007), http://www.nmc.org/pdf/2007_Horizon_Report.pdf (retrieved January 26, 2009)
[9] Freitas, S.: Learning in Immersive Worlds (2006), http://www.jisc.ac.uk/media/documents/programmes/elearninginnovation/gamingreport_v3.pdf (retrieved February 26, 2009)
[10] Loureiro, A., Bettencourt, T.: Building Knowledge in the Virtual World – Influ-ence of Real Life Relationships. In: Boa-Ventura, A., Morgado, L. e Zagalo, N. (org.) Proceedings of the SLACTIONS 2009 - Research Conference in the Second Life® World (2009)
[11] Vaill, P.: Learning as a Way of Being. Jossey-Blass Inc., San Francisco (1996)
[12] Cobb, J.: A Definition of Learning (2009), http://www.missiontolearn.com/2009/05/definition-of-learning/ (retrieved January 25, 2010)
[13] Downes, S.: Learning Networks and Connective Knowledge (2009), http://www.downes.ca/post/36031 (retrieved January 25, 2010)
[14] Bessenyei, I.: Learning and Teaching in the Information Society. E-learning 2.0 and Connectivism (2007), http://www.ittk.hu/netis/doc/ISCB_eng/12_Bessenyei_final.pdf (retrieved January 25, 2010)
[15] Lester, J.: Artistic expressions in Second Life. Journal of Virtual Worlds Re-search (2009), http://jvwresearch.org/v1n3.html (retrieved March 20, 2009)
[16] Johnson, N.: The Educational Potential of Second Life® (2006), http://digitalunion.osu.edu/showcase/virtualenvironments (retrieved February 2, 2008)
[17] Wagner, J.: The School of Second Life®: Creating new avenues of pedagogy in a virtual world (2007) http://www.edutopia.org/school-second-life (retrieved February 1, 2008)
[18] Stephenson, K.: What Knowledge tears apart, networks make whole. International Communication Focus, 36 (1998), http://www.netform.com/html/icf.pdf (retrieved January 25, 2010)

[19] Kemp, J., Livingstone, D.: Putting a Second Life® "Metaverse" Skin on Learning Management Systems (2007), `http://www.sloodle.org/whitepaper.pdf` (retrieved February 2, 2008)

[20] Hayes, G.: Virtual Worlds, Web 3.0 and Portable Profiles (2006), `http://www.personalizemedia.com/virtual-worlds-web-30-and-portable-profiles` (retrieved February 2, 2008)

[21] Veen, W., Vrakking, B.: Homo Zappiens – Growing up in a digital age. Network Continuum Education, London (2006)

[22] Loureiro, A., Bettencourt, T.: The use of Immersive worlds for learning contexts: – A Connectivism Approach. In: Proceedings of the INTED 2010 International Technology, Education and Development Conference, pp. 002459– 002467 (2010)

[23] Castells, M.: A sociedade em rede. In: Cardoso, G., et al. (eds.) A sociedade em rede em Portugal, pp. 19–29. Campo das Letras, Porto (2005)

[24] Lima, J., Capitão, Z.: E-Learning e e-Conteúdos – Aplicações das teorias tradicionais e modernas de ensino e aprendizagem à organização e estruturação de e-cursos. Centro Atlântico, Lisboa (2003)

[25] Dias, P., Gonçalves, A.: PICTTE: um projecto de formação a distância para professores. In: Dias, P., e Freitas, C. (org.) Proceedings of II Conferência Internacional de Tecnologias de Informação e Comunicação na Educação, Challenges', pp. 301–312. Centro de Competência Nónio Século XXI, Universidade do Minho, Braga (2001)

ICT-Supported Education; Learning Styles for Individual Knowledge Building

Harald Haugen[1], Bodil Ask[2], and Sven Åke Bjørke[3]

[1] Stord/Haugesund University College, Norway
harald.haugen@hsh.no
[2] University of Agder, Norway
bodil.ask@uia.no
[3] University of Agder, Norway
sven.a.bjorke@uia.no

Abstract. School surveys and reports on integration of ICT in teaching and learning indicate that the technology is mainly used in traditional learning environments. Furthermore, the most frequently used software in the classrooms are general tools like word processors, presentation tools and Internet browsers. Recent attention among youngsters on social software / web 2.0, contemporary pedagogical approaches like social constructivism and long time experiences with system dynamics and simulations, seem to have a hard time being accepted by teachers and curriculum designers. How can teachers be trained to understand and apply these possibilities optimally that are now available in the classroom and online, on broadband connections and with high capacity computers? Some views on practices with the above-mentioned alternative approaches to learning are presented in this paper, focusing particularly on the options for online work and learning programmes. Here we have first hand experience with adult and mature academics, but also some background with other target groups.

Keywords: Learning styles, social software, Web 2.0, social constructivism, system dynamics, simulation.

1 Introduction

In international comparative surveys, e.g. PISA[1], researchers ask whether today's students are prepared for future challenges?

- *Can they analyse, reason and communicate effectively? Do they have the capacity to continue learning throughout life? The OECD Programme for International Student Assessment (PISA) answers these questions and more, through its surveys of 15-year-olds in the principal industrialised countries. Every three years, it assesses how far students near the end of compulsory education have acquired some of the knowledge and skills essential for full participation in society.*

Findings vary throughout the OECD world. Norwegian results in reading, scientific and mathematical literacy appear to be very disappointing, while Finnish students

M.D. Lytras et al. (Eds.): WSKS 2010, Part I, CCIS 111, pp. 215–224, 2010.

score among the highest. At the same time, Norway is on top using ICT in schools, while Finland is a bit behind. Norwegian educational authorities have been searching for ways and means to mend the failing knowledge level among students - and perhaps taking advantage of the investments made in new technology for schools.

How can these facts be explained? Is it the introduction and applications of ICT that causes the low academic scores in Norway?

1.1 Low Integration of ICT

A recent survey, *Education, Curricula & Technology* (ECT, 2007-10)[2], among teachers in Norwegian secondary schools reveals that ICT is abundantly present in schools, but there are hardly any signs that its full potential is approached. Traditional learning environments are copied into the new technology, standard software is the most common ICT activity reported. There seem to be a lack of competent role models for teachers; they are hampered by their own background and traditions in learning and teaching.

In Mathematics for instance, the survey[3] shows that teachers are very confident in their own competence in mathematics, and that their command of ICT tools is sufficient. Spreadsheets are useful for calculations, for making tables and drawing graphs, but are rarely used for simulations, testing of hypotheses or applications that are more advanced. Dedicated software e.g. for geometry, is rarely used, and it seems that teachers lack the experience and insight to see the learning potential in application of advanced software. A mere knowledge of the software and competence within mathematics are not sufficient, however; it also requires ability to use the software in proper didactical and subject oriented ways.

Similarly in social sciences[4], Internet is used for finding maps and statistical facts, PowerPoint is used to show photos and group work and Word is used to write up reports. But dedicated geographical information systems (GIS) are rarely used; simulations of populations or economic systems are hardly mentioned. 70% of the responding teachers claim that they are *interested* or *very interested* in applying ICT in their teaching. But a much lower fraction is actually using it more than as a communication or distribution tool through Internet and LMS.

Also in natural sciences,[5] the findings are in the same categories. Reports from excursions are written in Word, illustrated by digital photos, but no simulations of e.g. food chains or marine balances are applied. Subject specific software and web sites are rarely used, and many teachers claim that there are many other and more important activities to fit into restricted time frames, than to *waste time on ICT*.

Reports on findings within *practical and aesthetical curriculum subjects* [6] [7] [8] and in *languages*[9] also indicate findings in the same direction.

General conclusions from this first part of the ECT project is that teachers are positive to the use of ICT in schools, they are fairly confident about their own skills both in subject matters and in ICT, but they stick to general software, parts of an LMS and Internet. Teachers only integrate fractions of the new technology into their methodology and learning environment for students. Reasons they give for low infusion of ICT varies, but are very often related to lack of time and doubts about the learning effect of ICT; other activities are deemed more important for the learning outcomes.

2 Contemporary Pedagogical Approaches

The main pedagogical approaches the last decades have been based on behaviourism, cognitivism, and constructivism[10]. With the development of online learning, constructivism has emerged as the more appropriate for the creation of online learning environments[11]. Collaborative learning in communities has opened up ways to deeper learning and gaining of insight through the necessity of formulating own tentative points of view, the negotiation of meaning and construction of new knowledge. Social constructivism seems to fit the online learning environment perfectly.

Bruner's[12] constructivist theory is a framework for instruction based on the study of cognition and child development research. Bruner claims that learning is an active process in which the learner constructs new ideas and concepts based on his or her current and past knowledge. Rather than being a passive recipient of information, the learner must select and transform information, construct hypotheses, make decisions and rely on a cognitive structure to do so[13] Constructivism has been further developed and adapted to different learning environments, in particular social constructivism.

Social constructivism emphasizes the collaborative nature of learning. This approach is partly based on the work of the Russian psychologist Vygotsky, who insisted that learning takes place in a social context. As a consequence, students join a knowledge-generating community and in collaboration with others solve problems and assignments in a context as close to reality as possible. Processing and assessing information, negotiation of meaning and co-constructing new knowledge are important tasks. The students use information they gather actively by applying it in discussion with others. Studies should in principle be undertaken for a purpose, and the participants should critically assess information according to relevance and usefulness in solving the task at hand.

3 Learning Styles

Information is not knowledge,
Knowledge is not wisdom,
Wisdom is not truth,
Truth is not beauty,
Beauty is not love,
Love is not music,
and Music is THE BEST.
from Frank Zappa, "Packard Goose"

The DIKW pyramid: Data, Information, Knowledge, Wisdom[14] indicates that there is a clear distinction between data and information, between information and knowledge and again between knowledge and wisdom or insight. We all 'drown' in data and pieces of information. According to this view and to traditional constructivist philosophy, teaching by merely disseminating information is rather futile. Information can be compared to water. You can throw it on students by the buckets, but most will run off or evaporate. To construct knowledge, the students must be in a learning mode. Understanding and insight does not occur automatically. Learning is a cognitive activity taking place in the student's brain. Focus must be on learning processes rather than on teaching.

There are several approaches to the creation of good learning environments, where students are encouraged to engage in learning activities with knowledge construction, deep learning, insight and wisdom as goals. Socio-constructivism emphasizes the negotiation of meaning leading to deeper learning and insight. Then students obtain and discuss information in order to construct knowledge.

To obtain and select information, it is claimed that learning increases with the number of senses activated. If we can hear, see, taste, smell, touch and feel, we remember and understand better than if only one of our senses is in use. Some are more visual in their approach to learning, others more auditive or maybe tactile[15]. A person who prefers a tactile approach learns better if he or she can move around, touch things and learn through their fingers so to speak. If a student can apply his or her preferred learning style, learning becomes easier according to this theory.

David Kolb [16] introduces another approach with four learning styles: The 'converger', the 'diverger', the 'assimilator' and the 'accomodator'.

'Convergers' prefer working with abstract conceptualization and active experiments. They like making practical applications of ideas and solve problems. The 'divergers' like concrete experience and reflective observation. They prefer finding different perspectives. Characteristic for 'assimilators' is that they like making theoretical models and reason inductively. 'Accomodators' according to this theory prefer concrete experience. They engage with their surroundings and do things rather than read about them.

Kolb developed the 'Learning Style Inventory', an assessment method used to determine an individual's learning style.

Other more controversial approaches to learning, like neuro-linguistic programming [17] and 'Accelerated learning' [18] also emphasize the learning style approach. 'Accelerated learning' introduces the 'multiple intelligences', like visual, kinesthetic, linguistic, social, naturalist and musical intelligences. According to this theory, learning increases with several intelligences activated.

The efficiency of various approaches to learning can always be discussed. Anyway, it is fairly obvious that the traditional one-way lecturing or teaching has its weaknesses. Modern learning environments should probably look more like a 'smorgasbord' of learning resources and learning methods, where students have the opportunity to pick and choose, rather than the teacher serving one ready made, same style dish to all.

The application of ICT in education can facilitate this. However, it must be clear that computers are just tools. The tools alone can not make the various learning activities and resources. The teachers; the pedagogues, must be properly trained for building these kinds of learning environments. Solid subject knowledge, pedagogical skills, empathy and engagement are still the important factors for the 'CREAM' strategy for learning[15]. This strategy involves *C*reativity and confidence to use individual learning styles, *R*eflections on own learning, *E*ffective organization of the learning environment, *A*ctivity; physically and mentally, and *M*otivation. Technology can just facilitate when appropriate, never substitute for the good teacher.

4 Social Software/Web 2.0

According to Wikipedia the term "**Web 2.0**" is commonly associated with web applications that facilitate interactive information sharing, interoperability, user-centered design, and collaboration on the World Wide Web[19]. The important characteristic of Web 2.0 is to remove the perception of interaction between human and computer to the benefit of social interactions between humans, where the technology has been "blackboxed". Typical tools are hosted services like blogs, Facebook, twitter, video-sharing sites and wikis. The point is that the website is interactive. Instead of just passively reading a text the user is encouraged to contribute with texts, pictures, additional information, opinions etc. The O'Reilly Media arranged a conference on the topic on the topic in 2004 and Tim O'Reilly is therefore associated with the concept Web 2.0[20]. Professor Tim Berners-Lee who has been credited with inventing the World Wide Web, thinks that the concept of Web 2.0 is a "*piece of jargon*"[21], as the social tools were embodied in the first place.

5 System Dynamics and Simulations

System thinking and system dynamics with simulations seem to have a hard time being broadly accepted by teachers and curriculum designers. The visions of the developers of *system thinking* and software tools to study the dynamics of real world models were also opening up for new approaches to learning. Class discussions of models with flows and accumulations, mutual interactions of dependent variables etc seemed an activating and student engaging exercise.

It is all based on theories by Jay Forester[22] at MIT and others, starting with his speech at The Club of Rome in 1970, where he introduced the *World Model*[23]. His ideas continued to develop through several phases, e.g. by his work with Gordon Brown [24] on learning strategies for all school levels (K-12), for better integration and involvement of ICT in the learning of several school subjects. Important for the wide-spread interests in system thinking is also P. Senge's book *The Fifth Discipline*[25].

New and more flexible tools have replaced the old versions of Dynamo[26], Stella[27], PowerSim[28] that introduced graphical interfaces for simpler implementation of models and simulations. Both teacher trainers and teachers of today should be offered the possibility to exploit system dynamics as an educational method. This is a way of investigating, studying and learning about complex systems, particularly in social and natural sciences, but also in other subjects like mathematics, physical education etc.

Already at the WCCE 90 in Sydney, Australia, in a paper on *System dynamics as an Educational Method*, it was claimed that

> *Our surrounding world consists of complex systems, too complex to be grasped by our minds without assistance. . . . Building and manipulating models help us to understand the dynamics of such systems. . . . Computer technology has made manipulation and calculations much easier, while authoring systems for simulations have made model construction simpler*[29].

Here experiences and recommendations were presented, including the three stages:

- Simple simulations of dynamic processes where students study effects of changing different parameters; the model is hidden, prepared by the software producer
- Model and simulation studies, where the model is graphically and/or mathematically visible, relations/equations may be altered and parameters adjusted for repeated running of the simulations
- Development of their own system dynamic models, based on subject knowledge, ability or creativity to see relations between involved variables and constants, then testing hypothesis through simulations of the model to see what is in agreement with nature or with other experiences[29].

These stages are meant to gradually introduce teachers and students to complex systems related to subjects in question or cross-curriculum topics. The first stage, the black-box simulation, demonstrates - assuming that the model is correct and realistic - what the consequences are when changing one or more of the variable parameters, and provides training in systematic thinking and testing of models. It is a well known method and is the basis for a lot of computer games and training scenarios.

The real system thinking comes when students are able to enter stage two, having proper software and visible models available. They discover relations between variables in nature or other systems; they may play with the model construction and see what alterations lead to. Running the simulation for each change reveals what the results are. It is a perfect tool for group discussions and collaborative learning.

The real deep learning comes with the third stage, when students are challenged to construct their own models of complex systems they shall study, e.g. balance between prey and predators in an isolated system, or the economy of a youth club. This part requires access to a simplified interface of a software system, an authoring tool that makes model construction simple even if the model is complex. It requires solid subject or cross curricular knowledge by the students! Not only superficial knowledge is required, but an understanding of the system to be modelled. The role of the teacher is important, as a guide and provider of hints and ideas during the process. A simulation of the model follows to see if the results appear reasonable. The final proof of the pudding is a comparison or testing of the simulation versus the real world system.

By introducing these stages and methodology to teachers they may be convinced that there are options for learning environments that may lead to better and more efficient use of the technology. The ideas were tested with students in the 1990-ies, using the existing versions of Stella and PowerSim at the time. The responses and results were positive - even with the technology and software existing twenty years ago.

Today's increased computer capacity, broadband connections and better teacher knowledge of ICT, should count in favour of even better results in 2010. For support and professional development there is a System Dynamics Society[30]. There are annual conferences, particular providers for K-12 adapted learning environments, CLE[31], for researchers and educators at all levels working with system dynamics for learning purposes. There are also lots of online simulation games, e.g. Sim City, and many improved tools are available, both commercially and as freeware.

The above "marketing" of system dynamics is only meant as an example of how certain tools and educational methods can benefit learning outcomes and usefulness of ICT in education. There are many other dedicated methods and tools that work in particular subjects, topics and learning situations that can provide similar advancements towards better integration. Hopefully teacher educators, in-service providers and others that work with ICT in schools can demonstrate and offer introductions and access to such possibilities. This may widen the teachers' visions and practice beyond application of word processors and presentation software in their classes. May be we will then find better learning results related to the technology?

6 How to Train Teachers

Teachers who are already out in schools or universities will have a constant need for professional upgrading. This is particularly true for professors and academic staff who are dealing with higher education and meant to be models for their students in future careers.

6.1 Professional Development

Adults and mature academics are in constant need for professional development. The introduction of ICT and its proper application in modern learning environments are important measures in that respect. Shorter and less formal courses may be an option for academic staff who does not want to take a leave in order to be updated.

The need for access to education on a global scale requires new and flexible ways to offer education, also at university level. This has encouraged the globalisation of some ideas initiated during the NITOL project [32], further developed in European projects, i.e. courses on how to tutor and develop online learning.

An online programme for in-service and upgrading of teachers, particularly aiming at university and college staff, including teacher trainers, has been offered and tested in a global setting. This set of two courses at master's level, named *E-teaching I* and *II*, awarding 10 + 10 ECTS credits, has been very well received. Reactions from course participants document both initial lack of competencies in the field of e-learning, and the acquirement of new knowledge and skills.

6.2 The E-Teaching Courses

The growing demands for higher education around the world render particularly universities in developing countries vulnerable. Economy, campus facilities as well as access to qualified staff set limits for enrolment of new students far below national and regional demands. Vast masses of knowledge-hungry candidates are knocking on the university gates. Available resources are insufficient to meet the needs through traditional systems and organisations.

Most developed countries have programmes for foreign aid, financing education etc. in developing countries. There is almost no end to the needs for solving the most urgent situations. Much of the efforts towards education go into primary and adult education in order to overcome illiteracy. By the time these obvious and urgent needs are met, there are hardly any means left for higher education, let alone for in-service or further education of already qualified teachers and other academics. In some cases bursaries or grants are offered for further studies or post graduate work at institutions in developed countries, thus taking the grantees away from important duties and students at their home institutions. The training in a different cultural setting may even be of less value when they return, or still worse, may tempt the grantees to continue working under better conditions in the developed parts of the world.

Could net based study programmes, developed and anchored locally, be a way to keep the academics at their home institutions, thus creating new learning environments for larger masses of their countrymen? This may improve capacity, accessibility and cost effectiveness for more students, and reduce the brain-drain from already scarce resources.

Two dedicated courses on e-learning, both at master's degree level, each awarding 10 credits (ECTS), are offered globally online to professors and teaching staff.

- E-teaching 1, basic online methodology and pedagogical principles for tutors [33]
- E-teaching 2, planning, designing and development of online courses [34]

The courses were developed on the basis of material and experiences from collaborative EU projects on e-learning (MENU) and take advantage of expertise at partner institutions. In principle, the courses are to be financed through student fees. During the pilot period, however, available funding has allowed to establish bursaries to cover greater parts of the fees for participants from developing countries. Economy has thus not been a major obstacle for interested staff members so far. The major challenges that remained are related to lack of time and to the unstable infrastructure, causing some of the registered students to drop out without completing the course.

The lack of infrastructure and access to modern technology is often argued against this strategy for offering higher education to target groups in developing countries. Statistics now show, however, that the situation is changing drastically. It is thus reason to believe that within a few years' time the access to Internet will be rather widespread also in the developing world. Therefore, preparing the present and future teaching staff at universities and schools in these regions for the new learning arenas may be of particular value to strategies, plans and activities. Despite the present low coverage, the relative growth is rather impressive[35].

Pedagogical approaches to effective learning are changing with trends and time, also for online learning. The online E-teaching courses have both presented and practiced a *social constructivist* approach, a method that has caught great interest among the highly qualified *students,* i.e. professors and teachers. This method is claimed to be a suitable method to make online learning an attractive alternative for higher education, particularly in lifelong learning perspectives.

An extra asset here is the high level of knowledge among the participants, all of them being well qualified academics. It is thus a matter of tutoring and guidance to make collaboration, peer tutoring and constructive criticism among peers constitute a strong learning resource. To many of the participants this way of studying and learning is new, and it has taken both time and efforts to break their academic habits and convince them of the benefits. The final results, however, have come out very positive.

References

[1] PISA - OECD Programme for International Student Assessment, http://www.pisa.oecd.org/pages/0,2987,en_32252351_32235731_1_1_1_1_1,00.html
[2] Education, Curricula & Technology (ECT), http://www.hsh.no/fou/forskningsprogram/ect.htm
[3] Tuset, G.A.: Matematikkfaget og bruk av IKT på ungdomstrinnet: - Hvem er lærerne som bruker IKT i matematikkundervisningen? In: SHUC (2010) (in print)
[4] Andersland, S.: Skulefagundersøkinga 2008/2009 - Fagrapport samfunns-fag. In: SHUC (2010) (in print)
[5] Fadnes, P.: Skolefagundersøkelsen i ECT-prosjektet - Fagrapport Naturfag. In: SHUC (2010) (in print)
[6] Liten bruk av IKT-verktøy i kunst og håndverk – fornuftig bortvelging eller vegring og inkompetanse? In: SHUC (2010) (in print)
[7] Espeland, M., Arnesen, I.G.: Musikkundervisninga på ungdomstrinnet og bruk av IKT - eit tenleg instrument for heile musikkfaget? In: SHUC (2010) (in print)
[8] Arnesen, T.E.: IKT i kroppsøving på ungdomstrinnet - som lærarane ser det. In: SHUC (2010) (in print)
[9] Flatøy, I.: Bruk av IKT i norskfaget på ungdomstrinnet: ei styrking eller ei svekking av faget? In: SHUC (2010) (in print)
[10] Siemens, G.: Connectivism: A learning theory for the digital age (2004), http://www.elearnspace.org/Articles/connectivism.htm (accessed February 2010)
[11] Net Pedagogy Portal, http://www.thewebworks.bc.ca/netpedagogy/Evolution/evolution.html (accessed February 2010)
[12] Bruner, J.: The Process of Education. Harvard University Press, Cambridge (1960); Bruner, J.: Going Beyond the Information Given. Norton, New York(1973)
[13] Kerlins.net, http://kerlins.net/bobbi/education/teachonline/pedagogy.html, link to Constructivist theory, Bruner, http://tip.psychology.org/bruner.html (viewed February 2010)
[14] Rowley, J.: The wisdom hierarchy: representations of the DIKW hierarchy. Journal of Information Science 33(2), 163–180 (2007)
[15] Cottrell, S.: The study skills handbook, Palgrave (2008)
[16] Kolb, D.: Experiential learning: Experience as the source of learning and development. Prentice-Hall, Englewood Cliffs (1984)
[17] Beaver, D.: NLP for lazy learning, how to learn faster and more effectively, Vega (2002)
[18] Gardner, H.: Theory of Multiple Intelligences, http://www.accelerated-learning.net/multiple.htm (accessed February 16, 2010)
[19] http://en.wikipedia.org/wiki/Web_2.0 (accessed February 22, 2010)
[20] http://oreilly.com/web2/archive/what-is-web-20.html (accessed February 22, 2010)
[21] http://en.wikipedia.org/wiki/Web_2.0#cite_note-developerWorks_Interviews:_Tim_Berners-Lee-3#cite_note-developerWorks_Interviews:_Tim_Berners-Lee-3 (accessed February 22, 2010)

[22] Forrester, J.W.: World Dynamics. Productivity Press, Portland (1970)
[23] ISEE, System dynamics for kids, http://www.iseesystems.com/community/connector/Zine/MayJune04/hight.html
[24] Origin of system dynamics, http://www.systemdynamics.org/DL-IntroSysDyn/origin.htm
[25] Dynamo language, http://www.eric.ed.gov/ERICWebPortal/custom/portlets/recordDetails/detailmini.jsp?_nfpb=true&_&ERICExtSearch_SearchValue_0=EJ351446&ERICExtSearch_SearchType_0=no&accno=EJ351446
[26] Dynamo language, http://www.eric.ed.gov/ERICWebPortal/custom/portlets/recordDetails/detailmini.jsp?_nfpb=true&_&ERICExtSearch_SearchValue_0=EJ351446&ERICExtSearch_SearchType_0=no&accno=EJ351446
[27] Stella software, http://www.mpassociates.gr/software/catalog/sci/ithink/stella.html
[28] Powersim homepage, http://www.powersim.com/
[29] Haugen, H.: System Dynamics as an Educational Method. In: McDougall, Dowling (eds.) Proceedings from IFIP WCCE 1990, Computers in Education. C. North Holland, Amsterdam (1990)
[30] System dynamics Society, http://www.systemdynamics.org/
[31] CLE - the Creative Learning Exchange, http://www.clexchange.org/
[32] NITOL, http://ans.hsh.no/nitol/
[33] E-teaching 1, http://w.uia.no/videre/e-teaching1 (viewed May 2, 2009)
[34] E-teaching 2, http://w.uia.no/videre/e-teaching1 (viewed May 2, 2009)
[35] Internet World Stats http://www.internetworldstats.com/stats.htm (Viewed January 03, 2008)

Effective Design and Evaluation of Serious Games: The Case of the e-VITA Project

Dimitra Pappa[1] and Lucia Pannese[2]

[1] National Centre for Scientific Research (NCSR) "Demokritos", 15310 Agia Paraskevi, Greece
[2] Imaginary srl. Via Mauro Macchi, 52 - 20124 Milano, Italy
dimitra@dat.demokritos.gr, lucia.pannese@i-maginary.it

Abstract. Learning and training are presently facing new challenges and a strong transformation. The use of electronic games for education (game-based learning) promotes an agile, immersive and stimulating form of learning that fosters learner engagement and motivation. Nonetheless, the design of effective and engaging educational games is a creative process that is unique to each situation. This paper discusses the inherent challenges of building intellectually appropriate and engaging games and presents the methodology adopted in the case of the e-VITA project that applies GBL to promote knowledge sharing and transfer for intergenerational learning. The paper analyses the e-VITA framework for SGs evaluation, which is central to the project's iterative development approach. Early findings stemming from the validation of the e-VITA prototype game are also presented.

Keywords: Serious games, game-based learning, evaluation, design, framework, informal learning.

1 Introduction: Learning and Serious Games

Learning and training are presently facing new challenges and a strong transformation: a swiftly growing knowledge society in which knowledge acquisition and transfer are major elements of human activities and definitely the main creative force, demands new approaches to learning as well as to knowledge sharing and management.

At the same time the demographic changes in Europe's population, as well as the rapid changes in the market that businesses have to face, as well as the needs of "generation Y" – the digital natives [1], children born with technology shaping their minds - request innovative concepts and pedagogical models for effective knowledge sharing and management in society, in business and in schools. Traditional learning methods that have worked in the past have proven ineffective for the students of today. The current generation of students, having grown up with technology, are developing "new forms of evaluation skills and strategies"[2] and seek interactivity and fast-paced, visually stimulating and engaging learning experiences, in stark contrast to the content traditional educational systems are designed to offer [2].The development of methods for engaging different generations, kinds of people, company roles,… in simultaneous learning processes becomes also crucial for today's society. Modern technologies are

M.D. Lytras et al. (Eds.): WSKS 2010, Part I, CCIS 111, pp. 225–237, 2010.

transforming learning, changing where, what and how we learn. Learning is becoming ubiquitous, a life-long process that can also take place outside the classroom. Nowadays non-formal and informal learning methods are becoming widely used in very many different contexts.

Serious games (SGs), i.e. games in which education is the primary goal, rather than entertainment [3], can facilitate learning from the experiences of others. According to Kolb's [4] learning cycle, the process of learning involves four stages: concrete experience, observational reflection, abstract conceptualisation, and active experimentation. SGs have learning goals and structure, but in addition are adaptive and interactive and most importantly they provide enjoyment, pleasure, motivation, ego gratification (through competition and wining) and emotion, in order to achieve learner engagement and involvement. Games create simulated environments that facilitate immersion, allowing learners to explore alternative approaches to situations virtually, in order to directly experience practical and emotional consequences of their actions, rather than wondering "what would happen if ...?"

Other studies have shown that computer games can assist players to acquire certain cognitive abilities and skills and improve understanding in topics [5],[6],[7]. In games, players have to manage multiple inputs and objectives at the same time, different resources, and to make instant decisions. Players are also required to complete a number of specific tasks to win. People who play such video games exhibit and even increase what is called fluid intelligence [8] which is associated with problem solving [9]. Nevertheless, in the modern technological world of fast decision-making, e-mail, blog and various collaborative tools and environments, games might be helping develop the kinds of skills children need to succeed.

In this context the use of Serious Games (SGs) for learning is rapidly establishing its space, although in different forms that span from videogames, to casual games, to virtual worlds. What brings them all together is the characteristic of making learning an engaging, immersive experience, that is attractive to all generations, and that fosters deep reflection about the context the learner is interacting with. It moreover puts the learner at the centre of the learning experience and changes his or her role from "passive vessel" to "active participant" [10], making the learning experience much richer and meaningful [11].

The debate continues about **what makes a game effective** and **how it should be used.** Making "intellectually appropriate, challenging and enriching" games is a relatively under-researched topic, and still today is considered a key research challenge, as is the integration of SGs into the learning process [12]. Effective game-based learning calls for applications that have defined learning outcomes and are designed to promote active participation and interaction, balancing the subject matter with the game play, in order to enhance the ability of the learner to retain and apply the knowledge gained to the real world. Consequently, designing effective, engaging SGs draws on several disciplines, calling for theoretical understanding of learning, cognition, emotion, and play. Along with great game design, SGs need content and pedagogy expertise, design research, and impact research. In complex application settings the development of theoretical models about what the games should look like is not sufficient. Instead active user involvement is required, throughout the development process.

In the present paper

The paper discusses the inherent challenges of building intellectually appropriate and engaging games and presents the methodology adopted in the case of the e-VITA project ("European life experience") that applies game-based learning as a means to promote knowledge sharing and transfer for intergenerational learning. The following section provides additional information regarding the scope and objectives of the e-VITA project and presents the complexity of SGs design in the context of an informal process such as intergenerational learning, which usually takes place during regular everyday exchanges with older relatives and friends. Subsequently, Section 3 analyses the e-VITA frameworks for SGs development and evaluation. Game development is regarded as a c process that builds on **continuous evaluation and improvement** and the **active involvement of users**. The e-VITA evaluation framework includes three main analysis dimensions: technical verification, User Experience evaluation and pedagogical aspects evaluation (evaluation of learning outcome). Section 4 presents early findings stemming from the validation of the e-VITA prototype game.

2 The e-VITA Project

The e-VITA project – European life experience, www.evitaproject.eu - co-funded by the Education and Culture DG under the Lifelong Learning Programme, aims at developing and testing SGs that allow younger generations to "live" stories told by older people. This way the complexity of the past can be experienced directly and understood while playing a game that once used to be a real story.

The e-VITA project wants to test and investigate new ways of knowledge sharing and knowledge transfer in an intergenerational setting. To do this, in E-VITA the principles of Game-Based-Learning and Storytelling are combined for the creation of different serious games focusing on the transfer of life experiences of older people to younger ones. Typically, intergenerational learning is an informal and incidental process that refers to the sharing of information, thoughts, feelings and experiences between different generations. With games allowing for the creation of simulated environments that facilitate immersion, engagement and involvement, SGs emerge as an effective solution for supporting intergenerational learning. However, the development process introduces an additional challenge, namely that of capturing the knowledge of older generations (both tacit and explicit) and transposing it into games. This complex objective can be achieved through the use of storytelling. Storytelling is a process and a mean for sharing, interpreting and offering knowledge and experiences to an audience. Told stories are giving a context, they are embedding knowledge into a concrete situation; they are not only comprising pure facts, but also connections and emotions. In this light, the combined use of SGs and storytelling was deemed necessary as a means facilitate intergenerational learning.

Overall, the e-VITA methodology for GBL for intergenerational learning involves the following steps:

- Storytelling for capturing the knowledge of senior citizens
- Definition of instructional design methodologies for SG design
- SGs development

Viewed in the light of the SECI model for knowledge creation proposed by Nonaka and Takeuchi [13], conceptually, the Storytelling process covers the first two steps of the knowledge conversion process i.e. the conversion of the tacit knowledge of senior citizens to explicit knowledge (socialisation and externalisation). The resulting explicit knowledge is subsequently analysed and organised in the form of SGs (combination) which is internalised by learners during game playing. As part of this process explicit knowledge transforms to tacit and becomes a part of individual's basic information. The knowledge conversion process is illustrated in Figure 1.

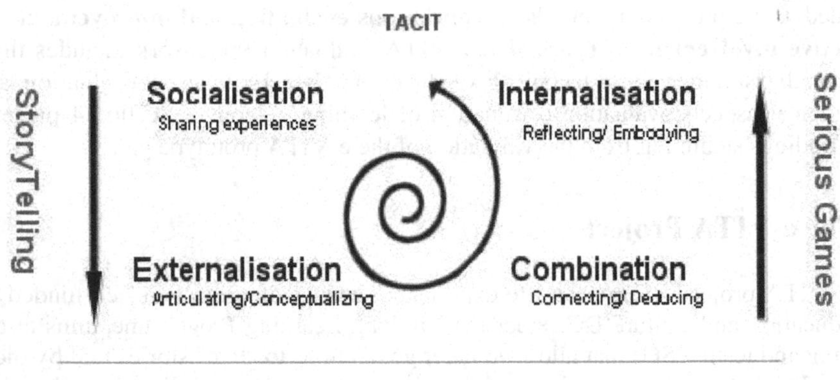

Fig. 1. The e-VITA knowledge conversion process

The e-VITA project promotes and investigates pedagogy-driven innovation by defining new approaches to problem-based and contextualised learning as well as knowledge transfer integrating Game Based Learning [GBL] with intergenerational learning concepts. A set of 'European cultural games' about cross-border experiences of older Europeans is being developed, allowing users to experience a past Europe of e.g. strict travelling and migration rules, different economic and monetary systems, uncertainties towards intercultural aspects in an engaging way, promoting self- reflection on the achievements of the European Integration process outside a formal instructional context.

Knowledge creation and transfer can be promoted in different settings, but when it comes to the transfer of life experiences into real-life situations a game-based-approach can be the most effective one as it is already an experiential method based on interactivity. Serious games (virtual, interactive web-based simulations of real situations, in which the player takes the role of one of the main figures) integrated into training environments can play a crucial role for promoting knowledge transfer.

The four e-VITA Serious Games will be related to episodes that should not go further back than the 1960s and not having to do with the war. Specifically the outcomes will be:

- An experiential game about the topic "East and West block" and in particular about experiences from a divided Europe. In countries like Poland or Germany the European divide was observable every day. The contacts between East and West Europe were often a complicated challenge, and often experienced as a contact to a different, an "outlandish world". The game will be set-up in the form of a branching story and its prototype is already available in the project website under www.evitaproject.eu in the section "e-VITA games".
- A narrative based game about the topic "Tourism and Travelling in Europe", hosting tourists including both perspectives: from the guest and from the host. This is the game of the four, where the component of the Storytelling will be strongest emphasized.
- A problem-based game about the topic "Working abroad". It will be about business trips and migration: travelling for business is not the same as travelling for tourism, and settling in another country gives a far deeper insight in traditions and culture.
- An exploratory game about the topic "Former times without technology and media". For young adults and teenager a world without mobile phones, Internet, Computers is unthinkable. Before the information and communication revolution other ways of recreation, meeting people, exchange with others were prevailing. "How was my social life as I was a teenager?", "How were social contacts taking place?", "How were communication and meetings organised?".

3 The Development of the e-VITA Serious Games

The design of effective and engaging SGs of educational games is a creative process that is unique to each situation. Furthermore, the process draws on several disciplines, since it requires a theoretical understanding of learning, cognition, emotion, and play., While theories of SGs design are starting to evolve, issues including how a specific game should be structured and used and what makes it effective for a specific target group and a specific application context still remain part of research. Overall, the game design for educational games is dependent on the learning objective, the intended user group and under what circumstances the game will be used.

SGs build on the principle that a purposeful interaction of learners with their learning environment can create deeper levels of personal change and growth. Games allow for the creation of fictive environments that help demonstrate the complexity of the situation and the point of view and the constraints of different actors. In this context rational problem-solving and exploration can be promoted. Player motivation and engagement are critical to the success of SGs. Ideally players should be immersed in the action: identify themselves with player tokens, have an emotional response to events and outcomes.

In this light, particular attention should be placed on the game's educational approach and visualisation, namely to the definition of the game's underlying pedagogical concept and workflow, the development of an appropriate story board and selection of graphical deign. Overall, the applied learning methods must adhere to the way students select, organise, and store information according to their learning styles [14]. The designers of GBL should consider the varying learning styles of their indented user group while developing training solutions. Given that a student's depth of understanding can range from the recitation of superficial descriptions of facts to deeper insights in interpretation, application, and self-understanding [15], ideally, instructional approaches should attempt to guide students toward a penetrating understanding of subject matter. Furthermore, SGs should promote critical reflection as a means to effect changes in students' attitudes and belief systems and hence to change perceived relationships to their life situations.

In the case of the e-VITA project the goal of promoting intergenerational and intercultural learning for a heterogeneous target group that features learners of different ages and from several European countries, students and professionals, experienced and inexperienced game players etc increase the complexity of the task. Given the complexity of game design, the e-VITA project adopts a development approach that builds on **continuous evaluation and improvement** and the **active involvement of users** throughout the development process. This approach is inspired after Deming's model for continuous quality improvement in product development (the Deming Cycle or PDCA Cycle), which builds on the principle that business processes should be analysed and measured to identify sources of variations that cause products to deviate from user requirements. The model consists of a logical sequence of four repetitive steps for continuous improvement and learning: Plan, Do, Study (Check) and Act, where:

1. PLAN: Design or revise business process components to improve results
2. DO: Implement the plan and measure its performance
3. CHECK: Assess the measurements and report the results to decision makers
4. ACT: Decide on changes needed to improve the process

In accordance to Deming's model the game creation process should feature the following steps, as illustrated in Figure 2:

1. **Requirements analysis:** The collection and analysis of requirements, which are related to this game, in conjunction with the overall learning objective to be achieved, the target group and the context of learning.
2. **Design:** The translation of the requirements into concrete design specifications, featuring: selection of the most relevant pedagogical model, definition of storyboard, design of workflow, graphical definition.
3. **Creation and testing:** Creation and verification / validation of the games.
4. **Improvement & Finalisation:** Definition and implementation of changes needed to improve the quality of the game.

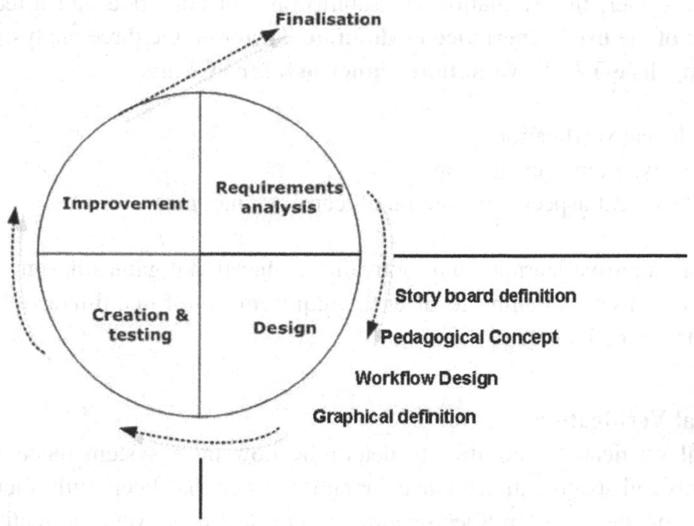

Fig. 2. The e-VITA game development process

Overall, each genre of game has its own evaluation system or evaluation criteria. There can be significant differences, even among games serving educational purposes. In addition to the lack of consensus about what makes a game effective, the evaluation of SGs is a challenging task, particularly with respect to the educational outcome. Several approaches exist with respect to SGs evaluation. For example, de Freitas & Oliver [16] proposed a four dimensional framework for the evaluation of games- and simulation-based education. The evaluation perspectives include: i) the context, ii) the learner, iii) the internal representational world and iv) the processes of learning. The first perspective deals with where the play/learning takes place and how that influences the way the game will be played. The second dimension focuses on the learner or learner group, studying how e.g. their background influences their learning. The third dimension aims at the game itself, i.e. how well the game world establishes interactivity, immersion and the level of fidelity used. Finally, the last dimension deals with learning methods, models and frameworks used to support learning practice.

Overall, SGs combine pleasure with education, being designed to "engage, entertain and educate". The e-VITA project proposes an **evaluation framework** that emphasises the threefold nature of SGs as: (a) IT products, (b) Games and (c) Learning Instruments, three critical dimensions can be distinguished with respect to both the development and the evaluation of educational games: effective SGs need to be (a) technically sound and easy-to-use IT products, (b) fun and engaging games and (c) effective learning instruments that lead to the achievement of the desired learning outcome. This translates into requirements concerning the game's:

Technical solidity & Usability
Cognitive & affective aspects
Pedagogical aspects (achievement of learning outcome)

Viewed together, the evaluation of usability and of cognitive and affective aspects form part of the **user experience evaluation**. Therefore the three analysis dimensions composing the **e-VITA evaluation framework for SGs** are:

Technical verification
User Experience evaluation
Pedagogical aspects (evaluation of learning outcome)

In order to improve learning and motivation, educational games design should target all three dimensions. Failing to meet the requirements of one dimension could compromise the effectiveness of learning.

Technical Verification

Technical verification and aims to determine how far a system meets technical requirements and specifications. Once the entire system has been built, then it has to be tested against the "System Specification" to check if it delivers the features required. In the context of E-VITA, the verification of the **technical solidity** of the produced SGs needs to be verified before they are released for use.Technical verification is primarily a laboratory testing exercise, aimed at identifying and record potential software problems.

User Experience Evaluation

A game must be understood in terms of its rules, interface, and the concept of play that it deploys. User experience evaluation evolves around the evaluation of usability and cognitive & affective aspects form part of the **user experience evaluation.** Critical aspects to be investigated include:

- How easy the system is to use for the intended purpose, as determined mainly by the human-machine interface design (usable).
- The extent to which the user views the system as useful and satisfactory (acceptance).
- The extent to which the SGs are compelling/engaging for the target audience (realism, satisfaction).

Garris et al. [17] analysed the motivational characteristics of games in six dimensions: fantasy, rules/goals, sensory stimuli, challenge, mystery and control. Addressing these categories or dimensions when designing games will spur motivation and improve the training outcome [17].

The overall aim of this analysis dimension is to *bridge* SG development work with the users' expectations (Figure 2).

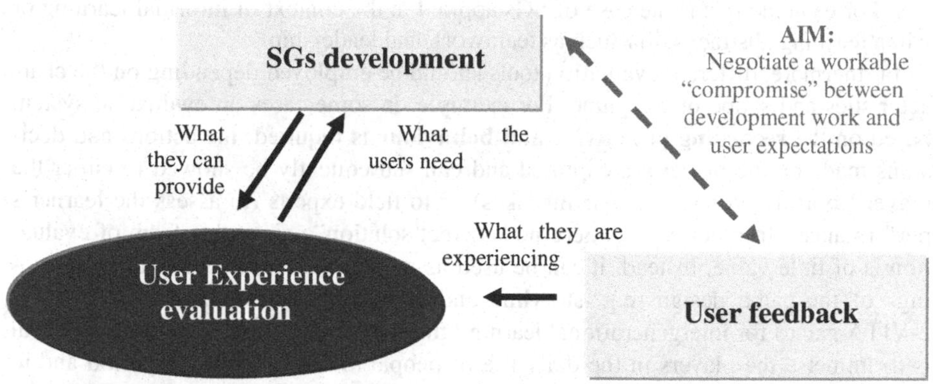

Fig. 3. User Experience Evaluation

Evaluation of Learning Outcome

Serious games, like every other tool of education, must be able to show that the necessary learning has occurred. According to Kevin Corti Serious games "will not grow as an industry unless the learning experience is definable, quantifiable and measurable". While the efficacy of games in studies, like e-learning in general, has been inconclusive, with 'no significant difference' being reported in some studies where face-to-face and game-based approaches are set head to head, the potential of educational games to improve learning and motivation is increasingly accepted [18].

SGs provide an environment for active, critical learning, allowing users to explore skills, methods, and concepts rapidly within a safe experiential environment designed with behavioural learning components. The potential Learning outcomes include changes in participants' behavior, knowledge, skills, attitudes, and/or levels of functioning, and as such they can be:

- **Short-term,** outcomes are relatively immediate changes that occur within a few days or weeks or participation (science workshop).
- **Medium-term**, outcomes that may occur within a few months of participation
- **Long-term**, outcomes that may occur months or years after participation.

Critical elements to be investigated include:

- What are the learning goals?
- How well do the learners achieve those goals?
- Are learners able to remember facts?
- Are they able to make "correct" decisions?
- What else are they learning?

However, measuring learning and/or improvements is a particularly complex task. With SGs placing less emphasis on rote memorisation of facts, the results obtained from traditional learning assessment methods may not accurately reflect the learning gained from serious games. Qualitative indicators about what and how appear to be more relevant in this case, compared to traditional quantitative learning success statistics. For example this is the case of SGs applied in the context of informal learning or when teaching abstract skills such as teamwork and leadership.

Furthermore, different evaluation tools should be employed depending on the characteristics and scope of the game. For example, in some cases an evaluation system based on the **recording** of **activity and behaviour** is required: the actions and decisions made by the player are captured and can subsequently be showed to either the player (to analyse/compare their mistakes) or to field experts (to assess the learner's performance). In other cases where no "correct solution" exists, this form of evaluation is of little value. Instead, it can be used as a way to discover eventual shortcomings of the game design (e.g. storyline and workflow issues). In the case of the e-VITA games for intergenerational learning this aspect is less relevant, since the goal is to immerse the players in the daily life of people in a different time period and to allow them to internalize and absorb the tacit knowledge of older generations.

In the light of the above, types of assessment often used in serious games include:

Completion Assessment, about whether the player was able to complete the game
In-Process Assessment, about the way players choose their actions
Teacher Evaluation of the student's understanding of the material proposed in the game

As a generic approach the Kirkpatrick's evaluation model [19] could be employed. The model which is used to evaluate learning in organisations, includes four levels of evaluation, namely measuring:

LEVEL 1: reaction, what the learners thought and felt about the training
LEVEL 2: learning, the resulting increase in knowledge or capability
LEVEL 3: behaviour, extent of behaviour and capability improvement and implementation/application
LEVEL 4: results, the effects on the business or environment resulting from the trainee's performance

The e-VITA project focuses mainly on intercultural comprehension, understanding the concepts behind the European process, the organization of the European society etc, aiming to provide factual knowledge on the subject and increase learners' comprehension of related situations and their ability to act accordingly. Therefore, the e-VITA SGs target several learning objectives:

- **Knowledge:** Increasing knowledge of historical facts around Europe
- **Affect:** How do learners feel about European integration
- **Motivation:** Making learners want to learn more about European integration

Another important element in the validation of the e-VITA games is **Fidelity validation**, namely the verification of the validity of the games with respect to the **accuracy of the facts** presented in the game (historical data and facts), and the **visual fidelity** in representing a certain historical period etc.

4 Prototype Evaluation

The preliminary validation of the e-VITA prototype game has clearly demonstrated the importance of this factor. The evaluation involved a broad target group from several European countries (Spain, Portugal, Poland, Italy, Greece, UK) and combined the use of questionnaires with targeted interviews. Although debated by several research studies (e.g. [20]), stereotypical gender and age differences that are often evident in leisure gaming were reflected on the validation results, clearly stressing the need to take gender and age into consideration during GBL planning.

The use of technology for instruction is in its infancy. Every form of technology has its strengths and weaknesses and for less digitally literate users could be a frustrating process and a barrier hindering the adoption of GBL. To address this risk, game content must be solid, substantial, and clear.

Similarly, the patterns of game-play of the intended target group should be taken into consideration during SGs design. In this study the players' previous experience with games emerged as both an enabling and a hindering factor. Experienced gamers (mostly under 20, male participants) could easily get familiarised with the game, finding their way around intuitively without need for guidance, but at the same time had "false" expectations of the game, stemming from their experience with entertainment-oriented games and their inability to grasp the difference between serious games and leisure games. During the survey, these players demonstrated lower motivation rates and reluctance in repeating the gaming experience, being disappointed by the "lack of action" in the game. Nonetheless, when they were asked whether they would accept such a game as part of their school curriculum, their views shifted and the acceptance rate rose. Clearly a large part of the appeal of SGs is that they provide a familiar environment for the latest generation of students. However, games that act too much like a classroom, with pop quizzes interrupting the player's experience can disrupt their appeal.

This result stresses the need for a balance between education and entertainment in educational games: although a serious game is a game in which education is the primary goal, rather than entertainment, the potential of technology to create engaging experiences should be exploited, always taking into consideration the expectations of the players. Furthermore, this result justifies existing concerns about the use of the term "serious" in conjunction to games [21] . Once this distinction is made clear and players understand the concept of serious games, the potential of educational games as a tool to be used with mixed age, gender and cultural groups rises considerably. Clearly, 'immersive world' applications have the potential to support communications between learners, to support problem-based learning opportunity and to support exploratory learning experiences [22]

Another important aspect of GBL that emerged in this work relates to the applicability of educational games for fostering learning and motivation in complex learning situations, like intergenerational and cultural learning, which evolve mainly around the sharing of information, thoughts, feelings and experiences. While GBL has a clear value for transmitting explicit, factual knowledge, perhaps its greater strength relates to the transferring of tacit knowledge, skills, behaviours that can be embedded in games. In this light, the effective capturing of tacit knowledge emerges as a critical success factor in building SGs. While considerable effort and significant research work has been done in the direction of developing quality games, in terms of pedagogic approaches and technologies to be applied depending on the application setting and the specific educational objective, little has been said about the importance of groundwork, namely about the quality of material upon which the game development is based.

The work of the e-VITA project has already demonstrated that SGs used in the context of intergenerational learning, need not only to appeal to younger generations of players, or convey practical or historical information about past decades, but rather to immerse players in the life of older generations. In order to achieve this objective GBL design needs to employ a holistic methodology that enhances the potential of SGs by combining them with other instruments. In the case of intergenerational learning the combined use of SGs and Storytelling can cater for the knowledge conversions that take place during the learning process, from the point where a senior externalises their experience to the point where a the player assimilates and internalises this knowledge.

Given that SGs can be extremely diverse in terms of audience, specific learning goals, topic etc, the biggest challenge for future research in the field is probably to collect evidence from diverse game and context-specific observations to systematically contribute to the development of a generic theory for GBL.

This innovative learning methodology is set to address primarily the challenge of transferring tacit knowledge through gaming and as such it could be adopted in other application settings with similar requirements (e.g. organisational learning). Overall the e-VITA project promotes and investigates pedagogy-driven innovation, defining new approaches to problem-based and contextualised learning as well as knowledge-transfer, integrating GBL with intergenerational learning concepts. In that sense, these outcomes (pedagogical models, GBL development and implementation process, intergenerational approach) can be transferred to other learning scenarios applicable in other contexts.

5 Conclusion

The requirements of serious games design are discussed in this paper in conjunction with an integrated evaluation framework that takes into account the different facets of SGs as applied in the context of the e-VITA project for intergenerational learning. The project work has entered its second year and is presently focusing on a comparative investigation of different pedagogical methods: experiential, narrative, problem-based and exploratory. This exercise is also expected to provide additional insight regarding the application of the proposed evaluation methodology.

Acknowledgments

This research has been co-funded by the European Commission within the Lifelong Learning Programme, KA3 (www.evitaproject.eu).

References

1. Prensky, M.: Digital game-based learning. McGraw-Hill, New York (2001a)
2. Conole, G., De Laat, M., Dillon, T., Darby, J.: Jisc lxp: Student experiences of technologies. University of Southampton, Southampton (2006)
3. Michael, D., Chen, S.: Serious games: Games that educate, train and inform. Thomson, Boston (2006)
4. Kolb, D.A.: Experiential learning: Experience as the source of learning and development. Prentice-Hall, Englewood Cliffs (1984)
5. Aguilera, M., Mendiz, A.: Video games and education: Education in the face of a "paralel school". Computers in Entertainment 1(1), Article 8 (2003)
6. Becta. Computer games in education (2006), http://partners.becta.org.uk/index.php?section=rh&rid=13588 (retrieved 25/01, 2010)
7. Jenkins, H., Klopfer, E., Squire, K., Tan, P.: Entering the education arcade. Computers in Entertainment 1(1), 17–28 (2003)
8. Perez, R.: Researchers examine video gaming's benefits. In: Defence, D.o (ed.) (2010)
9. Cattell, R.B.: Intelligence: Its structure, growth, and action. Elsevier Science Pub. Co., New York (1987)
10. Iverson, K.: E-learning Games: Interactive Learning Strategies for Digital Delivery. Pearson Prentice Hall, Upper Saddle River (2005)
11. Jonassen, D.: http://www.accesswave.ca/~hgunn/special/papers/hypertxt/cle.html
12. de Freitas, S.: Using games and simulations for supporting learning. Learning, Media and Technology Special Issue on Gaming 31(4), 343–358 (2006)
13. Nonaka, I., Takeuchi, H.: The Knowledge-Creating Company: How Japanese Companies Create the Dynamics of Innovation. Oxford University Press, New York (1995)
14. Kerka, S.: Learning Styles and Electronic Information: Trends and Issues Alert (1998)
15. Williams, G., McTighe, J.: Understanding by design. Association for Supervision and Curriculum Development, Alexandria (1998)
16. de Freitas, S., Oliver, M.: A four dimensional framework for the evaluation and assessment of educational games. Computer Assisted Learning (2005)
17. Garris, R., Ahlers, R., Driskell, J.E.: Games, motivation, and learning: A research and practice model. In: Simulation & Gaming, vol. 33(4), Sage Publications, Thousand Oaks (December 2002)
18. de Freitas, S., Jarvis, S.: Towards a development approach for serious games. In: Connolly, T.M., Stansfield, M., Boyle, E. (eds.) Games-Based Learning Advancements for Multi-Sensory Human-Computer Interfaces: Techniques and Effective Practices. IGI Global, Hershey (2008)
19. Kirkpatrick, D.L.: Evaluating Training Programs. Berrett-Koehler Publishers, Inc., San Francisco (1994)
20. de Freitas, S.: Emerging technologies for learning, Research Report, vol. 3 (2008), http://partners.becta.org.uk/upload
21. Huizinga, J.: Homo Ludens: A Study of the Play Element in Culture. Beacon Press, Boston (1955, originally published in 1938)
22. Saunders, R.L.: The genesis of a virtual world revisited. International Journal of Web-Based Communities 3(3), 271–282 (2007)

A Method for Group Extraction in Complex Social Networks

Piotr Bródka[1], Katarzyna Musial[2], and Przemysław Kazienko[1]

[1] Institute of Informatics, Wrocław University of Technology
Wyb.Wyspiańskiego 27, 50-370 Wrocław, Poland
[2] School of Design, Engineering & Computing, Bournemouth University, Poole, Dorset, BH12 5BB, United Kingdom
piotr.brodka@pwr.wroc.pl, kmusial@bournemouth.ac.uk,
kazienko@pwr.wroc.pl

Abstract. The extraction of social groups from social networks existing among employees in the company, its customers or users of various computer systems became one of the research areas of growing importance. Once we have discovered the groups, we can utilise them, in different kinds of recommender systems or in the analysis of the team structure and communication within a given population.

The shortcomings of the existing methods for community discovery and lack of their applicability in multi-layered social networks were the inspiration to create a new group extraction method in complex multi-layered social networks. The main idea that stands behind this new concept is to utilise the modified version of a measure called by authors multi-layered clustering coefficient.

Keywords: Multi-layered social network, groups discovery in social network, multi-layered clustering coefficient, social network analysis.

1 Introduction

In the recent few decades, the area of complex networks has attracted more and more scientists from different research fields. All complex networked systems have some common features such as: (i) skewed distribution of connections, (ii) small degree of separation between vertices, (iii) high clustering rate, (iv) non-trivial temporal evolution and last but not the least (v) presence of motifs, hierarchies and communities [3], [10]. The feature that is investigated by authors in this paper is the last enumerated one, i.e. the existence of communities whereas the subset of complex systems that is analysed are social networks.

A social network (SN) is one of the type of complex networks in which nodes are people (social entities) and the edges denote the relationships between various people [13]. The concept of SN, first coined in 1954 by J. A. Barnes [1], has been in a field of study of modern sociology, geography, social psychology, organizational studies

M.D. Lytras et al. (Eds.): WSKS 2010, Part I, CCIS 111, pp. 238–247, 2010.

and computer science for the last few decades. Social networks and social network analysis supported by computer science provide the opportunity to expand other branches of knowledge. Lately, we have experienced the rapid growth of social structures supported by communication technologies and the variety of Internet- and Web-based services. This article focuses on discovering the communities within the complex multi-layered social networks (CMSN) extracted from different systems based on communication technologies, in which users interact or cooperate with each other by means of various dedicated services. The main characteristic of CMSN is that they consist of many layers, corresponding to different kinds of relationship.

The extraction and analysis of groups in social networks is not a new concept and as presented in Related Work section has been investigated by many scientists. However, none of the research addresses this issue for networks where more than one type of relationship exists and this is a goal of the presented research.

The next, second section of the article includes the description of the most commonly utilised methods to group extraction. In section 3, the concept of multi-layered social network is presented. After that the new method and its characteristics together with preliminary experiments are described. Finally, the conclusions and future work in the area of group extraction are depicted.

2 Related Work

Many approaches to the problem of community identification in social networks which consist of one type of connections have been developed. The existing methods origin both from the graph theory and data mining techniques. In the former, the notion of a group is formalised by the general property of cohesion among community members and the evaluation of this feature determines whether the set of people can be seen as a group or not. The assessment of cohesion can be made based on the complete mutuality, reachability, diameter and nodal degree [13]. Other methods that are used in extracting communities are fuzzy clustering approaches and specifically clique percolation methods that will allow the groups to overlap [8], [7].

Girvan and Newman analyzed a network of scientific collaboration [4]. Scientific collaboration is associated to co-authorship: two scientists are connected if they have written at least one paper together. The authors invented and used a new method on a collaboration network of scientists working at the Santa Fe Institute. Obtained groups reflect research divisions at the Santa Fe Institute. The community structure of scientific collaboration networks has been investigated by many other authors. Radicchi et al analyzed network of scientific collaborations and network of college football teams to test improved version of Girvan and Newman method [9]. Some other types of collaboration networks have been studied as well. Gleiser and Danon investigated a collaboration network of jazz musicians [5]. Musicians are connected if they have played in the same band. Extracted, by Girvan and Newman method, communities reflect both racial segregation and geographical separation.

Tyler et al. also used modified version of Girvan and Newman algorithm to study a network of e-mail exchanges between workers of HP Labs [12]. The method enables to measure the degree of membership of each member within a community and allows communities to overlap. The extracted groups matched quite closely the organization of the Labs in departments and project groups. The same method have been used to find communities of related genes [15].

Blondel et al. developed a fast hierarchical modularity optimization technique and used it to analyze a huge network of mobile phone communications between 2.6 million users of a Belgian phone operator [2]. The group extraction and analysis, performed, reveals six hierarchical levels. The 1st level consists of 261 groups with more than 100 vertices. Users are split in two main groups which reflect the linguistic division of Belgian population.

Traud et al. used data from Facebook and created a network of friendships between students of different American universities; students were connected if they were friends on Facebook [11]. Newman's spectral optimization of modularity was used to detect the communities. The results were compared to demographic information on the students' populations, one finds that communities are organized by class year or by House (dormitory).

However, the domain analysis has indicated that there is no group extraction method dedicated to the multi-layered social networks. Moreover, there is lack of research that would point out whether the existing methods for community discovery in regular social networks can be utilized in multi-layer social networks.

3 Complex Multi-layered Social Networks

The structure that will be analysed in this research is *a network*, i.e. set of interconnected nodes. In this paper, the networks extracted from different systems based on communication technologies will be investigated. The units (nodes) in such CMSNs are digital representations of people who use email services, telecommunication systems, multimedia sharing systems, access blogosphere etc. The node is also called identifier (*id*). Based on interactions between users their mutual relationships are extracted and in the next step the communities can be identified. Due to diversity of communication channels the analyzed networks are *multi-layered,* i.e. they consist of more than one type of relationship. Different relations can emerge from different communication channels, i.e. based on each communication channel separate relation that can be also called a layer of a network is created. These various relations between two users can be grouped into tie. The concept of multi-layered complex social network is presented in Fig. 1.

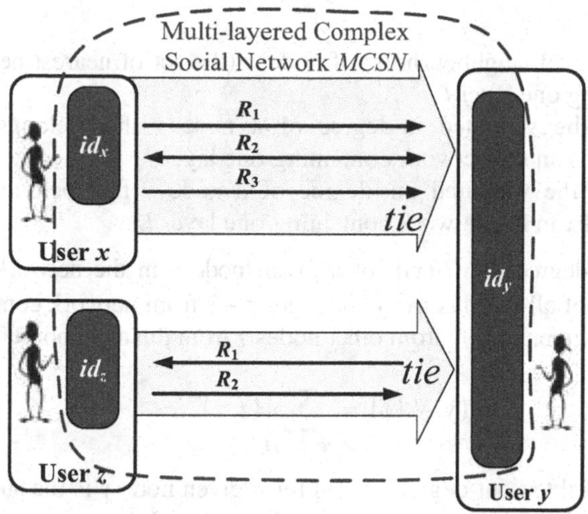

Fig. 1. The concept of multi-layered complex social network extracted from systems where users are represented by their digital identities

4 Multi-layered Clustering Coefficient in the Complex Multi-layered Social Network

Before the general concept of the method can be presented, three new measures need to be described: local clustering coefficient tailored for the needs of CMSN – multi-layered clustering coefficient (*MCC*) and two measures that respect either extended nearest neighbourhoods (*MCCEN*) or reduced nearest neighbourhoods (*MCCRN*). All these concepts were developed to be utilized in the group extraction within CMSN, see Sec. 5. Their detailed description is presented in this section.

4.1 Local Clustering Coefficient in the 1-Layered Social Network

The regular local clustering coefficient is a measure of degree to which nodes in the network structure tend to cluster together. It quantifies how close the node's neighbours are to being a fully connected graph. Local clustering coefficient was introduced by Duncan J. Watts and Steven Strogatz who utilized it in order to determine whether a graph is a small-world network [14].

The local clustering coefficient $CC_l(x)$ for node x in the network that contains single layer l in which the relationships are weighted and directed, is calculated as follows:

$$CC_l(x) = \frac{\sum_{y \in N_l(x)} \left(in_l(y, N_l(x)) + out_l(y, N_l(x))\right)}{2 \cdot card(N_l(x))}, \tag{1}$$

where:

$N_l(x)$ – the 1–level neighbourhood of node x (the set of nearest neighbours) in the network containing one layer l,

$in^l(y,N_l(x))$ – the weighted in-degree of a node y that belongs to the 1-level neighbourhood of x in the network containing one layer l,

$out_l(y,N_l(x))$ – the weighted out-degree of a node y that belongs to the 1-level neighbourhood of x in the network containing one layer l.

The weighted in-degree $in_l(y,N(x))$ for a given node y in the network containing one layer l is the sum of all weights $w(z,y)$ of edges $z \rightarrow y$ from network containing one layer l that income to a given node y from other nodes z from the neighbourhood $N_l(x)$.

$$in_l(y, N_l(x)) = \sum_{z \in N_l(x)} w(z, y), \tag{2}$$

Similarly, the weighted out-degree $out_l(y)$ for a given node y is the sum of all weights $w(y,z)$ of the outgoing edges $y \rightarrow z$ that come from x's neighbours z.

Note that if the sum of weights of outgoing edges for a given node is always 1, then $CC_l(x)$ is from the range (0;1]. It reaches 1, if the neighbours $y \in N_l(x)$ have outgoing relationships only towards other nodes $z \in N_l(x)$. It means that there does not exist edges $y \rightarrow x$ or $y \rightarrow k$, where k is a node outside $N_l(x)$.

4.2 Multi-layered Local Clustering Coefficient for Complex Multi-layered Social Networks

A measure called the multi-layered local clustering coefficient $MCC(x)$ needs to be introduced as not the simple one-layered social networks but the multi-layered social networks are investigated in this paper. The measure $MCC(x)$ in the multi-layered environment, is the average of clustering coefficients $CC_l(x)$, see Eq. 1, from all component layers l. Thus, each layer is treated here as a separate network containing one, lth layer. The value of $MCC(x)$ is computed in the following way:

$$MCC(x) = \frac{\sum_{l \in L} CC_l(x)}{card(L)}, \tag{3}$$

where: l is the index of the lth layer from the set L of all layers in a given CMSN.

Note that $CC_l(x)$ is calculated separately for each layer l, i.e. it takes into account only the neighbourhood of x that exists only in layer l.

4.3 Multi-layered Clustering Coefficient in the Extended Neighbourhood

The second measure – multi-layered clustering coefficient in the extended neighbourhood (*MCCEN*) is in its concept similar to the multi-layered clustering coefficient *MCC* but the neighbourhoods used by *MCCEN* are defined differently. The measure *MCCEN*(x) denotes, to which extent the nearest neighbourhoods existing in different layers for a given user x overlap each other. First, we need to define the extended, multi-layered neighbourhood *EN*(x) for a given node x in the set L of layers. It is a union of neighbourhoods from all layers:

$$EN(x) = \bigcup_{l \in L} N_l(x), \tag{4}$$

where: $N_l(x)$ – the nearest neighbours of node x in the layer l.

The multi-layered clustering coefficient in the extended neighbourhood $MCCEN(x)$ for a given node x, respects the extended neighbourhoods $EN(x)$ instead of neighbourhoods from only one layer $N_l(x)$, compare Eq. 1, as follows:

$$MCCEN(x) = \frac{\sum_{l \in L} \sum_{y \in EN(x)} \left(in_l(y, EN(x)) + out_l(y, EN(x)) \right)}{2 \cdot card(EN(x)) \cdot card(L)}. \tag{5}$$

4.4 Multi-layered Clustering Coefficient in the Reduced Neighbourhood

Similarly to multi-layered clustering coefficient in the extended neighbourhood (*MCCEN*), we can define multi-layered clustering coefficient in the reduced neighbourhood (*MCCRN*). It takes into account yet another reduced neighbourhood $RN(x)$ of a given node x, i.e. the set of neighbours who occur in every layer. Hence, the reduced neighbourhood $RN(x)$ is an intersection of sets – neighbourhoods from all layers:

$$RN(x) = \bigcap_{l \in L} N_l(x). \tag{6}$$

The multi-layered clustering coefficient in the reduced neighbourhood $MCCRN(x)$ for a given node x, is computed in the following way:

$$MCCRN(x) = \frac{\sum_{l \in L} \sum_{y \in EN(x)} \left(in_l(y, RN(x)) + out_l(y, RN(x)) \right)}{2 \cdot card(RN(x)) \cdot card(L)}. \tag{7}$$

5 A New Method for Group Extraction in the Complex Multi-layered Social Network Based on Multi-layered Clustering Coefficients

5.1 Why Do We Need Yet Another Method for Group Extraction

The concept of group and methods for its extraction is not fully addressed even in the networks where only one type of relationship exists as the definition of a term 'group' in the literature is inconsistent and sometimes even researchers use a group concept without giving it a precise formal definition [13]. This task is even more challenging in CMSN as it is very hard to establish which types of relationships determine that a set of users and their connections can be called 'a group'. Thus, the main contribution of the research within this topic to the field of community extraction and analysis would be to create a definition of 'a group' within the multi-layered environment and to develop the methods that enable to extract these groups from the gathered data about users and their interactions. On the other hand, the groups can be discovered and investigated in each of the layer separately (each layer is created based on one type of relation).

5.2 General Concept of Method for Group Extraction

There are two general approaches to extract groups in multi-layered environment: (i) extracting groups in each layer separately and then merge the communities throughout the layers, (ii) first flatten the network into one layer and then discover groups within it. In the new method proposed in this article, the communities are extracted from the network as a whole not from each layer separately.

The general concept of clustering is selection of "strong nodes", i.e. nodes with strong enough multi-layered clustering coefficients, create a group from their neighbourhoods and join to this group the neighbourhoods of "strong neighbours". The process proceeds as follow:

STEP 1: Calculate all three multi-layered clustering coefficients for multi-layered social network, namely, $MCC(x)$, $MCCEN(x)$, and $MCCRN(x)$ separately for each node x in the network, see Section 4.
STEP 2: Extract set A of "strong nodes x", for which all three multi-layered clustering coefficients exceed appropriate thresholds: α, β, γ, i.e. $MCC(x)>\alpha$, $MCCEN(x)>\beta$, and $MCCRN(x)>\gamma$. For all nodes in A, identify their 1-level extended neighbourhoods $EN(x)$, see Eq. 4. Neighbourhoods $EN(x)$ are achieved as by-products while computing $MCCEN(x)$, see Sec. 4.3. Initialize an empty set B of already processed nodes.
STEP 3: The entire ith group is created within this step, starting from the extended neighbourhoods of a strong node from set A, next going throughout the neighbourhoods of the neighbours.

a) Create a new empty group $G_i = \varnothing$ and initialize set T_i with node x taken from set A: $T_i=\{x\}$. T_i is a set of strong and leading nodes to be processed for G_i.
c) Take the first/next node y from T_i and fill group G_i with the extended neighbourhood of y: $G_i=G_i \cup EN(y)$ and add node y to already processed nodes: $B=B\cup\{y\}$. Remove node y from set A: $A=A\setminus\{y\}$. At the first run $y=x$.
d) Identify not yet processed leading nodes z within $EN(y)$ using the following criteria: $MCC(x)>\alpha'$, $MCCEN(x)>\beta'$, $MCCRN(x)>\gamma'$, $\alpha'\leq\alpha$, $\beta'\leq\beta$ and $\gamma'\leq\gamma$. Create set S from these nodes.
e) Remove from S all already processed nodes: $S=S\setminus B$ and add new set S to T_i for further processing: $T_i=T_i\cup S$. The neighbourhoods of S members will be joint to G_i.
f) Remove the just processed node y from T_i: $T_i=T_i\setminus\{y\}$.
g) Go to step 4c unless set T_i is empty.

STEP 4: Repeat entire step 4 until set A of "strong nodes" for processing is empty.
STEP 5: Create a separate group of outliers from all nodes that do not belong to any group G_i.

Note that a new group is created with each iteration of step 3. Finally, we achieve as many groups as many times step 3 is invoked, plus eventually one group of outliers created in step 5.

6 Experiments

The main goal of the experiments was to investigate the characteristics of proposed in the paper metrics that serve to assess the extent to which the neighbourhoods of user are clustered within the complex multi-layered social networks.

The experiments were performed on 1000 users from the Flickr system where eleven different layers have been identified. These layers include: tags used by more than one user R^t, user groups R^g, photos added by users to their favourites R^{fa}, R^{af}, R^{ff}, opinions about photos created by users R^{oa}, R^{ao}, R^{oo}, and the relations derived from the contact lists R^c, R^{ac}, R^{cac}. The detailed information about the data set can be found in [6].

The outcomes of the experiments have shown that the value of *MCC* coefficient varies from 0 to 0.53, the value of *MCCEN* is from the range 0 to 0.61 and the value of *MCCRN* from 0 to 0.19. There were only 7 users whose *MCCRN* was greater than 0. All the results are presented in Fig. 2, 3, and 4.

It can be noticed that the multi-layered clustering coefficient for reduced neighbourhood equals 0 for most users and it means that there are only few users who have similar neighbourhoods on all layers. This implicates that a user maintains the relationships with different neighbourhood on different layers. This is also confirmed by the relatively high *MCCEN* value (average is 0.48).

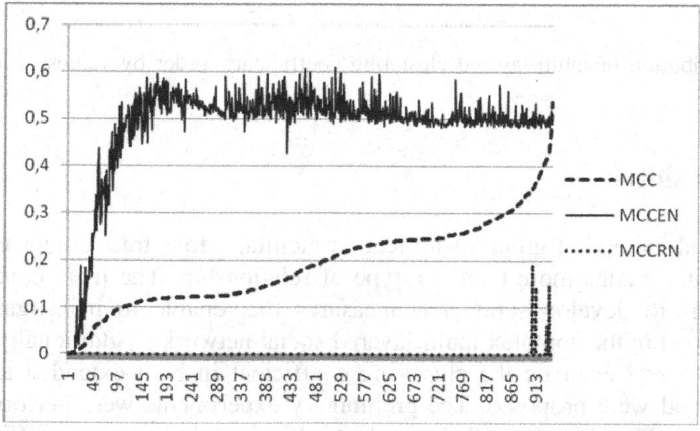

Fig. 2. Distribution of multi-layered clustering coefficients; order by value of *MCC*

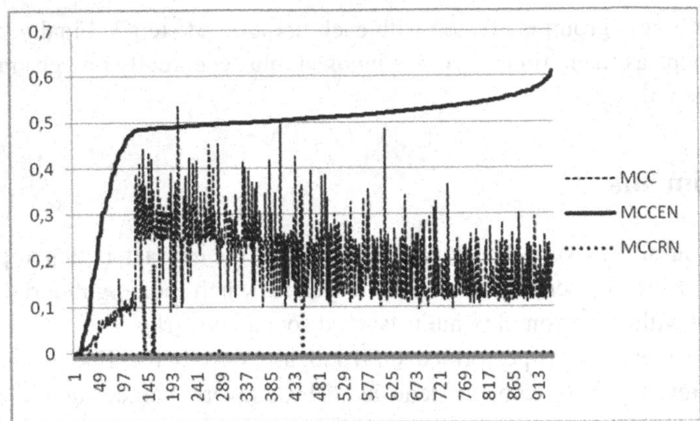

Fig. 3. Distribution of multi-layered clustering coefficients ; order by values of *MCCEN*

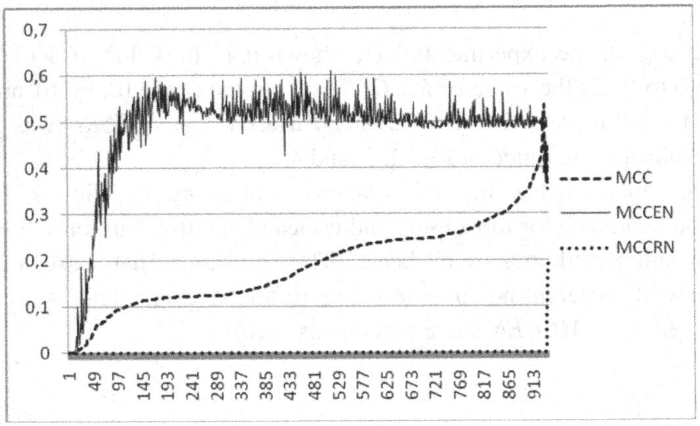

Fig. 4. Distribution of multi-layered clustering coefficients; order by values of *MCCRN* and *MCC*

7 Conclusions

The proposed method of group identification facilitates to extract groups in the social network that contains more than one type of relationship. The main contribution of this paper is to develop some new measures that enable to investigate the user neighbourhood in the complex multi-layered social networks. Additionally, the methods to create and evaluate the clustering coefficient in both extended and reduced neighbourhood were proposed. The preliminary experiments were performed on the Flickr system. They have revealed that the multi-layered clustering coefficient in the extended neighbourhood *MCCEN* is relatively high and reaches in average the level of 0.61, whereas the multi-layered clustering coefficient in reduced neighbourhood *MCCRN* equals 0 for most users. The values of multi-layered local clustering coefficient *MCC* vary from 0 to 0.53.

The interesting extension of current work will be to investigate the influence of these coefficients on the size and structure of the groups discovered. Future work will also focus on the comparison of the communities extracted using the proposed method and the investigation of correlation between these groups. This will enable to define which types of relations are utilized in the process of group formation and based on which of them the more or less sustainable groups emerge.

Acknowledgments. This work has been supported by the Polish Ministry of Science and Higher Education, the development project, 2009-11.

References

1. Barnes, J.A.: Class and Committees in a Norwegian Island Parish. Human Relations 7, 39–58 (1954)
2. Blondel, V.D., Guillaume, J.-L., Lambiotte, R., Lefebvre, E.: Fast unfolding of communities in large networks. J. Stat. Mech. P10008 (2008)
3. Caldarelli, G., Vespignani, A. (eds.): Large Scale Structure and Dynamics of Complex Networks, From Information Technology to Finance and Natural Science, Complex Systems and Interdisciplinary Science, vol. 2. World Scientific Publishing Co. Pte. Ltd., Singapore (2007)
4. Girvan, M., Newman, M.E.J.: Community structure in social and biological networks. Proc. Natl. Acad. Sci. USA 99(12), 7821–7826 (2002)
5. Gleiser, P., Danon, L.: Community structure in jazz. Adv. Complex Syst. 6, 565 (2003)
6. Kazienko, P., Musial, K., Kajdanowicz, T.: Multidimensional Social Network and Its Application to the Social Recommender System. IEEE Transactions on Systems, Man and Cybernetics - Part A: Systems and Humans (2010) (in press)
7. Palla, G., Barabasi, A.-L., Vicsek, T.: Quantifying social group evolution. Nature 446, 664–667 (2007)
8. Palla, G., Derenyi, I., Farkas, I., Vicsek, T.: Uncovering the overlapping community structure of complex networks in nature and society. Nature 435, 814–818 (2005)
9. Radicchi, F., Castellano, C., Cecconi, F., Loreto, V., Parisi, D.: Defining and identifying communities in networks. PNAS 101, 2658–2663 (2004)
10. Strogatz, S.H.: Exploring complex networks. Nature 410(6825), 268–276 (1998)
11. Traud, A.L., Kelsic, E.D., Mucha, P.J., Porter, M.A.: Community structure in online collegiate social networks, eprint arXiv:0809.0690
12. Tyler, J.R., Wilkinson, D.M., Huberman, B.A.: Email as spectroscopy: Automated discovery of community structure within organizations. In: Communities and Technologies, pp. 81–96. Kluwer, B.V., Deventer (2003)
13. Wasserman, S., Faust, K.: Social network analysis: Methods and applications. Cambridge University Press, New York (1994)
14. Watts, D.J., Strogatz, S.: Collective dynamics of 'small-world' networks. Nature 393, 440–444 (1998)
15. Wilkinson, D.M., Huberman, B.A.: A method for finding communities of related genes. Proc. Natl. Acad. Sci. U.S.A. 101, 5241–5248 (2004)

Usability Evaluation of Web-Based Collaboration Support Systems: The Case of CoPe_it!

Nikos Karousos[1], Spyros Papaloukas[1], Nektarios Kostaras[1], Michalis Xenos[1], Manolis Tzagarakis[2], and Nikos Karacapilidis[3]

[1] Software Quality Research Group, Hellenic Open University
26 222 Patras, Greece
{karousos,s.papaluk,nkostaras,xenos}@eap.gr

[2] Dept. of Economics, University of Patras
26 504 Patras, Greece
tzagara@upatras.gr

[3] IMIS Lab, MEAD, University of Patras
26 504 Patras, Greece
nikos@mech.upatras.gr

Abstract. Usability is considered as a very significant factor towards the wide acceptance of software applications. Although the usability evaluation can take place in different forms, the entire evaluation procedure usually follows predefined ways according to a classification of the common characteristics of software applications. However, contemporary Web 2.0 applications, which aim at both social network development and collaboration support, reveal the need for modifying the settings of the evaluation procedure. This is due to some unique characteristics of these applications, such as the support of both synchronous and asynchronous collaboration, the use of common spaces for working and information exchanging, and the advanced notification and awareness services. This paper explores these applications' particularities with respect to the way the whole usability evaluation procedure is affected and proposes a composite evaluation technique based on the development of appropriate heuristics that is suitable for such cases. The aforementioned issues are elaborated through the case of CoPe_it!, a Web 2.0 tool that facilitates and enhances argumentative collaboration.

Keywords: Collaboration Support Systems; Usability; Evaluation.

1 Introduction

Usability remains a critical issue in both the design and implementation of any software application with high interactivity. Usable systems have great potential to become widely accepted, while systems with very rich functionality may become useless if they are difficult to be used. In order to ensure a high level of usability in software applications, researches have developed an open set of usability evaluation methods that can be followed in different phases of the software lifecycle and can be

M.D. Lytras et al. (Eds.): WSKS 2010, Part I, CCIS 111, pp. 248–258, 2010.

also combined for optimal results. These methods are categorized – according to their characteristics – as analytic, empirical and inquiry [1], [2], [3]. The selection of the appropriate method (or set of methods) to be applied in a particular system's evaluation still remains an open research issue. Until now, the most common way to evaluate software is first to classify it to a predefined software class and then to follow an evaluation procedure that best fits to this class (according to empirical facts).

However, recent advances in computing and Internet technologies, together with the advent of the Web 2.0 era, resulted to the development of online web-based collaboration support tools that cannot be easily classified under the traditional software classes, since they offer a wide set of novel functionalities and diverse visual representations to an open set of potential users. Such tools offer people an unprecedented level of flexibility and convenience to participate in complex collaborative activities such as communication, online debates, distance learning, co-authoring, decision support, mind maps, common workspaces, problem solving etc. The usability factor of these tools cannot be evaluated by following an existing evaluation methodology and has to be revised based (but not limited) on their unique characteristics.

This paper explores the particularities of web-based collaboration support systems, with respect to the way the whole usability evaluation procedure is affected, and proposes a composite evaluation technique that is suitable for such cases. More specifically, Section 2 sketches the most widely accepted usability evaluation methods classified under two main categories and discusses the ways they could combine for the evaluation of applications. Section 3 elaborates critical issues that affect the settings of the evaluation methodology for contemporary web-based collaboration support systems, while section 4 presents the proposed evaluation approach for such cases. Finally, Section 5 presents a case study for the proposed methodology; this study concerns CoPe_it! [4], a Web 2.0 tool that facilitates and enhances argumentative collaboration.

2 Usability Evaluation: Methods and Techniques

The term usability is described in the ISO 9241-11 standard [5] as "*the extent to which a product can be used by specified users to achieve specified goals with effectiveness, efficiency and satisfaction in a specified context of use*". Effectiveness is defined as the accuracy and completeness with which users achieve specified goals. Efficiency measures the resources expended in relation to the accuracy and completeness with which users achieve goals. Finally, satisfaction is the freedom from discomfort, and positive attitudes towards the use of the product. Nielsen [6] further described usability according to five basic parameters, namely: (a) ease and speed of learning of system use, (b) efficiency to use, (c) easiness to remember system use after a certain period of time, (d) reduced numbers of user errors and easy recovery from them, and (e) subjective satisfaction of users.

The evaluation of usability has three main goals: the assessment of software's functionality, the assessment of users' experience during interaction with the interface and the identification of specific problems of the software. Usability evaluation can be performed using various methods. The most common categories these methods belong to are the *analytic* and the *empirical* [1], [2], [3].

Analytic methods are based either on standards and rules or on theoretical models that simulate a user's behavior. These methods are often used in a usability laboratory at the stage of the syntax of specifications before the development of the prototypes and without the participation of users. This category includes two types of evaluation methods: (i) *inspections*, which include heuristic evaluation and walkthroughs, and (ii) *theoretically-based models*, which are used to predict user performance. Heuristic evaluation employs mainly usability experts, but typical users may be used as well to identify any usability problem. This is achieved with the guidance of heuristics, which is a mixture of rules that use common sense knowledge, usability guidelines and standards. Walkthroughs involve mainly usability experts walking through scenarios with prototypes of the application. Finally, theoretically-based models are used for comparing the efficacy of different interfaces of the same system and the optimal arrangement and location of features on the interface base [7]. A main characteristic of analytical evaluation is that users do not need to be present [8].

Empirical methods are based on the development and evaluation of the behaviour and the characteristics of a prototype or a completed system. These methods can be employed either in a usability laboratory or wherever the system is in full operation. The participants of the evaluation process can be both representative users and usability experts. The empirical methods can be further divided into two main categories: *experimental* and *inquiry*. The most commonly employed experimental methods are *performance measurement*, *thinking aloud protocol* and *user actions logging*. Performance measurement provides quantitative measurements of a software system's performance when users execute predefined actions or even complete operations. Thinking aloud protocol is a method that focuses on the measurement of the effectiveness of a system and the user's satisfaction. According to this method, users interact with the system, while they state aloud their thoughts, opinions, emotions and sentiments regarding the system. Finally, user actions logging involves techniques that record the actions of users while they interact with a software product. The most common of them are note taking, voice recording, video recording, computer logging and user logging.

Finally, *inquiry methods* focus on the examination of the usability characteristics of a software system by measuring users' opinion. The most popular of them are *user questionnaires*, *user interviews*, *focus groups* and *field observation*. The use of questionnaires provides valuable feedback and obtains answers to specific questions from a large group of people, especially in the case that the target group is spread across a wide geographical area [7]. Interviews form a structured way of evaluating a software system, where the researcher is in direct contact with the user. The questions of the interview follow a hierarchical structure, through which the general opinion of the product is formed, while more specific quality characteristics are also considered. Focus group is a method according to which a group of about 10 users is formed under the supervision of a coordinator, who is in charge of the topics of the conversation. At the end of this conversation, the coordinator gathers their conclusions on the quality of the software product. Finally, in field observation the researcher observes the users at their working place, while they are using and interacting with the software product.

In general, usability evaluation can be performed using methods from the above-mentioned two broad categories (analytic and empirical). Each of these categories comprises several methods that may be performed independently, in order to evaluate a specific usability aspect of a system. The settings of a complete evaluation procedure that includes the selection of the appropriate methods, the implementation of the evaluation stage and the results analysis usually depend on the type of the software applications. Based on evaluators' experience, the existing infrastructure and the applications' main characteristics, the settings may be modified in order to develop a suitable evaluation procedure for a particular application. However, the development of innovative software applications, such as the contemporary web-based collaboration support systems, raises the need for a deep pre-evaluation analysis of their characteristics in order to determine an appropriate usability evaluation procedure.

3 Critical Issues about Usability Evaluation in Contemporary Web-Based Collaboration Support Systems

The selection of the evaluation techniques is usually based on the type of software applications. However, contemporary collaboration support systems cannot be easily classified as an ordinary type of applications with respect to the evaluation purpose. These systems usually cover a wide range of functionalities and offer different visual representations in the same environment. Moreover, the exploitation of the Web 2.0 capabilities in such systems increased the level of complexity since social networks and different semantics over the same data can be supported. In this context, these systems should be examined with respect to their particularities towards the extraction of a set of important characteristics that may aid the determination of a suitable evaluation procedure.

The main idea, in which collaborative software is based on, is that such systems should focus on the support of both individual and team work. It is required to design environments that can handle and represent different kinds of interactions while they can provide intelligent functionality in order to assist participants to problem solving. Furthermore, as contemporary collaborative software evolves and migrates into the Internet itself, it contributes to the development of the so called Web 2.0, bringing a set of web-based collaborative features within corporate networks. These include document sharing and group authoring, group calendar, instant messaging, web conferencing, etc. Apart from the above features, Web 2.0 collaborative applications are nowadays characterized by their ability to work with and manage a large number of participants organized by themselves in social networks. In such cases, issues like awareness, personalization and adaptation are also playing a critical role for the systems' exploitation; at the same time, they may complicate the usability evaluation process. Below is a non-exhaustive list of critical characteristics of contemporary Web-based collaboration support systems that have to be taken into consideration for the design of an effective evaluation procedure:

- *Context of a system's use* [9]. Individuals may collaborate while being co-located or geographically dispersed; besides, they may collaborate in a synchronous or asynchronous mode (not depending on others to be around at the same time). The above can affect both the human interface and the types of interactions between participants.
- *Individuals' and teams' work.* Collaborative work usually aims at the establishment of a solution in a team's problem. For this purpose, individuals may work alone or as a part of a team. For each case, the evaluation method may consider the role of each single user inside the context of the team's objectives.
- *Appropriation.* An individual or group adapts a technology to their own particular situation; the technology may be appropriated in a manner completely unintended by the designers [10], [11]. In such cases, the more generic purpose the collaborative applications are, the more different scenarios for collaboration they may support. However, the overall evaluation procedure on generic purpose software is not an easy task since it highly depends on the selection of one or more representative scenarios.
- *Awareness.* Individuals working together need to be able to gain some level of shared knowledge about each other's activities [12]. Awareness may be achieved with various techniques within and outside the scope of an applications' environment and may include different technological means (email, mobile notification etc) that have to be considered while evaluating the whole application.
- *Cognitive overhead and information overload [13].* Diverse types of data and knowledge resources may appear during the exchange of numerous ideas about the solution of a specific issue. In such cases, individuals usually have to spend much effort to conceptualize the current state of the collaboration and grasp its contents. Specifications for providing multiple projections, scalable filtering and timely processing of the associated big amounts of data should be considered and supported while evaluating the application.
- *Social behavior [13].* The representation and visualization of dynamically changing social structures, relationships and interactions taking place in a collaborative environment with multiple stakeholders are of major importance. Perception and modeling of actors, groups and organizations in the diversity of collaborative contexts are usually supported. What is required is development and utilization of appropriate mechanisms that perceive given structures in order to extract useful information and enable adaptation.
- *Expression of tacit knowledge [13].* A community of people is actually an environment where tacit knowledge (i.e. knowledge that the members do not realize they possess or knowledge that members cannot express with the means provided) predominantly exists and dynamically evolves. Such knowledge must be efficiently and effectively represented in order to be

further exploited in a collaborative environment. However, the subjectivity of such representation may lead to misunderstandings.

Past studies in the area of available practices in usability measuring revealed a lack of existing methodologies in such Web-based tools [14]. Thus, the adoption of new evaluation methodologies became crucial.

4 The Proposed Usability Evaluation Methodology

A set of evaluation methods for the measurement of usability of the games Civilization and Second Life were carried out in the Software Quality Evaluation Laboratory of Hellenic Open University (HOU) by the Software Quality Research Group [15-17]. The results and the experience gained have shown that the combination of methods amplifies the progress of the experimental procedure, providing that the conducting conditions simulate reality adequately and the users could interact and simultaneously express their thoughts in a very easy and spontaneous manner [18]. These methods were used to categorize usability problems through the observation of users and validate them by the use of an integrated experiment. The combined methods were used both in HOU's laboratory, under the discrete attendance of the usability experts, as well as in the users' own places.

The development of the proposed methodology consists of four main stages:

- Analysis of existing scientific studies, identification and classification of usability problems for web-based collaboration systems, and extraction of a set of specifications that deals with both user interface principles and application specific characteristics.
- Observing users interacting with the system, while the evaluation expert records the usability problems they may encounter (some of these problems already exist in a list produced in the previous stage). At this stage, known heuristics are extended to more specific ones, according to the particular requirements.
- Description of how usability problems can be resolved through the creation of heuristics. Although some heuristics have derived from previous studies, they can be adapted for Web-based collaboration support systems. It is, therefore, imperative at this point to categorize heuristics.
- Usage and validation of heuristics by an integrated experimental procedure using three different methods. First, heuristic evaluation by usability experts, during which most usability problems of the software are detected (thus indicating the effectiveness of our heuristics). The heuristics verification is achieved by using a new observation and logging combined with the thinking aloud protocol and, finally, questionnaires adapted upon the above heuristics.

5 Evaluating CoPe_it!

CoPe_it! is an innovative web-based tool that complies with collaborative practices to provide members of communities with the appropriate means to manage individual and collective knowledge, and collaborate towards the solution of diverse issues (Figure 1). CoPe_it! achieves this by introducing the notion of *incremental formalization* of argumentative collaboration, in which the tool considers semantics as an emergent aspect and gives control over formalization to the user [13]. As the collaboration proceeds, more advanced services can be available. Once the collaboration has been formalized to a certain point, CoPe_it! can exhibit an active behavior facilitating the decision making process. CoPe_it! enables synchronous and asynchronous collaboration. It adopts a spatial metaphor to depict collaboration in a 2-dimensional space and supports the process of *information triage* [13].

Although CoPe_it! is a tool that can be used in several scenarios – from informal discussions and content structuring and sharing to medical decision support and diplomacy – its usage remains at a low level. Traffic reports (using Google Analytics) show that there are many users that visit CoPe_it! but only a small percentage of them revisits it again. The tool's usability evaluation was expected to give valuable results that will aid its designers to a forthcoming user interface revision.

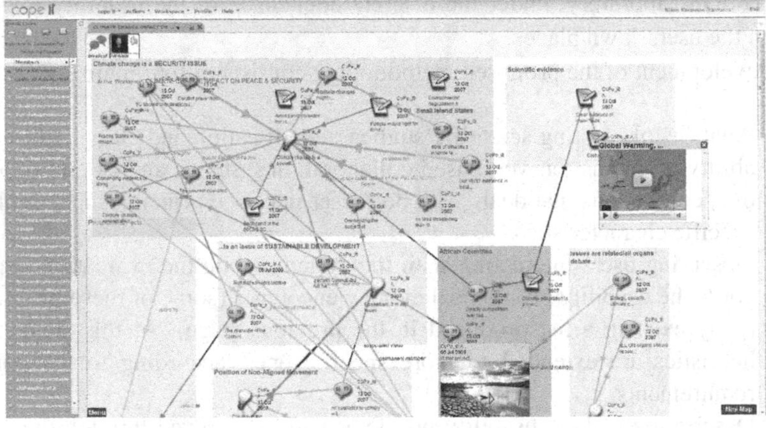

Fig. 1. Collaboration taking place in a workspace of CoPe_it!

The evaluation of CoPe_it! is based on the proposed methodology, in which a set of heuristics, adapted according to the requirements of the software under evaluation, was developed. Usability experts using the heuristic evaluation method have detected a number of usability errors. The results of heuristic evaluation will be validated and extended in the future by the use of experimental and inquiry evaluation methods like users logging, thinking aloud protocol and questionnaires. More precisely, the idea was that heuristics can be developed for specific software categories like Web-based collaboration support systems. The validation of our heuristics can be made by evaluating CoPe_it! and by developing principles that describe the usability problems that may occur.

Table 1. Usability Heuristics

Heuristic Rule	*Summary*
H1.1. Visibility of system status	The system should always keep users informed about what is going on through appropriate feedback within reasonable time.
H1.2. Match between system and the real world	The system should speak the user's language, with words, phrases and concepts familiar to the user, rather than system-oriented terms. Follow real-world conventions, making information appear in a natural and logical order.
H1.3. User control and freedom	Users often choose system functions by mistake and will need a clearly marked "emergency exit" to leave the unwanted state without having to go through an extended dialogue. Support undo and redo.
H1.4. Consistency and standards	Users should not have to wonder whether different words, situations, or actions mean the same thing. Follow platform conventions.
H1.5. Error prevention	Even better than good error messages is a careful design which prevents a problem from occurring in the first place. Either eliminate error-prone conditions or check for them and present users with a confirmation option before they commit to the action.
H1.6. Recognition rather than recall	Minimize the user's memory load by making objects, actions, and options visible. The user should not have to remember information from one part of the dialogue to another. Instructions for use of the system should be visible or easily retrievable whenever appropriate.
H1.7. Flexibility and efficiency of use	Accelerators - unseen by the novice user - may often speed up the interaction for the expert user such that the system can cater to both inexperienced and experienced users. Allow users to tailor frequent actions.
H1.8. Aesthetic and minimalist design	Dialogues should not contain information which is irrelevant or rarely needed. Every extra unit of information in a dialogue competes with the relevant units of information and diminishes their relative visibility.
H1.9. Help users recognize, diagnose, and recover from errors	Error messages should be expressed in plain language (no codes), precisely indicate the problem and constructively suggest a solution.
H1.10. Help and documentation	Even though it is better if the system can be used without documentation, it may be necessary to provide help and documentation. Any such information should be easy to search, focused on the user's task, list concrete steps to be carried out, and not be too large.

Our methodology suggests the development of heuristics adapted according to both the Nielsen's approach [6] (Table 1) and the specific particularities of Web-based collaborative systems (Table 2). This was conducted by studying usability problems in existing scientific surveys, by exploiting experience gained during the development of this kind of heuristics for specific software [16],[19], and through the observation of users by usability experts. The heuristics produced are classified into two categories which concern: (i) *The user interface:* a set of usability heuristics [8] derived from a factor analysis of 249 usability problems was used (see Table 1); (ii) *The*

Web-based collaboration support systems characteristics: heuristics derived from such characteristics have been analyzed in Section 3 and are presented in Table 2. Furthermore, in the case of CoPe_it!, additional heuristics have been included to address the argumentation related features and functionality.

Table 2. Heuristics derived from the system's particularities

Heuristic	*Summary*
H2.1. Context of a system's use	The system may support both synchronous and asynchronous collaboration mode, as well as co-located and distributed cooperation.
H2.2. Individuals' and Teams' work	Individuals work should be considered by the system within the context of a team's work.
H2.3. Awareness	The system should provide a variety of awareness services in order to keep the user informed about the whole status of the collaboration.
H2.4. Appropriation	Users should have the ability to adapt their environment to best fit to their special use case.
H2.5. Cognitive overhead and information overload	The system should support the provision of multiple projections, scalable filtering and timely processing of the associated big amounts of data.
H2.6. Social behavior	The system should represent and visualize dynamically changing social structures, relationships and interactions and should also perceive given user structures in order to extract useful information and to enable adaptation.
H2.7. Expression of tacit knowledge	Users should be able to efficiently and effectively discover and represented tacit knowledge as well as to give and understand semantics added by other individuals or teams.
H2.8. Argumentation	Users should be able to express their thoughts as arguments in a well formed discussion towards the problem solving.
H2.9. Decision Support	The system should aid users to problem solving through decision support mechanisms.

The next stage of our methodology concerns the heuristic evaluation. It is worth mentioning that the evaluation will take place in two different stages for each of the two tables and by different teams of evaluation experts. For the heuristics of Table 1, some user interface experts will be used, while for those of Table 2 some experts on Web-based collaborative systems will be involved. Based on the initial results of the evaluation, some scenarios of usage will be created. These will lead users to some potential usability problems. Next, these scenarios will be given to the users in order to start observe and record their actions. In this way, it will be possible to confirm both the initial results of heuristic evaluation and the validity of the heuristics derived from the web-based collaboration support systems' characteristics. The results of the observation are expected to uncover usability flaws, which may not be detected in the first stage of the evaluation. In order to achieve this task, specialized software that records the activity on the computer screen will be used. This software will allow us to record the user interactions, facial expressions and users' verbal reactions when the thinking aloud protocol is used.

In the final stage of the proposed methodology, a questionnaire-based form will be offered to users in order to have the ability to get some particular comments about their experience. This is expected to be an extra confirmation about the result of the heuristic evaluation. As the evaluation takes place, the produced errors in the first table's heuristics will highlight the need for corrections in the user interface, while the second table's heuristics will bring out functional errors that may occurred in the earlier stages (design phase) of the system's development.

Three main issues were pointed out during the first stages of the evaluation process of CoPe_it!:

- The usage of heuristics in the usability evaluation of such tools seems to be promising enough, since the evaluation turned to be focused on the main problems of the tool, while users may later bring up new unnoticed problems.
- Generic purpose collaboration tools are too difficult to be evaluated by using a single scenario of usage. Unaware users may choose wrong functionality for their tasks and fail to reach their target. Such systems have to be evaluated using a plethora of scenarios of usage.
- Observing user-machine interaction requires a rich infrastructure that can support parallel recording of multiple user workstations. The gap between the theory and the implementation of such a method increases when synchronous collaboration is taking place.

Finally, the usability experts observed some crucial issues while using the abovementioned heuristics:

- Heuristics may enable evaluators to identify problems that they would have otherwise failed to notice.
- It is easy to use separate heuristics for each category of usability errors. In this work, separation concerns user interface and the Web-based collaboration support systems characteristics.
- Flexibility in heuristics determination may result to a high level of adaptation in the evaluation procedure as far as the application's particularities are concerned.

6 Conclusion

This paper presents an innovative usability evaluation technique that is based on the combination of existing evaluation methods and takes into account the particularities of contemporary Web-based collaboration support systems. In such systems, which are difficult to be classified under a predefined software application class, the application of a traditional evaluation procedure may not be efficient. The usage of heuristics that concern user interfaces and application's particularities seems to be suitable in cases of applications with complicated functionality. This is due to the flexible heuristics determination, which makes the entire evaluation process adaptable and can also help the evaluators (both experts and users) to focus on critical application problems.

References

1. Avouris, N.: Human Computer Interaction. Hellenic Open University Publications (2003) (in Greek)
2. Crosby, P.: Quality is still free. McGraw-Hill, New York (1996)
3. Lindgaard, G.: Usability Testing and System Evaluation: A Guide for Designing Useful Computer Systems. Chapman and Hall, London (1994)
4. CoPe_it! Available at http://copeit.cti.gr
5. ISO 9241 Part 11, Ergonomic Requirements for Office Work with visual display terminals (1998)
6. Nielsen, J.: Usability Engineering. Academic Press, London (1993)
7. Sharp, H., Rogers, Y., Preece, J.: Interaction Design: beyond human-computer interaction, 2nd edn. Wiley, Chichester (2007)
8. Nielsen, J., Mack, R.L.: Usability Inspection Methods. John Wiley & Sons, Inc., New York (1994)
9. Shen, H.H., Dewan, P.: Access control for collaborative environments. In: Proceedings of the 1992 ACM Conference on Computer-Supported Cooperative Work, pp. 51–58. ACM Press, New York (1992), http://portal.acm.org/citation.cfm?id=143461
10. Tang, J.C., Isaacs, E.A., Rua, M.: Supporting distributed groups with a Montage of lightweight interactions. In: Proceedings of the 1994 ACM Conference on Computer Supported Cooperative Work, pp. 23–34. ACM Press, New York (1994), http://portal.acm.org/citation.cfm?id=192861&dl=GUIDE
11. Neuwirth, C.M., Kaufer, D.S., Chandhok, R., Morris, J.H.: Issues in the design of computer support for co-authoring and commenting. In: Proceedings of the 1990 ACM Conference on Computer-Supported Cooperative Work, pp. 183–195. ACM Press, New York (1990), http://portal.acm.org/citation.cfm?id=99354
12. Patterson, J.F., Hill, R.D., Rohall, S.L., Meeks, S.W.: Rendezvous: an architecture for synchronous multi-user applications. In: Proceedings of the 1990 ACM Conference on Computer-Supported Cooperative Work, pp. 317–328. ACM Press, New York (1990)
13. Karacapilidis, N., Tzagarakis, M., Karousos, N., Gkotsis, G., Kallistros, V., Christodoulou, S., Mettouris, C., Nousia, D.: Tackling cognitively-complex collaboration with CoPe_it! International Journal of Web-Based Learning and Teaching Technologies 4(3), 22–38 (2009)
14. Hornbæk, K.: Current practice in measuring usability: Challenges to usability studies and research. International Journal of Human-Computer Studies 64(2), 79–102 (2006)
15. Papaloukas, S., Xenos, M.: Usability and Education of Games through Combined Assessment Methods. In: Proceedings of the 1st ACM International Conference on Pervasive Technologies Related to Assistive Environments (PETRA 2008), Athens, Greece, July 15-19 (2008)
16. Papaloukas, S., Xenos, M.: Enhanced socializing through the usability of a videogame - virtual environment: a case study on Second Life and SimSafety. Technical Report 30-01-10, Hellenic Open University (2010)
17. Software Quality Research Group, Hellenic Open University (2009), http://quality.eap.gr
18. Xenos, M., Papaloukas, S., Kostaras, N.: Games' Usability and Learning – The Civilization IV Paradigm. In: Proceedings of the IADIS Game and Entertainment Technologies, Conference (GET 2009), Algarve, Portugal, June 17 - 19, pp. 3–10 (2009)
19. Papaloukas, S., Patriarcheas, K., Xenos, M.: Usability Assessment Heuristics in New Genre Videogames. In: Proceedings of the 13th Panhellenic Conference on Informatics (PCI 2009), Corfu, Greece, September 10 - 12, pp. 202–206. IEEE Press, Los Alamitos (2009), ISBN: 978-0-7695-3788-7

User Interface Composition with COTS-UI and Trading Approaches: Application for Web-Based Environmental Information Systems

Javier Criado, Nicolás Padilla, Luis Iribarne, and Jose-Andrés Asensio

Applied Computing Group
{javi.criado,npadilla,liribarne,jacortes}@ual.es
http://www.ual.es/acg
University of Almeria, Department of Languages and Computing
Ctra Sacramento s/n, 04120 Almeria, Spain

Abstract. Due to the globalization of the information and knowledge society on the Internet, modern *Web-based Information Systems* (WIS) must be flexible and prepared to be easily accessible and manageable in real-time. In recent times it has received a special interest the globalization of information through a common vocabulary (i.e., *ontologies*), and the standardized way in which information is retrieved on the Web (i.e., powerful search engines, and intelligent software agents). These same principles of globalization and standardization should also be valid for the user interfaces of the WIS, but they are built on traditional development paradigms. In this paper we present an approach to reduce the gap of globalization/standardization in the generation of WIS user interfaces by using a real-time "*bottom-up*" composition perspective with COTS-interface components (type interface *widgets*) and trading services.

1 Introduction

In a world that is more and more open, where globalization of information and the knowledge society on the Internet proliferate, *Web-based Information Systems* (WIS) must be flexible and prepared for easy adaption, extensible, accessible and manageable in real time by different persons and/or groups of persons with common interests located in different places. Recently, special interest has been given to globalization of information through a common system vocabulary using ontologies and web semantics. A great effort has also been devoted to recalling information on the Web, with powerful search engines based on ontologies and intelligent software agents, a mechanism known in the literature as "*information retrieval*". However, at present, WIS user interfaces (UI) are still being constructed on the basis of traditional software development paradigms, without taking into account in their construction (or in the knowledge managed by the systems) the main criterion of globalization, that they must be distributed, open and changing. This means that a WIS UI must be able to be dynamically reconstructed in real time depending on the type of interaction (individual

M.D. Lytras et al. (Eds.): WSKS 2010, Part I, CCIS 111, pp. 259–266, 2010.

or collective) and the purpose of the interaction (management, technical, etc.). A WIS example requiring a solution for this situation gap are *Environmental Management Information Systems* (EMIS) [1]. EMIS are social and technical systems with a variety of final users and actors (i.e., politicians, technicians, administrators, etc.) that cooperate with each other and interact with the system by means of powerful and strict UI for decision-making, problems resolution, etc.

SOLERES is a Web-based EMIS which sets up a framework for correlating satellite maps and ecological cartography using neural-networks (`http://www.ual.es/acg/soleres`). This information system, like other current WIS, must be flexible and allow simple, quick access to promote globalization of the information. To accomplish this goal, our environmental information system was basically designed in two large subsystems. On one hand all of the infrastructure and platform supporting the information system knowledge base (SOLERES-KRS), and on the other, all human-computer interaction (SOLERES-HCI). The system for representing knowledge, implemented in SOLERES-KRS, was modeled using ontologies, which allows the system to have meta-information repositories of satellite images and cartography, with the original information in repositories outside of the system. The platform was prepared to incorporate information from correlating satellite images and cartography. This subsystem, and also the system for representing the knowledge that it implements, has been widely described elsewhere [2] [3] [4]. On the other hand, the SOLERES-HCI subsystem manages exploitation of the information (in this case environmental), facilitating interaction with user interfaces that mediate for the users in searching for and exploiting the information and facilitating decision-making tasks (environmental), and prediction/prevention. Our proposal for building WIS/EMIS user interfaces is a real-time approach inspired on "*bottom-up*" composition perspective with COTS-interface components (type interface *widgets*) and trading services.

This article deals with the SOLERES-HCI subsystem. To do this, in Section 2 we describe the *state-of-the-art* most related to this part of our system. In Section 3 we introduce a simple scenario to explain the cotsget architecture. In continuation, in Section 4, we describe a proposal for construction of UIs based on the use of COTS (*Commercial Off-The Shelf*) [5] [6] components and real-time UI regeneration techniques through trading services. Finally, in Section 5 we come to some conclusions and identify some future work to be undertaken.

2 Related Work

This section briefly reviews areas related to the main parts of this work: (a) EMIS works; (b) UI modeling and construction; (c) trading services and COTS components.

An EMIS is a special kind of *Geographic Information System* (GIS) [1]. There are several different kinds of EMIS in the literature, which use some of the technologies in our system. For instance, InfoSleuth [7] is a distributed EMIS based on agents, able to offer complex consulting services on heterogeneous resources, and is based on ontologies, services or interaction templates. EDEN-IW [8] is an EMIS, which allows information recall, treatment and location with an intelligent UI and support tools depending on the access profile. NZDIS [9] is an EMIS based on a multi-agent system describing the architecture for constructing distributed information systems based on existing sources of heterogeneous information. FSEP [10] is a weather prediction EMIS based on agents and components for distributed execution. None of these systems combine traders and COTS components for building user interfaces.

They're also many model-based tools for generating UIs in the literature: IDEAS (*Interface Development Environment within OASIS*) [11], a model-based UI development methodology that allows the UI to be specified in UML diagrams formally using the OASIS specification language [12]; OVID (*Object, View and Interaction Design*) [13], a methodology that uses a set of UI design techniques for objects developed by IBM; WISDOM (*Whitewater Interactive System Development with Object Models*) [14], a methodological proposal for UML-based UI development; UMLi [15], a UML notation extension for designing UIs.

In the field of Software Engineering, there are many publications on COTS software development methodologies, methods and techniques, e.g., [16] [17] [18]. There are also publications in which COTS are used for modular design of information system applications, such as the one in [19]. In [22] we developed a composition experiment with commercial *Geographic Translator Service* (GTS) components used in GIS. The trend in the last few years in component-based software application development research is to facilitate automatic integration of commercial components (COTS) through composition (or assembly) of their parts. To solve this task, a selection criterion must be determined that can be approached in different ways, intuitively, by direct assessment or by indirect methods. In [21] the authors develop an indirect assessment method based on domains (domain-based COTS-product selection method: DBCS), which reduces the complexity and improves efficiency, by taking the relationships between the components and the system into consideration. Another indirect method for selection and composition of components is based on the use of trading services. Inspired by the OMG trading model, in [20] we developed a trading model for COTS components in open-distributed systems, which is later integrated in a spiral model methodology and used to develop COTS-based software [22].

Although many studies use the COTS paradigm, few describe realistic information systems development cases making use of these components, and fewer still COTS multi-component user interfaces. [23] presents a product that makes use of COTS as clients of an activated Bluetooth device which uses these available components to construct a graphic interface which is originally empty, treating each component as an element of the interface that summarizes the functionality of the service it offers. Another example of a UI constructed by assembling graphic components is the iGoogle user interface [24] (Figure 1), which offers an extensive catalogue of services that can be added to our personalized interface, keeping in mind that these elements are not dependent on each other and any combination is possible. For instance, the iGoogle UI contains five *widgets*: a calendar, a calculator, a translator, a weather service, and a Google map service.

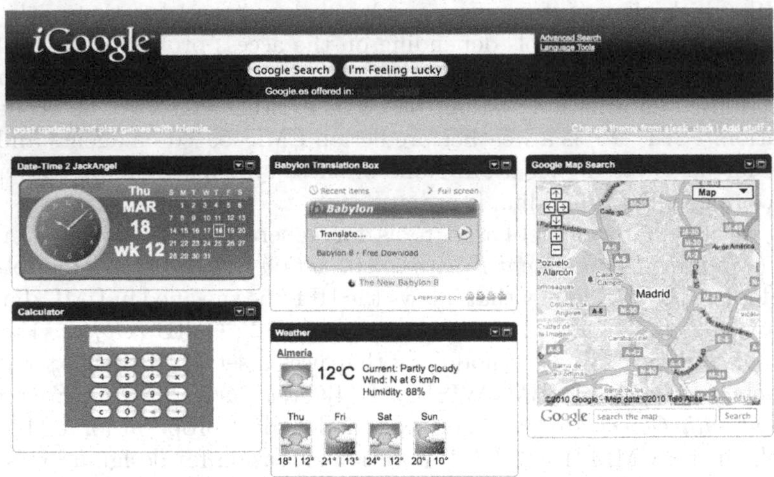

Fig. 1. A piece of an iGoogle User Interface

3 An Example Scenario

To explain the proposal let us suppose the scenario (advanced before) of a simple converter service of spatial images known as *Geographic Translator Service* (GTS). This type of service is very usual in distributed GIS and EMIS, where the whole of the information is distributed and interconnected using object-oriented techniques. Figure 2 shows the conceptual behaviour of a GTS, and written also in UML-RT notation: a language for modeling complex real-time systems (e.g., telecommunications, automatic control and aerospace applications, among others). Although it is a visual modeling language with formal semantics for specifying, visualizing, documenting and automating the construction of complex, event-driven, and distributed real-time systems, we use this notation only as a conceptual way to describe the *cotsget architecture* because it uses simple notation. UML-RT notation uses: capsules, ports and connectors. Capsules represent a graphical notation to refer to the whole component. Ports mediate the interaction of the capsule with the outside world by means of small black box, to describe the components provided behaviour, and small white boxes to describe those components required behaviour. Connectors are represented by means of lines that unite two ports. If a connector unites more than one port, it must be duplicated in the capsule that requires it, shown as a double small box.

The behaviour of a GTS component is as follows. Using a XML message, the a offering component (Sender in the figure) delegates the conversion process to the GTS component (step 1 in the figure). The XML message contains the conversion information. The translated image is stored in a buffer (step 2), and then the GTS returns an UDDI identifier to the origin component (step 3). After that, this UDDI is sent to the requiring component (step 4), which uses the UDDI as a code to extract the converted file from the buffer (step 5).

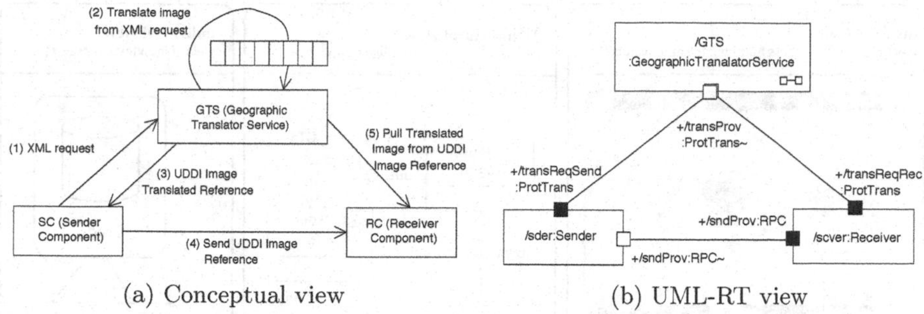

(a) Conceptual view (b) UML-RT view

Fig. 2. The Geographical Translator System (GTS) example

4 Automatic *Cotsget*-Based User Interfaces

Implementation of dynamic WIS UIs (such as the SOLERES) can be done by component composition in real time. To do this, there must be a market (an industry) of UI components, known in the literature as a CBSD (*Component-Based Software Development*) as a COTS component. Based on this component market, and with the intervention of a trading process, the system will be able to generate in real-time the user interface based on established criteria: an user-interface architecture.

SOLERES-HCI includes the construction of simple WIMP (*Windows, Icons, Menus and Pointers*) user interfaces [25] based on "*bottom-up*" composition of COTS interface components like *widgets* or *gadgets* in real time. We call these user interface components *cotsgets*, and they could be resident in public repositories. Each UI component (*cotsget*) has a concrete functionality and is prepared for assembly and operation with others (Figure 3). Concrete *cotsget* components reside in trader repositories. Component's provided/required services are used by traders in selecting processes to fulfill the *dependences* requirements fixed by the cotsget architecture.

Definition 1 (concrete cotsget). *A concrete cotsget* $\mathcal{CG} = (s, n, P, R)$ *consists of: (i) a stereotype* << *cotsget* >>*; (ii) a component name n; (iii) a finite set P of provided services* $P = \{P_1, \ldots, P_n\}$*; (iii) and a finite set R of required services* $R = \{R_1, \ldots, R_n\}$.

Each *cotsget* has a series of properties of dependency. Some of these properties are related to visual aspects, behavior, etc. The dependences can be spatial, temporal, etc. These properties depend in turn on individual and/or group factors related to the system users. All of these aspects define the specification of each *cotsgets* and are described by a specification language. Therefore, the whole WIMP-*cotsgets* user interface will respect some composition principles (e.g., dependences between components, use restrictions, availability, visibility, etc.). In our case we will only consider dependences between component in a general way (i.e., for interoperability issues).

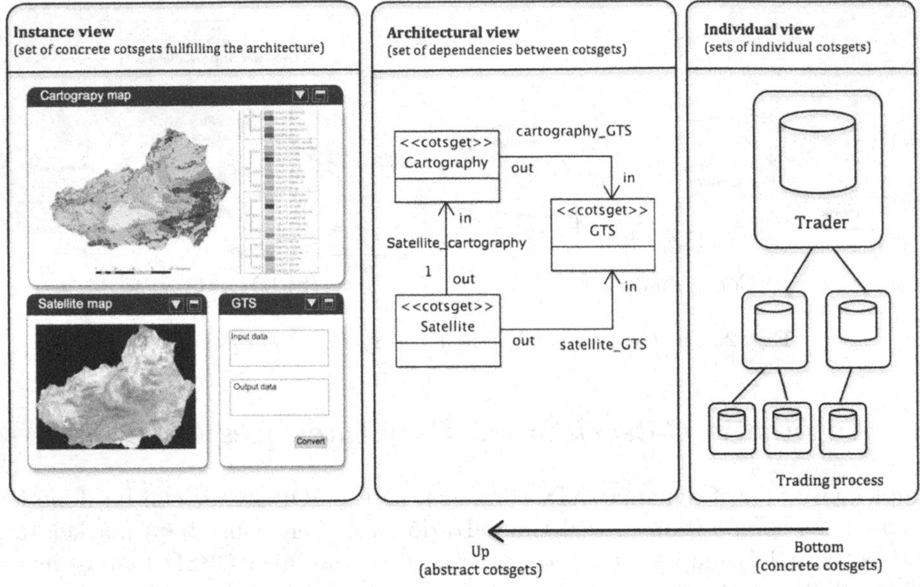

Fig. 3. A WIS *cotsget*-based interface following a "bottom-up" perspective

Definition 2 (Dependency). *A dependency D =(n,in,out) between cotsget component is a connector between two cotsget components which consists of: (i) a connector name n; (ii) a connector rol "in" as a input to a provided service of cotsget; (iii) and connector rol "out" as a output from a required service of cotsget.*

Dependences between components are described in an architecture. We use UML notation to describe cotsget architectures. The user-interface automatic generation process is a part of a methodology for evolutive user interfaces inspired on Model-Driven Development perspectives. The methodology defines the cotsget architecture by means of metamodel, which is a conceptual representation written in UML class diagram.

Definition 3 (Cotsgets Architecture). *A cotsgets architecture A =(n,C,D) consists of: (i) an architecture name n; (ii) a finite set C of cotsget components* $p, q, r, \ldots$; *(iii) and a finite set D of dependences* $u, v, w, \ldots$, *where* $D \subseteq (C \times C)$. *As usual, we write* $p \rightarrow q$, *rather than* $(p, q) \in \rightarrow$.

User interface generation is an automated process that is performed once the specifications of the components that are to be part of the interface have been determined (i.e., in the architecture). The purpose of this process is the selection of the best component configuration to meet with the new specification of *cotsgets* components. To carry out this task, the subsystem includes a trading service. A trading service, according to ISO/IEC 13235 [26] (trading ODP), basically allows users to offer and discover instances of interfaces that provide certain services. Therefore, a trader is a component through which one series of components can make their capabilities known (*export*), and others can acquire those services (*import*). In our case, the trader will manage a *cotsgets* component repository to select those, which best fit the specification instructions obtained from the transformation. Each of the components in the repository is described in detail to provide information on its characteristics and specifications. With this information, the trader is able to obtain the interface component configuration that best fits the needs and regenerate the UI model that will meet the requirements imposed by the transformation process.

5 Conclusions and Future Work

This paper presents the architecture of the SOLERES *human-computer interaction* sub-system, called SOLERES-HCI, which includes the construction of simple WIMP user interfaces based on the real-time composition of COTS-UI (*cotsgets*) user interface components. Through a concrete UI constructed using these components, new user interfaces can be generated in execution time. Using a user interface regeneration process, the best configuration of *cotsgets* that meets certain specifications is selected.

Future work will study different possibilities for interaction, cooperation and dependences between components that could arise considering the different user profiles that intervene in the system and the set of user interface components offered. Furthermore, the optimum solution search strategy in the *cotsgets* repository managed by the trader must be determined, with special interest in the use of *neural-networks*, *decision trees*, *Bayesian networks* and *influence diagrams*.

Acknowledgment. This work has been supported by the EU (FEDER) and the Spanish MICINN under grant of the project I+D TIN2007-61497 "SOLERES. A Spatio-Temporal Environmental Management System based on Neural-Networks, Agents and Software Component" (http://www.ual.es/acg/soleres).

References

1. ISO. Environmental Management Systems. Specification with guidance for use (Noviembre 2004)
2. Asensio, J.A., Iribarne, L., Padilla, N., Muñoz, F.J., Ayala, R.M., Cruz, M., Menenti, M.: A MDE-based Satellite Ontology for Environmental Management Systems. Springer book, Heidelberg (2010) (in press)
3. Iribarne, L., Padilla, N., Asensio, J.A., Muñoz, F.J., Criado, J.: Involving Web-Trading Agents & MAS. In: An Implementation for Searching and Recovering Environmental Information. In: ICAART 2010, Valencia, Spain, pp. 268–273 (2010)
4. Padilla, N., Iribarne, L., Asensio, J.A., Muoz, F.J., Ayala, R.: Modelling an Environmental Knowledge-Representation System. In: Lytras, M.D., Carroll, J.M., Damiani, E., Tennyson, R.D. (eds.) WSKS 2008. LNCS (LNAI), vol. 5288, pp. 70–78. Springer, Heidelberg (2008)

5. Heineman, T.H., Council, W.T.: Component-Based Software Engineering. In: Putting the Pieces Together, pp. xlii+818. Addison Wesley, Reading (2001)
6. Lau, K.K.: Component-Based Software Development: Case Studies, p. 303 (2004)
7. InfoSleuth, http://www.research.telcordia.com/InfoSleuth/
8. EDEN-IW, http://www.eden-iw.org
9. Cranefield, S., Purvis, M.: Integrating environmental information: Incorporating metadata in a distributed information systems architecture. Advances in Environmental Research 5, 319–325 (2001)
10. Dance, S., Gorman, M., Padgham, L., Winikoff, M.: An evolving multi agent system for meteorological alerts. In: Proc. 2nd Int. Joint Conf. on Autonomous Agents and Multiagent Systems, pp. 966–967 (2003)
11. Lozano, M.D., Ramos, I., González, P.: User Interface Specification and Modeling in a Object Oriented Environment for Automatic Software Development. In: Int. Conf. on Tech. of Object-Oriented Languages and Systems, pp. 373–381 (2000)
12. Letelier, P., Ramos, I., Sánchez, P., Pastor, O.: OASIS version 3: A Formal Approach for Object Oriented Conceptual Modeling. UPV, Spain (1998)
13. Roberts, D., Berry, D., Isensee, S., Mullaly, J.: Designing for the User with OVID: Bridging User Interface Design and Software Engineering. New Riders Pub., Indianapolis (1998)
14. Nunes, N.: Object modeling for user-centered development and user interface design: The WISDOM apprach. Thesis. University of Madeira, Portugal (2001)
15. Pinheiro, P.: Object Modelling of Interactive Systems: The UMLi Approach. Thesis. University of Manchester (2002)
16. Wallnau, K.C., Hissam, S.A., Seacord, R.C.: Building Systems from Commercial Components, pp. xv+379. Addison-Wesley, Reading (2002)
17. Meyers, B.C., Obendorf, P.: Managing Software Acquisition. Open Systems and COTS Products, pp. xxvii+360. Addison Wesley, Reading (2001)
18. Heineman, T.H., Council, W.T.: Component-Based Software Engineering. Putting the Pieces Together, pp. xlii+818. Addison Wesley, Reading (2001)
19. Alencar, P.S.C., Cowan, D.D., Luo, M.: A framework for community systems. Annals of Software Engineering 13(1-4), 381–411 (2002)
20. Iribarne, L., Troya, J.M., Vallecillo, A.: A Trading Service for COTS Components. The Computer Journal 4(3), 342–357 (2004)
21. Leung, H.K.N., Leung, K.R.P.H.: Domain-Based COTS-Product selection method. In: Cechich, A., Piattini, M., Vallecillo, A. (eds.) Component-Based Software Quality. LNCS, vol. 2693, pp. 40–63. Springer, Heidelberg (2003)
22. Iribarne, L., Troya, J.M., Vallecillo, A.: Trading for COTS Components to Fulfil Architectural Requeriments. In: The Development of Component-Bases Information Systems, vol. 11, pp. 202–222. M.E. Sharpe, Inc. (2005)
23. Wagner, S., Nielsen, C.C.: Usability and Implementation Experiences with COTS Products used as a Distributed Client Platform. In: 3rd Int. Conf. on Pervasive Computing and Applications, vol. 1, pp. 399–404 (2008)
24. iGoogle, http://www.google.es/ig
25. Almendros, J., Iribarne, L.: An Extension of UML for the modeling of WIMP user interfaces. J. of Visual Lang. and Computing 19(6), 695–720 (2008)
26. ITU/ISO. ODP Trading Function Specification. ISO/IEC 13235 (1997)

A Module for Adaptive Course Configuration and Assessment in Moodle

Carla Limongelli[1], Filippo Sciarrone[2], Marco Temperini[3], and Giulia Vaste[1]

[1] Department of Computer Science and Automation, Roma Tre University
Via della Vasca Navale, 79 00146 Roma, Italy
{limongel,vaste}@dia.uniroma3.it

[2] Open Informatica s.r.l., E-learning Division
Via dei Castelli Romani, 12A - 00040 Pomezia, Italy
f.sciarrone@openinformatica.org

[3] Department of Computer and System Sciences, Sapienza University
Via Ariosto, 25 00184 Roma, Italy
marte@dis.uniroma1.it

Abstract. Personalization and Adaptation are among the main challenges in the field of e-learning, where currently just few Learning Management Systems, mostly experimental ones, support such features. In this work we present an architecture that allows MOODLE to interact with the LECOMPS system, an adaptive learning system developed earlier by our research group, that has been working in a stand-alone modality so far. In particular, the LECOMPS responsibilities are circumscribed to the sole production of personalized learning objects sequences and to the management of the student model, leaving to MOODLE all the rest of the activities for course delivery. The LECOMPS system supports the "dynamic" adaptation of learning objects sequences, basing on the student model, i.e., learner's *Cognitive State* and *Learning Style*. Basically, this work integrates two main LECOMPS tasks into MOODLE, to be directly managed by it: Authentication and Quizzes.

All in all, and so far, the advantage of the presented integration is in the real possibility to deliver and take personalized courses, residing and basically remaining into the MOODLE environment.

1 Introduction

Personalization and Adaptation are among the main challenges in the field of e-learning. However, just few Learning Management Systems (LMSs) support such features, mostly as experimental ones. As a matter of facts, the integration of personalization aspects into state-of-the-art and widely used LMSs is a complex task and it is taken into consideration from the scientific community. For instance, the *Grapple* Project[1] is a three years European project involving 14 partners from 9 European countries, and aims at delivering to learners a technology-enhanced learning environment that guides them through a life-long

[1] http://www.grapple-project.org/

M.D. Lytras et al. (Eds.): WSKS 2010, Part I, CCIS 111, pp. 267–276, 2010.

learning experience, automatically adapting to their personal preferences. In [10] an extended discussion is presented about personalization and adaptation in e-learning and on the development of suitable tools for the authoring of learning material and its use in adaptive courses. Two main aspects of the work in this area of adaptive systems are related to the ways the learning material (usually embedded and specified into learning objects) is automatically sequenced in a course, and the ways teachers and content developers can define such material and express learning (or teaching) strategies to sequence and deliver it. In several systems, such as AHA! [3] and ELM-ART [9] the learning objects sequence is actually produced and delivered step by step, for example through the *link-annotation* technique [2]; in other systems the sequence is completely set initially, and then maintained, modified and possibly reproduced on occurrence [1,7]. The LECOMPS system, presented in [8], follows an approach of the latter type. Here we cope with the complexities of the integration of personalization aspects into the MOODLE LMS. We present an architecture that allows MOODLE to interact with an adaptive system, the LECOMPS system, that we developed earlier, and that has been working stand-alone so far. The LECOMPS system supports the "static" configuration and the "dynamic" adaptation of sequences of learning objects, basing on a student model constituted by learner's *Cognitive State* (CS) and *Learning Style* (LS). Basically, the work we present here is the integration of the following two LECOMPS tasks into the MOODLE LMS. The first task is the Authentication management: the learner is a "MOODLE student" and interacts mainly with it. The second task is Quizzes management, that, thanks to LECOMPS, are personalized basing on the learning objects taken by the learner: in the LECOMPS environment they are first designed and then imported-in and delivered-through MOODLE; then the results of quizzes are sent back to LECOMPS, to allow for student model updating. LECOMPS updates the student model by updating its CS an LS [8]. In particular the CS is updated by either adding new knowledge ("certified" by right answers to quizzes), or increasing/decreasing the degree of *certainty* for knowledge that were already in the CS, or canceling knowledge from CS (when it drops below a stated degree of certainty). The delivery of a course to the particular learner it was configured for, is performed completely into the MOODLE environment. Conversely, the thorough import of the questions defined in LECOMPS into the MOODLE databases, allows for the delivery of quizzes through MOODLE, also allowing teacher and students to access a complete history of the quizzes taken and maintained to support item and performance analysis. The advantage of the presented integration is in the real possibility to deliver and take personalized courses by the MOODLE environment only. This integration brings two main advantages: MOODLE is enriched with personalization, allowing for a different sequencing of learning materials for different students; the LECOMPS personalization process could be enriched using both the MOODLE quiz management and logging, characteristics that make MOODLE one of the most used LMS. Our work is still to enhance: LECOMPS is still needed for certain activities that should be better managed in an LMS such as MOODLE such as authoring and management of learning objects repositories.

However, the final aim in this line of work is to circumscribe the LECOMPS responsibilities to the sole production of personalized sequences of learning objects together with the management of the student model. In Section 2 we describe the LECOMPS system. In Section 3 the integrated architecture of the resulting system is presented with some example of quizzes management. Finally, in Section 4 conclusions are drawn.

2 The Lecomps Learning Management System

LECOMPS is a web-based e-learning environment, in which learners and teachers get support to the following activities:

- authoring of learning material, i.e. learning component, as described in the following definition 2
- creation of learning environments (the framework in which students enroll to get personalized courses about a stated subject matter, and teachers state the general aims of such courses, i.e. the target knowledge common to all students)
- enrollment of learners and monitoring (from both teachers and learners) of the learning activities and results
- automated construction and adaptive delivery of the personalized courses, tailored over learning goals, student's knowledge and learning styles.

A personalized course is a sequence of learning objects, picked up from a repository. The sequence is defined specifically over the present state of the student model.

For experimental reasons the system is available in different versions, each one basing on a particular *engine*, responsible for learning object selection and sequencing; the first engine issued (which is also the one running into the version of LECOMPS referred to by this article) used a graph traversing algorithm, specifically designed; a second version [6] was redesigned to exploit a planning-based approach; a third version is being studied, in parallel, using a constraint-logic-programming-approach [8].

The concept of learning object is implemented in LECOMPS by the structure of Learning Component (LC). The representation of knowledge, occurring in the definition and management of LCs and in other areas of the system, is expressed by *knowledge items* (*kis*), which are basically nouns for concepts. To manage Learning Styles we adopt the Felder and Silverman's model [4,5], which allows us to qualify a learner by a combination of two possible values for each one of four dimensions.

Definition 1. *Student Model The Learner's Cognitive State (CS) is the set of pairs $< ki, certainty >$, listing the kis presently owned by the learner, each one qualified by its level of certainty (as determined by the system basing on learners answers to tests).*

The Learner's Learning Style (LS) is represented by a 4-tuple of couples, $< d_1, v_1; d_2, v_2; d_3, v_3; d_4, v_4 >$, where each d_i is one of the basic values in a *dimension of the Felder-Silverman model (d_1 = active/reflective, d_2 = sensing/intuitive, d_3 = visual/verbal, d_4 = sequential/global) and the $v_i \in [0, 11]$.*

Definition 2. *Learning Component A Learning Component (LC) comprises:*

Required Knowledge. *A set of* kis *denoting the knowledge that is supposed to be needed in order to take the learning content of the LC.*

Acquired Knowledge. *A set of* kis *denoting the knowledge that is supposed to be gained after taking the LC.*

Learning Content. *Defined as an XHTML resource, possibly in four versions (one for each combination of the LS dimensions sensing/intuitive and visual/verbal, each one weighted by values e.g. to state how much sensing and how much verbal is the fourth version).*

Annotations. *Notes (one for each value in the LS dimensions active/reflective and sequential/global) devised to be submitted to the learner during the taking of the LC. Except the global annotation, they are shown together with the learning material of the LC. The global annotations, instead, are used to provide the learner with a summary of each lesson (i.e. subset of the LCs in the course).*

Questions. *A set of quizzes, deemed to be used during the verification process of a course. Each question can be labeled, if reasonable, by a* ki *(so right answer to such question will give possession of the related* ki*). Questions are embedded in the LC because this allows to contextualize them to the actual learning material of the LC, which we suppose makes them more effective.*

Index and Effort. *A name for the LC and an informal quantification of the effort needed to take the LC content (effort is used to balance the partition of the course in lessons).*

The system builds a personalized course as a selection of LCs; the selection (which is called *configuration*) is based on the Target Knowledge (TK) and on the individual Starting Knowledge (initial state of CS). TK is a set of *kis*, as well. The set of LCs (a course configuration) is linearized in lessons, according to appropriate constraints on lesson length. Then the learning path is administered, by presenting the material in different ways, depending on the personal learner's learning styles.

In Figure 2 the functional schema of LECOMPS is depicted. A *Learning Environment* defines the part of the system from where the courses about a certain subject matter will be constructed and delivered, under the administration of a certain teacher. It comprises:

Domain of knowledge. All *kis* used in the definition of the LCs (the corpus of knowledge - or, better, the names of the concepts in the corpus - possibly managed by the courses).

LC Pool. The repository of LCs, managed by the (authors and) teachers, through the authoring tools available in LECOMPS.

Basic TK. A set of *kis*, designing the target knowledge that is common to all the learners' personalized courses; the TK of each individual course might be varied by the teacher, at configuration time.

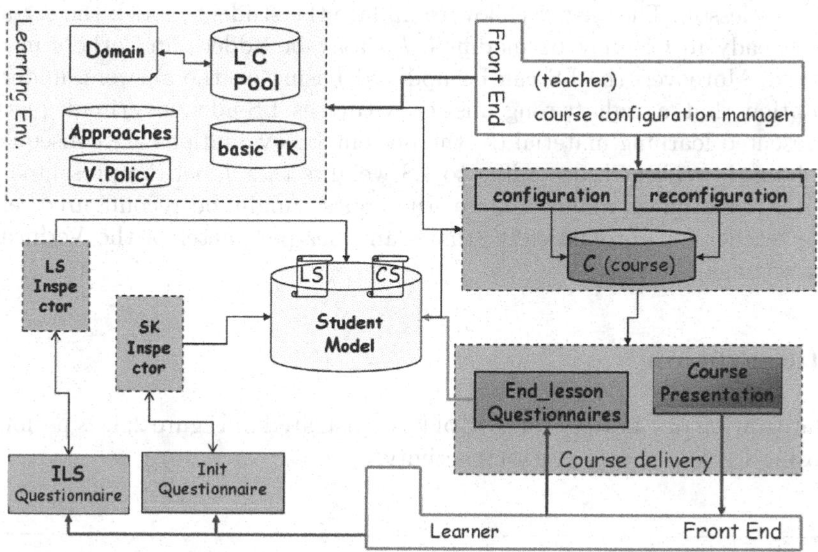

Fig. 1. Functional schema of the LECOMPS system

Approaches. A set of *approaches* designed by the teacher. An Approach is a way to express special preferences of the teacher with respect to the content of a personalized course. It can be described either as a set of *kis*, or as a set of LCs, which will be *forced* in the course configuration. An approach can be used to constrain a course in such a way it will use a certain terminology, or just will contain a certain set of learning material, in spite of the possibility it is not indispensable to reach the basic aims of the course.

Verification Policy. This is a set of parameters that drives the management of the CS during the taking of an individual course. Such parameters say what certainty is given a *ki* when it enters the CS after a right answer in a test, or how much such certainty increases or decreases after answers to further questions about that same *ki*, or what certainty thresholds are assumed for the *kis* to be extracted or permanently joined to the CS (under a threshold the *ki* is lost by the learner; above another threshold, no further questions will be met by the learner about that concept).

When a student enrols at a course, the Initial Questionnaire and the ILS Questionnaire initialize, resp., the CS and the LS in her/his model. Then, basing on the present (initial) student model and on the basic TK (possibly augmented by the teacher through some approaches), the personalized course is configured. The course is a sequence of LC, suitably partitioned in Lessons. When a component is presented, the learning content and the annotation versions are selected appropriately from the LC, with respect to the present evaluation of the LS. After each lesson an intermediate quiz is defined dynamically, by randomly selecting questions from the LCs in the lesson, so to check about the *kis* "apprehended" during the lesson. The answers allow to update the student model: the certainty of *kis* already in CS may be modified; *kis* may be added, and others may be extracted. Moreover, the LS can be updated basing on the answers, under the assumption that a right/wrong answer witnesses LS-adequacy/inadequacy of the presented learning material (so the present LS evaluations are consequently strenghtened/weakened, according to LS weights that label the presented material). After student model update, the course might be reconfigured, either by the teacher, or automatically (that's another parameter of the Verification Policy settings).

3 Integration

The integration of LECOMPS in MOODLE is illustrated in Figure 2; it is performed proposing LECOMPS as a MOODLE activity.

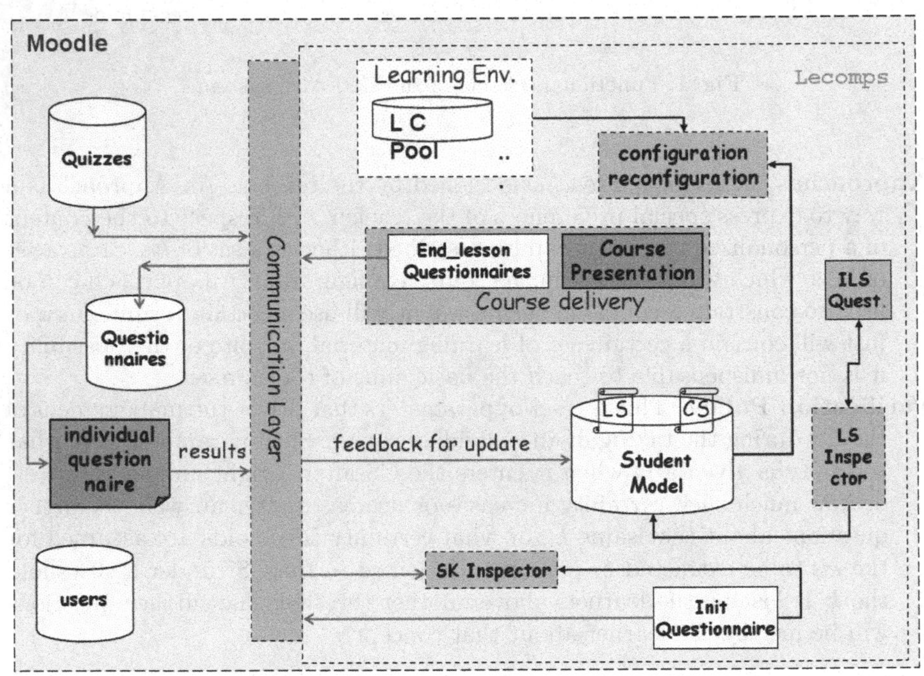

Fig. 2. Integration of LECOMPS in MOODLE: functional view

The basic management of users registration and authentication is provided by MOODLE. The integration proceeds through a communication layer, set up between MOODLE and LECOMPS. The first task of such communication layer is to maintain synchronized the MOODLE database of quizzes with the LCs repository: basically each time a question is added to a component, it can be transferred to the MOODLE database; this is a semiautomatic process, presently. A learner, registered in MOODLE, can enroll in a course and be presented with an initial questionnaire. The initial questionnaire is designed by LECOMPS (SK Inspector module) and communicated to MOODLE. MOODLE presents the questionnaire and collects the results. Then feedback is sent back to LECOMPS, in order to initialize the Cognitive State. The Learning Style is initialized in this stage as well, yet the process is carried on entirely by LECOMPS. After the configuration of the personalized course is done, it is presented to the learner.

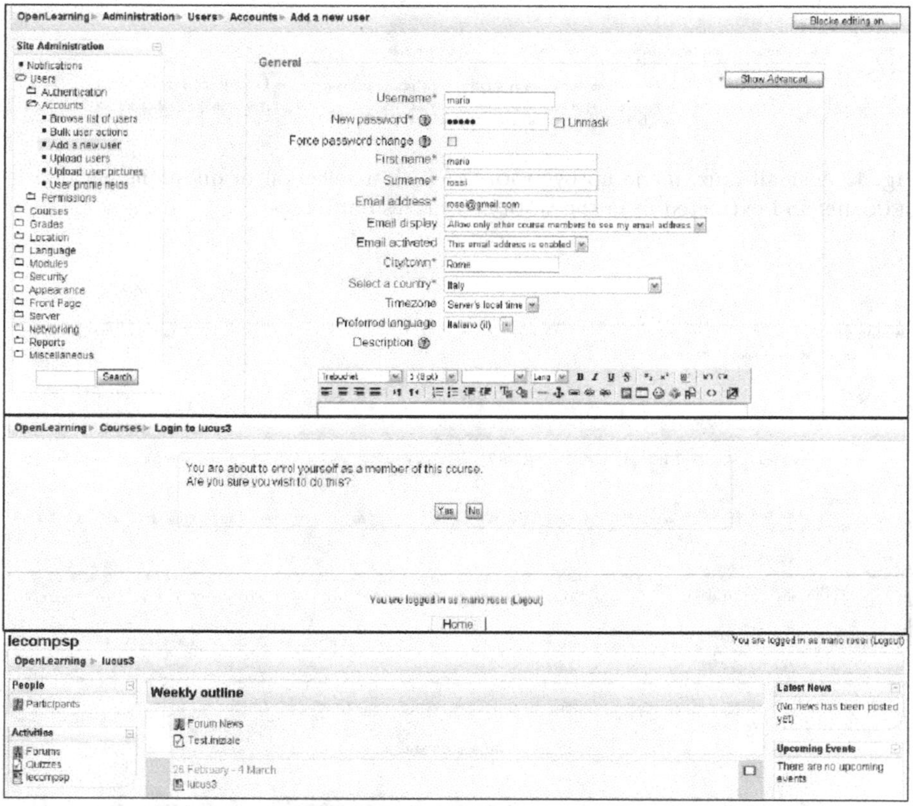

Fig. 3. Users' access into the integrated system: above, the registration phase is shown; below, the access to the MOODLE LECOMPS-Activity (related to a course called "lucus3")

When a (intra lessons) quiz has to be delivered, LECOMPS produces its specification and transfers the data to MOODLE, which will 1) prepare the test extracting the questions from its database; 2) present it to the learner; 3) collect results. Then the results are transferred back again to LECOMPS, and the student model is updated accordingly.The quiz will be stored, for possible further analysis from the teacher.

lecompsp

You are logged in as mario rossi (Logout)

OpenLearning ▸ lucus3 ▸ Quizzes ▸ Test.iniziale ▸ Review of attempt 1

Test.iniziale

Review of attempt 1

Finish review

Started on Monday, 1 March 2010, 02:20 PM
Completed on Monday, 1 March 2010, 02:20 PM
Time taken 46 secs
Marks 3/21
Grade **1.43** out of a maximum of 10 (**14%**)

1 Marks: 1/1

An epigraph convey information to be preserved as long as possible about [the author or main responsible in the construction of a building] ✓

Correct
Marks for this submission: 1/1.

2 Marks: 0/1

The Amphitheatrum was a small construction, compared to others known, yet completely functional

Choose one answer. a. The "vomitoria"were secluded places, behind the marble tiers, where sick people could (hastily) search for relief. ✗
b. The tiers were built with marble following the natural slope of the terrain ground. However there were also additional tiers, built with wood, movable and usable upon necessity.

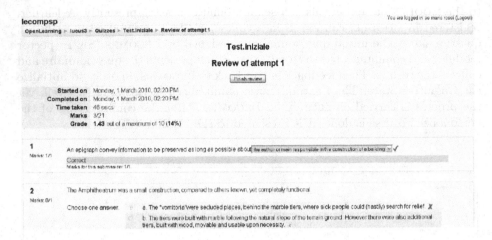

Fig. 4. A small quiz, made up by MOODLE, with a selection of questions decided by LECOMPS and extracted from the MOODLE quizzes databases

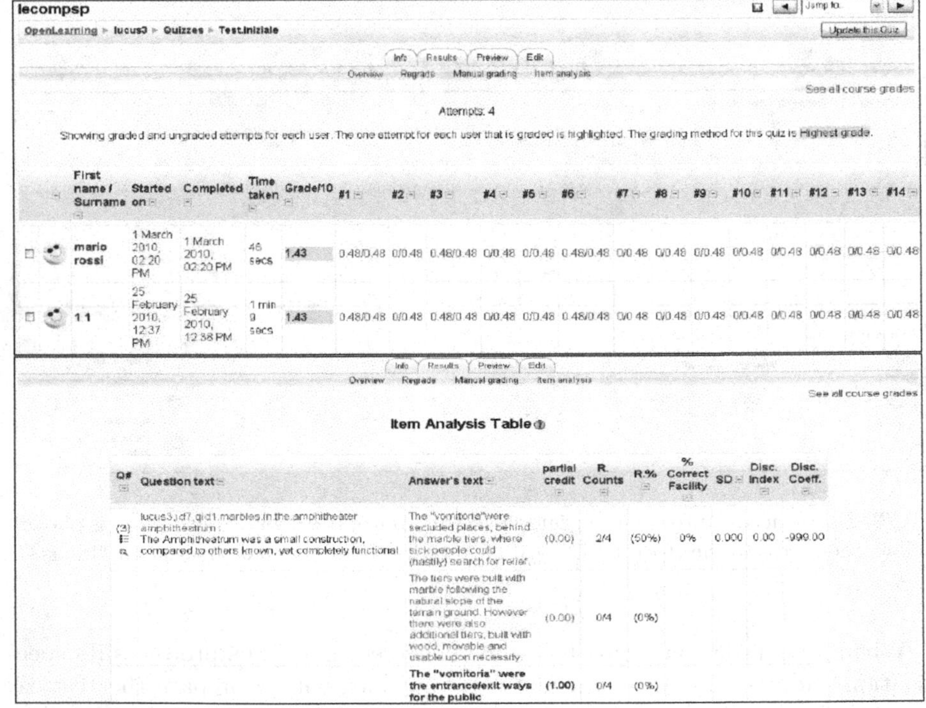

Fig. 5. Report about questions and questionnaires

This approach exploits MOODLE modularity: LECOMPS is installed in MOODLE in the directory *mod* as a new module. The teacher logs in MOODLE; (s)he can introduce a LECOMPS activity in his courses, and navigate the LECOMPS environment. Figure 3 shows the student's functionalities performed in MOODLE: the student is registered as a MOODLE user, (s)he enrolls the course through MOODLE authentication and MOODLE course registration, and (s)he obtains her/his personalized course through the LECOMPS personalization engine, seen as an activity of the course ("lucus3" in the bottom of the figure).

Figure 4 shows a quiz delivered to a learner. As mentioned above, LECOMPS produces the list of questions for a quiz, by selecting randomly from the questions contained into the learning components seen in a lesson. Such specification is automatically imported in MOODLE, where the real quiz is composed (by accessing the quizzes database), and presented to the learner.

The feedback coming from the answers to a quiz go back to LECOMPS, in order to perform the necessary updates over the student model. Meanwhile the quiz is stored with its results. When a further analysis of quizzes is required, the teacher can access them, as shown in Figure 5.

4 Conclusions and Future Work

Our research is aiming at the development of a full integration of capabilities, for the support to personalized and adaptive courses, in a state-of-the-art LMS. In particular we are working on MOODLE, due to its well known modularity and extendibility, and on a standalone LMS that we developed earlier, LECOMPS, in which we implemented our approach to personalization and adaptation in e-learning.

In this paper we propose a step in such integration. We have developed a first level embedding of the LECOMPS system in a MOODLE module (namely an *activity*). Yet, by no means we claim that a complete integration has been reached.

The integration, so far, is limited to the management of enrolling and authentication, and to the automated import of the questions defined in the learning components, into the MOODLE database. As limited as it is, the simple communication implemented between MOODLE and LECOMPS let us gain something relevant: the quizzes defined by LECOMPS after each lesson of the course, are stored, with their answers, for future consultation; history of the learner's participation in the course (through answer to questions) is recorded; the records of the answers given by all the students to a same question, are stored and can be evaluated, allowing for an analysis of the questions defined in the learning components.

Presently the personalized courses are presented through the MOODLE interface, yet it is still the original LECOMPS system acting to select the material to be actually presented (basing on the definition of the course, as a sequence of Learning Components, and on the actual evaluation of the learner's learning style). All the other functionalities of LECOMPS, such as the authoring tools, the graphical interface to the repositories of learning components, and the interaction of the teacher with the configuration interface (to manage learning environments and to actually produce courses), are still visibly in LECOMPS.

In terms of future work, we plan to advance along the integration path. While working on the lacks mentioned in the previous paragraph, we intend to devolve to MOODLE several tasks, related to the presentation of the courses, the storing of the previous versions of a same adaptive course, and the collection of data relevant to the student model update, so to leave to LECOMPS software only the kernel of personalization activities. Another aspect we plan to work upon, is the accomodation of the learning components in the framework of the SCORM standard for e-learning. We plan to use such result in order to allow the definition of a personalized course as a SCORM package, and let MOODLE receive it and present it through its implementation of the SCORM API.

References

1. Baldoni, M., Baroglio, C., Brunkhorst, I., Marengo, E., Patti, V.: Reasoning-Based Curriculum Sequencing and Validation: Integration in a Service-Oriented Architecture. In: Duval, E., Klamma, R., Wolpers, M. (eds.) EC-TEL 2007. LNCS, vol. 4753, pp. 426–431. Springer, Heidelberg (2007)
2. Brusilovsky, P.: Adaptive Hypermedia. Journal of User Modeling and User-Adapted Interaction 11, 87–110 (2001)
3. De Bra, P., Smits, D., Stash, N.: Creating and delivering adaptive courses with AHA! In: Nejdl, W., Tochtermann, K. (eds.) EC-TEL 2006. LNCS, vol. 4227, pp. 21–33. Springer, Heidelberg (2006)
4. Felder, R.M., Silverman, L.K.: Learning and teaching styles in engineering education. Engineering Education 78(7), 674–681 (1988)
5. Felder, R.M., Spurlin, J.: Application, reliability and validity of the index of learning styles. Int. Journal of Engineering Education 21(1), 103–112 (2005)
6. Limongelli, C., Sciarrone, F., Temperini, M., Vaste, G.: Lecomps5: a Framework for the Automatic Building of Personalized Learning Sequences. In: Lytras, M.D., Carroll, J.M., Damiani, E., Tennyson, R.D. (eds.) WSKS 2008. LNCS (LNAI), vol. 5288, pp. 296–303. Springer, Heidelberg (2008) ISBN/ISSN: 978-354087780-6
7. Sangineto, E., Capuano, N., Gaeta, M., Micarelli, A.: Adaptive course generation through learning styles representation. Universal Access in the Information Society (UAIS) 7(1-2), 1–23 (2008)
8. Sterbini, A., Temperini, M.: Adaptive construction and delivery of web-based learning paths. In: Proc. 39th ASEE/IEEE Frontiers in Education Conf. (2009)
9. Weber, G., Brusilovsky, P.: Elm-art: An adaptive versatile system for web-based instruction. Int. Journal of AI in Education 12(4), 351–384 (2001)
10. Wolpers, M., Grohmann, G.: PROLEARN: technology-enhanced learning and knowledge distribution for the corporate world. Int. Journal of Knowledge and Learning 1(1-2), 44–61 (2005)

User Acceptance of a Software Tool for Decision Making in IT Outsourcing: A Qualitative Study in Large Companies from Sweden

Christoffer Andresen, Georg Hodosi, Irina Saprykina, and Lazar Rusu

Department of Computer and Systems Sciences
Stockholm University, Sweden
christoffer.andresen@gmail.com, hodosi@dsv.su.se,
irina.saprykina@gmail.com, lrusu@dsv.su.se

Abstract. Decisions for IT outsourcing are very complex and needs to be supported by considerations based on many (multiple) criteria. In order to facilitate the use of a specific tool by a decision-maker in IT outsourcing, we need to find out whether such a tool for this purpose will be accepted or rejected or what improvements must be added to this tool to be accepted by some IT decision makers in large companies from Sweden.

Keywords: IT outsourcing, decision makers, ITO tool, user acceptance, decision making.

1 Introduction

A systematic analysis was often absent in early stages of IT outsourcing decisions [14]. Outsourcing decisions will have long term effect on the IS strategy, and therefore a systematic analysis should be performed [14]. It is an important business change whether a company should outsource IT or not. For this purpose, the large companies could learn from their best practices and the way to improve the ITO process [11]. Decisions in IT Outsourcing are complex decisions, so in order to facilitate this process the IT tools should be used. However, there is an issue of acceptance of such systems and tools by companies/decision makers. Why should manager accept this tool, when over a long time many decisions on IT outsourcing have been taken successfully without such tools followed the established at that time processes and practices. Thus, there is need for such a tool to be accepted by IT decision makers in order that the get expected (advantages) benefits. In addition, there is a need to understand the way a decision is made and the processes implemented. Since there is a lack of available tools for IT outsourcing decisions in the market [10] there is a need to investigate if the accepted tool would contribute to the decision making, which we believe will increase the effectiveness of decision process and ensure more reliable decision making.

There is a need for a framework for making decision in IT outsourcing [7]. In our study, we will contribute with an IT Outsourcing Tool (ITO Tool) to see if a software tool can be useful and helpful for IT outsourcing decisions [10]. We believe that such

M.D. Lytras et al. (Eds.): WSKS 2010, Part I, CCIS 111, pp. 277–288, 2010.

a tool developed for IT outsourcing decisions can facilitate and improve the decision making in that area. This will help to structure the way for analysing the enterprise situation and help to decide whether the IT outsourcing should be performed or not. In addition, we are of opinion that improvements of the decision making process will relate to time saving, performance of the decision making and the transaction cost of IT outsourcing. Due to the fact that human's willingness to accept and adopt new artefacts is challenging, and has been studied over long time, there is a need to investigate if the ITO Tool would be accepted by decision makers. In this study, we will make use of adoption theory from [8]. The adoption theory is called the Technology Acceptance Model (TAM), which is a well used instrument to find out whether a system will be accepted or rejected. The ITO Tool must contribute and improve today situation to be accepted [8], There are many frameworks/models, which could be used for decision, however not all frameworks/models can be equally applicable for the established outsourcing processes. The main purpose of the study is to find out, with use of the Technology Acceptance Model (TAM), whether the ITO Tool for decision making of IT outsourcing would be accepted or not, and if negative – to understand the reasons for rejecting it. Our research questions are; In which way (to which extent) can the ITO Tool be accepted for some decision makers in IT outsourcing in Swedish companies of a global scale, and what contribution can be provided to the ITO Tool?

2 Research Background

2.1 Description of the IT Outsourcing Tool (ITO Tool)

To not mix up the definition "ITO Tool" as a general tool in this paper, we will use the term "ITO Tool" for the specific software product we will evaluate. The main purpose of the ITO Tool is to provide assistance to the managers to make decisions at initial phase about IT outsourcing without having external consultancy. The ITO Tool according to the researches is business neutral, which means that it is not made for any specific business area, like manufacturing, banking or other [10]. Thus, by being business neutral, the tool can be used by managers in many different outsourcing cases. Furthermore, the ITO Tool is neutral because, there is no algorithm that encourage or discourage to outsource IT or not. Transaction Cost Theory (TCT), according to Williamson is rather conservative and does not encourage IT Outsourcing if there are no strong reasons showing the advantages [20]. ITO Tool is based on TCT. ITO Tool can "*highlight the potential risks, which may be hidden by the cost savings regarding IT outsourcing*" and gives description about them [10]. Moreover, this helps the managers to get information regarding ITO considerations which they do not think to consider.

A risk assessment contains four dimensions, the risk factors, scenarios of what can happen, the consequences and risk mitigation mechanism [5]. The ITO Tool is developed in MS Excel application and a screenshot of the tool is presented in Figure 1. The ITO Tool lists 80 questions from different risk areas and the scenarios are the answers the users select. In the end the consequences are shown in a graph, where the risk exposures are calculated. The mitigation mechanism is handled by highlighting the high risks that must be mitigated before further proceeding of IT outsourcing. The

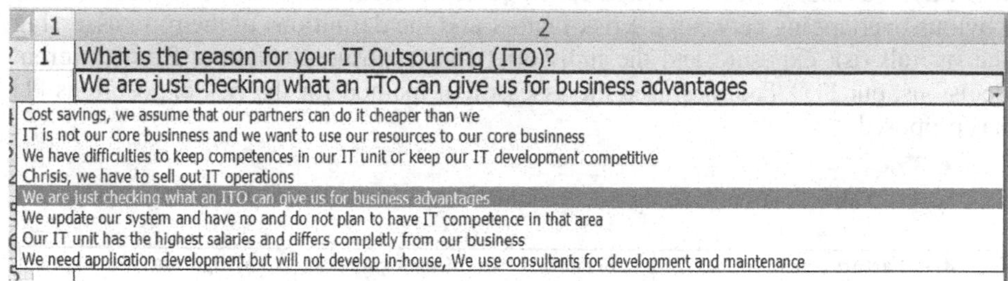

Fig. 1. Screenshot from the ITO tool [10]

ITO tool is presented with a graphical view of the risk exposure from the risk assessment with recommendations about to do the IT outsourcing or not [10].

2.2 Risk Assessment of IT Outsourcing

Risk management of decision making for IT outsourcing have been studied intensively in the last ten years, and still new risk factors appear according to new fields of type of outsourcing, for instance cloud computing [15]. Both financial benefits and risks are elements for making decisions of IT outsourcing [12]. Making decision for IT outsourcing includes high degree of uncertainty according towards price/performance, underlying economic shift, business and IT alignment and supplier selection and its contract negotiation [19].

Enterprises should be aware to outsource too much, due to decreasing grade of successful outsourcing [13]. On the other hand, selective outsourcing is not more successful than total outsourcing even if that is more uncommon [16]. Anyhow, Outsourcing is a risky endeavour. Outsourcing enables the companies to refocus on their core business [16], and the initial agreements must consider the risk profile of the unique deal [6].

Risk management are assessed or analysed as a probability and effects (consequences), which are mapped according to the very high, high, moderate (medium), low and very low scale [18][17]. Effects can be assessed in catastrophic, serious, tolerable or insignificant [18]. Risks should be considered as a negative event [2], but also a potential negative outcome due to uncertainty future developments [21]. "Managers are making decisions with respect to IT and outsourcing is often overly optimistic, according to [9]. They take their decisions to outsource based on a best case scenario". On the other hand, [2] noticed that "once risk exposure is explicit, and the possible compromises clear to the managers, risk becomes a lot more manageable".

In the review of the research literature, we have found different ITO frameworks. In our research, we have selected and adapted from [4] the ITO risk assessment framework. Our decision model, implemented in the ITO tool, is covering the risk factors presented in Table 1. In fact, as a matter of the problem complexity with interlinked risks and mutual dependencies of different events it is not possible to isolate each risk, therefore in the ITO Tool a question can cover one or more risk factors[1]. In

[1] We want to keep the number of questions for assessing the risk exposure as low as possible. Therefore, we try to also to combine different ITO risk areas.

this way, the result will have a high coverage of different risk factors. There is also an obvious overlapping between the risk factors and the definitions of them. In assessing the overall risk exposure and the individual risk exposures resulting from different decisions, our ITO Tool has used the assessment method for the risk exposure as [1] has proposed.

Table 1. IT outsourcing risk assessment framework (adapted from [4])

Risk Factors (The figures within the brackets are the numbers of questions that are referring to the risk factors used in our ITO Tool)	**Scenarios**	**Consequences**	**Mitigation mechanisms**
• Asset specificity (6) • Small number of Suppliers (1)	Lock-in	Cost Escalation and Service Debasement	• Mutual hosting • Dual sourcing
• Uncertainty (2)	Costly contractual amendments		• Sequential contracting • Contract flexibility • Short term contracts
• Uncertainty (2) • Client's degree of expertise in IT operations (5) • Client's degree of expertise in outsourcing contracts (4) • Relatedness (functional and organizational) (2) • Ex-ante imperfection (24)	Unexpected transition and management costs		• Clan mechanisms • External expertise procurement
• Measurement problems (2) • Supplier's degree of expertise in IT operations (5) • Supplier's degree of expertise in outsourcing • Contracts (4)	Disputes and litigation		• Alternative methods of dispute resolution • Clan mechanisms • Procurement of external expertise

The risks from the ITO tool are calculated for each question and represented in the end as sum of these risks and the tool calculates the risk exposure (RE) according to the next formula [10]:

$$RE_{tot} = \sum_{i}^{N} Pr(UO_i)*L(UO_i),$$

The formula: $Pr(UO_i)$ means: the probability of an undesirable outcome *i*, and $L(UO_i)$ is the loss of undesirable outcome *i*. RE_{tot} is the accumulated risk exposure for the N number of risks. In IT outsourcing context the losses of undesirable outcome are losses about outsourcing contract and probability of an undesirable outcome is function of such losses [2].

The risk exposure in the ITO Tool is presented on the figure below as a plane graph. The number of items is the questions, which user answered are stated on the vertical line. The calculations of risks are presented on horizontal line, according to scale they are weighted as small losses - 0, 2, medium losses – 0,5 and critical losses- 0,95. The decision about outsourcing has been presented according to calculation of losses, which has been provided by decision maker.

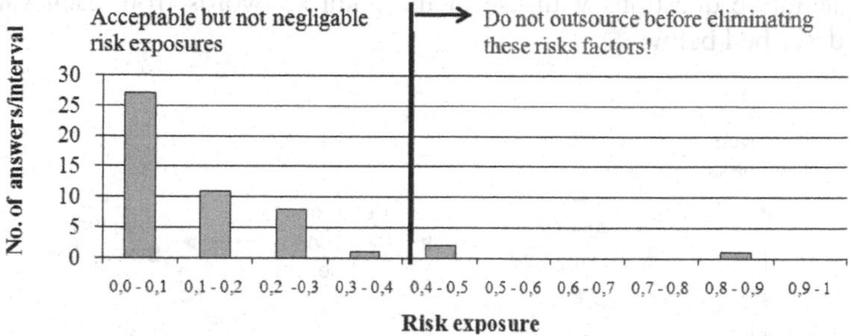

Fig. 2. Distribution of the questions that generate RE from the ITO tool [10](for a particular example)

2.3 Research Methodology

For assessing the acceptance of the ITO Tool, we have done interviews with executives' experts in IT outsourcing in large companies from Sweden, with experience in IT outsourcing. The interviewees are mentioned in Table 2 regarding their position, experience in IT outsourcing, type of relationships from the four companies' part of our research analysis.

Table 2. Research sampling

Position in the company of the interviewee	Years of IT outsourcing experiences	Type of company: All large companies	Companies
Executive	14 years	Advisory service	Company A
CIO	1,5 years	Buyer	Company B
Head of Procurement	7 years	Buyer	Company C
Senior sales manager	Not provided	Both Seller and Buyer	Company D

We believe that our sampling size cannot make any generalization, but we will get useful information of what best practises from some decision makers consider to make decisions in IT outsourcing. Due to type of methodology, we have got deep interviews of executives in Swedish global companies, which have knowledge and experience in this topic. Our findings regarding the technology acceptance of the ITO Tool will provide great value towards further development of this tool, or if such tool is not accepted at all into decision making in IT outsourcing.

Before we collected data of technology acceptance, we introduced the ITO Tool to the decision makers, so that they could touch and feel how the tool worked in decision making of IT outsourcing. We shortly described the purpose of the ITO Tool, and that the tool was based on 80 questions with multiple options of answers, and the algorithm behind for assessing the risk exposure [10].

The computer with the ITO Tool installed was given to the interviewee, where the interviewee tested the ITO Tool with a case in their mind. The duration time of answering all the questions was given up to 20 minutes for all four companies.

After the software tool was tested, we asked questions from the TAM [8], which we had rephrased from quantitative questions with answering in a seven point Likert scale to qualitative questions with use of the main keywords from each variable of TAM and described below.

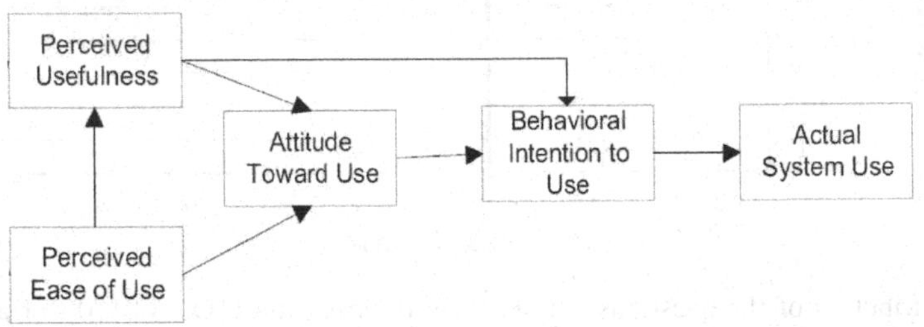

Fig. 3. Technology Acceptance Model, TAM [8]

2.4 Perceived Usefulness

The keywords from TAM for the variable Perceived usefulness are "useful", "helpful", "performance", "effectiveness", and "provide" [8], and the questions we created were:

a) What do you think the purpose/advantage of this tool can provide you? (Provide)
b) How can use of the tool provide advantage in IT outsourcing decisions? (Performance and effectiveness)
c) Do you think the risks are listed with values of Risk Exposure was helpful? (Helpful)

2.5 Perceived Ease of Use

The keywords from TAM for the variable Perceived ease of use are "easy to use", "understandable", "easily find" and "learn" [8] and the questions we created were:

a) Did you like the interface of this tool? Why or why not? (easy to use and understandable)
b) Will it be easier to use if the risk-types would be grouped? (easily find)

2.6 Attitude towards Use Are the Impressions from Perceived Usefulness and Ease of Use

The keywords from TAM for the variable Attitude toward use are "good idea", "advantage" and "pleasant experience" [8] and the questions we created were:

a) As a person, do you easy adopt new technology? (Regarding personal adoption)
b) In what way gives the tool you a pleasant experience? (pleasant experience)

c) Do you think the tool is a good idea, why? Suggestion for improvements?(good idea).

2.7 Behavioural Intention to Use, Are Dependent on the Attitude of the Decision Tool

The keywords from TAM for variable Intention to use are "thought to use", "going to" and "recommend" [8] and the questions we created were:

a) After testing the tool, do you think you will use it, why and why not? (Thought to use)
b) Will you recommend this tool for other colleagues? Why and why not? (Recommend).

3 Results from User Acceptance of IT Outsourcing Tool (IT)

3.1 User Acceptance of Company A

The interviewee from the Company A finds the tool useful, since anything that can make the decision makers to think and assess the readiness for the IT outsourcing is good. Moreover, he/she finds that all questions are relevant, and the tool can be used as an advanced check list, but also be useful to provide objective. For instance the CIO needs a good argument for not outsourcing, and then the objective tool gives the CIO a winning argument. However, the Company A finds the tool useful, but only as a readiness tool such, as a check list that can be used to get useful objective viewpoints. We do not think the Company A accepts that the ITO Tool is a tool for making decision, but rather a tool for assessments.

As concerns disadvantages, the Company A finds it difficult to see if the ITO Tool covers all different criteria, and provides the ranking from important questions to less important ones, and how the questions are relevant to each other. The tool looks more like a readiness, or may be a subsidiary, back-up tool rather than a decision tool. Therefore, the ITO Tool should have been divided into parts, first where one assesses the readiness, next a "yes"/ "no" decision or cancel and full stop. Moreover, the output should be descriptive instead of digits, where the output make classification by risks level, for instance like virus scanning software, where it is "two very high", "five high", "three medium" risks, and so on. Moreover, the interface works fine, but a web-based interface would be preferred, instead. However, the Company A stated that decision makers should use a tool like a robot, and cannot use only one tool for making a big outsourcing, but the tool can be used for interpretation with the view to get another perspective to assess the risks.

The Interviewee from the company A is a medium adopter of new Information Technology. However, the interviewee was not in a position to accept the tool how it was now, but he/she would accept the ITO tool with some improvements introduced.

3.2 User Acceptance of Company B

The interviewee from the Company B thinks that the ITO Tool is good enough and provides the needed help. On the other hand, the interviewee does not have trust in the tool 100% and wants to have a possibility to check whether the tool was the right one or not, based on earlier experiences. Moreover, as he/she assumed it should be possible to customise the tool. Regarding the technical side of the user interface, the questions should be shown without scrolling, and the answers should be possible to see straight away. Anyhow, regarding Company A and E thinks that the ITO Tool will have more need for such a tool, when he/she is inexperienced in the decision making which he/she is.

The Interviewee from the Company B is a medium adopter of new Information Technology, and will accept the tool and recommend the tool to other colleagues. Moreover, we did not get any other feedback of the perceived usefulness of what the advantages or disadvantage were, and whether the ITO Tool was useful for the purpose of the decision making in IT outsourcing, but instead, information about cosmetic changes from the perceived ease of use. There was one feature he/she wanted is a possibility to check whether one can trust the tool or not in the decision making. A reason of not having any new suggestions or improvements of the functionality of making decision can be related to the low working experience of the interviewee - 1.5 years in IT outsourcing, on the other hand we think that Company B easily will accept the tool since the Company B do not have any formulized sourcing processes, only supporting guidelines.

3.3 User Acceptance of Company C

The interviewee from the Company C finds the user interface fine where the questions and answers are shown in a good format and the decision makers can assess the risks visually instead of engaging into a mathematic exercise. Moreover, he/she liked to look at various risk types by reviewing risk, where he/she got a clear review. The ITO Tool could be deployed in different steps of the sourcing process since this tool covers a lot of different perspectives, where the question and answers need to be interpreted. The numeric figures are a good way of showing the result. However, the tool can be deployed as it is, and be useful, but the ITO Tool can also be used in communication with various stakeholders, and to create joint work and discuss the risks around.

On the other hand, in the decision making, some risks cannot be mitigated, since it depends on the risk profile of how much risk he/she can accept. Moreover, it should be possible to customise the tool according to the risk profile for the decision case, but he/she will recommend the tool to other colleagues after improvements.

The interviewee is a medium adopter of the new Information Technology; and accepted the ITO Tool. We have got an important feedback from him/her, namely, on the concept of reviewing risks, on the question and answering exercise instead of calculating the risks, and on the criteria, which were broad and could be used in different steps in the sourcing process. The only drawback was that the decision maker would have different risk profiles and might not mitigate certain risk depending on the sourcing case.

3.4 User Acceptance of Company D

The interviewee from the Company D thinks that the ITO Tool is a good help to structure the thoughts regarding decision making, and can be used as a check list, but the risks could be assessed alone. Moreover, it was for the first time when the interviewee has seen such a decision tool, and he/she believes that it would help decision makers, if they start from the scratch. On the other hand, the interviewee does not like that; the ITO Tool had a mathematical decision model, considering it a too complicated design. The interviewee thinks the risks should be grouped to see which area of risks is under the assessment. Even if the Interviewee looking at the same risks in a group meeting, to see if the outsourcing process should continue or not, the number of 80 questions that have to be addressed in the tool seem to be too excessive and need to be considerably reduced.

The interviewee is a late adopter of new Information Technology, and does not want to accept the ITO Tool due to the fact that the interviewee was looking at the same risks but in another way, as we know from the best practises as well. On the other hand, the interviewee sees the potential in the tool and finds it useful and helpful for decision makers without any way of doing risk assessment. We think the reason of not accepting the ITO Tool by the interviewee was rather subjective one and depended on the personal perception and experience, and not on the quality of the ITO Tool itself.

4 Conclusions and Recommendations

First of all, for the purposes of the study we would refrain from any generalization, due to the small sample size, but we believe that our "lessons learned" of the user acceptance from our interviewees with executives from large Swedish companies experts in IT outsourcing, will contribute with usefully information whether a such ITO Tool will be accepted or not for decision makers in IT outsourcing.

4.1 In Which Way Can the ITO Tool Be Accepted for Some Decision Makers in IT Outsourcing in the Large Swedish Companies?

The Company A expressed itself for the tool to be divided in the following two parts: assessment of readiness and decision making - "yes", "go" and "not-to-go" for IT outsourcing. Due to the problem of a lack of a distinctive difference between readiness and decision making in the ITO Tool, it is also difficult to see if this tool covers all different criteria, and to see whether the questions are relevant to each other, let alone, ranking between important and less important questions. These deficiencies should be improved before the Company A will accept the ITO Tool in its work.

The Company B asked for mostly cosmetic changes to be able to accept the tool. We did not understand this position clear since, to our firm understanding, cosmetic change, as we think do not affect the decision making purposes of the tool, but we think that the perceived easiness of using the ITO Tool had effect on the acceptance of the tool by the said Company.

The Company C has accepted the tool as of the outset. In particular, it liked the way of assessing risks from a list, where various types must be reviewed to get a clear view. According to the company's the tool can also be used in communication with various stakeholders to create joint work and discussion around the risks.

The Company D noted the usefulness in the ITO Tool for the decision making, since the Company D has been practicing the risk assessment in the similar way in group meetings. At the same time, the Company D did not accept the tool, which, to our clear perception, was motivated by a personal attitude of the interviewee and, namely, his/her recent personal adoption of new information technology.

4.2 What Contribution Can Be Provided to the ITO Tool?

A contribution for the ITO Tool acceptance is a list of suggestions of new improvements in the user interface functionality, but also some new features in the ITO Tool.

Functionality

- Should be possible to customise the tool.
- The ITO Tool questionnaire should be divided into two parts. The first is readiness, - if you are ready or not, and the second part, given that you are ready, - go to outsource or not, then full stop
- Reduction of the number of questions.

User interface

- All questions should be displayed without scrolling, and it should be possible to view the answers straight away.
- The ITO Tool should in a more clear way cover all criteria, and to reflect the ranking between the most important questions and less important ones, as well as to show the interrelation between the questions.
- The output in a descript way should replace the digits and a summary like a virus scanning software, where the classification of how may high risks, medium risk, low risks.
- The question could be grouped by risk types, but the graphical result does not need to be grouped. The purpose of grouping risks is to find the problem area, but also as Company C suggested, use the ITO Tool as a communication tool, where you can use different parts from the tool, you can assess with different professions.

New features

- Want to compare own experience with the tool, to see if the taken risk was consider right or not. If this feature will increase the trustfulness to the ITO Tool, then it is needed to get higher opportunities for use acceptance.
- The tool would be extended with evaluations criteria for supplier selection.
- Type of Risk Profile will be introduced, having in mind that some risks cannot be mitigated and one has to accept certain risks.
- From best practises, check the suppliers financial stability, in supplier selection
- From best practises, it seems that selections of different type of relationships is part of the sourcing process, but maybe implement interdependencies between criteria that can make suggestions of what type of relationship should be selected.

References

1. Aubert, B., Dussault, S., Patry, M., Rivard, S.: Managing the risk of IT outsourcing, System Sciences. In: Proceedings of the 32nd Annual Hawaii International Conference - HICSS-32 (1999)
2. Aubert, B., Patry, N., Rivard, S.: Managing IT outsourcing risk: Lesson learned, CIRANO, Montreal, 2001s-39 (2001), http://www.cirano.qc.ca/pdf/publication/2001s39.pdf (accessed on May 2007)
3. Aubert, B., Patry, N., Rivard, S.: A framework for information technology outsourcing risk management. The DATA BASE for Advances in Information Technology 36(4) (2005)
4. Bahli, B., Rivard, S.: Information Technology Outsourcing Risk: A Scenario-Based Conceptualisation. HEC Montréal, Cahier de la Chaire de gestion stratégique des technologies de l'information, Octobre 02-04, pp. 1–22 (2002), http://neumann.hec.ca/chairegestionti/cahiers/cahier0204.pdf, (accessed on May 2007)
5. Bahli, B., Rivard, S.: The information technology outsourcing risk: a transaction cost and agency theory-based perspective. Journal of Information Technology 18, 211–221 (2003)
6. Corbitt, B.J., Tho, I.L.: Toward an economic analysis of IT outsourcing risks. In: 16th Australasian Conference on Information Systems (2005)
7. Cronk, J., Sharp, J.: A framework for deciding what to outsource in information technology. 10th Journal of Information Technology, 259–267 (1995)
8. Davis, F.D.: Perceived usefulness, perceived ease of use and user acceptance of information technology. MIS Quarterly 13(3), 319–340 (1989)
9. Hirscheim, R., Lacity, M.: The Myths and Realities of Information Technology Insourcing. Communication of the ACM 43(2), 99–107 (2000)
10. Hodosi, G., Rusu, L.: A Software Tool that Supports Decisions for Companies to Outsource Information Technology or Not. In: Proceedings of the Mediterranean Conference on Information Systems - MCIS 2007, University of Trento, Venice, Italy, October 4-8, vol. 1, pp. 69–78 (2007)
11. Hodosi, G., Rusu, L.: Information Technology Outsourcing: A Case Study of Best Practices in two Swedish Global Companies. In: Proceedings of the Mediterranean Conference in Information Systems - MCIS 2008, Hammamet, Tunisia, October 23-26 (2008)
12. Jurison, J.: The role of risk and return in information technology outsourcing decisions. Journal of Information Technology, 239–247 (1995)
13. Lacity, M., Kahn, S.A., Willcocks, L.P.: A review of the IT outsourcing literature: Insight for practice. Journal of Strategic Information Systems 18, 130–146 (2009)
14. Looff, L.A.: Information systems outsourcing decision making: a framework, organizational theories and case studies. Journal of Information Technology, 281–297 (1995)
15. Martens, B., Teuteberg, F.: Why management matters in IT outsourcing – a systematic literature review and elements of a research agenda. In: 17th European Conference on Information Systems (2009)
16. Rouse, A.: Testing some myths about I.T. outsourcing: A survey of Australia's top 1000 firms. In: 16th European Conference on Information Systems (2008)
17. Tho, I.: Managing the risk of IT outsourcing. Butterworth-Heinemann Publications, Elsevier, Oxford (2005)
18. Sommerville, I.: Software Engineering. Addison-Wesley Publishers Limited, USA (2007)
19. Willcocks, L.P., Lacity, M.C.: Information systems outsourcing in theory and practice. Journal of Information Technology 10, 203–207 (1995)

20. Williamson, O.: The Economic Institutions of Capitalism - Firms, Markets, Relational Contracting, pp. 52–63. The Free Press, London (1985)
21. Wüllenweber, K., Jahner, S., Kromar, H.: Relational Risk Mitigation: The Relationship Approach to Mitigating Risk in Business Process Outsourcing. In: Proceedings of the 41st Hawaii International Conference on System Science -2008. IEEE, Los Alamitos (2008)

Cubic Satellites, Vanguard Technology Integration, an Educational Opportunity of Modernization in Mexico

Olmo A. Moreno-Franco[1], L.A. Muñoz-Ubando[2], Prudenciano Moreno-Moreno[3], and Eduardo E. Vargas-Méndez[4]

[1] Universidad Modelo, Ingeniería Mecatrónica
Carretera a Cholul, 200 mts. después del Periférico, Mérida, Yucatán, 97305, México
[2] The Robotics Institute of Yucatán, http://www.triy.org/ (CITI), Calle 60 Norte # 301
Colonia Revoluciones, Mérida, Yucatán, 97118, México
[3] Universidad Pedagógica Nacional, CCAA: Políticas Públicas y Educación. Área I
Carretera al Ajusco No. 24, Col. Héroes de Padierna, México, D. F., 14200, México
[4] Universidad del Valle de México, Campus Mérida, Laureate International Universities, Ingeniería Mecatrónica
Calle 79 No.500, Col. Dzitya Polígono Chuburna, Mérida, Yucatán., 97110, México
olmo.moreno@triy.org, alberto.munoz@triy.org,
pmoreno@ajusco.upn.mx, eduardo.vargasme@uvmnet.edu

Abstract. This paper provides a theoretical approach on the CubeSat standard making a cost-benefit analysis in the use of pico-satellites at the education and technology integration model for educational modernization. With the CubeSat format is planned to develop an orbit LEO pico-satellite as part of a multidisciplinary project led by the Robotics Institute of Yucatan (TRIY), assisted with previous experience in Mexico and Colombia, to build a satellite capable of stabilizing through a robotic device, which will be a training model for human resources in Mexico. The CubeSat initiative represents a technological development of more than 10 years who is still alive and growing, attracting new participants from different educational institutions and global business, which has proven to be a project that would be made and successful results with a significant low budget compared to other space missions, and finally is an opportunity to bring students and teachers to the aerospace industry, through a convergence of technology, and academic discipline.

1 Introduction

Passed away 53 years since it was launched into orbit by the Russians the first artificial satellite called Sputnik I from the Baikonur Cosmodrome in Tyuratam, Kazakhstan (1957). Their mission: to obtain information on the concentration of electrons in the ionosphere, having a shelf life of 3 months [1].

Eleven years later, Mexico enters the satellite era in 1968 when the TV signals are transmitted via satellite to the Olympic Games in Mexico, through the satellite ATS-3 [2] property of NASA [3] and hired by the company INTELSAT [4]. Until 1985, Mexico placed into orbit its first satellite called Morelos I, with the mission of unifying telecommunications in rural areas and urban areas in the nation, and at a cost of $92 million [5].

M.D. Lytras et al. (Eds.): WSKS 2010, Part I, CCIS 111, pp. 289–296, 2010.

The need for telecommunications, micro-gravity experiments, multidisciplinary academic participation and the miniaturization of technology has made the dream closer to reality space for academic institutions (public and private) and business through technology integration designed for size, resources, and costs reduction of artificial satellites. This process will involve Cubic Satellite, known as CubeSat.

A CubeSat is a type of miniature satellite for space research, which has a volume of exactly one liter, weighs no more than one kilogram, and typically uses commercial electronics. Since 1999, California Polytechnic University (CalPoly) by Prof. Jordi Puig-Suari [6] and Stanford University by Professor Bob Twiggs [7] developed the CubeSat specifications to help universities worldwide to conduct space science and exploration [8], this is known as the CubeSat standard [9] (See Fig.1).

There are four different types of CubeSats: a) 0.5U: which specifies a half of unit, given the unit in decimeters, b) 1U: including the unit and the standard of cubic decimeters, c) 2U: describes a pico-satellite consists of two units, and d) 3U: is the maximum size that may have a pico-satellite under the standard [10].

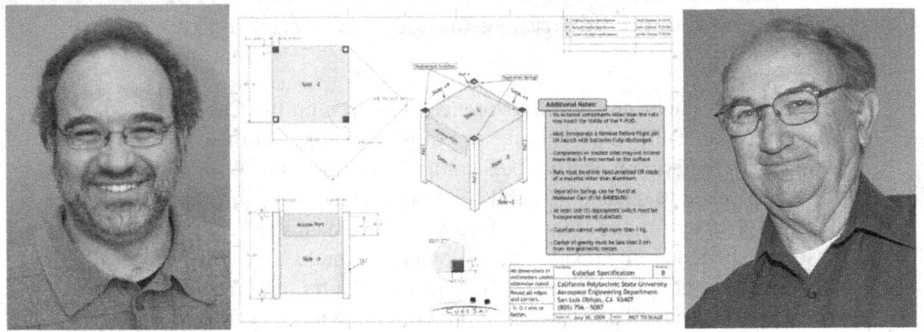

Fig. 1. Left Prof. Jordi Puig-Suari in the center the CubeSat Standard, and right Prof. Bob Twiggs

Its main objective is to reduce the costs of design, development, launch and operation for experimental processes in space compared to the costs of commercial satellites in the same or higher orbits and to reduce the times of this process flow. These costs does not include the operation from a ground station, the range is from $65 thousand USD to $100 thousand USD, depending on the experimental payload will and the technological characteristics of the system [11]. The costs are relatively low compared with costs exceeding $100 million USD [12] that require the commercial satellites, military and explorative.

To send a CubeSat in space, is necessary flow of process from the design and manufacture of the pico-satellite, a test phase (extreme temperatures and vibration), and finally an institution (normally closed) will be responsible for placing through a system of peak-satellite deployment in space.

The design and development stage of the CubeSat is possible through parts and components from suppliers dedicated to the Pico-Satellite, where the market leader is the company Pumpkin Inc. [13] with the integrated development CubeSat Kit [14], these kits are used by 60% of developers in the world CubeSats [16]. Tests can be conducted in such institutions backed up by aerospace international agencies, in the case of temperature tests, the International Research Institute of Stanford (IRIS) [17] performed measurements of extreme temperature under vacuum in cameras designed for CubeSat, where pico-satellites are tested in conditions of -30 ° to + 50 degrees Celsius [18].

In the design and construction of CubeSats coexistence of an ideal multidisciplinary involving to be developed in academic environments that permit exploration of science as a trigger for opportunities mechanism in research groups and work, bringing a technology impact of participating institutions while preserving the philosophy of standardization and open source. The education sector is fully aware that the awakening vocations for students in an early time generate human resources capable of performing scientific research in industry demanded by society to meet new challenges, take up old projects and make changes and improvements to existing systems; the technology boom presents an overview of resource use to study and understand the means and mechanisms that move in the vicinity of the coexistence of mankind and his environment.

2 An Opportunity at the Education Sector

For its experimental condition, the CubeSat offer great opportunities for the participation of the educational environment for its realization, as the aircraft design is divided into the CubeSat standard specifications, which presents that reliability is backed up by various satellites launched under this protocol. Furthermore, technologies are available for development and achievable, this means that most educational institutions interested in implementing the project, can achieve goals and objectives on time less than two years from the time the project starts to date release, bringing its work to a LEO orbit (Low Earth Orbit) located between 300km and 800km above Earth's surface [19].

Building CubeSats, converge in a synergistic force between educational institutions and business, which generates a technology push to the institution as well as the motivation of the group of project partners in the design. When developing CubeSats designers should be aware that the project has a potential for failure due to inclement weather and other phenomena present in space, one of the advantages of the standard is that it is possible to test equipment (pico-satellite earth stations) across distances shorter than LEO either a balloon or a means and mechanism to raise the satellite without leaving the atmosphere.

Within the epistemological areas which are enhanced using pico-satellites are: Biology (GeneSat 1 Research Center NASA Ames, genetic experiments) [20]; Meteorology (study of weather), Seismology (QuakeSat , study of earthquakes) [21], Geosciences, Physics and Chemistry (the study of nano-materials); Cartography; Astronomy and finally performing science technology integration: Aerospace Engineering, Electronics, Informatics and Mechanics.

3 CubeSat Statistics 2003 – 2008

Since its inception in 1999, the CubeSat project has focused on promoting the participation of universities, research institutes and development agencies, aerospace and telecommunications companies as a means of exchanging information and a forum for developers of pico-satellites. More than 27 countries top the list of nations cooperating with the project through its academic institutions, where 48% of the collaborators are from institutions in the United States, followed by 6% for employees in Germany and 5% of participants from Japan [19]. In the future Hispanic American countries like Mexico and Peru will join the list of CubeSat project partners, in turn, more countries will enter the development of pico-satellites and that is a proposed increase in force and which has proved capable of producing success stories in various space missions.

Within the global participation, 76% of employees correspond to higher-level academic institutions, with projects of undergraduate, graduate and doctorate who top the list. 11% of participants belong to business groups dedicated to the telecommunications, space experiments, and image processing, among others; in this group are also collaborating world's space agencies. Suppliers of components and services for CubeSats occupy 7% interest, are mostly companies engaged in the sale and distribution of electronic and mechanical (hardware systems: batteries, solar cells, chassis, electronic hardware, etc.) at the United States. Because of the versatility, ease of integration, and availability of resources, more and more educational institutions of secondary levels are involved in the production of pico-satellites, these collaborative groups begin their projects as part of scientific roots programs or introduction to the science and research, it is noteworthy that although they have put into orbit the satellite peak, the experience that makes each participant impacts on their own motivation for choosing to study a degree of technological sciences, this group represents 4% of participants worldwide, the United States is the only country where being performed. Finally with 2% for the group of amateurs who make up by people without scientific profile or not belonging to any school, realize self-made design, development and technology exploration with the CubeSat standard [19].One of the most notable features that make attractive CubeSat initiative are the costs of the project, is more representative of its release which includes an approximate $40 billion USD [22] under companies like Eurokote and Kosmotras [23]. Because manufacturing costs ranging from $ 25 thousand USD to $60 thousand USD depending on the technological characteristics of the system and the payload or experiment to send into microgravity orbit. The payloads carry the experiment in space, the experiments range from telecommunications testing, to testing of biological species in microgravity. The space presents a hostile environment for devices that are sent. Extreme temperatures, radiation exposure to collisions and other celestial bodies are some of the dangers that can suffer when a satellite is in orbit, as well as a failure during the rocket launch from the Earth, or in the deployment process through mechanisms that put it in orbit. Coupled with this, miniaturization of components becomes more difficult the task of resolving the possible default or failure caused to the CubeSat; when designing pico-satellites, developers must be aware about the possibility of mission failure due to the large number of factors that affects them away from Earth. The proportion of cases of success and failure cases for CubeSats released from 2003 to 2008 makes clear that 65% of these failed and only 35% were successful [10]. Most failures are due to launch because the rocket had a mechanical failure which precluded his arrival out of orbit. Other failure is lack of communication between the CubeSat and the ground station. Among the success stories are records of pico-satellites with longer operating time than they were designed.

4 Human Resource Generation

Within the design of Pico-Satellites is the training of human resources as part of the dynamic integration of the project. These human resources will be individuals able to solve proposed problems, work in teams and participate in different stages such as design, development, construction, assembly, launch, operation and documentation.

With the use of pico-satellites in schools may include academic subjects that were previously beyond grid, now careers as electronics engineering and computer science are enhanced with modules for the aerospace technologies, leading to a modernization in the Academic Staff of the institution, and not only affected the previous careers; in the design and development CubeSat philosophy remains open source, so that these technologies can bring a diversity of individuals who are different from activities engineering, whether fans, artists, middle and high school students or anyone who wants to integrate their work into space. While the lifetimes of a CubeSat is relatively short compared to the commercial telecommunications satellite, the pico-satellite project with an average 3-year period provides a great opportunity for students to participate from the beginning to the release, allowing enough time to produce the necessary documentation that may be useful in certification processes, thus contributing to the production of scientific material that describes the development of a CubeSat experience.

5 CubeSat State of the Art in México

Since 1982 Mexico has six satellites in geostationary orbit: Morelos I and II, Solidaridad I and II and SATMEX 5 and 6, which include exclusive telecommunications tasks (Internet, Telephony, Distance Learning, TV, Radio and Video conferencing, business and government) [5]. Mexico launched the scientific-experimental satellite UNAMSAT-B in a LEO orbit in 1996 [5]. The start of the project was through a group of amateurs who in 1970 began experimenting with satellite telecommunications, it was not until 1995 when the National Autonomous University of Mexico in association with the University of Moscow, launched the first Mexican scientific satellite from the Plesetsk Cosmodrome, in Russia, the mission: gather information on distances and transport of meteorites impacting the Earth, unfortunately the launch mission failed, hitting the rocket after launch [24].

Through the leadership of Dr. David Liberman UNAMSAT-B [25] is the product of years of work and research by the University Program for Space Research and Development (PUID) [26], whose purpose is to train and educate students and UNAM academic staff in the areas of technology and space development. The tasks and Mexican space projects that are aimed at developing research and space exploration, as well as phenomena of the Earth's magnetic field. In the area of pico-satellites,

Mexico has a group of seven researchers from the National Autonomous University of Mexico who developed the CubeSat called SATEDU [27]. This pico-satellite was designed to teach and train students in classrooms, schools and laboratories in various areas of operation of the device, it was developed and validated by the Engineering Institute of UNAM.

For Vicente [28], Mexico has made in the past a couple of projects with micro-pico satellites, which not only try to end the industrial and technological backwardness of the country, if not complete these projects for the implementation of the Agency Mexican Space (AEXA), which is a public agency with legal personality and its own technical and managerial autonomy, which will form part of the Secretariat of Communications and Transport.

According to the experience of Dr. Esau Vicente, the development of an experimental satellite in Mexico requires 4 to 8 years of work depending on financial aid, and the magnitude of technological and scientific progress. It was noted that this type of project allows the participation of 25 to 200 people according to the challenges and the magnitude of the technological demands led satellite mission. Taking into account the cost of this type of project (half a million to 5 million U.S. dollars) the relationship between staff numbers of participants against the project cost is very low. Considering the way the young Mexican through his university is integrated into the project, this is motivated by the satellite and space projects, is notably a very low efficiency in the ranks of the participation and training of new resources humans in this area [28].

6 Involvement and Proposal of the Robotics Institute in Yucatan CubeSat Program

During the days of 22 to 25 April 2009, held the Annual Workshop of Developers CubeSats in its sixth edition in the University of California located in San Luis Obispo, in the southwestern United States. The workshop aims to gather new participants and experts to show different developments, proposals, success stories and unsuccessful missions that have been developed.

Mexico had a presence in CubeSats Developers Workshop sixth version through participation from the Robotics Institute of Yucatan (TRIY) [29], who intend to pursue the design, construction, technology integration, launch and tele-operation of CubeSat standard for a 3U pico-satellite which carries a robotics payload as an experimental model of orbital stabilization, called TRIY-SAT I. The idea is to perform an operations center (earth stations) located in the Yucatan Peninsula, which offers features ideal for tele-operate satellites due to geographical location and topography of the place. The Robotics Institute of Yucatan has highly qualified personnel in the area of telecommunications, microelectronics, robotics and software development, who joined the project as a multidisciplinary research team. One goal is to link together with the Sergio Arboleda University in Colombia, who are an experienced group in the area of pico-satellites, they have already in orbit pico-satellite Libertad I [30], so the TRIY team may seek advice on the various steps of the satellite design flow. This project aims to be a starting point for future missions where the objectives are the development and integration of new technologies for future exploitation and use and marketing to benefit the community.

7 Conclusions

The CubeSat standard is hard work in design, miniaturization and integration technology. Not only is a means to carry a payload into space, but also a mechanism for convergence of multidisciplinary groups worldwide, who have the opportunity to participate in an aerospace engineering project, which in the past was for agencies specializing in branch. The protocol offers a generation of highly skilled human resources and scientific production may be effective in various educational institutions in the various projects undertaken.

With the standard approach is easier to make closer space student communities, acting as a trigger of opportunity, a learning channel where they can generate links and partnerships at national and international level, obtaining advice from experts who are already done CubeSat launch experience, and thus able to provide a consultancy service to institutions or companies interested in sending pico-satellites into space.

In Mexico, the pico-satellite project is a modernization of technology for educational institutions, not only for the design and use of new technologies, but also by the training received by participants and knowledge gained through experience. It is advantageous to the rapid development cycle of a CubeSat, which belongs to a standardized international community and where other staff have made scientific contributions to the philosophy of open source and have succeeded in their missions. Technology integration for CubeSats represents a unique category in their field, which positions the institutions and people participating in a globally recognized standard of excellence.

The CubeSat standard technology integration is within the growing trends of educatronics and its relationship to the educational and productive synergy between agencies, companies, universities and scientific-technological research. The CubeSat project is developing a trend of technological convergence and academic disciplines through the various areas of study. It is a leading example of the information society and knowledge economy.

References

1. Wikipedia: Sputnik (2009), http://es.wikipedia.org/wiki/Sputnik/
2. NASA: ATS-3 16 Years in Orbit Evaluation. Goddar Space Fligth Center. Greenbelt, Maryland, USA (1986), http://ntrs.nasa.gov/archive/nasa/casi.ntrs.nasa.gov/19860066768_1986066768.pdf
3. Nacional Aeronautics and Space Administration: NASA Web Page (2009), http://www.nasa.gov/
4. INTELSAT Web Page (2009), http://www.intelsat.com/
5. Tun, D., Beaujean, P.: Satélites Mexicanos. CiberHábitat, Ciudad de la Informática. Página Web. México (2006), http://www.ciberhabitat.gob.mx/medios/satelites/mexicanos/
6. Prof. Jordi Puig-Suari: Personal Web Page at Calpoly (2008), http://aero.calpoly.edu/faculty/jordi-puig-suari/
7. Prof. Bob Twiggs: Personal Web Page at Stanford (2008), http://aa.stanford.edu/aeroastro/Twiggs.html/
8. Wikipedia: CubeSat (2009), http://en.wikipedia.org/wiki/CubeSat/
9. CubeSat Calpoly Project: Background (2009), http://cubesat.atl.calpoly.edu/pages/home/background.php/

10. Wikipedia: List of CubeSats (2009), http://en.wikipedia.org/wiki/List_of_CubeSats#cite_note-CP-Rockot-1
11. Leonard, D.: Cubesats: Tiny Spacecraft, Huge Payoffs at Space.com (2007), http://www.space.com/businesstechnology/cube_sats_040908.html/
12. Celorio, M.: El Nuevo Satélite Mexicano, un Impulso para la Educación a Distancia. Revista Entérate, Año 1, Número 10, Julio de 2002. Universidad Nacional Autónoma de México, México (2002), http://www.enterate.unam.mx/Articulos/2002/julio/satelite.htm/
13. Pumpkin Inc., Web Page (2009), http://www.pumpkininc.com/
14. CubeSat Kit, Web Page (2009), http://www.cubesatkit.com/
15. CubeSat Calpoly Project: The CubeSat Kit (2009), http://cubesat.atl.calpoly.edu/pages/suppliers/pumpkin-inc..php
16. Citado en el 6th Annual CubeSat Workshop por Andrew Kalman. Universidad Politécnica de California, San Luís Obispo California, Estados Unidos (2009)
17. Stanford Research Institute, Web Page (2009), http://www.sri.com/
18. Klofas, B., van Dyk, K., Doe, R.: CTEC: CubeSat Thermal Environment Chamber. In: SRI International. CubeSat Developers' Workshop 2009. San Luis Obispo California, USA (April 2009)
19. CubeSat Calpoly Project: Ground Operators (2009), http://cubesat.atl.calpoly.edu/pages/ground-operators.php
20. Santa Clara University: GeneSat-1 Mission (2007), http://genesat.arc.nasa.gov/
21. Stanford University: QuakeSat Nano-Satellite (2004), http://www.quakefinder.com/services/quakesat-ssite/
22. CubeSat Calpoly Project: Background (2009), http://cubesat.atl.calpoly.edu/pages/home/background.php
23. Kosmotras, International Space Company, web Page (2009), http://www.kosmotras.ru/
24. Nuñez, G.: Entrevista a David Liberman, XE1TU. Publicado en la revista QST de la ARRL, http://www.arrl.org/, http://www.xe1rcs.org.mx/colabora/unamsatb.html
25. Simón, M.: El Satélite UNAMSAT-B ya está en órbita. Revista Digital Sidereus Nuncius No. 0, Universidad Nacional Autónoma de México (1996), http://sidereus.safirunam.org.mx/index.php/revistas/9-no-0/10-unamsat-b
26. Memoria UNAM 1996, Programa Universitario de Investigación y Desarrollo Espacial, Universidad Nacional Autónoma de México (1996), http://www.planeacion.unam.mx/Memoria/anteriores/1996/puide.php
27. Satélite Educativo Mexicano: SATEDU. Página Web (2009), http://proyectos.iingen.unam.mx/satedu/
28. Vicente-Vivas, E., Jiménez, E.A., Carizales, Z.L., Sánchez, R.C.A., Alba, C.R., García, M.A., Islas, G.: Successful Development of a Portable Didactic Satellite for Training and Research in Satellite Technology. In: CORE-2009, 10th Computing Congress, CIC-IPN, México City, May 27-29 (2009)
29. The Robotics Institute of Yucatán, Web Page (2009), http://www.triy.org/
30. Universidad Sergio Arboleda: CubeSat Libertdad I (2007), http://www.usergioarboleda.edu.co/proyecto_espacial/index.htm

Using Learning Objects in Games

Miroslav Minović, Miloš Milovanović, and Dusan Starcevic

Faculty of Organizational Sciences, Laboratory for Multimedia Communications, University of Belgrade
{mminovic,milovanovicm,starcev}@fon.rs

Abstract. Our research in game based learning area is moving from traditional web-based Learning Management Systems towards game-based Learning Management Systems, with the intention of integrating upsides of using games in university education. This paper gives insight in to our recent work in area of reusability of Learning Objects between web-based LMSs and game-based LMSs. One of the major issues was how to use classical Learning Objects in development of educational games. We decided to apply a Model Driven Approach to Learning Objects repurposing, which represents a two-step process. Web based Learning Object is transformed into more abstract model and then returned enriched with game specific attributes to a platform specific model. For that purpose we propose a new term Educational Game Learning Object (EGLO). Different games that use different environment and settings can simply reuse Educational Game Learning Objects. Another contribution of our work is a software tool that can be used to import, transform, edit and add metadata, store and export Learning Objects. Applicability of this approach is demonstrated in one simple example.

Keywords: Game-Based Learning, Learning Objects, MDA content repurposing.

1 Introduction

Game based learning promises to be a new successful approach in conducting university education. Motivating today's students with traditional teaching methods such as lectures and written materials proves to be a difficult task. Universities are searching for new role in changing context of education. Gaming is becoming a new promising form of interactive content, worth of exploration [1].

Finding the right way to model the knowledge for use in educational games presents an important issue. The purpose of this paper is to propose a model that will attempt to establish the balance between knowledge integration on one side, and its reusability on other. Our model driven approach is relying on use of Learning Objects (LO) as constructing pieces of knowledge resources which are specialized for educational game design purpose. Learning objects represent a small, reusable pieces of content relevant for learning (for example, an online exercise; a coherent set of introductory readings on a specific topic; or an assessment test) [2].

On the other hand, the problem of reusability is more complex in the area of educational games then in the classical web based LMS systems. Games require much better integration of Learning Objects into virtual environments, in the context of

M.D. Lytras et al. (Eds.): WSKS 2010, Part I, CCIS 111, pp. 297–305, 2010.

Learning Object presentation as well as interaction. That is why we will propose a use of Educational Game Learning Objects (EGLO) and attempt to solve a reusability problem by applying the method of MDA (Model Driven Approach) content repurposing EGLO represents a formally specified model, enriched in comparison to classical Learning Object with attributes necessary for application in educational games. In this case EGLOs can be reused in different educational games as well as other eLearning forms, online classes, tests etc.

In second section we briefly address games developed and applied for education. Third section is focused on the new subject of Educational Games Learning Object. Fourth section contains our solution proposal. Finally, we finish with a conclusion.

2 Literature Review

The ever-increasing importance of knowledge in our contemporary society calls for a shift in thinking about innovation in e-learning. Important factor for the success of e-learning lies in knowledge management [3, 4].

In the context of e-learning, ontologies serve as a means of achieving semantic precision between a domain of learning material and the learner's prior knowledge and learning goals [5]. Ontologies bridge the semantic gap between humans and machines and, consequently, they facilitate the establishment of the semantic web and build the basis for the exchange and re-use of contents that reaches across people and applications [6].

It is important to be able to separate content from expression within a LO in order to be able to clearly distinguish two important types of questions: those dealing with the meaning that has to be conveyed by the LO, and those dealing with how meaning is to be expressed [7].

On the other side, main purpose of educational games is to teach and pass knowledge. That is why a majority of educational games is focused mainly on knowledge.

Regardless of the rapid growth of this research field, knowledge modeling for the purpose of educational games is still in its initial phases. While there are many examples of practical work in knowledge modeling and knowledge management, there is very little practical work done in the field of knowledge modeling and integration with educational games. While there are numerous efforts that games can be applied to learning, relatively few attempts can be found where principles of learning and knowledge management were explicitly followed a priori in design [5].

How to use classical Learning Objects in development of educational games presents a major issue of our research. We will utilize Model Driven Approach for the purpose of Learning Objects repurposing. Problem we will focus on is finding suitable structure for LO's in order to be used in Game-Based LMS. Additionally, we will invest an effort to maintain reusability of existing LO's and keep compatibility with existing LO standards.

3 Educational Game Learning Object

3.1 Background

Today's eLearning systems consist mainly from two parts: Learning Objects (LO) and Learning Management Systems (LMS). Initial approach in using games in education was to create games that represent Learning Objects [8, 9] and use them in LMS. Unfortunately only edutainment level of gameplay can be reached this way [10]. Since learning objects should represent small, reusable pieces of content relevant for learning [2], games created this way would be too simple. Even though complex games can be produced as LO's, basic principles of LO's wouldn't be honored. Additionally, games have higher interaction levels with users than LMS's do.

During our effort to model world of educational games, and to apply these models in game-based learning field, we reached a conclusion that a different approach is required. Our proposition as a potential solution to this problem is to build a Game-Based Learning Management System (GB-LMS). It will be a new form of LMS that is mainly based on educational games. Such LMS will provide game environment with all learning management functionalities, and will require different kind of Learning Objects in order to fully integrate knowledge into the game, without losing game characteristics.

In following sections focus will be directed on how to structure LO for Game-Based LMS, how to reuse existing LOs, and how to keep compatibility with existing LO standards.

3.2 Learning Object Attributes

Today Learning Objects are described by Learning Object Metadata (LOM). LOM is a data model, usually encoded in XML, used to describe a learning object and similar digital resources used to support learning. The purpose of learning object metadata is to support the reusability of learning objects, to aid discoverability, and to facilitate their interoperability, usually in the context of online learning management systems (LMS).

Based on the experience from practice, members of BELLE project [11] recommend minimal elements set from LOM which should be implemented. We will rely on this set of elements for the purpose of this paper.

Table 1. Minimal set of LOM elements identified by BELLE project

Name	LOM number	LOM name
Title	1.2	General.Title
Description	1.5	General.Description
Description	1.6	General.Keyword
Author or Contributor	2.3.2	Lifecycle.Contribute.Entity- N or ORG
Location, Address or URL	4.3	Technical.Location
Date	2.3.3	LifeCycle.Contribute.Date
Learning Resource Type	5.2	Educational.Learning Resource Type
Learner Level	5.6	Educational.Context

Learning Objects described with LOM satisfy the needs of web based LMS systems, because they are presented to the student without substantial modifications. Formatting applied by author of LO will be preserved, such as: chosen fonts and size for textual elements of LO, given size, resolution and colors for graphical elements, etc. On the other side, LOs have very limited reusability in game environment, since learning content should be embedded into the game. Another problem that occurs is that every new game requires different presentation of LO. Besides formatting, interaction with student differs between game-based and web-based LMS. For that purpose, it is necessary to expand existing LO model. Our proposal constitutes of creating a specific Learning Object that encapsulates traditional LO with additional elements that provide LOs the ability to be reusable in game settings. In our model we named it Educational Game LO (EGLO).

3.3 Educational Game Learning Object Attributes

Educational Game LO (EGLO) consists of LO elements. Each element posses five groups of attributes (Table 2). Educational holds additional data, such as LearningResourceType and Layer. LearningResourceType classifies LO by purpose, and Layer

Table 2. Set of additional EGLO elements

Attribute name	Possible values
Educational.Learning ResourceType	info, cognition, assessment, exercise
Educational.Layer	Each element of LO can be placed in a different layer, which enables game-based environment to decide where and how to display elements of LO
Media.ContentType	text, graphic, video, sound, complex
Media.Format	media formats, like: ascii, html, gif, png, jpg, mp3, avi, ...
Graphic.Type	vector, raster
Graphic.DimensionsX	Picture width in pixels
Graphic.DimensionsY	Picture height in pixels
Graphic.ResX	number of dots per inch for X dimension
Graphic.ResY	number of dots per inch for Y dimension
Graphic.Colors.BitDepth	number of bits used to represent colors on picture
Graphic.Colors.Number	number of different colors used on picture
Graphic.Size	Number of bytes that picture occupies in memory
Text.Font	Font, example: Times New Roman
Text.Size	Text size
Text.Color	Text color
Sound.SampleRate	Sound sample rate
Sound.Length	Sound length in seconds
Sound.Size	Sound length in bytes
Video.Length	Video length in seconds
Video.Size	Video length in bytes
Video.FrameRate	Number of frames per second
Video.Dimension	Video Resolution
Interaction.Input	Mouse, Keyboard, GamePad, Voice, GPS position, other
Interaction.Output	Screen, Vibration, other

classifies LO by presentational importance. These two attributes provide important information to Game-Based LMS in order to properly decide where and how to present LO elements to the player. Attributes in Media group define concrete Content-Type and Format for each LO element. Further groups are used to describe relevant metadata for each of the supported content types, such as Graphic, Text, Sound and Video, enabling GB-LMS to properly transform content and integrate it adequately into game world. Last one group target Interaction between LO element and student, defining possible Input and Output interaction styles.

4 Tranformation of Learning Object for Games

Since the problem of using existing LOs occurred also a problem of returning EGLOs back to the community can be identified. Once the Learning Object is created for use in an educational game there is no reason why it shouldn't be used in some other purpose. This raises a problem of standardization. A relation between Learning Objects that are used in educational games and standard Learning Objects described by a known standard (such as LOM) must be found. For this purpose we decided to apply a concept of content repurposing. Main idea is to select an existing standardized LO, raise it to a higher level of abstraction and enrich it for use in educational games.

Our approach is inspired by the model-driven development, which uses a platform-independent base model (PIM), and one or more platform-specific models (PSM), each describing how the base model is implemented on a different platform [12].

Understanding of the proposed model can easily be reached through couple of simple examples. Since the course of Computer Networks belongs to our Laboratory research group we decided to use the examples from that specific area. Initially we will start from a traditional LO that constitutes of a text and image, and is presented in HTML format. That LO explains a concept of TCP synchronization through performing of three-way handshake (Figure 1.).

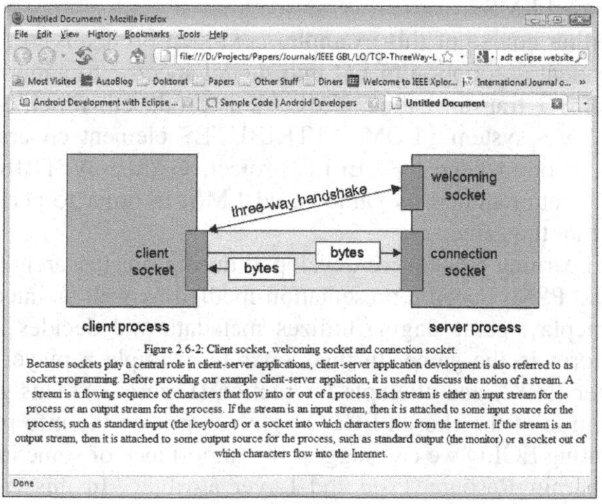

Fig. 1. TCP Three Way Handshake HTML

First step requires us to transform existing platform specific model expressed as HTML Learning Object into a more abstract specification level. For that purpose we developed a software tool for Educational Game Learning Object Management. Some of its functionalities include: importing of HTML LO's, transformation to EGLO's, creation of new EGLO's, automatic and manual completion of LO meta-data, storing of EGLO's into repository (Figure 2.).

During the import phase, system populates values from LOM elements if they exist. Upon that, it analyzes HTML code, and identifies LO elements (text paragraphs, images, videos etc.) and attempts to extract as much metadata information as possible.

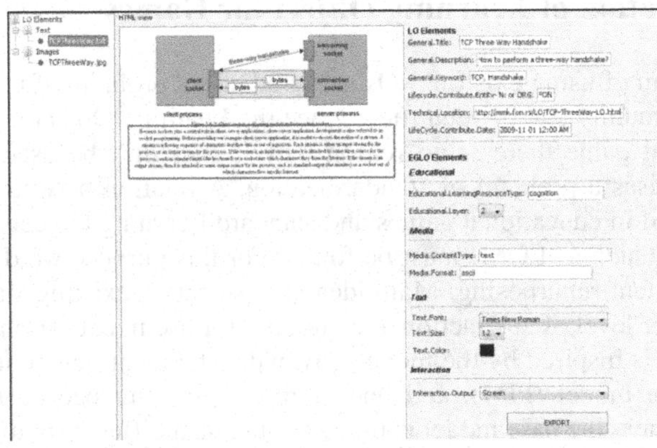

Fig. 2. Editor – Transforming from LO to EGLO

User can manually define LO elements as well as change or fill in missing metadata. Final result is PIM model expressed as a XML document structured by formally defined XML schema. This XML Document contains enough information to enable later transformation into platform specific LO description, which can be used in web-based or game-based LMS.

Following further course of this example, next step brings us to transforming the platform independent description of LO into model specific to game based platform. Upon applying XSLT transformation, XML file is produced, which can now be used by game-based LMS systems. LOM_ATTRIBUTES element covers a basic set of LOM attributes recommended by BELLE project. GAME_ATTRIBUTES element carries additional data required by game-based LMS, in order to perform integration of LO elements into the game.

Game Based Learning System we developed during our research has built in support for generated PSM. Specific presentation method as well as interaction strongly depends on gameplay, game engine utilizes metadata and decides in runtime how EGLO will perform in the game. In this concrete example a player reaches a Non Playing Character (NPC) and attempts interaction (Figure 3.). This game decides to present a description of the chosen EGLO by placing it on the info panel next to the NPC. When creating EGLO we can suggest the importance of some information from LO by using LearningResourceType and Layer attribute. In this case since image element has attribute LearningResourceType set to "info" this game decides it should present the image in the info dialog panel. Since Layer is set to "1" game decides it has to be shown to player in any case scenario. On the other hand, since Layer attribute for text is set to "2", player can decide whether it will read the content. By simple clicking on the image right information panel will pop up and provide player the ability to read the content.

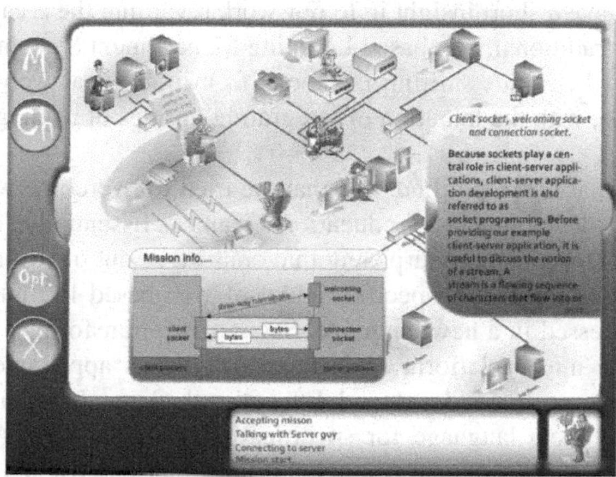

Fig. 3. TCP Three Way Handshake LO in a game executed in Java Applet environment

Another upside of using this method is simpler adaptation of EGLO presentation depending on device platform. Figure 4 shows same game and same EGLO interpreted on a JME platform. In this case also based on Layer and LearningResourceType attributes game engine decides to present the image on the first screen, upon meeting the NPC, and provides the text after clicking on the Info option from the menu.

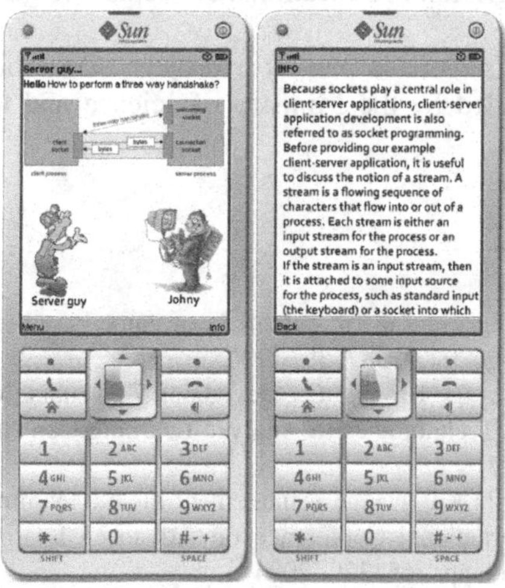

Fig. 4. TCP Three Way Handshake LO in JME Mobile Game

By doing so, the life cycle of LO from HTML, to integration into game environment is completed.

5 Conclusion

In this paper we gave a short insight in to our work regarding the area of using Learning Objects from traditional web-based Learning Management Systems in games. Our research is directed towards shifting the focus from traditional web-based LMSs to game-based LMSs, with the intention of integrating upsides of using games in university education.

Specific issue that was identified, and that we tried to overcome was how to use a classical LO's in development of educational games. Essentially, our approach is based on using MDA content repurposing that constitutes out of two main steps. First step is to transform a platform specific model of web based LO into more abstract model that is expressed in a new language. Second step transforms a resulting model from the step one into a platform specific model that is applicable in educational games. For that purpose we developed Educational Game Learning Object Metamodel and related meta language for specification of such LO's. Additionally, we introduced a new term Educational Game Learning Object (EGLO).

Another contribution of our work is a software tool that can be used to import, transform, edit and add metadata, store and export Learning Objects.

In our further research we intend to examine the reusability and create transformations from EGLO back to LO standard. Also we plan to investigate using this approach with commercially developed games. We intend further development of new game types by using EGLO's is intended as well as development of EGLO metamodel and language in order to support new features required by new game types. Future activities for improvements should include development of knowledge engine, to act as a proxy between EGLO repository and game engines. Such engine should enable much easier integration of educational concepts into games.

Acknowledgments. This work is part of a project "Corporate portal for employee long life learning", funded by the Ministry of science and technology Republic of Serbia, grant no: 006221.

References

1. Pivec, M.: Editorial: Play and learn: potentials of game-based learning. British Journal of Educational Technology 38(3), 387–393 (2007)
2. Jovanović, J., Gašević, D., Brooks, C., Devedžić, V., Hatala, M., Eap, T., Richards, G.: Using Semantic Web Technologies to Analyze Learning Content. IEEE Internet Computing 11(5), 45–53 (2007)
3. Ronchetti, M., Saini, P.: Knowledge management in an e-learning system. In: Proceedings of the 4th IEEE International Conference on Advanced Learning Technologies ICALT 2004, Joensuu, Finland, pp. 365–369 (2004)

4. Kostas, M., Psarras, J., Papastefanatos, S.: Knowledge and information management in elearning environments: The user agent architecture. Inf. Manage. Comput. Security 10(4), 165–170 (2002)
5. Kickmeier-Rust, M., Albert, D.: The ELEKTRA Ontology Model: A Learner-Centered Approach to Resource Description. In: Leung, H., Li, F., Lau, R., Li, Q. (eds.) ICWL 2007. LNCS, vol. 4823, pp. 78–89. Springer, Heidelberg (2008)
6. Antoniou, G., van Harmelen, F.: Web ontology language: OWL. In: Staab, S., Studer, R. (eds.) Handbook on Ontologies, pp. 67–92. Springer, Heidelberg (2004)
7. Brajnik, G.: Modeling Content and Expression of Learning Objects in Multimodal Learning Management Systems. In: Stephanidis, C. (ed.) HCI 2007. LNCS, vol. 4556, pp. 501–510. Springer, Heidelberg (2007)
8. Teixeira, J.S.F., Sá, E.D.J.V., Fernandes, C.T.: A taxonomy of educational games compatible with the LOM-IEEE data model. In: Proceedings of Interdisciplinary Studies in Computer Science SCIENTIA 2008, pp. 44–59 (2008)
9. Torrente, J., Moreno-Ger, P., Martínez-Ortiz, I., Fernández-Manjón, B.: Integration and Deployment of Educational Games in e-Learning Environments: The Learning Object Model Meets Educational Gaming. Educational Technology & Society 12(4), 359–371 (2009)
10. Egenfeldt-nielsen, S.: Beyond Edutainment: Educational Potential of Computer Games. Continuum International Publishing Group Ltd. (2007)
11. Best Practice Metadata Guidelines, The Belle project (2002) `http://belle.netera.ca`
12. Obrenovic, Z., Starcevic, D., Selic, B.: A Model Driven Approach to Content Repurposing. IEEE Multimedia 11(1), 62–71 (2004)

E-MEMORAe2.0: A Web Platform Dedicated to Organizational Learning Needs

Adeline Leblanc and Marie-Hélène Abel

Heudiasyc CNRS UMR 6599
University of technology of Compiègne
BP 20529 , 60 205, Compiègne, France
{adeline.leblanc,marie-helene.abel}@utc.fr

Abstract. In the current economic environment, learn became the best means, for a company, to be competitive in preserving knowledge and experiments of each collaborator and each team. Such companies are called learning organizations because they build structures and strategies in order to increase and to maximize the organizational learning. An organizational learning is a process which can be seen as a collective capability based on experiential and cognitive processes and involving knowledge acquisition, knowledge sharing and knowledge utilization. In this paper, we specify the concept of organizational learning in identifying its needs. Then we present how the web platform E-MEMORAe2.0 answers to each needs.

1 Introduction

Due to the growth and development of information and communication technologies, information takes a more and more important place in our society which can be qualified of information society. This context implies new working forms and new learning forms that constitute an integral part of industrial challenges. Becoming a learning organization is a way to an organization to stay competitive. Such an organization is an organization in which work is anchored in an organizational culture that allows and encourages the training at various levels: individual, group and organization. Each organization actor is a kind of continuous learner. He has to use the good resource at the right moment. In other words, a learning organization tries to maximize organizational learning. Organizational learning presents specific needs. It needs at least three processes in order to take place: a learning, a social and a knowledge management processes. In this sense it is necessary to take into account both formal learning (definition, organization, sharing and capitalization of resources and explicit knowledge) and informal learning (tacit knowledge externalization and competences transmitting). Different types of environment are used in an organizational learning context but no one is able to answer to all the organizational learning needs. Within the MEMORAe approach, we chose to model and develop an environment that take into account all the organizational learning needs from the modeling and design beginning.

M.D. Lytras et al. (Eds.): WSKS 2010, Part I, CCIS 111, pp. 306–315, 2010.

In the following, we specify the concept of organizational learning by underlining its needs. Then we present different platforms used in an organizational learning context and we show their limits. Finally, we present our environment and how it answers to all organizational learning needs.

2 Organizational Learning

The organizational learning is distinguished from the individual learning although it is dependent from the latter. It is an emergent property of the interactions between the organization members. Thus organizations form a place of synergies allowing the creation of knowledge higher than the one of their members. It is a question of collective intelligence. This one can be defined in terms of ideas circulation, of practices diffusion. It is a question of being interested in how organization members develop capacities of acquisition, storage, processing and use of information. Therefore, the organizational learning does not relate to the private knowledge of the individuals but to the collectives knowledge that they mobilize in the organization. This type of knowledge is at the intersection of private knowledge and public knowledge and come from interaction, competences and knowledge management.

2.1 Definition

Obviously, there are different points of view of organizational learning and many works in this research field. Claus Neergaard has developed a model in which four major types of learning have been identified, each represents a specific point of view [14]. Organizational learning regroups all of these learning types (called perspectives by Neergaard, cf. Figure 1).

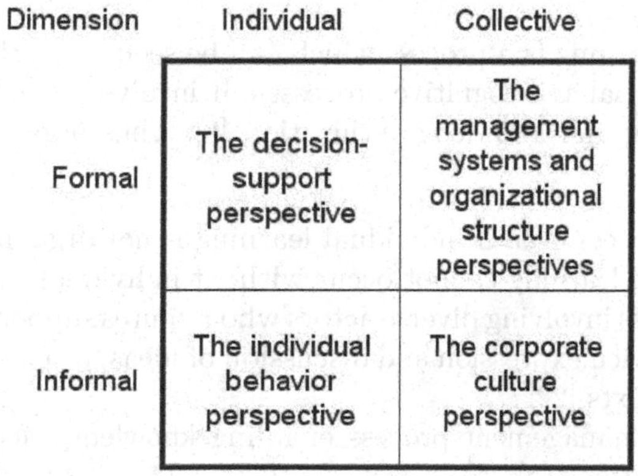

Dimension	Individual	Collective
Formal	The decision-support perspective	The management systems and organizational structure perspectives
Informal	The individual behavior perspective	The corporate culture perspective

Fig. 1. Several view points according to different dimensions [14]

In his model:

- the *decision support perspective* focuses on formal and individual learning processes in organizations. The main interest is how an individual decision maker learns in connection with problem-solving situations. This includes the use of information technology and decision models to support decision making. The perspective is mainly used to study and understand how individual learning is influenced by available information technology and its institutionalized knowledge [3] [7].
- the *individual behavior perspective* deals with informal learning processes of an individual. It captures information about human behavior - for example how individuals react in given situations and under specific conditions - as well as the personal interactions among people. Attention is focused on the informal, unconscious behavior of a single organizational member and the interpersonal interactions among members of an organization [4].
- the *management systems and organizational structure perspectives* concentrate on collective learning processes that are guided by formal organizational structures and by management systems through formal planning and control processes, operating procedures and reward systems [6] [16]. The allocation of responsibility and authority, and the structure of divisions, departments and sections, also regulate organizational learning processes.
- the *corporate culture perspective* represents what an organization knows, which is neither codified nor formalized in systems [19]. The focus is on social, informal relations, collective habits, behavioral patterns and attitudes existing in an organization.

This definition of organizational learning shows that a learning organization must favor formal/informal learning and also individual/collective learning.

2.2 Organizational Learning Process

Organizational learning is a process which can be seen as a collective capability based on experiential and cognitive processes. It involves knowledge acquisition, knowledge sharing and knowledge utilization [8]. Thus organizational learning process needs:

- a learning process even if individual learning is not organizational learning, organizational learning cannot occur without individual learning [9]
- a social process involving diverse actors who requires support of collaboration that allows a rich expression and discussion of ideas/proposals under specific problem contexts [22]
- a knowledge management process enabling knowledge acquisition, sharing and capitalization [15].

Figure 2 shows the organizational learning needs that we have identified. This needs take into account formal/informal and individual/collective learning and are rely on:

- Manage the expertise field of the organization: explicit knowledge, formal competences and resources,
- Favor collaboration: define communities of practice and their aims: facilitate resources sharing, communication (externalization) and coordination.

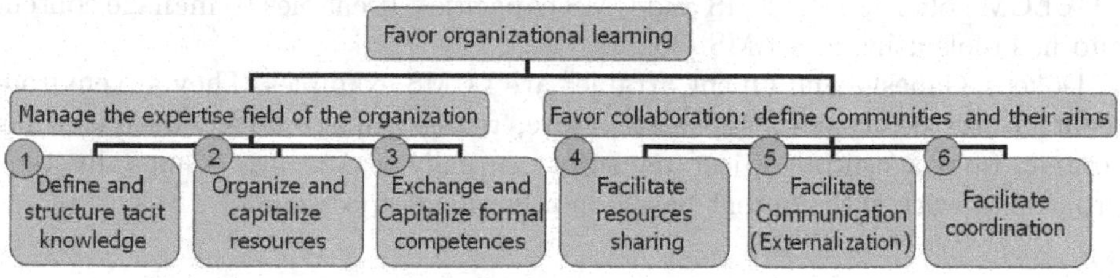

Fig. 2. Organizational learning needs

3 Platform Used in an Organizational Learning Context

Different platform types can favor organizational learning and can answer to a part of its needs. We can mentioned two platform families: platform favoring creation and management of content and platform favoring collaboration between communities members.

3.1 Content Management Platform

E-learning spreads progressively in system dedicated to teaching and also in system dedicated to attendance, distance and blended learning. Moreover Content Management System (CMS) and Learning Management System (LMS) are in constant development. In this context, they gain functionalities and becomes Learning Content Management System (LCMS).

A CMS is a dynamic website, it aims to manage and publish contents quickly, easily and user-friendly in the Web by using only a web navigator. Generally in a CMS we find:

- Content Management: used by contributors in order to write several contents and by administrator in order to create users accounts,
- Content Delivery: used by Web master and publish chief in order to publish content.

Spip, Joomla and Typo3[1] are CMS examples. They are used by private and public organization in order to manage their professional Website. They enable to create quickly and easily content in a Website. The main advantage of these platforms is their capacities to separate the form and the substance.

A LMS is a platform of training management and organization. It regroups necessary tools for the three actors of the training: the administrators, the teachers and the learners.

[1] `http://www.spip.net/ http://www.joomla.org/ http://typo3.org/`

Claroline, eFront and Moodle[2] are LMS examples. They are use today in many organizations (universities, schools, corporations). Generally, they provide a content repository for course materials as well as facilities for student tracking and management. They propose authoring, assessment and communication, such as email and discussion groups.

A LCMS offers all the LMS and CMS capacities. It enables to manage content and has tools using in a LMS [20].

Dokeos, Ganesha and OpenCartable[3] are LCMS examples. They are environments where developers can create, store, reuse, manage and deliver learning content from a central object repository, usually a database. Generally they propose to work with content based on a learning object model.

3.2 Collaborative Platform

A web platform can favor collaboration, it can enable to exchange and share resources, knowledge or competences in order to, for example, solve a common problem. Thus we can mentioned collaborative learning, working, training, etc. [13]. A collaborative web platform, thanks to different tools, enables users to realize their collectives tasks (working or learning) [18].

We can note that different types of collaborative web platform exist, we can mentioned Computer-Supported Cooperative Work (CSCW), Computer-Supported Collaborative Learning (CSCL).

The research field on CSCW covers the information technologies application as a support for collaborative work. It concerns at the same time the desire to understand the group work and also the study of web technologies which enable to favor this group work [17]. This research field has four faces: Work, Cooperative Work, Support Cooperative Work and Computer-Supported Cooperative Work. It regroups different research fields like computer science, cognitive science, psychology, sociology, etc. [17]. The aim of CSCL is to organize knowledge in order to access, share and capitalize them.

The CSCL research field is interested in the tools favoring collaborative learning (attendance, distance and blended learning). Computer becomes a tool to save the collective memory and the principal media for communication [5].

3.3 Limits of the Existing Platform

Figure 3 represents how each platform can answer to organizational needs (needs are presented in Figure 2). Even if platforms can favor organizational learning, they are not modeled and developed in order to answer to all its needs. Thus, they stress on one need but require additions or adaptations for other needs. These additions or adaptations are often plugins that are disconnected to the rest of the platform.

---

[2] `http://www.claroline.net/ http://www.efrontlearning.net/ http://moodle.org/`

[3] `http://www.dokeos.com/ http://www.ganesha.fr/ http://adullact.net/projects/opencartable`

Platform	Manage			Favor		
	Knowledge	Resources	Competences	Resources sharing	Communication	Coordination
CMS	X	X				
LMS		X		X		
LCMS	X	X		X		
CSCW		X		X	X	X
CSCL		X		X	X	X
Wiki	X	X		X	X	X

Fig. 3. Platform and organizational learning needs

4 MEMORAe2.0

Our aim, within the approach MEMORAe, is to answer to all the organization learning needs and to take into account all these needs from the modeling to the development of the platform.

To answer to these needs we propose to operationalize connections between e-learning and knowledge management in an organizational learning context. We chose to associate: a) knowledge engineering and educational engineering; b) Semantic Web and Web 2.0 technologies to model and build a collaborative learning environment as organizational learning support.

In order to assess our approach, we chose to build learning organizational memory for academic organization: a course on applied mathematics at the University of Picardy (France). In the remainder of this paper, we present through examples of our environment E-MEMORAe2.0[4] (cf. Figure 4) how we answer to the organizational learning needs (cf. Figure 2).

4.1 Manage the Expertise Field of the Organization

In this section we show how we manage the expertise field of the organization. In the section 2.2 we identified four needs to enable this management (cf. Figure 2 numbers 1 to 3).

Need 1. Define and Structure Explicit Knowledge. In order to define, structure and capitalize explicit knowledge we chose to use a learning organizational memory [1].

Our learning organizational memory is structured by means of ontologies that define knowledge within the organization. We distinguished two types of ontology: the domain ontology and the application ontology.

The domain ontology represents specific conceptualizations of a domain. This representations is reusable for several applications of this domain. In the framework of our projects, the domain is a learning organization. Domain ontology allows to model knowledge concerning the domain (persons, resources, groups, etc.) [10].

The application ontology represents specific knowledge to a given application. In the framework of our project we built the ontology for applied mathematics

[4] `http://www.hds.utc.fr/memorae/`

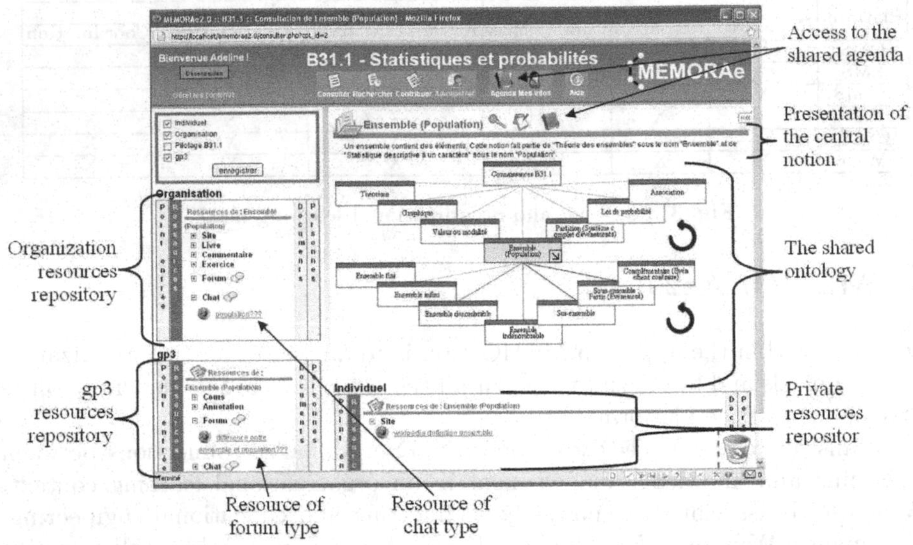

Fig. 4. The E-MEMORAe2.0 platform

course. The construction of the application ontology is presented in [1]. It allows to represent learning knowledge like 'Set', 'Finite Set', etc. (see the shared ontology in Figure 4).

Need 2. Organize and Capitalize Resources. In order to organize and capitalize resources of a learning organization, we used notions of the application ontology to semantically index these resources. Thus a resource is capitalized and can be indexed by all the application ontology notions that are treated in the resource. Moreover an application ontology notion can index all resources that treat of itself [2].

Thus users can navigate through the notion of the ontology, have a presentation of the selected notion and access to resources indexed by the selected notion (see the resources in Figure 4).

Need 3. Exchange and Capitalize Formal Competences. Our learning organizational memory modeling is structured by means of ontologies that define knowledge within the organization. Like knowledge we distinguished two types of ontology: the domain ontology and the application ontology.

On the one hand, competence domain ontology allows to model organizational learning competences thanks to knowledge they put into practice. Stader and Macintosh [21] proposed an ontology of organizational competences. We adapted this ontology within our context. On the other hand, competence application ontology allows to model applied mathematics course competences [12].

The competence application ontology is linked to knowledge application ontology by the relation 'Put into practice'. Thus a competence like 'Summarize a random variable' puts into practice knowledge like 'random variable', 'real random variable', etc.

4.2 Favor Collaboration: Define Communities of Practice and Theirs Aims

In order to motivate users to exchange and transfer tacit knowledge and competences we chose to take into account community of practice. That is why we chose to define groups, groups member, group memory and we developed semantic model to design web platform functionalities in order to favor and facilitate resources sharing, communication and coordination in the community (cf. Figure 2 numbers 4 to 6) [10].

Need 4. Facilitate Resources Sharing. In order to facilitate exchange and transfer of resources we designed the learning organizational memory around three types of sub-memory that constitute the final memory of the organization:

- organization memory: it enables all the members of the organization to access knowledge and resources without access right. These resources and knowledge are shared by all the organization members.
- group memory: it enables all the group members to access knowledge and resources shared by them. The group is at least made of two members.
- individual memory: it is private. Each member of the organization has his own memory in which he can organize and capitalize his knowledge and resources.

All these memory levels are represented in E-MEMORAe2.0 by spaces (repositories) that share the same ontologies but store different resources. They can be visualized at the same time. Figure 4 illustrates the visualization of three spaces: one dedicated to organization members, one dedicated to gp3 members (the user is a gp3 member) and one dedicated to the connected user.

Thus, users can make a drag and drop to transfer a resource from a specific repository to another.

Need 5. Facilitate Communication. In order to favor externalization of tacit knowledge and competences transfer, we chose to model exchange resources from Web2.0 technologies which consist in semantic forum and chat.

A semantic forum (see the resources of forum type in Figure 4) is an Internet forum that has an underlying model of the knowledge described in its content [2]. Such content is formed by users questions and answers about specific topics concerning the forum themes. All the questions and their answers are micro-contents that we can described by the author, the date of posting but also by the theme and the topic it is about. In our context, in order to not be disconnected with the learning context, topics are defined by ontology concepts. All this knowledge is defined semantically.

Thus users do not access to the forum itself but to the repository resources space. Then he can select resources of Forum type to participate to the forum about the selected concept (knowledge or competence) which represent the topic [11]. Consequently, users can exchange ideas about specific topics.

In the same way we defined the semantic chat that is form by users messages about specific concept and we indexed the chat session by this concept (see the resources of chat type in Figure 4).

Need 6. Facilitate Coordination. In order to facilitate coordination we chose to model and develop a semantic shared agenda (see the access to the shared agenda in Figure 4). Each meeting of the shared agenda can be semantically indexed by the ontology notion in the same way of each other type of resources.

5 Conclusion

In this paper we presented organizational learning needs and how we take them into account within the E-MEMORAe2.0 platform. We considered that organizational learning can be divided into three intertwined sub processes: a learning, a social and a knowledge management process. We decided to model and build a learning organizational memory as a support for all these processes. The advantage of our approach is that each tool are linked to the whole by the means of the shared ontology. Thus formal/informal training and the individual/collective dimensions are considered in the same collaborative web platform.

E-MEMORAe2.0 evaluations gave us good results [10]. Users used their different memories and forums. Currently our environment is used by academics. We have contact with industrials in order to evaluate such an environment in their organization.

References

1. Abel, M.H., Barry, C., Benayache, A., Chaput, B., Lenne, D., Moulin, C.: Ontology-based Organizational Memory for e-learning. Educational Technology & Society Journal 7(4) (2004)
2. Abel, M.-H., Leblanc, A.: A web plaform for innovation process facilitation. In: Proceedings of the International Conference on Knowledge Management and Information Sharing, KMIS 2009 part of IC3K 2009 International Joint Conference on Knowledge Discovery, Knowledge Engineering and Knowledge Management, Madeira Portugal, pp. 141–146 (2009)
3. Alter, S.L.: Decision Support Systems: Current Practice and Continuing Challenge. Addison-Wesley, Reading (1980)
4. Argyris, C.: On Organisational Learning. Basil Blackwell, Oxford (1993)
5. Benali, K., Bourguin, G., David, B., Derycke, A., Ferraris, C.: Collaboration/Coopration. Secondes assises nationales du GdRI3 (2002)

6. Cyert, R.M., March, J.G.: A Behavioural Theory of the Firm. Basil Blackwell, Oxford (1963)
7. Duncan, R., Weiss, A.: Organizational learning: Implications for organizational design. In: Research in Organizational Behavior Greenwich, pp. 75–123. JAI Press, CT (1979)
8. Huber, G.P.: Organizational learning: The contributing processes and literatures. Organization Science 2, 88–115 (1991)
9. Kim, D.H.: The Link between Individual and Organizational Learning. Sloan Management Review 35, 37–50 (1993)
10. Leblanc, A., Abel, M.-H.: E-MEMORAe2.0: an e-learning environment as learners communities support. International Journal of Computer Science and Applications, Special Issue on New Trends on AI Techniques for Educational Technologies 5(1), 108–123 (2008)
11. Leblanc, A., Abel, M.-H.: Linking Semantic Web and Web 2.0 for Learning Resources Management. In: Lytras, M.D., Damiani, E., Carroll, J.M., Tennyson, R.D., Avison, D., Naeve, A., Dale, A., Lefrere, P., Tan, F., Sipior, J., Vossen, G. (eds.) WSKS 2009. LNCS (LNAI), vol. 5736, pp. 60–69. Springer, Heidelberg (2009)
12. Leblanc, A., Abel, M.-H.: Competences Management in an Organizational Learning Context. In: Proceedings of the International ACM Conference on Management of Emergent Digital EcoSystems, MEDES 2009, pp. 353–360 (2009)
13. Lehtinen, E., Hakkarainen, K., Lipponen, L., Rahikainen, M., Muukkonen, H.: Computer Supported Collaborative Learning: A Review (1999), `http://etu.utu.fi/papers/clnet/clnetreport.html`
14. Neergaard, C.: Creating a learning organisation: a comprehensive framework. PhD Thesis. Denmark: Department of Production, Aalborg University (1994)
15. Reamy, T.: KM and elearning: A powerful combination. EContent 26(10), 18–22 (2003)
16. Riis, J.O.: Design of Management Systems - An Analytical Framework. Akademisk Forlag (1978)
17. Rodden, T.: A survey of CSCW Systems. Interacting with Computer 3(3), 319–353 (1991)
18. Coutaz, J., Nigay, L., Salber, D., Blandford, A., May, J., Young, R.: Four Easy Pieces for Assessing the Usability of Multimodal Interaction: The CARE Properties. In: Proceedings of the INTERACT 1995 Conference, pp. 115–120 (1995)
19. Schein, E.H.: Organisation Culture and Leadership. Jossey-Bass, San Francisco (1992)
20. Sem Prospective: Rapport annuel 2004-2005 du groupe de travail Prospective éducative et bases de données pédagogiques (PE-BDP). Secteur Prospective (2005)
21. Stader, J., Macintosh, A.: Capability Modelling and Knowledge Management; Applications and Innovations. In: The 19th International Conference of the BCS Specialist Group on Knowledge-Based Systems and Applied Artificial Intelligence, Cambridge, pp. 33–50 (1999)
22. Zhang, Z., Tang, J.: Information Retrieval in Web 2.0. In: Wang, W. (ed.) International Federation for Information Processing, IFIP, Integration and Innovation Orient to E-Society, vol. 1, pp. 663–670. Springer, Boston (2007)

Approaches to Learning and Kolb's Learning Styles of Undergraduates with Better Grades

Patrícia Almeida[1], José Joaquim Teixeira-Dias[2], Mariana Martinho[3], and Chinthaka Balasooriya[4]

[1] Research Centre for Didactics and Technology in Teacher Education (CIDTFF), Department of Education, University of Aveiro, 3810-193 Aveiro, Portugal
[2] Department of Chemistry, University of Aveiro, 3810-193 Aveiro, Portugal
[3] Escola EB 2,3/S de Oliveira de Frades, Portugal
[4] School of Public Health & Community Medicine, University of New South Wales, Sydney, Australia
patriciaalmeida@ua.pt

Abstract. The purpose of this study is to investigate if the teaching, learning and assessment strategies conceived and implemented in a higher education chemistry course promote the development of conceptual understanding, as intended. Thus, our aim is to analyse the learning styles and the approaches to learning of chemistry undergraduates with better grades. The overall results show that the students with better grades possess the assimilator learning style, that is usually associated to the archetypal chemist. Moreover, the students with the highest grades revealed a conception of learning emphasising understanding. However, these students diverged both in their learning approaches and in their preferences for teaching strategies. The majority of students adopted a deep approach or a combination of a deep and a strategic approach, but half of them revealed their preference for teaching-centred strategies.

Keywords: Learning styles, approaches to learning, Kolb's learning styles, teaching strategies, learning strategies, assessment strategies, scholarship of teaching and learning.

1 Introduction

This paper is based upon a growing body of work shaped by a research project aiming to promote the advancement of the scholarship of teaching and learning (SoTL), through the implementation of classroom research, at the University of Aveiro, in Portugal [1], [2].

The project reported here is based within a programme for 1st year students in sciences and engineering, at the University of Aveiro, in Portugal. This work relies upon the belief that it is possible to:

M.D. Lytras et al. (Eds.): WSKS 2010, Part I, CCIS 111, pp. 316–321, 2010.

- enhance SoTL through the implementation of classroom research projects involving science university teachers and educational researchers;
- promote active, integrated and deep learning in chemistry through student-centred teaching approaches, namely by the encouragement of question-asking between teachers and students.

With this in mind, an action research project aiming to promote student-centred teaching approaches, and ultimately to enhance SoTL, is being developed with 100 chemistry students, in full collaboration between an educational researcher from the Education Department, and a professor from the Chemistry Department.

The teaching, learning and assessment strategies at the chemistry course for 1st year students were conceived, designed and implemented in order to support integration [3] and foster deep learning [4]. It was our intention that students' perceptions of the learning environment should be centred on the need for conceptual understanding. These strategies comprised several formats, such as:

(1) small pauses during lectures to encourage students' oral questions. In the middle of the lesson, the teacher stopped lecturing for two or three minutes, and invited the students to think about or to discuss the class topics with their colleagues. At the end of the break, students had the opportunity to raise oral questions. If the students felt more comfortable, they could write their questions instead, and the teacher would answer orally at the beginning of the next lesson.

(2) teacher's written questions during lectures to facilitate the organisation of teaching and learning and to serve as a role model to students. For instance, throughout the 'Water' topic, the teacher presented seventeen written questions. These had diverse degrees of difficulty and served different functions.

(3) practical laboratory sessions were conceived in order to promote the development of concepts and understanding and not merely as a handmaid of lectures. Having this in mind, these sessions were used for problem solving and development of concepts. In laboratory classes, the students have opportunities to: (a) identify the main objectives of the work; (b) identify and overcome any conceptual and practical difficulties encountered; (c) plan and execute the work; (d) record and discuss the results and observations in their lab book; (e) answer the questions raised in their laboratory manual.

(4) 'Questions and answers in Chemistry' online forum to encourage and facilitate students' questioning. Students could use this tool to raise written questions related to the topics taught during lectures and practical laboratory sessions. The teacher answers all questions within two days, also on the online forum. All questions and answers are available to all chemistry students.

(5) 'Problem-based cases' online forum to encourage students to ask questions and suggest possible explanations for the phenomena proposed by the teacher.

In order to promote the alignment between teaching, learning and assessment [5], the following assessment strategies were considered:

(1) *multiple-choice test* due to the large number of students in the chemistry course;

(2) participation in the two online forums considering both the number and the quality of the participation;

(3) performance in practical laboratory work considering both students' performance in practical classes and the content of the lab book.

2 Research Questions

According to Case and Marshall [6], the way students perceive the learning context significantly influences their use of a specific approach. Then, *in a chemistry course intentionally conceived and designed to promote higher-order thinking, do students with better grades adopt a deep approach? Or is it possible to obtain high grades using a strategic or a surface approach?* It also known that chemistry' students exhibit a tendency to adopt an assimilator style [3]. So, *do chemistry students with better grades possess an assimilator learning style?*

3 Method

3.1 Participants

The main sample was composed of 100 undergraduate students (56 female, 44 male; mean age 19 years old) who were tackling foundation chemistry, although following different degree programs, such as physics, environmental engineering and materials engineering; this class did not include students following a chemistry degree program. For this particular research, the eight chemistry students with the highest grades (all over 75%) were selected and then analysed in a deeper way.

3.2 Data-Gathering

Data were gathered by means of observation of all Chemistry classes, students' interviews, documental analysis and the administration of the Portuguese version of the Learning Styles Inventory [7] and the Portuguese version of the ASSIST [8].

4 Findings and Discussion

4.1 Kolb's Learning Styles and Students with Better Grades

The results of the LSI for the eight students show that these learners fall into two camps: assimilating (7 students) and accommodating (1 student). As shown in Figure 1, only one of these students presents a clear preference for AC and AE, being a converger. The other seven students were identified as assimilators, showing a preference for grasping information through AC and processing it through RO. These results concur with those obtained by Kolb [3], [7] and Nulty and Barret [9], suggesting that the typical chemist is an assimilator. Assimilators usually possess the abilities to create theoretical models, to compare alternatives, to define problems and to formulate hypotheses [3].

If considering the group of eight students with better grades, Fábio was the one with lower marks. It is possible that this student had to struggle more to obtain better grades, since his learning style was different from the one usually associated to chemistry.

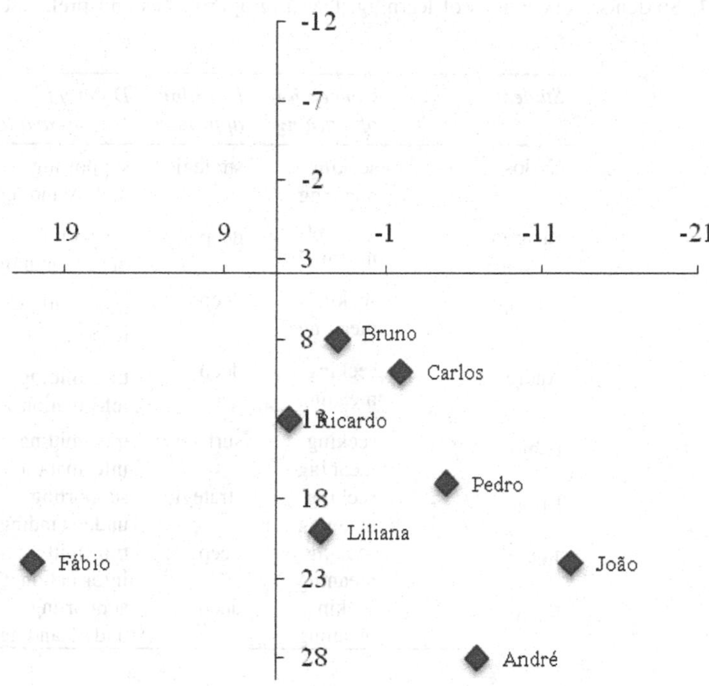

Fig. 1. Distribution of the eight students' learning styles according to LSI

4.2 Approaches to Learning and Students with Better Grades

The results of the ASSIST, including conceptions of learning, learning approaches and preferences for different types of courses and teaching, are presented in Table 1.

The eight students showed a conception of learning associated with a deep learning approach. During interviews, all the students remarked that it was important to memorise and apply knowledge, but all agreed that learning could not be, and should not be, only memorizing and applying.

All students emphasised the role of understanding in the learning process. Bruno and Carlos went beyond this and also stressed the importance of questioning and critical thinking in the learning process.

Five students adopted a deep learning approach (Liliana, André, João, Ricardo and Pedro); two used a strategic approach (Carlos and Bruno) and only one was identified as a surface learner (Fábio).

Carlos and Bruno were identified as strategic learners through the ASSIST; the interviews showed that these students associated the strategic approach with a deep approach. This seems to be the most successful way to cope with the learning and assessment tasks in this course, since these learners were the ones with the highest grades. All the students that participated in the online discussions said that the bonus on the final grade was an interesting stimulus, but also referred that they would participate anyway.

Table 1. Students' conceptions of learning, learning approaches and preferences for types of teaching

Student	*Conception of learning*	*Learning approach*	*Different types of courses and teaching*
Carlos	seeking meaning	strategic	supporting understanding
Ricardo	seeking meaning	deep	supporting understanding
Liliana	seeking meaning	deep	transmitting information
André	seeking meaning	deep	transmitting information
Fábio	seeking meaning	surface	transmitting information
Bruno	seeking meaning	strategic	supporting understanding
João	seeking meaning	deep	transmitting information
Pedro	seeking meaning	deep	supporting understanding

Fábio was the only surface learner. He did not participate in the online discussions and did not attend all classes, because "*it was not compulsory*".

Even if the eight students have a conception of learning that is associated with a deep approach, and if the majority of learners adopt a deep or strategic approach to learning, their preferences in what concerns types of teaching are divided: four students show a preference for types of teaching that emphasise the transmission of information, while the other four prefer teaching strategies that enhance understanding (see Table 1).

5 Conclusions

From this study it is clear that it is possible to create a learning environment focused on conceptual understanding. This research also shows that, with appropriate and diversified strategies, stimulus and motivation, students can enhance their interest and engagement with learning chemistry and, consequently, adopt a deep learning and obtain higher grades.

From the eight students selected, seven were identified as assimilators, the learning style associated to the archetypal chemist. Carlos and Bruno, both identified as balanced learners [10] were also characterised as strategic-deep learners. It seems that these learners are at a higher level of development, having the ability to display different abilities, according to the demands of the learning environment. We believe that it is worth to analyse, with a larger sample, the possible existence of a relationship between the balanced style [3] and the strategic approach [4], when this is associated with a deep approach to learning. This could enhance the relationship already established between these two distinct theories of learning styles [11].

Due to the specific context and to the small number of students interviewed, it is not possible to generalise the results. Thus, one of our purposes for future research is to develop a similar study with a larger sample of students, as well as with students with different kinds of grades (from the lower to the highest marks). We also intend to clearly specify the kind of strategies conceived, as well as the context in which these were implemented, in order to promote discussion about the kind of teaching, learning and assessment strategies that can be used to promote deep learning.

References

1. Albergaria Almeida, P.: Scholarship of teaching and learning: an overview. Journal of the World Universities Forum 2, 143–154 (2010)
2. Almeida, P., Teixeira-Dias, J.J., Medina, J.: Enhancing the Scholarship of Teaching and Learning: the interplay between teaching and research. International Journal of Teaching and Case Studies 2, 262–275 (2010)
3. Kolb, D.A.: Experiential Learning: experience as the source of learning and development. Prentice Hall, Englewood Cliffs (1984)
4. Entwistle, N.J., McCune, V., Walker, P.: Conceptions, styles and approaches within higher education: analytic abstractions and everyday experience. In: Sternberg, R.J., Zhang, L.F. (eds.) Perspectives on Cognitive, Learning and Thinking Styles, pp. 103–136. Erlbaum, New Jersey (2001)
5. Biggs, J.: Teaching for quality learning at university. The Society for Research into Higher Education & The Open University Press, Buckingham (1999)
6. Case, J., Marshall, D.: Approaches to learning. In: Tight, M., Mok, K.H., Huisman, J., Morphew, C.C. (eds.) The Routledge International Handbook of Higher Education, pp. 9–19. Routledge, New York (2009)
7. Kolb, D.A.: The Kolb Learning Style Inventory version 3. Hay Resources Direct, Boston (1999)
8. Valadas, S., Gonçalves, F., Faísca, L.: Approaches to studying in higher education Portuguese students: a Portuguese version of the approaches and study skills inventory for students. Higher Education 59, 259–275 (2009)
9. Nulty, D.D., Barrett, M.A.: Transitions in students' learning styles. Studies in Higher Education 22, 333–345 (1996)
10. Kolb, A., Kolb, D.A.: Learning styles and learning spaces: enhancing experiential learning in Higher Education. Academy of Management Learning & Education 4, 193–212 (2005)
11. Almeida, P., Pedrosa de Jesus, H., Watts, M.: Developing a mini-project: students' questions and learning styles. Psychology of Education Review 32, 6–17 (2008)

Semantically Enriched Tools for the Knowledge Society: Case of Project Management and Presentation

Jakub Talaš, Tomáš Gregar, and Tomáš Pitner*

Masaryk University, Faculty of Informatics,
Botanická 68a, 60200 Brno, Czech Republic
173016@mail.muni.cz, xgregar@fi.muni.cz, tomp@fi.muni.cz
http://www.fi.muni.cz

Abstract. Working with semantically rich data is one of the stepping stones to the knowledge society. In recent years, gathering, processing, and using semantic data have made a big progress, particularly in the academic environment. However, the advantages of the semantic description remain commonly undiscovered by a "common user", including people from academia and IT industry that could otherwise profit from capabilities of contemporary semantic systems in the areas of project management and/or technology-enhanced learning. Mostly, the root cause lays in complexity and non-transparency of the mainstream semantic applications. The semantic tool for project management and presentation consists mainly of a module for the semantic annotation of wiki pages integrated into the project management system *Trac*. It combines the dynamic, easy-of-use nature and applicability of a wiki for project management with the advantages of semantically rich and accurate approach. The system is released as open-source (OS) and is used for management of students' and research projects at the research lab of the authors.

Keywords: Web 2.0, project management, semantic wiki, RDF, Fresnel.

1 Motivation

We have reached the point where there exist many language specifications, ontologies for many domains, specialized knowledge repositories, and respective tools. One of main goals of current semantics-related development is to recommend the advantages of semantics to common users. That requires hard work, because users are often conservative and accustomed to their habits, they mostly do not experiment with new applications or work processes. So it is important to find methods, how to integrate new paradigms with the existing tools.

Another important success determinant for any semantic project is to work in an appropriate application domain where the semantic categories (classes)

* This research has been supported by the Student Research Project No. MUNI/G/0121/2009 of Masaryk University.

M.D. Lytras et al. (Eds.): WSKS 2010, Part I, CCIS 111, pp. 322–328, 2010.

and properties are reasonably well known, formally described, and/or mapped to existing ontologies. We identified the project management and presentation as one of such domains (see formats like *FOAP* [1] and *DOAP* [2]). They are also vital from a practical point of view for both teaching and practice, and can easily be tested and valorized. Other aspects of project management can be inspected elsewhere – like team building issues [8] or quality of the management surveys [9].

2 Semantic Wiki

Any modern system for *Computer-aided* (not just software) *project management* covers the area of collaborative content creation, sharing, and publication. In a university environment targeted to students, these requirements are even amplified, cf. [3]. The members of a project team must share a common environment, see relevant analytical documents, and contribute to discussions. All these activities intensively deal with content. For instant content creation, wiki systems became a de-facto standard as a mean to share, present and exchange information, and are present in nearly all project hosting and management platforms (Sourceforge.net, Codeplex.com, github.org etc.).

There exist many implementations of such interface, based on different languages and storage databases[1]: *MediaWiki* (PHP, MySQL), *Dokuwiki* (PHP), *Twiki* (Perl) etc. An integrated Wiki is also an inevitable part of the project management system *Trac*[2] being used by many OS projects as referred later.

However, the vast majority of systems run without support for semantics [4]. Most of current semantic wiki engines are developed in academic environment. That brings some advantages (open source and free distribution), as well as drawbacks (lots of them is currently abandoned; sometimes, they even do not ever reach a usable milestone)[3]. Existing semantic wikis can stand as the functionality model:

ACE wiki – defines concepts and properties in natural language (like "every country is an area"). It is easy and well-arranged wiki with wide capabilities in building the semantics. The statements are checked for potential semantic collisions like *"Country has one capital"* vs. *"The capital of Germany is Berlin" and "The capital of Germany is Bonn".*

KiWi – stands for *Knowledge In Wiki.* This system is intended for sharing and managing the knowledge.

OntoWiki – very advanced and user friendly wiki-engine, cf. `http://ontowiki.net/Projects/OntoWiki`.

Semantic MediaWiki – is an extension of the popular MediaWiki, cf. `http://semantic-mediawiki.org/wiki/Semantic_MediaWiki`. It adds possibility to add properties to pages and semantic searching.

[1] `http://www.wiki.org/wiki.cgi?WhatIsWiki`
[2] `http://trac.edgewall.org/`
[3] `http://semanticweb.org/wiki/Tools`

TaOPis – easy wiki system for project and contributors' listing, cf. `http://autopoiesis.foi.hr/wiki.php?name=TOP+Administration`.

Wikidsmart – communicates with project management system Jira. Wiki authoring can create bug/feature/feature document in Jira (or other connected management system), cf. `http://semanticweb.org/wiki/Wikidsmart`.

KnowWE – this system annotate content of wiki pages analogically to our *Trac Semantic Extension*. It also recommends pages with semantically related topics or topics with similar attributes. It features an easy-to-use semantic search functionality, cf. `http://semanticweb.org/wiki/KnowWE`.

3 Project Management and Presentation Using a Wiki

An academic environment as well as most commercial ones needs a web-based system capable to present software developed done *in situ*, e.g. non-fully-public projects that are not appropriate to be hosted on remote platforms like Sourceforge. Examples from the university environment include *in-term projects*, *bachelor or diploma theses*, or some *research projects*. As a result of an extensive survey [5], the web-based system *Trac* (mentioned above) has been selected. An important factor determining the selection of a right project management system was its semantic capabilities that are substantial for working on project-based tasks [7]. Trac includes a wiki, allows synchronization with a Subversion repository, contains modules for bug tracking, issue reporting etc.

The use in programming-related courses at a university primarily demanded serious improvements in the system structure and design in order to supports multiple projects and localization. The installation implemented in the research lab of the authors is called *Deep Thought* (DT). A fundamental advantage of Trac/DT is a wide support for extensions. There exist two types of extensions — *plugins* and *macros*. Plugins can, thanks to their low-level interface to other Trac modules, extend whole system functionality. Macros are direct components of the Trac wiki-subsystem for dynamizing wiki pages.

4 Semex — Semantic Annotations in the Wiki

However, from the semantic point of view, the core contribution has been done in the *Semex* (Semantic extension) project. *Semex* allows annotations of wiki content according to ontological definitions in the knowledge database *Sesame 2*. It also enables visual highlighting of the tagged parts of text and viewing their context. This functionality brings the possibility of browsing pages via semantic relations; e.g. *person* — his/her *projects*; or *"show all project contributors, who are older than 18 years"*. It can integrate the content with other services (e-mail), mine concept definitions from the repository or other web-service, or list other instances of the same concept [6]. It is composed of a Trac plugin assuring the administrative functions and communication with the knowledge repository and a set of wiki macros. Macros visualize semantic data instantly on the wiki pages and interact with the users; they are capable to wrap the authoring of semantic statements directly in the user interface, cf. Fig. 1.

Fig. 1. Popups with semantically precise information from the wiki

4.1 Technology

Extension uses library *RDFLib*[4] for work with RDF triples (i.e. inner representation of sources, statements, relations, ontologies). Interface with Sesame 2 (via its REST protocol interface) could be offered by *RDF Alchemy*[5]; Sesame is just one of triple-stores the library can communicate with.

The important part of the Semex development was also the selection (to preserve not to "reinvent the wheel") of ontologies to work with. DT, as multi-project management system cope with information about persons (`foaf`, `http://xmlns.com/foaf/0.1/`), projects, developers (`doap`, `http://usefulinc.com/ns/doap#`), documents (`dc`, `http://purl.org/dc/elements/1.1/`), wiki pages (`wiki`, `http://sw.deri.org/2005/04/wikipedia/wikiont.owl#`), events, deadlines, meetings (`event`, `http://purl.org/NET/c4dm/event.owl#`), or places (`geo`, `http://www.w3.org/2003/01/geo/wgs84_pos#`) etc. This ontological structure allows describing semantics of the wiki documents.

4.2 Functionality

The solution covers all basic use-cases required for a computer-aided project management and presentation using wiki. The administrative section allows creating, editing and deleting persons, projects, events, places and documents via a form-based web interface. The module also automatically creates wiki pages

[4] `http://www.rdflib.net/`

[5] `http://www.openvest.com/trac/wiki/RDFAlchemy`

for the respective objects — names of these wiki pages start with `Semex:`. In the prototype, access to the sections is authenticated and authorized via *Kerberos* and the users can use their Faculty accounts credentials.

Wiki macros are the "visible" part of the module, cf. Fig. 2. A common visitor of DT sees only them. Trac macros could be written in wiki page as short tag enclosed in doubled square brackets (with optional parameters in parentheses).

Editing info

```
[[SemexCommon()]]

== Info about presentation ==
Bc. [[Semex(info, foaf:jakub_talas, Jakub Talaš)]] will have a presentatic
[[Semex(info, event:konference, DiVAI conference)]] in [[Semex(info, geo:S


=== List of all events ===
[[Semex(query , SELECT ?name ?source WHERE {?source rdf:type event:Event;
```

Fig. 2. Writing complex queries in wiki

We developed various macros for Semex:

Info it shows popup menu with options and information about selected object. It also allows user to see all statements of this object.

Query returns a list of RDF sources according to entered SPARQL query. Suitable for automatic lists.

Calendar prints out simple calendar with upcoming events

Allabout prints out all information about a source and similar ones.

SemexCommon prerequisition for other semantic macros (semantic methods, GUI forms).

GUI of macros (popup menus, simple user-centered wizards) is created via the *jQuery 1.3* library. With wizards, even common user with minimal notion of formal semantics can exploit the semantics. Macros have also possibilities to utilize fully-fledged queries in SPARQL.

5 System Integration

One of the usage patterns of the semantically enhanced project management system Deep Though is the university teaching. Choosing the right pattern of integration into the whole study process and administration is crucial, it was necessary to integrate the extension module and the whole system with the *University's study administration information system* (IS) in order to ensure smooth application in software development oriented courses. Students in these courses have to *build a team*, sign up for some *project assignment* and then *work on it*. This integration allows to get needed data from the IS, and automatically

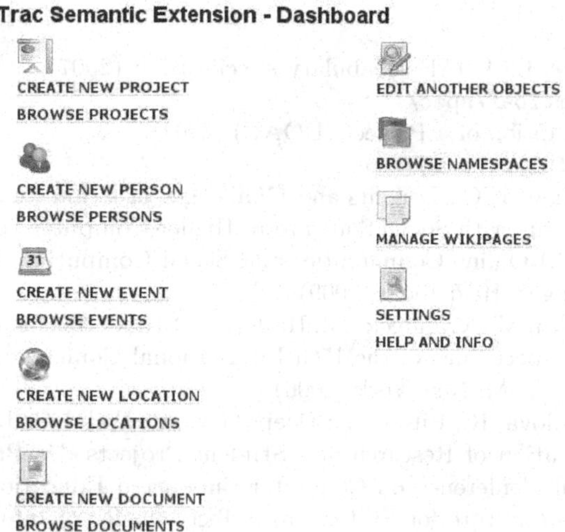

Fig. 3. Entities common for all projects in Deep Though

create an environment for projects. Metadata is also imported into the semantic repository and utilized via the semantic module of Deep Thought, cf. Fig. 3.

The most visible features and contributions of this semantically-enhanced project management system in comparison with tradition PM systems is a common knowledge base consisting of concepts (entities) maintained centrally and reusable in all projects wherever it is relevant, see Fig. 3. A clear advantage of this approach is in its flexibility — once the DOAP ontology schema is replaced by a newer standard for project description, the transition will be significantly easier that in a classical database system where the relational or object/class schema must be modified — with all the undesired consequencies it might have.

6 Conclusion

Mentioned wiki systems have proven that semantic extensions and semantic features make a sense. Semantic features are useful more in narrower and well known domains — where the ontologies and specialized tools for users can be identified and constructed. Deep Thought belongs to such tools. For comparison, the best practical example known in this category is the connection between *Wikidsmart* and *Jira* where semantics brings really an added value recognizable at the first look. Semex is being developed with this in mind.

Though in its early state, it contributes to better usability of the Deep Thought Trac-based multi-project management system. It shows the way to easy-of-use semantically rich applications that are substantial for the coming knowledge society. It has also clearly demonstrated that the way to fully-semantic applications is not an easy one and will require a lot of effort.

References

1. Brickley, D., Miller, L.: FOAF vocabulary specification (2007), http://xmlns.com/foaf/spec/
2. Dumbill, E.: Description of a Project (DOAP) (2004), http://trac.usefulinc.com/doap
3. Kadenbach, D., Kleiner, C.: Benefits and Challenges of Using Collaborative Development Environments with Social Software in Higher Computer Science Education. In: Schuler, D. (ed.) Online Communities and Social Computing. LNCS, vol. 5621, pp. 479–487. Springer, Heidelberg (2009)
4. Völkel, M., Krötzsch, M., Vrandecic, D., Haller, H., Studer, R.: Semantic Wikipedia. In: WWW 2006: Proceedings of the 15th International Conference on World Wide Web, pp. 585–594. ACM, New York (2006)
5. Gregar, T., Pospíšilová, R., Pitner, T.: Deep Thought: Web based System for Managing and Presentation of Research and Student Projects. In: Proceedings of the First International Conference on Computer Supported Education, CSEDU 2009, p. 5. INSTICC — Institute for Systems and Technologies of Information, Control and Comunication, Lisboa, Portugal (2009)
6. Geurts, J., et al.: Towards Ontology-driven Discourse: From Semantic Graphs to Multimedia Presentations. In: Fensel, D., Sycara, K., Mylopoulos, J. (eds.) ISWC 2003. LNCS, vol. 2870, p. 16. Springer, Heidelberg (2003)
7. Landaeta, R.E., Pinto, C.A., Kotnour, T.: Assessing faulty knowledge management systems in project-based organisations. International Journal of Knowledge and Learning 5(2), 122–143 (2009)
8. Herández-López, A., Colomo-Palacios, R., García-Crespo, Á., Soto-Acosta, P.: Trust Building Process for Global Software Development Teams. A review from the Literature. International Journal of Knowledge Society Research (IJKSR) 1(1), 65–82 (2010)
9. Bodea, C.-N., Dascalu, M.: Quality of Project Management Education and Training Programmes. International Journal of Knowledge Society Research (IJKSR) 1(2), 13–25 (2010) ISSN: 1947-8429

Application of Scientific Approaches for Evaluation of Quality of Learning Objects in eQNet Project

Eugenijus Kurilovas[1,2,3] and Silvija Serikoviene[1]

[1] Institute of Mathematics and Informatics, Akademijos str. 4, 08663 Vilnius, Lithuania
[2] Vilnius Gediminas Technical University, Sauletekio al. 11, 10223 Vilnius, Lithuania
[3] Centre of Information Technologies in Education, Suvalku str. 1, 03106 Vilnius, Lithuania
eugenijus.kurilovas@itc.smm.lt, silvija.serikoviene@gmail.com

Abstract. The paper is aimed to analyse the application of several scientific approaches, methods, and principles for evaluation of quality of learning objects for Mathematics subject. The authors analyse the following approaches to minimise subjectivity level in expert evaluation of the quality of learning objects, namely: (1) principles of multiple criteria decision analysis for identification of quality criteria, (2) technological quality criteria classification principle, (3) fuzzy group decision making theory to obtain evaluation measures, (4) normalisation requirement for criteria weights, and (5) scalarisation method for learning objects quality optimisation. Another aim of the paper is to outline the central role of social tagging to describe usage, attention, and other aspects of the context; as well as to help to exploit context data towards making learning object repositories more useful, and thus enhance the reuse. The applied approaches have been used practically for evaluation of learning objects and metadata tagging while implementing European eQNet and te@ch.us projects in Lithuanian comprehensive schools in 2010.

Keywords: Learning object, multiple criteria decision analysis, optimisation methods, expert evaluation, quality criteria.

1 Introduction

eQNet is a three-year (September 2009-2012) Comenius Multilateral Network [3] funded under the European Commission's Lifelong Learning programme (LLP). The project is coordinated by European Schoolnet (EUN) and involves 9 Ministries of Education or agencies nominated to act of their behalf. The primary aim is to improve the quality of learning objects (LOs) in European Schoolnet's Learning Resource Exchange (LRE) [8] which currently offers almost 130,000 LOs and assets from over 25 providers. As a pan-European service, the LRE particularly seeks to identify LOs that "travel well" (i.e., reusable) across national borders and can be used in a cultural and linguistic context different from the one in which they were created [3].

eQNet will do this by establishing a network consisting of researchers, policy makers and practitioners (teachers) that will develop and apply "travel well" quality criteria to both existing LRE content as well as that to be selected in future from national repositories. The vision driving the LRE is that a significant percentage of high

M.D. Lytras et al. (Eds.): WSKS 2010, Part I, CCIS 111, pp. 329–335, 2010.

quality LOs developed in different countries, in different languages and to meet the needs of different curricula can be re-used at European level.

eQNet will provide a forum for joint reflection and co-operation related to the exchange and re-use of educational content and allow network members to: (1) better share information and expertise particularly related to "travel well" quality criteria (pedagogical, technical and intellectual property rights (IPR) factors); (2) develop new frameworks to improve the quality of LOs and metadata in both national repositories and the LRE, including the growing volume of user-generated content and metadata, as well as to improve the multilinguality of LRE content as a result of the translation of metadata, making use, where appropriate, of automatic metadata translation approaches and technologies; (3) enable schools to participate in a Community of Practice related to the use LOs at European level.

Major results will include: the development of "travel well" quality criteria to more easily identify LOs with the potential for cross-border use (this work package is coordinated by Lithuanian partner, in particular by the author of the paper); the practical application by teachers of these criteria to >3,500 LOs in the LRE; 'showcases' of the best of these LOs in a "travel well" section of the LRE portal; where necessary, the enrichment of selected LOs with new or better metadata; a Community of Practice for teachers around these LOs [3].

2 Methodology of the Research

One of the main features achieving the high LOs effectiveness and efficiency level is LOs reusability. The need for reusability of LOs has at least three elements: (1) interoperability: LO is interoperable and can be used in different platforms; (2) flexibility in terms of pedagogic situations: LO can fit into a variety of pedagogic situations, and (3) modifiability to suit a particular teacher's or student's needs: LO can be made more appropriate to a pedagogic situation by modifying it to suit a particular teacher's or student's needs [4].

Reusability of LOs (or their ability to "travel well" between different contexts and education systems) is considered by the authors as a part of the overall quality of LOs. This means that any high quality LO has some reusability level (or potential to "travel well"), but this does not mean that any reusable LO is quality one.

The main problem analysed in the paper is how to establish (1) a 'proper' set of LOs "travel well" quality evaluation criteria which should reflect the objective scientific principles of construction a *model* (criteria tree) for LOs "travel well" quality evaluation, and also (2) a 'proper' *method* for evaluation of LOs quality.

Expert evaluation is referred here as the multiple criteria evaluation of LOs aimed at selection of the best alternatives (i.e., LOs) based on score-ranking results [6]. If the set of decision alternatives (LOs) is assumed to be predefined, fixed and finite, then the decision problem is to choose the optimal alternative or, maybe, to rank them. But usually the experts have to deal with the problem of optimal decision in the multiple criteria situation where the objectives are often conflicting. In this case, an optimal decision is the one that maximises the expert's utility. These principles of identification of quality evaluation criteria have been analysed in multiple criteria decision analysis (MCDA) theory related research works, e.g., [2].

Evaluation of LOs quality is a typical case where the criteria are conflicting, i.e., LOs could be very qualitative against several criteria, and not qualitative against the other ones, and vice versa. Therefore, the authors propose to use MCDA approach for creation of LOs quality evaluation model and method.

LOs multiple criteria evaluation method is referred here as the experts' additive utility function represented by formula (1) below including LOs evaluation criteria, their ratings (values) and weights [6]. This method is well-known in the theory of optimisation methods and is named "*scalarisation method*". A possible decision here could be to transform multi-criteria task into one-criterion task obtained by adding all criteria together with their weights. It is valid from the point of view of the optimisation theory, and a special theorem exists for this case [6].

Therefore, here we have the experts' additive utility function:

$$f(X)=\sum_{i=1}^{m}a_i f_i(X), \sum_{i=1}^{m}a_i=1,\ a_i>0. \tag{1}$$

where $f_i\ (X_j)$ is the rating (i.e., non-fuzzy value) of the criterion i for the each of the examined LOs alternatives X_j. The weights here should be 'normalised' according to the *'normalisation' requirement.*

$$\sum_{i=1}^{m}a_i=1,\ a_i>0. \tag{2}$$

The major is the meaning of the utility function (1) the better LOs meet the quality requirements in comparison with the ideal (i.e., 100%) quality.

3 Literature Analysis and Research Results

This section is aimed (1) to apply the aforementioned scientific approaches to propose a suitable scientific model and method for evaluation of quality of LOs, (2) to present LOs experimental evaluation results, and (3) to present social tagging approach to enrich multilingual LOs metadata in eQNet.

3.1 Learning Objects Quality Evaluation Model

The following *principles of identification of quality evaluation criteria* are relevant to all MCDA approaches: (1) value relevance; (2) understandability; (3) measurability; (4) non-redundancy; (5) judgmental independence; (6) balancing completeness and conciseness; (7) operationality; (8) simplicity versus complexity [2].

On the other hand, according to the *technological quality criteria classification principle*, we can divide technological quality criteria into 'internal quality' and 'quality in use' criteria of the educational software such as LOs. 'Internal quality' is a descriptive characteristic that describes the quality of software independently from any particular context of its use, while 'quality in use' is evaluative characteristic of software obtained by making a judgment based on criteria that determine the worthiness of software for a particular project. Any LOs quality evaluation model (set of criteria) should provide the experts (decision makers) the clear instrumentality who (i.e., what kind of experts) should analyse what kind of LOs quality criteria in order to select the best LOs suitable for their needs. According to aforementioned *principle*, 'internal quality' criteria should be mainly the area of interest of the software engineers, and 'quality in use' criteria should be mostly analysed by the programmers and users taking into account the users' feedback on the usability of software [6].

The authors have applied these two principles in their papers [5], [6] on technological evaluation of the learning software, and thus have identified a number of LOs technological quality evaluation criteria presented in the technological part of the LOs quality evaluation model presented in Fig. 1.

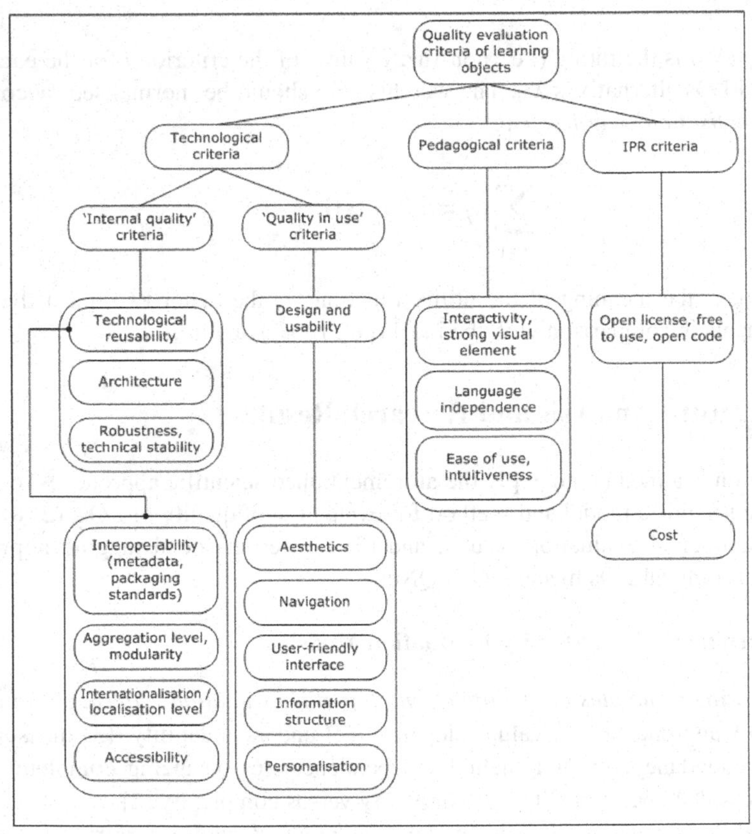

Fig. 1. LOs quality evaluation model (criteria tree)

On the other hand, the authors have analysed a number of existing models (sets of quality evaluation criteria) for evaluation of pedagogical quality of LOs, e.g., [1], [7], [9], [10], and [13].

The suitable criteria based on MCDA principles [2] are: (1) interactivity, strong visual structure (animations, images and short videos are travelling best); (2) language independence or low language dependence (easily translatable) or multilinguality; (3) ease of use, intuitiveness. Intellectual property rights (IPR) criterion should also be considered here [5].

Therefore, the authors propose to construct the LOs quality evaluation model (see Fig. 1) based on the literature analysis, MCDA principles of identification of quality evaluation criteria, and technological quality criteria classification principle.

3.2 Learning Objects Quality Evaluation Method

The widely used measurement criteria of the decision attributes' quality are mainly qualitative and subjective. Decisions in this context are often expressed in natural language, and evaluators are unable to assign exact numerical values to the different criteria. Assessment can be often performed by linguistic variables: 'bad', 'poor', 'fair', 'good' and 'excellent'. These values are imprecise and uncertain: they are commonly called 'fuzzy values'. Integrating these different judgments to obtain a final evaluation is not evident. Therefore, the authors have proposed to use *fuzzy group decision making theory* to obtain final assessment measures [11]. Linguistic variables conversion into non-fuzzy values of the evaluation criteria is as follows: 'excellent'=0.850; 'good'=0.675; 'fair'=0.500; 'poor'=0.325; 'bad'=0.150 [6].

The weight of the evaluation criterion reflects the experts' opinion on the criterion's importance level in comparison with the other criteria for the particular needs. For example, for the most simple (general) case, when all LOs evaluation criteria are of equal importance (i.e., we pay no especial attention to LOs reusability criteria), the experts could consider the equal weights a_i = 0.125 according to the normalisation requirement (2).

But if we pay especial attention to LOs reusability criteria, we can, e.g., consider the increased weights for the 1st and 6th LOs quality evaluation criteria (see Fig. 1 and Table 1), because these criteria deal with LOs reusability mostly. In this case these increased weights could be, e.g., twice higher in comparison with the other ones – 0.2, and all other criteria weights according to normalisation requirement (2) should be equal 0.1.

Lithuanian Mathematics expert teacher (the co-author of the paper) has applied the presented evaluation model and method in eQNet project (see Table 1). A number of probably qualitative reusable LOs have been identified in Lithuanian LOs repositories and evaluated against the aforementioned model and method (see formula (1).

There are three examples of these LOs presented in Table 1: (1) LO1: "Coordinate Method", available online at http://mkp.emokykla.lt/imo/lt/mo/250/; (2) LO2: "Polygon area", available online at http://mkp.emokykla.lt/imo/lt/mo/431/; and (3) LO3: "Interval Method", available online at http://mkp.emokykla.lt/imo/lt/mo/316/.

Table 1. Results of experimental evaluation of LOs general quality (q) and "travel well" quality (twq)

LOs evaluation criteria	LO_1q	LO_2q	LO_3q	LO_1twq	LO_2twq	LO_3twq
Technological criteria:						
1. Technological reusability	0.675	0.850	0.675	*0.1350*	*0.1700*	*0.1350*
2. Design and usability	0.675	0.850	0.850	0.0675	0.0850	0.0850
3. Working stability	0.675	0.500	0.675	0.0675	0.0500	0.0675
4. Architecture	0.675	0.500	0.500	0.0675	0.0500	0.0500
Pedagogical criteria:						
5. Interactivity level	0.850	0.500	0.325	0.0850	0.0500	0.0325
6. Language independence	0.675	0.850	0.325	*0.1350*	*0.1700*	*0.0650*
7. Ease of use, intuitiveness	0.850	0.850	0.500	0.0850	0.0850	0.0500
IPR criteria:						
8. Open licence, cost	0.850	0.850	0.850	0.0850	0.0850	0.0850
Evaluation results:	***0.7406***	***0.7188***	***0.5875***	***0.7275***	***0.7450***	***0.5700***

These results mean that LO_1 meets 74.06% general quality (q) in comparison with the ideal, LO_2 – 71.88%, and LO_3 – 58.75%. They also mean that LO_1 meets 72.75% "travel well" quality (twq) in comparison with the ideal, LO_2 – 74.50%, and LO_3 – 57.00%. Therefore, LO_1 is the best alternative (among the evaluated) from general quality point of view, but LO_2 is the best from "travel well" quality point of view.

3.3 Social Tagging in eQNet

In eQNet, the partners consider that context comprises the LO usage situation and environment as well as persistent and transient properties of the user. They concentrate on teachers using LO repositories as an important use-case example and focus on language and country as context variables. We can use such context information to improve the use and reuse of LO repositories by making them more useful in a multilingual and multicultural context. The central role that social tagging can play in this process is outlined in eQNet: on the one hand, tags describe usage, attention, and other aspects of context; on the other hand, they can help to exploit context data towards making LO repositories more useful, and thus enhance the reuse.

This approach could be especially useful for user generated content and Web 2.0 communities while implementing the other ongoing LLP project te@ch.us aimed at the creation and analysis of the learning communities for Web 2.0 teaching [12].

4 Conclusion and Recommendations

The presented research results show that MCDA approach-based LOs evaluation model presented in Fig. 1 and method represented by formula (1) are applicable in real life situations when education institutions have to decide on purchase of LOs for their education needs in the market. The proposed approaches are quite objective, exact and simply to use for choosing the qualitative LOs alternatives.

On the other hand, the proposed LOs "travel well" quality evaluation approach is applicable for the aims of eQNet project in order to select "travel well" LOs from LRE or elsewhere to use them in the other education contexts and countries.

References

1. Becta: Quality principles for digital learning resources (2007)
2. Belton, V., Stewart, T.J.: Multiple criteria decision analysis: an integrated approach. Kluwer Academic Publishers, Dordrecht (2002)
3. eQNet: Quality Network for a European Learning Resource Exchange project website (2010), `http://eqnet.eun.org`
4. Kurilovas, E.: Interoperability, Standards and Metadata for e-Learning. In: Papadopoulos, G.A., Badica, C. (eds.) Intelligent Distributed Computing III, Studies in Computational Intelligence, vol. 237, pp. 121–130. Springer, Heidelberg (2009)
5. Kurilovas, E., Dagiene, V.: Learning Objects and Virtual Learning Environments Technical Evaluation Criteria. Electronic Journal of e-Learning 7(2), 127–136 (2009)
6. Kurilovas, E., Serikoviene, S.: Learning Content and Software Evaluation and Personalisation Problems. Informatics in Education 9(1), 91–114 (2010)
7. Leacock, T.L., Nesbit, J.C.: A Framework for Evaluating the Quality of Multimedia Learning Resources. Educational Technology & Society 10(2), 44–59 (2007)
8. LRE: European Learning Resource Exchange service for schools web site (2010), `http://lreforschools.eun.org/LRE-Portal/Index.iface`
9. MELT: EU eContentplus programme's Metadata Ecology for Learning and Teaching project web site (2008), `http://melt-project.eun.org`
10. Paulsson, F., Naeve, A.: Establishing technical quality criteria for Learning Objects (2006), `http://www.frepa.org/wp/wp-content/files/Paulsson-Establ-Tech-Qual_finalv1.pdf`
11. Ounaies, H.Z., Jamoussi, Y., Ben Ghezala, H.H.: Evaluation framework based on fuzzy measured method in adaptive learning system. Themes in Science and Technology Education 1(1), 49–58 (2009)
12. te@ch.us: Helping teachers integrate Web 2.0 into the classroom. EU LLP te@ch.us project (Learning community for Web 2.0 teaching). European Schoolnet (2010), `http://www.europeanschoolnet.org/web/guest/about/release/-/asset_publisher/0Tqh/content/20655?redirect=%2Fweb%2Fguest%2Fabout%2Frelease`
13. Vargo, J., Nesbit, J.C., Belfer, K., Archambault, A.: Learning object evaluation: Computer mediated collaboration and inter-rater reliability. International Journal of Computers and Applications 25(3), 198–205 (2003)

Appendix

The work presented in this paper is partially supported by the European Commission under the LLP – as part of the eQNet project (project number 502857-LLP-1-2009-1-BECOMENIUS-CNW) and te@ch.us project (project No. 504333-LLP-1-2009-1-DE-COMENIUS-CMP). The authors are solely responsible for the content of this paper. It does not represent the opinion of the European Commission, and the European Commission is not responsible for any use that might be made of data appearing therein.

Empowering the Design and the Sharing of Learning Plans by Means of Net Technologies: The IAMEL System

Rosa Maria Bottino, Michela Ott, and Mauro Tavella

Istituto Tecnologie Didattiche – CNR
Via De Marini, 6, Genoa Italy
{bottino,ott,tavella}@itd.cnr.it

Abstract. This paper reports on the research work carried out by the authors in the framework of the IAMEL project, supported by the Italian Ministry of Education. The project was mainly aimed at enhancing the teaching/learning of mathematics by providing teachers with specific e-learning platforms endowed with a number of dedicated tools supporting the setting-up and the carrying-out of specific in-field experiments. One of the main results of the project was the development of a methodology to carry out the design of educational interventions; such a methodology was based on a conceptual goal-oriented framework and on different authoring tools among which the IAMEL system, an online tool fully described in the paper that allows both the production and the sharing of pedagogical plans and consents the design and the modeling of educational interventions with different levels of granularity and scope.

Keywords: Technology Enhanced Learning, Pedagogical Planning, Net – Technologies, Learning Innovation, Formal Education.

1 Introduction

Nowadays a new learning/teaching panorama is emerging [1]. A number of important novelties are around and deeply involve the main actors in the educational scene: learners and teachers. The learners of the new Knowledge society [2] are increasingly felt as being at the centre of the educational process and, as a consequence, the ways in which they tackle educational tasks appreciably change and the role of teachers is also being radically transformed [3].

Indeed, the teacher's primary role shifts from that of information giver, to that of facilitator and guide [4], the teacher's function incorporates mediation, modeling, and coaching, and this requires a high degree of adaptivity to new learning/teaching schemes, models and tools (e.g. managing technology may take up a great deal of time and intellectual energy).

Even in this emerging new learning landscape the relevance of a teacher-driven pedagogy cannot be questioned [5], and the pedagogical choices made by the teachers and the overall pedagogical approach they adopt are increasingly felt as having a concrete value to broaden the students' learning opportunities and foster learning [6].

M.D. Lytras et al. (Eds.): WSKS 2010, Part I, CCIS 111, pp. 336–342, 2010.

As a matter of fact, pedagogical planning intended as the process of producing "a blueprint for the enactment of learning activities" [7] or even "a description of the playing out of a learning situation or a unit of learning aimed at the acquisition of a precise body of knowledge through the specification of roles and activities" [8] continues to play a fundamental role in contemporary education.

In the new educational landscape, teachers and all those involved in designing and enacting learning processes (trainers, pedagogical experts, designers, researchers etc…) are increasingly required to take into account a huge variety of different elements, in an effort to ensure that these form part of a coherent, manageable whole that responds effectively to learners' needs and that consents the full attainment of the intended educational objectives.

Current research in the field of pedagogical planning mainly focuses on defining which tools and methods better serve the scope since a wide number of different tools and different approaches are adopted to assist "teachers in the thought processes involved in selecting appropriate methods, tools, student activities and assessments to suit the required learning objectives" [9].

ICT-based environments and tools aimed at supporting and backing the process of pedagogical planning are widely considered extremely useful resources and recently, a number of significant attempts to use ICT to describe and share pedagogical ideas have been carried out [10, 11]. The availability of such ICT-based tools has given strong impulse to the formalisation of pedagogical plans [12] and this fact, on the one hand, increases the possibility of sharing and re-using pedagogical ideas/methods, on the other, makes the process of pedagogical planning conceptually simpler and offers the possibility of better managing complexity [13].

This paper aims at giving a contribution to the research field by presenting an on line environment devoted to pedagogical planning. This environment was designed and implemented in the framework of the research project IAMEL, supported by the Italian Ministry of Education and Research under the PRIN 2007 (Research Projects of National Interest) programme, the main aim of which was that of supporting the teaching/learning of mathematics by enhancing the potential of e-learning platforms at these ends.

In this project pedagogical planning was broadly felt as a key aspect and a specific ICT-based tool was produced, following previous experiences [10] carried out by the authors, who were partners of the consortium.

In the following, an overall description of the IAMEL system is provided and its main features are illustrated by focusing on key innovative aspects.

2 The IAMEL System at a Glance

The IAMEL system was designed and implemented with the main aim of allowing the production and sharing of structured pedagogical plans; it is content and subject-independent although it was conceived and created to address the needs of researchers and teachers working in the field of mathematics.

In the following the structure and the main features of the IAMEL pedagogical plans are presented and subsequently the overall computing architecture of the system is briefly described by focusing on its main innovative characteristics.

2.1 The IAMEL Pedagogical Plans

Figure 1 shows the main screen of an exemplary pedagogical plan, called PLAN X, that gives a global idea of the overall structure and contents of the IAMEL Pedagogical Plans.

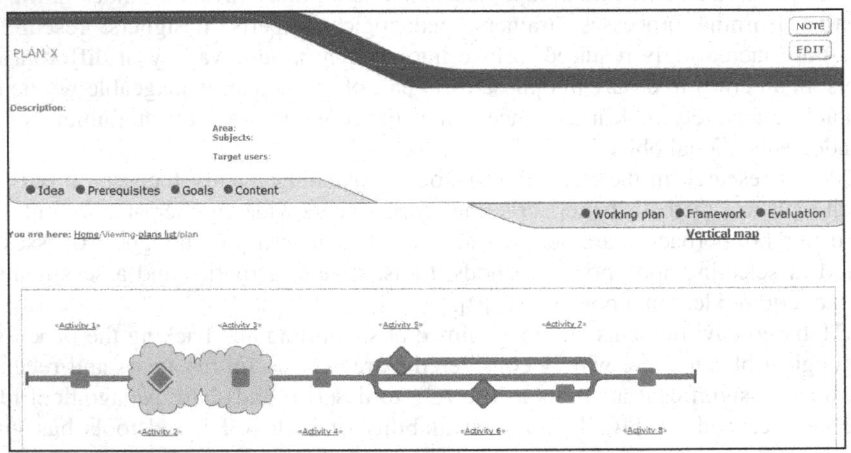

Fig. 1. Main screenshot of an exemplary IAMEL Pedagogical Plan

The main upper part of the screen contains some basic data (description, authors, target population…) aimed at providing key information about the plan; the map at the bottom of the screen shows, instead, the sequence of the different activities to be carried out. Each activity is then further described in detail in a separate section where its relevant functional aspects are highlighted.

Basic Data/Key Information

Key information provided in the upper part of the screen (Fig.1) mainly aim at providing a general overview of the plan by giving a basic idea of its features, constraints and overall feasibility. The underneath ribbon gives further general detail on the plan at hand by means of seven small tabs that can be expanded by clicking on them, thus providing access to a text box containing detailed information about: the underpinning *idea*, the *prerequisites* demanded to the students in order to perform the required activities, the *goals* to be achieved by the learner population, the specific *content* addressed, the *working plan*, the theoretical *framework* that has informed the process of the plan design and, finally, the methods, parameters and specific tools adopted to carry out the *evaluation* of the envisaged activities.

Activities: Flow and Description

The core of the whole plan are, nevertheless, the activities to be carried out; as shown in Fig.1, the map containing the flow of the activities appears in the main screen shot of the plan.

As to the type of the activities, the IAMEL system distinguishes among "mandatory/obligatory activities", namely those that are considered necessary to fulfill the intended educational objectives and "optional activities" or activities that are not to be carried out by all students in a classroom or discretionary activities non essential to the learning/teaching scope.

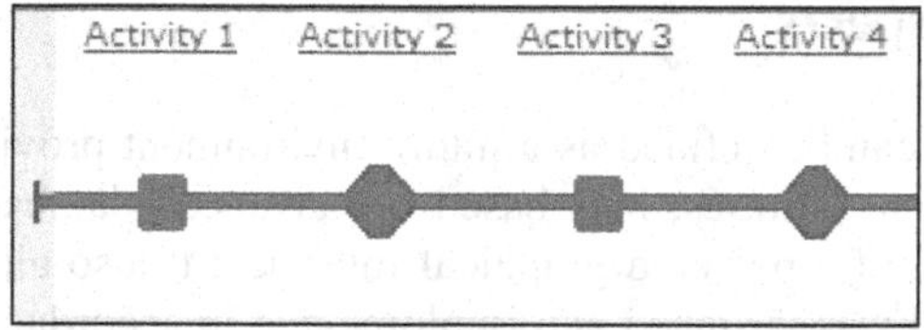

Fig. 2. Map of the activities (flow: obligatory-optional-obligatory-optional)

Figure 2 shows an exemplary simple map of activities. The represented sequence is composed by obligatory activities (squares) and optional activities (rhombuses). The actual flow is linear and sequential: an initial obligatory activity is followed by an optional one, subsequently the third activity is again obligatory while the last one is, once more, optional. IAMEL, nevertheless, allows the building up of very complex and articulated plans where the sequence of the activities can be far more variegated and diversified. For instance, as shown in figure 3, it offers the possibility of setting up "two routes" (Fig.3, left part) or even "three routes" paths (Fig.3, right part), where the user can autonomously choose among different alternatives. As an example, the flow represented in the left part of figure 3 envisages that after performing the mandatory "Activity 1" and before performing the mandatory "Activity 5" the users have the possibility to follow the upper route (where only one optional activity is foreseen) or to follow the lower route where one mandatory activity and an optional one (to be performed in a linear sequence) are foreseen.

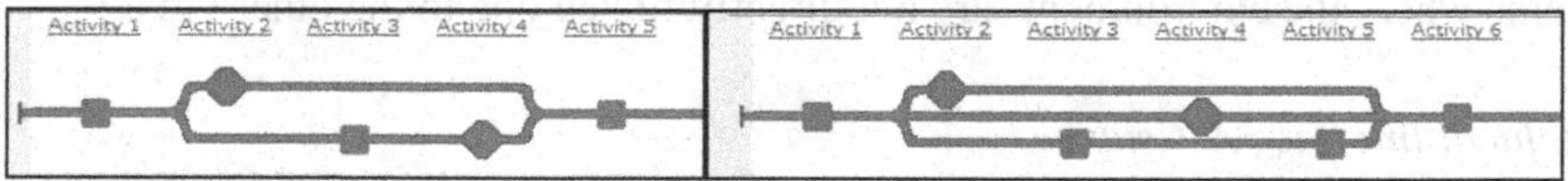

Fig. 3. Map of the activities: "two routes" and "three routes" flow

As a further opportunity the map also encompasses the possibility of defining a set of activities to be caried out in a random, not strictly sequential order.

In order to allow full comprehension and, possibly, reusability and modifications/adaptations, each activity of the plan is further described in details in a separate section, where its relevant aspects are highlighted. A full description of the activity at hand is provided, together with its main learning objectives and the needed prerequisites. The tools and resources needed (or even suggested) to perform the activity are described and, possibly, made available, linked or provided for downloading; detailed information about the educational method adopted is given as well with a specific focus on the evaluation methods, tools and measures to be used. An accurate description of the teaching methodology, the work organization, the teaching/learning strategy adopted, the overall time required etc...is also provided and, in addition, all relevant documents and reports are available in the "Documentation" section.

3 The IAMEL System: Relevant Technical Features and Key Innovative Aspects

The IAMEL system can be defined as a multi-environment providing different kinds of users with different facilities; it is based on advanced database technologies and exploits the potential of a powered graphical interface; it also allows customized access by the users and was designed and implemented in accordance with the "Design for All" [14] principles.

To date, the pilot experiments conducted seem to confirm that the IAMEL system is endowed with a number of significant features that contribute to make it a widely usable and accessible tool. Among these features it is worth highlighting:

Data-Base Facilities
IAMEL is powered by PHP and based on a MySQL database whose structure is the result of the common work of the researchers involved in the project.

Increased flexibility and augmented search facilities are some of the key added values provided by the fact that the pedagogical plans are in a database compatible format.

Multi-Environment Features
The IAMEL system encompasses two different environments: the "authoring environment" and "viewing environment; it allows direct and immediate "commuting" between the authoring and the viewing environment, thus *de facto* functioning as a multi-environment system; this represents a relevant novelty with respect to other systems where the environments are not directly linked one to the other [15].

Graphical Interface Assistance
The system includes a graphical interface which greatly enhances the system usability. Thanks to this feature the users, in a few steps can modify the map of the activities of a plan (flow of the activities)

Customization Features
The system comprises a number of features allowing a high degree of customization and personalization. This aspect is particularly important to sustain and improve the software accessibility by persons with special needs.

The architecture of the entire system is fully compliant with the required accessibility standard (use of validated XHTML and CSS) and meets the requirements of the Italian law in force (law 4/2004 or Stanca Act[1]).

---

[1] Italian Law 4/2004 Provisions to support the access to Information Technologies for the disabled `http://www.pubbliaccesso.gov.it/normative/law_20040109_n4.htm`

4 Conclusive Remarks

Pedagogical plans and wider learning scenarios of different levels of granularity and scope can be designed, modelled and retrieved by means of the IAMEL tool: e.g. scenarios modelling the specific articulation of a learning activity, scenarios modelling a set of learning activities, scenarios modelling the orchestration of different learning activities or sets of activities, etc.

The approach adopted to build up the IAMEL system differs from the standard approach adopted for instance by the IMS-LD main stream movement [16]; IAMEL, in fact, defends the idea of providing teachers with means to build high-level models rather than offering a ready-to-use modelling language.

We can see the pedagogical plan approach as a potential answer to the complexity and intricacy of the issues inherent to "educational design". We also hope that it can foster new practices and cultures of describing pedagogical practice, thus also allowing making further steps in the direction of concretely building a shared "knowledge culture" [17].

This research line appears productive and opens perspectives related to the introduction of intention-based modelling and seems crucial, in particular, in TEL research since is strictly linked with the idea that the design of new technological tools is always to be complemented with the design of specifically designed pedagogical plans to specify how those tools are to be integrated in the teaching and learning processes.

The first results of the in-field experimentations of the IAMEL system, carried out in the framework of the above mentioned research project, suggest that pedagogical planning, which is actually a traditional practice for educators, when it is mediated by new technologies and in particular by net-technologies, acquires new potentialities for the propagation of innovation among teachers. The success of tools of such kind depends not only on their ergonomic quality but also on the appropriateness of underlying concepts of users practice and representation. IAMEL has been designed taking into account pre-existing practices but it is also a flexible system that can be adapted to users' specific needs. From one hand, it offers a more systematic approach to the design of pedagogical plans, an activity often suffering of a low degree of formalization, and, on the other hand, it supports the modification and reuse of previously developed plans.

References

1. Punie, Y.: Learning Spaces: an ICT-enabled model of future learning in the Knowledge-based Society. European Journal of Education 42(2), 185–199 (2007)
2. Lytras, M.D., Sicilia, M.A.: The Knowledge Society: a manifesto for knowledge and learning. International Journal of Knowledge and Learning 1(1/2), 1–11 (2005)
3. Sharma, R., Ng, E., Dharmawirya, M., Ekundayo, S.: A Policy Framework for Developing Knowledge Societies. International Journal of Knowledge Society Research (IJKSR) 1, 122–145 (2010)
4. Lytras, M.D.: Teaching in the knowledge society: an art of passion. International Journal of Teaching and Case Studies 1(1/2), 1–9 (2007)
5. Conole, G., Dyke, M., Oliver, M., Seale, J.: Mapping pedagogy and tools for effective learning design. Computers & Education 43(1-2), 17–33 (2004)

6. van Es, R., Koper, R.: Testing the pedagogical expressiveness of IMS LD. Educational. Technology & Society 9(1), 229–249 (2006)
7. Falconer, I., Beetham, H., Oliver, R., Lockyer, L., Littlejohn, A.: Mod4L Final Report: Representing Learning Designs. Joint Information Systems Committee, JISC (2007), http://mod4l.com/tiki-download_file.php?fileId=7
8. Pernin, J.P., Lejeune, A.: Models for the re-use of learning scenarios (2006), http://dspace.ou.nl/bitstream/1820/580/1/Models.pdf
9. Bailey, C., Zalfan, M.T., Davis, H.C., Fill, K., Conole, G.: Panning for Gold: Designing Pedagogically-inspired Learning Nuggets. Educational Technology & Society 9(1), 113–122 (2006)
10. Earp, J., Pozzi, F.: Fostering reflection in ICT-based pedagogical Planning. In: Philip, R., Voerman, A., Dalziel, J. (eds.) Proceedings of the First International LAMS Conference 2006: Designing the Future of Learning. LAMS Foundation, Sydney, pp. 35–44 (2006)
11. Dalziel, J., McAndrew, P., Goodyear, P.: Patterns, designs and activities: unifying descriptions of learning structures. International Journal of Learning Technology 2(2-3) (2006)
12. Bottino, R.M., Earp, J., Olimpo, G., Ott, M., Pozzi, F., Tavella, M.: Pedagogical plans as communication oriented objects. Computers & Education (2010) (in press), doi:10.1016/j.compedu, 02.011
13. Reigeluth, C.M.: A New Paradigm of ISD? Educational Technology 3(36), 13–20 (1996)
14. Klironomos, I., Antona, M., Basdekis, I., Stephanidis, C.: EDeAN Secretariat for 2005 White Paper: Promoting Design for All and e-Accessibility in Europe. Universal Access in the Information Society 5(1) (2006)
15. Benigno, V., Ott, M., Puddu, F., Tavella, M.: Netform: An online support system for teachers. In: Callaos, N., Lesso, W., Sanchez, B. (eds.) Proceedings of the 8th World Multi-Conference on Systemics, Cybernetics and Informatics (SCI 2004), pp. 85–90. IIIS, Orlando (2004)
16. Koper, R.: Current research in Learning Design. Educational Technology & Society 9(1), 13–22 (2006)
17. Bakry, S., Alfantookh, A.: Toward Building the Knowledge Culture: Reviews and a KC-STOPE with Six Sigma View. International Journal of Knowledge Society Research (IJKSR) 1, 46–64 (2010)

Survey on Intelligent Assistance for Workplace Learning in Software Engineering

Eric Ras[1] and Jörg Rech[2]

[1] Centre de Recherche Public Henri Tudor, John F. Kennedy avenue 29, L-1855 Luxembourg-Kirchberg, Luxembourg
[2] SAP Research CEC Karlsruhe, Vincenz-Prießnitz-Str. 1, 76131 Karlsruhe, Germany
Eric.Ras@tudor.lu, Joerg.Rech@sap.com

Abstract. Technology-enhanced learning (TEL) systems and intelligent assistance systems aim at supporting software engineers during learning and work. A questionnaire-based survey with 89 responses from industry was conducted to find out what kinds of services should be provided and how, as well as to determine which software engineering phases they should focus on. In this paper, we present the survey results regarding intelligent assistance for workplace learning in software engineering. We analyzed whether specific types of assistance depend on the organization's size, the respondent's role, and the experience level. The results show a demand for TEL that supports short-term problem solving and long-term competence development at the workplace.

Keywords: Technology-enhanced learning, software engineering, intelligent assistance, survey.

1 Introduction

Once they finish their education and training and start on a real job, novice software engineers are faced with having to work with the latest technology, complex software systems, software integrated into business processes or other technologies (e.g., embedded systems), and software projects with a multidisciplinary character. To cope with these challenges, they need specialized, up-to-date skills [1-2]. Not all of these skills can be acquired in an academic setting. Instead, continuous education, practicing, and experiential learning at work are required. Educational settings are needed that are viable during their day-to-day work (i.e., on-work). Burgess and Russel state that technology-enhanced learning (TEL) allows organizations to update training content easily, deliver training to all employees, provide training to personnel on demand, anytime, and anywhere, and reduce travel costs to outside training facilities [3].

The learning material offered has to be appropriate in a given working context and be in line with the short- and long-term learning goals of the software engineer. In order to embed learning into a software engineer's daily work, the latest collaboration, communication, and learning technologies can be used. Social software (e.g.,

M.D. Lytras et al. (Eds.): WSKS 2010, Part I, CCIS 111, pp. 343–349, 2010.

Wikis, blogs), semantic Web technologies, as well as so-called personal learning environments [4], have opened up new ways for developing intelligent assistance systems [5] that can be blended into daily work environments [6]. However, a lot of research remains to be done in order to find out how these systems can support short-term training and long-term competence development.

Intelligent assistance systems [7] support software engineers in solving problems in a specific context during their work. Giving support to the software engineers in requirements, design, programming, or other software-related phases is necessary, as the work product is typically very complex, large, and influenced by many persons.

In order to better understand the usage of intelligent assistance for learning, we conducted a survey that explored how we can shape and improve educational R&D activities and extend the body of knowledge about TEL systems in the domain of software engineering.

In Section 2, we describe the structure of the survey as well as the characteristics of the participants. The findings of the survey, as presented in Section 3, showed that there is a high demand and acceptance for unobtrusive, quickly executable, and reactive findings in core learning phases. The conclusion in Section 4 summarizes our survey results.

2 The Survey

With regard to the learning-related aspects, the survey about intelligent assistance in software engineering [7] focused on learning behavior, assistance preferences for learning, tool environments available for the integration of TEL, and information sources for learning content and activities. The survey was conducted with German enterprises. In order to reflect the industrial standpoint on TEL at the workplace, the following evaluation only used the results from the companies, which means 89 complete data sets out of 460 responses in total. As far as differentiating characteristics for statistical group comparisons are concerned, we used the company size, the position, as well as the experience of the participants in this evaluation.

Company size was differentiated using four categories based on the SME definition of the European Union and varied from micro (1-9, 21% in the sample) via small (10-49, 44%) and medium (50-249, 24%) to large enterprises (more than 250, 11%). The *participants' position* was differentiated into four specific categories ranging from employees (32% in the sample) via project managers (15%) and middle management (28%) to the board of directors (25%). The large number of participants from higher hierarchies might be caused by the large number of micro and small enterprises with flat hierarchical levels. The *participants' experience* measured in years of practice in software development was used to differentiate between four levels of experience. We used the levels beginner (1-5 years, 20% in the sample), intermediate (6-10, 20%), advanced (11-15, 28%), and senior (more than 16, 32%) based on an equidistant range of years.

The full survey consisted of 38 questions (including additional explanatory information) that could be answered in about 30 minutes. Results more focused on the assistance part of the survey are available in [7].

3 Findings

In order to analyze the data, we generated the distributions of the answers by all participants and compared the different groups mentioned above by conducting an analysis of variance for independent samples (ANOVA) with a significance level of 10% ($\alpha = 0.1$).

Based on our analysis, we found that, in general, people evaluate the understandability of the information and its suitability for learning as mediocre (29.2% saying it is good or very good, 50.6% calling it mediocre, and 20.2% considering it bad or very bad) – independent of their position, experience, and company size. We identified a trend that the learning content is less and less understandable with increasing experience and decreasing position. However, the differences were not statistically significant. The more experience people collect and the more technical jobs they have, the more they require learning material to keep them up to date.

The following sub-sections summarize further findings regarding learning behavior, assistance preferences for learning, tool environments available for integration into TEL, and information sources for learning activities.

3.1 Learning Behavior

Software engineers are often confronted with new application areas and technologies, which requires them to learn continuously. But why are they learning and gathering information? We investigated the respondents' retrieval rationales and present the results in Fig. 1 (next page). It shows that the main learning rationales are solving concrete problems at hand, closing knowledge gaps about technologies, and personal motivation. TEL systems should therefore focus on the user's current demands, problems, and knowledge gaps.

3.2 Preferences for Learning Assistance

The survey further investigated what kind of learning assistance the participants prefer. Overall, people seem to prefer textual representations for assistance over audio-visual ones – 79.5% prefer short textual descriptions such as tooltips. Likewise, 70.5% of the participants prefer textual assistance in the form of lists and 69.3% would like to have visual assistance in the form of pictures, graphs, or icons. However, animated assistance (e.g., avatars) were rejected by 85.3%, audio assistance by 82.7%, and video was rejected by 59.1%.

Regarding the reactivity of assistance systems, more than half of the participants prefer reactive systems (53.4%) that are triggered by the user and more than one third prefers proactive systems (40.9%) that automatically provide learning assistance to the user. This view on interactivity was also confirmed by the results of another question regarding types of intelligence assistance. The participants prefer to see all (52.8%) or at least a filtered selection of potential assistant alternatives. The realization of the proposed assistance should then be triggered by the user (52.8%) and should neither be conducted automatically after a specific period of time nor instantly. Feedback, however, seems to be not that important and was only requested by 23.6%, who want it on demand.

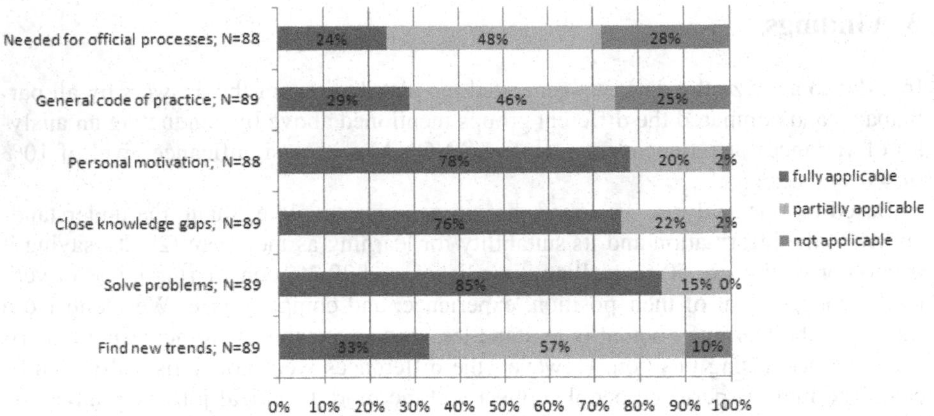

Fig. 1. Learning Rationales

Furthermore, participants were asked which learning-specific aspects intelligent assistance should improve (fully applicable=3, partially applicable=2, not applicable=1). Short-term problem solving was rated the highest with an average mean of 2.81. No significant difference was found for the different experience levels (beginner, intermediate, advanced, senior). As can be seen from Table 1**Error! Reference source not found.**, beginners and seniors rated long-term competence development statistically more significant than the intermediate and advanced groups did.

Table 1. Preferred Purposes of Assistance Systems

	Short-term problem solving	Long-term competence development	Learning at the workplace	Integration of knowledge mgt., learning, and work
Mean 1 (Beginner)	2.65	2.53	2.53	2.41
Mean 2 (Intermediate)	2.88	2.04	1.96	2.08
Mean 3 (Advanced)	2.86	2.07	2.07	2.25
Mean 4 (Senior)	2.86	2.33	2.37	2.44
Mean difference (1 vs. 2)	0.23	**0.49**	**0.57**	**0.33**
p-value (1 vs. 2)	0.13	**.034**	**.006**	**.069**
Mean difference (3 vs. 4)	0.00	0.26	**0.30**	0.19
p-value (3 vs. 4)	1.00	0.26	**.099**	0.31

This might indicate that beginners lack competencies at the beginning of their careers and that seniors need to refresh their competencies. Regarding the preference for learning at the workplace, beginners and seniors are both significantly more interested. Beginners rated the importance of integrating knowledge management, learning, and working as significantly more important than the intermediates did. 37% of all participants rated information about and links to experts important as information resource. It is interesting that beginners rate links to experts as being much more relevant (65%) than people with an intermediate experience level did (21%), with a statistical significance of .004. People with advanced experience level rate it at 29% and seniors at 41%.

3.3 TEL Integration

Besides getting people to use TEL systems, it is also crucial that these systems get integrated into existing corporate communication systems. Social interaction and exchange of knowledge with other peers is essential in TEL systems. Table 2. shows which communication systems are used within companies. Email and groupware systems are used most often, and a third of the participants are using Wiki systems for communication purposes. Hence, we should integrate these systems for connecting people in collaborative TEL systems. Less experienced people (i.e., the "Net generation" [8]) are using electronic communication systems such as email, chats, groupware, or Wikis more frequently than people with a higher level of experience (i.e., older people). This means that people's level of experience should be considered in the design of TEL systems.

Table 2. Communication Systems Used

	Chat system	Content mgt. system	Groupware	Newsgroups	Video conferencing	Wiki system	Web portal	Email
Average	21.3%	10.1%	49.4%	16.9%	7.9%	34.8%	23.6%	76.4%
Beginner	41.2%	11.8%	58.8%	17.6%	0.0%	41.2%	23.5%	94.1%
Intermediate	20.8%	4.2%	54.2%	12.5%	8.3%	37.5%	16.7%	87.5%
Advanced	5.9%	11.8%	41.2%	23.5%	0.0%	41.2%	23.5%	76.5%
Senior	17.2%	13.8%	44.8%	17.2%	17.2%	27.6%	31.0%	55.2%

Fig. 2 shows phases in software engineering where the participants frequently need information or support by colleagues in order to make decisions, solve problems, or enhance their competencies. The data shows that the early development phases such as project management, requirements engineering, software design, and programming are the phases with the highest need for additional information, and therefore, the most relevant phases to be addressed by TEL systems.

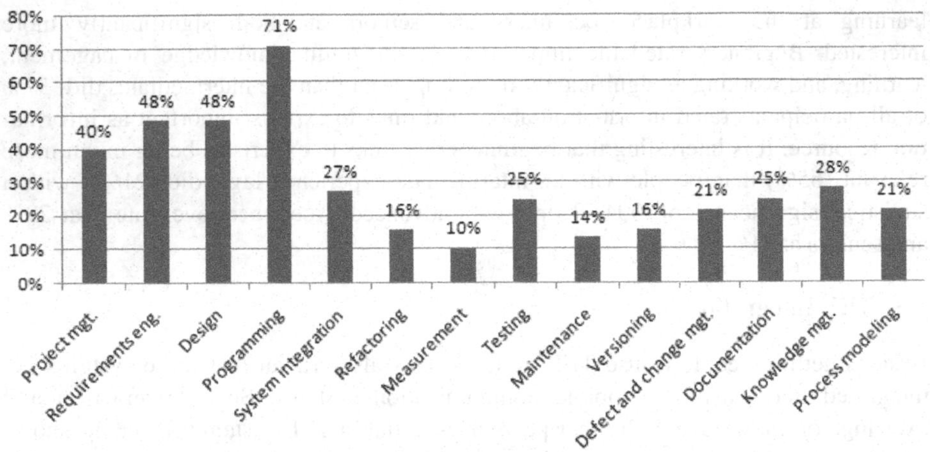

Fig. 2. Information Need in SE Phases

3.4 Information Sources for Learning

Finally, we investigated which information sources are used that can be integrated into TEL systems at the workplace. Not surprisingly, most people are using Internet search and personal contacts as their sources of information.

Table 3. Information Sources Used During Work (mean is measured in hours per week)

	Internet Search	Chats, Forums	News, Blogs, etc.	Knowledge bases on the Internet	Company-specific Knowledge Bases	FAQs, Tutorials, Books, etc.	Help systems in the applications	Training videos	Audio books, podcasts, etc.	Magazines, Journals, etc.	Colleagues and Friends	Conferences, Fairs, Seminars, etc.
Mean	2.9	1.3	1.2	1.1	2.2	2.0	1.,6	.05	.,05	1.3	2.4	.60
Std. dev.	2.3	1.6	1.5	1.3	2.2	1.7	1.7	.21	.27	1.3	1.,8	.83

However, as presented in Table 3**Error! Reference source not found.**, training videos, audio books, and even seminars only represent a very small percentage of weekly information gathering activities. Regarding our three differentiation groups (i.e., experience, position, and company size), we could not find any significant differences in the use of information sources.

4 Conclusion

To keep software engineers up to date, we need technology-enhanced learning systems that will provide them with competence-, activity- and problem-centered learning material at their workplace.

The findings of this survey provide a general characterization of learning behavior, assistance preferences, available tool environments, and information sources to complement TEL systems. The findings are particularly interesting for companies developing intelligent tools for software engineers as well as for managers responsible for the tool infrastructure and for employee competence development.

We are currently in the process of combining intelligent assistance for software developers that help them with short-term problem solving with TEL systems that support the software engineer's long-term competence development in a context-sensitive and problem-centered way. The combination of these two similar technologies will be used for integration into state-of-the-art software development environments using semantic technologies.

References

1. Ghezzi, C., Mandrioli, D.: The challenges of software engineering education. In: Inverardi, P., Jazayeri, M. (eds.) ICSE 2005. LNCS, vol. 4309, pp. 115–127. Springer, Heidelberg (2006)
2. Shaw, M., Herbsleb, J., Ozkaya, I.: Deciding what to Design: Closing a Gap in Software Engineering Education. In: Inverardi, P., Jazayeri, M. (eds.) ICSE 2005. LNCS, vol. 4309, pp. 28–58. Springer, Heidelberg (2006)
3. Burgess, J.R.D., Russell, J.E.A.: The Effectiveness of Distance Learning Initiatives in Organizations. Journal of Vocational Behavior 63, 289–303 (2003)
4. Wilson, S., Liber, O., Beauvoir, P., Milligan, C., Johnson, M., Sharples, P.: Personal Learning Environments: Challenging the dominant design of educational systems. In: Tomadaki, E., Scott, P. (eds.) 1st Joint International Workshop on Professional Learning, Competence Development and Knowledge Management (LOKMOL 2006 and L3NCD 2006), CEUR Workshop Proceedings, Crete, Greece, vol. 213, pp. 67–76 (2006)
5. Rich, C., Waters, R.C.: The programmer's apprentice. ACM, New York (1990)
6. Rech, J., Ras, E., Decker, B. (eds.): Emerging Technologies for Semantic Work Environments: Techniques, Methods, and Applications. IGI Global (2008)
7. Rech, J., Ras, E., Decker, B.: Intelligent Assistance in German Software Development: A Survey. IEEE Software 24, 72–79 (2007)
8. Ras, E., Rech, J.: Using Wikis to Support the Net Generation in Improving Knowledge Acquisition in Capstone Projects. Systems and Software 82, 553–562 (2009)

V-NIP Ceaser: Video Stabilization System

Kamran Manzoor[1], Atique Ahmed[1], Sohail Ahmad[1],
Umar Manzoor[2], and Samia Nefti[2]

[1] Department of Computer Engineering,
University of Engineering and Technology, Taxila, Pakistan
[2] Department of Computer Science, School of Computing, Science and Engineering,
The University of Salford, Salford, Greater Manchester, United Kingdom
kami.manzoor@yahoo.com, atique.cp27@yahoo.com,
ssohail15@yahoo.com, umarmanzoor@gmail.com,
s.nefti-meziani@salford.ac.uk

Abstract. In this paper, we propose a practical and robust approach of video stabilization that produces full-frame stabilized videos with good visual quality. While most previous methods end up with producing low resolution stabilized videos, our completion method produces full-frame videos by temporally filling in missing frame parts by locally aligning required data from neighboring frames. The proposed system has been evaluated on large number of real life videos; results were very promising and support the implementation of the solution.

Keywords: Video Stabilization, Video enhancement, Background segregation, Rudimentary replication, Jitter removal.

1 Introduction

Due to the lack of stability in human anatomy, video stabilization is sometimes must to achieve good results. This is something manufacturers of video cameras have dealt with for a long time. However, today we are swiftly getting closer to a situation where video cameras are becoming an integrated part of mobile phones and this will raise the need for video stabilization even more, not only in the physical design of the device. Video cameras are designed for filming, while mobile phones are designed for phoning. Also when it comes to the possibility to do good video stabilization, the mobile equipment falls short of the larger devices. So an efficient video stabilization system is required which can produce good quality stabilized videos and should be cheap in the context memory usage and processing power. Video stabilization is not only required for mobile equipment but has very vast applications.

Assume a camera rigidly mounted on a vehicle in motion, if the motion of the vehicle is smooth so will be the corresponding image sequence taken from the camera. In the case of small unmanned aerial imaging system, and off road navigating ground vehicles, the onboard cameras experience sever jitter and vibration. Consequently, the video images acquired from these platforms have to be preprocessed to eliminate the jitter induced variations before human analysis. The task at hand is to detect the jitter and eliminate its effect. A major problem of current software video stabilizers is that they cannot differentiate between an intentional and an un-intentional jitter in the video.

M.D. Lytras et al. (Eds.): WSKS 2010, Part I, CCIS 111, pp. 350–356, 2010.

In this paper, we propose a practical and robust approach of video stabilization that produces full-frame stabilized videos with good visual quality. While most previous methods end up with producing low resolution stabilized videos, our completion method can produce full-frame videos by temporally filling in missing frame parts by locally aligning required data from neighboring frames. In addition our system can also differentiate between an intentional and an un-intentional jitter so that only the un-intentional jitters can be operated. Experimental results are included from real life situations and result shows the efficiency of the proposed system.

2 Background

Many methods for video stabilization have been reported over the past few years. There are three types of image stabilizers currently available [1]: Digital Image Stabilization (DIS), Optical Image Stabilization (OIS), and Mechanical Image Stabilization (MIS). Digital Image Stabilization (DIS) systems use electronic processing to control image stability. A major disadvantage of this system is that if there is a large object moving in the frame, it may be interpreted as camera vibration and the camera will attempt to stabilize the subject causing a blurring of the image and reduction in picture resolution.

The Optical Image Stabilization (OIS) system, unlike the DIS system, manipulates the image before it gets to the Charge Coupled Device (CCD). When the lens moves, the light rays from the subject are bent relative to the optical axis, resulting in an unsteady image because the light rays are deflected. By shifting the IS lens group on a plane perpendicular to the optical axis to counter the degree of image vibration, the light rays reaching the image plane can be steadied [2], but it makes the lens very complex and very vulnerable to mechanical damage.

Mechanical image stabilization involves stabilizing the entire camera, not just the image. This type of stabilization uses a device called “Gyros”. Gyros consist of a gyroscope with two perpendicular spinning wheels and a battery pack. Gyroscopes are motion sensors. When the gyroscopes sense movement, a signal is sent to the motors to move the wheels to maintain stability. The gyro attaches to the camera’s tripod socket and acts like an "invisible tripod" [3]. The vibration gyro was improved by employing a tuning fork structure and a vibration amplitude feedback control [4]. But they are heavy, consume more power, and are not suitable for energy sensitive and payload constrained imaging applications.

3 System Design

Many methods for video stabilization have been reported over the past few years. Most proposed methods compensate for all motion [5, 6, 7], producing a sequence where the background remains motionless. Our proposed process consists of three independent but closely related phases as shown in figure 1. These phases are as follow:

- Motion Estimation
- Background Segregation
- Rudimentary Replication

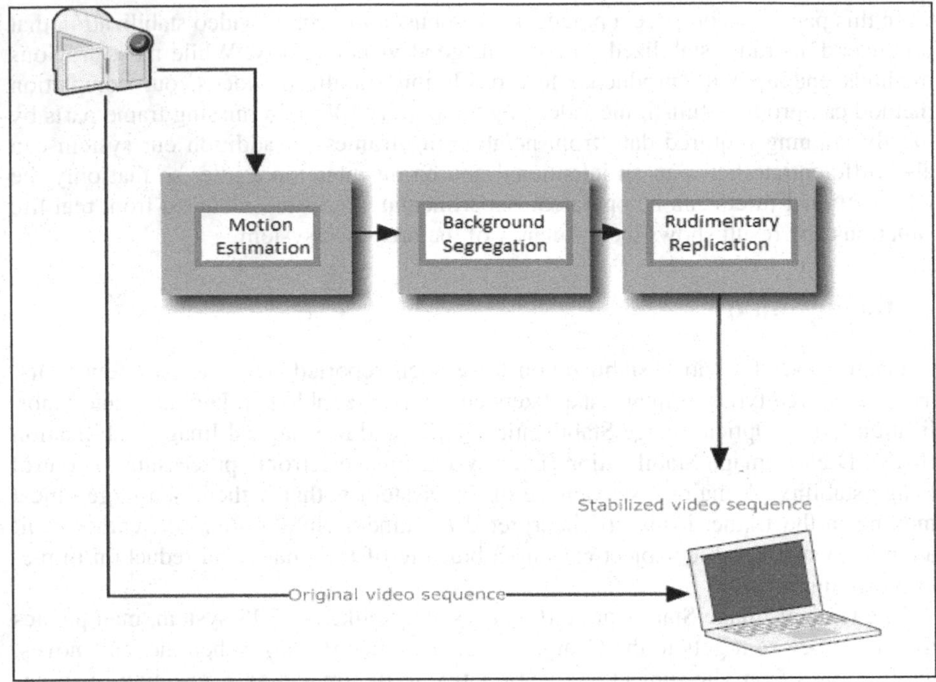

Fig. 1. Process Model of V-NIP Ceaser

3.1 Motion Estimation

Motion estimation is the process which generates the motion vector that determines how each motion prediction frame is different from the previous frame. In general there are following four cases of motion 1) Still camera, single moving object, constant background 2) Still camera, several moving objects, constant background 3) Moving camera, relatively constant scene 4) Moving camera, several moving objects.

Computing Motion Vectors: A two-dimensional vector used for inter prediction that provides an offset from the coordinates in the decoded picture to the coordinates in a reference picture. *A motion vector is the key element in the motion estimation process.* It is used to represent a macro block in a picture based on the position of this macro block in another picture, called the reference picture. Motion Vectors can be used for determining any sort of motion in the video. This motion may be intentional or unintentional i.e. jitter motion. This technique is also used in video compressions. In motion estimation optical flow is the methodology which is used to estimate motion in video subsequent frames.

The concept of motion vectors is illustrated in figure 2, where the picture in the third right column is the corresponding motion vectors of the pixels from frame1 to frame2. Since all the pixels in frame1 move towards right so are the corresponding motion vectors.

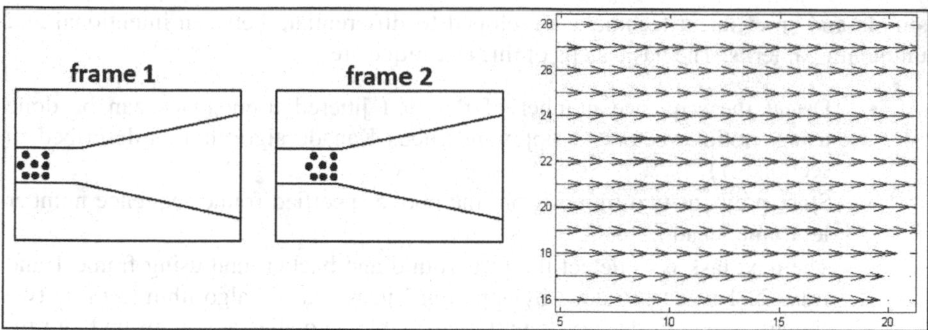

Fig. 2. Motion Vectors

Optical Flow Calculation: Optical flow or optic flow is the pattern of apparent motion of objects, surfaces, and edges in a visual scene caused by the relative motion between an observer and the scene. Optical flow has many different generic classes in which it can be categorized: 1) Matching Techniques: The principle is to divide the image into small blocks and to match them between two successive images based on similitude criterion. 2) Differential Techniques: Based on the hypothesis that the brightness of a particular moving point is constant in time. Based on extensive experiments, we have applied Lucas Kanade **[LK]** algorithm which belongs to differential technique for finding motion vectors.

Jitter in any video can be detected by using *motion vectors (LK algorithm)*. In case of jitter-less video the corresponding motion vectors will be smooth and regular as the velocities of pixels lies within a certain range as shown in figure 2 but in case of jittered video, the corresponding motion vectors will be very irregular as illustrated in figure 3.

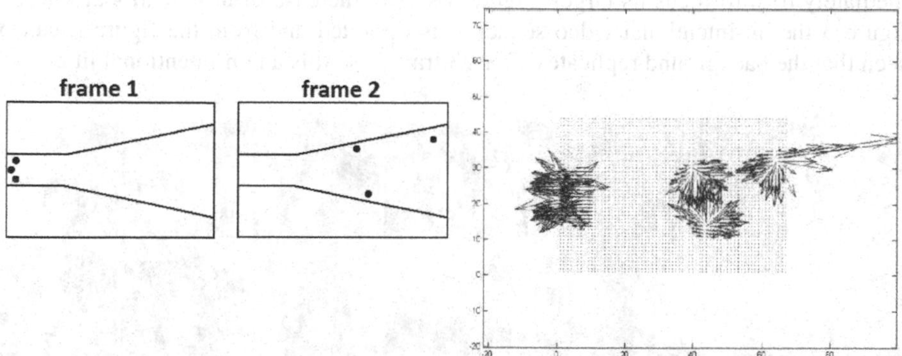

Fig. 3. Motion Vectors (jittered)

3.2 Background Segregation

Once the jitters are detected in the incoming video frames, the next task is to differentiate between an intentional and unintentional jitter. Background segregation is a simple and an efficient technique developed to differentiate between intentional and unintentional jerks. The basic steps of this technique are:

- Detect the sequence number of the first jittered frame.(This can be done using motion vectors i.e applying Lucas Kanade algorithm as described in section 3.1).
- Store previous two frames from the above specified frame sequence number let frame 1 and frame 2.
- The next task is to detect the foreground and background using frame 1 and frame2. This can be done by applying Lucas Kanade algorithm to these two frames. We consider pixels with reasonable velocities as foreground and remaining with negligible velocities as background.
- Save the background as a new image with foreground as zeros.
- Subtract this new image with upcoming frames and start a counter for counting the number of frames. Trace the minimum subtraction result and stop the counter. This minimum subtraction result shows the replication of background.
    - If minimum subtraction result is found then check
        - If the counter value is less than or equal to 15 then the jerk is considered to be *unintentional* and it should be operated.
        - If the counter value is greater than 15 then the jerk is considered to be an *intentional* jerk.
    - If minimum subtraction result is not found then it is also considered to be an *intentional* jerk but now in this case the cameraman is capturing a new scenario so that's why expected background does not replicate.

Based on experimental results and probabilistic theorems, in case of unintentional jitters background replicates after limited number of frames because cameraman immediately tries to focus its target. Figure 4 shows the case of un-intentional jitter. In figure 5 the un-intentional video sequence is operated and from the figure it can be seen that the background replicates after 13 frames so it is an un-intentional jitter.

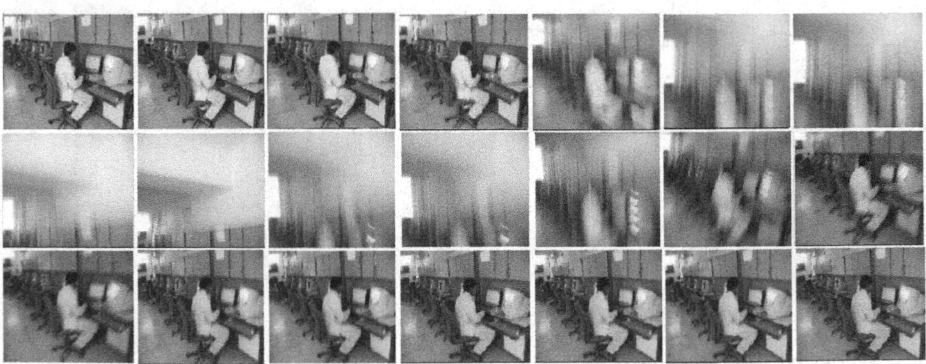

Fig. 4. Un-intentional jittered video sequence

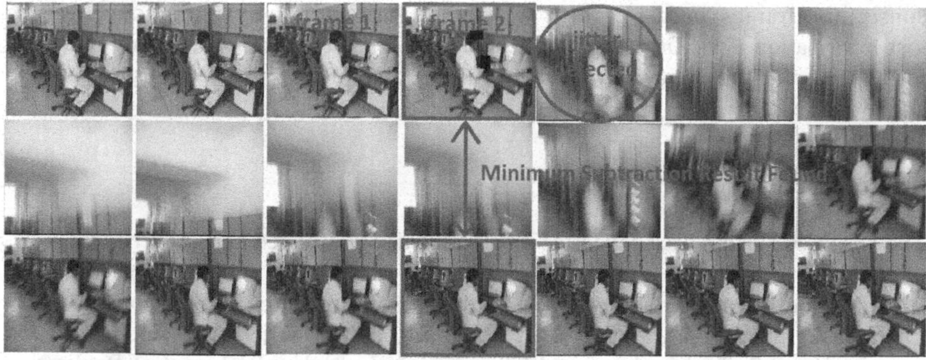

Fig. 5. Background Segregation Result (**count=13**)

3.3 Rudimentary Replication

Background segregation provides us a path to discriminate between intentional and unintentional jitters. The next step is to eliminate only the unintentional jitters to stabilize the video. The major goal is to recover the lost information in the frame. Various techniques have been proposed. In [8], technique called motion inpainting is used for this purpose but the major drawback of this technique is that it is based on image inpaiting [9,10, 11] which involves complex computation so it is not efficient in video completion.

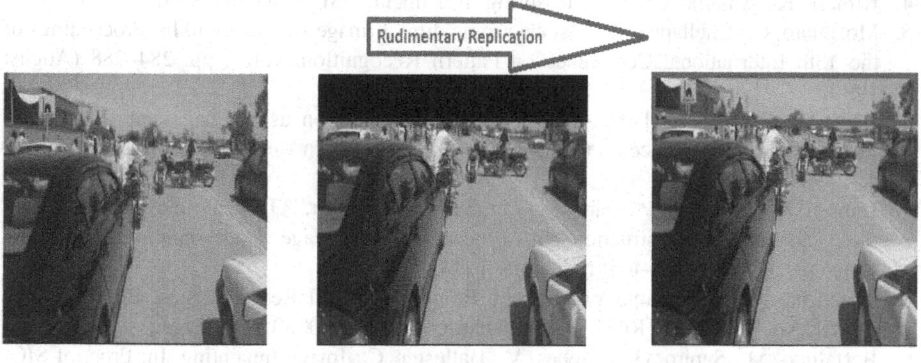

Fig. 6. Rudimentary Replication

Wexler et al. [12] filled in the holes in a video by sampling spatio-temporal volume patches from different portions of the same video. This non-parametric sampling based approach produces a good result; however, it is highly computationally intensive. Also, it requires a long video sequence of a similar scene to increase the chance of finding correct matches, which is not often available in the context of video stabilization. Our proposed methodology **"Rudimentary Replication"** is based on motion vectors of individual pixels which are calculated by optical flow(Lucas Kanade Algorithm). Optical flow provide us the distance travelled by individual pixels between consecutive frames. In case of jitter, *there is irregular motion of pixels*. To recover the lost information, specific area is replicated from previous frame. The only overhead for this approach is of memory. The result of rudimentary replication is shown in the above figure 6.

4 Conclusion

The proposed system has been tested on a wide variety of video clips to verify its effectiveness. The three phases of the system are explained along with their real-world results. Motion Estimation is used to detect the presence of jitter in the incoming video. Then Background Segregation is used to identify either the jerk is intentional or un-intentional and finally if jerk is found to be un-intentional then Rudimentary Replication is being used to compensate the loss of information in the jittered frame.

References

1. Robert, G.: VideoMaker Magazine The End Of ShakyCamera, `http://www.videomaker.com/scripts/article_print.cfm?id=9999` (accessed January 13, 2006)
2. Canon Digisuper 100xs, Product Manual, `http://www.canon.com/bctv/products/pdf/100xs.pdf` (accessed May 20, 2006)
3. iMultimedia, Use Image Stabilization – Gyroscopic Stabilizer, `http://www.websiteoptimization.com/speed/tweak/stabilizer` (accessed January 13, 2006)
4. Kimura, K.: Angular Velocity Measuring Instrument, USP 2544646 (1985)
5. Morimoto, C., Chellappa, R.: Fast electronic digital image stabilization. In: Proceedings of the 13th International Conference on Pattern Recognition, vol. 3, pp. 284–288 (August 1996)
6. Irani, M., Rousso, B., Peleg, S.: Recovery of ego-motion using image stabilization. In: Proc. of IEEE conference on Computer Vision and Pattern Recognition, Seattle, WA, pp. 454–460 (June 1994)
7. Hansen, M., Anandan, P., Dana, K., van der Wal, G., Burt, P.J.: Real time scene stabilization and mosaic construction. In: Proc. DARPA Image Understanding Workshop, Monterey, CA, pp. 457–465 (November 1994)
8. Matsushita, Y.: Full-frame Video Stabilization, Microsoft Research Asia, Beijing Sigma Center, No.49, Zhichun Road, Haidian District Beijing 100080, P. R. China
9. Bertalmio, M., Sapiro, G., Caselles, V., Ballester, C.: Image Inpainting. In: Proc. of SIGGRAPH, pp. 417–424 (2000)
10. Criminisi, A., Perez, P., Toyama, K.: Object Removal by Exemplar-Based Inpainting. In: IEEE Conf. on Computer Vision and Pattern Recognition, vol. 2, pp. 721–728 (2003)
11. Litvin, A., Konrad, J., Karl, W.C.: Probabilistic video stabilization using Kalman filtering and mosaicking. In: Proc. Of IS&T/SPIE Symposium on Electronic Imaging, Image and Video Communications, pp. 663–674 (2003)
12. Wexler, Y., Shechtman, E., Irani, M.: Space-time video completion. In: Proc. of IEEE Conf. on Computer Vision and Pattern Recognition, vol. 1, pp. 120–127 (2004)
13. Jia, J., Wu, T.P., Tai, Y.W., Tang, C.K.: Inference of foreground and background under severe occlusion. In: Proc. of IEEE Conf. on Computer Vision and Pattern Recognition, vol. 1, pp. 364–371 (2004)

Using Wikis to Learn Computer Programming

David González-Ortega, Francisco Javier Díaz-Pernas, Mario Martínez-Zarzuela, Míriam Antón-Rodríguez, José Fernando Díez-Higuera, Daniel Boto-Giralda, and Isabel de la Torre-Díez

Department of Signal Theory, Communications and Telematics Engineering, Telecommunications Engineering School, University of Valladolid, Valladolid, Spain
{davgon,pacper,marmar,mirant,josdie,danbot,isator}@tel.uva.es

Abstract. In this paper, we analyze the suitability of wikis in education, especially to learn computer programming, and present a wiki-based teaching innovation activity carried out in the first course of Telecommunication Engineering during two academic courses. The activity consisted in the creation of a wiki to collect errors made by students while they were coding programs in C language. The activity was framed in a collaborative learning strategy in which all the students had to collaborate and be responsible for the final result, but also in a competitive learning strategy, in which the groups had to compete to make original meaningful contributions to the wiki. The use of a wiki for learning computer programming was very satisfactory. A wiki allows to monitor continuously the work of the students, who become publishers and evaluators of contents rather than mere consumers of information, in an active learning approach.

Keywords: Wiki, computer programming learning, collaborative learning.

1 Introduction

Spanish universities are involved in a convergence process toward the EHEA (European Higher Education Area) [1]. The adaptation to EHEA implies the implementing of a university system with similar features in many European countries with very different societies and educational cultures.

One of the key factors in the implementing of new university degrees is the series of competences that each subject has to contribute to develop. A competence can be defined as the knowledge, skills, and attitudes which a person has to be able to apply, in order to act effectively in response to the needs of a particular context [2]. The development of cognitive, affective, socioemotional, and physical abilities has to support the competences. These competences have to qualify students to get by suitably in varied contexts, both vital and professional [3]. On the basis of either cross competences or those specific of a degree, both the aims to develop them and the learning outcomes embodied in the assessment procedures of each subject have to be set out.

Three new graduate degrees (Degree in Telecommunication Technologies Engineering, Degree in Telecommunication Systems Engineering, and Degree in

M.D. Lytras et al. (Eds.): WSKS 2010, Part I, CCIS 111, pp. 357–362, 2010.

Telematics Engineering) are going to be implemented in the Telecommunication Engineering School in the University of Valladolid. With a view to implementing the new graduate degrees, several professors devoted to the teaching of subjects related to computer programming have carried out a teaching innovation activity in the subject "Introduction to Computers" (2008-2009 and 2009-2010 courses). This subject belongs to the first course of Telecommunication Engineering. The activity consisted in the creation of a wiki in which the students had to include, in a collaborative way, common errors made in the coding of C language programs and explain them, their causes, and consequences. Some code lines causing the error could also be included together with the way the error was corrected. No very restrictive rule to contribute to the wiki was given.

The activity had to do with one of the applications of the Web 2.0, namely a wiki, which is a website whose pages can be created and edited via a web browser. The aim of the wiki is to promote active learning and collaborative work of the students with a view to developing competences related to computer programming, which first-course students usually find arduous.

The rest of the paper is organized as follows. Section 2 explains the implications of the EHEA and how wikis can help to achieve its aims. Section 3 talks about the subject in which a wiki activity was proposed. Section 4 describes the wiki activity and the analysis of the results using open questions and Likert scale questionnaires fulfilled by the students. Finally, Section 5 draws the main conclusions about the paper.

2 Wikis in Learning

The adaptation of the university degrees to the EHEA has to involve changes in the teaching paradigm. A subject planning focused on the teaching of the professor has to be replaced by a planning focused on the learning of the student. In this scenario, a great interest in the use of Web technologies to create flexible learning environments has been aroused. The advent of Web 2.0 technologies has offered professors an opportunity to exceed traditional teaching methodologies and develop student-centered personalized learning environments [4]. Web 2.0 includes applications such as blogs, discussion forums, social tagging, content management systems (CMS), and wikis. All these applications turn users into publishers rather than readers. They can edit existing material in such a way that new content is created and used in collaboration with other users. These forms of collaboration and knowledge sharing provide professors with a great opportunity to develop activities that require active student participation and knowledge building rather than memorization [4][5].

A wiki is a website hosted in a server that can be accessed via a web browser. Wiki users are able to add contents and edit existing information. The most popular wiki is Wikipedia, which is an encyclopedia with a huge amount of information [6]. Wiki users can add or edit its content without any knowledge about programming. To prevent undesired modifications, wikis store the changes in a history. Thus it is possible to return to a previous version of the wiki given that inappropriate content has been added.

The features inherent to wiki technology (creation and incremental improvement of knowledge, version management, and multiuser participation) make them suitable for group work and creation of content repositories. Sigala [4] stated that democratic participation, personal reflection, gradual evolution of wiki material through the contributions, and individual efforts help to humanize student learning through social interaction with other students.

The educational uses of wikis can provide several pedagogical benefits [7][8]. Among them, evolutionary knowledge building, progressive problem-solving, the explanation of diverse and often contradictory ideas, critical reflection, the ability to avoid premature judgment, and the engagement in complex and nuanced analysis of others' work can be mentioned.

Regarding experiences about using wikis in education, Grant [9] stated that the teacher should make sure that the aim and the essential points of wiki activity are understood by the students to have a meaningful collaborative participation. Raman and Ryan [10] suggested that the teachers have to prepare efficient designs to ensure a proper working of the wiki and also stated that the most important objectives of a wiki are to improve communication and to enable knowledge sharing.

3 Computer Programming Learning

A computer programming subject is included in the first course of Telecommunication Engineering. In this subject, C, which is a high-level programming language, is studied, dealing with the development of error free programs, clearly written and structured following a programming methodology. The same happens with the three previously mentioned degrees that will be implemented in the 2010-2011 course in the University of Valladolid. Being a subject that will be taught at the beginning of the degree, it has to develop only one specific competence related to Telecommunication Engineering. On the contrary, it has to develop nine cross competences related to the engineering education. Among them, the ability to communicate knowledge, procedures, results, and ideas and the ability to work in group, taken part actively, collaborating with the partners, and focusing on the whole result can be mentioned. The inclusion of an activity based on a wiki where all the students, in a collaborative way, add programming errors, represents a significant contribution to the development of those competences.

Moreover, unlike subjects such as Mathematics and Physics, in which the novel university students have a background, whether good or bad, from previous educational stages, computer programming is a new topic for most of them. While the students are learning to program in a high-level language, such as C, they make many errors, repeating some of them frequently. These errors can make lose much of the time devoted to the development of programs and can influence on the student motivation, which is a key factor in the learning process. When a student receives negative feedback from a computer, e.g. caused by an erroneous compilation, anxiety situations are likely to take place. This programming anxiety, from the McInereny's definition of computer anxiety [11], is defined as a psychological state engendered when a student experiences or expects to lose self-esteem in confronting a computer programming situation. The use of a wiki where students can read the errors that their partners made and how they corrected it, makes the students participate in the global learning experience of them all and allow them to help and be helped in a collaborative learning strategy. Besides, the wiki can be useful to greatly lessen the computer anxiety of the students.

4 Teaching Innovation Wiki Activity

A teaching innovation activity has been carried out in the four-month subject named "Introduction to Computers" in the first course of the Telecommunication Engineering in the University of Valladolid (Spain) during the 2008-2009 and 2009-2010 academic courses. The students had to create a wiki collecting the errors in the development of C language programs. A wiki was created in Wikispaces [12], accessible through the URL http://io-lenguajeC.wikispaces.com, so that the students could work collaboratively in a document that collected programming errors. Wikispaces is a free hosting service for wikis.

All the activities planned in the subject "Introduction to Computers" were made in two-student groups, just as the wiki. In the wording of the activity, the students were indicated that the point was not to comment on errors in the coding of a particular program, but common errors that can be made in different programs. Far from including many code lines, the error had to be classified (including it in a category among the different ones appearing in the document), its cause and consequences had to be explained, and how it was corrected. Before including an error, the students had to make sure that the error was not in the wiki yet. On the other hand, the students were encouraged to edit the information about any error present in the wiki, modifying or including additional information. As contributions were inserted in the wiki, its history included them, with information about the author and the deleted and inserted text in each one. The professors were the wiki organizers and the students were invited to subscribe to it through an e-mail sent to all the work groups. The students could make contributions to the wiki during one month each academic year.

In the 2008-2009 course, the wiki was presented to the students with one contribution from the professors to avoid student reluctance to contribute due to a blank wiki. In the 2009-2010 course, the students found the wiki in the state after the contributions made in the previous course. For this reason, just as the students in the 2008-2009 course focused on including novel contents in the wiki, the students in the 2009-2010 course had to focus on correcting and completing the information already present in the wiki to avoid including redundant information. Regarding the activity assessment, the students were told that the final result of the wiki, together with the particular contributions of each group, were taken into account. Thus the activity was proposed in a collaborative learning approach where the groups had to collaborate and be responsible for the final result, but also in a competitive learning approach where the groups had to compete to make original contributions.

The students did not have technical problems using the wiki, which is very simple. Although some students were firstly reluctant to work and get involved in the wiki, their resistance was decreasing just as they were observing the behavior of the remaining groups. The professors have observed a positive impact of the wiki on the involvement and active attitude of the students during lectures and laboratory sessions. The final result of the wiki in both courses was satisfactory, with a large number of quality contributions.

At the end of the activity, the students were asked about the creation of the wiki, the contributions of the remaining groups and its utility. The great majority of the students considered the creation and collaboration in the wiki very useful. Some particular commentaries were: "*It can be useful for many students that begin to study C programming, just as future students of this subject*", "*It was a query book when we made some error that we were not able to correct*", "*We find it useful because other students can learn from you and you can learn from them*".

Some students were reflected in commentaries made by others: "*we frequently identified with the errors inserted by other groups because we made the same errors*". The students were conscious of the progressive enrichment of the wiki due to the consecutive contributions that, "*as times goes by, the wiki improves and the result is more useful thanks to the new contributions and modifications*". The students can play a leading role in their learning process, turning them from mere recipients into active participants: "*We have realized about the things we know, where we make errors and what we have to do to improve our knowledge while we find errors in the wiki that we are able to correct*". Some mentioned that "*it took us much time to read the entire wiki and to include new information*". Others stated that "*if the wiki is used in the following years, it would improve little by little, leading eventually to a very practical wiki to begin to program in C language*". In other commentaries, the students thought that "*a wiki should be used in other subjects to improve learning*".

The wiki enabled that the students have collaborated continuously during the time period assigned to the activity, not only in the subject laboratory but also at home. Moreover, the work could be monitored by the professors via the wiki history that includes a detailed record of all the contributions. Regarding the group work, the best groups have made contributions distributed in time along the activity period, which was expected by the professors as they encouraged students to include errors in the wiki while they were programming, facing errors, and correcting them.

5 Conclusions

In this paper, we have presented a teaching innovation activity based on a wiki for the programming learning of Telecommunication Engineering students. The activity has been carried out during two academic courses. The activity had very positive results. Although the initial reluctance of the students, they have contributed meaningfully to the creation of the wiki dealing with C language programming errors that take place in the first stage of its programming learning. These errors can make students lose their motivation and have programming anxiety, thus making the learning process more difficult. The use of a Web 2.0 application, such as a wiki, for the students to share their programming learning experiences collaboratively, to comment their errors, and to correct them, make them active players in their learning process.

Although some students were reluctant to edit other partners' contributions, it must be interpreted as part of the habit of only reading information, encouraged by the traditional education and in the Web 1.0 environment. This reluctance can be overcome with the consciousness-raising carried out by the professors, who are helped by the unavoidable implementing of the new teaching-learning processes of the EHEA.

Today's students need to be comfortable in a variety of online environments, understand the Web behavior rules, and learn to assess different information sources. Using a wiki can develop all these abilities. Moreover, a wiki helps the students to understand the implications of group work and the individual responsibility toward the group. Concerning the subject about programming in the new graduate degrees to be implemented in the next course in the Telecommunication Engineering School in the University of Valladolid, a wiki would contribute to the development of competences assigned to this subject such as the ability to work in group collaboratively and the ability to communicate knowledge and results in writing.

A wiki activity has to be carefully planned and monitored by the professors in order to achieve successful learning. A wiki is framed in a participation architecture, where the students are encouraged to add value to the application while they are using it. Moreover, continuous monitoring of the students work can be carried out. The students become publishers and evaluators of contents working collaboratively with their partners rather than mere consumers of information.

References

1. Bologna Declaration: Ministers of Education of 29 European Countries (1999)
2. Perrenoud, P.: Diez nuevas competencias para enseñar. Graó, Barcelona (2004)
3. Mérida Serrano, R., García Cabrera, M.M.: La formación de competencias en la universidad. Revista electrónica interuniversitaria de formación del profesorado 8(1) (2005)
4. Sigala, M.: Integrating Web 2.0 in e-learning environments: a socio-technical approach. International Journal of Knowledge and Learning 3(6), 628–648 (2007)
5. Cych, L.: Social networks. Emerging Technologies for Learning 1, 32–41 (2006)
6. Wikipedia, http://www.wikipedia.org
7. Fountain, R.: Wiki pedagogy. Dossiers Technopedagogiques (2005)
8. Lin, B., Hsieh, C.: Web-based teaching and learner control: a research view. Computers and Education 37, 377–386 (2001)
9. Grant, L.: Using Wikis in Schools: a Case Study (2006), http://www.futurelab.org.uk
10. Raman, M., Ryan, T.: Designing Knowledge Management Systems for Teaching and Learning with Wiki Technology. Journal of Information Systems Education 16(3), 1–10 (2005)
11. McInereny, V.: Computer anxiety: Assessment and treatment. The University of Western Sydney, Sydney (1997)
12. Wikispaces, http://www.wikispaces.com

The Enterprise 2.0 Concept: Challenges on Data and Information Security

Ana Silva[1], Fernando Moreira[2], and João Varajão[3,4]

[1] EGP – University of Porto Business School, Portugal
[2] University Portucalense, Portugal
[3] University of Trás-os-Montes e Alto Douro, Portugal
[4] Centro ALGORITMI, Portugal
anamachadosilva@gmail.com, fmoreira@uportu.pt, jvarajao@utad.pt

Abstract. The Web 2.0 wave has "hit" businesses all over the world, with companies taking advantage of the 2.0 concept and new applications stimulating collaboration between employees, and also with external partners (suppliers, contractors, universities, R&D organizations and others). However, the use of Web 2.0 applications inside organizations has created additional security challenges, especially regarding data and information security. Companies need to be aware of these risks when deploying the 2.0 concept and take a proactive approach on security. In this paper are identified and discussed some of the challenges and risks of the use of Web 2.0 tools, namely when it comes to securing companies' intellectual property.

Keywords: Enterprise 2.0, Web 2.0, security, data, information.

1 Introduction

What started as a Web phenomenon, much led by the proliferation of social networks and the growing use of tools such as *blogs*, *wikis* and *mashups*, is now gaining wide acceptance at an enterprise level. Several companies are beginning to understand the benefits that the Web 2.0 concept and tools can bring in terms of internal collaboration, staff engagement and knowledge sharing.

Tim O'Reilly, as cited by Ross Dawson (2009), views the Web 2.0 as "the business revolution in the computer industry caused by the move to the Internet as platform, and an attempt to understand the rules for success on that new platform. Chief among those rules is this: build applications that harness network effects to get better the more people use them."

Users started experiencing the advantages of the Web 2.0 tools in their personal life recently, connecting with friends on social networks, sharing their views through *blogs* or collaborating through *wikis*. Concepts such as *commenting*, *microblogging*, *tagging* and *rating*, became part of their "regular" vocabulary.

But soon users began to make use of these tools to connect with co-workers, or with other people sharing the same interests, on more "professional" social networks such as *LinkedIn*. They started sharing work documents through *web applications*

M.D. Lytras et al. (Eds.): WSKS 2010, Part I, CCIS 111, pp. 363–368, 2010.

such as *Google Docs* or using their personal email accounts for professional reasons because they find these web-based email services much more appealing and flexible. And it did not take long before people started demanding, inside their companies, the same user experience, tools and networking.

With the blurring of the frontier between personal and professional use of web-based tools companies are currently facing additional security challenges, namely in what concerns the protection of intellectual property. In this paper we will reflect on some of these challenges and risks and provide some guidelines for managing them.

Following, in section 2, are discussed the implications of the Web 2.0 phenomenon for enterprises. In section 3, are identified some of the main challenges of Enterprise 2.0 on data and information security. Section 4 is about security recommendations. Finally, in section 5, some final remarks are made.

2 Implications of the Web 2.0 Phenomenon for Enterprises

Citing an example from the United States, Jim Till (2008) pointed that "researchers estimate that more than half of US employees abandon enterprise tools when they need to work with applications outside of their organization to complete a project or task." And a recent press release from IDC (2010), highlighting some key findings of a research on the intersection of the topics of Web 2.0, Enterprise 2.0 and collaboration, stated that last year "57% of U.S. workers use social media for business purposes at least once per week".

As companies began deploying the Web 2.0 concept and tools inside their organizations, the notion of Enterprise 2.0 emerged. This is a term largely attributed to Andrew McAfee (2006) that described it as "the use of emergent social software platforms within companies, or between companies and their partners or customers."

Today, if someone was asked to give a definition of Enterprise 2.0, it would probably be something like "the deployment of Web 2.0-style tools and practices with the purpose of fostering collaboration and collective intelligence inside organizations". The concept has to go beyond technology in order to truly reflect a new way of working and collaborating, both inside (between co-workers) and outside (with partners) the company.

At the moment the question for several companies, especially the larger ones with a wide geographic present, does not seem to be whether or not to deploy the Enterprise 2.0 concept, but rather when and how.

As Ross Dawson (2009) referred "key issues in adapting Web 2.0 tools to the enterprise include scale, IT security, identity, information loss, and auditability." And in the latest Enterprise 2.0 conference, Whitney Michael (2009) published a small article where it highlighted that security concerns were appointed, by 31,5% of respondents to a survey conducted in May 2009, as the greatest challenge in E2.0 adoption.

Dawson (2009) summarized the main risks and concerns usually associated with the implementation of the Enterprise 2.0 concept, categorizing it in: security; loss of control; reputation; and reliability. But the author also points to the risks of taking no action, such as the unauthorized use of external tools to perform work tasks, leading to IT security risks and lack of integration with existing systems, or the scattering of information with users placing information outside a coherent firm structure.

Presently it seems that companies can no longer escape the side effects that the Web 2.0 wave has on the way employees work, collaborate and network. One of the key security issues arising from this trend is the loss of intellectual property occurring either by a naive use of Web 2.0 applications or due to the fragility that these applications have in terms of security. In fact, security experts draw attention to the fact that the open nature of the Web 2.0 makes it naturally more vulnerable to breaches.

3 Enterprise 2.0: Challenges on Data and Information Security

One of the key characteristics of the open and collaborative environment of the Web 2.0 is trust: people trust the recommendation of others and freely disclose information about themselves. As expressed by McClure (2008), citing Jordan Frank, "there's a sense of security in a Web 2.0 world where people trust their personal information to others… they trust these sites."

In the collaborative, informal and easy 2.0 environment, people share opinions, ideas, thoughts and personal information. They install applications or widgets without much consideration and understanding of the implied risks, and they don't really take the time to read licensing agreements.

The blurring of the limits between personal and professional uses of Web 2.0 tools, and the increasing use of web applications to exchange work information, is raising some concerns on data and information security with serious repercussions at the enterprise level.

People often post information on the web (*blogs*, *social networks*, etc.) regarding what they are working on at a professional level, without being fully aware that most of these web applications default to public access, and that even without citing the name of the employer people might still link the information back to the company. This can result in the leakage of sensitive information to the exterior of an organization, namely to competitors. Other times employees make negative comments about their companies, or make statements that can be seen externally as representing the views of that company, with severe consequences for a company's reputation and for themselves.

Another challenge on information security is the increasing use of Web 2.0 tools in the workplace for performing regular work tasks or exchanging professional data, thus increasing the vulnerability of the network to security breaches leading to "silent" attacks that could result in data leakage or destruction. According to Will Dormann, cited by George Lawton (2007), "Web 2.0 sites inherently carry more risk than traditional Web sites because they let users upload content and require scripting capabilities — which can run code or carry malware — to function properly... hackers have exploited Web 2.0 to launch worms that execute harmful operations outside the browser, leaving users unaware of their activities." Websense Inc. (2009) conducted a survey called "Web 2.0 @ work" and found that 95% of companies surveyed allowed access to some types of Web 2.0 sites or applications, though 91% stated that they did not have the necessary security to protect their organizations from all Web 2.0 threat vectors across Web, email and data security. In its research Websense also concluded that "the exposure of confidential information is now the single greatest threat to enterprise security" referring that "57 percent of data-stealing attacks are conducted over the Web".

Security issues also arise when implementing enterprise *mashups* that pull information from multiple sources, including web sites, company databases and emails. The use of *mashups* in companies is rapidly growing since it enables non-technical users to gain greater insights from information coming from several applications, and because "non-developers" can easily create them.

The risks here are two-fold: one is having the wrong people accessing sensitive information and the other is having malicious code creeping into the company's systems. If a strong security architecture is not built with the development of the *mashup* then there is a risk of one person's *mashed-up* application giving transitive privileges to another person that shouldn't have them, whether inside or outside the organization.

4 Security Recommendations

Experts on security suggest several measures when implementing the Enterprise 2.0 concept, or Web 2.0 applications inside the organization, namely to deal with the issues surrounding data and information risks.

The first recommendation is to raise the awareness of employees regarding these threats and provide training in the safer handling of new web technologies. Companies should also clearly state the rules of Web 2.0 usage inside the organization by preparing and communicating well understood policies, with examples of do's and don'ts. Companies such as Sun Microsystems are, for example, implementing specific policies to deal with the implications of the blogging activities of their employees. Cited by Mary Brandel (2007), Arabella Hallawell, an analyst at Gartner Inc., thinks that "organizations are more likely to use policy rather than technology to control the risks raised by Web 2.0 technologies".

On the technical side, companies will have to focus increasingly on user authentication and content encryption methods, which for many organizations means investing more in directory management in order to guarantee that information is accessed only by the persons with the right access role. In fact Jordan Frank from Traction Software, cited by Marji McClure (2008), stated that "the matter of security goes beyond simple authentication (am I who I say I am?) and privacy control (who can see what information)". Frank also noted that other important aspects of security include permissions/access control ("What can you see and do in the environment?"), an audit trail ("What happened over time? When was a document emailed? What comments were included on it?"), and monitoring (the ability for users to keep up-to-date on new activity).

When it comes to the development of *mashups*, the advice given when it comes to dealing with the risk of unwanted access to sensitive information, is to have a system that enforces security at the data level.

Experts such as Mark Kraynark from Imperva, cited by McClure (2008), also point to the need of applying security on the server side, because that is where the company has the highest control, and to take a proactive approach through the continuous monitoring of its Web 2.0 systems, sending alerts and applying corrective measures whenever a breach is detected.

One major recommendation is for companies to select providers of Web 2.0 tools with security built-in since there are now several enterprise-focused versions of applications such as *wikis*, *blogs*, *web conferencing*, *document sharing* and even *social networks*. As pointed by Jesse Wilkins (2009) "many of these can be implemented behind the organization's firewall and integrated into the identity infrastructure such as *Active Directory*. They generally use open protocols and data structures (often XML-based), so organizations should have minimal difficulty exporting from one solution to another or applying retention controls and policies."

Major software companies are already releasing their versions of "social software for the enterprise" in order to take advantage of the increasing demand for collaborative applications. Customers, especially larger corporations, are looking for solutions that can also be integrated with their existing systems and applications.

According to Mary Ann Davidson and Elad Yoran (2007), the use of Information Rights Management (IRM) will be essential to the security of the Enterprise 2.0. IRM can be described as new form of information security technology that secures and tracks sensitive digital information everywhere it is stored and used. This differs from "conventional" information management that traditionally only manages documents, emails and web pages, while they remain stored within server-side repositories. But once information leaves a secure server environment it becomes more vulnerable to modification, theft or piracy.

Companies will thus have to guarantee the security of data using encryption to extend the management of information beyond the repository on end user desktops, laptops and mobile wireless devices, in other repositories, inside and outside the firewall.

5 Conclusions

It seems that the Web 2.0 wave has come to the Enterprise helping to create a collaboration-enhanced environment. As Gartner (2010) referred in the press release highlighting the latest findings on their research on social software in the enterprise "A lot has happened in a year within the social software and collaboration space. The growing use of platforms such as Twitter and Facebook by business users has resulted in serious enterprise dialogue about procuring social software platforms for the business".

But the use of Web 2.0 applications also generates additional security challenges, namely at the level of intellectual property.

Enterprises have to be able to establish a good balance between enabling the increasing trend for collaborative environments and practices inside organizations, while still guaranteeing the security of information and also in some cases of a company's reputation.

As Davidson and Yoran (2007) referred, companies need to implement Security 2.0, a concept that means "finding an adaptive security model that will facilitate collaboration without making it the fatally weak link in the security chain." These authors point to the fact that "the implications of Security 2.0 will be felt in virtually every dimension of IT, ranging from data security to device security (on all end points) to connectivity security (all networks and perimeters)".

A clear understanding of the risks implied by the deployment of the Enterprise 2.0 concept, coupled with a proactive approach on security, the training of employees in order to raise awareness for security issues and the clear definition of procedures, seems to be the best way to guarantee that companies can fully benefit from a collaborative environment whilst safeguarding their intellectual property.

References

Davidson, M.A., Yoran, E.: Enterprise Security for Web 2.0. Computer 11, 117–119 (2007)
Cunningham, P., Wilkins, J.: A Walk in the Cloud. Information Management Journal, 22–30 (2009)
Taft, D.K.: IBM 'Smashes' Web 2.0 security risks. eweek 36(40) (2008)
Brandel, M.: Keeping Secrets in a WikiBlogTubeSpace World. Computerworld, 26–30 (2007)
McClure, M.: Web 2.0 Security: Getting Collaborative Peace of Mind. Econtent, 36–41 (2008)
Lawton, G.: Web 2.0 Creates Security Challenges. Computer 10, 13–16 (2007)
Cluley, G.: New internet brings security challenges. Infosecurity 2(41) (2007)
Till, J.: Using Web 2.0 safely in the enterprise. NetworkWorld 13(26) (2008)
Nene, B., Swanson, T.: Information Rights Management Application Patterns. Microsoft White Paper. In: Michael, W. (ed.) Enterprise 2.0: What, Why and How. Enterprise 2.0 Conference (2009)
McAfee, A.: Enterprise 2.0, version 2.0. Andrew McAfee blog (2006)
Dawson, R.: Implementing Enterprise 2.0. Advanced Human Technologies, Sidney (2009)
IDC, http://www.idc.com/
Websense: State of Internet Security, Q1 - Q2. Websense White Paper (2009)
Gartner, http://www.gartner.com

Development of a Sensor Network System for Industrial Technology Education

Chi-Chia Liu[1], Din-Wu Wu[2], Min Jou[3], and Sheng-Jia Tsai[4]

[1] Associate Professor, Department of Industrial Education, National Taiwan Normal University, Taiwan
[2] Instructor, Department of Industrial Education, National Taiwan Normal University, Taiwan
[3] Professor, Department of Industrial Education, National Taiwan Normal University, Taipei, Taiwan
[4] Graduate Student, Department of Mechatronic Technology, National Taiwan Normal University, Taiwan
joum@ntnu.edu.tw

Abstract. Technology of e-learning has been gradually applied to all kinds of professional teaching fields. However, practicing and operation in real environment cannot be replaced by the method of e-learning such as multimedia and interactive simulations. The present e-learning system has very limited benefit for course of experiment and practical training, especially for the course which requires to experiment in clean room (ex. MEMS). Thus, the quality and quantity of industrial technology education cannot be improved. In order to overcome obstacles of traditional experiment and practical training course and enhance functions of present e-learning system, the study is going to take sensor network technology as foundation to developed web services system. The system is able to present the students 'operation and results right away, thus students can be guided appropriately when they face problems during experiment and practical training. Besides, the system is able to record students' learning process of experiment and practical training. These data of learning process will be helpful for building adaptive u-learning environment for skill-training.

Keywords: Technological education, sensor network, u-learning environment.

1 Introduction

With recent advances in micro-electro-mechanical systems (MEMS) and wireless communication technologies, wireless sensor networks have come out from laboratories and will be used everywhere to change our future lives. Wireless sensor networks are more attractive and useful than traditional wired sensing systems because of their ad-hoc and easy deployment. This new technology expands our sensing capabilities by connecting the physical world to the communication networks and enables a broad range of applications (Akyildiz, Su, Sankarasubramaniam, and Cayirci, 2002). Sensor networks are the integration of sensor techniques, distributed computation, and wireless communication techniques. The network can be embedded in our physical environment and used for sensing, collecting data, processing information of monitored objects, and transferring the processed information to users. The architecture of the

M.D. Lytras et al. (Eds.): WSKS 2010, Part I, CCIS 111, pp. 369–374, 2010.

sensor node's hardware consists of five components, i.e., sensing hardware, processor, memory, power supply, and transceiver (Tubaishat, Madria, 2003). For many applications, a sensor network operates in three phases. In the first phase, sensors take measurements that form a snapshot of the signal field at a particular time. The measurements are stored locally. The second phase is information retrieval in which data are collected from individual sensors. The last phase is information processing in which data from sensors are processed centrally with a specific performance metric (Dong, Tong, and Sadler 2007). Such a network is composed of many tiny low-power nodes, each consisting of actuators, sensing devices, a wireless transceiver, and possibly a mobilize (2002). These sensor nodes are massively deployed in a region of interest to gather and process environmental information.

The higher capital cost of acquiring MEMS's equipment within each university presents a considerable financial challenge. Much time and cost are used to teach these techniques. Particularly, computerized machines are continuously increasing in use. The development of educating engineers on computerized machines becomes much more difficult than with traditional machines. This is because of the limitation of the extremely expensive cost of teaching. The quality and quantity of teaching cannot always be promoted in this respect. The traditional teaching methods cannot respond well to the needs of the future. Most of technology education relies on "cookbook"-oriented experiments that provide students with a technical question, the procedure to address the question, the expected results of the experiment, and even an interpretation of those results. By contrast, self-directed learning is to encourage students to learn inductively with the help of teaching systems. This method gives students more freedom to come up with a question to investigate, devise an experimental procedure, and decide how to interpret the results. Long pointed out that there are at least six kinds of cognitive skills appear to be particularly important in successful self-directed learning. They are as follows: goal setting skills, processing skills, other cognitive skills, some competence or aptitude in the topic or a closely related area, decision making skills, and self-awareness. Effective, or successful, self-directed learning depends on information gathering, information monitor students' processing and other cognitive activities, and in the way they react to information. The evolution of computer and Internet technologies has made it easy to access learning contents from almost anywhere, anytime, and at user pace. Self-directed e-learning focuses on the independent learner, one who engages in education at his own pace, free from curricular obligation. A number of tools, some purposefully and others serendipitously, have become key enablers of this learning paradigm. For example, tools such a Google Scholar, CiteSeer Research Index, etc. make it possible to do literature search without stepping out of one's room (Desikan, DeLong, Beemanapalli, Bose, and Srivastava). The advance in the optical-fiber network makes real-time transmission of a large amount of data, such as three-dimensional models or video images, possible between remote places. In particular, by connecting virtual environments through the broadband network (Paquette, Ricciardi-Rigault, Paquin, Liegeois, Bleicher, 1996), a three-dimensional virtual world can be shared between remote places. The field oú virtual reality (VR) initially focused on immersive viewing via expensive equipment, is rapidly expanding and includes a growing variety of systems for interacting with 3D computer models in real-time (Sung & Ou, 2003). Various applications in fields including education, training, entertainment, medicine and industry have been developing, and more and more areas will gain benefits from using VR (Craig, Sherman, 2003). In the past few years, a number of interactive VR systems have been developed. An educational virtual environment (Bouras, Philopoulos, Tsiatsos, 2001) is a special case of a VR system where the emphasis is more on education and collaboration than on simulation.

2 Development of Sensor Network Environment

The new technology of wireless sensor network expands sensing capabilities by connecting the physical world to the communication networks. In order to support self-directed learning in MEMS technology, many sensor devices need to be deployed in the laboratory to collect real-time information of students' motion and machine operation conditions. The Zigbee modules were used to build a wireless sensor network in this research. The proposed architecture of the sensor network system is shown in Figure 1. The overall system architecture consists of a Web camera, a Zigbee dongle (base node), a server, and wireless sensor nodes. The wireless sensor nodes consist of two key parts, referred to as the static and the mobile nodes. The static sensor nodes are scattered in the laboratory and they form a multi-hop mesh networking topology. A key role of the static node is to transfer all the data packets coming from the mobile node back to the dongle. The other key role of the static node is to provide a sufficient number of anchor points for the localization. Each of these sensor nodes has the capability of collecting data and routing data peer-to-peer to the Zigbee dongle. The Zigbee dongle is used to bridge the sensor network to Internet. It provides a serial interface and a wireless connection for node programming and data transfer. The server is connected to the Internet to enable remote users to access the laboratory monitoring system. The mobile node, comprising an accelerometer worn by students, is for monitoring student motion and position in an indoor environment.

During the process of experiment and practice, student needs to rotate hands by hands while operating machines, and adjust machining parameters. Also, there are some machines require students to touch pedals by feet and adjust machining parameters. Therefore, the study intends to incorporate ultra-thin force sensing unit (0.127mm) into a Zigbee node, make flexible force sensors, and then install handles and pedals. "Are students able to use tools correctly?" is the necessary subject needs to be trained during experiment and practice. Therefore, the study plans to connect Zigbee node with PIR325 infrared sensing unit to make wireless infrared sensor, and then install it in the tool box.

Besides, the study connects Zigbee node with three-axis micro electro-mechanical system (MEMS)-based accelerometer to make wireless accelerometer (Figure 2). An accelerometer is a device measuring proper acceleration. It is available to detect magnitude and direction of the acceleration as a vector quantity. The sensor is worn on student; it can not only detect and record student's position inside the laboratory but also know their movement.

3 Implementation

A graphical user interface (GUI) was designed for remote users to carry out the desired operations such as sending commands and parameters to drive the sensor nodes and visualizing the measurement results. The thesis use ASP.NET and Microsoft Visual C#

to write an internet program in order to achieve the goal of quick and convenient information process. Figure 3 shows the Web GUI when a user is monitoring the laboratory environment at the remote client side. A remote user is able to adjust the view angle of camera to get required video data by click on the mouse.

This interface accepts remote client side to get information about which node he/she wants to monitor by clicking on the buttons and checkboxes on the panels. After that, click the sensor which has been installed on the node, and observe sensors' signal. The data of selected sensors are collected and sent to the Web GUI at fixed time intervals. Figure 4, the top-right corner is the information measured by IR sensor, as time's changing, top-center shows force sensor's instant information. On the other hand, the middle is the information measured by accelerometer, as time's changing, top-left corner shows student's current position in laboratory.

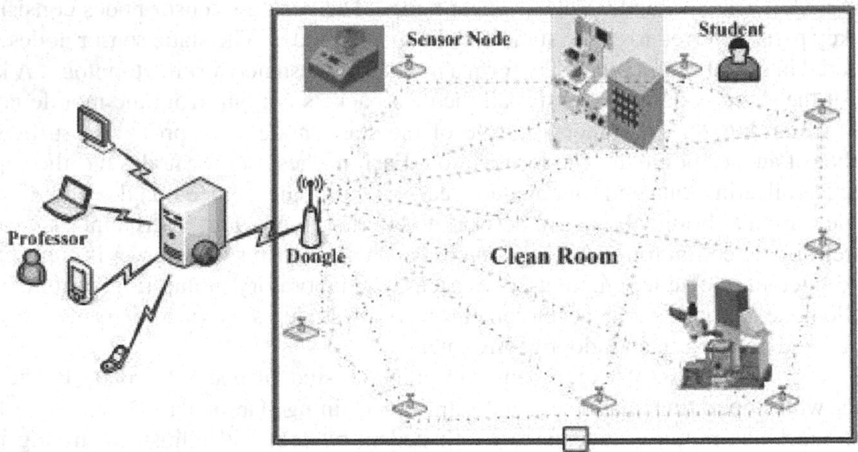

Fig. 1. Architecture of the wireless sensor network system

Fig. 2. Wireless accelerometer

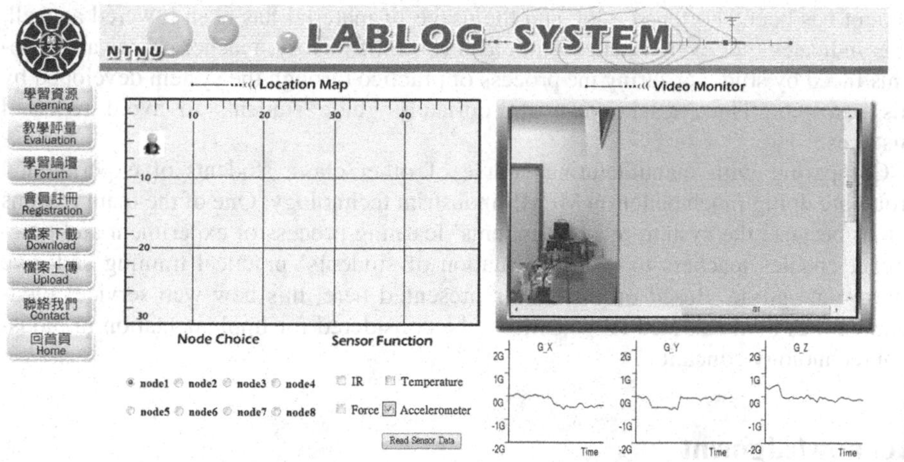

Fig. 3. GUI of the wireless sensor network system at the remote client side

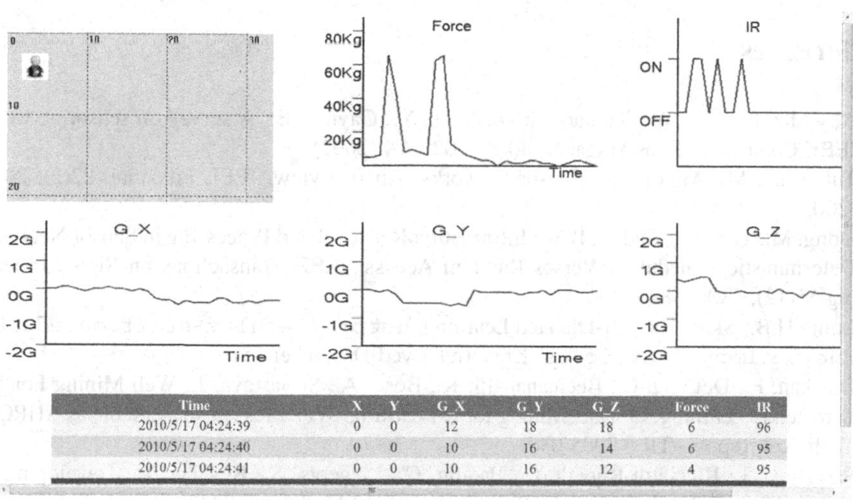

Time	X	Y	G_X	G_Y	G_Z	Force	IR
2010/5/17 04:24:39	0	0	12	18	18	6	96
2010/5/17 04:24:40	0	0	10	16	14	6	95
2010/5/17 04:24:41	0	0	10	16	12	4	95

Fig. 4. Real time monitoring of sensors at the remote client side

4 Conclusions

Practical training is the important teaching strategy to improve students' industrial technology competence. The study uses sensor network technology to develop ubiquitous learning and teaching web services environment for industrial technology education. The developed system was applied to the course of MENS manufacturing. According to related data, teacher shows high satisfaction to this system. Comparing to manufacturing course in previous years, average time of practical training of each student has been shortened a lot, and the usage of material has been lowered as well. This indicates that even practicing in clean room of factory, teacher can aware problems faced by students during the process of practice through the system developed by this research. Thus, teacher can appropriately guide students to avoid repeated mistakes.

Comparing with manufacturing course of other class, students of experimental group are doing much better on MEMS industrial technology. One of the main reasons is that because the system records students' learning process of experiment and practice, it enables teachers to analyze situation of students' practical training and give appropriate guide. Based on the results presented here, this new web services environment has demonstrated its potential to be considered for implementation in industrial technology education.

Acknowledgment

The authors gratefully acknowledge the support of this study by the National Science Council of Taiwan, under the Grant No. NSC98-2511-S-003-015-MY2.

References

1. Akyildiz, I.F., Su, W., Sankarasubramaniam, Y., Cayirci, E.: A survey on sensor networks. IEEE Communications Magazine 40(8), 102–114 (2002)
2. Tubaishat, M., Madria, S.: Sensor networks: An overview. IEEE Potentials 22(2), 20–23 (2003)
3. Dong, M., Tong, L., Sadler, B.M.: Information Retrieval and Processing in Sensor Networks: Deterministic Scheduling Versus Random Access. IEEE Transactions on Signal Processing 55(12), 5806–5820 (2007)
4. Long, H.B.: Skills for Self-Directed Learning, `http://faculty-staff.ou.edu/L/Huey.B.Long-1/articles.htm` (retrieved December 15)
5. Desikan, P., DeLong, C., Beemanapalli, K., Bose, A., Srivastava, J.: Web Mining For Self Directed E-Learning. In: Data Mining for E-Learning. WIT Press (also available as AHPCRC Technical Report –TR # 2005-030)
6. Paquette, G., Ricciardi-Rigault, C., Paquin, C., Liegeois, S., Bleicher, E.: Developing the Virtual Campus Environment. In: Proceedings of Ed-Media, pp. 244–249 (1996)
7. Sung, W.T., Ou, S.C.: Using Virtual Reality Technologies for Manufacturing Applications. Int. J. Com. Applications Tech. 17(4), 213–219 (2003)
8. Craig, A.B., Sherman, W.R.: Understanding Virtual Reality – Interface, Application, and Design. Elsevier Science (Morgan Kaufmann Publishers, Calif., USA (2003)
9. Bouras, C., Philopoulos, A., Tsiatsos, T.: E-learning through distributed virtual environments. J. Netw. Comput. Appl. 24(3), 175–199 (2001)

A Study of Successful and Unsuccessful Online Learning Environment Experiences

Katrina Maxwell and Albert A. Angehrn

INSEAD, boulevard de Constance, 77300 Fontainebleau, France
{katrina.maxwell,albert.angehrn}@insead.edu

Abstract. This paper presents the lessons learned from a collection of 18 different experiences of implementing online skill-based learning management systems and collaborative environments in higher education and enterprises. These experiences were collected in order to guide the design and implementation of a new internet-based service, OpenScout, which aims to help learners find, improve and share open content for management education and training.

Keywords: Best practices, collaborative environments, learning management systems.

1 Introduction

Many online collaboration systems fail to deliver the value expected (Barrett et al, 2009; Labianca et al, 1998; Miles and Snow, 1992; Shenkar and Yan, 2002). Thus the objective of this study was to try to understand why some systems fail and others succeed, in order to guide the design and implementation of a new internet-based service, OpenScout, which aims to help learners find, improve and share open content for management education and training. OpenScout is a 3 year project co-funded by the European Commission within the eContentplus Programme (www.openscout.net) and was launched in September 2009. In this paper we share the lessons we have learned from collecting the actual experiences of OpenScout project consortium members (i.e. Partners) with real life, productive, skill-based learning environments in higher education and enterprises.

2 Methodology

OpenScout partners were asked to provide examples of interesting experiences, both good and bad, of implementing online management learning environments in higher education and enterprises. We collected information not just about good practices but also about unsuccessful practices, in order to be aware of possible pitfalls and try to avoid them. In order to collect these experiences we developed an intelligence gathering framework. Partners were asked to classify the overall success (i.e. the use of the system) of each experience as a: Success (A), Took off then died (B), Got stuck at a low level (C), Never took off (D).

M.D. Lytras et al. (Eds.): WSKS 2010, Part I, CCIS 111, pp. 375–382, 2010.

The classification of the success pattern of a case was made by the experience contributor. This classification was verified by the authors by reviewing all the information provided, followed by a discussion with the experience provider for further clarification if necessary. We collected information about the context of the system experience including purpose, type of users, why chosen, key features, license, and staff costs; the key features on a technical level including all aspects of content (type, rating, quality control, reuse, organization, connection to competences), search/browse functionalities, use of recommendation agents and games, and user profiles; and the key features on a social level including motivation, incentives, and stakeholder relationships. We also asked the respondents to share their success measures, their opinion of the key factors which contributed to the success or failure of the system and the main lessons they learned. We then categorized, summarized and analyzed all of the experiences in order to extract relevant information.

3 Overview of Collected Experiences

OpenScout partners provided information about 18 different experiences of implementing online skill-based learning environments in higher education and enterprises. Ten experiences concerned Learning Management Systems (LMS), four experiences were about Collaborative Environments (CE), and four experiences concerned systems that included both a LMS and a Collaborative Environment. In addition, information about LMS systems being developed in two ongoing EC projects was provided, and one partner provided information about a digital content repository which offers support for some collaborative features. Table 1 shows the breakdown of experiences by context and system type.

Table 1. Experiences by Context and System Type

	LMS	**CE**	**LMS+ CE**	**TOTAL**
Higher Education	7	1	3	11
Enterprises	1	2	0	3
Higher Education + Enterprises	2	1	1	4
TOTAL	10	4	4	18

Eight of these systems require commercial or educational licenses. The other ten did not require licenses and include seven University systems of which six are based on OpenSource software (4 Moodle, 1 LCMS/dotLRN, 1 Open eClass) and three systems developed in past EC projects. We found very few experiences with competence based education in the consortium. Experiences were broadly categorized as successful or not successful (took off then died, got stuck at low level, never took off). Overall 67% of the experiences were considered to be successful. Learning Management Systems experienced the highest success (80%) and the least successful experiences concerned Collaborative Environments (25%).

4 Main Learnings by System Type

In this section we summarize the main learnings by system type. More details about the experiences can be found in a publicly available OpenScout deliverable (Maxwell et al, 2010).

4.1 Learning Management System (LMS) Experiences

The ten LMS experiences concern formal, closed online and blended learning, mainly given to students at Universities. They include both commercial (5) and non-commercial systems (5). Eight of these experiences were considered to be successes.

The main lessons learned from the successful experiences are:

- Lots of staff needed to make this work.
- System is successful when supported by the University or Company.
- Key factor of success is teachers. Teachers must be motivated to learn how to create content. Teachers/tutors need to motivate students to use the system by providing their lectures and writing messages in group forums.
- Success may be mainly because the obligation to use level is very high – students must use the platform to take these courses.
- Integration with other internal information systems was mentioned as being important in choosing a system in three cases.

Two systems were considered less successful. Some reasons given are:

- System was no longer supported by University. It is easier for professors to use platforms supported by the University and they may be required to do so (took off then died).
- The students were not obligated to use it. Just a place to access further readings for the course (stuck at low level).

4.2 LMS and Collaborative Environment (CE) Experiences

Four very different experiences concerned using both an LMS and a CE. Three of these were considered a success and one got stuck at a low level. It is interesting to note in these combined systems that the LMS component is more successful than then CE component.

Successful
Virtuoso
The Cisco Academy platform Virtuoso was used by one university professor who is also a Cisco Certified associate instructor (http://www.cisco.com/web/learning/netacad/index.html). The Virtuoso environment is very tightly controlled and is a closed environment for formal learning. In order to become an instructor, you must teach at an organization which participates in the program. She reports that the courses provided are of very high quality, and that the sharing of additional materials such as teaching aids and ideas, presentations, and good practices by instructors is widely used. One motivation to do this is to be included in the next course design team. This mainly gives the instructor prestige. However, although there is no money

directly involved, Cisco has a complex system allowing people with important input to benefit from additional programs and schemes so there could be some indirect financial benefit. In this case the main lesson is that collaboration happens because:

- There is a strong incentive for instructors to share content and experiences.

OpenLearn

Of all the experience collected, OpenLearn is the closest to OpenScout. OpenLearn is the Moodle-based open content initiative of the Open University, UK which includes courses, archived materials and collaborative spaces (http://www.open.ac.uk/openlearn/home.php). OpenLearn is divided into two areas LearningSpace and LabSpace. LearningSpace is an informal and open system used by learners of all ages and backgrounds to improve skills, take free courses and try out online learning. This is very successful. All LearningSpace materials are taken from existing academically quality controlled OU course materials. In addition, dedicated OpenLearn Academic staff assessed these materials for reuse as open content and repurposed them for delivery in LearningSpace as Open Educational Resources. Faculty Liaison representatives work with Academic staff to locate, acquire and develop sets of materials. Main factors of its success are:

- Fully supported by the University.
- High quality content controlled by University.
- Very well publicized.
- Very easy to start taking a course – no registration in system required.

LabSpace is the dedicated area for reuse of OpenLearn and other open content. It is considered to be less successful than LearningSpace. Registered users anywhere can reuse LearningSpace units in the LabSpace area as well as adding and/or mixing in their own content. Registered users can also use the system's communication tools such as Flashmeeting and Flash Vlog. Main learnings are:

- Provide useful services without registration.
- Provide registered users with tempting extra benefits.
- Keep the quality controlled content in a separate area from freely uploaded material.

eRoom

OUNL used eRoom in their online learning environment as a place for a small number of BSc students (16 per year) to undertake online team collaborative work during a remote internship (http://www.emc.com/products/detail/software/eroom.htm). Although they consider it a success, this is because there is no other alternative. As various components of the system are not integrated, it is not easy to use. Users need some time to get familiar with it. It is also labor intensive for tutors and difficult to scale up. Finally, although better solutions are now available, the University has stuck to a choice made 10 years ago. Its success is thus due to these factors:

- Students are obliged to use it.
- It has University support.

Less Successful
Moodle & Wikispaces
The less successful experience was a combination of Moodle and Wikispaces (www.wikispaces.com) used by one professor for her University course. In this case, it was the collaborative environment Wikispaces which did not meet with much success. Main lessons learned are:

- Students did not want to change from the collaborative platforms they were already using.
- Students did not do anything beyond what they were obliged to do.

4.3 Collaborative Environment Experiences

There were four collaborative environment experiences. Three of these systems were the results of EC projects, and one is a commercial system. Only one system has open content (Slidestar). A main difference between the CE experiences and the LMS experiences is that the staff needs to run the CE are low. The idea being that once you set up a collaborative environment it runs itself.

Successful
KLAB
KLAB (Knowledge and Learning Among Business) is an advanced knowledge management tool specifically designed for enhancing communication, information and knowledge exchange within an existing inter-organizational learning network (PLATO™) (Angehrn et al, 2003). It is used by the groups of SME owner managers and coaches (managers in a multinational company) who meet regularly. The platform is closed to the community. It started as a pilot in the context of an EC project and is still used today. The main reason to use KLAB is to access all information used in the PLATO™ group. New information and content provided by speakers can only be retrieved via the platform.

Lessons learned from this experience are that SME owners need an easy to use system. Local language is a must. They are very busy with their day to day business and rarely use the online help manual. They prefer to be guided by phone, or face-to-face. Although they can communicate within the system via email, skype, instant messages and forums, they do not use these features. They mainly download documents and look at contact details of people in their PLATO™ group. In order to attract them to the platform new information is needed regularly.

In summary SME users:

- Need an easy to use system in their local language.
- Want to talk to a real person when they need help.
- Do not use the system more than absolutely necessary (information retrieval only).

Less Successful
AtGentNet
AtGentNet is a Web2.0 collaborative learning platform with embedded agents (Angehrn, 1997; Nabeth et al, 2008). It was developed as part of an EC research project aimed at designing ICT solutions to support attention. It was used in a 6 month

off-line executive vocational training program for SMEs. In addition to providing supplementary course material the platform was also used as a place to exchange knowledge, and support decision making in an online game. The platform was closed to program participants. This system took off and then died. Once the program finished people returned less and less often to the platform.

The main lessons learned from this experience are:

- Must control quality when anyone can add content.
- Organizing an online game increased user participation.
- The system was not used more than necessary (i.e. not beyond program end)
- Program coordinators now use Facebook to develop the social community aspect.

GMPTube

GMPTube is a video-based Web2.0 platform used for extending the learning and networking of participants in an executive general management program beyond the classroom (Maxwell and Angehrn, 2010). Participants were 33 - 55 years old. The platform was closed and participation was optional. The main reason to use the platform was to share videos and experiences about implementing what they learned during the program back in their company during program breaks, to view profiles of the other participants, and to exchange information about group projects. This platform never took off. Participants mainly watched videos, and looked at user profiles, but did not share new material.

This experience identified three main barriers to Web2.0 inter-organizational learning and collaboration in executive education: technological barriers, motivational barriers and the inter-organizational aspect itself. Many executives were unable to access the platform from their companies. This is a major barrier. Organizations can't expect to profit from Web2.0 tools if they forbid access to them, and managers can not be expected to spend time doing something which is not rewarded. The fact that the platform is video-driven posed a problem both with company firewalls, and with the need for managers to buy webcams.

Motivation is key. If they were motivated, participants could have bought a webcam and accessed the platform from home. However, there are easier alternative ways to collaborate and keep in contact with classmates such as email and LinkedIn that are not video-driven. Finally, the inter-organizational aspect is a barrier because of confidentiality issues. It is one thing to share an experience in class, and quite another thing to have some lasting proof that you said something about your company that you should not have. How much can you safely say about your experience implementing ideas from executive training in your company to people in other organizations? Even people used to face-to-face inter-organizational exchanges hesitate to extend this to an online environment.

The main lessons from this experience are:

- Inter-organizational collaborative systems should be designed to be accessed from within companies. Potential problems with company firewalls should be considered.
- Executives will probably only access inter-organizational collaborative systems to obtain information, not to share information.

Slidestar

Slidestar is a free open content webservice provided by IMC, a German company (www.slidestar.de). It was developed to complement the company's lecture and presentation recording tool with a video lecture repository and related community. Users are students and professors from 18-65 years old. The main reason to use Slidestar is to have free access to and free of charge space to keep video lectures and learning materials. Its success is currently stuck at a low level. This is because it is hard to establish a content community as an open Web2.0 application. The market is already dominated by a few large platforms to keep lectures namely YouTube Edu and iTunes U even though they provide less functionality. IMC has thus found that it works better to license their technology to educational institutions that want their own lecture portal.

Main learnings from this experience are:

- People do not want to change from the collaborative platforms they already use.
- Users appreciated ability to create groups for private publishing.
- Users appreciated RSS feeds on new content from "my professor" or subscribed authors.

5 Conclusions

The objective of this study was to try to understand why some systems fail and others succeed, in order to guide the design, community involvement and organizational aspects of a new internet-based service, OpenScout, which aims to help learners find, improve and share open content for management education and training. Here we have presented the lessons learned from a collection of 18 different experiences of implementing online skill-based learning management systems and collaborative environments in higher education and enterprises.

Acknowledgements

This work was sponsored by the OpenScout Project funded by the European Commission's eContentplus Programme as a Targeted Project in the area of Educational Content. The contribution of experiences from OpenScout Consortium members is gratefully acknowledged.

References

1. Barrett, B.F.D., Grover, V.I., Janowski, T., van Lavieren, H., Ojo, A., Schmidt, P.: Challenges in the adoption and use of OpenCourseWare: experience of the United Nations University. Open Learning: The Journal of Open and Distance Learning 24(1), 31–38 (2009)
2. Labianca, G., Brass, D., Gray, B.: Social networks and the perception of intergroup conflict: the role of negative relationships and third parties. Academy of Management Journal 41, 55–67 (1998)
3. Miles, R.E., Snow, C.C.: Causes of failure in network organizations. California Management Review 34(4), 53–72 (1992)

4. Shenkar, O., Yan, A.: Failure As a Consequence of Partner Politics Learning From the Life and Death of an International Cooperative Venture. Human Relations 559, 565–601 (2002)
5. Maxwell, K., Angehrn, A., Bastiaens, Y., Connolly, T., Holtkamp, P., Kalz, M., Klobučar, T., Luccini, M., Mejeryte–Narkeviciene, K., Nadolski, R., Pappa, D., Parodi, E., Pawlowski, J., Pipan, M., Pirkkalainen, H., Schwertel, U., Stefanov, K., Terrasse, C., Volungeviciene, A.: OpenScout report D6.1 Good Practice Scenario Collection. In: ECP 2008 EDU 428016 (2010)
6. Angehrn, A.A., Gibbert, M., Nicolopoulou, K. (eds.): Special Issue on Understanding Learning Networks. European Management Journal 21(5), 559–562 (2003)
7. Angehrn, A.A.: An Agent-Centered Framework for the Analysis and Diagnosis of Organizational Groupware Platforms. In: Salvendy, G., et al. (eds.) Design of Computing Systems: Cognitive Considerations, pp. 289–292. Elsevier, Amsterdam (1997)
8. Nabeth, T., Karlsson, H., Angehrn, A.A., Maisonneuve, N.: A Social Network Platform for Vocational Learning in the ITM Worldwide Network. In: Proceedings of IST Africa 2008, Windhoek, Namibia (2008)
9. Maxwell, K., Angehrn, A.A.: Lessons Learned from Deploying a Video-Based Web2.0 Platform in an Executive Education Context. In: Lytras, M.D., Ordonez De Pablos, P., Avison, D., Sipior, J., Jin, Q., Leal, W., Uden, L., Thomas, M., Cervai, S., Horner, D.G. (eds.) Technology Enhanced Learning: Quality of Teaching and Educational Reform, TECH-EDUCATION 2010, Communications in Computer and Information Science, vol. 73, pp. 195–201. Springer, Heidelberg (2010)

Assistance System for Disabled People: A Robot Controlled by Blinking and Wireless Link

Lara del Val, María I. Jiménez, Alonso Alonso, Ramón de la Rosa, Alberto Izquierdo, and Albano Carrera

Departamento de Teoría de la Señal y Comunicaciones e Ingeniería Telemática, Universidad de Valladolid, España
lara.val@tel.uva.es

Abstract. Disabled people already profit from a lot of technical assistance that improves their quality of life. This article presents a system which will allow interaction between a physically disabled person and his environment. This system is controlled by voluntary muscular movements, particularly those of face muscles. These movements will be translated into machine-understandable instructions, and they will be sent by means of a wireless link to a mobile robot that will execute them. Robot includes a video camera, in order to show the user the environment of the route that the robot follows. This system gives a greater personal autonomy to people with reduced mobility.

Keywords: Assistance technology, blinking, disability, robot, wireless.

1 Introduction

One of the clearest attributes of human dignity refers to liberty. Liberty is the ability to choose among possibilities, to be accountable for one's action. Autonomy principle is closely related to this responsible liberty. People attach more and more importance to personal autonomy as the only way of treating disabled people fairly and equally.

Nowadays 9% people in the world have some disability [1]. They can be caused by several reasons, such as accidents, population ageing or congenital causes. Assistance or Rehabilitation Technology (AT or RT) arises in response to disability problem and the loss of personal autonomy, reaching into expanding disabled people abilities [2].

RT develops assistive robots, which are included in three groups: smart wheelchairs [3], telecare systems [4] and assistive robots over mobile platforms [5]. Most of these systems are controlled through traditional control methods: a joystick, a mouse or a keyboard. The problem arises with people who control only head movements. For these severe physically disabled people, there are systems that are controlled by voice [6], by brain waves [7], by head tilt [8], or even by electrooculography [9]. The disadvantage of these systems is their electrodes, which work out uncomfortable for some users, and their training work is long and complex [10]. Furthermore, most of these systems have a PC connecting the user and the device to be controlled. Development of a portable system, which controls mobile objects through stimuli, comes up with the purpose of remove this intermediate device. So the system could be easily carried

M.D. Lytras et al. (Eds.): WSKS 2010, Part I, CCIS 111, pp. 383–388, 2010.

and could be applied to countless daily life devices. Furthermore, hardware that comes into contact with the user is removed due to comfort reasons.

This paper proposes the design and implementation of an assistance prototype system for disabled people. This system will favor people with reduced mobility. It tries to promote and take advantage of movements that the patient preserves in order to execute those tasks that he cannot carry on by himself. The system tries to extend control and influence of this patients over their usual environment; this gives them greater autonomy and quality of life. Developed system consists of a robot whose movements are controlled by some voluntary action that the disabled person is able to execute. The system is very flexible and is included in pervasive computing thanks to the use of wireless links and to its modular structure. Like this, the designed prototype can be fitted to include more devices that could make human-environment interaction easier, such as a mechanical arm or a wheelchair.

2 System Objectives

Some principal system objectives are imposed, in order to establish the specifications over the design. First, this system must achieve generic objectives of assistance systems:

- Functionality: System must be useful for disabled people and must help them to make tasks that they cannot make on their own.
- Usability: System operation must be easy to learn and use.
- Comfort: System must be comfortable to use, in order to avoid user's rebound.
- Portability: The more portable the system is, the more easy to use it is and if the system has a stand-alone operation.
- Economy: Final product must have a moderate cost to be available to everyone that need it or want to use.
- User satisfaction.

Apart from these generic objectives, some specific objectives are pursued with this system:

- Providing severe disabled people with a means of interaction and environmental exploration is the final purpose of this system. The purpose of this system development is that severe disabled people will recover independence and liberty through interacting and exploring the environment by means of the limited gestures that they are still able to carry out. Some of these disabled people only keep mobility over the neck, or even only blinking capacity. That is the reason why the developed prototype has a human–machine interface (HMI) based on blinking detection.
- The system must be flexible to adapt itself to different disabilities by means of several user interfaces. So it could be used as a training system for the rehabilitation of disabled people. These users will be able to exercise the movements that they can execute, just like that changing the system input interface. Blinking detection interface could be changed for buttons or even for a manipulative arm. This objective is closely related with pervasive computing.

- The system must also be able of being employed as an entertainment system, mainly for disabled children. The possibility of interacting with the environment, which this system offers, is a key factor on the feasibility of the system acceptance as a game by disabled children. This system could also be use as a rehabilitation one. Play has an important role in children's development, a crucial vehicle to learn about themselves, the environment, and to develop social relationships.

3 System Structure

Figure 1 shows system general structure, on a functional level. The system is composed, mainly, of four blocks:

- The first subsystem is the user interface and is used to detect stimuli. It detects user's voluntary movements through a sensor; particularly, this article explains blinking detection sensor.
- This subsystem is the input interface of the second subsystem: the processing and transmission block. It interprets stimuli and sends them to the reception unit placed on the robot through a wireless link.
- This robot is the third subsystem. The reception unit adapts the stimuli to be understood by the robot, which moves according to them.
- Finally, this robot has a video camera that is added to its frontal side. This video camera transmits on UHF to the TV set that is placed in front of the disabled person. With this video camera, the user can watch the environment of the robot's route.

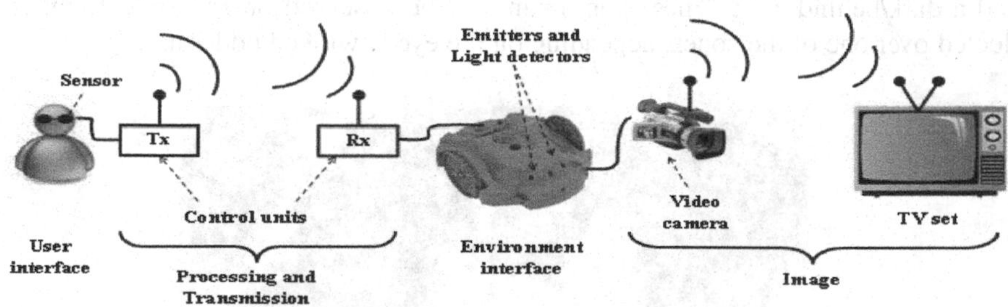

Fig. 1. System general structure, on a functional level

4 System Implementation

Once system structure and operation are defined, components of each system block have to be specified for each block task. Finally, the system is assembled. This stage takes into account that the system must have a reduced size and a friendly physical appearance, so circuits are hidden as much as possible.

Voluntary blinking is produced by a contraction of orbicularis muscle that surrounds the eye [11]. With this action, an ahead/behind movement comes about on eye external angle. This movement is the basis for blinking detection. Interface block achieved two tasks: getting the user order and fitting it for transmission. Produced signals could be simple or complex. The simple ones are generated through one action. There are three types of these simple signals: right eye blinking, left eye blinking and both eyes blinking. Complex signals are generated by means of two consecutive actions: right eye and then left eye blinking, or left eye and then right eye blinking. It is taken into account that second blinking must be within a predefined time interval. Table 1 shows these simple and complex actions, i.e., the relation between user blinking and corresponding robot movements.

Table 1. Relations between blinking, actions and instructions identification

Instruction ID	Blinking*	Action	Previous instruction
1	REB	Advance	Any
2	LEB	Move back	Any
3	REB»LEB	Turn right	Any
4	REB»LEB	Turn left	Any
5	REB+LEB	Stop	1,2,3 or 4
6	REB+LEB	Advance	5

*REB = right eye blink, LEB = left eye blink, » = consecutive stimuli, + = simultaneous stimuli.

Blinking reception block consists of glasses and optic sensors that are placed on the glasses arms, as can be observed on Figure 2. These optic sensors consist of an infrared emitter and a photodetector. Signal reception is based on measuring changes on light that comes from a source. Infrared emitter gives infrared light our towards eye external angle, where two different zones have been defined: a light/ahead zone and a dark/behind zone. These zones can also be observed on Figure 2. Light is reflected over one of the zones, depending on the eye is winked odder not.

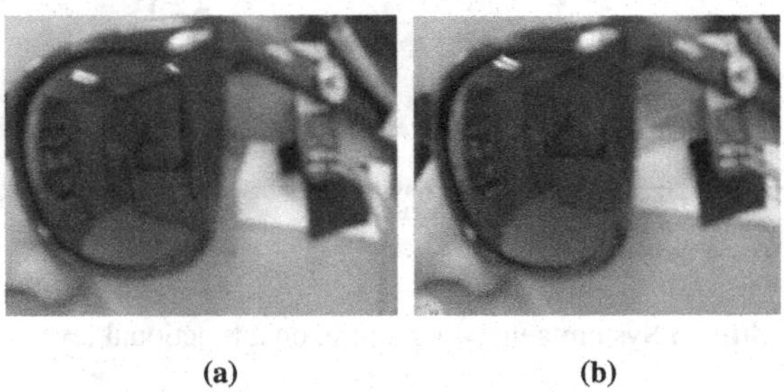

(a) **(b)**

Fig. 2. Sensor positioning and reflection area definition: (a) Resting-state and (b) Blinking

The environment interface is a commercial robot, in order to avoid designing and making a specific robot. Like this, developing a low-cost and flexibly programmable solution is achieved, so that the system reaches a larger number of people.

The image block captures images through a video camera that is placed on the front part of the robot, as can be observed on Figure 3, and sends them through a UHF channel. Finally, these images are displayed on a TV set.

Fig. 3. Final robot appearance

5 System Performance Evaluation

In this section, the operational tests that have been carried out with our prototype are presented. Five people with no disabilities were asked to follow a use and learning protocol, which was developed to measure system usability and time that is necessary to control robot activity.

After testing the system, users were asked to answer a questionnaire, in order to assess their opinion regarding some system features. Their answers were coded according to a 5-level Likert scale (from -2 to 2), and are shown on Figure 4. All these features have positive evaluations. System response delay is the only feature that does not seem positive. Fortunately, these delays can be improved if the patient is trained enough in interface use.

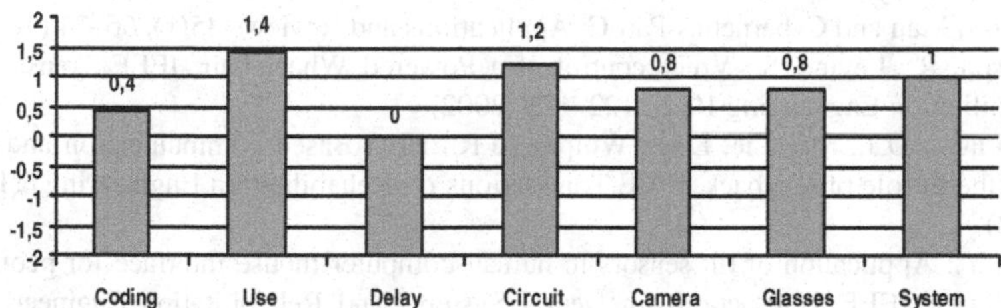

Fig. 4. Average users' evaluation

6 Conclusions

This is an easy to use system for people that have reduced mobility, but are able to execute voluntary actions with their facial muscles, particularly those related with blinking. This system can also be used by people that need support on their interaction with the environment, because they are immobilized, for example, in bed.

This system has different uses, such as trainer of communication capabilities that disabled people have. These capabilities can be used to manipulate a wheelchair, a robotic arm or even a computer mouse with the same interface. This use allows them to watch some home areas where they cannot move due to their physical disabilities.

Our system can also be used as a communication means to allow disabled people to demand medical assistance to their carers.

The system is very inexpensive and is within reach of any disabled person. The cost of elements that are part of the system does not exceed 200$, without including the TV set. At present, a new version of this system is being developed. It has a wireless TV set, in order to improve system performance, being able to send captured images to several TV sets: to the disable person's one and to the carer's one.

In any case, its ease of installation, handling and its use without a PC make this system being suitable for people with no technical education. Some system functions can be programmed, such as transmitting certain sounds or certain light signals. These changes can be done because the robot is very flexible and easy to be programmed.

References

1. Disabled Peoples' International, Strategic plan (2005), `http://www.dpi.org`
2. Association for the Advancement of Assistive Technology in Europe, AAATE. A 2003 View on Technology and Disability, (2003), `http://www.aaate.net`
3. Mihailidis, A., Elinas, P., Boger, J., Hoey, J.: An intelligent powered wheelchair to enable mobility of cognitively impared older adults: An Anticollision System. IEEE Trans. on Neural Systems and Rehabilitation Engineering 15(1), 136–143 (2007)
4. Cortés, U., Annicchiarico, A., Vázquez-Salceda, J., Urdiales, C., Cañamero, L., López, M., Sánchez-Marrè, M., Caltaginore, C.: Asistive technologies for the disabled and for the new generation of senior citizens: The e-Tools architecture. AiCommunications. The European Journal on Artificial Inteligence 16(3), 193–207 (2003)
5. Volosyak, I., Kouzmitcheva, O., Ristic, D., Gräser, A.: Improvement of Visual Perceptual Capabilities by Feedback Structures for Robotic System FRIEND. IEEE Transactions on Systems, Man and Cybernetics-Part C: Applications and Reviews 35(1), 66–74 (2005)
6. Simpson, R., Levine, S.: Voice control of a Powered Wheelchair. IEEE Transaction on Rehabilitation Engineering 10(2), 122–125 (2002)
7. McFarland, D.J., McCane, L.M., Wolpaw, J.R.: EEG-Based communication and control short-therm role of feedback. IEEE Transactions on Rehabilitation Engineering 6(1), 7–11 (1998)
8. Chen, Y.: Application of tilt sensors in human-computer mouse interface for people with disabilities. IEEE Transactions on Neural Systems and Rehabilitation Engineering 9(3), 289–294 (2001)
9. Barea, R., Boquete, L., Mazo, M., López, E.: System for Assisted Mobility Using Eye Movements Based on Electrooculography. IEEE Transaction on Rehabilitation Engineering 10(4), 209–218 (2002)
10. Wolpaw, J.R., Birbaumer, N., Heetderks, W.J., Mcfarlands, D.J., Peckham, P.H., Schalk, G., Donchin, E., Quatrano, L.A., Robinson, C.J., Vaughan, T.M.: Brain-computer interface technology: a review of the first international meeting. IEEE Transactions on Rehabilitation Engineering 8(2), 164–174 (2000)
11. Berardelli, A., Cruccu, G., Kimura, J., Ongerboer de Visser, B.W., Valls-Sole, J.: The orbicularis oculi reflexes. The International Federation of Clinical Neurophysiology. Electroencephalogr. Clin. Neurophysiol. Suppl. 52, 249–253 (1999)

Security System Technologies Applied to Ambient Assisted Living

Juan J. Villacorta, Lara del Val, Mª Isabel Jimenez, and Alberto Izquierdo

E.T.S.I. Telecomunicación, Universidad de Valladolid
Camino del Cementerio s\n, 47011 Valladolid, Spain
{juan.villacorta,larval,marjim,alberto.izquierdo}@tel.uva.es

Abstract. The increasing elderly population has increased interest in the Ambient Assisted Living systems. This article presents a system for monitoring the disabled or elderly developed from an existing surveillance system. The modularity and adaptability characteristics of the system allow an easy adaptation for a different purpose. The proposed system uses a network of sensors capable of motion detection that includes fall warning, identification of persons and a configurable control system which allows its use in different scenarios.

Keywords: Disabled people, elderly, Ambient Assisted Living, sensor network.

1 Introduction

Most of the industrialized countries tend to an increasingly aging population, causing a rising in the percentage of elderly and disabled population. This growing group of people usually requires a greater number of medical and social attentions. Programs like AAL (Ambient Assisted Living) of the European Commission [1] promote the application of information and communication technologies to enable that elderly or disabled people can remain longer living independently in their own house with a improved quality of life. At the time that the costs to public health and social systems are reduced by avoiding the need to go to medical or social centers frequently.

The Ambient Assisted Living systems, also called Home Care Systems, are based on the use of a set of sensors interconnected by different types of communication systems in order to get information about the status of the patient and to provide care in his own home.

In [2] Ambient Assisted Living solutions are defined as the application of Ambient Intelligence (AmI) technologies to allow the adaptation of home environment so people with specific demands, such as disabled and elderly, can live longer in their own homes. These AmI systems are composed of a top-level control entity which provides intelligence to the system and network of sensors whose goal is to get information from the environment.

As AmI systems, security systems have a network of sensors that gather information from the environment in order to perform the tasks of surveillance and intrusion detection and to control the access, among other tasks. The difference is in the actions that the top-level module performs from the information obtained. In the case of AmI

M.D. Lytras et al. (Eds.): WSKS 2010, Part I, CCIS 111, pp. 389–394, 2010.

systems the top-level entity uses that information to improve the quality of life of the users, while security systems are designed to ensure the integrity of the persons and objects monitored. The flexibility of the top-level module can transform a system designed for surveillance or AmI into an Ambient Assisted Living system. In this article presents how a multisensor surveillance system [3] can be adapted to the area of AAL.

2 System Architecture

The designed system presents a modular and distributed structure that can be easily modified to suit the particular conditions of the operating environment and expanded by adding new modules, depending on the specific needs or the future advances in technology.

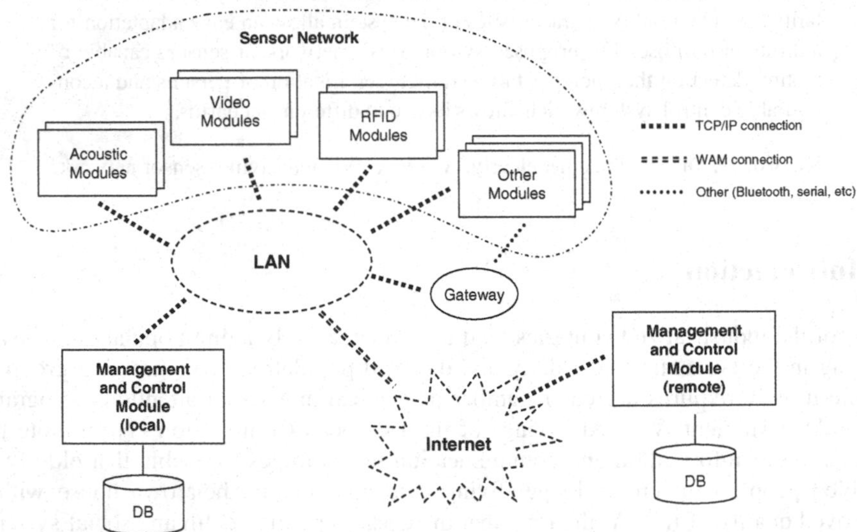

Fig. 1. Block diagram of the system

The system shown in figure 1 consists of two types of modules: management and control modules and sensor modules, such as the acoustic, image or RFID modules.

The control and management modules are the top-level entity of the system. All implementations must have at least one of these modules that are the central and indispensable element of the system. Its function is to establish communication with the other modules and to manage the tasks performed by each of them. During its operation this module uses a database that stores all information from the system, both its configuration and the data obtained from the various sensor modules.

The sensor modules are used to interact with the environment. Primarily they provide information to the system about what is happening but, in some cases, these modules are also actuators because they can modify the operating environment, e.g. allowing or not to open a door.

Communication between the different modules of the system is performed using the TCP/IP protocol through a local area network (LAN). The system also contemplates the connection of modules that do not include network capabilities by the use of gateways [4] that allow the translation other connection interfaces such as USB or Bluetooth to the system transparently.

2.1 Management and Control Module

The management and control module, or MCM, is the central and most significant element of the system. It is the responsibility of providing intelligence to the system by controlling the operation of other modules and the fusion and management of all information provided by all them.

To perform its functions, the MCM uses the following concepts [5]:

- A task is the execution of a series of actions by a module or device.
- An event is the response to an incident that happens during the accomplishment of a task. Events are generated by the sensors modules and received by the MCM.
- Policies of action: define the actions to be taken after the arrival of each event occurred. With the arrival of an event the MCM selects the set of policies associated with it and takes the decision of which policy to implement.

All the information about tasks, events and policies associated with a concrete system implementation is stored in a database connected to the management and control module. Likewise, in the database is also stored the system configuration including the modules that compose it and their properties. Thus, the individualization and adaptability of the system is based on the information stored in this database. On one hand, the modification of the stored policies will influence directly in the behaviour of the system, but also the inclusion of new modules in the database and/or the modification of the existing ones will provide with new functionalities to the system.

In the block diagram of the system shown in the figure 1 there are two management and control modules: a local module and a remote one. For proper operation of the system it is only indispensable to have the local module that is responsible for receiving events and applying the suitable policies. The remote MCM is an optional element and it can be viewed as a backup system of the local MCM storing a copy of all information of the local module. The second function of the remote MCM is to act as an alarm centre, since the local MCM can invoke a task in the remote MCM as a result of the application of a policy. For example, in case that the system detects an accident it can invoke an alarm in the remote module, allocated in a hospital, to request the sending of aid to the address where the system is located.

2.2 Sensor Network

2.2.1 Acoustic Module

This module is a application of SODAR (SOund Detection And Ranging) technologies that use arrays of sensors to realize the location and tracking of objects. Although based on the philosophy of RADAR systems, these systems differ for using acoustic waves instead of electromagnetic ones [6].

The use of an array of sensors allows, through beamforming techniques [7], positioning the monitoring beam electronically. The ability to change the pointing angle quickly allows these systems to carry out several tasks simultaneously, being able to track multiple objects while detecting the presence of new ones.

The main functions performed by the acoustic module are:

- Surveillance: with the purpose of detecting the presence of new objects.
- Tracking: updating the position of every object detected in the vigilance.

Taking into account the purpose of the system, we have adapted the module to enable the detection of a falls. The fall of a person supposes an abrupt change of his position, from a vertical position to a horizontal one [8]. The absence of later movement can also be used for the detection of a serious fall. These considerations have been taken into account in the processing algorithms to enable the fall detection in this module.

2.2.2 Video Module

The video module is responsible for the capture and processing of images from the room in which the module is located. Their integration into the system allows corroborating the information obtained by the acoustic module providing greater reliability to the system.

This module is divided into two subsystems: the acquisition subsystem that takes charge of controlling the camera itself and capturing images and the processing subsystem that is responsible for managing the sequence of images in order realize a detection of movement. The implemented algorithm uses a variation of the Sakbot algorithm [9] as it provides good results without a high computational load.

The main function of the video module is the confirmation of the detections made with the acoustic module due the more accuracy of it. This module is also used for fall detection using an algorithm for extracting vertical-horizontal dimensions of the detected objects [10] and generating a fall event when a sudden change is detected.

2.2.3 RFID Module

The purpose of this module is mainly for identification but also for access control. Each person who usually enters the house has a bracelet that includes a passive RFID tag. The RFID readers are distributed at the doors of the rooms. When a person crosses a door, the RFID reader detects the bracelet and identifies the person who wears it. This module is complementary to the acoustic and video modules, since it allows assigning an identity to people detected by these other modules.

Besides to this identification functionality, each RFID reader controls the operation of the electronic lock of the door, allowing or not the access to the room depending on the identity of the person that is going to use it.

2.2.4 Other Modules

The flexibility of the system architecture allows adding different devices depending on the needs of each particular case. Some examples of other modules included in the system are:

- Panic button: it is a large button positioned in an easily accessible place. Its pulsation indicates that an emergency has occurred.

- GSM module: the purpose of this module is to alert when an emergency takes place by sending an SMS to a telephone number previously stored in the system.
- Display module for notices: to notify important information to the patient or caregiver.

3 Case of Study: Nurse at Home

This case study is applicable to disabled persons or elderly who have a nurse to assist them living in the same house. The purpose of the system in this case is to provide to the patient greater privacy and freedom, since it is not necessary the presence of the nurse at all time, but in case of emergency the system will alert the nurse that will come quickly.

An example of a house implementing this usage scenario can be the following: the patient has two interconnected rooms for their personal use. Each room is equipped with an acoustic module and a video module. Also in the access doors of each room there is an RFID module. In the room assigned to the nurse there is placed a computer that integrates the MCM and a display module. The patient's rooms and the nurse's one are connected by a corridor that has a video module.

Action policies can be adjusted depending on the needs of the patient. The following examples of patients are contemplated:

- Patient who for his deficiencies or diseases should remain lying down. Such patient should stay in bed all the time. When the patient is alone, there should be no movement in either of the two rooms. Motion detection by the acoustic module, checked with the video module will generate an alarm on the screen of the nurse.
- Patient with episodes of disorientation: in this case the patient movement within his private rooms is allowed, so that the detection of movement does not generate an alarm to the nurse. Depending on the severity of the patient it is allowed to go out from his private area to the common corridor.
- Patient in relative good health: this is the simplest case. The patient can move without restrictions for their rooms and even go out to the common area. The system will record his movements for if an accident like a fall takes place.

The tests realized on the proposed scenarios have verified the correct functioning of the whole system including the detection and tracking of moving objects and the detection of falls and the usefulness of the double video-acoustic check to reduce the number of false alarms. We also found that the accuracy in the monitoring of patients with symptoms of disorientation allows the identification of such events by detecting erratic movements by the patient.

4 Conclusions

This article presents a system for monitoring the disabled or elderly developed from an existing surveillance system. The system includes different types of sensors for the detection, identification and tracking of persons in the workspace. Among these sensors it is necessary to emphasize, for its innovation, the acoustic sensor, which makes use of beamforming techniques, and its integration with the video module.

This is an open system that can be adapted for different situations as shown in the explained case of study. This flexibility is due to the management and control module that, through the use of policies of action, is responsible for merging the information from all existing modules and taking suitable decisions. The use of policies of action allows the modification and adaptation of the system behaviour to each particular case.

At this time the work team is focused on several lines of development, including the integration of new modules or the identification of episodes of disorientation. Likewise, we have experimented with acoustic signature techniques to identify people in order to assign an identity to the targets detected by the acoustic module, the obtained results, although promising, are still too preliminary for its inclusion in the developed system presented in this paper.

References

1. The Ambient Assited Living (AAL) Joint Programme, http://www.aal-europe.eu/
2. Kleinberger, T., Becker, M., Ras, E., Holzinger, A., Müller, P.: Ambient Intelligence in Assisted Living: Enable Elderly People to Handle Future Interfaces. In: Stephanidis, C. (ed.) UAHCI 2007 (Part II). LNCS, vol. 4555, pp. 103–112. Springer, Heidelberg (2007)
3. de Jesus, J.D., Calvo, J.J.V., Fuente, A.I.: Surveillance system based on data fusion from image and acoustic array sensors. IEEE, Aerospace and Electronic Systems Magazine 15(2), 9–16 (2000)
4. Hou, J.C., et al.: PAS: A Wireless-Enabled, Sensor-Integrated Personal Assistance System for Independent and Assisted Living. In: 2007 Joint Workshop on High Confidence Medical Devices, Software, and Systems and Medical Device Plug-and-Play Interoperability pp.64–75 (2007)
5. Rao, S., Cook, D.J.: Predicting Inhabitant Actions Using Action and Task Models with Application to Smart Homes. International Journal of Artificial Intelligence Tools 13(1), 81–100 (2004)
6. Strobel, N., Spors, S., Rabenstein, R.: Joint audio-video signal processing for object localization and tracking. In: Brandstein, M.S., Ward, D.B. (eds.) Microphone Arrays: Signal Processing Techniques and Applications, pp. 203–225. Springer, Heidelberg (2001)
7. Van Veen, B., Buckley, K.: Beamforming: A versatile approach to spatial filtering. IEEE ASSP Magazine, 4–24 (1988)
8. Noury, N., et al.: Fall detection - Principles and Methods., Engineering in Medicine and Biology Society. In: 29th Annual International Conference of the IEEE, pp. 1663–1666 (22-26, 2007)
9. Cucchiara, R., Grana, C., Piccardi, M., Prati, A.: Detecting moving objects, ghosts, and shadows in video streams. IEEE Transactions on Pattern Analysis and Machine Intelligence 25(10), 1337–1342 (2003)
10. Miaou, S.-G., Sung, P.H., Huang, C.Y.: A Customized Human Fall Detection System Using Omni-Camera Images and Personal Information. In: 1st Transdisciplinary Conference on Distributed Diagnosis and Home Healthcare, D2H2, pp. 39–42 (2006)

E-Commerce Sites: Use Intention by Brazilian Users

Cayley Guimaraes, Lucas Lacerda, and Diego R. Antunes

UFPR, Curitiba, Brazil
profcayley@yahoo.com.br, lacerdabh@gmail.com, drantunes@gmail.com

Abstract. This article discusses the behavior of Brazilians intention of use e-commerce sites. To explain its use, or not, the Unified Theory of Acceptance of Technology (UTAUT) was used. A survey was conducted through a questionnaire based on variables from UTAUT available for twenty days over the Web, that prompted 1900 responses. The results indicate that Effort and Social Influence are the variables of the model that better explain Brazilian users intention to use e-commerce sites.

Keywords: E-commerce, UTAT, Intention to use.

1 Introduction

According to Magalhaes [7], the Internet is the media with the highest growth rate, and a vehicle that has an ever increasing value to all fields of human activities. And it was in this environment that e-commerce sites emerged, as a tool for commerce and trade of merchandize and services.

Kalakota & Whinston [5] define e-commerce as a modern technology of business, one that directs the needs of organizations, markets and consumers, lowering costs and enhancing the quality of services, thus speeding the overall trade process. One type of e-commerce is the Business-to-Consumer (B2C), that provides information from sellers to user to mediate the commerce [6].

In Brazil, 44% of Internet users declared to have used sites to browse for products and prices, but only 13% have actually concluded the buying. Additionally, only 29.54% of users, who have expressed interest in buying a product from an e-commerce site, have purchased [4]. It is, then, important to find out why more than 71% of potential buyers hesitate to do so using e-commerce sites. The UTAUT, as proposed by [11], may be used for this purpose [10]. The findings may be used to develop better sites in order to help sales increase.

A survey, based on the UTAUT model, was conducted, via one of the largest e-commerce sites in Brazil. The questionnaire was available for twenty days, and it received 1900 voluntary responses. The remainder of this paper describes the model, the working assumptions, the questionnaire and the results.

M.D. Lytras et al. (Eds.): WSKS 2010, Part I, CCIS 111, pp. 395–400, 2010.

2 Unified Theory of Acceptance Use of Technology (UTAUT)

Venkatesh [11] studied several models of use behavior and technology acceptance models to compile the Unified Theory of Acceptance Use of Technology (e.g. Technology Acceptance Model TAM, TAM2 among others). The UTAUT model has four determinant constructs, that directly influence in the acceptance of technology and use behavior: Performance Expectation, Effort Expectation, Social Influence and Facilitating Conditions. There are other four constructs that are moderators, and have an indirect influence: Gender, Age, Experience and Voluntary Use.

According to the UTAUT model [11] Performance Expectation is the degree to which an individual believes that the use of the system will aid her to obtain gains in the execution of a task. This construct is derived from five different constructs of the eight theories used by the author. They are: Perceived Usefulness (the degree a person believes that using a certain system will aid her performance from TAM [2]. Extrinsic Motivation (the perception that users will want to perform an activity because it would aid performance, remuneration and promotions MM [2]. Job Fit (the belief a user has that the use of a certain technology will enhance her job performance MPCU [9]. Relative advantage (the degree to which an innovation is perceived as an improvement in the way of doing things IDT [8]. Outcome Expectation Performance (the consequences related to performance. Outcome Expectation Personal (the consequences related to personal performance SCT [3].

Effort Expectation is the degree of easiness of use associated with the use of the system. It was derived from: Perceived Ease of Use (the degree a person believe that using a system would be free of effort TAM [2]. Complexity (the degree to which an innovation is perceived as somewhat difficult to comprehend and use MPCU [9]. Ease of Use (the degree in which using an innovation is perceived as being difficult IDT [8].

Social Influence is the pressure a person believes is exerted by other people, regarded as important to her, for her to use a new system. This construct is derived from: Subjective Norm (the perception an individual has of the opinion of other people, considered important by her, about using or not a system TAM [2]. Social Factors (the appropriation of the subjective culture of the group of reference and interpersonal agreements an individual makes with others in specific social situations MPCU [9]. Image (the use of a system improves the individuals image in social settings IDT [8].

Facilitating Conditions are the degree to which a person believes that there are organizational and technical infra-structure to support the use of a system. This construct comes from: Perceived Behavioral Control (perceptions of internal and external constraints over behavior, including auto-efficiency and resources and technologies conditions TPB [1]. Facilitating Conditions (objective factors in the environment that observers consider that allow a certain act to be performed MPCU [9]. Compatibility (the degree to which an innovation is perceived as being consistent with existing values, needs, past experiences and potential adopters IDT [8].

Gender, Age, Experience and Voluntary Use are considered by [11] as moderators. Gender and Age moderate Performance Expectation (stronger effect for men and younger workers). Gender, Age and Experience moderate Effort Expectation (stronger effect for women, older workers, and those with limited experience). Gender, Age, Voluntary Use and Experience moderate Social Influence (stronger effect for women, older workers, in mandatory use condition and with limited experience. Age and Experience moderate Facilitating Conditions (stronger effect for older workers and experience).

3 Working Assumptions

The survey was made available through the Internet, via one of the largest Brazilian e-commerce sites, over a period of twenty days (from 05/02/2010 to 05/23/2010). There were 1900 spontaneous responses. 60% of the respondents are males, and the average age is 27.8 years. A five-point Likert Scale (ranging from 1- totally disagree, 2 disagree, 3 neutral, 4 agree, to 5 totally agree) was used. The variables of the model, combined with the constructs from which they derived, were used to elaborate a series of testing assumptions. The Voluntary Use construct was not used, because it was considered that the use of e-commerce site was voluntary (i.e. not an obligation of any sort).

A1: Performance Expectation influences the intention of use of an e-commerce site the greater the performance of expectation, the greater is the intention of use.

A2: Effort Expectation influences e-commerce site intention of use the lesser the expectation, the greater the intention of use.

A3: Social Influence plays a role in the intention of use of e-commerce sites the greater the social influence, the greater the intention of use.

A4: Facilitating conditions influence intention of use of e-commerce sites the greater the social influence, the greater the use.

A5: Gender and Age are moderator factors in Performance Expectation.

A5A: The effect on Performance Expectation on intention of use is more intense for men than for women.

A5B: The effect on Performance Expectation varies with age: the younger the individual, the more intense is the effect.

A6: Gender, Age and Experience are Moderating Factors in Effort Expectation.

A6A: The effect on Effort Expectation on intention of use is more intense for women than for men.

A6B: The effect of Effort Expectation varies with age the older the individual, the more intense the effect.

A6C: The effect of Effort Expectation is more intense on individuals with limited experience than on more experienced individuals.

A7: Gender, Age and Experience are moderating factor on Social Influence.

A7A: The effect on Social Influence is more intense for women than for men.

A7B: The effect on Social Influence on intention of use varies the older the individual, the more intense the effect.

A7C: The effect on Social Influence on intention of use is more intense on individuals with limited experience than on individuals with more experience.

A8: Age and Experience are moderating factors on Facilitating Conditions.

A8A: The effect on Facilitating Conditions on intention of use varies with age the older the individual, the more intense the effect.

A8B: The effect on Facilitating Conditions on intention of use is more intense on individuals with limited experience than on individuals with more experience.

Table 1. Questionnaire

Construct		ID	Questions
Moderating Factors	Gender	Q1	Male
			Female
	Age	Q2	Open
	Experience	Q3	Did you use e-commerce sites in the last six months?
	Experience	Q4	Did you buy?
Performance Expectation	Perceived Usefulness	Q5	Compared to traditional buying process, with the use of the e-commerce site you had a better performance
	Relative advantage	Q6	The task of buying products and services is better executed when an e-commerce site is used than when the traditional process is used.
	Job Fit	Q7	Your work performance is better when you e-commerce sites.
	Personal results expectation	Q8	The use of e-commerce sites brings you personal realization.
Effort Expectation	Perceived Ease of Use	Q9	Buy through e-commerce sites does not generate effort.
	Complexity	Q10	E-commerce sites are ease to understand and use.
	Ease of use	Q11	E-commerce sites are difficult to use.
Social Influence	Subjective Norm	Q12	A friend's recommendation would influence you to buy a certain product or service through an e-commerce site.
	Social Factors	Q13	The fact that some people from your social group have bought products and services through an e-commerce site would make you decide to also buy.
	Image	Q14	You feel that the use of an e-commerce site improves your image in your social group.
Facilitating Conditions	Perceived Behavioral Control	Q15	You have total control of your actions when using an e-commerce site.
	Facilitating Conditions	Q16	You would use an e-commerce site if technical support were available.
	Compatibility	Q17	Given your context, the e-commerce site adapts to your needs.

4 Results, Analysis and Conclusion

For Assumption A1, Q5 had an average of 3.22 and standard deviation of 1.15; Q6 had an average of 2.89 and standard deviation of 1.24 and Q8 had an average of 2.78 and standard deviation of 1.13. The results seem to indicate that A1 does not hold. Further investigation must be performed to understand this result.

As for Assumption A2, Q9 had an average of 3.59 and standard deviation of 1.23; Q10 had an average of 3.23 and standard deviation of 1.20 and Q11 had an average of 3.69 and standard deviation of 1.00. The results seem to indicate that A2 does hold. Therefore, it is important to take Effort Expectation into account when designing e-commerce sites.

As for Assumption A3, Q12 had an average of 3.47 and standard deviation of 1.31; Q13 had an average of 3.18 and standard deviation of 1.33 and Q14 had an average of 2.21 and standard deviation of 1.07. The results seem to indicate that A3 does hold. Therefore, it is important to take Social Influence into account when designing e-commerce sites.

As for Assumption A4, Q15 had an average of 2.71 and standard deviation of 1.37; Q16 had an average of 3.20 and standard deviation of 1.30 and Q17 had an average of 2.37 and standard deviation of 1.30. The results seem to indicate that A4 does not hold. Further investigation must be performed to understand this result.

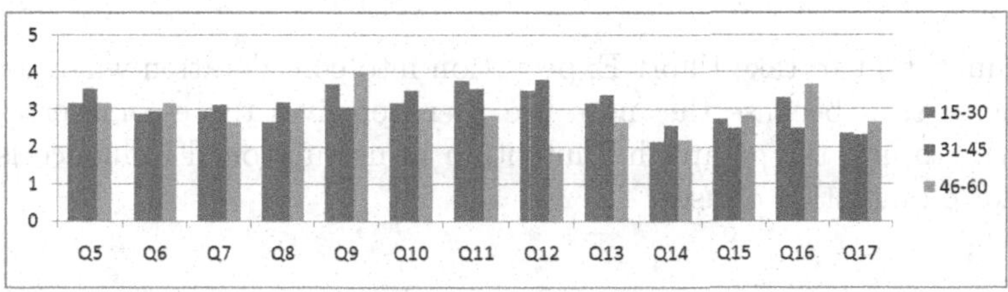

Fig. 1. Response averages for different groups

In Figure 2, as for Assumption A5A, the results for Q5, Q6, Q7 and Q8 tells us that the effect of Performance Expectation is more intense for males. But A5B, in Figure 1, as per the averages from Q5, Q6, Q7 and Q8, the averages show no decrease of Performance Expectation as age increases.

In Figure 2, as for A6A, averages for Q9, Q10 and Q11 show little variation between gender. Also, in Figure 1, as for A6B, there was no decreasing variation on the averages among the between age groups. Further investigation is necessary. As for A6C, the averages for people with experience are higher than that for people without experience.

In Figure 2, as for A7A, the averages for Q12, Q13 and Q14 shows a more intense effect for males. In Figure 1, A7B, the averages for Q12, Q13 and Q14 for the various age groups considered was not consistent, therefore, it is hard to make a definite conclusion. A7C showed a higher average (3.89) for persons with experience than that for people without experience (2.79).

In Figure 2, A8A, the averages for questions Q15, Q16 and Q17 are below the expected average (3.00), which indicates that A8A does not hold. Also, for A8B, the averages for people with experience (3.23) were higher than that for people without experience (3.13).

This research had a goal to verify the intention of use of Brazilian e-commerce sites using the UTAUT. The results show that the greater the Effort Expectation, the higher the intention of use by the subjects (A2). Gender influences this relation in a different way than that proposed by the model, as for A6A. Experience and age also influence this construct, albeit with some unexpected results. A3 does hold: the greater the Social Influence, the greater the intention of use. H7A shows that the effect is more intense for males than for females. And A7C shows that the effect is less intense on individuals with limited experience.

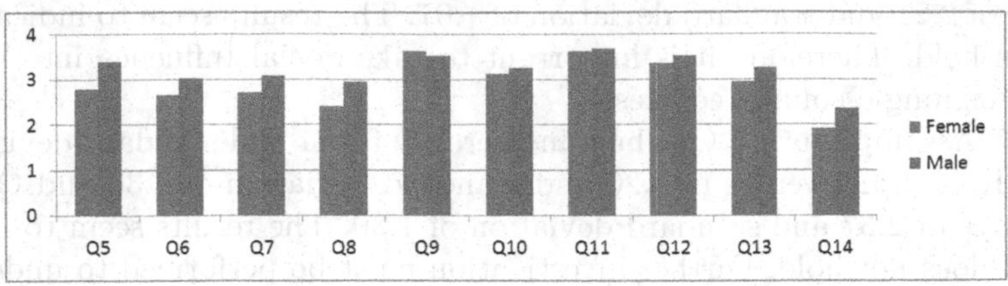

Fig. 2. Response averages for different sex

It is important to take Effort Expectation into consideration when designing e-commerce sites because the more the user perceives the e-commerce site as being easy to use, the greater her intention in use it. Social Influence is also a motivator on intention of use.

References

1. Ajzen, I.: The Theory of Planned Behavior. Organizational Behavior and Human Decision Processes 50(2), 179–211 (1991)
2. Davies, F.D., Bagozzi, R.P., Warshaw, P.R.: Extrinsic and Intrinsic motivation to use computers in the workplace. Journal of Applied Social Psychology 22, 11–32 (1992)
3. Compeau, D.R., Higgins, C.A., Huff, S.: Social Cognitive Theory and Individual Reactions to Computing Technology: A Longitudinal Study. MIS Quarterly 23(2), 145–158 (1999)
4. Comite Gestor da Internet no Brasil - CGI, Pesquisa sobre o uso das tecnologias da informacao e da comunicacao no Brasil de 2008. So Paulo 2009, `http://www.cetic.br/tic/2008/index.html`
5. Kalakota, R., Whinston, A.B.: Eletronic Commerce. A Managers Guide. Addison-Wesley, Berkeley (1997)
6. Lobler, M.L., Monize, S.V., Kelmara, M.V.: A Aceitacao do Comercio Eletronico Explicada pelos Modelos TAM e TTF Combinados, Sao Paulo (2006)
7. Magalhaes, A.S.: E-Commerce e E-Banking no Brasil: Uma perspectiva do Usuario. Sao Paulo (2007)
8. Moore, G., Benbasat, I.: Development of an instrument to measure the perceptions of adopting an information technology innovation. Information Systems Research 2, 173–191 (1991)
9. Thompson, R.L., Higgins, C.A., Howell, J.M.: Personal Computing: Toward a Conceptual Model of Utilization. MIS Quarterly 15(1), 124–143 (1991)
10. da Silva, J.M.B.: Aplicacao do modelo UTAUT na avaliacao da intencao de uso de sistemas ERP. Dissertacao de Mestrado Profissionalizante em administracao IBMEC, Rio de Janeiro (2009)
11. Venkatesh, V., Morris, M.G., Davis, G.B., Fred, D.: User acceptance of information technology: Toward a unified view. MIS Quarterly 27(3), 425–478 (2003)

Instructional Leadership and Schools Effectiveness

Daisy Kee Mui Hung[1] and Premavathy Ponnusamy[2]

[1] School of Management, Universiti Sains Malaysia, 11800 Penang, Malaysia
[2] Aminuddin Baki Institute, Ministry of Education, 06000 Kedah, Malaysia
daisy@usm.my, prema_usm@hotmail.com

Abstract. With the influx of information technology through the Internet and the use of ICT in our daily lives, our future generation has traversed from a mere change of era to a dynamic era of change. Thus, the role of school leaders is becoming more challenging than ever. They need to make greater strides to ensure that they are able to make adjustments and readjustments in instructional practices to cater for the changing elements in their organization. In brief, the school leaders have to be creative, innovative with entrepreneurial drive in order to steer their subordinates (teachers) towards school excellence. Leadership of principal is therefore considered as a main criterion to create successful schools in country's educational advancement. Besides, the school effectiveness plays a crucial role in country's academic advancement. This paper focuses on a comprehensive review of literature on the relationship between instructional leadership and school effectiveness.

Keywords: Instructional Leadership, School Effectiveness, Malaysian Education System.

1 Introduction

The development of a knowledgeable society has brought changes in economy and various societal structures. This can be obviously seen in the changes brought in the field of education. Globalization has led the Malaysian Education System to shift its educational focus that gives rise to the need to reflect and revisit its education growth strategies to ensure that they are relevant in today's world. In fact, the growing focus in this field is related to the development of competencies and knowledge among educational leaders. Moreover, as educational practitioners, it is also vital that all those concerned strive to build cooperation and synergies in education between all the related departments under the Ministry of Education (MOE) to reinforce education growth in Malaysia. What is lacking now is the commitment to follow-up with action.

It is crucial that we are attached to the issues revolving around educational leadership and management especially in the era of internationalization which demands new perspectives and practices in leading and managing the education system. Skilful school leaders play a key role in school improvement or school effectiveness. They are the most responsible personnel in the educational system for school improvement even though they do not have a direct effect. This statement affirms Hallinger's (2003) findings that school leaders indirectly influence school effectiveness. School

M.D. Lytras et al. (Eds.): WSKS 2010, Part I, CCIS 111, pp. 401–406, 2010.

leaders and teachers are regarded as the highly intellectual work force. Therefore, there is a need to examine or explore the relationship between instructional leadership behaviour of headmasters and school effectiveness.

2 School Effectiveness

Malaysian education system has been encountering increase in pressure to raise standards of learning and academic achievements of students for more than ten years. There are number of programmes and awards such as the National Aspiring School Award (NASA) aimed towards quality improvement that were initiated in search for excellence and assurance of quality in schools (Khuan, Chua & Abdul Razak, 2004).

There are two theoretical guidelines or models used in making the decision on school effectiveness. The models are the goal model of organizational effectiveness and system-resource model of organizational effectiveness. According to the goal model, the effectiveness of schools is based on the outcome of the activities to meet or to exceed its goals (Hoy & Miskel, 2001). The system-resource model delineates effectiveness as the ability of an organization to secure assets. Both the goal and system-resource models share the important assumption where the goal model defines effectiveness in terms of achieving the objectives of the organization that can be exchanged for other resources. The system-resource model is based on the open-systems viewpoint. It stresses more on the harmonious functions of the organization's internal components.

INPUTS →	TRANSFORMATION →	OUTPUT
Inputs Effectiveness Criteria	**Throughputs Effectiveness Criteria**	**Outcomes Effectiveness Criteria**
Teacher Capabilities Student Readiness Parental Support Policies & Standards Physical Facilities Fiscal Resources	• Instructional Quality • Leadership Quality • Curriculum Quality • School & Classroom • Learning Time • Climate Health • Motivational Levels • Harmony & Vision	Students Learning Academic Achievement Job Satisfaction Absentee Level Dropout Rate Performance Quality
	Added Perspective **Time Constraint**	
	Feedback	

Fig. 1. Integrated Model of Organizational Effectiveness (Hoy & Miskel, 2001)

These two theories are similar although their ideas are slightly different. The goal and system-resource effectiveness are integrated as a goal and system–resource model. This model uses specific indicators of the input, throughput or outcome concepts as operative goals. These goals are combined with the time frame and the constituencies applicable to each indicator (Hoy & Miskel, 2001). The model is illustrated in Figure 1.

3 School Leadership and Management

As the government aspires to make Malaysia a 'Centre for Educational Excellence', educational improvement is therefore crucial. In order to bring the nations aspiration into a reality, the achievement of advancement in national educational development can be enhanced effectively through knowledgeable, skilled and capable personnel in the field of leadership and management (Aminuddin Baki Institute, 2009). Besides, the fast-paced advancements in technology and communications affect the nature of teaching and learning process as well as leadership and management. School leaders have to be aware of the events around the organization and keep up-to-date in order to cater the demands of students and other stakeholders of the organization. Even though the main role of principals is to focus on the teaching and learning processes as their core tasks in school operations, they often allocate more time for managerial and administrative tasks. Leadership and management have to be considered equally in schools in order to operate effectively and achieve the objectives (Bush & Middlewood, 2005). According to Hallinger and Murphy (1987), principals are encouraged to be strong educational leaders. Hechinger, The New York Times President, commented that,

> "I have never seen a good school with a poor principal, or a poor school with a good principal. I have seen unsuccessful schools turn around into successful schools and regrettably outstanding schools slide rapidly into decline. In each case, the rise or fall could be traced to the quality of the principal."

This sharp observation by Hechinger illustrates that the rise or fall of the schools' performance is in the leaders' hands. Schools can generate the levels and kinds of learning that society desires as the leaders become more skilled at organizing teachers in various arrangements to work toward specific goals (Synder, 1983). Principal and headmaster leadership is the most important factor in school effectiveness, progress and excellence (Rusmini, 2006). Leadership is a process that influences an individual and brings all the members in the school organization towards the organizational strategy. Effective leaders are able to adjust the leadership style with the environment within the organization (Rusmini, 2006).

According to leadership theories and research findings, the characteristics of effective educational leaders are divided into leadership quality and curriculum leadership. For instance, findings of Hallinger and Murphy (1985) and Sammons, Hillman and Mortimore (1995) show that leadership quality comprises of the vision that is clearly shared among the organization's members. Quality leaders also work with high communication skills with many people (Sammons et al, 1995). Whereas, findings on curriculum leadership show that leaders play an important role as instructional leaders by creating the conducive environment suitable for learning (Hallinger & Murphy, 1985; Sammons et al, 1995). These leaders also support the various instructional methods practiced by teachers in the classrooms (Sergiovanni, 2001) and observe every actions carried out in school (Levine & Lezotte, 1990).

Since, the era of 21st century filled with hurdles and obstacles, it is indisputably an age characterized by nothing else but unprecedented changes. Thus, every party concerned should recognize the importance of the role of headmasters as leaders in school management.

4 Instructional Leadership

Hallinger and Murphy (1987) reported in their study that one of the main obstacles that hinder principals from exercising strong instructional leadership is the lack of knowledge about the curriculum and instruction. Thus, they need to have the best leadership and management practices and equip themselves with essential professional skills so as to face the challenges in their organization. This is because, school leaders have long believed that instructional leadership which consists of supervision, staff development and curriculum development facilitates school improvement (Blase & Blase, 2004).

In order to carry out their duties, the leaders of schools face many challenges especially on how to share and sustain ideas about change especially transform what was essentially a conservative system. The leaders need to practice instructional leadership to enhance their leadership competencies. For instance, Hallinger and Murphy (1987) had put forward ideas stating that leaders need to have understanding of the curriculum and instruction. Thus, it is very lucid that headmasters being school leaders should be equipped with knowledge and expertise in order to carry out practices in ways to contribute to the schools' improvement. They must be competent enough to practice the activities that enable instructional improvement. In fact, the leaders of schools are the key players to develop the instructional improvement of each school.

However, the importance of the role of the instructional leadership was deduced from the research on schools' effectiveness. Studies proved that the skilful leadership of school principals was the main contributing element in change implementation, school improvement or schools' advancement (Hallinger, 2003). In other words, instructional leadership mainly focuses on the roles of the school leaders as curriculum and instructional coordinators, controller supervisors and developers in schools (Hallinger & Murphy, 1985). Hallinger and Murphy (1985) developed the most well known model for instructional leadership. It is widely used by researchers because of its high validity and reliability. As classified and further discussed by Hallinger and Murphy (1985) and explained again in Hallinger (2008), this model comprises of three dimensions of instructional leadership such as defining the schools' mission, managing the curriculum and instruction and promoting a positive school-learning climate. The three dimensions of school instructional leadership consist of ten types of specific instructional leadership job functions (Hallinger and Murphy, 1985). They are further explained below:

> *Defining the schools' mission* consists of two specific job functions: frame goals and communicates goals.
> *Managing the curriculum and instruction* has four specific job functions: knows curriculum and instruction, coordinates curriculum, supervises and evaluates, and monitors progress.

Promoting the school learning climate also has four specific job functions: sets standards, sets expectations, protects time, and promotes improvement.

The past studies show that instructional leadership conceptual models exist in multitude form and researchers define instructional leadership through the traits, behaviour and processes a person needs to lead a school effectively (Alig-Mielcarek, 2003). In the early 1980's, instructional leadership models appeared when researches were carried out on effective schools (Hallinger & Murphy, 1985). It is considered as a strong, directive leadership and focuses directly on curriculum and instruction. Instructional leadership is important in the schools' effectiveness in terms of teaching and learning. Nevertheless, there were critics about this model. This model was said to be focusing highly on the school leaders who play an important role as the focus of expertise, power and authority (Hallinger, 2003).

5 Conclusions

It is difficult to make a linear connection between leaders' expertise, their related key practices and circumstances needed for the improvement of schools. However, the connections are very important for understanding how instructional leadership can contribute towards school effectiveness. The expert instructional leaders can use their competency to work with and through their subordinates to improve their school effectiveness. Furthermore, school leaders are viewed as key agents or key players in the reform of schools. The review of literature stressed that leaders of schools should be instructional experts and need to be educational visionaries to be able to give direction and expertise to the subordinates and move towards school success. This paper suggests that instructional leaders play a very important role in initiating and sustaining school improvement and hence the relationship between instructional leadership of principal and school effectiveness should be examined in the present education system in Malaysia.

References

Alig-Mielcarek, J.M.: A model of school success: Instructional leadership. Academic press and Student achievement. Unpublished doctoral dissertation, Ohio State University (2003)

Blase, J., Blase, J.R.: Handbook of instructional leadership, How successful principals promote teaching and learning, 2nd edn. Corwin Press, California (2004)

Bush, T., Middlewood, D.: Leading and managing people in education. Sage Publications Limited, London (2005)

Hallinger, P.: Leading educational change: Reflections on the practice of instructional and transformational leadership. Cambridge Journal of Education 33(3), 329–351 (2003)

Hallinger, P.: A review of PIMRS studies of principal instructional leadership: Assessment of progress over 25 years. Paper Presented at the Annual Meeting of the American Educational Research Association (AERA), New York (2008)

Hallinger, P., Murphy, J.F.: Assessing the instructional leadership behavior of principals. Elementary School Journal 86(2), 217–248 (1985)

Hallinger, P., Murphy, J.F.: Assessing and developing the instructional leadership of school principals. Educational Leadership 45(1), 55–61 (1987)

Hechinger: The New York Times President, `http://www.quotegarden.com/travel.html` (retrieved)

Hoy, W.K., Miskel, C.G.: Educational administration: Theory, Research and Practice, 6th edn. McGraw Hill, Singapore (2001)

Institut Aminuddin Baki.: KOMSAS, Course Directory 2010. Genting Highlands, IAB (2009)

Khuan, W., Chua, H.T., Abdul Razak, M.: Aspiring for school excellence: A Malaysian case. Jurnal Pengurusan dan Kepimpinan Pendidikan 14, IAB (2004)

Levine, D.U., Lezotte, L.W.: Unusually effective schools: A review and analysis of research and practice. The national centre for effective schools research and development, Madison (1990)

Ahmad, R.K.: Hubungan antara kepimpinan, komitment guru, kompetensi guru, amalan-amalan terbaik dan keberkesanan sekolah sekolah. Desertasi Ph.D., Universiti Utara Malaysia (2006)

Sammons, P., Hillman, L., Mortimore, P.: Key characteristics of effective schools: A review of school effectiveness research. Institute of Education, London (1995)

Sazali, Y., Rusmini, K.A., Abang Hut, A.E., Zamri, A.B.: Amalan kepimpinan instruksional guru besar. Paper Presented at National Colloquium on Instructional Leadership. IAB, Jitra, Kedah, Malaysia (2007)

Sergiovanni, T.: The principalship: A reflective research practice perspective, 4th edn. Allyn & Bacon, USA (2001)

Synder, K.J.: Instructional leadership for productive schools. Educational Leadership 9, 32–37 (1983)

Conversation Threads Hidden within Email Server Logs

Sebastian Palus and Przemysław Kazienko

Wroclaw University of Technology, Institute Informatics
Wyb. Wyspianskiego 27, 50-370 Wroclaw, Poland
sebastian.palus@gmail.com, przemyslaw.kazienko@pwr.wroc.pl

Abstract. Email server logs contain records of all email Exchange through this server. Often we would like to analyze those emails not separately but in conversation thread, especially when we need to analyze social network extracted from those email logs. Unfortunately each mail is in different record and those record are not tided to each other in any obvious way. In this paper method for discussion threads extraction was proposed together with experiments on two different data sets – Enron and WrUT..

Keywords: Email threads, email logs, email analysis.

1 Introduction

Millions of email messages are sent every second worldwide. Although most of them are considered as spam, there is still a huge number of non-useless emails written and read every day. Each message is an individual and can be compared to regular letters rather than direct talk. However, we can divide all messages to two groups: questions and answers [1,7]. A start of a conversation is very likely to be a question. Next steps in the time sequence are responses to the initial message with some additional inquiries. Altogether, they form a thread – group of messages exchanged between a group of people on one or more topics within the period of time. Grouping of emails into threads can add much more data for further analysis. We can not only consider individual messages but analyze them as a set of questions and replies which can lead to exploring new roles and activities within the group of people or, in other words, a social network [2,5,6,9].

2 Related Methods

2.1 Perceptual Method

It is very easy to detect threads of conversations in the room full of people. Birds of a feather flock together. So do people with an interest on given topic. They form themselves into groups. It is not so obvious in email communication, however. A sender and a receiver can be in different part of the world, it is not possible to group them visually.

M.D. Lytras et al. (Eds.): WSKS 2010, Part I, CCIS 111, pp. 407–413, 2010.

2.2 Email Specific Methods

The standard format of an email message described in [8] consists of several fields to enable mail and thread identification [4]. The most important field is Message-ID. It provides an unique identifier for each message. Note that an email message can be sent to more than one recipient. Its uniqueness is provided by the host, so each recipient of the message will receive exactly the same Message-ID. After that, while replying, additional two fields will be filled. These are In-Reply-To and References. The first one contains a Message-ID of the message to which it is a reply and only it. References field contains Message-IDs of all previous messages in the thread. So, if message B is a reply to message A and message C is a response to message B, then References field of message C will contain Message-ID of A and Message-ID of B (Fig. 1). Having this information we can built an exact thread tree [12].

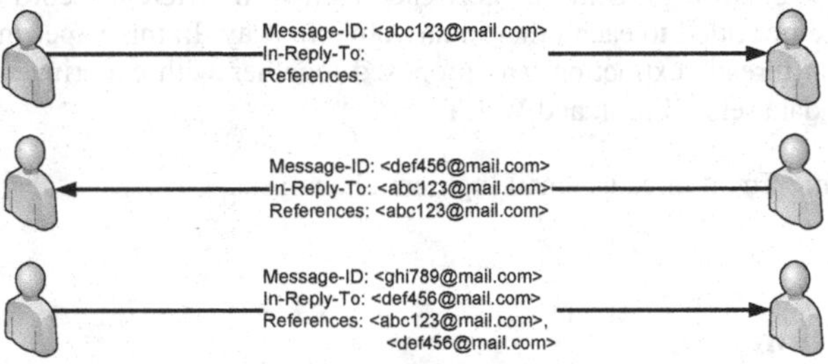

Fig. 1. Email message headers

It all looks great but it is not, though. *Message-ID* is not a mandatory field and its uniqueness is not global. Algorithms of generating these IDs vary between hosts, there are no global databases which can guarantee its uniqueness. It is easy to find more than one message with the same ID. *In-Reply-To* and *References* fields are also optional so it cannot be a certain and universal method for thread detection.

2.3 Text Recognition of Subject and Body

On the other hand, there are more fields in email message format which can be used to group emails into threads. The first one is a Subject field. It is the easiest way for a human to group emails by it. Consecutive messages have the same subject usually preceded by various prefixes like Re: (Reply to) or Fwd: (Forwarded). Moreover, there is a message body which include citation of the replied email. By comparing words from the subject and the body it is possible to group messages together [10,11]. However, the subject can be changed by any sender and still be in the thread. Same case with the body, where citations could be cut or pasted from completely other topic. Finally, there are data sets like email server logs which contain only sender and recipient addresses, date and *Message-ID*, where none of methods described in this section can be applied. This is where it is needed to provide a new method which focus on available factors.

3 The Method of Thread Detection for Email Communication

3.1 File Format

Email server logs are text files usually containing data only about individual fact of sending message, e.g. date, time, sender, recipient and *Message-ID.* (Fig. 2).

Mail sent date | Mail sent time | Sender email address | Recipient email address | Message-ID

```
1-May-2009 18:59:59.59 john@doe.com bogdan@kowalski.pl <YTEWSDXLCMNXO6324KNMOAS843@doe.com>
2-May-2009 08:07:35.21 jan@nowak.pl marysia@nowak.pl <OIUAS8OIHAS6XJUH56@nowak.pl>
2-May-2009 13:22:06.35 marysia@nowak.pl jan@nowak.pl <VBNMZ9HAS67GASA231@nowak.pl>
2-May-2009 09:31:36.11 john@doe.com tomek@nowak.pl <QOXZMNAS8OAS6SHA92N@doe.com>
2-May-2009 09:31:36.11 john@doe.com jane@doe.com <QOXZMNAS8OAS6SHA92N@doe.com>
```

Fig. 2. Mail log file format

3.2 Cleaning and Thread Extraction

The available data was very limited so this method will use all possible information. Thus, rows with one or more blank fields have to be deleted. All emails with corrupt date or time was removed as well. Then, log activities was grouped into messages, because each recipient of the same message forms a separate row in the log file. *Message-ID* field equivalency is not enough factor for message grouping. A tuple of *Message-ID, Date, Time*, *Sender* is a minimal key assuring that different messages will not be treated as one. However, Time field could vary between recipients of the same message because of the fact that these copies are not sent in the same time, so small tweaks are needed to not lose any recipient. Hence, Time should be compared with the neighbourhood of 5 minutes which is large enough to cover all cases.

In this concept, messages are considered to be in the same thread if two conditions are met: a) they are exchanged between the same group of people - a set of sender and recipients; b) the time difference between each pair of successive messages are not greater than n days. In other words, for each pair of *K* and *L* messages, where there are no message *M* between them, there cannot be a difference greater than n in the terms of sent date. To perform tests of this approach, T-SQL scripts was created.

4 Experiments

4.1 Enron Email Dataset

A first dataset chosen for this analysis is the Enron Corpus, which was made public during the legal investigation concerning the Enron corporation [3]. It is an almost complete set with message headers, subjects and bodies, without In-Reply-To and References, however. Klimt and Yang cleaned the corpus, removing certain folders, spam and duplicates which shrunk initial number of 619,446 messages to 200,339. Then they grouped them into threads, which were considered as a sequence of messages that contained the same words in subject and were among the same users. 30,091 threads were detected, consisting of 123,501 emails. The average thread size was 4.10 with a median of 2 (Table 1.).

Table 1. Enron Corpus Threads Distribution from [3]

thread size	2	3	4	5	6	7	8	9	10	(10-20]	20+
# of threads	16736	4782	3049	1282	879	903	378	214	178	1260	430
percentage	55.62%	15.89%	10.13%	4.26%	2.92%	3.00%	1.26%	0.71%	0.59%	4.19%	1.43%

In the analysis Subject or Body fields were not used, so it was not possible to detect spam or Trash folders. In fact, only duplicates were removed. All the operations were performed on dates and users. 246,011 messages left after process of cleaning, 45,672 messages more than in the previous example. Then the thread detection was run for seven different time frames – from one day to one week. (Table 2., Table 3., Fig. 3.).

Table 2. Number of threads detected in Enron epending on the size of the time frame

time frame (days)	1	2	3	4	5	6	7
# of threads	34495	36242	36654	36362	36136	35966	36018
# of messages	106906	120795	128032	133620	138221	142500	147291
percentage of all messages	43.46%	49.10%	52.04%	54.31%	56.18%	57.92%	59.87%

Table 3. Distribution of thread sizes in Enron depending on the size of the time frame

T.frame	2	3	4	5	6	7	8	9	10	(10-20]	20+
1	22567	5921	2573	1121	676	385	309	201	153	444	145
2	22008	6399	3049	1612	939	537	403	224	203	662	206
3	21888	6579	3188	1556	972	560	422	251	224	700	314
4	21503	6580	3071	1434	953	601	442	290	251	844	393
5	20953	6558	3076	1537	992	606	455	325	264	910	460
6	20516	6495	3101	1602	1059	640	464	339	259	983	508
7	20198	6518	3127	1638	1102	698	492	346	277	1060	562

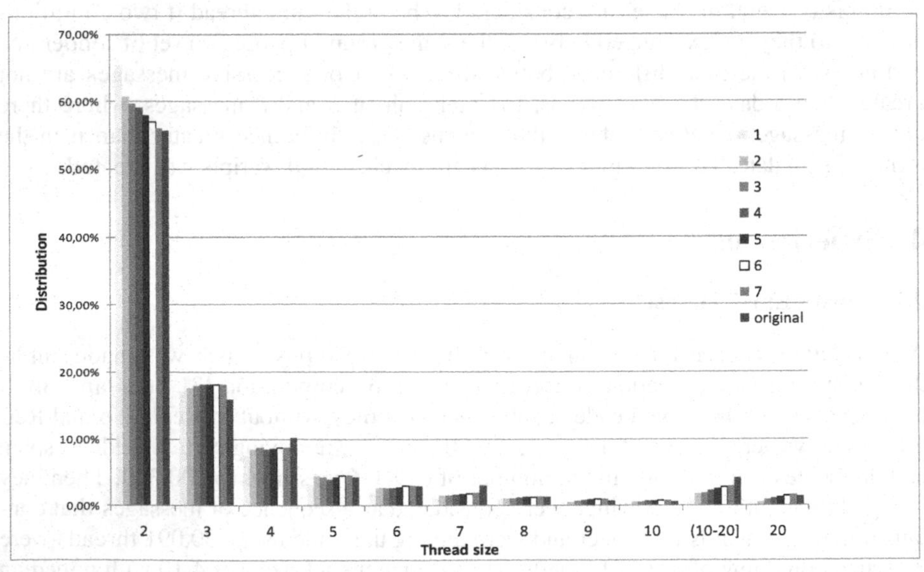

Fig. 3. Comparison of percentage distribution of thread sizes with original distribution

4.2 WrUT Email Logs

The second analyzed data set was the log file from Wroclaw University of Technology (WrUT) Email Server [2]. In fact, it was the main reason to find alternative thread detection method because of the lack of data provided. These logs looks exactly like the example from Fig. 2. After the process of eliminating duplicates and messages with bogus sender, recipient or date, there were 6,403,737 mail messages left. Then, the thread detection was applied to find discussions in different time windows (Table 4.).

Table 4. Number of threads detected in WrUT logs

time frame	1	2	3	4	5	6	7
# of threads	687201	769226	804336	812759	799772	782014	786347
# of messages	2541188	30022894	3271092	3483658	3626504	3792080	4025426
% of all messages	39.68%	468.83%	51.08%	54.40%	56.63%	59.22%	62.86%

The distribution of thread sizes is found to be similar to the Enron (Table 5.).

Table 5. Distribution of thread sizes in WrUT logs depending on the size of the time frame

T.frame	2	3	4	5	6	7	8	9	10	(10-20]	20
1	438662	119774	51072	24179	14090	8493	5894	3975	3401	11185	6476
2	472887	134765	59430	35232	18105	10621	7373	5105	4283	13987	7438
3	496747	141332	62498	32387	17967	11150	8004	5747	4598	15319	8587
4	483379	144913	71230	37148	18985	11999	8287	5996	4580	15998	10244
5	438952	155193	82365	40822	20900	13242	8833	6178	4928	17330	11029
6	385419	162215	82826	50176	34148	14125	10131	7242	5222	18771	11739
7	373954	158021	75728	51499	34200	24567	16555	9015	7376	22696	12736

There is lesser number of big threads (10-20 messages). (Fig. 4.).

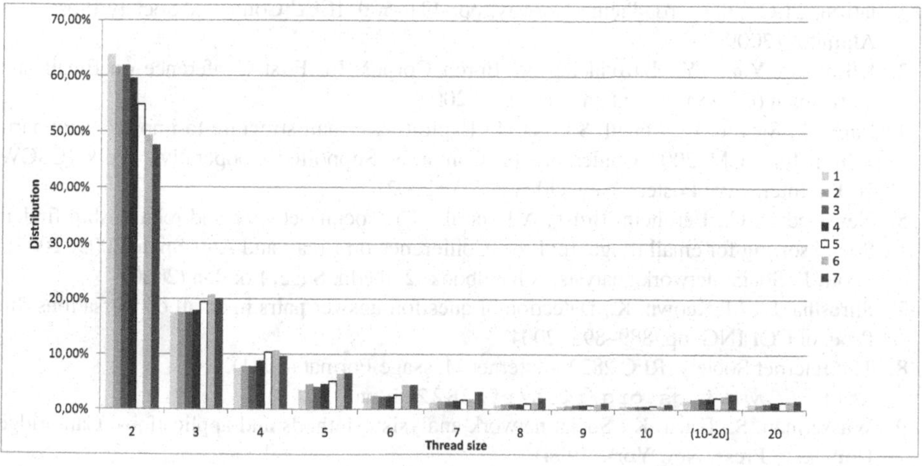

Fig. 4. Percentage distribution of thread sizes in WrUT logs

The method proposed in this paper is not completely accurate. With a big dose of certainty we can assume that it will detect threads that are not actual ones. It can lose some others. There can be too many or too few messages in a thread comparing to the real one. However, in such incomplete data, results are fairly good. Presented detection method effects differs from Klimt & Yang results (see Section 4.1) by only 2% to 4% depending on the time window size.

5 Conclusions and Future Work

The closest result to the real data was achieved by using the one week time frame. However, seven days period between two consecutive messages is probably too long to consider them as one discussion thread. The analysis of real Enron Corpus threads reveal that the time between messages was mostly not longer than 3-4 days. It makes sense when we look upon work week as 5 days from Monday to Friday. An answer to a question asked on Friday can be sent on Monday at the earliest. I believe that four-days time window is the closest to the reality.

Although this detection method cannot be considered as reliable, it still can be used to discover some deeper connections in social network. With a small dose of probability we can assume that some group of people discuss together and therefore their interests focus on some particular topic [5].

Acknowledgments. This work was supported by The Polish Ministry of Science and Higher Education, the development project, 2009-11.

References

1. Goffman, E.: Replies and responses. Language in Society 5, 257–313 (1976)
2. Juszczyszyn, K., Musiał, A., Musiał, K., Bródka, P.: Molecular Dynamics Modelling of the Temporal Changes in Complex Networks. In: IEEE Congress on Evolutionary Computation, CEC 2009, Trondheim, Norway, pp. 491–500. IEEE Computer Society Press, Los Alamitos (2009)
3. Klimt, B., Yang, Y.: Introducing the Enron Corpus. In: First Conference on Email and Anti-Spam (CEAS), Mountain View, CA (2004)
4. Lam, D., Steven, L., Rohall, S.L., et al.: Exploiting e-mail structure to improve summarization. In: ACM 2002 Conference on Computer Supported Cooperative Work (CSCW 2002), Interactive Posters, New Orleans, LA (2002)
5. Neustaedter, C., Bernheim Brush, A.J., et al.: The social network and relationship finder: Social sorting for email triage. In: Proc. Conference on Email and Anti-Spam 2005 (2005)
6. Scott, J.: Social network analysis: A handbook, 2nd edn. Sage, London (2000)
7. Shrestha, L., McKeown, K.: Detection of question-answer pairs in email conversations. In: Proc. of COLING, pp. 889–895 (2004)
8. The Internet Society. RFC 2822 – Internet Message Format (2001), `http://www.faqs.org/rfcs/rfc2822.html`
9. Wasserman, S., Faust, K.: Social network analysis: Methods and applications. Cambridge University Press, New York (1994)

10. Wu, Y., Oard, D. W.: Indexing Emails and Email Threads for Retrieval. In: Proceedings of the SIGIR 2005, Salvador, Brazil (2005)
11. Yeh, J.Y., Harnly, A.: Email thread reassembly using similarity matching. In: Proc. Conference on Email and Anti-Spam, CEAS 2006 (2006)
12. Zawinski, J.: Message Threading (2002), `http://www.jwz.org/doc/threading.html`

Mobile System to Guide Blind People in a Well-Known Environment

Luis M. Domene, José A. Piedra, and Manuel Cantón

Dpto. Lenguajes y Computación
Área de Ciencias de la computación e Inteligencia Artificial
University of Almeria
04120 Almeria
jpiedra@ual.es, mcanton@ual.es

Abstract. The system aids to low-vision disabled people to move in a well-known environment, at the University of Almeria. So, a 3G mobile phone has been used in order to help blind people to have a better standard of life because they could go from a building to other using his mobile phone. Therefore, audible instructions are used to inform the user, which will have been decided in advance by the computer vision module (the decision will be taken according to the environment). That module captures images in real time (using the camera of the mobile phone, which has to be over the chest of the user, fixed with a string) and recognizes static objects in the middle of the way. Moreover, it tries to avoid the situation in which the user is going out of the way. On the other hand, an application has been developed so as to supervise all the users of the system and even visualize their position.

Keywords: Blind people, system of guide, mobile phones, computer vision.

1 Introduction

In the field of blind disability, it cannot be found many projects which use computer vision due to the difficulty of the task. But, for instance, in 1977 it was created a Guide Dog Robot to enhance mobility aids for the blind. This robot used an ultrasonic sensor, an optical sensor and a landmark sensor [1]. Without a doubt, the use of sensors helped to solve the problems related with recognition of obstacles and positions which are really difficult in computer vision. By contrast, it is quite easy to find projects which connect the electrical device and PDA using Bluetooth. Even, some projects try to adapt the mobile phones to this kind of disability (using a big Braille keyboard) [2]. As well, scientists of the Utah State University have recently created a robot to help blind people when they are buying in a supermarket [3]. By contrast, and especially related with the guide of blind people, it has been developed some technologies based in global positioning using GPS [4], brain implants, neuronal prosthesis and systems based on a laptop [5]. Finally, it can be found some projects that use mobile phone and a computer vision system for the detection and identification of urban objects from mobile phone imagery [12], or even studies about mobile technology adoption and accessibility the interaction for Blind and Low-vision users [13].

M.D. Lytras et al. (Eds.): WSKS 2010, Part I, CCIS 111, pp. 414–420, 2010.

2 General Description and Methodology Used

The present system tries to guide a person from a building of the University of Almeria to another one through the pavement for pedestrians. Therefore, a mobile phone is used, which should be placed on the chest of the person (using a string or something similar) in order to focus correctly on the environment. This mobile phone will send, one by one, the snapshot of the path to a server. Additionally, it will detect static objects (benches, rotundas, streetlight and gardens) in an autonomous way. As a consequence, the system will give an audible order to guide the person.

The system (Figure 1) has been created using a WiFi network to communicate all the modules (Figure 1) and different open source technologies, such as a MySQL Database [6], monitor client application programmed with Java 2 standard Edition and a JDBC connection [6], server based in Apache Tomcat [6] and a client programmed with Java 2 Micro Edition.

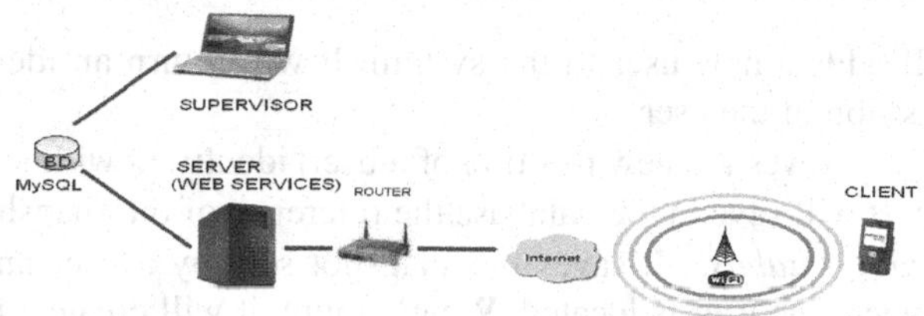

Fig. 1. System's arquitecture

2.1 Database

A MySQL database has been used with the aim of saving the position of each user of the system, the identifier and the last snapshot taken by the user. Therefore, three tables have been implemented in order to be accessed by the monitor application and the server using an easy architecture.

2.2 Monitor Client Application

The Java SE monitor application (Figure 2) will be in charge of showing to the administrator the position of all the users of the system. To do that, it will be built a

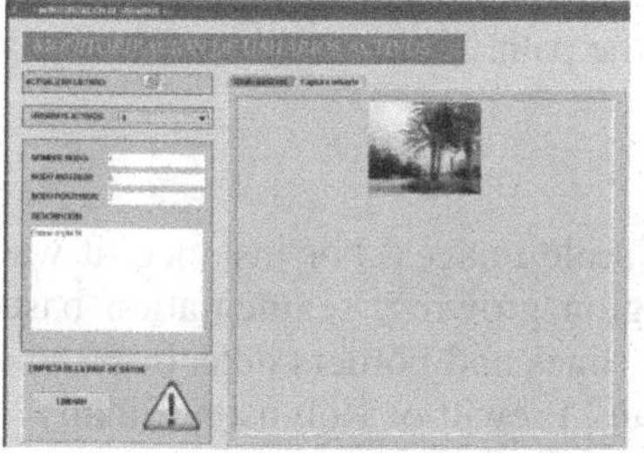

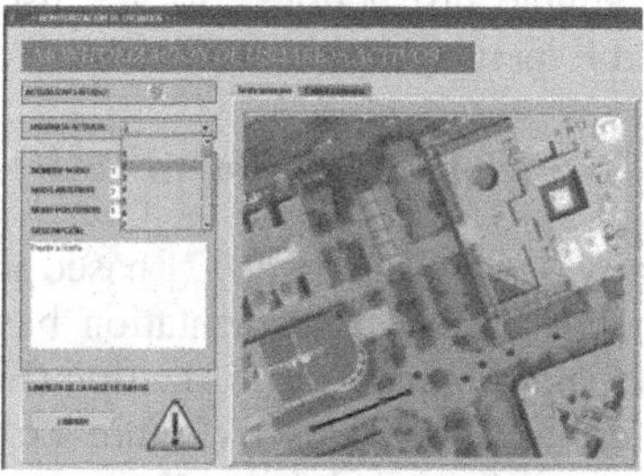

Fig. 2. Monitor client application's interface

graph with the path of the users. In addition, the application will provide to the administrator different tasks, for instance, erasing the database, supervising the position of the user in a well-know path or even getting the last snapshot taken by one user will be allowed. Only the last snapshot will be stored with the aim of avoiding saturation problems in the server side.

2.3 Server

All the Java ME clients have access to the server using Web Services. So, the Internet and an Apache Tomcat server to publish the Web Services will be essential. This server will connect with the database in order to update it with the information received from the clients. On the other hand, a Wi-Fi communication has been used to connect the mobile phones with the server. As a consequence, no firewall rules have been modified because port 80 is used.

Four services are offered in order to achieve the objective desired:

- *recordUser*. It adds a new user to the system. It will return an identifier and will update the position of the user.
- *recordPosition*. It saves the new position of a user, identified with a specific key.
- *saveSnapshot*. It will save in the database the reference of the snapshot of a user.
- *createKnowledgeDatabase*. It saves the snapshot sent by a user and also updates the position where the user is located. What's more, it will create a knowledgebase for the Artificial Vision module.

3 Java ME Client and Artificial Vision Module

3.1 Java ME Client

All the clients will be able to guide the user in an autonomous way. That's because it will be used an Artificial Vision system in order to avoid static objects and to recognize the position of the users. Therefore, the client will send his position and an image of the environment (one image per 5 seconds). As a consequence, it should be connecter to the Internet all the time. This image will be in a small size because it's not possible to take snapshot in the highest resolution because they are directly taken of the video camera. The mobile phone used in the system it was a Nokia's N80.

Furthermore, this application has a system of sound to guide the blind user with very simple instructions. So, the user will receive the decision taken by the Rule-Based Expert System to avoid object or follow the path.

3.2 Artificial Vision System

Initially, several methods [7] based in the grayscale images. For instance, it was implemented [8][9] a segmentation based on region growing, segmentation based on grey scale (Figure 3), Binarization (Figure 4.b), lines and borders detection and some operator as Sobel, Kirsch (Figure 4.c), Laplacian , Prewitt or Robinson. Finally, all of them were discarded due to the computational cost involved. As a result, we made up a segmentation based on the colors of the scene to be considered. Then, all the images were reduced in order to avoid delays in the process of decision (initially at 160x120 pixels). So, we only kept the central part of the image.

Fig. 3. Segmentation based on grey scale

Fig. 4. (a) Grey scale image, (b) Binarization of a scene and (c) Kirsch's filter

Once all the images were preprocessed it started the segmentation process (Figure 5) to locate the appropriate regions. Then, it was built a Rule-Based Expert System to recognize the different tonalities of the colors, and to take a decision (that it will be transmitted to the user). Therefore, four regions can be detected: red (normal path to be followed), blue (sky of the scene), green (vegetation of the scene) and White (undefined region to be used in future projects). Within these regions, the system could be able to decide if the user is going to crash with a static objet or even in which part of the scene the user is located.

Finally, and due to the difficulty of doing the segmentation processed, we had to be developed two methods so that the system could take the right decision. On the one hand, it was developed a method to evaluate the proximity to an object. On the other hand, it was developed a method to know if a user is going out of the well-known path.

Fig. 5. Segmentation based on the tonalities of the colors

For the first method, the system goes through the image, from the bottom to the upper part of the image, looking for a change from one region to another, that is to say, the system record the horizontal reference of the pixel where a different region starts). For example, it can seek for changes from red to green region (most common) or to the blue one (stranger to find). Thus, the image is divided into four equal parts (each guide starts in each one of the quarts that divide logically the image). So, this method can handle the proximity to objects and also, when the blind user is unwittingly leaving a safety zone (i.e. if you find that the value of the one guide is much higher than other one). In Figure 6, we can see that guide 3 has a higher value than guide 1, so the person is going out of the path (moving to the right part of the path).

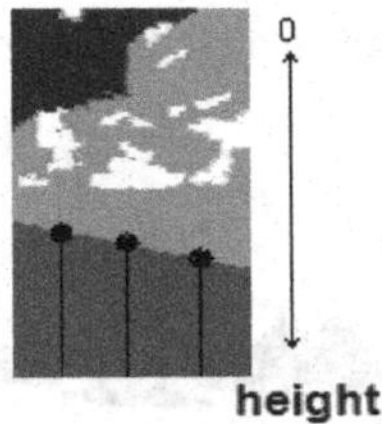

Fig. 6. First Method developed, where guide 1 < guide 3

In the second method (Figure 7), while the segmentation is been done, it counts the number of pixels classified as red region in two different parts of the image (only pixels situated at the bottom of the image). Thus, we can manage unwittingly departures from the safety zone.

Fig. 7. Second Method developed, where the amount of red pixels in subregion 1 is higher than in subregion 2

3.3 Rules-Based Expert System

It has been developed a rule-base expert system which contains several rules for each region. Therefore, a process to find the correct values of the RGB colors had to be done. The algorithm for the blue region is, for instance as follow: if you find a pixel that belongs to the upper-half of the image, the blue component of the RGB space is between the values 160 and 256 and that value is superior to the red component of the RGB space it has been found a pixel which belongs to the blue region (marked previously as sky) and so forth with the others regions.

4 Results and Contribution to the Field

The cost of the system is quite low in comparison with the cost of a guide dog (it could take many months to instruct this kind of dogs and almost 38.000$ [10]). That's because of the use of open source technologies which equilibrate the cost of buy a 3G mobile. In contrast, this system could improve the standard of life of the handicapped person because it avoids the long process of memorize the routes (what could take a considerably amount of time).

The system has presented a clear problematic related to the computer vision module, especially with the capacity of computation and the performance (some delays appeared in the response of the system). As a consequence, a different positioning system is needed, and as a result, all the resources could be dedicated to the object detection. Finally, the time dedicated to the whole process, that is to say, capturing images, segmentation image processing, making a decision and sending the image and contextual information to the server; take towards 2.1 seconds, so it could be used in some situations where enough time is available.

As it is shown in Table 1, the execution time varies due to the state of the device (whether it is busy or not). Furthermore, some others unexpected delays could appear during the execution of the system (i.e. Trying to access to the camera when it is no ready). As a consequence, the time for taking a snapshot could even rise to the 5 seconds approximately.

5 Conclusion

Firstly, a continuous optimization process has been done to the computer vision module in order to create a distributed client-server system. So, wasting operations and redundant image readings have been omitted [11] with the intention of static object detection in the route and also, in order to control when the user is going out of the known route. Meanwhile, the monitor application supervises the position of the users registered.

Secondly, a Nokia N80 has been used in this project, so the current mobile phones (for instance iPhone or HTC) would probably improve the final performance of our system. That is due to having better resources and predictably better operative system.

As a final conclusion, our suspicions about the difficulty creating a computer vision system for the external environment have been refuted. It's quite complicated due to the changes in the illumination and difficulty of recognize unexpected objects. Therefore, it is a complicated problem but doable whether it's used together with other engineering techniques. Thus, it could be viable in well-know indoor environment, where meteorological condition doesn't affect to luminosity and where sonar can be really effective.

With reference to future works, a positioning technology like GPS could give better results. Moreover, other jobs that can improve the system are, for instance, the recognition of new routes, Wi-Fi triangulation, dynamic object detection, face recognition system in order to avoid the authentication process or implementing a VoIp technology to communicate Supervisor with the blind person.

References

1. Tachi, S., Komoriya, K.: Guide dog robot. Mechanical Engineering Laboratory, Tsukuba Science City, Japan (1977)
2. OWASYS 22C, Teléfono móvil adaptado, http://www.owasys.com/accesible/owasys22c.php
3. Gharpure, C., Kulyukin, V.: Robot-Assisted Shopping for the Blind: Issues in Spatial Cognition and Product. Selection. International Journal of Service Robotics (1-3), 237–251 (2008)
4. Loomis, J.M., Golledge, R., Klatzky, R.L.: Navigation System for the blind: Auditosy Display Modes and Guidance. Teleoperators and Virtual Enviroments, 193–203 (1998)
5. Hub, A., Diepstraten, J., Ertl, T.: Design and development of an indoor navigation and object identification system for the blind, In: ACM SIGACCESS Accessibility and Computing, vol. 77-78, pp. 147–152 (2003)
6. Rodríguez, F.P.: Acceso a Base de Datos con JAVA-JDBC, del capítulo IV del P.FC, Entorno Cliente/Servidor Para El Acceso Remoto A Cámaras Mediante Tecnología Móvil. Universidad de Almería (2004)
7. Gonzalez, R.C., Woods, R.E.: Digital image processing. Prentice-Hall, New Jersey (2001)
8. Guindos Rojas, F., Piedra Fernández, J.A., Peralta López, M.: Visión Artificial con IMtdi. Universidad de Almería (2001)
9. Guindos Rojas, F., Piedra Fernández, J.A.: Tratamiento digital de imágenes con Imtdi. Universidad de Almería (2001)
10. Guide Dogs of America (GDA) - International Guiding Eyes Program, http://www.guidedogsofamerica.org/faq.html#cost
11. Tierno Alvite, J., y Campo Vázquez, M. C.: Aplicaciones de tratamiento de imagen en terminales J2ME con cámara. In: II Congreso JavaHispano (2004) ISBN: 84-689-0035-4
12. Fritz, G., Seifert, C., Paletta, L.: A Mobile Vision System for Urban Detection with Informative Local Descriptors. In: Fourth IEEE Conference on Computer Vision Systems (ICVS 2006), p. 30 (2006)
13. Jayant, C.: Mobile Accessibility: Camera Focalization for Blind and Low-Vision Users on the Go. ACM 37(96) (2010)

Indexing Moving Objects: A Real Time Approach

George Lagogiannis, Nikos Lorentzos, and Alexander B. Sideridis

Agricultural University of Athens, Iera Odos 75, 11855 Athens, Greece
{lagogian,lorentzos,as}@aua.gr

Abstract. Indexing moving objects usually involves a great amount of updates, caused by objects reporting their current position. In order to keep the present and past positions of the objects in secondary memory, each update introduces an I/O and this process is sometimes creating a bottleneck. In this paper we deal with the problem of minimizing the number of I/Os in such a way that queries concerning the present and past positions of the objects can be answered efficiently. In particular we propose a new approach that achieves an asymptotically optimal number of I/Os for performing the necessary updates. The approach is based on the assumption that the primary memory suffices for storing the current positions of the objects.

Keywords: Information Systems, Persistence, I/O complexity.

1 Introduction

Objects that change their position and/or shapes over time introduce large spatiotemporal data sets. The efficient manipulation of such data sets is crucial for an increasing number of computer applications (location aware services, traffic monitoring etc). In the real time version of our spatiotemporal problem, we can consider a client-server architecture where each moving client (object) sends its position to the server, at discrete times. The server collects information reports (messages) of the form (object Id, current-cell, current time) from the moving objects, every P seconds. We assume that the objects move in a 2 dimensional space. By *current position* of an object we mean the position indicated by the last message sent by the object. Note that the actual current position is unknown, and one can only guess, according to the latest position, and the speed vector of the object. The term "real time", is used to denote that the updates on the data structures (in secondary memory) caused by the messages (sent by the vehicles) are not postponed, but instead, these structures are updated with every incoming message.

In building a system to index moving objects, we have two alternatives for indexing the involved space (which is a 2-d space in our case), *static* and *dynamic* indexing. In this paper we present an approach based on static indexing of the involved space, that store the incoming messages by sparing an asymptotically optimal number of I/Os (in [6], which is an extended version of this work, we also present an approach based on dynamic indexing). By "asymptotically optimal", we mean that the incoming messages are stored by sparing O(1) I/Os per O(B) messages, where B is the number of messages that fit into a disk block.

M.D. Lytras et al. (Eds.): WSKS 2010, Part I, CCIS 111, pp. 421–426, 2010.

Optimizing the updates of existing multidimensional index structures (mainly the R-tree) is the target of many recent efforts (see [3], [4], [7], [8], [9], [11]). A common part of most of these solutions is a secondary index structure, used for accessing the leaf of the main indexing structure that contains a given object. This secondary index structure is used to avoid the multiple paths search operation in the R-tree during the top-down update. This way, a bottom-up approach is proposed.

Compared with the related work described above, our work differs because of the combination of the following three characteristics: i) we use a worst case efficient data structure instead of the R-tree, which is not very efficient under a large amount of updates, ii) we aim at storing not only the present positions of the objects, but also the past ones, and iii) we incorporate a theoretical framework for presenting asymptotically optimal solutions, in contrast with most of the related work, which are implementation oriented.

2 Problem Definition

As is obvious, storing the past positions of objects requires the use of secondary storage. Given that a large number of objects is being tracked, the main concern is facing the bottlenecks caused by the large volume of I/Os. The parameters involved are summarized as follows.

N: The maximum number of tracked objects.
M: The amount of main memory used.
P: The time period of communication between the objects and the base station, measured in seconds.
B: The number of messages that fit into a disk block.
W: The total number of messages received by the system during the tracking time.

Definition 1: An I/O may be of one of the following two types:

- *Message storing I/O*, which stores some (optimally $O(B)$) messages, into a disk block.
- *Rebalancing I/O:* This I/O is caused by the rebalancing operations of the indexing structure.

A solution that accomplishes efficient storage of the incoming messages in real time clearly satisfies the following property.

Property 1: The total number of message storing I/Os for storing the total number of messages (W) received by the system is $O(W/B)$.

Property 1 allows us to maximize the number of tracked vehicles, N, or to reduce the value of P. Our target in this paper is to provide solutions that satisfy property 1. For our purposes, it is assumed that the primary memory is sufficiently large to store the current position of tracked objects and it seems that this is a reasonable assumption (see [6]). We work on the external-memory model of computation (see [1]). This means that the only measurement of efficiency we use for the solutions of this paper is the number of I/Os i.e., we are not interested in measuring the time spent for actions in primary memory. Also, we assume that the position of an object at any time instance t, is the one dictated by the last message sent by the object, before t. Due to space limitations, many details are omitted. However, they can be found in [6].

The remainder of the paper can be summarized as follows: The partially persistent B-tree, briefly presented in Section 3, represents the base structure for the description of the proposed approach. Assuming that no rebalancing I/Os occur, Section 4 aims at reducing the message storing I/Os. The reduction of the rebalancing I/Os is addressed in Section 5.

3 Partial Persistence

The approaches to be presented in the next sections are based on the partially persistent B-tree (see [2], [10]), which is briefly presented in this section. In general, a partially persistent B-tree is a modified B+-tree. Its internal nodes contain index records and its leaves contain data records. A data record contains the fields *key, start* (the time instance that the record was inserted into the tree*), end (*the time instance that the record was "deleted"), and *info* (information associated with the *key*). An index record contains the fields *key*, *start*, *end* and *ptr*, where *ptr* is a pointer to a node of the next level. The node pointed by the *ptr* pointer contains keys no less than *key*, has been created at the time instance *start* and has been copied at the time instance *end*. A data record is *active* (*live*) if its *end* field has value '$', i.e. it has not been updated, "deleted" or copied to another node. If this is not the case, the data record is *inactive* (*dead*). Thus, to "delete" a record we just set its *end* value to the current time. An index record is active if it points to an active node at the immediately lower lever.

The space consumption of optimal partially persistent B-trees is $O(m/B)$ blocks (where m is the total number of updates) and updates can be performed in $O(\log_B(m/B))$ worst case time. In the amortized case, the update time is constant.

4 The Solution

We consider a grid on our 2-dimensional map. Each incoming message is a tuple (O_{id}, C_{id}, t), where O_{id} is the id of the object that sent the message, C_{id} is the id of the cell that contains O_{id}, and t is the time at which the message was sent. For simplicity, we assume that each object can determine its current cell, i.e., it has some computational power. If this is not the case, the current cell can easily be determined by the system, with a simple calculation. The objects inside each cell are indexed by a partially persistent B-tree. Each time an object leaves a cell C_2 and enters another cell C_1, its tuple, which is located in C_2 is set to inactive, by replacing the value $ of its *end* field by the time at which the object sent the message. Next, a new tuple for this object is inserted into the persistent B-tree of C_1. Its *start* value is set equal to the time at which the message was sent, and its *end* value is set to $. This approach is described in Subsections 4.1 and 4.2. To avoid complicated details, we assume that if an I/O is needed, it is performed immediately. Note that although this is an unrealistic assumption, it allows for simplifications. The realistic assumption is that if an I/O is needed, a request for this I/O is inserted into a buffer, and the I/Os are performed from this buffer, in a FIFO order. We call this buffer, the *I/O buffer*. In Subsection 4.3, we analyze the approach by taking into account this last, realistic assumption. Keep in mind that during Section 4, we assume that no rebalancing I/Os occur. We are going to deal with the rebalancing I/Os in Section 5.

The static indexing strategy is suitable for processing range queries based on *spatiotemporal range predicates*, i.e., pairs (S, T) where S is a spatial constraint and T is a temporal constraint which can be either a time instance or a time interval. The output of the query is either the set of objects inside S at the time instance T, or the set of objects inside S at some time instance during the time interval T. A detailed description of how such predicates can be processed by using the static indexing approach is omitted due to space limitations, but it can be found in [6].

4.1 Data Structures

For each cell C_i of the grid, we maintain in secondary memory a partially persistent B-tree, called PBC_i. In primary memory we maintain the following data structures:

- For each cell C_i of the grid, we maintain an indexing structure called *active_PBCi*,. Let C_i be a cell. PBC_i contains both active and inactive nodes. The *active_*PBC_i is the tree defined by the active nodes of PBC_i and the pointers that connect these active nodes. For every leaf V of the *active_*PBC_i, there is a leaf X in PBC_i which satisfies the following property. *At the time V was created, X was also created to be identical to V*. We call X, *image of* V, and we store into V a pointer to X.
- A table A with the tracked objects. Suppose that we receive a message from object i. Then entry A[i] contains the current cell of the object.

4.2 Algorithm to Handle Incoming Messages

Suppose we receive a message (O_i, C_k, t). The algorithm for the processing of this message is the following:

Step 1: We go to A[i] and find the current cell of O_i. Let C_j be that cell. If $C_k = C_j$, we do nothing. Otherwise we store C_k, in A[i] and proceed to Step 2.

Step 2: We find the appropriate leaf V in the *active_*PBC_k and insert into it the new tuple. If V is not full, we are done. If V is full we may have either to split, or merge V with a neighboring leaf. In either case, one or two new leafs must be created. Figure 1 shows the actions of Step 2, in the case at which V is split into two leafs, named V_1 and V_2. We execute the insertion algorithm of the partially persistent B-tree on the *active_*PBC_k, with one difference: we throw away all the inactive nodes. For example, in Figure 1, leaf V is thrown away when the algorithm finishes. By following the pointer from V we reach X, the image of V. We then update X, to be identical to V. Next, we proceed with the insertion algorithm on PBC_k, and we create the image leaf of each new leaf created by the insertion algorithm in the *active_*PBC_k (X_1 is the image leaf of V_1 and X_2 is the image leaf of V_2). We connect each new leaf in primary memory, with its image leaf in secondary memory.

Step 3: In the *active_*PBC_j, we find the leaf that contains the tuple of O_i. We execute the deletion algorithm of the partially persistent B-tree on the *active_*PBC_j, in order to delete the tuple of O_i, in the same way we executed the insertion algorithm in Step 2.

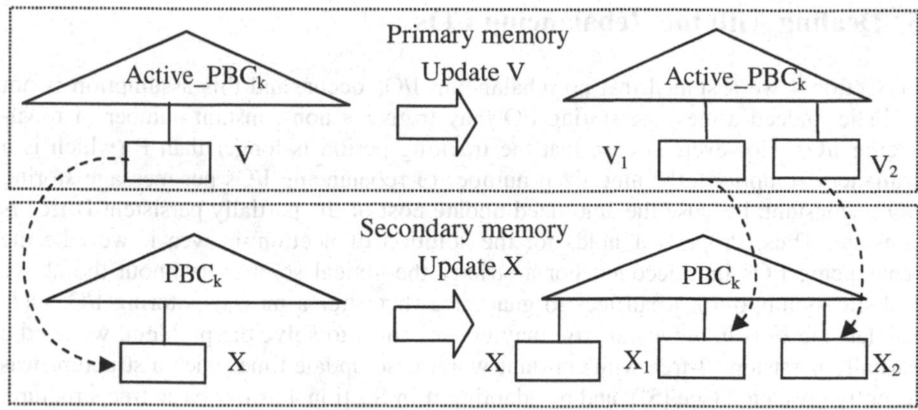

Fig. 1. Deactivating leaf V in cell C_k leads to updating its image leaf, X, on disk

4.3 Analysis of the Solution

In this subsection we add to the approach already presented in subsection 4.2, the realistic assumption that *an I/O buffer exists.* Whenever a leaf in main memory is deactivated, it is inserted into this I/O buffer. I/Os in this buffer are processed in a FIFO order. Once the I/O indicated by the leaf has been served, the space in main memory which was occupied by the leaf is set free. Due to this, the definition of active_PBs has to be revised as follows: *If Ci is a cell of the grid then the active_PBCi contains all the active nodes of PBCi plus the inactive nodes in the I/O buffer.*

Lemma 1: If W is the total number of messages received by the system, then the approach of this section, stores these messages in $O(W/B)$ message storing I/Os, i.e., property 1 holds:

Proof: Omitted (see [6]). □

To determine the amount of main memory consumed by the approach of this section, we notice that this amount is equal to the space (S_1) occupied by the active nodes, plus the space (S_2) occupied by the deactivated nodes. Each node inside the I/O buffer will be deleted from the active_PB when the I/O has been served.

Lemma 2: S_1 is $\Theta(N)$.

Proof: Omitted (see [6]). □

Lemma 3: S_2 is $O(N)$.

Proof: Omitted (see [6]). □

From Lemmas 2 and 3, it follows that $M = \Theta(N)$. The secondary memory used is $O(W/B)$ blocks.

5 Dealing with the Rebalancing I/Os

In Section 4 we assumed that no rebalancing I/Os occur, and this assumption is not realistic. Indeed a message storing I/O may trigger a non-constant number of rebalancing I/Os. However, in case that the tracking period is longer than P (which is a realistic assumption), the amortized number of rebalancing I/Os per message storing I/O is constant, because the amortized update cost of the partially persistent B-tree is constant. Thus, Property 1 holds for the solution of Section 4, even if we take the rebalancing I/Os into account. For a strictly theoretical solution (without the above realistic assumption), it suffices to guarantee that after a message storing I/O, O(1) rebalancing I/Os *in the worst case* may occur. Thus, to solve the problem, we need a partially persistent B-tree with constant worst case update time. Such a structure was recently presented (see [5]), and by adapting it in Section 4 as our basic tree structure, we achieve O(1) rebalancing I/Os per message storing I/O, in the worst case.

References

[1] Aggarwal, A., Vitter, S.J.: The input/output complexity of sorting and related problems. Communications of the ACM 31(9), 1116–1127 (1988)

[2] Becker, B., Gschwind, S., Ohler, T., Seeger, B., Widmayer, P.: An asymptotically optimal multiversion B-tree. The VLDB Journal 5(4), 264–275 (1996)

[3] Cheng, R., Xia, Y., Prabhakar, S., Shah, R.: Change Tolerant Indexing for Constantly Evolving Data. In: ICDE, pp. 391–402. IEEE Computer Society Press, Tokyo (2005)

[4] Kwon, D., Lee, J.S., Lee, S.: Indexing the current positions of moving objects using the lazy update Rtree. In: MDM, pp. 113–120. IEEE Computer Society, Singapore (2002)

[5] Lagogiannis, G., Lorentzos, N.: Partially Persistent B-trees with Constant Worst Case Update Time. Technical report 184, Informatics Laboratory, Department of Science, Agricultural University of Athens (May 2010)

[6] Lagogiannis, G., Lorentzos, N., Sideridis, A.B.: Indexing moving objects: A real time approach. Technical report 186, Informatics Laboratory, Department of Science, Agricultural University of Athens (July 2010)

[7] Lee, L.M., Hsu, W., Jensen, S.C., Cui, B., Teo, L.K.: Supporting Frequent Updates in R-Trees: A Bottom-Up Approach. In: VLDB, Berlin, pp. 608–619 (2003)

[8] Saltenis, S., Jensen, S.C.: Main memory operation buffering for efficient R-tree update. In: VLDB, pp. 591–602. ACM, Vienna (2007)

[9] Tung, H., Ryu, K.: One update for all moving objects at a timestamp. In: CIT, p. 6. IEEE Computer Society, Seoul (2006)

[10] Varman, P., Verma, R.: An Efficient Multiversion Access Structure. IEEE Transactions on Knowledge and Data Engineering 9(3), 391–409 (1997)

[11] Xiong, X., Aref, G.W.: R-trees with Update Memos. In: ICDE, pp. 22–22. IEEE Computer Society, Atlanta (2006)

The Study in Group: A Case

Óscar Angulo[1], Juan Carlos López-Marcos[2], and María del Carmen Martínez[1]

[1] Universidad de Valladolid, Departamento de Matemática Aplicada, Escuela de Ingenierías Industriales, C/Francisco Mendizábal, 1, 47014 Valladolid, Spain
oscar@mat.uva.es, carmen@mat.uva.es

[2] Universidad de Valladolid, Departamento de Matemática Aplicada, Facultad de Ciencias, Paseo del Cauce, s/n, 47005 Valladolid, Spain
lopezmar@mac.uva.es

Abstract. In this work, we present an activity developed for the practical lessons into the subject *Fundamentos Matemáticos de la Ingeniería* which belongs to the graduate program of *Ingeniero Técnico en Diseño Industrial (Industrial Design Technical Engineering)*.

In this one, the students are grouped with the aim of working together in the subject contents along the whole course. Every group has its duty and, as the result of the activity, they have to give back a writing form and to show the solutions in the classroom. We show that the results are amazing.

1 Introduction

The aim of a teacher must mainly consist on transmiting the specific knowledge of the studying planning of a particular subject (product). But, we sometimes forget the other side: the students. They are the clients, the persons whom the product is produced for. Therefore, there is a complementary activity which oughts us to verify the result of the process, i.e. we have to check if the student has lernt such knowledge and which is the quantity of knowledge they have. This last behaviour is related with the quality compromise or the client satisfaction with the product, in our case it is developed into the teach-learn process.

This task is heavier when the subject is about Mathematics in a Technical Career and the students are into the first course. These students who will become engineers think about Mathematics as an auxiliary tool instead of a main subject.

We also have to take into account that we are immersed into a main change into the spanish University. We are adapting the actual careers into new Graduate courses with the following introduction of the ECTS credit (European Credit Transfer System). Therefore we wanted to have an experience with

1. the way in which the students learn the subject,
2. the way in which we have to qualify the outwards activity of the student,
3. the activity of *Resolución de problemas (exercise solver)*, and
4. the competency of *Trabajo en grupo (work group)*.

M.D. Lytras et al. (Eds.): WSKS 2010, Part I, CCIS 111, pp. 427–431, 2010.

Here, we present our experience about the changes introduced in the practical lessons (practical credits of the subject). These were previously dedicated to the solution of problems with a symbolic solver, and the main responsable of the activity was the teacher. Now, we have organized the classroom into several groups, using the *Resolución de problemas (exercise solver)* technique. With the aim that this activity would be useful to verify the individual knowledge of every student. All the activity is proportionally included into the final qualification of each student. A large and rapidly growing body of research confirms the effectiveness of this kind of learning in higher education [1,2,3,4,5].

The paper is organized as follows: Section 2 indicate the scenary of the subject, next we will describe the proposed activity. In Section 4, we will introduce an example of a practice day and, in the final Section we will introduce the obtained results.

2 Preliminaries

We have developed this case study with the first year students of the Industrial Design Technical Engineering career. The name of the subject is *Fundamentos Matemáticos de la Ingeniería (Mathematical Preliminaries in Engineering)*. And the study is centered in the practical credits of such one.

The main difficulty of our students is their diversity: bachelor, technical formation, olders students that failed in previous years,.... So, the first day of the subject, we make a test about they mathematical background. Also we are interested in a new information: their previous studies. At least the 50% of the students are from a Scientific-Technical Bachelor, with a high level in Mathematics because this career has a number of students limitation. On the other hand we find people provided by Technical Studies with a very low level in mathematics. Finally, we have a new case, the students which reenter in the subject after several nonstuding years (job, other subjects in the career,...) with the aim of completing (or ending) the formation.

The subject *Fundamentos Matemáticos de la Ingeniería* is a whole year one, with 9 credits (6 of them are theoretical and 3 of them are practical). Its contents are classical in a first course in Engineering: Linear Algebra, Calculus (Differential and Integral) and Differential Equations. The level is slightly higher that the provided in the last courses of Bachelor and the novelty in the knowledge reaches half part of that one.

The proccess of learning is splitted into theoretical and practical credits. We use the theoretical credits to expose the theoretical contents of the subject. The last years the practical ones where employed to instruct them about symbolic calculus software. The results of this division were not satisfactory because we did not assure neither the success of the mathematical knowledge learning nor the learning of the software. Therefore, we thought about a different approach that we present here. This one transform the computer practical lessons into group work.

3 Activity

We planned for the practical credits of the subject the following activity. They have to elaborate six practical exercises along the whole course (it is a yearly subject). These practical exercises are distributed uniformely along the year. We try to make three exercises each quaterly, which means that every month the students have to prepare a practical activity.

This activity conforms the 30% of the final qualification of the subject. They are in the form of *Resolución de Problemas (problem solver)* and with the technique of *Trabajo en grupo (group work)*.

The groups are formed ramdomly. They are composed by at most six persons and built by the proper students and we respect their affinity, we only take a chance in trouble solution. In this year, 94.74% of the total of the students have taken part in the activity. They were distributed into 15 groups, the teachers have composed only three of them. We have tried that the students with low-level in mathematics would be distributed uniformly into the groups because this is the group of students which has higher possibilities of retiring from the activity. Of course, there were some of the students which abandon the subject but the percentage was lower than in previous years.

4 Practice Days

The work to make is divided into in-class exercises and out-of-class tasks. The period of a practice last four weeks, one month, along four two hours sessions. All of them take place at the theory classroom.

We have splitted groups in two parts, because of the number of groups. In such way, the exercises assignment is given to a part of the groups in the first practical session and in the second one to the rest. These two practical sessions consist on the solution of the exercises at the classroom employing all the knowledge they obtain along the theoretical classes. During this period of time one of us stays in the classroom as a technical support to solve all the doubts about the work. Also this teacher controls the work made by each group, not only to examine (the assistance of all the members of the group) but also to check the behaviour of each group. We observe that there are a diversity of behaviours, some of them divide individually the exercises and then they comment the doubts and the results; other groups solve the exercises all together and one of them take note of all the results, comments and calculus. The evaluable task of this first session is a draft of the final work where they include the solution of the problems and they will give the teacher to correct both the evaluation and the incorrect procedures.

From now on, the students has their out-of-class task. They have to solve all the problems they did not solve in-class. Also they have to answer all the doubts they have in the solutions. This work could be individual or cooperative. This one is common in almost all the groups of the subject. The second evaluative aspect consists on a talk with the teacher about the work, during the next week.

This is made by the whole group. All of them could take the option of making more reunions with the teacher both individually and collective. In this session, the draft is given back to the group with the corrected exercises. In such session, the teacher explains the exercises (the corrected and the uncorrected) and solve the errors. At this time, the teacher analyzes the activity of all the members of the group in the solution of the exercises. Once they make this meeting, they have to complete the right solution of the problems and to make a final form which includes both the complete and right solution and a work diary. In this one, they have to explain briefly the way in which they made the activity. This is a basic task because it allows us to have a feedback about the period of time that the activity lasts.

Last week the next in-class session takes place. Each student group must to give the teacher the form of the activity in which they have to complete the instructions given with the exercises. Also they have to make an exposition about the problems in the classroom. The teacher select the student and the exercise and all together give him a qualification which also corresponds to all the group. These two activities are evaluated. The oral exposition is considered at the moment with cooperative evaluation. The final form is evaluated following the norms given in the practical exercise. All the groups know previously what is going to evaluate.

Then all the studens assist for 5 hours each practice, i.e. 30 hours which complete exactly the three practical credits of the subject.

5 Results

Now we show the results of the activity. As a first remarkable result, we have obtain that all the students work the subject continuously. This is one of our aims because we consider that this subject needs a continuous effort to pass.

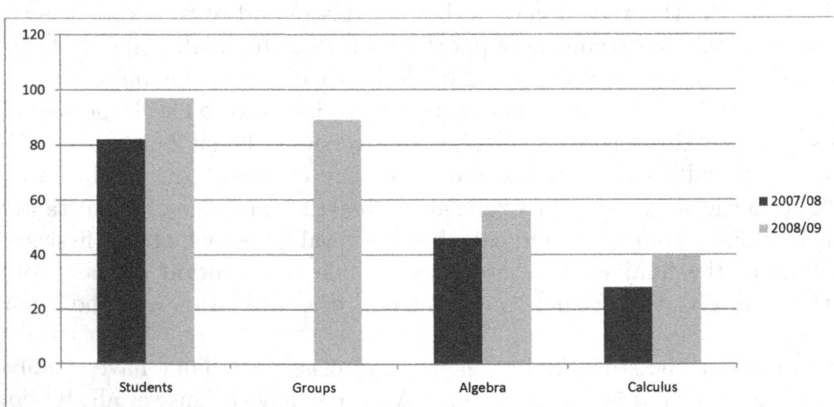

Fig. 1. Comparative number of students in the exams

We can observe in Figure 1 that the number of students which have continued working the subject until the second partial exam has been greater both quantity and percentage than the previous years.

With respect to the second aim, we have to celebrate the success, i.e. the number of students that passed the exam has been increased a lot as we can see in Figure 2.

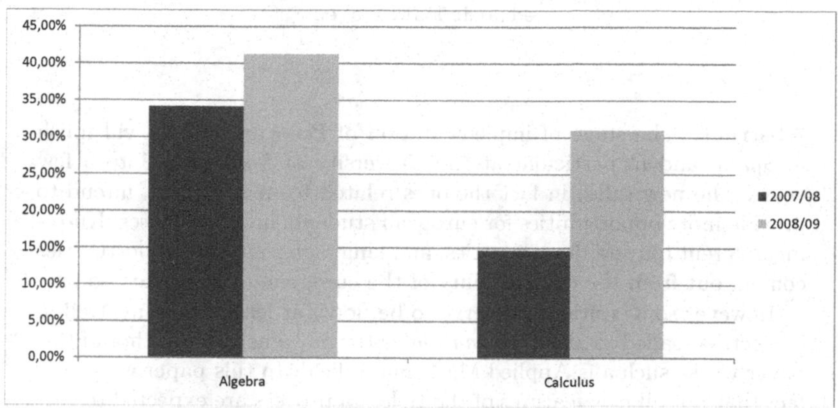

Fig. 2. Comparative percentage of students that pass the exams

Finally, we want to notice that the fact that the students give back a work diary allow us to verify the time that the students need to follow the subject. These data allow us to deduce that the mean time dedicated to each practice has been 10 hours in group work and 2 hours in an individual work. These quantities are into the parameters we managed when we propose this activity.

References

1. Astin, A.: What Matters in College: Four Critical Years Revisited. Jossey-Bass, San Francisco (1993)
2. Cooper, J., Prescott, S., Cook, L., Smith, L., Mueck, R., Cuseo, J.: Cooperative Learning and College Instruction. California State University Foundation, Long Beach, CA (1990)
3. Goodsell, A., Maher, M., Tinto, V.: Collaborative Learning: A Sourcebook for Higher Education. National Center on Postsecondary Teaching, Learning, and Assessment, University Park, PA (1992)
4. Johnson, D.W., Johnson, R.T., Smith, K.A.: Cooperative Learning: Increasing College Faculty Instructional Productivity, ASHE-ERIC Higher Education Report No. 4, George Washington University (1991)
5. McKeachie, W.: Teaching Tips, 8th edn. Heath & Co., Lexington (1986)

A Criticism on the Bologna's Learning Strategies

Eduardo Cuesta*

University of Valladolid, Department of Applied Mathematics
E.I.I. sede Francisco Mendizabal
C/ Francisco Mendizabal 1, Valladolid 47014, Spain
eduardo@mat.uva.es

Abstract. The stage of implementation of Bologna process will finish in Spain, and in particular at the University of Valladolid, into a few years. The new rules, in fact the ones related to new degrees, intend to provide more opportunities for european students in many senses: Knowing different universities, countries, and languages; new job opportunities coming out from the compatibility of the european degrees, and so on.

However some criticism deserve to be done, at least when involved in subjects so-called as *Basic Formation* as the one where the author of this paper works such a is Applied Mathematic field. In this paper we on the fact that not all new features of the Bologna process are expected to success, and that despite of several methodologies have been implemented and tried (even before Bologna process starts), the academic results are being not so good as expected.

1 Introduction

The University of Valladolid (Spain) is ready to finish the practical implementation of the new degrees according the Bologna's rules. These rules establish as founding philosophy the responsibility of all parts involved in the Higher Education in the european space. On the one hand the institutions promoting these changes as well as all education innovations leading to a successful implementation, and encouraging at the same time to the Universities to get the higher rates of quality in Europe and all around the world. On the other hand professors should change the way of doing applied up to now, i.e. adapting his mind to the new rules. The professors should offer to the students new learning tools in a wide sense: on-line information, academic help, tutorials, printed notes,...; laboratory practices, seminars, home-works,...; updating of learning methods, subjects, fields of research,...; contacts with other Universities to get fellows...; and many others. Finally, the students should realize about the importance and interest for themselves to make the most of his stay at the University, not only by the final qualifications, but also by the opportunities they can get while and after this period (jobs, fellows, learning opportunities,...).

* The author's research has been supported Department of Applied Mathematics of the University of Valladolid.

M.D. Lytras et al. (Eds.): WSKS 2010, Part I, CCIS 111, pp. 432–436, 2010.

The criticism of Bologna process is about this question: *After this kind of educational revolution, are the final results as good as expected?* Some answers are discussed in the next sections which come out in view of the results observed at the University the author works, and might be are of application in some others Universities and countries. In this case we will not focus on some other questions as for example *Are all involved parts right doing?*, which by chance are interesting question too.

2 Framework

From several years ago we (the author of this paper and some colleagues) are working on the Bologna process, which means adapting the higher education at the University of Valladolid to the new Bologna's framework.

That job has focused, from the beginning of this process, on the degrees in technical engineering (to be transformed into the new degrees) and has started several years ago. In particular, four years ago we decided to gradually adapt the learning methods with new strategies, in particular:

- Seminars, with public presentations
- Home-works involving a bit more complicate works that merely class-room exercises
- Lab practices and tasks for working groups
- ...among some others

This methodology intents to develop *transversal skills* in the students, such a the capability of doing public dissertations, of making reports on fixed subjects, of leading and manage working groups, and might be the most important and linking with the previous section, of taking some responsibility in his own learning capabilities.

This experiences haven been implemented for first and second year students, the subject has been basic mathematics: (in a few words) basic calculus, algebra, and numerics, and advanced calculus including differential equations. In this paper the discussion will mainly focus on the course Métodos Matemáticos I whose content is precisely Advanced Calculus. This course take part of the program of Technical Electronic Engineering, which is a three years degree. As we commented this degree will transform into the new engineering degree from the next season on.

3 Brief Description of Activities

The proposal of activities follows this methodology (without describing precisely contents which can be more specific and technical):

- Two home-works have proposed, none of them compulsory, under the following rules:

  - These works have to be done by working groups (4-6 peoples/group).
  - These works consist in solving a list of exercises and theoretical questions.
  - Students have to do a public dissertation on the development of such a task.
  - A six-pages report has to be presented, under certain rules fixed by the professor.
- The evaluation of these works is as follows:
  - In case of participating in this methodology the qualification of these works is up to 30% of the total qualification. The rest of qualification will correspond to the final exam (written, as classical).
  - The evaluation take into account several items: Public presentations and discussion of results, quality of the report, the methods to solve the problems, bibliography,...

Any way there will be a final exam, where the students participating in this methodology can avoid the parts of the exam afforded in the works. The rest of student can reach the whole qualification just by solving the whole exam.

This methodology, known as *cooperative learning*, intends to develop the *transversal skills* commented in the previous section.

4 Conclusions

Despite of the methodology has been followed each year by a high percentage of students (let us recall that the participation is not compulsory) the results has been not so good as expected. In particular, some data of the last courses (from 2007/08-2009/10, three years) where this methodology worked are shown in Table 1.

Table 1.

Course: Métodos Matemáticos I(*)			
Data	2007/08	2008/09	2009/10
Number of students	44	48	32
Partipants in the meth.	40 (90%)	33 (68%)	29 (90%)
Pass the course	30 (68%)	33 (68%)	20 (62%)
Pass the exam (no home-works)(**)	20 (45%)	14 (29%)	12 (37%)
Pass the home-works	26	27	23

(*) Data refers to qualifications in the first attemp.
(**) Pass the course without taking into account the home-works qualifications (the percentage is over the number of students).

The main conclusions one can notice, in view of Table 1, and in addition by my our teaching experience, can be briefly summarized as follows:

- First of all a high participation of students in the methodology we proposed is observed. This can interpreted as the student are very concerned with the Bologna process.
- The number of students passing the course improved with this methodology (despite Table 1 does not show a longer history of data) which turns out to be be very motivating.
- The most disappointing however is the data in the fourth row (Pass the exam without home-works). This looks like the students realize that the exam is not important and the most important are the home-works and complementary activities. In fact, it can be observed that the low qualifications in the exams is closely related with the low level in mathematics which is dramatically falling down. I understand that complementary activities we are promoting (in the Bologna language the *transversal skills*) are getting an overvalued importance, much more than the knowledge of the subjects of the course itself.

These thoughts open so many questions: *Are we right doing?, Are the student ready for new framework?, Is might be the philosophy of the Bologna process wrong? Are we "over–evaluating" the complementary activities? Shouldn't we mainly promote the students skills in the subjects of each course over other items?*

Acknowledgments

The author gratefully acknowledges to the colleagues participating in the Educational project *Adaptación de la E.U.P. de la Universidad de Valladolid al espacio europeo de educacin superior con la partipación de las Escuelas superiores de Valladolid, Burgos y Zamora.* The author gratefully acknowledge as well to the student for his participation in this methodology and his related feed-backs.

References

1. Alvarez, V., García, E., Flores, J., Romero, S., et al.: Guía para la planificación y ejecución de la docencia. Sevilla, Spain (2003)
2. Bará, J., Valero, M.: Evaluar la Universidad. Problemas y nuevos enfoques. Narcea, S.A. de Ediciones, Madrid (2003)
3. Brown, S., Glasner, A.: Evaluar en la Universidad. Problemas y nuevos enfoques, Narcea, S.A. de Ediciones, Madrid (2003)
4. Cuesta, E., Fernando, M.L.: Trabajo en grupo, aprendizaje cooperativo basado en problemas, exposición pública y evaluación alternativa en una asignatura de matemáticas en ingeniería técnica. Actas del XV CUIEET, Valladolid, Spain (2007)
5. European Ministers of Education: The European Higher Education Area Bologna Declaration, Bologna (1999)
6. Felder, R.M., Brent, R.: Effective Strategies for Cooperative Learning. J. Cooperation & Collaboration in College Teaching 10(2) (2001)

7. Group GREIDI: Profundización en la aplicación de experiencias de aprendizaje activo en el ámbito de la ingeniera. Proyecto UV31/04, Agencia para la Calidad del Sistema Universitario en Castillay Len (2005)
8. Monereo, C., Pozo, J.I.: La Universidad ante la nueva cultura educativa. Sntesis, S.A., Madrid (2003)
9. Nuñez, T., Loscertales, F.: El grupo y su eficacia. EUB, S.L. Barcelona (2003)
10. García, E., Jiménez, E.: Evaluación alternativa en la enseanza universitaria, Guía para la planificación y ejecución de la docencia elaborado por Alvarez, V., García, E. y otros. Sevilla, Spain (2003)

Retracted: Application of Scientific Approaches for Evaluation of Quality of Learning Objects in eQNet Project

Eugenijus Kurilovas[1,2,3] and Silvija Serikoviene[1]

[1] Institute of Mathematics and Informatics, Akademijos str. 4, 08663 Vilnius, Lithuania
[2] Vilnius Gediminas Technical University, Sauletekio al. 11, 10223 Vilnius, Lithuania
[3] Centre of Information Technologies in Education, Suvalku str. 1, 03106 Vilnius, Lithuania
eugenijus.kurilovas@itc.smm.lt, silvija.serikoviene@gmail.com

Abstract. The paper is aimed to analyse the application of several scientific approaches, methods, and principles for evaluation of quality of learning objects for Mathematics subject. The authors analyse the following approaches to minimise subjectivity level in expert evaluation of the quality of learning objects, namely: (1) principles of multiple criteria decision analysis for identification of quality criteria, (2) technological quality criteria classification principle, (3) fuzzy group decision making theory to obtain evaluation measures, (4) normalisation requirement for criteria weights, and (5) scalarisation method for learning objects quality optimisation. Another aim of the paper is to outline the central role of social tagging to describe usage, attention, and other aspects of the context; as well as to help to exploit context data towards making learning object repositories more useful, and thus enhance the reuse. The applied approaches have been used practically for evaluation of learning objects and metadata tagging while implementing European eQNet and te@ch.us projects in Lithuanian comprehensive schools in 2010.

Keywords: Learning object, multiple criteria decision analysis, optimisation methods, expert evaluation, quality criteria.

1 Introduction

eQNet is a three-year (September 2009-2012) Comenius Multilateral Network [3] funded under the European Commission's Lifelong Learning programme (LLP). The project is coordinated by European Schoolnet (EUN) and involves 9 Ministries of Education or agencies nominated to act of their behalf. The primary aim is to improve the quality of learning objects (LOs) in European Schoolnet's Learning Resource Exchange (LRE) [8] which currently offers almost 130,000 LOs and assets from over 25 providers. As a pan-European service, the LRE particularly seeks to identify LOs that "travel well" (i.e., reusable) across national borders and can be used in a cultural and linguistic context different from the one in which they were created [3].

eQNet will do this by establishing a network consisting of researchers, policy makers and practitioners (teachers) that will develop and apply "travel well" quality criteria to both existing LRE content as well as that to be selected in future from national repositories. The vision driving the LRE is that a significant percentage of high quality

M.D. Lytras et al. (Eds.): WSKS 2010, Part I, CCIS 111, pp. 437–443, 2010.

LOs developed in different countries, in different languages and to meet the needs of different curricula can be re-used at European level.

eQNet will provide a forum for joint reflection and co-operation related to the exchange and re-use of educational content and allow network members to: (1) better share information and expertise particularly related to "travel well" quality criteria (pedagogical, technical and intellectual property rights (IPR) factors); (2) develop new frameworks to improve the quality of LOs and metadata in both national repositories and the LRE, including the growing volume of user-generated content and metadata, as well as to improve the multilinguality of LRE content as a result of the translation of metadata, making use, where appropriate, of automatic metadata translation approaches and technologies; (3) enable schools to participate in a Community of Practice related to the use LOs at European level.

Major results will include: the development of "travel well" quality criteria to more easily identify LOs with the potential for cross-border use (this work package is coordinated by Lithuanian partner, in particular by the author of the paper), the practical application by teachers of these criteria to >3,500 LOs in the LRE, 'showcases' of the best of these LOs in a "travel well" section of the LRE portal, where necessary, the enrichment of selected LOs with new or better metadata, a Community of Practice for teachers around these LOs [3].

2 Methodology of the Research

One of the main features achieving the high LOs effectiveness and efficiency level is LOs reusability. The need for reusability of LOs has at least three elements: (1) interoperability: LO is interoperable and can be used in different platforms; (2) flexibility in terms of pedagogic situations: LO can fit into a variety of pedagogic situations, and (3) modifiability to suit a particular teacher's or student's needs: LO can be made more appropriate to a pedagogic situation by modifying it to suit a particular teacher's or student's needs [4].

Reusability of LOs (or their ability to "travel well" between different contexts and education systems) is considered by the authors as a part of the overall quality of LOs. This means that any high quality LO has some reusability level (or potential to "travel well"), but this does not mean that any reusable LO is quality one.

The main problem analysed in the paper is how to establish (1) a 'proper' set of LOs "travel well" quality evaluation criteria which should reflect the objective scientific principles of construction a *model* (criteria tree) for LOs "travel well" quality evaluation, and also (2) a 'proper' *method* for evaluation of LOs quality.

Expert evaluation is referred here as the multiple criteria evaluation of LOs aimed at selection of the best alternatives (i.e., LOs) based on score-ranking results [6]. If the set of decision alternatives (LOs) is assumed to be predefined, fixed and finite, then the decision problem is to choose the optimal alternative or, maybe, to rank them. But usually the experts have to deal with the problem of optimal decision in the multiple criteria situation where the objectives are often conflicting. In this case, an optimal decision is the one that maximises the expert's utility. These principles of identification of quality evaluation criteria have been analysed in multiple criteria decision analysis (MCDA) theory related research works, e.g., [2].

Evaluation of LOs quality is a typical case where the criteria are conflicting, i.e., LOs could be very qualitative against several criteria, and not qualitative against the other ones, and vice versa. Therefore, the authors propose to use MCDA approach for creation of LOs quality evaluation model and method.

LOs multiple criteria evaluation method is referred here as the experts' additive utility function represented by formula (1) below including LOs evaluation criteria, their ratings (values) and weights [6]. This method is well-known in the theory of optimisation methods and is named "*scalarisation method*". A possible decision here could be to transform multi-criteria task into one-criterion task obtained by adding all criteria together with their weights. It is valid from the point of view of the optimisation theory, and a special theorem exists for this case [6].

Therefore, here we have the experts' additive utility function:

$$f(X) = \sum_{i=1}^{m} a_i f_i(X), \sum_{i=1}^{m} a_i = 1, \ a_i > 0 \tag{1}$$

where $f_i\ (X_j)$ is the rating (i.e., non-fuzzy value) of the criterion i for the each of the examined LOs alternatives X_j. The weights here should be 'normalised' according to the *'normalisation' requirement*

$$\sum_{i=1}^{m} a_i = 1, \ a_i > 0. \tag{2}$$

The major is the meaning of the utility function (1) the better LOs meet the quality requirements in comparison with the ideal (i.e., 100%) quality.

3 Literature Analysis and Research Results

This section is aimed (1) to apply the aforementioned scientific approaches to propose a suitable scientific model and method for evaluation of quality of LOs, (2) to present LOs experimental evaluation results, and (3) to present social tagging approach to enrich multilingual LOs metadata in eQNet.

3.1 Learning Objects Quality Evaluation Model

The following *principles of identification of quality evaluation criteria* are relevant to all MCDA approaches: (1) value relevance; (2) understandability; (3) measurability; (4) non-redundancy; (5) judgmental independence; (6) balancing completeness and conciseness; (7) operationality; (8) simplicity versus complexity [2].

On the other hand, according to the *technological quality criteria classification principle*, we can divide technological quality criteria into 'internal quality' and 'quality in use' criteria of the educational software such as LOs. 'Internal quality' is a descriptive characteristic that describes the quality of software independently from any particular context of its use, while 'quality in use' is evaluative characteristic of software obtained by making a judgment based on criteria that determine the worthiness of software for a particular project. Any LOs quality evaluation model (set of criteria) should provide the experts (decision makers) the clear instrumentality who (i.e., what kind of experts) should analyse what kind of LOs quality criteria in order to select the best LOs suitable for their needs. According to aforementioned *principle*, 'internal quality' criteria should be mainly the area of interest of the software engineers, and 'quality in use' criteria should be mostly analysed by the programmers and users taking into account the users' feedback on the usability of software [6].

The authors have applied these two principles in their papers [5], [6] on technological evaluation of the learning software, and thus have identified a number of LOs technological quality evaluation criteria presented in the technological part of the LOs quality evaluation model presented in Fig. 1.

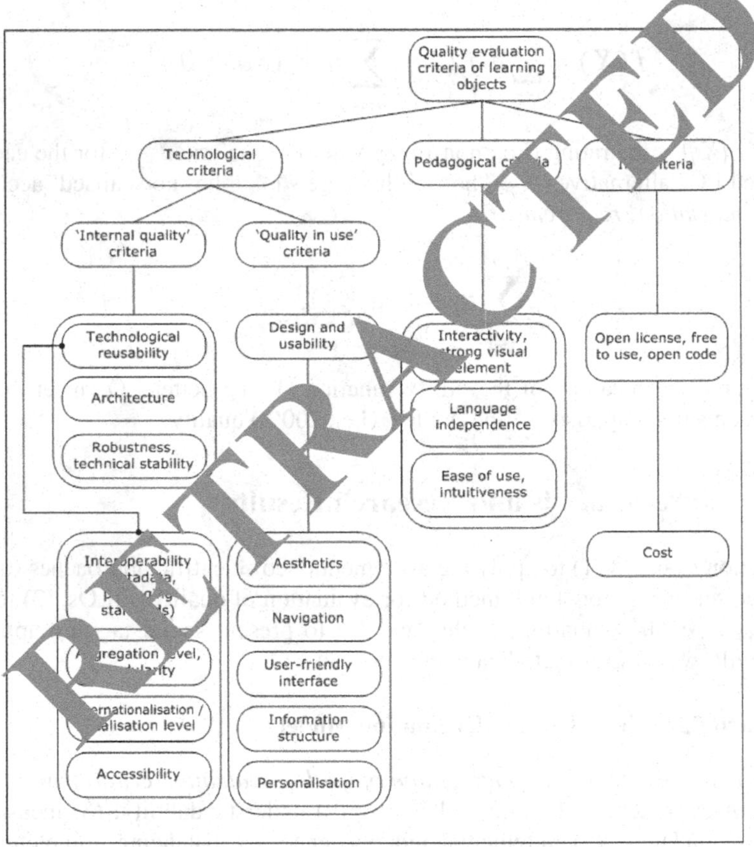

Fig. 1. LOs quality evaluation model (criteria tree).

On the other hand, the authors have analysed a number of existing models (sets of quality evaluation criteria) for evaluation of pedagogical quality of LOs, e.g., [1], [7], [9], [10], and [13].

The suitable criteria based on MCDA principles [2] are: (1) interactivity, strong visual structure (animations, images and short videos are travelling best); (2) language independence or low language dependence (easily translatable) or multilinguality; (3) ease of use, intuitiveness. Intellectual property rights (IPR) criterion should also be considered here [5].

Therefore, the authors propose to construct the LOs quality evaluation model (see Fig. 1) based on the literature analysis, MCDA principles of identification of quality evaluation criteria, and technological quality criteria classification principle.

3.2 Learning Objects Quality Evaluation Method

The widely used measurement criteria of the decision attributes' quality are mainly qualitative and subjective. Decisions in this context are often expressed in natural language, and evaluators are unable to assign exact numerical values to the different criteria. Assessment can be often performed by linguistic variables: 'bad', 'poor', 'fair', 'good' and 'excellent'. These values are imprecise and uncertain: they are commonly called 'fuzzy values'. Integrating these different judgements to obtain a final evaluation is not evident. Therefore, the authors have proposed to use *fuzzy group decision making theory* to obtain final assessment measures [11]. Linguistic variables conversion into non-fuzzy values of the evaluation criteria is as follows: 'excellent'=0.850; 'good'=0.675; 'fair'=0.500; 'poor'=0.325; 'bad'=0.150 [6].

The weight of the evaluation criterion reflects the experts' opinion on the criterion's importance level in comparison with the other criteria for the particular needs. For example, for the most simple (general) case, when all LOs evaluation criteria are of equal importance (i.e., we pay no especial attention to LOs reusability criteria), the experts could consider the equal weights a_i = 0.125 according to the normalisation requirement (2).

But if we pay especial attention to LOs reusability criteria, we can, e.g., consider the increased weights for the 1st and 6th LOs quality evaluation criteria (see Fig. 1 and Table 1), because these criteria deal with LOs reusability mostly. In this case these increased weights could be, e.g., twice higher in comparison with the other ones – 0.2, and all other criteria weights according to normalisation requirement (2) should be equal 0.1.

Lithuanian Mathematics expert teacher (the co-author of the paper) has applied the presented evaluation model and method in eQNet project (see Table 1). A number of probably qualitative reusable LOs have been identified in Lithuanian LOs repositories and evaluated against the aforementioned model and method (see formula (1).

There are three examples of these LOs presented in Table 1: (1) LO1: "Coordinate Method", available online at http://mkp.emokykla.lt/imo/lt/mo/250/; (2) LO2: "Polygon area", available online at http://mkp.emokykla.lt/imo/lt/mo/431/; and (3) LO3: "Interval Method", available online at http://mkp.emokykla.lt/imo/lt/mo/316/ .

These results mean that LO_1 meets 74.06% general quality (q) in comparison with the ideal, LO_2 – 71.88%, and LO_3 – 58.75%. They also mean that LO_1 meets 72.75% "travel well" quality (twq) in comparison with the ideal, LO_2 – 74.50%, and LO_3 – 57.00%. Therefore, LO_1 is the best alternative (among the evaluated) from general quality point of view, but LO_2 is the best from "travel well" quality point of view.

Table 1. Results of experimental evaluation of LOs general quality (q) and "travel well" quality (twq)

LOs evaluation criteria	LO_1q	LO_2q	LO_3q	LO_1twq	LO_2twq	LO_3twq
Technological criteria:						
1. Technological reusability	0.675	0.850	0.675	*0.1350*	*0.1700*	*0.1350*
2. Design and usability	0.675	0.850	0.850	0.0675	0.0850	0.0850
3. Working stability	0.675	0.500	0.675	0.0675	0.0500	0.0675
4. Architecture	0.675	0.500	0.500	0.0675	0.0500	0.0500
Pedagogical criteria:						
5. Interactivity level	0.850	0.500	0.325	0.0850	0.0500	0.0325
6. Language independence	0.675	0.850	0.325	*0.1350*	*0.1700*	*0.0650*
7. Ease of use, intuitiveness	0.850	0.850	0.500	0.0850	0.0850	0.0500
IPR criteria:						
8. Open licence, cost	0.850	0.850	0.850	0.0850	0.0850	0.0850
Evaluation results:	***0.7406***	***0.7188***	***0.5875***	***0.7275***	***0.[illegible]50***	***0.5700***

3.3 Social Tagging in eQNet

In eQNet, the partners consider that context comprises the LO usage situation and environment as well as persistent and transient properties of the user. They concentrate on teachers using LO repositories as an important use-case example and focus on language and country as context variables. We can use such context information to improve the use and reuse of LO repositories by making them more useful in a multilingual and multicultural context. The central role that social tagging can play in this process is outlined in eQNet: on the one hand, tags describe usage, attention, and other aspects of context; on the other hand, they can help to exploit context data towards making LO repositories more useful and thus enhance the reuse.

This approach could be especially useful for user generated content and Web 2.0 communities while implementing the other ongoing LLP project te@ch.us aimed at the creation and analysis of the learning communities for Web 2.0 teaching [12].

4 Conclusion and Recommendations

The presented research results show that MCDA approach-based LOs evaluation model presented in Fig. 1 and method represented by formula (1) are applicable in real life situations when education institutions have to decide on purchase of LOs for their education needs in the market. The proposed approaches are quite objective, exact and simply to use for choosing the qualitative LOs alternatives.

On the other hand, the proposed LOs "travel well" quality evaluation approach is applicable for the aims of eQNet project in order to select "travel well" LOs from LRE or elsewhere to use them in the other education contexts and countries.

References

1. Becta: Quality principles for digital learning resources (2007)
2. Belton, V., Stewart, T.J.: Multiple criteria decision analysis: an integrated approach. Kluwer Academic Publishers, Dordrecht (2002)

3. eQNet: Quality Network for a European Learning Resource Exchange project website (2010), http://eqnet.eun.org
4. Kurilovas, E.: Interoperability, Standards and Metadata for e-Learning. In: Papadopoulos, G.A., Badica, C. (eds.) Intelligent Distributed Computing III, Studies in Computational Intelligence, vol. 237, pp. 121–130. Springer, Berlin (2009)
5. Kurilovas, E., Dagiene, V.: Learning Objects and Virtual Learning Environments Technical Evaluation Criteria. Electronic Journal of e-Learning 7(2), 127–136 (2009)
6. Kurilovas, E., Serikoviene, S.: Learning Content and Software Evaluation and Personalisation Problems. Informatics in Education 9(1), 91–114 (2010)
7. Leacock, T.L., Nesbit, J.C.: A Framework for Evaluating the Quality of Multimedia Learning Resources. Educational Technology & Society 10(2), 44–59 (2007)
8. LRE: European Learning Resource Exchange service for schools web site (2010), http://lreforschools.eun.org/LRE-Portal/Index.iface
9. MELT: EU eContentplus programme's Metadata Ecology for Learning and Teaching project web site (2008), http://melt-project.eun.org
10. Paulsson, F., Naeve, A.: Establishing technical quality criteria for Learning Objects (2006), http://www.frepa.org/wp/wp-content/files/Paulsson-Establ-Tech-Qual_finalv1.pdf
11. Ounaies, H.Z., Jamoussi, Y., Ben Ghezala, H.H.: Evaluation framework based on fuzzy measured method in adaptive learning system. Themes in Science and Technology Education 1(1), 49–58 (2009)
12. te@ch.us: Helping teachers integrate Web 2.0 into the classroom. EU LLP te@ch.us project (Learning community for Web 2.0 teaching). European Schoolnet (2010), http://www.europeanschoolnet.org/web/guest/about/release/-/asset_publisher/0Tqh/content/20655?redirect=%2Fweb%2Fguest%2Fabout%2Frelease
13. Vargo, J., Nesbit, J.C., Belfer, K., Archambault, A.: Learning object evaluation: Computer mediated collaboration and inter–rater reliability. International Journal of Computers and Applications 25(3), 198–205 (2003)

Appendix

The work presented in this paper is partially supported by the European Commission under the LLP – as part of the eQNet project (project number 502857-LLP-1-2009-1-BECOMENIUS-CNW) and te@ch.us project (project No. 504333-LLP-1-2009-1-DE-COMENIUS-CMP). The authors are solely responsible for the content of this paper. It does not represent the opinion of the European Commission, and the European Commission is not responsible for any use that might be made of data appearing therein.

Exploring Learning through Audience Interaction in Virtual Reality Dome Theaters

Panagiotis Apostolellis and Thanasis Daradoumis

University of the Aegean, Department of Cultural Technology and Communication
Harilaou Trikoupi & Faonos Street, 811 00 Mytilini, Lesvos, Greece
{p.apostolellis,daradoumis}@aegean.gr

Abstract. Informal learning in public spaces like museums, science centers and planetariums is increasingly popular during the last years. Recent advancements in large-scale displays allowed contemporary technology-enhanced museums to get equipped with digital domes, some with real-time capabilities like Virtual Reality systems. By conducting extensive literature review we have come to the conclusion that little to no research has been carried out on the leaning outcomes that the combination of VR and audience interaction can provide in the immersive environments of dome theaters. Thus, we propose that audience collaboration in immersive virtual reality environments presents a promising approach to support effective learning in groups of school aged children.

Keywords: Audience Interaction, Informal Learning, Virtual Reality, Immersive Displays, Dome Theaters.

1 Introduction

The notion of free-choice or informal learning has become more and more popular over the last decade, especially for young children. It is a standard practice nowadays for classes to visit museums in order to provide out-of-school pedagogy to students. Technology-enhanced museums, like planetariums and science museums, which are increasingly equipped with dome screens[1], are considered adept sources of knowledge where large groups of children can simultaneously 'absorb' the information provided. But are those venues taking full advantage of the potential that this state-of-the-art technology offers for delivering knowledge to their audiences? Are there any ways to engage visitors in a greater extent with the content so as to increase motivation and, consequently, their capacity to learn?

By extensively reviewing related literature and practices from institutions around the world, we have come to the conclusion that there exist very few public spaces that offer to their visitors the ability to massively interact with real-time content in a dome theater, with the intent to facilitate learning. Thus, we propose in this paper that by providing a way to an audience to interact with the 'live' content projected on an immersive display (like a dome screen) can bear immense learning outcomes. In order

[1] The *LNP's Dome Theater Compendium ONLINE!* [1] offers a quite exhaustive list of institutions around the world, with full dome capabilities.

M.D. Lytras et al. (Eds.): WSKS 2010, Part I, CCIS 111, pp. 444–448, 2010.

to base our assumption we will start by briefly setting out the way that technology can effectively fulfill the learning needs of museum visitors. Then we will elaborate on the educational value that the combination of three advanced technologies can bring to the knowledge-hungry young visitors of such museums, referring to the most prominent related work on each field. We will conclude by referring to the work we have done so far, our future steps, and the desired outcomes of our ongoing research.

2 Learning in Technology-Enhanced Contexts

Current trends in technology are shifting learning from the typical classroom to virtual classrooms, emerging in free-choice learning settings such as museums, science centers and planetariums, mainly by way of exploiting their sociocultural properties. Children, as the core visitors of such spaces, derive meaning affecting their construction of knowledge through engaging in social interactions within cultural groups [2], such as classmates, teachers, parents, content experts, or co-participants in shared interactive experiences. Effective learning in such spaces is believed to be accomplished for two additional reasons: it is contextual and it takes advantage of visitors' prior knowledge [3]. Proper exploitation of those properties in appropriately designed interactive experiences can prove very efficacious in fostering learning in a large audience of people, especially school aged children. In order to achieve this, the harmonic integration of three modern technologies is of ultimate importance: *Virtual Reality*, *Immersive Displays* and *Audience Interactivity*.

2.1 Virtual Reality in Education

Virtual Reality (VR) is regarded by many scholars as one of the most notable tools of informal education. Its unique features of autonomy (imitating human behavior), interaction (real-time control and navigation) and presence (the sense of 'being' inside the artificial world) [4], constitute it a highly respectable medium for imparting knowledge through constructivist learning. However, the use of VR technology is by no means a guarantor of effective learning; it is only through rigorous design and the integration of other equally important learning elements that the true educational value of VR can unfold [5]. Such elements we consider to be the immersive attributes of dome displays and the social properties of audience interaction, which will be reviewed in the following sections.

Research on the field of VR in education has primarily included science-related subjects and attempted to access the technology's efficacy on conceptual learning. An extensive research conducted in this field is the project *ScienceSpace* [6], which concluded that VR enhanced students' abilities to conceptualize abstract scientific ideas. No matter how rigorous this study was, it lacked the unexplored potential of today's dome theaters: multi-user participation, social interaction, and collaborative play. Another example of virtual learning environments which included collaborative learning through play, was the *NICE* Project [7], in which two physically distributed groups of 7 to 8 children used different immersive VR setups (ImmersaDesk™, CAVE™), in order to cultivate and tend a virtual garden. Results revealed that, besides the hardware usability problems, the leaders-drivers of the experience were largely the ones who perceived the conceptual model and expressed higher degrees of presence and engagement. This finding supports our assumption that it is the meaningful interaction of all the participants of a shared experience which acts as a leverage for increased enjoyment and positive learning outcomes.

No matter how thorough some of the investigations about the learning benefits of VR have been, there are rare cases where researchers have tested the true potential of the technology on a large audience of people. Digital dome theaters have the capacity to provide a custom experience to each group of spectators through the manipulation of real-time synthesized imagery by a content expert [8]. Moreover, by providing branching paths through the content, spectators have the feeling of participating in the unraveling story. Nevertheless, the true power of the medium lies within its immersive and mass-interactive properties, which have been greatly left unexplored.

2.2 Immersive Displays and Learning

The majority of studies performed on VR and education mobilized head-mounted displays to facilitate individual immersion (the sense of 'being there') in the virtual world. The evolution of VR technology and immersive displays has brought up bigger setups which could accommodate a larger audience, the most popular of which being the ImmersaDesk™ (for 5 people maximum) and the CAVE™ (for up to 10 people). However, large-scale immersive displays like dome theaters attempt to promote the overall experience of a larger group of people (from 60 people to a few hundreds) by means of providing transparency of mediating technology, seating and viewing comfort for extended periods, theatrical surround audio, and interactive ergonomics [9].

The degree of awareness of the mediation (transparency) is the most significant determinant of the feeling of presence in the projected (virtual) world. Presence is, also, closely related to the audience's perception of the virtual environment, which is determined by the prior knowledge participants bring in the experience and contextual information [10]. Taking advantage of these characteristics of audience members are, as mentioned at the outset, important factors for informal learning. Despite the common belief that immersion aids learning, the majority of studies has mainly focused on conceptual learning. An exception to this is a research which evaluated the impact of an immersive panoramic display (partial dome) on learning about factual information (i.e. an Egyptian temple), and revealed that visually immersed students availed themselves of better support in their learning activities [11].

Besides the aforementioned technical advantages of dome theaters and their impact on learning, maybe the most prominent of their features is the capacity to provide a social experience. People and especially children are accustomed at learning in social contexts, like school classrooms, through instruction and tutoring. However, in order to unveil the full potential of these spaces, we need to provide the tools and the content for group interaction activities, where audience members can learn through collaborative decision making and problem solving. This type of *audience interactivity* and its impact on leaning has undergone scant research.

2.3 Audience Interactivity

Audience Interactivity is a fairly new and unexplored field, and refers to the process that a large number of co-located people engages in interacting meaningfully with the content presented to them on a large-scale display. Such practices can be usually found in digital planetariums and digital dome theaters, which have the capacity to accommodate such a large audience. No matter how rapidly such venues have proliferated over the last decade [1], they still lack either the infrastructure or the desire to implement and evaluate such mass interaction systems.

Various methods have been tried to achieve interaction in digital theaters, the most prominent of which are the mass-audience polling device Cinematrix™, motion analysis techniques and custom joypad setups. Among the very few examples in which researchers ventured to experiment with this technology, are two productions on science education [12] which employ Cinematrix™ paddles to selectively present information about cell biology and the brain, to an audience of 150 people situated in a planetarium. Although this work was very promising, as concluded by informal observations, there was no formal evaluation carried out to assess the efficacy of mass interaction for facilitating learning. Other research efforts with a larger audience participating in interactive games include the work of Maynes-Aminzade et al. [13], who experimented with facilitating mass-interaction by means of motion tracking techniques and laser pointers. Although this work still does not include any formal critique methods, we agree with its conclusions that "the greatest challenge lies not in developing the technology for audience interaction, but in designing engaging activities".

We have been experimenting with this subject for the past two years, developing immersive, interactive VR productions for the digital dome "Tholos", of the cultural center "Hellenic Cosmos", located in Athens, Greece. Although the used paradigms of audience interaction (using a keypad) are fairly simple so far [14], we find that the impact they have on school aged children is intense. Besides this indication acquired from observations, the effectiveness of audience interaction in learning stems from our belief that such social interactions of children in dome theaters lie within the "Zone of Proximal Development" (ZDP). The term ZDP, introduced by Vygotsky, determines the area between the level of the child's independent performance and the level of assisted performance, either by a tutor (instructor) or more capable peers [2].

Although audience interactivity constitutes a promising field, we believe that there is a considerable gap concerning its exploitation in VR dome theaters in order to facilitate learning, especially in children. Thus, our efforts are directed towards developing a framework that will guide the design and evaluation of a VR show with audience collaboration in a digital dome theater, processing the following properties:

- A combination of first and third person world view, according to the type of interaction (individual or group) and the task being performed.
- Individual avatar representation and manipulation in order to increase awareness in the virtual world, the feeling of empathy and, eventually, engagement.
- On-the-fly formation of groups which will be assigned with suited tasks, fulfilled only through collaborative or competitive activities.
- Allowance of wrong choices and provision of multiple paths, as a means of increasing free-choice interaction and providing alternative narratives.
- Guidance and interaction facilitation by a human agent impersonated as an avatar in the virtual world (a technique known in the field of HCI as the "Wizard of Oz").
- Creation of a narrative from the lived experience and distribution to participants, in order to foster discussion in other contexts (e.g. classroom, home, personal research).

3 Conclusion

Our ongoing research involves building and testing a theoretical framework which will ground our assumptions that, by providing meaningful interactive activities that facilitate collaboration in Virtual Reality dome theaters, we will manage to leverage learning in an audience of school aged children.

References

1. Loch Ness Productions: LNP Dome Theater Compendium Online!, http://www.lochnessproductions.com/lpco/lpco4.html
2. Vygotsky, L.: Mind in Society: The Development of Higher Psychological Processes. Harvard University Press, Cambridge (1978)
3. Falk, J.H., Dierking, L.D.: Learning from museums: visitor experiences and the making of meaning. AltaMira Press, Walnut Creek (2000)
4. Zeltzer, D.: Autonomy, interaction, and presence. Presence 1(1), 127–132 (1992)
5. Winn, W.D.: What we have learned about VR and learning and what we still need to study. In: Proceedings of Laval Virtual, Laval, France, pp. 8–17 (2005)
6. Dede, C., Salzman, M., Loftin, R.B., Ash, K.: Using Virtual Reality Technology to Convey Abstract Scientific Concepts. In: Jacobson, M.J., Kozma, R.B. (eds.) Learning the Sciences of the 21st Century: Research, Design, and Implementing Advanced Technology Learning Environments. Lawrence Erlbaum, Hillsdale (1997)
7. Roussos, M., Johnson, A., Moher, T., Leigh, J., Vasilakis, C., Barnes, G.: Learning and Building Together in an Immersive Virtual World. Presence 8(3), 247–263 (1999)
8. Gaitatzes, A., Papaioannou, G., Christopoulos, D., Zyba, G.: Media productions for a dome display system. In: Proceedings of the ACM symposium on Virtual Reality Software and Technology, Limassol, Cyprus, pp. 261–264 (2006)
9. Lantz, E.: Large-scale immersive displays in entertainment and education. In: 2nd Annual Immersive Projection Technology Workshop, May 11-12 (1998)
10. Carss, P., Hazelden, K.: The Perception of Domed Environments. Fulldome Summit, Chicago, Illinois (2008)
11. Jacobson, J.: Ancient Architecture in Virtual Reality: Does immersion really aid learning? PhD Thesis, University of Pittsburgh (2008)
12. Fisher, R., Vanouse, P., Dannenberg, R., Christensen, J.: Audience Interactivity: A Case Study in Three Perspectives Including Remarks about a Future Production. In: Proc. of the Sixth Biennial Symposium for Arts and Technology, New London, Connecticut (1997)
13. Maynes-Aminzade. D., Pausch, R., Seitz, S.: Techniques for interactive audience participation. In: Proceedings of the Fourth IEEE International Conference on Multimodal Interfaces, Pittsburgh, PA, USA (2002)
14. Christopoulos, D., Apostolellis, P., Onasiadis, A.: Educational Virtual Environments for Digital Dome Display Systems with Audience Participation. In: Proc. of the 13th Panhellenic Conference in Informatics - Workshop in Education, Corfu, Greece, pp. 265–275 (2009)

Students' Everyday Use of Web 2.0 Collaboration Tools and Use within Moodle

Lasma Ulmane-Ozolina*, Vineta Kulmane, and Marina Kazakevica

Liepaja University, Liela street 14, Liepaja, LV-3401, Latvia
luo@liepu.lv, vkulmane@gmail.com, marinaka@inbox.lv

Abstract. Moodle is the one of most popular learning management systems. Situation in Liepaja University shows that Moodle is used mainly for content delivery. To activate student learning in Moodle and enhance Moodle usage, collaboration supported tools will be present for academic staff. Research is made to choose the most popular tools from the student point of view to enhance their learning. Focus group interviews is conducted to find out what web 2.0 collaboration tools students are using in their everyday life and what tools using in Moodle. The idea is to transmit the students' everyday life skills with Web 2.0 in the learning activities.

Keywords: Collaboration tools, web 2.0, Moodle, skills' transmission, students.

1 Introduction

Moodle becomes the most popular learning platform for the higher education institutions. It is attractive for the higher education institutions not only as open source application but also because of wide offer of the tools to organize the content and learning. Today's buzzword is *web 2.0*. One of the main advantage of web 2.0 is it is free of charge. That allows researchers to think that young people use it in their everyday life and has raised an issue of its usability in education. Many researchers admit that more effective tools are those that students are already familiar with or at least have some experience and skills to work with (Dado & Beheshti, 2009; Jackson, 2003; Saunders & Klemming, 2003).The possibility to use or transmit student prior skills with web 2.0 collaboration tools in the educational settings could be very beneficial. This is one of the issues for research mentioned in Educational Science News by Christine Greenhow, Beth Robelia, and Joan E. Hughes (2009). It is important because if the student knows how to use tools and can use it in the time and place comfortable to him/her, then much more attention will be paid to the content (Ozsariyildiz, & Beheshti, 2007; Lomas et al., 2008). And some tools in Moodle (blog, chat, discussion forum ect.) can be recognized as web 2.0 tools just in "closed" environment. The research is done at Liepaja University (Latvia) to find out do really students use web 2.0 collaboration tools in their everyday life and which of these tools students see as potential ones to use within Moodle. The article shows the main findings.

---

* Corresponding author.

M.D. Lytras et al. (Eds.): WSKS 2010, Part I, CCIS 111, pp. 449–452, 2010.

2 Web 2.0 and Tools in Moodle

Technology itself cannot enhance or change the learning or the teaching process (Rogers,2004) but it can offer more flexibility for the teaching - learning process and approaches to learning (Saunders & Klemming, 2003; Jackson, 2003; Ozsariyildiz, & Beheshti, 2007). Technological tools cannot be used as a replacement for activities but rather as a complementary to a more traditional way of teaching-learning modes (Jackson, 2003). The complementary use of ICT tools should be well analyzed because the tools have to be used in an appropriate way and in the right circumstances to achieve a positive effect on learning (Saunders & Klemming, 2003). Tools must be used effectively and meaningfully (Tomei, 2008; Oteroet al, 2005).

The authors have to admit that web 2.0 tools promote interaction between people and content of information space. Literature describes web 2.0 tools as a "two-way web", a "participatory web", a "social web". These terms point to the presence of interaction. The most popular tools are blogs, wikis, social networking tools and others. Chris Dede (Dede, 2009) categorizes web 2.0 tools into three categories: those supporting sharing, thinking and co-creating. Tools that facilitate thinking (blogs, online discussion forums) and co-creating (wiki, collaborative file creation) are the ones that can be used for collaborative learning within Moodle because they are integrated in learning management system.

Moodle offers different tools. Some of the tools mainly support individual activities, like, test, exercise, lesson, advanced uploading of files, online text. Some tools mainly support collaborative activities, like, wiki, discussion forum, chat, and workshop. The lecturers' usage of these tools differs very much. Mainly they use Moodle tools for providing learning materials. Some of these tools can be classified as Web 2.0 tools as wiki, discussion forum and blog in the "closed" environment. The "closed" environment offers safe usage of these tools in the terms of the ability to use them and the safeness of content. Authors see this as an advantage because academic staff is not very skilled in using technology.

3 Research Methodologies

There are two focus group interviews. Six Master program (Information technology) students have participated in the first group (group IT). They are very experienced in the use of different technological tools. The second group (group ES) consisted of six students from the Master program "Educational Sciences". These students are not skilful in the use of technological tools. The first group consisting of advanced IT users allowed group interview to be recorded, but in the other one 2 out of 6 students disagreed on group interview recording.

4 Results

The aim of the interviews is to analyze the students' point of view on the usage of collaboration tools in their everyday life and on learning activities and to find out the students' suggestions on tools to use for learning in and out of Moodle.

The question about students' self-evaluation offers the evaluation scale from 1 (no skills) to 10 (advanced skills). Students' self-evaluation grades in each group are different, but with small dispersion in each. The average for group IT is 8,2 but for group ES this is 6,8. However in each group there is at least one student who has no experience with some tool and at least one who know one very well. For example, in the group IT one student is very optimistic about Twitter (microblog) and uses it every day. In comparison with group ES - nobody uses Twitter and not even try.

The results show that group IT evaluate their skills with different tools a little lower, for example, about blogs group IT evaluate themselves with 7, but group ES with 8. Discussion proves that they think about their skills not only as users but also as administrators. In comparison with the other group what evaluating their skills only from the user's point of view.

Questions about each of the tools and their usage in the students' everyday life shows different situation. In the focus group interviews Group IT decides, that they always use chat in their everyday actions. All students in the Group IT acknowledge that they use it (in the Skype program) for the problem questions appearing in their work; and also for personal communication with family members, peers and friends. Group ES in the interview indicate that they use chat in the Skype program, but not very often. As to other tools, both groups say that they rarely use discussion forums, blogs, wikis. Group ES answering to the questions about the usage of tools says that they use ICT tools only if they need very specific information on some issues and nobody use tools for communication with peers or friends, or just for fun. Group IT in opposition often says that they use tools for communication with peers, friends and read blogs because they are interested in some field, or just for fun.

There are differences between groups according to Moodle usage in the learning process. Group IT has a lot of study courses in the Moodle but group ES has only two and till the interview time they have not used them. Group IT admit that from the communication tools mentioned (discussion forum, chat, wiki, blog) they use nothing within Moodle. They say that there is a possibility to use discussion forum and the professor insists that they use it, but they described it as very "lifeless". The students decide that they like to manage discussions in Skype chat between each other and they want to see who is online. Students decide that for the professor it would be too difficult because of the large amount of students online in one time.

Asked for suggestions what tools to use for learning, group IT students offers the common e-mail account, Google calendar (for administrative issues, for homework timetable), Moodle calendar (for homework timetable) and those tools what supports immediacy. Group ES offers to use common e-mail account, virtual lessons, video-conferencing, but the main reasons were - time and money saving for travelling to the University.

5 Conclusion

Moodle is the one of the most popular learning management systems. But too often learning management systems are used mainly for content delivery. Some researchers communicate that students in the learning process like to use tools they are familiar with in their everyday life. Web 2.0 tools are seen as very popular in the young people life. That allows authors to think that if it would be possible to find alternative tools to web 2.0 within Moodle learning process can be enhanced.

Research is made to find out what tools students are already using in their everyday life. Focus group interviews show that students have some experience with web 2.0 tools – discussion forum, blog, wiki. Earlier research shows that it is important because then students pay more attention to the content and to learning itself and are not distracted by problems related to tool usage. However there are students with very different experience and skills so it has to be taken into account. On the other hand focus group interviews show that students see some tools as "lifeless" in Moodle. Probably it is because tools are not integrated sufficiently in the course. And a lot of focus is on immediate interaction with peers. Results shows students are not too much willing to use the same tools for everyday life activities and same in the educational settings. There has to be research done to find out barriers for that.

Acknowledgement. The article is written with financial support of ESF project "Development of doctoral studies at Liepaja University" project Nr.2009/0127/1DP/1.1.2.1.2./09/IPIA/VIAA/018.

References

Cox, G., Carr, T., Hall, M.: Evaluating the use of synchronous communication in two blended courses. Journal of Computer Assisted Learning 20, 183–193 (2004)

Dede, C.: Comments on Greenhow, Robelia, and Hughes: Technologies that facilitate generating knowledge and possibly wisdom. Educational Researcher 38(4), 260–263 (2009), http://er.aera.net (accessed February 10, 2010)

Jackson, P.: Ten Challenges for Introducing Web-Supported Learning to Overseas Students in the Social sciences. Active Learning in Higher Education 4, 87 (2003)

Lomas, C., Burke, M., Page, C.L.: Collaboration tools. Educause (August 2008)

Otero, V., Peressini, D., Meymaris, K.A., Ford, P., Garvin, T., Harlow, D., Reidel, M., Waite, B., Mears, C.: Integrating Technology into Teacher Education: A Critical Framework for Implementing Reform. Journal of Teacher Education 56(8) (2005)

Ozsariyildiz, S., Beheshti, R.: Effects of teaching environments and digital media: the case of a parametric design systems course. In: Rebolj, D. (ed.) Bringing ITC Knowledge to Work, pp. 763–768. University Library Maribor (TUD), Maribor (2008)

Tomei, L.: Adapting Information and Communication Technologies for Effective Education, pp. 1–12. Idea Group Inc. (IGI), USA (2007)

Rogers, G.: History, learning technology and student achievement: Making the difference? Active Learning in Higher Education 5, 232 (2004)

Saunders, G., Klemming, F.: Integrating Technology into a Traditional Learning Environment: Reasons for and Risks of Success. Active Learning in Higher Education 4, 74 (2003)

Enhancing Collaborative Learning through Group Intelligence Software

Yin Leng Tan and Linda A. Macaulay

Manchester Business School, University of Manchester, M15 6PB, United Kingdom
yin.tan@manchester.ac.uk, linda.macaulay@manchester.ac.uk

Abstract. Employers increasingly demand not only academic excellence from graduates but also excellent interpersonal skills and the ability to work collaboratively in teams. This paper discusses the role of Group Intelligence software in helping to develop these higher order skills in the context of an enquiry based learning (EBL) project. The software supports teams in generating ideas, categorizing, prioritizing, voting and multi-criteria decision making and automatically generates a report of each team session. Students worked in a Group Intelligence lab designed to support both face to face and computer-mediated communication and employers provided feedback at two key points in the year long team project. Evaluation of the effectiveness of Group Intelligence software in collaborative learning was based on five key concepts of creativity, participation, productivity, engagement and understanding.

Keywords: Collaborative learning, enquiry based learning, group intelligence tool, team work.

1 Introduction

Groupware and computer-mediated communication are a significant development in higher education where academics strive to respond to the ever growing call from employers for graduates who are effective team players.

Enquiry based learning (EBL) is widely reported in the literature as an approach that encourages participation and creativity among student teams. *"Creativity is a type of learning process where the teacher and pupil are located in the same individual." Arthur Koestler, Novelist* Thus highlighting the importance of providing frameworks such as EBL where students can map out their own learning process and 'learn by doing'.

In this paper we describe an enquiry based learning project where a commercial Group Intelligence tool was employed to enhance collaborative learning within student teams. The paper starts with an overview of the key concepts associated with team based EBL and Group Intelligence tools and then follows with a description of the team project. Employer involvement in the project and their assessment of the level of achievement of the teams is presented. The paper concludes with an evaluation of the effectiveness of the Group Intelligence tools in enhancing collaborative learning among student teams.

M.D. Lytras et al. (Eds.): WSKS 2010, Part I, CCIS 111, pp. 453–459, 2010.

2 Theoretical Framework

This paper is positioned against the literature on collaborative learning, "collaborative learning" refers to a situation where learning involves groups of students working together, "mutually searching for understanding, solutions, or meanings, or creating a product" [1]. Findings from Alavi [2] indicate that collaborative learning supported by groupware could lead to higher level of learning than groups not using groupware.

A review of a number of studies on teamwork and computer-supported collaborative learning suggests that five key concepts of participation, creativity, productivity, engagement, and understanding are important. The theoretical framework and related literature are shown in Table 1.

Table 1. Theoretical framework of collaborative learning

Concepts	Related Literature
Participation: level of teamwork, participation in discussion	[3], [7], [8], [9], [11] and [13]
Productivity: level of achievement, quality of outcome	[8], [11] and [13]
Creativity: level of contribution of ideas, novelty	[5] and [9]
Engagement: level of motivation, passion for their work, enthusiasm	[5], [8] and [10]
Understanding: level of understanding of the problem, and application of theory to practice	[4] and [9]

3 Method

This section describes the method used for the EBL project, including the task, team arrangement, structure of the project, the involvement of the tutors and business mentors, and teamwork supported by the Group Intelligence Tool. The project was undertaken by first year students on the B.Sc Information Technology Management for Business (ITMB) degree.

3.1 The Task and Groups Arrangement

The task set for the EBL project was to examine a university website from the point of view of a business seeking advice, consultancy or access to results from research conducted by university staff, to identify problems and to redesign the site to solve those problems. The 45 undergraduate students were divided into eight teams of five or six. Each team had the freedom to arrive at their own solution to the problem by following the stages; problem definition; user requirements; scope of the solution; high-level design; detailed design; implementation; testing and evaluation; and demonstration and documentation.

3.2 Structure of the Team Project

The structure of the EBL project was a one-hour lecture and a two-hour tutorial session each week throughout the whole academic year. A further two two-hour drop-in technical support sessions were arranged in the second semester. The one-hour lecture provided students with information about the team project; prepared them for the week-by-week tasks; introduced theories associated with group and team working skills and group facilitation skills; and introduced techniques for information gathering, interviewing and user and system evaluation. The aim of the tutorial was to enable and encourage students to adopt an EBL approach. Students met with tutors to discuss their ideas and used the Group Intelligence Tool 'ThinkTank' in the first semester for problem definition and requirements gathering; it was used again in second semester for decision making.

3.3 Group Intelligence Software and Group Intelligence Lab

A Group Intelligence tool ThinkTank[1] was used to support the teamwork among the student teams. ThinkTank is an interactive, web-based team-space for brainstorming, organizing ideas, prioritizing, voting, consensus building and documentation. A group intelligence lab was also set up to support both face to face and computer-mediated communication.

A ThinkTank session was set up for each team. Once the session has been set up, the students interact with each other to come out with the solution. The facilitator who set up the sessions for the teams in ThinkTank thus acts as the instructor controlling the overall process of the discussion, providing encouragement and support to enable the students to take responsibility for what and how they learn.

A typical ThinkTank session contains the following activities: brainstorming and commenting ideas (10-15 minutes), categorizing ideas (10-15 minutes), prioritizing ideas (10-15 minutes), voting and generating reports (10-15 minutes). For example, to get the student teams to 'identify the problems of an existing university website', a session called 'Problem definition' was set up to help brainstorms ideas about the users of the system and what types of business knowledge they might want access.

3.4 Academic Tutors and Employer Mentors

For EBL to be effective, apart from getting students to complete a task, it is important that the process is supportive [5] and [9]. Each team was also assigned an academic tutor and a business mentor. The role of the tutors was to provide support to the student teams regarding their project. Tutors also acted as assessors for the group presentations and provided individual assessment of each team member. The student teams met with their tutors on a weekly basis for an hour at the tutorial session. The business mentors provided extra-curricular support for the teams. Student teams met with their mentors twice a year. The meeting arrangements with the mentors were organised by the student teams. The business mentors in the academic year of 2007-08 were from Deloitte, BBC, Procter & Gamble and Unilever.

4 Outcomes

As a result of the EBL approach and teamwork supported by ThinkTank, six weeks into the team project the student teams were able to produce their interim results

[1] ThinkTank is the trademark of GroupSystems. See www.groupsystems.com

(problems, visions, target users and solutions) with ideas ranging from virtual library to social networking websites. The outcomes were presented at the first ITMB employers' event which was attended by members of ITMB Supporters Club. The ITMB Supporters Club is a group of employers who support the ITMB programme and meet twice a year to network with students and staff to exchange latest news and identify future opportunities for interaction.

The first ITMB employers' event was held on the 6th November 2007, the employers attending the event included IBM, Deloitte, Logica CMG, Royal Bank of Scotland (RBS), RM, Procter and Gamble, E-Skills UK, BT, SAP, Unilever, edge IPK, BBC and Accenture. At the event, the student teams presented their ideas and answered questions asked by employers.

The semester two ITMB employers' event was held on the 29th April 2008, employers attending included IBM, Accenture, LogicaCMG, Unilever, Deloitte, Network Rail, Procter and Gamble, e-Skills UK, Informed Solutions, RM, BT, and RBS. At this event, the student teams were required to produce posters and demonstrate their final software prototype to employers. An award of the Unilever Prize for best group poster and demonstration was presented at the end of the event. The judging of the group posters/demonstrations was carried out by a panel of employers based on the five concepts as outlined in section 2; creativity (idea originality and novelty), level of participation, engagement of the team members, productivity (completeness of the product), and level of understanding (by applying theory to practice).

5 Feedback

This section presents feedback gathered from students and employers.

5.1 Student Feedback

Questionnaires were distributed to students requesting feedback on their perception of the level of participation, creativity, productivity, engagement and understanding. The results from 35 responses are summarized below:

Participation: Over 90 percent of the students agreed that the feature of anonymity in ThinkTank allowed them to participate more freely when compared to traditional face-to-face meetings; despite this, 50 percent of the students indicated that they would have liked the level of their input to be recognised when using computer-mediated collaborative tools.

Productivity: Some 75 percent of the students agreed that the feature of parallel input in ThinkTank increased their productivity during a brainstorm session. Although more ideas meant that the quality of ideas might have been lowered, they also agreed that anonymity reduced social pressure and inputs were more honest.

Creativity: In a traditional meeting, very often ideas will emanate from one or two members of the group. The results showed that students were less likely to be influenced by fellow team members in ThinkTank; therefore, ideas can be freely expressed. However, students have a tendency to read other members' ideas during a brainstorm process, which could lower diversity of ideas as their inputs could be affected by other's ideas and time constraints for each activity in ThinkTank.

Engagement: Over 80 percent of the students generally felt that they were able to contribute individually to their team. Findings indicate lower motivation in teamwork when ThinkTank is used; however, students felt the task was more important to them when using ThinkTank compared to a traditional face-to-face meeting.

Understanding: Approximately 70 percent of the students agreed that they were able to directly convert the information/knowledge they gathered/learned into practice. The process of carrying out a ThinkTank session also allowed students to trigger a deeper understanding of their project.

5.2 Employer Feedback

The employer feedback of the EBL project was carried out at the ITMB employers' event which held on 29th April 2008. The employer feedback was conducted by student demonstration to the employers, and questions were then asked by the employers to the student teams. A feedback form based on the five concepts of participation, productivity, creativity, engagement and understanding for each team was completed by the employers.

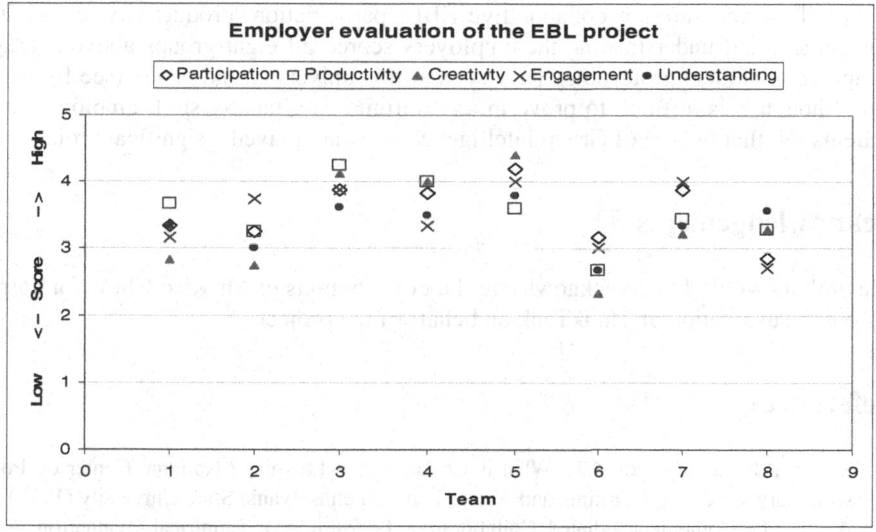

Fig. 1. Employer evaluation of the student teams based on the five concepts: participation, productivity, creativity, engagement, and understanding

Nine employers from IBM, Accenture, e-Skills UK, Deloitte, Unilever, BT and Informed Solutions participated in the project evaluation. A total of 51 copies of the evaluation forms were received. *Figure 1* shows the employers' feedback of the student teams based on their level of participation, productivity, creativity, engagement and understanding.

6 Conclusion

The Group Intelligence software enhanced collaborative learning in a number of important ways. The brainstorming sessions early in the project required each student to contribute via ThinkTank, contributions were anonymous and helped some students overcome the initial concerns about participating within their newly formed team. Students commented on each others ideas and the online discussion was followed by off-line discussion, thus encouraging participation in group discussion from the outset.

Each team session including all brainstorm ideas and comments were captured in the ThinkTank database and at the end of the session a report automatically generated. This contributed considerably to the productivity of the student teams and enabled them to spend time improving the quality of their reports rather than just capturing the basic outcome.

More students contributed ideas, more discussion of options took place during the ThinkTank prioritisation session leading in turn to the identification of new or new combinations of ideas and ultimately to students being more creative.

The level of debate increased and students certainly appeared more passionate than usual about the decisions made by their team, in particular, wanting to find out how their proposed solution would compare with that of their competitors i.e the other teams. Proposed solutions had to be converted into actual software based solutions, hence requiring a deep and full understanding of their proposal.

On all the measures of collaborative EBL: participation; productivity; creativity; engagement and understanding the employers scored all eight groups above average compared to student groups they have seen at this university and others (see figure 1) and although it is difficult to prove in any definite way faculty staff, employers and students felt that the use of Group Intelligence software played a significant role.

Acknowledgements

The authors would like to acknowledge the contributions of Mr Rico Chow for carrying out the evaluation of ThinkTank on behalf of the project.

References

1. Smith, B.L., MacGregor, J.T.: What is Collaborative Learning? National Center on Postsecondary Teaching, Learning, and Assessment at Pennsylvania State University (1992)
2. Alavi, M.: Computer-mediated Collaborative Learning: An Empirical Evaluation. MIS Quarterly 18, 159–174 (1994)
3. Aiken, M., Govindarajulu, C.D., Horgan, D.: Using a Group Decision Support System for School-based Decision Making. Education 115(3), 420–425 (1995)
4. Cocea, M., Weibelzahl, S.: Can Log Files Analysis Estimate Learners' Level of Motivation?. In: 14th Workshop on Adaptivity and User Modeling in Interactive Systems, October 9-11 (2006)
5. Edelson, D.C., Gordin, D.N., Pea, R.D.: Addressing the Challenges of Inquiry-Based Learning Through Technology and Curriculum Design. The Journal of Learning Science 8(3&4), 391–450 (1999)

6. Faulkner, R.: Wired Class Lets Everyone Talk at Once, The Hamilton Spectator, http://groupsystems.files.wordpress.com/2007/09/mohawk-college-class-participation.pdf
7. Guzzo, R., Dickson, M.W.: Teams in Organizations: Recent Research on Performance and Effectiveness. Annual Review of Psychology 47, 307–338 (1996)
8. Karau, S.J., Williams, K.D.: Social loafing: A meta-analytic review and theoretical integration. Journal of Personality and Social Psychology 65, 681–706 (1993)
9. Kahn, P., O'Rourke, K.: Understanding Enquiry-based Learning (EBL). In: Barrett, T., Mac Labhrainn, I., Fallon, H. (eds.) Handbook of Enquiry & Problem Based Learning Galway, CELT, pp. 1–12 (2005), http://www.nuigalway.ie/celt/pblbook/
10. Kravitz, D., Martin, B.: Ringelmann Rediscovered: The Original Article. Journal of Personality and Social Psychology 50, 936–941 (1986)
11. Nunamaker, J., Briggs, R., Mittleman, D., Vogel, D., Balthazard, P.: Lessons from a Dozen Years of Group Support Systems Research: a Discussion of Lab and Field Findings. Journal of Management Information Systems 13(3), 163–207 (1996)
12. Lee, V.S., Greene, D.B., Odom, F., Schechter, E., Slatta, R.W.: What is Inquiry-Guided Learning? In: Virginia, S.L. (ed.) Teaching and Learning Through Inquiry: A Guidebook for Institutions and Instructors Virginia. Stylus Publishing, Sterling (2004)
13. Manning, L.M., Riordan, C.A.: Using Groupware Software to Support Collaborative Learning in Economics. Journal of Economic Education, 244–252 (Summer 2000)

A Queuing Theory and Systems Modeling Course Based on Unified Modeling Language (UML)

Athanasios Perdos, George Stephanides, and Alexander Chatzigeorgiou

University of Macedonia, Applied Informatics, Egnatias 156,
54006 Thessaloniki, Greece
{perdos,steph,achat}@uom.gr

Abstract. This paper presents the implementation of a new teaching method in the way that a queuing theory and systems modeling or simulation course can be done. It also presents how this method was evaluated by the teachers and the students that attended the course and answered a questionnaire. This course is based on the use of Unified Modeling Language (UML) as the mean to teach modeling of discrete event systems such as queues and networks and not on Mathematics that sometimes is too difficult for students to understand.

Keywords: UML, Queuing Theory, Simulation, Network Modeling, Teaching Method.

1 Introduction

The great majority of courses relevant to network modeling and simulation or queues require very good knowledge of Mathematics. Lots of problems have arisen because students usually lack the demanded background in mathematics. The teaching method that has been followed in this area, involved the following aspects: a) Presentation of basic concepts of queuing theory, b) Presentation of the mathematical model, c) Evaluation of some simulation results. The disadvantages of this method are the following: a) It requires a very good knowledge of mathematics to understand the equations that describe the theoretical model, b) Some types of queues are very difficult to model using mathematics. For some other types it is rather impossible to use mathematics in order to model them, c) It demands a great amount of efforts to create a simulation software program.

Our emphasis in this paper is to describe and evaluate an innovating teaching method which purpose is two fold. First, it can serve as the basis for a course released from the problems that have been mentioned above. This method is based on the Unified Modeling Language and we believe that can ease the work both of educators and students because anyone that studies informatics has obtained the demanded knowledge for object oriented methods since the first or second year. Secondly, since UML is the tool to model it is possible to generate code for a simulation program using a tool such as Rational Rose [1].

M.D. Lytras et al. (Eds.): WSKS 2010, Part I, CCIS 111, pp. 460–464, 2010.

2 Course Schedule

2.1 Basic Concepts of Queuing Theory

Queuing theorists in order to classify queues use a shorthand notation called the Kendall notation [2], which defines the class A/S/m/c/p/SD as follows:

"A" is the interarrival time distribution. "S" describes the service time distribution. "m" denotes the number of servers available to give service to jobs in queue. "c" defines the capacity of the buffer. If c is unspecified, it is assumed to be infinite. "p" defines the maximum number of jobs. If p is unspecified, it is assumed to be infinite. "SD" stands for service discipline which is a very important aspect of queues and is related to the way that a server decides which job in the queue to pick next for service.

Some other significant variables of queuing theory are: "τ" = interarrival time. It is the time between two successive arrivals. "λ" = 1/E[τ] (E[τ] is the expectation of τ). It is the mean arrival rate. "s" =service time per job. "μ" =1/E[s]. It is the mean service rate per server. If there are m servers in a system then the total service rate is mμ. "n" = number of jobs in the system. This is also called queue length. "nq" =number of jobs waiting to start service. "ns" = number of jobs currently being served. "r" = response time. It is the time spent in the system, which includes both the waiting time for service and the service time. "w" = waiting time. It is the time interval between job's arrival time and the instant that the job starts service. Good references for queuing equations are the following: [3], [4], [5].

2.2 UML Diagrams

A short presentation of the diagram types and their characteristics must be presented before queues modeled using UML [6], [7], [8]. Some of the class diagrams that model this system are:

Queue Service Disciplines are specified in the following diagram.

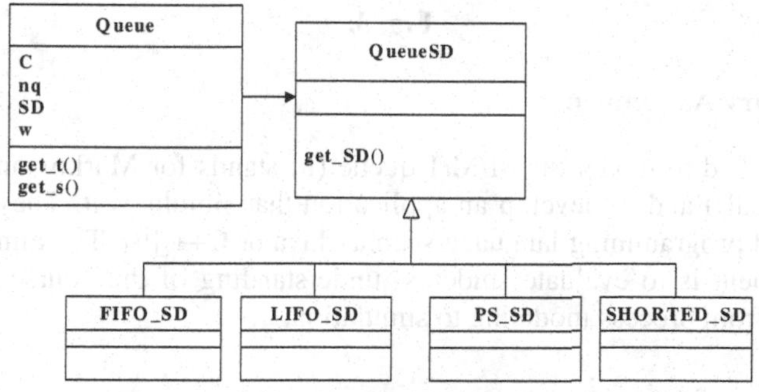

Fig. 1. Queue Service Discipline Class Diagram

For arrivals and service times the diagram for the distributions that produce random times is the following:

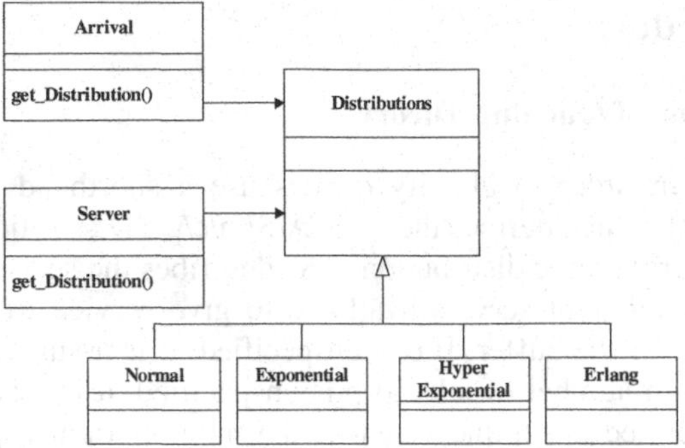

Fig. 2. Distributions

Beyond the class diagrams it is useful to show how the system is modeled using activities, and state diagrams.

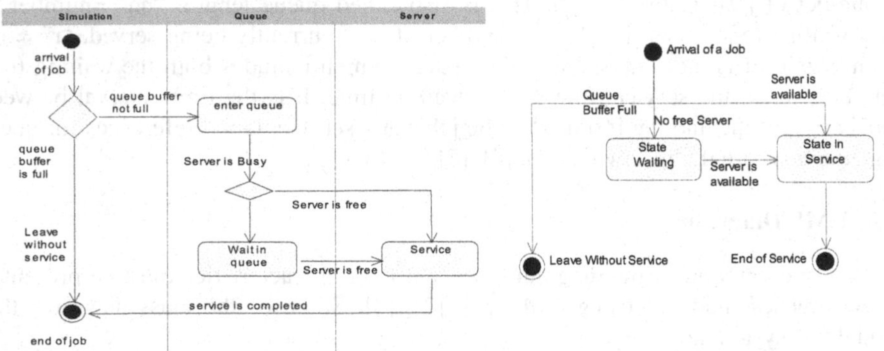

a) Activity Diagram Using Swimlanes b) State Machine Diagram for a Job

Fig. 3.

2.3 Laboratory Assignment

Students are asked to model the M/M/1 queue (M stands for Markovian or memoryless (exponential)) and to develop an application that simulates it. They can use any object oriented programming language such as Java or C++ [9]. The aim of this laboratory assignment is to evaluate students' understanding of the course and see how they can pass from process modeling to simulation.

3 Evaluation of the Teaching Method

From our side we believe that using UML to model not only queues and networks but any system gives a good understanding about the system properties and the interaction between its parts. Therefore students obtain the appropriate knowledge easily and without facing problems with the high level of mathematics that is required. Beyond the teaching process we consider that is easier for students to develop all the classes, that the system consists of and create an integrated application.

Our opinion about the way that the course was implemented is definitely influenced by our perceptions and beliefs. In order to obtain a more integrated feedback, a questionnaire was given to 81 students. Therefore, we had the opportunity to work out their answers and see how they evaluate our teaching method. A part of the questionnaire and the answers follow.

Table 1. Questions and Answers

	Question	1	2	3	4	5
Q1	It is not difficult to model systems using queuing theory mathematical model	Disagree				Agree
		1	2	3	4	5
		5	29	23	22	2
Q2	UML helps in understanding queuing theory	Disagree				Agree
		1	2	3	4	5
				2	39	40
Q3	There is a loss of information and there is a problem to understand queuing theory concepts when a system is modeled by UML	Disagree			Agree	
		1	2	3	4	5
		20	46	9	6	
Q4	Connection and interaction between the parts or objects of a system is presented better by mathematics or by UML	Mathematics				UML
		1	2	3	4	5
		1	4	7	27	42
Q5	Would you prefer to use UML or Mathematics, as basis in order to create simulation	Mathematics				UML
		1	2	3	4	5
				3	31	46
Q6	An economic model can be modelled and simulated better by the equations of the mathematical model or by UML diagrams	Mathematics				UML
		1	2	3	4	5
		2	8	15	34	22
Q7	Do you prefer a course about queuing theory based in mathematics or in UML	Mathematics				UML
		1	2	3	4	5
		3	4	16	38	20

It is obvious that students recognize from questions 1 and 2, that using UML compare to mathematics, is a better and easier way to model and understand queuing systems

In addition question 3 shows that students consider that there is not any loss of information when a system is modeled using UML and that there is not any problem understanding queuing theory concepts. They also strongly believe (question 4) that the connection and the interaction between a system's parts, is better presented by UML. Actually this question is very important for us, because a critical part of the teaching method relies in this concept.

The question 5 shows that students strongly believe that UML is better tool to design and develop software simulation for queuing systems. Students developed simulation software in the lab using the mathematical model in the beginning and using UML afterwards. Thus, they were able to see the differences and understand what method is more suitable for developing software.

Since our department of Applied Informatics has a lot of economic courses we wanted to see what students' opinion is about modeling an economic system. It is obvious from question 6 that students believe that UML and queuing theory can easily combined to model economic systems.

The last question that is presented in this paper was about students' opinion about the course schedule. We came in conclusion that students would like to see some mathematical equations from queuing theory but it seems that they believe it is better to hide the high level mathematical equations and focus on UML diagrams

4 Conclusion and Future Work

The outcomes from the questionnaire were really encouraging to continue this transition from the mathematical model to UML, as a mean to teach queuing theory or systems. Beyond the teaching process that has to be improved since we have much more experience, our aim is to develop a software tool that will be able to combine UML and object – oriented programming languages. This software will give the user the opportunity to design and model any queuing system such as networks, computer processors, and economic systems using UML.

References

1. http://www.rational.com/uml
2. Jain, R.: The Art of Computer Systems Performance Analysis: Techniques for Experimental Design, Measurement, Simulation, and Modeling. John Wiley & Sons, Inc., Chichester (1991)
3. Leigh, J.R.: Modelling and Simulation. Peter Peregvinus Ltd., London (1983)
4. Hoever Stewart, V., Perry Ronald, F.: Simulation, A Problem-Solving Approach. Addison-Wesley Publishing Company, Reading (1989)
5. Morse Philip, M.: Queues, Inventories and Maintenance. John Willey, New York (1967)
6. Quatrain, T.: Visual Modeling with Rational Rose and UML. Addison Wesley Longman, Inc., Reading (1998)
7. Kruchten, P.: The Rational Unified Process – An Introduction. Addison Wesley Longman, Inc., Reading (1998)
8. Booch, G., Rumbaugh, J., Jacobson, I.: The Unified Modeling Language User Guide. Addison Wesley Longman, Inc., Reading (1999)
9. Perdos, A., Chatzigeorgiou, A., Stephanides, G.: Simulation Software for a Network Modelling Lab. In: Third IEEE International Conference on Advanced Learning Technologies (ICALT 2003), p. 290 (2003)

`The Lived Experience of Climate Change´: An Interdisciplinary and Competence-Based Masters Track Using Open Educational Resources and Virtual Mobility

Dina Abbott, Joop De Kraker, Paquita Pérez, Catharien Terwisscha van Scheltinga, Patrick Willems, and Gordon Wilson[1,*]

[1] Development Policy and Practice, The Open University, Walton Hall, Milton Keynes, MK7 6AA, UK

Abstract. Drawing on the authors' involvement in a European Union Erasmus project, this paper explores a new holistic approach to climate change education which uses as a source of active/social learning and knowledge construction the diversity of different disciplinary and sectoral approaches. We further argue for a corresponding pedagogy based on developing transboundary competences where the communicative engagement across space and time, and between diverse perspectives and standpoints, is ICT-enabled. Meeting these challenges is a normative goal, not only for this expanded interdisciplinary approach to climate change education, but also for a global resolution of the climate change issue itself.

Keywords: Climate Change, Diversity, Interdisciplinary, Lived Experience, Communicative Engagement, Transboundary Competence, Virtual Mobility.

1 Introduction

Climate Change is strongly contested, and not only in well-publicized debates between most climate scientists who contend that anthropogenic activity is causing global warming and the skeptical minority. It occurs within the former group over the extent and rate of change, and its ecological and socio-economic impacts.

Contestation tends to take place *within* disciplines – for example, within climate science and within economics. In the world of policy and action, however, contestation also occurs *between* disciplines, between academics and practitioners, and between interest-based knowledge systems. The argument of this paper is that we should celebrate such diversity. Following Hulme [1], we see contestation as a crucial resource for learning and 'better' action rather than as an impediment to action..

What does our argument mean for climate change education? The paper authors are currently addressing the question through a European Union (EU) Erasmus project, 'The lived experience of climate change: elearning and virtual mobility', which brings together 8 Universities across 6 EU countries to support Masters study in the area. The project is creating curriculum resources (which will become open educational

* Corresponding author.

M.D. Lytras et al. (Eds.): WSKS 2010, Part I, CCIS 111, pp. 465–469, 2010.

resources), technology-supported learning communities and a platform for virtual mobility of students

Three imperatives drive the project: firstly, as educators, it is our duty to expose students to the range of perspectives and knowledges about climate change. Secondly it is particularly important to expose them to knowledge of the sectors on which climate change impacts directly: the natural resource sectors where water is of paramount importance. Thirdly, we should enable student interaction with diverse knowledges by developing competences for communicative engagement.

These imperatives form Sections 2, 3 and 4 below, while in Section 5 we examine the common motif of 'engagement' which runs through the previous sections.

2 Expanding the Knowledge Base of Climate Change Education

Climate change and its consequences for the functioning of human societies represent a defining challenge in the 21st century. Led initially by natural scientists, latterly other sciences have addressed the climate change theme: political science with respect to governance issues [2] and economics with respect to its costs and livelihood impacts [3].

Just as research on climate change has been dominated by the sciences, so too has University teaching. However, while reproduction of disciplinary specialists through teaching is both inevitable and also commendable in order to gain in-depth insights into particular aspects of climate change, the question arises as to what is missing.

To answer this question we start with the subject, the global challenge of climate change. Such challenges rarely fall neatly within the epistemological boundaries established by academic disciplines. This observation remains the most compelling reason for interdisciplinary approaches to the study of real-world problems [4] such as climate change, where exploration at the boundary interfaces of academic disciplines represents opportunities for gaining insights which would otherwise remain hidden.

The 'Lived experience of climate change' (LECHe) project does not only involve several institutions and countries, but also natural science, engineering and social science to create an interdisciplinary Masters curriculum. As implied by the title, however, 'The lived experience' expands the notion of interdisciplinarity to recognize the validity of the knowledges of professional practitioners and ordinary citizens. In contrast to academic disciplines, such knowledges are primarily tacit, being based on experience and shaped by socio-economic factors and life events.

Incorporating lived experience into curriculum alongside academic disciplinary knowledges is a challenge. In our project, and in academic deliberation generally, the challenge raises the question of how to conceptualize 'lived experience'. As a starting point we postulate that it is knowledge shaped by the temporal dimension of personal and collective histories gathered over generations, the broader political and economic influences which shape our lives both in the global North and South, our engagements with other knowledges, and our perceptions of biophysical impacts associated with climate change that challenge our lives and livelihoods. The dynamics of how these factors interact to generate, perpetuate and evolve 'lived experience' have not been explored in depth. Thus even at the starting point of deconstructing the concept of lived experience, there is a huge potential to expand and develop our knowledge of climate change.

Equally, the methodological complexity of building a research design of 'lived experience' offers further potential to move from known, safe disciplinary boundaries for Masters students to cross-disciplinary, unfamiliar ones and adopt multi-method approaches. Students also realize that research does not stop at the empirical or writing stage and that knowledge continues to be created through action, sometimes action that generates policy. For example, scientific data can be complemented by participatory action research (PAR) which includes a range of stakeholders throughout the research process to capture knowledge from diverse voices, in turn generating potential to feed into policy on mitigation and adaptation. Alongside are questions on how to build methodological rigor. Underlying all are ethical and moral questions of fieldwork led by relatively affluent academics and students investigating lived experiences of marginalized groups in both Europe and developing countries. Of course such investigations are needed as otherwise these groups tend to be forgotten, but reflection of this kind inevitably leads to a wider understanding of climate change.

We do not, however, have to build the above conceptual and methodological understandings anew. They are at least latent in the natural resource sectors on which climate change impacts directly, to which we now turn.

3 Incorporating Natural Resource Expertise: The Case of Water

There are particular reasons for including natural resource expertise in curriculum on the lived experience of climate change. Firstly, our basic human needs are dependent on access to natural resources, such access being critically affected by climate change. Secondly, natural resource expertise is directly concerned with real-world problem solving to enable continuing access. Following on and thirdly, the expertise is inherently multi-disciplinary, leading to the possibility of interdisciplinary solutions.

In the LECHe project we focus on expertise associated with the water sector as water is arguably the most basic of natural resources as the source of food and life. More specifically, this sectoral expertise contributes to climate change curriculum and our understanding of its lived experience in the LECHe project through combining:

Earth System Sciences and the impact of climate change on rainfall, its spatial patterns, frequency and severity, whether in the form of droughts or floods.

Technology, where environmental authorities and engineers play an important role in the enhanced control of water systems which are necessary for successful climate change adaptation.

Management, especially decentralized water management based on multiple-stakeholder cooperation and flexible adaptation to uncertainty induced by climate change.

Decentralized water management recognizes the potential of multi-stakeholder cooperation for creativity and innovation through active (or social) 'learning alliances' [5]. Active learning (or "social learning" [6]), for example within citizen user groups, or between these groups and scientists and policy makers, aspires to a shared understanding of the water system and the challenges to it in order to deal with complexity and uncertainty. The concept of active/social learning is particularly appropriate to the LECHe project where the envisaged learning communities and engagement through virtual mobility may be seen as directly experiencing social (or active) learning 'by doing'.

4 Virtual Mobility and Open Access in a Competence-Based Approach

As argued above, students should be exposed to a range of climate change perspectives. Moreover, to use diversity as a source of inspiration and better solutions instead of conflict and political paralysis, students should think, communicate, collaborate and integrate across knowledge boundaries. We call this 'transboundary competence' [7], on which social learning in professional practice is based.

In the LECHe project, this means that we need a learning environment that enables students to communicate, collaborate and reflect with their peers, teachers and supervisors and with the diverse experiential knowledges of climate change. Such a learning environment should build on the principles of virtual mobility and open access to educational resources. Virtual mobility, defined as 'using information and communication technologies (ICT) to obtain the benefits [of] physical mobility, but without the need to travel' (eLearningEuropa.info), allows, through an integrated Virtual Learning Environment, the formation of 'learning communities' [8]. Here, Masters students and staff across Europe meet, study, discuss and compare 'lived experiences of climate change' and scientific analyses thereof. In addition, we envisage 'open' learning communities at the science-society-policy interface where, students, teachers and researchers can engage with non-academics.

In view of the climate change topic, a major added advantage is the reduction in carbon footprint achieved with online development and exploitation of the modules. This reduction may amount to factor 8-20 [9, 10], if virtual mobility is used in the design instead of face-to-face delivery. The environmental impact (in terms of energy use and CO2-emissions) of internationalisation in higher education has scarcely been investigated, and its effect seems to be underestimated (or disregarded). Thus, in our approach virtual mobility is both the medium and (part of) the message.

5 Conclusion

Common to the above sections is that the lived experience of climate change is a process of engagement between diverse influences and perspectives. In the LECHe project, 'engagement' is:

- An object of study, being important for cooperative approaches to natural resource management and for evolving lived experience. 'Engagement' is key to the argument in Sections 2 and 3, being the means which turns diversity of knowledges into resources for social learning and action
- The subject of study, being the foundation of the transboundary competence approach to learning which is described in Section 4.

We adopt a broadly analytical approach to communicative engagement as an object of study, there being a wealth of both promotional writing [11] and critical studies [12]. As subject, we adopt a more normative stance – we are actively promoting knowledge construction through learning communities and virtual mobility as the basis of our pedagogy. The challenge of using ICTs to support this pedagogy goes beyond formal education, however. It is at the heart of whether or not we can, as one world, rise to the challenge of global issues such as climate change. This is the ultimate aim of the LECHe project – to develop ways of building the necessary cross-ontological capabilities to respond to the global climate change challenge.

References

1. Hulme, M.: Why we disagree about climate change: understanding controversy, inaction and opportunity. Cambridge University Press, Cambridge (2009)
2. Breitmeier, H.: The Legitimacy of International Regimes. Ashgate, Aldershot (2008)
3. Stern Review.:The economics of climate change. Cambridge University Press, Cambridge (2006)
4. Mohan, G., Wilson, G.: The antagonistic relevance of development studies. Progress in Development Studies 5(4), 261–278 (2005)
5. Ashley, R.M., Newman, R., Molyneux-Hodgson, S., Blanksby, J.: Active learning: building the capacity to adapt urban drainage to climate change. In: Proceedings of the 11th International Conference on Urban Drainage, Edinburgh, Scotland, August 31-September 5, p. 10 (2008)
6. Pahl-Wostl, C.: Requirements for adaptive water management. In: Adaptive and Integrated Water Management. Coping with Complexity and Uncertainty, pp. 1–22. Springer, Heidelberg (2008) ISBN 978-3-540-75940-9
7. De Kraker, J., Lansu, A., Van Dam-Micras, M.C.: Competences and competence-based learning for sustainable development. In: de Kraker, J., Lansu, A., van Dam-Mieras, M.C. (eds.) Crossing Boundaries. Innovative Learning for Sustainable Development in Higher Education, pp. 103–114. Verlag für Akademische Schriften, Frankfurt am Main (2007), http://dspace.ou.nl/handle/1820/2409 (retrieved)
8. De Kraker, J., Cörvers, R., Ivens, W., Lansu, A., Van Dam-Mieras, R.: Crossing boundaries – competence-based learning for sustainable development in a virtual mobility setting. Paper Presented at the 4th World Environmental Education Congress, Durban, South Africa (2007), http://dspace.ou.nl/handle/1820/2375 (retrieved)
9. Roy, R., Potter, S., Yarrow, K.: Designing low carbon higher education systems. Environmental impacts of campus and distance learning systems. International Journal of Sustainability in Higher Education 9(2), 116–130 (2008)
10. Pérez Salgado, F.: Online onderwijs en duurzaamheid: een groene inktvlek', School of Science, Open Universiteit Nederland (2008)
11. Chambers, R.: Whose Reality Counts? Putting the last first. Intermediate Technology Publications, London (1997)
12. Hickey, S., Mohan, G. (eds.): Participation. From Tyranny to Transformation? Zed Books, London (2004)

Student Performance in Online Project Management Courses: A Data Mining Approach

Constanta-Nicoleta Bodea, Vasile Bodea, and Radu Mogos

The Academy of Economic Studies, Calea Dorobanti, no. 15-17, Sector 1, 010552 Bucharest, Romania
bodea@ase.ro, vbodea@ase.ro, mogos.radu@gmail.com

Abstract. The paper presents the application of data mining for analyzing performance of students enrolled in an online two-year master degree programme in project management. The main data sources for the mining process are the survey made for gathering students' opinions, the operational database with the students' records and data regarding students activities recorded by the e-learning platform. More than 180 students have responded and more than 150 distinct characteristics/ variable per student were identified. Due the large number of variables data mining is a recommended approach to analysis data. Clustering, classification and association rules were employed in order to identify the factor explaining students' performance. The results are very encouraging and suggest several future developments.

Keywords: Data mining, e-learning, project management, student performance.

1 Introduction

The research in e-learning domain is facilitate by the extensive amount of data stored by the e-learning systems, Most of these systems have the ability to collect data about the student activities, tracking navigational pathways through educational resources, time spent on various topics, or number of visits. Also, the e-learning systems capture data about the amount and type of resources usage. This data often are the basis of the e-learning research.

One way to do research in e-learning is data mining. By data mining, it is possible to discover patterns to be used in predicting student behavior and efficient allocation of resources. Many case studies on data mining techniques in education are cited in the literature (Luan, 2002), (Ma & al, 2000), (Barros & Verdejo, 2000), (Ranjan & Malik, 2007). These case studies aim at predictions of student performance, mainly through cluster analysis to identify relevant types of students. (Delavari & al, 2005) proposed a model for the application of data mining in higher education. (Shyamala & Rajagopalan, 2006) developed a model to find similar patterns from the data gathered and to make predication about students' performance.

(Luan, Zhai, Chen, Chow, Chang & Zhao, 2004) presented different case studies on educational data mining. One of these studies intended to highlight factors that determine the academic success of first-year students. The methods used are: classification and regression trees and neural networks. There were generated decisions trees,

M.D. Lytras et al. (Eds.): WSKS 2010, Part I, CCIS 111, pp. 470–479, 2010.

and association rules. A sensitivity analysis was performed to analyze factors. Variables considered were demographic variables and performance indicators before college. By this analysis can be achieved overall average prediction in the year. The analysis carried out by two classes of methods showed that the most important factors for academic success in first year of college are SAT scores (average of high school equivalent) and position in the rankings achieved on average in high school.

2 Research Objective and Methodology

The research objective is to identify the main factors affecting the student's performance in e-learning environment. The main research questions are:

- Which are the most important factors affecting the student performance in e-learning environments?
- How overall student satisfaction influences the students' e-learning performance and which are the specific situations?
- How knowledge background, graduated faculty and student activity on the platform affect the students' performance and in which cases?
- Which is the relation between evaluation relevancy and performance in e-learning (relation based on communication involvement, communication efficiency, online activities involvement and the teacher impact) and how can be described this relation?
- How the time spent in front of the computer influence the activity on the platform and the performance in e-learning environments (for the second year)?
- Which are the most important factors affecting the students. performance regarding the platform satisfaction?
- Which are the association rules between attributes that describe the way in which the students' initial requirements were met? Which is the difference between the situation when general association rules were generated and the one where class association rules are mined?

The research is done using the data gathering from students enrolled in an online master degree programme in project management. This programme is delivered as an online programme and a traditional one by the Academy of Economic Studies, the biggest Romanian university in economics and business administration.

A survey was made to collect students. opinions about the online programme, in general, and specifically, regarding the e-learning platform, the educational resources available online, the communication with trainers, the assessment, the practical approach of different disciplines. The questionnaire was developed in order to collect a large amount of interesting information. The questionnaire is structured into five main parts:

- questions regarding organization aspects and technical platform;
- trainee's needs (motivation to participate into an online education programme);
- trainee's commitment towards the project management educational programme;
- syllabus and expectations from training providers;
- trainers' involvement - trainers' involvement.

Both open and multiple-choice questions were addressed. The questionnaire was given to 400 students enrolled in a two-year master programme of project management. 52 students enrolled in their 1st year of study and 129 students in their last year responded. The data included in filled questionnaires was processed and recorded in an excel database, for further analysis.

The performance measures are defined based on the following elements:

- The grades at all 14 disciplines scheduled in the first academic year and 6 disciplines included in the curricula for the second year.
- The practical scores at all 14 disciplines scheduled in the first academic year and 6 disciplines included in the curricula for the second year.
- Number of failures at first academic year exams
- Number of failures at second year exams

This data, except project scores was taken from **the operational database**, administered at university level. The practical scores, as part of grades, were available on the **e-learning platform**, all the professor reporting on the platform all assessment components, such as: tests, project, and final exam, at all disciplines.

The performance measures are:

- Grade Point Average in the first academic year (GPA_I)
- Grade Point Average in the second academic year (GPA_II)
- Practical Score Average in first academic year (PSA_I)
- Practical Score Average in the second academic year (PSA_II)
- Aggregated Performance in first academic year (EVALUATION_PERFORMANCE_CLASS_I)
- Aggregated Performance in the second academic year (EVALUATION_PERFORMANCE_CLASS_I)

EVALUATION_PERFORMANCE_CLASS_I is defined as follow:

EVALUATION_PERFORMANCE_CLASS_I = 0, if GPA_I is between 6 and 7
EVALUATION_PERFORMANCE_CLASS_I = 1, if GPA_I is between 7.01 and 8 and over 3 failed exams
EVALUATION_PERFORMANCE_CLASS_I = 2, if GPA_I is between 7.01 and 8 and less than 2 failed exams
EVALUATION_PERFORMANCE_CLASS_I = 3, if GPA_I is over 8.01 and less than 2 failed exams

EVALUATION_PERFORMANCE_CLASS_II is similarly defined, using GPA and number of failures from the second academic year.

In order to identify the main factors affecting the student's performance in e-learning environment some additional data regarding student activities on the virtual space was gathering based on the statistics provided by the e-learning platform.The Moodle platform offers analytical and graphical statistics regarding the student activity, such as: the number of platform access, per day, month, semester, year, entire programme, the number of new subject initiated by a student, the time spent on the virtual space, the area of virtual space visited by the student. Figure 1 presents some of the facilities offered by Moodle. As we can see, some students have a uniform platform accessing pattern, others access platform only during the exam period, and others did not use the platform, using additional communication solutions (e-mail groups) in order to be informed.

Based on the information provided by the e-learning platform, the following characteristics were defined for each student:

- Maximum_access_number_Class,
- Platform_access_total_number_Class
- Uniformity_Class
- Maximum_access _number per semester
- Number of subject _initiatives
- Platform_access_total _number,

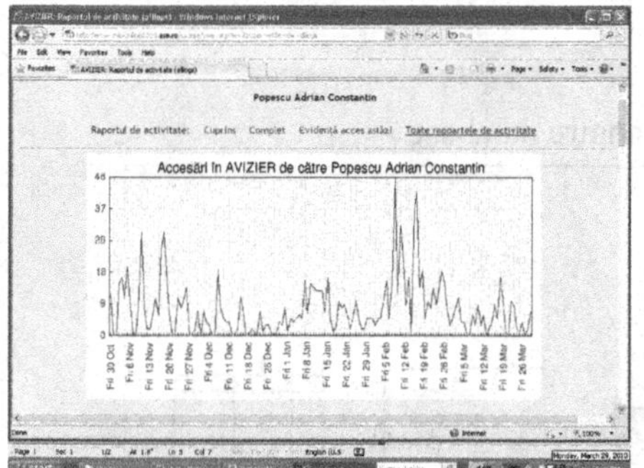

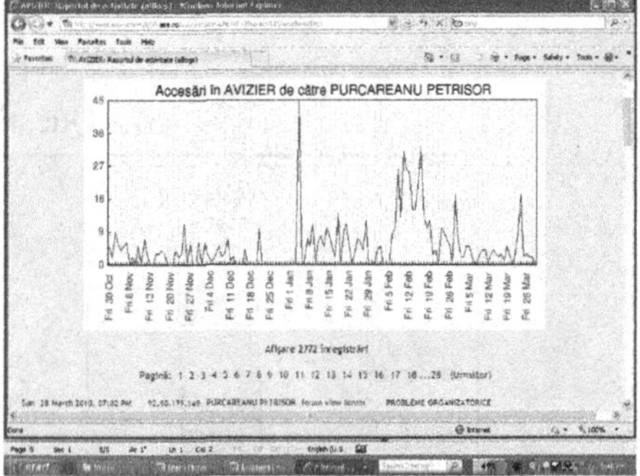

Fig. 1. Statistics regarding the student activities provided by e-learning platform

Figure 2 presents this three main data sources used in the data mining process. During the Data preparation and Data modeling phases, only data related to master students in second year were consider. The reason is there is not so many data on performance for freshmen. Or data mining is focused on performance analysis, so there is not useful to include all students in data mining analysis. The collected data will be used on a further longitudinal analysis of students' satisfaction, when it will be possible to analyze how perceived satisfaction is changing during the programme, when students pass into the second year.

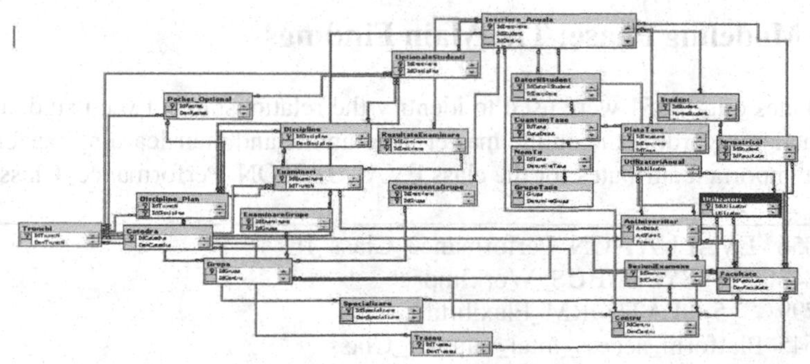

a) Operational database

Fig. 2. Data sources for data mining

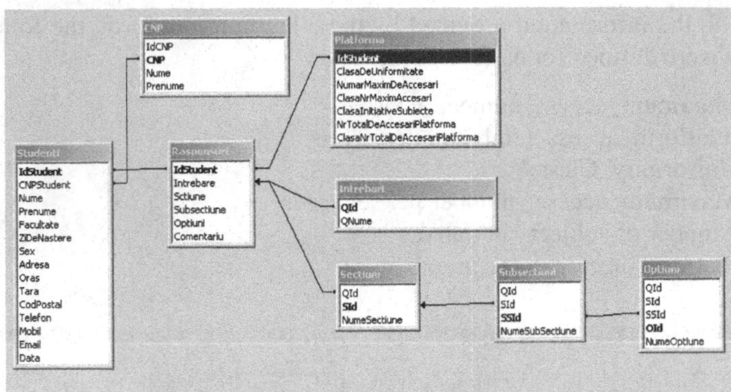

b) Questionnaire database

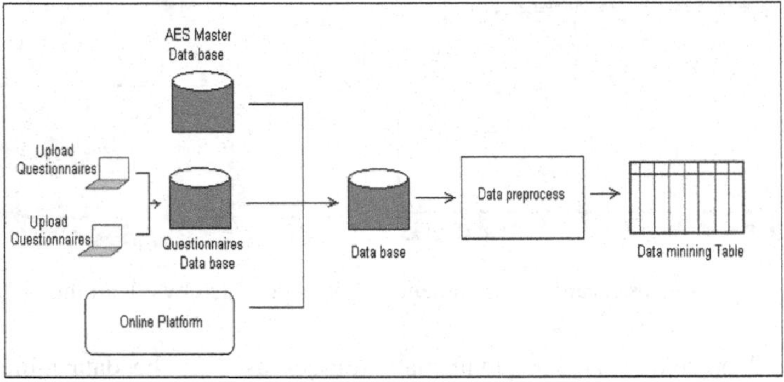

c) Data flow in data mining process

Fig. 2. *(continued)*

A preliminary data analysis was done in a traditional manner, as part of a larger and more detailed process of data exploratory analysis, organized as a data mining project. This kind of project is structured according the DM – CRISP methodology.

3 The Modeling Phase; The Main Findings

Ten attributes out of 151 were used to identify the relationship between students overall satisfaction regarding the online master programme and their learning performance. The most important attributes for the class EVALUATION_Performance_Class_I are:

0.1856	EVALUATION_Performance_Class_II
0.0846	2_8_SYLLABUS_WorkImpact
0.0799	3_5_PLATFORM_Flexibility
0.0645	Platform_access_total_number_Class
0.0534	2_6_SYLLABUS_RessourceSufficiency
0.042	1_5_NEEDS_InitialRequirements
0.0385	5_5_INSTRUCTORS_CommunicationEffeciency

0.0368 3_1_PLATFORM_Adequacy
0.0181 Maximum_access_number_Class

The most important attributes for the class EVALUATION_Performance_Class_II are:

0.1856 EVALUATION_Performance_Class_I
0.0762 1_5_NEEDS_InitialRequirements
0.0683 3_5_PLATFORM_Flexibility
0.0626 2_8_SYLLABUS_WorkImpact
0.0574 3_1_PLATFORM_Adequacy
0.0563 5_5_INSTRUCTORS_CommunicationEffeciency
0.0514 Platform_access_total_number_Class
0.0416 Maximum_access_number_Class
0.0327 2_6_SYLLABUS_RessourceSufficiency

To develop a **clustering model**, the Simple K-Mean algorithm is applied using Weka platform (Bouckaert, Frank, Hall, Kirkby, Reutemann, Seewald & Scuse, 2010). The cluster analysis experiment is related to the overall student satisfaction and the way in which this satisfaction influences student's learning performance. The cluster analysis results are presented in figure 3.

Attribute	Cluster 0	Cluster 1
1_5_NEEDS_InitialRequirements	3	1
2_6_SYLLABUS_RessourceSufficiency	2	1
2_8_SYLLABUS_WorkImpact	3	2
3_1_PLATFORM_Adequacy	To_some_exte nt	YES
3_5_PLATFORM_Flexibility	Involve-ment_in_any_deci sion	Choose his own_ homework_deadlines
5_5_INSTRUCTORS_CommunicationEf ficiency	3	2
EVALUATION_Performance_Class_I	3	2
EVALUATION_Performance_Class_II	3	2
Maximum_access_number_Class	1	2
Platform_access_total_number_Class	0	2

Fig. 3. Cluster centroids using Simple K-Means

The student profile for Cluster 0, according to cluster centroid is:

- The student considers that the online programme meets the initial requirements that he had when he enrolled for it in a satisfactory mode (3);
- The student considers that the resources provided at the courses are sufficient (2) to acquire the knowledge he needs
- The theme of the master projects correspond to the work activities in to some extend (3);
- The study platform used in online programme is appropriate to some extend;

- The student that he must be involve in any decision regarding the learning activity;
- The communication between teachers and student is efficient enough.
- The performance class for the first and second year is 3, meaning the average exams grades is over 8 and number of failed exams is less than 2.
- The maximum access platform number is between 26 and 40.
- The platform access total number is less than 600.

This profile denotes a student whose expectations were less satisfied at the end of programme, at the enrolment the student has already knowledge in project management domain, so the student is easily learning. That is why the performance of the students from this cluster is high.

The student from cluster 1 has a high level of satisfaction. The programme has offered a good understanding of the project management domain. The performance class is not as good as the one from cluster 0, but still is a good one, the average for the both years being between 7 and 8 and the failed exams number less 2.

Cluster 0 has 62% of instances, meaning 80 instances up to 129. The cluster 1 has 38 % of instances having the other 49 instances. The majority of the students enrolled for this master degree programme were initiated into the basics aspects of its domain. Most of the students, belonging to cluster 0, do not need much time to spend on the platform, for communication, information extraction and resources checking.

The classification experiment was developed using J48 algorithm. The result is a decision tree having the goal to classify the instances based on a specified attribute (class attribute). The objective of the experiment is to show when the overall satisfaction is accomplished and how it influences the performance.

1_5_NEEDS_InitialRequirements
2_6_SYLLABUS_RessourceSufficiency
2_8_SYLLABUS_WorkImpact
3_1_PLATFORM_Adequacy
3_5_PLATFORM_Flexibility
5_5_INSTRUCTORS_CommunicationEffeciency
EVALUATION_Performance_Class_I
Maximum_access_number_Class
Platform_access_total_number_Class

The experiment results are presented in figure 4. The characteristics of the results are:

- Correctly Classified Instances = 108, meaning 83,7 %;
- Incorrectly Classified Instances = 21, meaning 16.2 %;
- Kappa statistic (means “fulfil prediction level”) = 0,73. It is a good value (maximum is 1);
- Mean absolute error = 0,107;
- Root mean squared error = 0,2322;
- Relative absolute error = 34,9 %;
- Root relative squared error = 59,34%

Confusion matrix:

```
 a  b  c  d  <-- classified as
14  0  0  3 |  a = 0
```

0 1 0 0 | b = 1
4 0 46 7 | c = 2
3 0 4 47 | d = 3

Confusion matrix shows that for the first line, 14 instances were correct classified in class 0 (a), 3 instances were incorrect classified in class 3 instead of the class 0 (A).

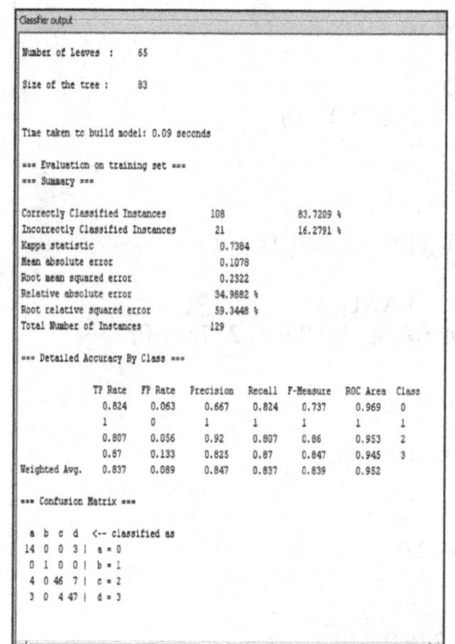

```
Classifier output

Number of Leaves  :     65

Size of the tree :      83


Time taken to build model: 0.09 seconds

=== Evaluation on training set ===
=== Summary ===

Correctly Classified Instances         108               83.7209 %
Incorrectly Classified Instances        21               16.2791 %
Kappa statistic                          0.7384
Mean absolute error                      0.1078
Root mean squared error                  0.2322
Relative absolute error                 34.9882 %
Root relative squared error             59.3448 %
Total Number of Instances              129

=== Detailed Accuracy By Class ===

               TP Rate   FP Rate   Precision   Recall  F-Measure   ROC Area  Class
                 0.824     0.063      0.667     0.824     0.737      0.969    0
                 1         0          1         1         1          1        1
                 0.807     0.056      0.92      0.807     0.86       0.953    2
                 0.87      0.133      0.825     0.87      0.847      0.945    3
Weighted Avg.    0.837     0.089      0.847     0.837     0.839      0.952

=== Confusion Matrix ===

  a  b  c  d   <-- classified as
 14  0  0  3 |  a = 0
  0  1  0  0 |  b = 1
  4  0 46  7 |  c = 2
  3  0  4 47 |  d = 3
```

a) J48 Results

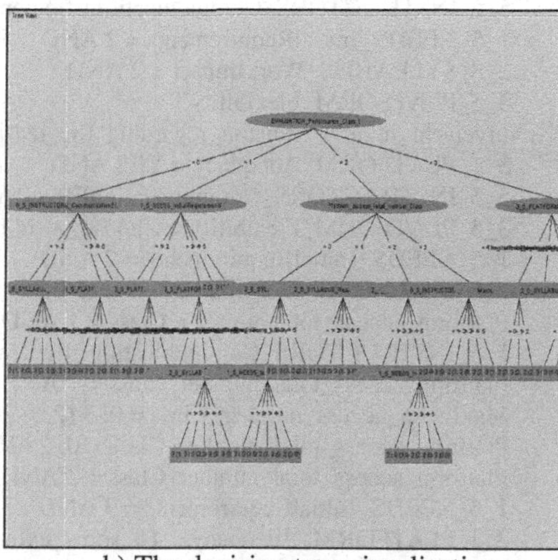

b) The decision tree visualization

Fig. 4. Results of the classification experiment using J48

Based on confusion matrix, some indicators can be compute, such as:

- **TP rate** (Rata true - positive); It represents the proportion in which the examples were classified in class x according to the whole examples number that belong to that class. In our case, for class a we have 14/(14+0+3); It represents the proportion in which the examples were classified in class x according to the whole examples number that belong to another class.
- **Precision,** representing the proportion of instances that belong to class x from the whole number of instances and classified in class x. For class a, Precision = 1.
- **Recall = TP rate**
- **F-Measure (Measure F)** is computing as: **2*Precision*Recall/(Precision + Recall).**

In order to obtain a rule set, the PART algorithm is used. The generated rule list is the following:

EVALUATION_Performace_Class_I = 3 AND 3_5_PLATFORM_Flexibility = Involvement_in_any_decision_regarding_the_learning_activity: 3 (18.0/3.0)

EVALUATION_Performace_Class_I = 3 AND
3_5_PLATFORM_Flexibility = Choose_own_homework_deadlines AND
2_6_SYLLABUS_RessourceSufficiency = 2: 3 (5.0/1.0)
EVALUATION_Performace_Class_I = 3: 3 (11.0/4.0)
3_5_PLATFORM_Flexibility = The_instructor_decides_the_educational_activities: 2 (7.0/3.0)
Platform_access_total_number_Class = 3 AND
EVALUATION_Performace_Class_I = 2: 2 (11.0/1.0)
1_5_NEEDS_InitialRequirements = 1 AND
2_6_SYLLABUS_RessourceSufficiency = 1 AND
5_5_INSTRUCTORS_CommunicationEffeciency = 2: 2 (7.0/1.0)
1_5_NEEDS_InitialRequirements = 2 AND
2_8_SYLLABUS_WorkImpact = 2 AND
3_5_PLATFORM_Flexibility = Involvement_in_any_decision_regarding_the_learning_activity: 2 (6.0/3.0)
3_1_PLATFORM_Adequacy = YES AND
5_5_INSTRUCTORS_CommunicationEffeciency = 3 AND
3_5_PLATFORM_Flexibility = Choose_own_homework_deadlines: 2 (7.0/1.0)
1_5_NEEDS_InitialRequirements = 2 AND
2_8_SYLLABUS_WorkImpact = 3: 3 (5.0)
Platform_access_total_number_Class = 1 AND
5_5_INSTRUCTORS_CommunicationEffeciency = 4: 2 (4.0)
Platform_access_total_number_Class = 1 AND
Maximum_access_number_Class = 0: 3 (2.0)
Platform_access_total_number_Class = 0: 2 (22.0/12.0)
Platform_access_total_number_Class = 2 AND
1_5_NEEDS_InitialRequirements = 3 AND
3_1_PLATFORM_Adequacy = To_some_extent: 3 (6.0/2.0)
3_1_PLATFORM_Adequacy = Not_good_enough: 3 (5.0/2.0)
5_5_INSTRUCTORS_CommunicationEffeciency = 3 AND
Platform_access_total_number_Class = 2: 0 (4.0/1.0)

The class attribute is EVALUATION_Performace_Class_II. Let suppose we consider the rule: EVALUATION_Performance_Class_I = 3 AND
3_5_PLATFORM_Flexibility = Involvement_in_any_decision_regarding_the_learning_activity: 3 (18.0/3.0)

This rule says that if the performance class for the first year is 3 (GPA over 8 and less than 2 failed exams) and the student thinks that he must be involved in any decision regarding the learning activity, then the Performance class for the second year is 3 (GPA over 8 and less than 2 failed exams).

4 Conclusions and Further Development

An improvement to the current data set would be if some attributes will be added. These attributes will be used to describe students' performance during their faculty years. An interesting analysis is to see if the students profile maintains the same during faulty period as during in the master period and in which cases. Based on this, many predictions could be made helping to identified better the students target profile.

Also, a new analysis direction could be based on some new attributes that describe the teachers point of view regarding students activity, projects quality, the quality of their questions and answers. Analyses about teachers' expectations from their students will help to configure an initial check/test for the future students that will enroll to this online master programme

Some new attributes could be used to describe exactly the platform potential and its actual exploitation level.

References

1. Barros, B., Verdejo, M.F.: Analyzing Student Interaction Processes In Order To Improve Collaboration: The Degree Approach. International Journal of Artificial Intelligence in Education 11, 221–241 (2000)
2. Bodea, C.: Project management competences development using an ontology-based e-learning platform. In: Lytras, M.D., Damiani, E., Carroll, J.M., Tennyson, R.D., Avison, D., Naeve, A., Dale, A., Lefrere, P., Tan, F., Sipior, J., Vossen, G. (eds.) WSKS 2009. LNCS (LNAI), vol. 5736, pp. 31–39. Springer, Heidelberg (2009)
3. Bodea, C., Dascalu, M.: A parametrized web-based testing model for project management. In: Spaniol, M., Li, Q., Klamma, R., Lau, R. (eds.) ICWL 2009. LNCS, vol. 5686, pp. 68–72. Springer, Heidelberg (2009)
4. Bodea, V.: Application and Benefits of Knowledge Management in Universities – a Case Study on Student Performance Enhancement. In: Informatics in Knowledge Society, The Proceedings of the Eight International Conference on Informatics in Economy, May 17-18, pp. 1033–1038. ASE Printing House (2007)
5. Bouckaert, R., Frank, E., Hall, M., Kirkby, R., Reutemann, P., Seewald, A., Scuse, D.: WEKA Manual for Version 3-6-2, University of Waikato, Hamilton, New Zealand (2010)
6. Delavari, N., Beikzadeh, M.R., Amnuaisuk, S.K.: Application of Enhanced Analysis Model for Data Mining Processes in Higher Educational System. In: Proceedings of ITHET 6th Annual International Conference, Juan Dolio, Dominican Republic (2005)
7. Luan, J.: Data Mining and Its Applications in Higher Education. In: Serban, A., Luan, J. (eds.) Knowledge Management: Building a Competitive Advantage for Higher Education. New Directions for Institutional Research, vol. 113. Jossey Bass, San Francisco (2002)
8. Luan, J., Zhai, M., Chen, J., Chow, T., Chang, L., Zhao, C.-M.: Concepts, Myths, and Case Studies of Data Mining in Higher Education. In: AIR 44th Forum Boston (2004)
9. Ma, Y., Liu, B., Wong, C.K., Yu, P.S., Lee, S.M.: Targeting the right students using data mining. In: Proceedings of the Sixth ACM SIGKDD International Conference on Knowledge Discovery and Data Mining, Boston, pp. 457–464 (2000)
10. Ranjan, J., Malik, K.: Effective Educational Process: A Data Mining Approach. VINE 37(4), 502–515 (2007)
11. Shyamala, K., Rajagopalan, S.P.: Data Mining Model for a better Higher Educational System. Information Technology Journal 5(3), 560–564 (2006)

Effects of Digital Footprint on Career Management: Evidence from Social Media in Business Education

Vladlena Benson and Fragkiskos Filippaios

Kingston Business School, Kingston University, Kingston Upon Thames, KT2 7LB, United Kingdom
v.benson@kingston.ac.uk, f.filippaios@kingston.ac.uk

Abstract. As online social media gain immense popularity among Internet users, we would like to explore the implication of social networking on career management. This paper links social capital theories and the impact of online social networks on ties between individuals in social and business uses. Social media contributes to building up individual digital footprint, or Internet content linked to individual names. We then propose a typology of the digital footprint based on the evidence from a survey of business students. Discussion of the implications of the study and arising research questions conclude the article.

1 Introduction

Online social media has become one of the most popular Internet applications of the decade. Social networks have been linked with creation and exploitation of social capital in recent literature. However, the effect that individual digital footprint has on the career prospects of students has remained underestimated in the social networks literature. This paper will construct a typology of the digital footprint left behind from different social networking activities undertaken by business students of different levels. It will start by defining the two dimensions of the digital footprint and then associate the dimensions with specific characteristics of the footprint. Finally the study will provide a typology of effects that digital footprint may have on career management of younger generation of business graduates.

2 Social Capital Theories and Career Success

Social capital theory and career success have been linked by Seibert, Kraimer and Liden (2001) who connected three competing theories of social capital: weak tie theory (Granovetter, 1973), structural hole theory (Burt, 1992) and social resource theory (Lin, 1999). Connections or ties between individuals in a network help provide the basis for analysis of social networks. Both the weak tie theory and the structural holes theory deal with the structure of social networks and the advantages that network topology offers. The weak tie theory considers the strengths of ties between individuals and proves that weak ties are indispensible to individuals' opportunities. In particular (Granovetter, 1973) shows that ties between members of a given network can be intense or weak. For instance, in a network with intense/strong ties information

M.D. Lytras et al. (Eds.): WSKS 2010, Part I, CCIS 111, pp. 480–486, 2010.

dissipates quickly and loses its value to members, e.g. friends, co-workers, members of local community, whereas infrequent and emotionally uninvolved relationships or weak ties commonly link networks with networks with unique information and resources. Granovetter (1973) argues that weak ties were more useful than strong ties as a source of information about job openings helping individuals with connections to external networks to gain access to better job opportunities. Another view on social capital is provided by the structural hole theory Burt (1992, 1997) the structural hole argument is that "social capital is created by a network in which people can broker connections between otherwise disconnected segments" (Burt, 2001, p. 202). Social networks rich in structural holes provide an individual with better access to information, bargaining power and therefore exercising greater control over resources and opening career opportunities throughout the social system. Finally, the social resource theory focuses on the content rather than the structure or strength of ties in a network. According to Lin (1999) social capital is formed via the capability to use ties between individuals in a network to reach a particular resource embedded in it to fulfil individual's instrumental objectives.

The diversely expressed but converging perspectives cited above concur that social capital is a metaphor in which social network is a type of asset which can create certain competitive advantage to some individuals or groups in pursuing their goals. With the general agreement that " better connected people enjoy higher returns" (Burt, 2001, p. 203) we proceed to the discussion of the digital footprint generated as a the result of networking on social media.

3 Digital Footprint

A growing number of publications (e.g. Barnes & Barnes, 2009, Lange 2007, Livingstone 2008, Lewis & West 2009) continuously draw attention to issues of privacy of individual information available as a result of social networking use. Some researchers (e.g. Weintraub & Kumar, 1997) argue that technology may be significantly changing boundaries between 'publicity' and 'privacy'. SNS increase the amount of private information shared online and possibly present a hazard to those users who overlook adjusting their SNS privacy settings. The old saying 'Choose your friends wisely' cannot be more relevant as in the context of online social networking. Increasingly, there are warnings that individuals should be careful of their use of networks generally as employers are more and more using information gleaned from social networks to assess future employees (Peluchette & Karl, 2010). However, there is also an increasing level of concern from the businesses themselves, regarding legal challenges and the risks involved in using social networks for building business, leading to policy developments (Wilson, 2009).

4 Typology

For the purposes of our study, one can classify the key characteristics of a digital footprint using two dimensions. The first one is related to the nature of the activity undertaken by the student. This can range from a pure social one to a strictly business activity. The goals of each activity differ substantially as we would expect students to make different use of their time, language and networking for social or business activities.

The second dimension is related to the level of studies and how far or close this is to the labour market. We would expect students that attend a foundation degree or early stages of an undergraduate degree not to be too much work oriented. Alternatively one could argue that the timing between joining the workplace and the impact of a digital footprint might be different between a full time undergraduate and a part-time postgraduate student.

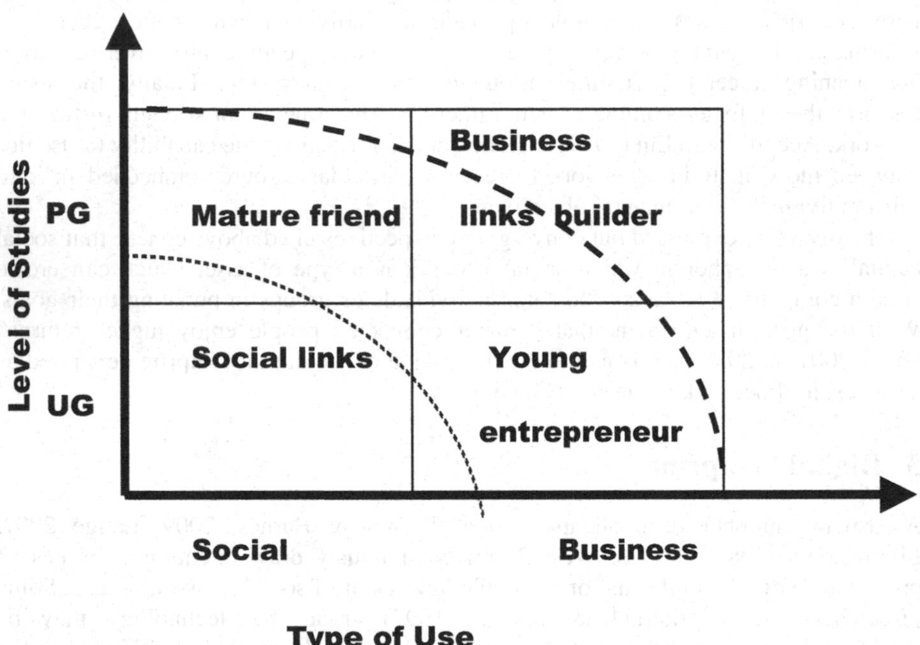

Fig. 1. Typology of Digital Footprint

5 Method

As a part of a wider study of online social networking in HE, a two phase approach to data collection was adopted, with two focus groups informing the development of a survey. The sample for the focus group was drawn ad-hoc from the student population at a post-92 University in the UK. Each focus group discussion was structured around nine open ended questions and lasted for approximately an hour. The discussions were digitally recorded and transcribed. The analysis of the focus group transcripts provided the starting point for developing a range of questions covering various aspects and concerns of social networking use. In the second stage of data collection a draft survey was piloted on twenty individual students at the research site. Based on the feedback from the pilot the questionnaire was amended and formatted into its final version. The questionnaire in paper format was distributed to a random sample of undergraduate and postgraduate students including UK and European universities.

The sample was drawn entirely from students studying on business courses. The total number of respondents comprised of 272 individuals, which gives a representative sample. The demographic data collected included information on age, nationality, number of years of work experience, first language, year and type of degree. Further questions covered a range of expectations and motivation for persistent use of various networks. The questions worded ('Why did you join this social network ' with answer options including ' Find a job', 'Make business contacts' as well as 'To find contacts at the University' and 'To be generally sociable', etc.) were provided for each network type. A Likert scale was used (1- Strongly Agree to 5- Strongly Disagree). Average age of respondents for Masters was 29 years, for Undergraduates – 22 years. By gender the sample comprised of 48% female respondents and 47% of males, 5% did not provide their answers. Dominant nationalities were as follows: British – 33%, Cypriot – 7%, Russian – 6,5%, Indian – 6%.

6 Empirical Evidence

The purpose of this section is to provide empirical evidence regarding the use of social networks from undergraduate and postgraduate students. We decided to use two key dimensions that demonstrate the difference between the two groups on the use of SNS. The first dimension is related to the use of social networks for socializing since the original opening of the account. Students answered using four discrete answers, i.e. not at all, less, about the same, more. We have assigned a numerical value on each dimension from 1 to 4 with 1 being not at all and 4 being more. The oneway ANOVA results for the social and business use are presented in tables 1 and 2 below. Results show a clear difference between the undergraduate and postgraduate students regarding the use of SNS for social purposes. The undergraduate students use more now, than when they originally opened their account, the SNS. There is a clear difference in the way they approach the SNS use by logging in more than the postgraduate students. This difference between the two groups is not evident though in the Business use of the SNS. Although postgraduate students log on more, there is no clear statistically different relationship between the two groups and the use of SNS for business use.

Table 1. Oneway Anova between Type of Degree and Use of network for Social Purposes

Type of degree	**Mean**	**Std. Dev.**	**Freq.**		
Undergraduate	1.99	1.61	132		
Postgraduate	1.60	1.55	99		
Total	1.82	1.59	231		
Source	**SS**	**Df**	**MS**	**F**	**Prob > F**
Between groups	8.44	1	8.44	3.34	0.0688
Within groups	578.62	229	2.52		
Total	587.07	230	2.55		

Table 2. Oneway Anova between Type of Degree and Use of network for Business Purposes

Type of degree	Mean	Std. Dev.	Freq.		
Undergraduate	1.21	1.27	132		
Postgraduate	1.34	1.47	99		
Total	1.26	1.36	231		
Source	**SS**	**Df**	**MS**	**F**	**Prob > F**
Between groups	0.97	1	0.97	0.52	0.4699
Within groups	426.38	229	1.86		
Total	427.35	230	1.85		

This result although not totally surprising, contradicts our key argument that postgraduate users would be more orientated towards the use of SNS for business purposes. We decided therefore to explore another dimension of our sample which is related to the amount of time the different groups of users spend online in the two activities, i.e. social purposes and business purposes. Tables 3 and 4 present the oneway ANOVA results between the type of user and the amount of time they spend on a weekly average basis. From table 3 one can see a difference between the undergraduate and the postgraduate students but this difference is not statistically significant. On the other hand table 4 gives a very different picture around the amount of time spent on business related use. The postgraduates spend more than twice the time than the undergraduate students using SNS from a business perspective. This difference is statistically significant and demonstrates that there are other more qualitative characteristics that might explain the use of SNS between the two groups.

Table 3. Oneway Anova Type of Degree and Use of network for Social Purposes (Time)

Type of degree	Mean	Std. Dev.	Freq.		
Undergraduate	4.52	4.87	89		
Postgraduate	4.02	5.76	60		
Total	4.32	5.23	149		
Source	SS	Df	MS	F	Prob > F
Between groups	9.21	1	9.21	0.33	0.5641
Within groups	4051.94	147	27.56		
Total	4061.15	148	27.44		

Table 4. Oneway Anova Type of Degree and Use of network for Business Purposes (Time)

Type of degree	**Mean**	**Std. Dev.**	**Freq.**		
Undergraduate	1.14	1.94	49		
Postgraduate	2.46	5.03	37		
Total	1.71	3.65	86		
Source	SS	df	MS	F	Prob > F
Between groups	37.07	1	37.07	2.84	0.0956
Within groups	1096.02	84	13.04		
Total	1133.09	85	13.33		

7 Conclusions

As a result of online social networking individuals tend to generate content associated with their name linking them to other individuals into a formal or informal network. Online networking has been positively linked to building and reinforcing social capital. In turn "better connected people" (Burt, 2001) are thought to enjoy an advantage in career management. Thus besides simple socialising, online social networks have an impact on business relations. The purpose of this study was to build a typology for the digital footprint. Analysis of data on the use of SNS from Business and Management Undergraduate and Postgraduate students provided an empirical lens on the online behaviour. The study concluded that there are four types of digital footprint with the key motivations for the use of SNS. These are: social links reinforcement, mature friend, young entrepreneur and business link builder. Undergraduate students primarily use SNS for social purposes whilst postgraduates focus primarily on the business use of SNS. It has become evident that social networking awareness is missing in HE curriculum. More research attention is needed to identify contribution of the digital footprint towards career management and business opportunities. Issues of privacy and security are likely to intensify with the growth of user generated content on the Internet. It is important to address these issues through further research studies into social media and its business applications.

References

Barnes, N.D., Barnes, F.R.: Equipping Your Organization for the Social Networking Game. Information Management 43(6), 28–33 (2009)

Burt, R.: Structural holes: The social structure of competition. Harvard University Press, Cambridge (1992)

Burt, R.: The contingent value of social capital. Administrative Science Quarterly 42, 339–365 (1997)

Burt, R.: The Social Capital of Structural Holes. In: Guillen, M., Collins, R., England, P., Meyer, M. (eds.) New Directions in Economic Sociology. Russell Sage Foundation, New York (2001)

Granovetter, M.: The Strength of Weak Ties. American Journal of Sociology 6, 1360–1380 (1973)

Lange, P. G.: Publicly private and privately public: Social networking on YouTube. Journal of Computer-Mediated Communication 13(1) (2007), http://jcmc.indiana.edu/vol13/issue1/lange.html (retrieved September 12, 2009)

Lewis, J., West, A.: 'Friending': London-based undergraduates' experience of Facebook. New Media Society 11(7), 1209–1229 (2009)

Lin, N.: Social Networks and status Attainment. Annual Review of sociology 25, 467–487 (1999)

Lin, N.: Social Capital: A Theory of Social Structure and Action. Cambridge University Press, New York (2000)

Livingstone, S.: Taking risky opportunities in youthful content creation: teenagers' use of social networking sites for intimacy, privacy and self-expression. New Media Society 10, 393–411 (2008)

Peluchette, J., Karl, K.: Examining Students' Intended Image on Facebook: "What Were They Thinking?!". Journal of Education for Business 85(1), 30–37 (2010)

Seibert, S., Kraimer, M., Liden, R.: A Social Capital Theory of Career Success. Academy of Management Journal 44(2), 219–237 (2001)

Weintraub, J., Kumar, K. (eds.): Public and Private in Thought and Practice. University of Chicago Press, Chicago (1997)

Wilson, J.: Social networking: the business case. Engineering & Technology 4(10), 54–56 (2009)

Design of a Learning Environment for Management Education
The Case of EduORG2.0 at the University of Pisa

Maria Cinque[1] and Antonella Martini[2]

[1] Fondazione Rui – Viale XXI Aprile, 36
00168 - Roma
[2] Faculty of Engineering – L.go L. Lazzarino, 2,
56100 - Pisa
m.cinque@fondazionerui.it, a.martini@ing.unipi.it

Abstract. There has been a vast debate in recent years about usage patterns of social computing and web 2.0 tools in learning contexts. A growing number of researchers suggest that certain pedagogical approaches are best suited in these contexts, since they involve active engagement, social learning, continuous feedback, enabling students' autonomous understanding and the transfer of those skills to useful or real-life settings. In this article we present the use of a social network as part of a formal course of Management at the University of Pisa. The institutional VLE – based on Moodle – has been integrated with a student support group hosted on Ning. Problems and opportunities for using Ning have been discussed in small groups and students feedback will be reported. The shift from Learning Management System (course centric) to a Personal Learning Environment (people centric) and then to Personal Learning Network is also been discussed and a framework for Education 2.0 is provided.

Keywords: Management education; Technology enhanced learning; Social networking; VLE (Virtual Learning Environment), PLE (Personal Learning Environment).

1 Introduction

As a part of the larger educational environment, technology provides a context that is shaped in part by the ways teachers enable their students' uses of technological tools. Technological contexts include the actual devices students use and the systems that support these devices. These technology contexts are in a state of almost constant change as a result of both innovation and a deliberate effort to expand access to technology in schools and universities. This is why the concept of "disruptive technology' was also applied to education. Katrina A. Meyer [1] points out that "although not a magical way to transform higher education, disruptive technology must interrupt our usual policies, practices, and assumptions. Consequently, 21st century education will be: student-centered, with learning put first, and flexible enough to accommodate

M.D. Lytras et al. (Eds.): WSKS 2010, Part I, CCIS 111, pp. 487–492, 2010.

different styles and interests; designed to offer options, motivate students, and provide connections to students' lives, jobs, and communities; able to capitalize on the willingness of faculty and students to experiment and fail, to improve, and to keep at problems until solutions are crafted.

A growing number of researchers suggest that certain pedagogical approaches are best suited for instruction that makes use of digital technological tools. These pedagogical approaches typically involve active engagement, social learning, continuous feedback, and real world application [2]. Constructivist theory suggests that learners construct their own knowledge, but facilitating such knowledge construction in the classroom is complex. In an effort to further define the problem, Mishra and Koehler [3] have theorized about a specialized form of knowledge called Technological Pedagogical Content Knowledge (TPCK) that represents the manner in which teachers integrate technology into instruction within the context of constructivist learning goals.

When teachers use 21st century technologies to facilitate student learning, evidence suggests that the learning that occurs is dynamic and multi-dimensional. This is learning (or e-learning) 2.0, which is not only "student-centered" but "community-centered", based on community of practice formed by "people who engage in a process of collective learning in a shared domain of human endeavour" [4]. In this sense it is "immersive" (learning by doing) and "situated" [5] and, basically, connected, networked learning [6].

Thinking on teachers' side McLoughling and Lee [7] outlined the 3 P's of 2.0 pedagogy: personalization (learner choice, learner agency, customization, self-regulation and management); participation (communication, collaboration, connectivity, community); productivity (learner created content, contribution to knowledge, generativity, creativity and innovation).

2 A Framework for Education 2.0

Using the 3P's as background and building on Enterprise 2.0 literature, we define Education 2.0 as "*a set of educational and technological approaches steered to enable new educational models, based on open involvement, emergent collaboration, knowledge sharing, internal/external social network development and exploitation*".

From an organisational point of view, Education 2.0 is a point of discontinuity that breaks the boundaries of the PLE both in terms of opening up the organisation to 'external' players (customers, suppliers, partners) and of re-thinking the traditional schemes of collaboration, knowledge sharing, and management of functional and hierarchical relations, so questioning the rigid stereotypes regarding the workspace and working hours. We modeled the emerging needs of learners from the emerging needs of knowledge workers 2.0 [10]. These needs can be divided into six key dimensions, as shown in Fig. 1.: *open belonging* (to supply secure and selective access to information, tools and connections that go beyond the Institutional's boundaries); *social networking* (learners increasingly need to develop and maintain that network of relations that is becoming a more and more important asset for their professional efficiency); *knowledge networks* (to prevent their knowledge and skills from being "surpassed" soon, learners must be able to build their own network to have access to knowledge and information from different sources, both explicit and implicit); *emergent collaboration* (in an increasingly fast and unpredictable competitive scenario, learners need to create cooperative settings in a fast, flexible way, even outside the formal organisational patterns); *adaptive reconfigurability* (students need to quickly reconfigure their own processes and activities); *global mobility* (learners spend an increasingly large share of their time far from the workplace and often in a state of mobility; new ICT enables them to be connected in any place and at any time of day through their own network of tools, thus making the workspace and working time more flexible).

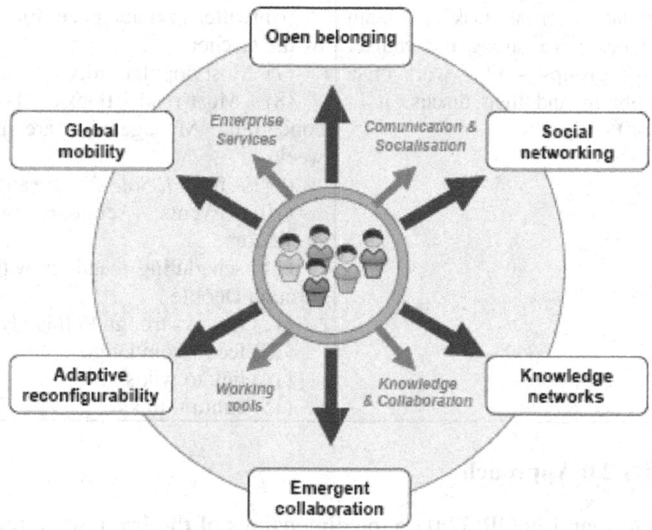

Fig. 1. Education 2.0 framework

3 The Case of EduORG2.0

3.1 Integrating the Institutional VLE

EduORG2.0 was created in 2009 for the course of Management – one of the Management Engineering degree – at the University of Pisa. It is based on two platforms: Moodle, which was already present in the Institution, and Ning[1]. While the first is used for the delivery of the programme (presentation of the course, calendar, slides etc.) and for formal communication (exams, calendar, mid-term tests etc.), Ning is used as a sort of 'laboratory', an environment in which students can enhance their learning through interaction and availability of further, non-compulsory, resources. See table 1.

[1] Ning.com (http://www.ning.com) is a free web-based platform that allows users to create their own social networking sites.

Table 1. The structure of EduORG2.0[2]

Moodle	On Ning
(1) the calendar of the course (Google Calendar) (2) the course presentation with a link to the teacher's website (3) resources (slides, handouts, exercises, links, lessons videoclips); the resources are ordered by module (4) sign up for exams (link to faculty service) (5) assignment on a task (a team competition takes place along the course: every week the groups – 14 – work on a given task/problem and then discuss it in plenary session)	(1) blog with post concerning daily lessons or team competition (2) forum, with are 3 pre-fixed categories (3) groups: every group has its own page with logo (4) *case histories of entrepreneurship*: an article is available every week and can be downloaded with BoxNet (integrated in Ning) (5) useful links (6) twitter in home page: for rapid prompts by the teacher (7) Most popular videos (8) Must-read books: books review concerning Management are posted every week (9) rss from *Il Sole-24 Ore* and *Ansa news* (10) Events: seminars with visiting professors (11) scheduling meetings with the teacher through Doodle (12) surveys trough Polldaddy (13) feeds from Diigo (14) link to wikis (15) cultural links

3.2 EduORG 2.0 Approach

It is possible to map EduORG2.0 on the dimensions of the framework reported in Fig. 1. It results that EduORG2.0 is an educational space that can be named 'social' since it creates an environment that is not targeted to the Institution population at large but to specific groups or communities. The level of users' participation and proactive involvement is high since they see the community as an important element to increase their wealth of knowledge, create new relations and increase their "learning" effectiveness and visibility. In addition, a number of users proactively participate in the creation of contents, take part in discussions and create interpersonal relations of trust and *mutual engagement*. At the same time, the teacher's commitment is very high, but the Institution does not 'see' and recognise the community as an important means to achieve its purposes, by proactively supporting it and allocating it some resources.

The platform has been customized in order to outline a path for guided learning: a message is posted by the teacher after every lesson, describing what has been done, where and how to study. The idea is to offer opportunities and resources beyond the mere 'technical knowledge', a support that could enhance student learning and encourage them to develop not only their 'hard' but also their 'soft' skills. Although the

[2] There is some integration between the social network and the VLE. There is a form on the Moodle course page, which allows participants to log on to Ning network, and an RSS feed displays news about the current module on the social networking site.

use of the social networking space is optional, all course participants have accessed it at least once. About a half of the participants are regularly (almost daily) active in the network and share information, resources and messages. The Ning platform has been presented with the metaphor of football camp, where students can train themselves. All the items of the network are inspired by this metaphor: a football team, composed by different players (the students with their distinctive abilities); a coach (the teacher); a training program; a to a football match (the exam).

3.3 Students' Feedback

As we said before, although not mandatory, Ning was accessed at least once by all course participants[3]. Each year, during the course, two meetings with team leaders are held to discuss on the following subjects: groups internal management (learning process and state of the art, learning difficulties, participation of all group members at the project works); evaluation of didactical resources (book, slides, handouts and exercises); suggestions.The opinions gathered during these meetings are very useful to the teacher, that asks the team leaders to express freely any problem arisen during group activities. Answers focus also on classmate and group feedback: sometimes – due to different problems – groups are not so tight and so collaborative as the team leader would expect. Some responses stress ease-of-use and practical application of Ning. Finally, some students (not all) show awareness of the 'additional value' of EduORG2.0 network for personal growth. Other important elements emerging from meeting report are related to the affordances offered by EduORG2.0 network and, generally, to functionalities and features a social network should contain in order to encourage students participation, to allow them develop competencies and to motivate them to learn. Didactical web sites are very much appreciated and aspects or features that motivate to learn were found to be related to the boundary (clear expectations, functionalities, goals), and usability aspect (ease of use, reliability, user-friendly, appealing interface), more than to particular aspects of learning or competence development (trace learning paths, progress indicator, test skill development, the idea that there is something to learn). These opinions show that powerful, intuitive social media tools represent and facilitate fundamental shifts in human interaction—shifts that can improve university learning.

4 Helping Students View Ning as a Personal Learning Network

In technology-enhanced learning discussion there is a strong trend that promote the change from Learning Management System (course centric) to a Personal Learning Environment (PLE) (people centric) [8] and then to Personal Learning Network [9].

"Learning networks capture an essential element in learning today, the simple fact that we don't know what we want to teach" [9]. Indeed, it is often suggested that the best we can manage is to teach students how to learn, and to encourage them to manage their

---

[3] EduORG2.0 in numbers: (2009) 156 enrolled, 13 groups, 87 posts, 49 forum discussions, 11 videos (each 30 views), 200 comments for each group (average rate); 41.285 log-in; (2010) 318 members, 14 groups, 85 forum discussions, 112 posts, 18 videos, more than 50.000 log-in.

own learning thereafter. The main purposes for implementing Ning community into the Management course were two-fold. First, we wanted to try to create a virtual classroom — an online community where students could converse and collaborate, and where the teacher could support and enrich their learning. Secondly, the teacher was hoping to enhance the course curriculum in a way that would help prepare students for the literacy demands of the 21st century. On both accounts, the experience has by far overwhelmed the original purposes, and we have just begun to glimpse its ultimate potential. As a virtual classroom, EduORG2.0 is in many ways a much more flexible and dynamic space than a physical classroom. Students can interact with any member about any topic or question at any time. And rather than being limited to a classroom where only 20 to 30 students are able to collaborate with one another, the virtual space enables students to interact with all 100 plus of their classmates, as well as alumni who continue to participate on the site. Furthermore, EduORG2.0 is a learning context in which the teacher can be the kind of educator 21st century students need—a facilitator, collaborator, and co-learner.

References

1. Meyer, K.A.: The Role of Disruptive Technology in the Future of Higher Education. EQ (Educause Quarterly) 33, 1 (2010), http://www.educause.edu/EDUCAUSE+Quarterly/EDUCAUSEQuarterly MagazineVolum/TheRoleofDisruptiveTechnologyi/199378 (verified on 24.04.2010)
2. Doolittle, P., Hicks, D.: Constructivism as a theoretical foundation for the use of technology in social studies. Theory and Research in Social Education 31(1), 71–103 (2003)
3. Mishra, P., Koehler, M.J.: Technological pedagogical content knowledge: A framework for teacher knowledge. Teachers College Record 108(6), 1017–1054 (2006)
4. Wenger, E.: Communities of Practice: Learning, Meaning, and Identity. Cambridge University Press, Cambridge (1998)
5. Lave, J., Wenger, E.: Situated Learning: Legitimate Peripheral Participation. Cambridge University Press, Cambridge (1991)
6. Downes, S.: E-learning 2.0. eLearn Magazine (October 17, 2005), http://elearnmag.org/subpage.cfm?section=articles&article=29-1 (verified on 23.04.10)
7. McLoughling, C., Lee, M.J.W.: The Three P's of Pedagogy for the Networked Society: Personalization, Participation, and Productivity. International Journal of Teaching and Learning in Higher Education 20(1), 10–27 (2008)
8. Wilson, S.: Future VLE – The Visual Version (2005), http://www.cetis.ac.uk/members/scott/blogview?entry=20050125 170206 (retrieved April 23, 2010)
9. Downes, S.: New Technology Supporting Informal Learning. Journal Of Emerging Technologies In Web Intelligence 2(1), 27–33 (2010)
10. Corso, M., Martini, A., Pesoli, A.: Enterprise 2.0: What Models are Emerging? Results from a 70 case-based research. International Journal of Knowledge and Learning 4(6), 595–561 (2008) ISSN 1741-1009

An Approach to Curriculum Design for Computer Science

Igor Schagaev[1], Elisabeth Bacon[2], and Nicholas Ioannides[1]

[1] London Metropolitan University, Faculty of Computing,
166-220 Holloway Road, London, N7 8DB, UK
{i.schagaev,n.ioannides}@londonmet.ac.uk
[2] University of Greenwich, School of Computing and Mathematical Sciences,
Maritime Greenwich Campus, Old Royal Naval College,
Park Row, Greenwich, London, SE10 9LS, UK
e.bacon@greenwich.ac.uk

Abstract. An approach to curriculum design for Computer Science and similar disciplines as a formal model is introduced. Functions of education process as knowledge delivery and assessment are considered. The structural formation of curriculum design using definitive, characteristic and predictive functions is presented. Influences on the process of changes in a discipline are described and functions of the core moving and merging are introduced. Initial considerations on the development of the algorithm to determine the core of a discipline are presented.

Keywords: Curriculum Design, Curriculum Core, Computer Science, Theory of Classification, Formalisation, Multiple Choice Answer Approach.

1 Introduction

Computer Science, though a relatively new and fast growing discipline for teaching, is, in fact, the theoretical base for the fastest ever growing area of technological development, that of Information Technology (IT). At first glance, as a discipline, Computer Science should absorb its own technical applications but previous attempts to do this failed. What is certain, however, is that Computer Science absorbs different theoretical and technical elements from different disciplines and influences many aspects of human life.

The idea behind this work is to build an algorithm of *Curriculum design* and development for *Computer Science* disciplines by attempting to form a logical *core* of *curriculum design* for computer science and similar disciplines. It starts by recognizing the fact that education is a driving force in the improvement of life for society at large. It then considers existing models of *curriculum development*, analyses curriculum design as *information processing* and introduces three main functions in discipline construction: *definitive, characteristic* and *predictive*. It then discusses ways of selecting the core of a discipline and its main features: *moving* and *merging*, and finally considers assessment as a part of curriculum development.

M.D. Lytras et al. (Eds.): WSKS 2010, Part I, CCIS 111, pp. 493–499, 2010.

The concept of *Curriculum design* was analysed by Aristotle: "*For the formal nature is of greater importance than the material nature*" [1] and Confucius: "*He who learns but does not think is lost; He who thinks but does not learn is in great danger*" [2], clearly identifying the necessity of reflecting on what one has learned. The cycle of education is thus completed when its outcome has been returned back to society (Figure 1).

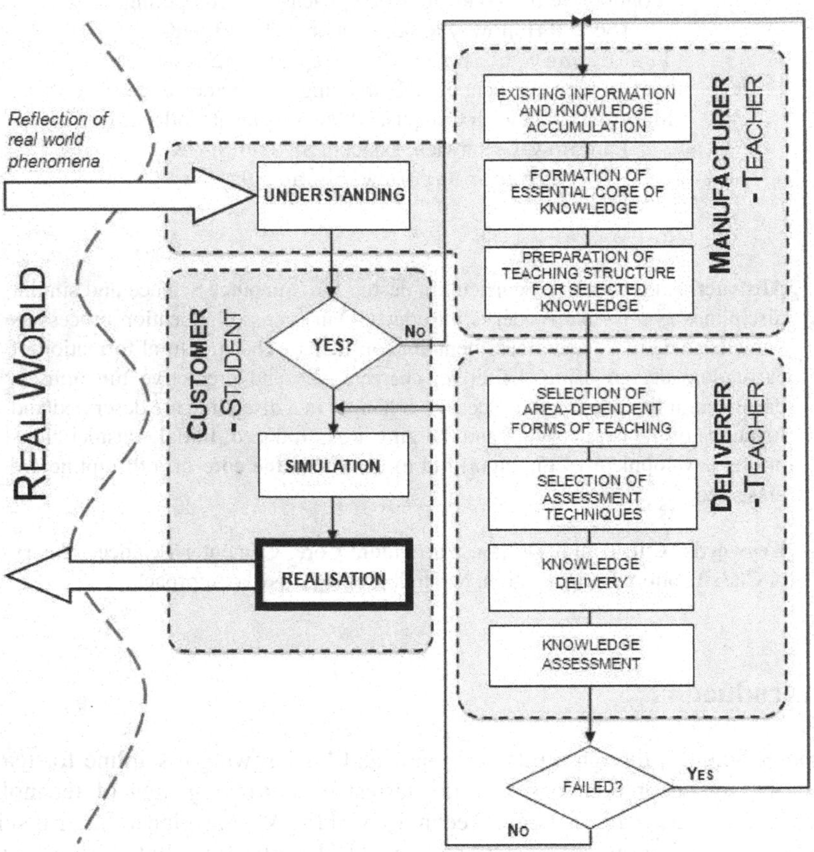

Fig. 1. 'Return the Results of Education to Society' Algorithm

Figure 1 also shows the roles of the main agents (student and teacher) in the framework of the education process with feedback being the main measure of teaching success. During teaching the lecturer is the main ***deliverer*** of the products: *Knowledge* and *Skills*. The main ***consumer*** or ***customer*** is the student. The cycle of education is completed when ***a customer*** returns his/her results back to the society and, therefore, becomes ***a deliverer***.

2 Science, Knowledge, Skills and Curriculum

The specific meaning of the main terms used here is defined below. Complete description of each term can be found in The New Penguin English Dictionary [3].

- Science - 1. The study, description, experimental investigation and theoretical explanation of the nature and behaviour of phenomena in the physical and natural world; 2. Branch of systematized knowledge of study.
- Knowledge - 1. Information, understanding acquired through learning or experience; 2. The total body of known facts or those associated with a particular subject; 3. Justified or verifiable belief, as distinct from opinion *(Phil).*
- Skills - Special abilities in particular field acquired by learning or practice.
- Curriculum - The courses offered by an educational institution or followed by an individual or group; *Latin* - running, course, course of study, programme.
- Computer Science - Study of the construction, operation, and use of computers.

Science differs from *Knowledge* by the indirect introduction of *the Subject* (an agent) to receive *Knowledge.* We define the relation between *knowledge* and *information* as:

$$Knowledge = Information + Algorithm\ of\ its\ Application \quad (1)$$

Any discipline of Computer Science assumes a certain amount of *Knowledge* (K) and *Skills* (S) in some proportion necessary in discipline design and curriculum development. *Skills* are different from *Knowledge* as they concern a special ability not a wide understanding of an area. *Skills* are concerned with the application of particular *Knowledge* or experience in a specific, well known environment, whereas *Knowledge* is about the application of experience and learning outcomes in an uncertain and wide environment. Rigorous separation of *Knowledge* and *Skills* helps balance discipline structure by means of using the most appropriate instruments of the teaching/learning circle: lectures, tutorials, practicals, courseworks, and assessment techniques. Both *Knowledge* and *Skills* are essential components of education:

$$Knowledge + Skills = Successful\ Application\ of\ Education \quad (2)$$

Disciplines where $K > S$ (Software Engineering, Algorithm Design, Problem Solving, Network Technologies, Theory of Programming, Discrete Math, etc.) require much more active lectures and seminars and must be built with a wide area of knowledge, be more abstract and, where possible, general in order to show the limits of the existing knowledge, as well as its place in the context of science.

Disciplines where $K < S$ (Web Design, HTML, Java, Visual Basic, Modula-2, Pascal, Applications of Databases, etc.) require many more practical sessions focussed on one narrow area of skills and their applicability, supported by small introductions of elementary or essential theory.

Disciplines where $K = S$ (Human Computer Interaction, Computer Aided Design, Computer Graphics, etc.) allow for a more balanced approach to instruments of the teaching/learning circle.

As far as the word *curriculum* is concerned, a more holistic approach may assume that this should be placed between the *aim of education* (what we want to achieve), and the *learning outcome* (what we are able to measure, the result of education) even though the measurability of the latter may be questionable. *Curriculum,* in turn, is just another name for the program of study which must be complete, efficient and reliable in order to provide *Education* in the selected area or discipline.

It is clear from the above that new research is required in the area of structuring of knowledge delivery and derivation of schemes in order to measure the result of discipline delivery. The research work presented here focuses on schemes of knowledge delivery and assessing and in this context *Curriculum Development.*

3 Modelling of Educational Program Development

Three very complex entities are involved in the process of education: *Science, Science Deliverer* (Lecturer) and *Science Consumer* (Student). Various authors [4], [5] and [6] described the main elements of the course design process, their interrelation in time and their logical order. However, the models that they put forward are too generic and concerns are raised with regards to their applicability, usefulness, efficiency and their measurement in the course design process. Moreover, they don't even mention the resource dependence of the discipline and possible ways for its delivery.

It is imperative that the context of the discipline is involved, embedded and reflected in and during the *curriculum design process*. The need to develop a new model of the discipline and, therefore, curriculum design is obvious. The order is also very important: at first, one has to develop *a discipline*, and *then* the way of delivery. Below is such a sequence of discipline development:

I. Determination and definitions of the main elements in the discipline
   - Description of connections between definitions
   - Selection of main features of definitions

II. Analysis of the schemes for discipline delivery (either existing, or new)

III. Specification of discipline delivery main elements
   - Course structure
   - Assessment instruments
   - Performance issues and scheme of its measurement

A development of the *Theory of Information Processing*, [7], [8] and [9], described at the level of the main categories and resources can help model education program development. In these papers, *input information* goes through an algorithm (processing), *new information* is created on the way and *the result* is produced and delivered. The process *of Learning* can also be analysed as *Information Processing* and vice versa:

The Processes of Teaching and Learning are in fact one entity:
Information Processing

4 Curriculum Development as Information Processing

By applying terms and results from the *theory of information processing* for various aspects and areas of pedagogy principles of classification for information systems can help build a course of learning with the highest possible understanding as well as a measure of this. Analysis of all possible resources necessary to form a *discipline* and its *curriculum* must follow and rigorous classification of resources and ways of their use and processing should be built to form the framework for all further steps. A well-known sequence of steps to deliver knowledge includes:

a) *Knowledge* delivery,
b) Delivery of practical (application of knowledge),
c) An assessment.

All steps in this sequence should be completed at the right time and should also be transparent to the system (University). In reality, many more steps (in the *Knowledge Delivery Algorithm*) are needed to eliminate malfunctions and avoid student failures or even their withdrawal from a course.

According to [7], [8] and [9] the options and resources that we have when creating a discipline and curriculum suitable for efficient teaching and learning are *structure*, *time* and *information*. At the same time, it is clear that testing time (assessment) should be eliminated from the algorithm of knowledge delivery even though without assessment it will be impossible to receive feedback on the quality of education, either at the macro level – from the society at large (see Fig.1) or from the university. To resolve this issue well-known hardware design techniques of self-checking [10] could help and should be used. In our case the most important feature of self-checking is <u>concurrency</u>, or near concurrency, with functioning and *self-checking* even though the term *self-checking* in pedagogy has a one-to-one synonym: *self-assessment*. The difference lies in the quality of self-assessment which is very weak in comparison with self-checking as described by the Boolean logic function. As far as resources for *knowledge delivery* are concerned *time* cannot be counted, as it is beyond our control! Figure 2 classifies resources for the delivery of knowledge with the two shaded boxes presenting IT elements involved in the process of *Knowledge* delivery.

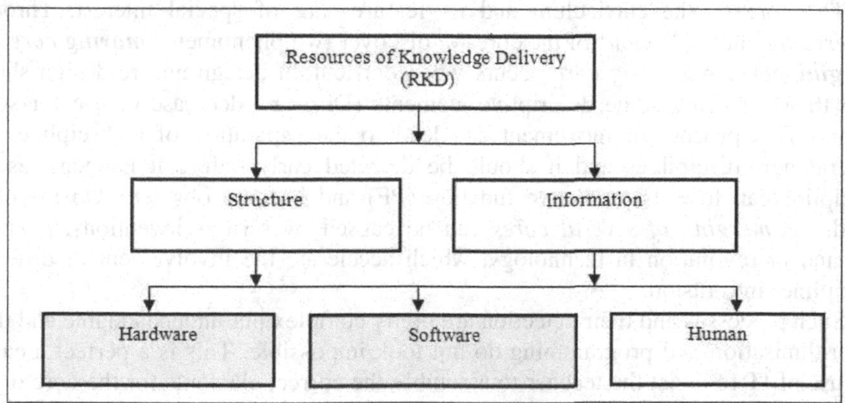

Fig. 2. Classification of Resources to deliver *Knowledge* excluding *Time*

5 Principles of Curriculum Design

The requirements for the formation of a new curriculum identify that:

1. By direct analogy with [7], [8] and [9], any discipline, as an introduction of a theory, should be considered from the point of view of performance of three interconnected functions: *Definitive* (what is it?), *Characteristic* (how are these definitions connected?) and *Predictive* (what if?).
2. The discipline must be constructed with the strict principle of aim integrity, i.e. with the selection of the single feature (predictive function) necessary to achieve and maximise.
3. Each phase of introduction, presentation and detailed analysis of a discipline development must be rigorously analysed. Otherwise, the success of the course built around this discipline will be problematic.
4. Only really essential features and details of the analyzed discipline objects and phenomena must be included.

The applicability of the three functions mentioned above is the key to successful discipline and curriculum development. Essentially, the resources available should be analyzed, including any new technologies such as information processing. IT involvement in the process of course construction should be considered from the beginning.

6 Curriculum Core

To build the core of a curriculum on a subject a set of Definitive Functions {DF} and one of Characteristic Functions {CF} must be constructed. The {DF} should contain the set of terms, in the same way as the Glossary of a book does, and the {CF} should contain the set of topics describing how definitions are connected, in the same way as the Index of a book does. By combining terms from the Glossary with the Index we have a semi-automatic procedure to form a set of essential questions required for *Assessment*.

The core of the curriculum and its features are of special interest. Through *observation* and *behaviour* of the core we discover two phenomena: ***moving core*** and ***merging core***. A *moving core* occurs when curriculum design and re-design shows growth when using some descriptive elements (DF_i) and decrease of use for some others. This process of movement can lead to the separation of a discipline into several new disciplines and it should be detected early before it happens, as the discipline can lose its predictive function (PF) and become obsolete. On the other hand, the *merging of several cores* can be caused by serious inventions, practical demand or revolution in technology, which accelerate the involvement of different disciplines into fusion.

Such processes and their detection are pretty complex but understandable and their algorithmisation and programming do not look impossible. This is a perfect area for the use of IT to assist the teacher to assemble the correct elements for the core of the discipline.

7 Conclusions

We attempted to form a logical *core* of *curriculum design* for computer science and similar disciplines. Initially, the main terms used were defined and the role of education in the improvement of life for the society at large was identified.

Existing models of curriculum development were briefly discussed and were found to be of a very generic nature. Their drawbacks were also identified as being applicability, usefulness and efficiency, and their measurement in the course design process. Curriculum design as information processing was then introduced along with the definitive, characteristic and predictive functions in discipline construction.

The principles of curriculum design, the core of the discipline, the way of its selection and its main features: moving and merging, were also discussed. The automatic formation of Glossary, Indexes, tracing their modifications, formation of assessment procedure and its realization was shown to be one of the roles of IT. The two processes (moving and merging) can help detect changes in scientific areas related to the discipline automatically and assist the teacher to almost automatically adjust the curriculum and assessment to these changes.

The next step in this work will incorporate further extensive analysis of the concepts introduced here. We will then focus in the development of assessment as part of curriculum development with analysis of its features and a new approach: *Multiple Choice Answers Approach* (MCAA) will be introduced along with the scheme for its realisation. This approach will enable us to achieve better reliability, validity and consistency of knowledge delivery.

References

1. Jeans, J.: The Mysterious Universe, pp.106–138. Macmillan, New York (1930)
2. ChinaCulture.org, Ministry of Culture, P. R. China, `http://www.culturalink.gov.cn/gb/en_aboutchina/2003-09/24/content_23084.htm` (accessed April 08, 2010)
3. Penguin, The New PENGUIN English Dictionary (2001)
4. Toohey, S.: Designing Courses for Higher Education, Buckingham. The Society for Research into Higher Education & Open University Press (1999)
5. Ramsden, P.: Learning to Teach in Higher Education. Routledge, London (1992)
6. Diamond, R.M.: Designing and Improving Courses and Curricula in Higher Education: A Systematic Approach. Jossey-Bass Inc., San Francisco (1989)
7. Schagaev, I.: Yet Another Approach to Classification of Redundancy. In: IMEKO Congress, Helsinki, Finland, pp. 485–490 (1990)
8. Schagaev, I.: Redundancy Classification For Fault Tolerant Computer Design. In: Proceedings of the 2001 IEEE Systems, Man, and Cybernetics Conference, Tuscon, AZ (2001)
9. Schagaev, I., Buhanova, G.: Comparative Study of Fault Tolerant RAM Structures. In: Proceedings of IEEE DSN Conference, Sweden, Goteborg (July 2001)
10. Carter, W.: Digital Designing with Programmable Logic Devices. Prentice Hall, Englewood Cliffs (1996) ISBN: 0133737217

3D Visualization in Elementary Education Astronomy: Teaching Urban Second Graders about the Sun, Earth, and Moon

Zeynep Isik-Ercan[1], Beomjin Kim[2], and Jeffrey Nowak[1]

[1] Department of Educational Studies, Indiana University-Purdue University Fort Wayne
[2] Department of Computer Science, Indiana University-Purdue University Fort Wayne, 2101 E. Coliseum Blvd. Fort Wayne, IN 46805-1499 U.S.A.
{isikz,kimb,nowakj}@ipfw.edu

Abstract. This research-in-progress hypothesizes that urban second graders can have an early understanding about the shape of Sun, Moon, and Earth, how day and night happens, and how Moon appears to change its shape by using three dimensional stereoscopic vision. The 3D stereoscopic vision system might be an effective way to teach subjects like astronomy that explains relationships among objects in space. Currently, Indiana state standards for science teaching do not suggest the teaching of these astronomical concepts explicitly before fourth grade. Yet, we expect our findings to indicate that students can learn these concepts earlier in their educational lives with the implementation of such technologies. We also project that these technologies could revolutionize when these concepts could be taught to children and expand the ways we think about children's cognitive capacities in understanding scientific concepts.

Keywords: Stereoscopic vision, astronomy, early childhood education, technology in elementary education, virtual environments.

1 Introduction and Theoretical Background

There are strong arguments from theories of developmentally appropriate practice and from maturationist beliefs that young children cannot comprehend most scientific concepts due to their limited reasoning abilities [1, 2]. Some researchers claim that young children are unable to explain astronomical ideas [3, 4], and that even fewer children can explain the scientifically correct relationship among Sun, Earth, and Moon.

On the other hand, there is a big push for increased science and math learning in elementary schools as outlined in the state standards for science, math, and technology. Moreover, taking a social constructivist perspective to curriculum, several researchers have pointed out that children as young as preschool age may be able to reason around scientific concepts [5, 6, 7] with scaffolding, modeling, and collaboration. Photos, videos, and software were often used in specifically supporting young children's understanding of the relationship among Earth, Sun, and Moon. One hesitation for teaching young children about the universe and objects in sky is that there is no possibility for children to fully understand that these objects are 3D in the videos

M.D. Lytras et al. (Eds.): WSKS 2010, Part I, CCIS 111, pp. 500–505, 2010.

since they do not see the depth of the objects. Sometimes, even after teaching, students might gain new misconceptions about Moon, Sun, and Earth, such as their shapes, orbits, and relationships relative to one another.

Perhaps due to these constraints, Indiana state standards for astronomy learning in second grade (2010) suggest the scope of learning about astronomy in second grade should be limited as rationalized by the following statements on the learning standard website: "During these years, learning about objects in the sky should be entirely observational and qualitative, for the children are far from ready to understand the magnitudes involved or to make sense out of explanations. The priority is to get the students noticing and describing what the sky looks like to them at different times. They should, for example, observe how Moon appears to change its shape. But it is too soon to name all Moon's phases and much too soon to explain them." [8]

2 The Study

Is it possible to support young children in their understanding of Earth, Sun, and Moon using technology, particularly through 3D virtual environments? 3D technologies already captivate young students' attention in entertainment contexts such as TV and video games. We wonder what 3D visualization might offer young students in their school learning, particularly in learning about Sun, Earth, and Moon in their science lessons.

2.1 Research Questions

In an interdisciplinary team composed of an early child educator, a computer scientist, and a science educator, we investigate whether younger children understand the shape of space objects and relationship among Moon, Sun and Earth when they are supported by active exploration through 3D visualization in northeast Indiana, in an urban school context. We specifically explore these research questions:

1. Do 3D visualization help urban second graders understand (a) the shape of Sun, Moon, and Earth, (b) how day and night happen, (c) how and why seasons happen, and (d), why Moon appears to change its shape?
2. Do urban second graders' motivation and attitude towards science learning increase as a result of the study?

3 Literature Review

3.1 3D Stereoscopic Vision and Virtual Reality Systems

Recent advancements in technology enable computer graphics capabilities to create further photorealistic images. Unlike the traditional 2D display devices, the 3D stereoscopic device uses two images of the same scene that are captured from slightly different perspectives. By using specially designed eyeglasses, each eye captures a different image from two superimposed images. The human brain combines two images into one particular image that allows us to perceive the depth.

The stereoscopic vision has been mainly used in technological fields in the past. Perhaps due to their high cost, constructing realistic 3D stereoscopic virtual environments (VE) in the past was limited to research centers for high computational visualization, automotive industry for prototype design, and defense-related companies for training and therapy [9, 10]. However, the recent advancement in computer technology significantly cut down hardware cost for rendering the stereoscopic images. By using modern computer graphics devices, one can even generate VEs on a Personal Computer that is viewable through 3D-compatable projectors.

Education is another emerging area that could utilize this technology. Introduction of stereoscopic vision into the education field has so far been proven as an effective tool to improve students' participation and also increase their understanding of the subject. The virtual reality environment has often been used for e-learning applications. In two different studies, a web-enabled interactive system implemented two subsystems of online virtual chemistry lab and online English language education system involved natural learning environments [11]. In another study, the VE was used for geometry education. A system utilized the collaborative augmented reality to teach geometry for high school students. The experimental tests showed positive results using the VEs in high school or university education [12].

3.2 3D Visualization and Elementary Education

Based on a recent literature review, we observed a scarcity of studies focusing on the use of VE, particularly utilizing 3D stereoscopic vision with younger children in different educational contexts. Fewer studies explored the ways 3D models could support children's school learning in elementary school. Hwang, Huang and Dong found that six graders rated the use of a multi-representative construction model as helpful, easy to use and useful in solving geometry problems [13]. A study in Scotland that explored the use of virtual environment in the context of a virtual interactive fantasy tale called Magic Cottage in 13 primary school children's imaginative writing and motivation in literacy learning has produced positive results as expressed by teachers and students [14]. Researchers also developed of a virtual 3D marine museum for science teaching in elementary schools that enhanced students' interest and learning motivation particularly due to its visual effects and game-based learning model [15]. Finally, a study aimed to develop a 3D VE model named Sun and Moon System with 128 Taiwanese fourth graders and found that students in the treatment group had significantly better grades as well as satisfaction with the use of this method of instruction in as reported by more than two thirds of the students [16].

3.3 Virtual Reality Systems in K-16 Astronomy Education

The 3D stereoscopic vision is an ideal resource to teach subjects like astronomy education that explains relationships among objects in 3D space. Several researchers evaluated the effectiveness of virtual reality systems for astronomy education in the classroom [17, 18]. They implemented a VE simulating the solar system to enhance students' understanding of astronomical concept. Moreover, experimental studies conducted with middle school, secondary students and college students showed improvement of learning results and participants expressed positive opinions on the proposed systems [19, 20]. In these studies with VE, students' understanding of astronomical concepts related to planets, and other astronomical objects proved to have fewer misconceptions after instruction and their mental models seemed more scientifically accurate [17, 18, 19, 20]. It is our hope that a similar result will be indicated by our research using this technology at the elementary level.

4 Methodology

4.1 Prototype System Configuration

In this research, our team is in the process of developing the software for 3D visualization via projectors and special goggles to observe Sun, Moon, and Earth, in a virtual reality environment in the classroom settings.

We first constructed a prototype system that displays a solar system -particularly focusing on Sun, Earth, and Moon as central objects- using 3D stereoscopic devices. The 3D VE showing a primitive solar system was constructed using the OGRE (Object-Oriented Graphics Rendering Engine), C++ programming language, and SketchUp for modeling planetary objects. Users are able to navigate the astronomical image in the stereoscopic vision using two special display devices, 120 Hz Samsung SyncMaster 3D LCD monitor and NVIDIA GeForce 3D Vision Kit including wireless active shutter glasses and USB-based IR Emitter for the synchronization. We're working to enhance the realism of the VE and develop intuitive interaction mechanisms for students in the early education. The completed system will project the image using a short-throw DLP Projector that allows students to experience 3D stereoscopic images using a low cost 3D polarized glass.

4.2 Implementation

We will collaborate with second grade classroom teachers to create the science lessons in order to implement 3D technology. The timeline of the research study is approximately 3-4 weeks of instruction in assigned science lessons. Students will be shown a big screen as they are also given 3D goggles to observe Sun, Moon, and Earth, and the interactions among them. Students will be able to explore the software and manipulate objects in the sky in small groups. Therefore, they will either be in the position of audience, or participators. The students will continue to observe, manipulate, and learn about the interactions and the relationships among Sun, Earth, and Moon with the guidance of the teacher.

4.3 Assessment

Pre and post interviews with students will be conducted as a means of qualitatively measuring their knowledge about the interactions and the relationships among Sun, Earth, and Moon, and exploring their attitudes and motivation towards science learning. Students' school work, specifically writing and drawing pieces will be collected, coded, and quantified to assess the impact of the intervention. A questionnaire to measure students' attitude and motivation towards science learning will also be used.

5 Conclusions

In this research we propose that it might be possible for younger children to learn about Sun, Moon, and Earth, particularly their shapes, the relationship among them, such as day and night, Moon's changing appearance and seasons with the help of 3D visualization. Therefore, this research hypothesizes that second graders can have an understanding about the shape of Sun, Moon, and Earth, how day and night happens, and how Moon changes its shape earlier in their educational lives if they are able to visualize their movement in a 3D VE.

The choice of focusing on an urban low achieving school aligns with our goal of providing children from disadvantaged communities with opportunities to use new visualization technologies in their education. This approach will also help us determine whether supporting children's school learning with these technologies also improves their motivation and confidence as successful learners. If our findings indicate that students can learn these concepts earlier in their educational lives with the implementation of such technologies, we believe these technologies could revolutionize when these concepts could be taught to children and expand our thinking about children's cognitive capacities in understanding scientific concepts.

References

1. Kuhn, D., Dean, D.: Connecting Scientific Reasoning and Causal Inference. Journal of Cognition and Development 5(2), 261–288 (2004)
2. Kuhn, D.: Children and Adults as Intuitive Scientists. Psychological Review 96, 674–689 (1989)
3. Sharp, J.G.: Children's Astronomical Beliefs: A Preliminary Study of Year 6 Children in South-west England. International Journal of Science Education 18(6), 685–712 (1996)
4. Jones, B.L., Lynch, P.P., Reesink, C.: Children's Conceptions of the Earth, Sun and Moon. International Journal of Science Education 9(1), 43–53 (1987)
5. Kamii, C., DeVries, R.: Physical Knowledge in Preschool Education: Implications of Piaget's Theories. Prentice-Hall, Englewood Cliffs (1978)
6. Russell, T., Harlen, W., Watt, D.: Children's Ideas about Evaporation. International Journal of Science Education 11(5), 566–576 (1989)
7. Ravanis, K.: The Discovery of Elementary Magnetic Properties in Pre-school Age: A Qualitative and Quantitative Research within a Piagetian Framework. European Early Childhood Education Research Journal 2(2), 79–91 (1994)
8. Indiana's Revised Academic Standards for Science in 2010 (2010), `http://www.indianascience.org/`
9. Crison, F., Lécuyer, A., Irisa, I.R., D'huart, D.M., Burkhardt, J., Michel, G., Dautin, J.: Virtual Technical Trainer: Learning How to Use Milling Machines with Multi-Sensory Feedback in Virtual Reality. In: IEEE Virtual Reality Conference, pp. 139–146 (2005)
10. Pair, J., Allen, B., Dautricourt, M., Treskunov, A., Liewer, M., Graap, K., Reger, G., Rizzo, A.: A Virtual Reality Exposure Therapy Application for Iraq War Post Traumatic Stress Disorder. In: IEEE Virtual Reality Conference, pp. 62–72 (2006)
11. Abdul-Kader, H.M.: E-Learning Systems in Virtual Environment. In: The 18th International Conference on Computer Theory and Applications, pp. 71–76 (2008)

12. Kaufmann, H., Schmalstieg, D.: Designing Immersive Virtual Reality for Geometry Education. In: IEEE Virtual Reality Conference, pp. 51–58 (2006)
13. Hwang, W.-Y., Su, J.-H., Huang, Y.-M., Dong, J.-J.: A Study of Multi-Representation of Geometry Problem Solving with Virtual Manipulatives and Whiteboard System. Educational Technology & Society 12(3), 229–247 (2009)
14. Patera, M., Draper, S., Naef, M.: Exploring Magic Cottage: a virtual reality environment for stimulating children's imaginative writing. Interactive Learning Environments 16(3), 245–263 (2008)
15. Tarng, W.-Y., Change, M.-Y., Ou, K.-L., Chang, Y.-W., Liou, H.-H.: The Development of a Virtual Marine Museum, for Educational Applications. J. Educational Technology Systems 37(1), 39–59 (2008-2009)
16. Sun, K.-T., Lin, C.-L., Wang, S.-M.: A 3-D Virtual Reality Model of Sun and Moon for E-Learning at Elementary Schools. International Journal of Science and Mathematics Education (2009)
17. Lee, H., Park, S., Kim, H., Lee, H.: Students' Understanding of Astronomical Concepts Enhanced by an Immersive Virtual Reality System (IVRS). In: International Conference on Multimedia and ICT in Education, pp. 1–5 (2005)
18. Ni, L., Krzeminski, M., Tuer, K.: Application of Haptic, Visual and Audio Integration in Astronomy Education. In: IEEE International Workshop on Haptic Audio Visual Environments and their Applications, pp. 152–156 (2006)
19. Chen, C.H., Yang, J.C., Shen, S., Jeng, M.C.: Desktop Virtual Reality Earth Motion System in Astronomy Education. Educational Technology & Society 10(3), 289–304 (2007)
20. Bakas, C., Mikropoulos, T.A.: Design of virtual environments for the comprehension of planetary phenomena based on students' ideas. Int. J. Sci. Educ. 25(8), 949–967 (2003)

Applying CIPP Model for Learning-Object Management

Erla M. Morales Morgado[1], Francisco J. García Peñalvo[2], Carlos Muñoz Martín[1], and Miguel Ángel Conde Gonzalez[1]

[1] GRIAL Research Group - University of Salamanca
[2] Computer Science Department / Science Education Research Institute / GRIAL Research Group - University of Salamanca
{erlamorales,fgarcia,carlosmm,mconde}@usal.es

Abstract. Although knowledge management process needs to receive some evaluation in order to determine their suitable functionality. There is not a clear definition about the stages where LOs need to be evaluated and the specific metrics to continuously promote their quality. This paper presents a proposal for LOs evaluation during their management for e-learning systems. To achieve this, we suggest specific steps for LOs design, implementation and evaluation into the four stages proposed by CIPP model (Context, Input, Process, Product).

Keywords: Metadata, Learning objects, Knowledge Management.

1 Introduction

In pedagogical area, there is an old model CIPP (Context, Input, Process and Product) attuned to evaluate the teaching/learning process into four stages. The stages mentioned above can be applied for LOs management in order to promote their quality during their life cycle.

To achieve this, we suggest specific things to take into consideration for each evaluation stage. Section 1 explains context evaluation where we suggest key issues to design LOs taking into account the specific educational situation where they are going to be reused. Section 2 explains input evaluation, attuned to ensure LOs elements are enough to achieve the specific leaning goal. On this basis, we propose a normalization process where it is possible to design LOs taking into account pedagogical and technical issues.

In order to ensure LOs quality design, we suggest an instrument for expert evaluation "HEODAR", which contains rubrics and specific criteria for pedagogical and technical issues. Section 3 explains how we think to promote process and product evaluation, to achieve this we take into account the students' interaction with LOs and the teachers LOs evaluation as a product using HEODAR, in this way they can be able to improve and reefed the LOs quality continually. Finally it presents our conclusions and plans for the next stages of our work (section 4).

M.D. Lytras et al. (Eds.): WSKS 2010, Part I, CCIS 111, pp. 506–511, 2010.

2 Learning Objects Context Evaluation

The opportunity offered by the LOs to be reused, indicating a high probability that they are imported, that is, acquired from external sources. On the other hand, may be the case that the LO requested does not exist and it has created. In both cases to determine the LOs needed in a learning situation, teachers should be based on the learning context on which to select the objectives, content and educational activities.

In case they are imported or created, they need to be suitable for the new context in which to reuse them. Williams [8] defines context evaluations that investigate the socio-political, organizational, and other contextual variables associated with the need for learning objects, courses, and support efforts.

Taking into account these arguments, we suggest the following things to take into account for context LOs evaluation: Learning goals, contents, learners' characteristics and didactic strategies. As shows Figure 1, we think it is necessary to normalize LO according to a specific model that aim to ensure their suitable characteristics as a LO and their pedagogical and technical issues [4].

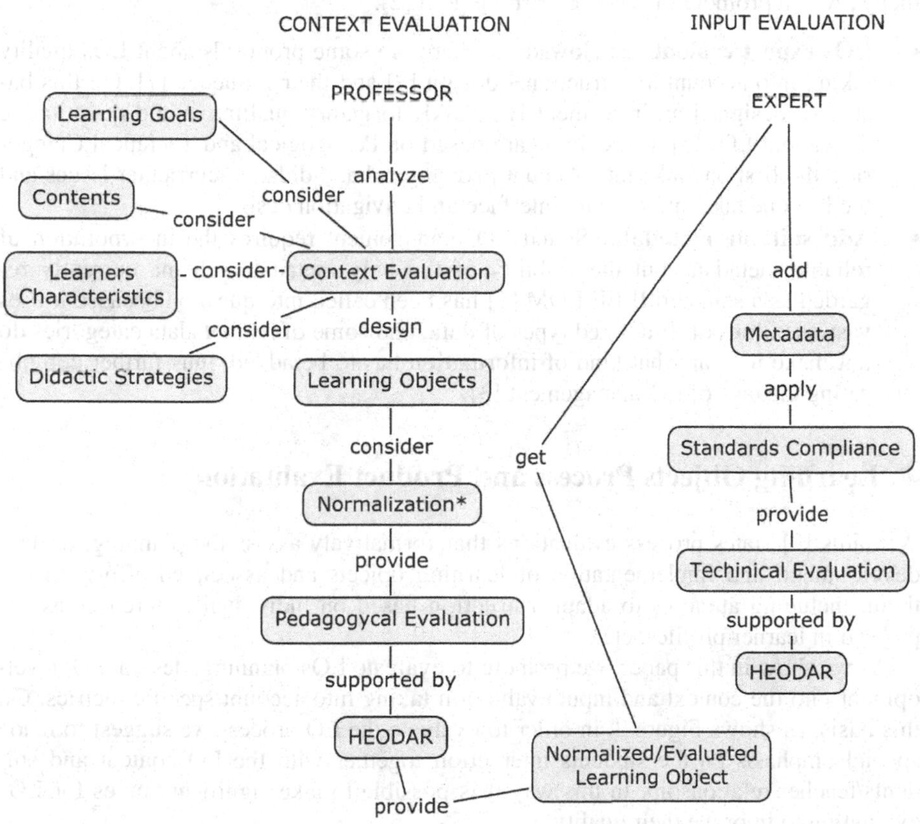

Fig. 1. Context and Input Learning Objects Evaluation

In this context, normalization means that although LO instructional design is currently a much-discussed topic, there are certain aspects that must be considered to ensure a quality LO instructional design [4]. The model promotes to consider the minimal required elements to support a LO as a reusable didactic source, where it is needed to establish all the context issues mentioned above.

Once we have the LOs design it is needed to valuate if they have the pedagogical and technical requisites to reuse them, according to this we suggest the next evaluation stage: Input evaluation, as we are going to explain in the next section.

3 Learning Objects Input Evaluation

CIPP model establish the input evaluation as a way to detect alternative necessities in the context evaluation. According to [8] input evaluations compare alternative inputs or means for meeting the needs identified in context evaluations, including but not limited to learning objects. On this basis, we suggest to apply an input evaluation directed to ensure the LOs have all the elements for their reuse and the didactic elements, which promotes a specific learning goal [2].

- **LOs expert evaluation:** Nowadays, there are some proposals about LOs quality taking into account a instructional design [8] and their sequence [7]. On this basis, we designed an instrument HEODAR to gather qualitative and quantitative data about LOs [5], [6]. Criteria are based on Pedagogical and Technical Categories, the first one take into account pedagogical and didactic-curricular issues and the last one take into account interface and navigation design.
- **Add suitable metadata:** Sound LO management requires the incorporation of reliable metadata, but the viability of the only metadata schema currently regarded as a standard IEEE LOM [1] has been called into question because it uses vast quantities of ill-defined types of data, and some of its metadata categories do not make it clear what kind of information has to be added, thus further complicating the task of LO management [3].

4 Learning Objects Process and Product Evaluation

Williams [8] states process evaluations that formatively assess the planning, design, development, and implementation of learning objects and associated efforts to use them, including attempts to adapt instruction based on individual differences as expressed in learner profiles, etc.

As we show in this paper, we promote to evaluate LOs planning, design and development into the context and input evaluation taking into account specific metrics. On this basis, as shows Figure 2, in order to evaluate the LO process we suggest to made special emphasis on the students interaction together with the LO content and students/teacher relationship. In this way it is possible to take significant notes for LOs evaluation to improve their quality.

As we said before we promotes the process evaluation to valuate the LOs implementation and collect information about the attitude of the students and comments. In this process teacher can realize if their students are understanding and learning about the specific contents. In order to obtain specific users data we suggest to make a product evaluation through HEODAR that can be use to collect quantitative and qualitative information.

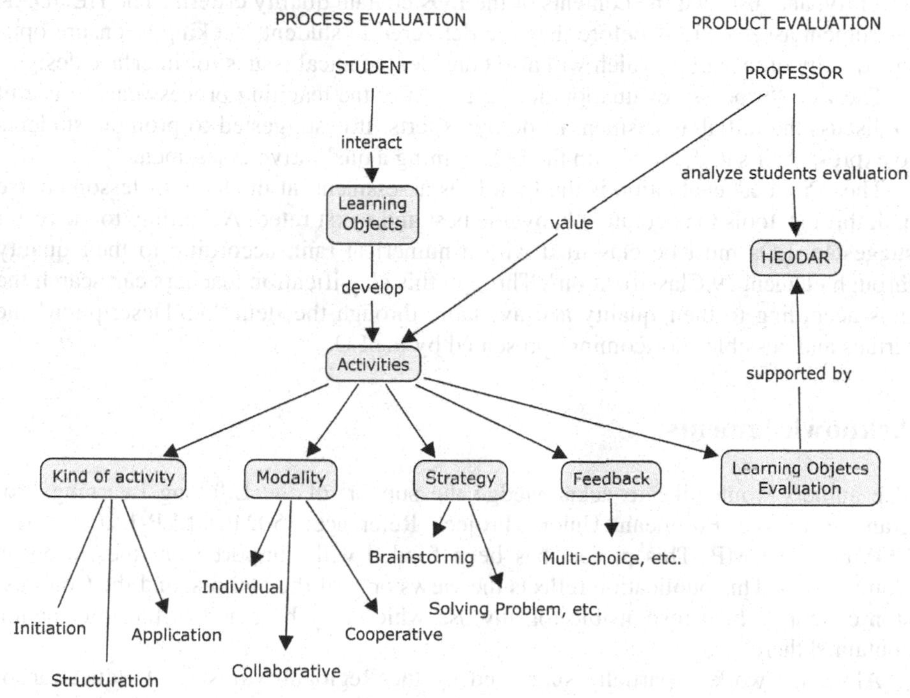

Fig. 2. Process and Product Learning Objects Evaluation

In order to get a balanced LO quality value we suggest to average the final score from each one of the four instrument parts, in this way it is possible to add a specific value to LO metadata into 9.classification IEEE LOM metadata [4]. This category aims to add quantitative and qualitative values in order to search and manage LOs according to their quality.

5 Conclusions

Williams rescues the CIPP approach to assess LOs promotes reuse because they are used in processes for a variety of contexts. Into the "Context" evaluation we had mentioned certain aspects to consider in determining whether the LOs to reuse adapting to the new educational situation. To ensure a proper LOs design, we suggest a normalization process where LOs was proposed to classify them according to criteria to different kind of goals and contents to facilitate their management. The classification of the LOs according to the cognitive level allows teachers to facilitate the LOs searching according to their educational goals, which indicate what the student is able to do and estimated the level of complexity. The "Content Type" classification help to better define the type of LO for reuse.

The “Input evaluation”, ensures that the LOs met with the interoperability and reusability, and also that the contents of the LOs contain quality criteria. The HEODAR instrument assesses LOs before they are delivered to students seeking to ensure optimal quality of teaching, which will also consider technical issues for interface design.

The LOs “Process” evaluation during and after the teaching process can be useful to discuss the initial assessment made by experts. It is suggested to promote students to express their satisfaction with the LOs gaining a qualitative assessment.

The "Product" evaluation is the final LOs assessment, at the level of lesson course and, through tools to accurately know the best and worst rated. According to the result suggested, LOs must be classified with a numerical rank according to their quality through element "9.Classification". Through this classification teachers can search the LOs according to their quality and available through the item "9.3.Description" the virtues and possible shortcomings presented by the LO.

Acknowledgments

The authors would like to acknowledge the support of the Lifelong Learning Programme of the European Union. Project Reference: 502461-LLP-1-2009-1-ES-COMENIUS-CMP. This project has been funded with support from the European Commission. This publication reflects the views only of the authors, and the Commission cannot be held responsible for any use which may be made of the information contained therein.

Also, this work is partially supported by the Regional Ministry of Education of Junta de Castilla y León through project GR47.

References

1. IEEE LOM: IEEE 1484.12.1-2002 Standard for Learning Object Metadata, http://ltsc.ieee.org/wg12
2. Morales, E.M., García, F.J., Barrón, Á.: Key Issues for Learning Objects Evaluation. In: Proceedings of the 9th International Conference on Enterprise Information Systems (ICEIS 2007), vol. 4, pp. 149–154. INSTICC Press (2007)
3. Morales, E.M., García, F.J., Barrón, Á.: Quality Learning Objects Management: A proposal for e-learning Systems. In: 8th Int. Conf. on Enterprise Information Systems Artificial Intelligence and Decision Support Systems, pp. 312–315. INSTICC Press (2006)
4. Morales, E.M., García, F.J., Barrón, A.: Improving LO Quality through Instructional Design Based on an Ontological Model and Metadata. J.UCS. Journal of Universal Computer Science 13(7), 970–979 (2007)
5. Morales, E.M., García, F.J., Barrón, A.: An evaluation instrument for learning object quality and management. In: 10th Int. Conf. on Enterprise Information Systems, pp. 327–332. INSTICC Press (2008)

6. Morales, E.M., Gómez, D., García, F.J.: HEODAR: Herramienta para la Evaluación de Objetos Didácticos de Aprendizaje Reutilizables. In: X Simp. Int. de Informática Educativa (2008)
7. Zapata, R.M.: Calidad en entornos virtuales de aprendizaje y secuenciación de Learning objects (LO). In: Actas del Virtual Campus 2006 (2006)
8. Williams, D.D.: Evaluation of learning objects and instruction using learning objects. In: Wiley, D.A. (ed.) The Instructional use of LOs (2000), `http://reusability.org/read/chapters/williams.doc`

An Interactive Learning Environment for Teaching the Imperative and Object-Oriented Programming Techniques in Various Learning Contexts

Stelios Xinogalos

Department of Technology Management, University of Macedonia, Greece

Abstract. The acquisition of problem-solving and programming skills in the era of knowledge society seems to be particularly important. Due to the intrinsic difficulty of acquiring such skills various educational tools have been developed. Unfortunately, most of these tools are not utilized. In this paper we present the programming microworlds Karel and objectKarel that support the procedural-imperative and Object-Oriented Programming (OOP) techniques and can be used for supporting the teaching and learning of programming in various learning contexts and audiences. The paper focuses on presenting the pedagogical features that are common to both environments and mainly on presenting the potential uses of these environments.

1 Introduction

The acquisition of problem-solving and programming skills in the era of knowledge society seems to be particularly important. However, teaching and learning programming is a difficult topic. A popular teaching approach that is used in order to overcome the underlying difficulties is based on using microworlds or mini-languages (Brusilovsky et al., 1997). Karel and objectKarel are based on the well-known microworlds of Karel (Pattis et al., 1995) and Karel++ (Bergin et al., 1997) respectively. So, these two programming environments share the usual pedagogical benefits of microworlds:

- The programming language consists of a limited instruction set with simple syntax and semantics.
- The metaphor used is an existing metaphor that students are – usually – familiar with, minimizing in this way the cognitive distance between the mental models or descriptions of algorithms in natural language and their description in the programming language.
- The problems solved usually attract students' attention, since they refer to real world problems and not to number and symbol processing.
- The execution of the program is visible on the screen, revealing this way the semantics of the taught concepts, as well as the concepts related to the structure and execution of programs.

M.D. Lytras et al. (Eds.): WSKS 2010, Part I, CCIS 111, pp. 512–520, 2010.

Besides these benefits the environments of Karel and objectKarel, which were designed for clearly didactical purposes, have further pedagogical benefits that stem from their technology enhanced design. Specifically, objectKarel that supports the object-oriented programming technique was developed in the context of a PhD dissertation and was a result of extended research regarding students' difficulties and misconceptions when introduced to programming, teaching approaches, educational programming environments, didactical tools, and educational technology. objectKarel was evaluated positively by two groups of undergraduate students of an Informatics Department (Xinogalos et al., 2006c) and instructors that used objectKarel in other institutes. This resulted in our decision to develop the identical environment Karel for supporting the imperative/procedural programming technique, which is used extensively in Greek Educational Institutes. Karel was developed recently in the context of a research regarding the teaching of programming with microworlds and funded by the Greek Ministry of Education and the European Union as part of the project "Pythagoras II – Funding of research groups in the University of Macedonia".

In this paper we describe briefly: (1) the pedagogical features that both environments share; (2) the potential uses of the environments for teaching programming concepts and/or techniques to various audiences and different learning contexts; (3) experiences from using them in the classroom, and (4) plans for further research.

2 The Pedagogical Features of Karel and objectKarel

In this section we describe briefly the pedagogical features of Karel and objectKarel that make these microworlds ideal for teaching programming concepts.

A familiar metaphor. Karel and objectKarel are based on the microworlds Karel (Pattis et al., 1995) and Karel++ (Bergin et al., 1997), which use a familiar metaphor. The metaphor used is that of a world of robots. The actor of Karel is a robot named Karel and the actor/s of objectKarel one or more robots (objects) assigned various tasks in a world that consists of: (1) crisscrossing horizontal streets and vertical avenues forming one block intervals; (2) wall sections between adjacent streets or avenues used to represent obstacles (hurdles, mountains, mazes etc); and (3) beepers – small plastic cones that emit a quiet beeping noise – placed on street corners (Figure 1). Students write programs that instruct robots how to perform their tasks. Robot Karel and robots of the base class in objectKarel can move forward a block, turn left in place (90° to the left), pick beepers from the current corner or put beepers from their bag to the corner. If a robot with such primitive abilities is not appropriate for a task, then students can implement new subprograms in Karel, or create a new class of robots that extends the base or a previously declared class in objectKarel.

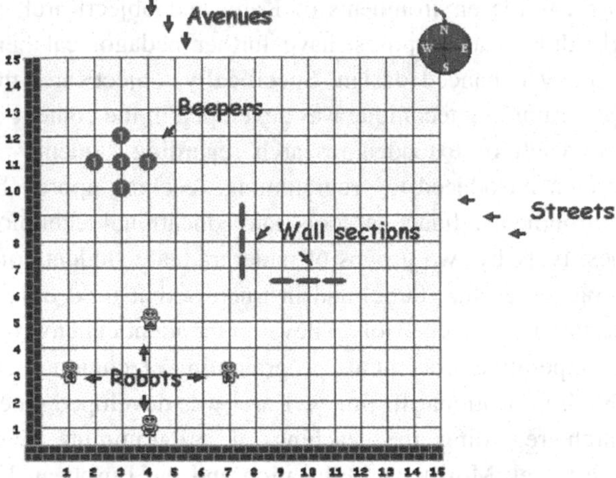

Fig. 1. The metaphor of objectKarel

A learning module with hands-on activities. Both environments have a learning module containing the necessary didactical material: a brief and concise text for the intended programming concepts and hands-on activities for familiarizing users with these concepts (Xinogalos and Satratzemi, 2005) (Figure 2). In the context of these activities students interact with robots by pressing buttons and executing in their own pace specially designed examples. The material covered in this module is presented in Table 1 for both the programming techniques supported. According to the audience and the purpose of a specific teaching some or all the didactical units can be used, in the specific order or an order that suits better.

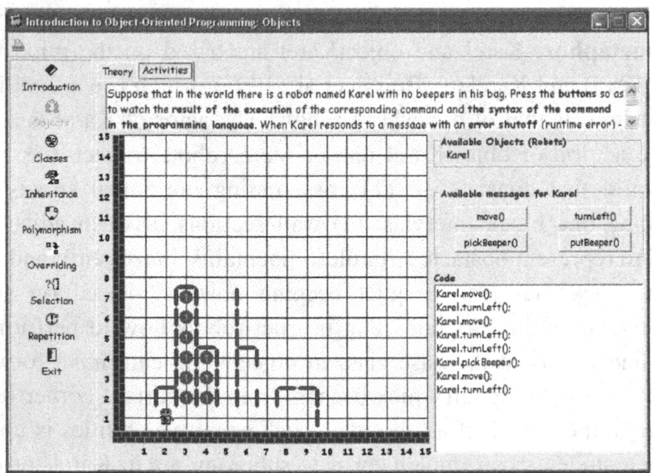

Fig. 2. The learning module consisting of a *theory* tab and an *activities* tab

Table 1. The didactical units of Karel and objectKarel

Karel	objectKarel
Introduction	Introduction
Basic instructions	Objects
Functions	Classes
Selection	Inheritance
Repetition	Polymorphism
	Overriding
	Selection
	Repetition

A structure editor. Users develop programs not by writing the source code without guidance, as is usually the case, but instead by interacting with the special structure editor (Figure 3). Users develop the program by selecting statements from a menu and interacting through dialog boxes. In this way users do not have to memorize the syntax of the language and can concentrate on the concepts.

A "friendly" compiler. Due to the use of the structure editor the errors that can arise are very few. The few error messages that can occur are user-friendly and highly informative: (1) the actual line of the error is presented; (2) the message uses natural language; (3) the source of the error is explained. Users interact with the error messages by double clicking on them. In this case the line of the error in the source code is highlighted by changing the color of its background.

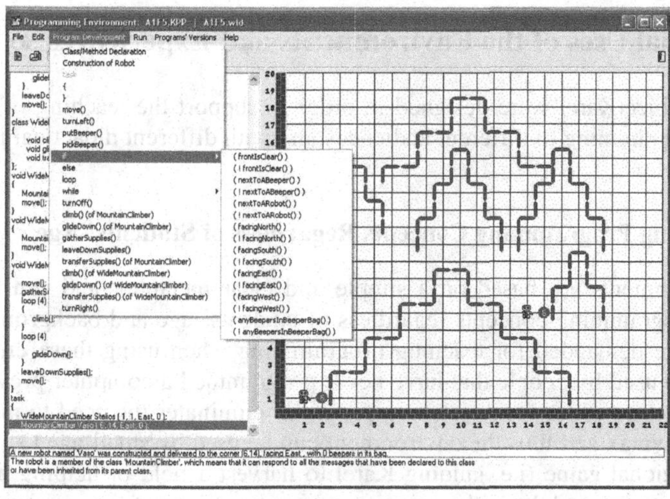

Fig. 3. Developing a program with the structure editor of Karel/objectKarel

An execution system enhanced with program animation & explanatory visualization abilities. Users can run their programs, execute them step-by-step, or trace through them with a speed they choose on their own. The current statement is highlighted by changing the color of its background, while users watch the robot/s executing it in the microworld. Furthermore, a message explaining the semantics of the executing statement in natural language is presented in order to assist users in comprehending the principles of the programming technique used, an ability known as explanatory visualization.

An open environment. In both environments, instructors during the presentation of concepts through examples and users during experimentation with programs can manipulate directly the situation of the world and continue executing the program. This feature helps instructors present the dynamic behavior of programs and flow of control structures for different situations of the world (program's input).

A tool for monitoring difficulties and assessing problem-solving techniques. The environments were supplemented with the ability of saving each compiled version of a program, along with the compiler output. The list of versions is presented in a tree form, and each version can be selected and studied by just clicking on it. This feature was initially developed in order to assist instructors in studying students' difficulties and misconceptions, as well as their problem-solving techniques (Xinogalos and Satratzemi, 2004). However, it can be used by users too in case they want to assess their problem-solving path, study their errors and develop their own improved problem-solving patterns.

A tutorial. Both environments incorporate a brief tutorial (in html format) containing everything the user might need regarding the use of the environment.

3 Potential Uses of the Environments and Experiences so Far

Karel and objectKarel were designed in order to support the teaching of various aspects of programming to different audiences and with different didactical purposes, as described below.

3.1 Teaching Programming Concepts Regardless of Students' Age

Both environments are based on a simple and clear metaphor and can be used for teaching programming concepts regardless of students' age and background. No prerequisites are demanded for teaching programming when using these environments. They can be used by people that have never programmed a computer previously. The use of a structure editor for developing programs eliminates the need to memorize the language's syntax and thus the environment can be used by small-aged students more as an educational game (i.e. guiding Karel to harvest a field or helping him find the way home), or even adults with no programming experience for acquiring basic problem-solving and programming skills.

Recently, the environments were presented to Secondary Education teachers that are going to educate 3200 Informatics teachers - in Greek Secondary Education Schools - on emerging Informatics technologies, pedagogical utilization of ICT with application in Didactics of Informatics, as well as pedagogical use of educational software (microworlds like Karel and objectKarel included). The project is funded by the Greek Ministry of Education and the European Union (http://edu19-20.cti.gr/).

3.2 Teaching Basic Programming Concepts and Principles of the Procedural or/and the Object-Oriented Programming Techniques

Both environments can be used for teaching the main programming concepts: sequential, conditional and repetitive programming structures. Karel can be used for teaching the main principles of the procedural/imperative programming technique: developing programs in modules, functions. Finally, objectKarel can be used for teaching the main principles of the object-oriented programming technique – objects, classes, inheritance -, or even more advanced concepts, such as multilevel inheritance, polymorphism, overriding, and refactoring. Such a teaching can aim at acquiring general programming knowledge or a deeper and more elaborate knowledge on object-oriented programming. For example, students can be involved in projects that demand the application of a rigorous design process resulting in a multilevel class hierarchy, application of polymorphism and overriding, or even in refactoring existing projects with poor class design.

objectKarel was used in two distinct teachings with quite different content, which will be described in the next section.

3.3 Helping Students Overcome the Difficulties Faced in a Conventional Teaching

The teaching of programming is accompanied by many difficulties and misconceptions. These difficulties and misconceptions are much more severe when students are introduced to programming in the conventional way, which is based on a conventional programming language and a professional programming environment. Some students do not manage to overcome their difficulties and the worst outcome is their frustration and dropping out of classes. In our opinion, Karel and objectKarel can provide great help in such circumstances too. Although, someone could think that these environments are intended just for introducing students to programming, they can – as well – be used after an unsuccessful conventional introduction to programming for helping students overcome their difficulties and gain confidence in their ability to program.

objectKarel was used twice for helping undergraduate students of an Informatics Department that had previously been unsuccessfully introduced to programming to overcome their difficulties. All the students had been taught the principles of procedural programming with Pascal and had all failed the exams. Some of them had been taught OOP with Java too. The first teaching took place in 2002 (Xinogalos et al., 2006a) in the context of evaluating objectKarel, while the second teaching took place in 2006 in the context of evaluating a redesigned more advanced series of lessons based in objectKarel (Xinogalos et al., 2006b). Both teachings consisted of five two-hour lessons carried out exclusively at the laboratory. The taught concepts were presented using the material incorporated in the environment, while students developed programs in pairs of two. The rigorous study of students' programs (the consecutive versionsof programs), the final test and the questionnaire for evaluating objectKarel made clear that the goal of the teachings was accomplished: students managed to face many difficulties and misconceptions regarding basic programming concepts that are technique independent, such as sequential, conditional and repetitive structures, and also comprehended the principles of the OOP technique.

3.4 Preparing Students for Their Transition to a Conventional Procedural or Object-Oriented Language

When the goal is not just teaching programming concepts and/or techniques, but preparing future software developers, teaching with a microworld is not enough. However, introducing them to procedural or object-oriented programming with a microworld is not just possible, but highly recommended. In a comparative study of students' answers on a common test taken by two independent undergraduate groups of students in the context of a teaching with objectKarel (10 hours) and a more conventional teaching based on BlueJ and Java (44 hours), showed that students' conceptual grasp of OOP concepts was much deeper in the objectKarel group (Xinogalos, 2008). The question that remains, however, is whether the knowledge acquired in objectKarel is transferred afterwards in the conventional language used for presenting the real thing.

Although, we do not have empirical data we have implications that this approach works well. Professor Rüdiger Lunde mentioned in a personal contact that he used objectKarel with his students in the first two and a half week of a lecture on "Programming in C/C++" for technical computer scientists (first semester, 6 hours per week) at the University of Applied Sciences in Ulm. The general feed-back of his students (about 35) was very positive and most of them recommended the use of objectKarel for the next lecture of this kind.

3.5 Presenting Comparatively the Principles of the Procedural and OO Programming Techniques

Karel and objectKarel are ideal for teachings that aim at presenting comparatively - in a short time – the principles of the two most popular programming techniques: the OO and the procedural technique. The basic control structures can be taught once, nomatter with which technique the instructor will choose to begin. Furthermore, the GUI and the functionalities of Karel and objectKarel are identical and no additional time will be spent for familiarizing students with the environment. What is more important is that the principles of the two techniques are presented in a clear way, while the same problems can be solved using both techniques – clarifying in this way their differences.

3.6 Presenting Problem-Solving Techniques

Problem-solving is part of everyday life. Even if someone is never going to program a computer, it is likely that s/he will have to use some sort of computer and do something beyond the 'usual' (solve some sort of computer problem), and it is sure that s/he will have to solve many problems. So, acquiring problem-solving skills is important for everyone. In this sense, Karel or objectKarel can be used just for teaching problem solving techniques even to non CS majors. Also, the two environments can be used for teaching advanced problem-solving techniques and program-design processes to students with programming experience. Techniques for designing, such as *design trees*, techniques for designing, analyzing and implementing a program, such as *stepwise refinement*, and tools for supporting students in selecting the appropriate structures for implementing their algorithms, such as *decision maps*, can be taught effectively in these environments. According to the audience and the learning context problems of varying difficulty can be used.

3.7 Self-learning of Programming Concepts/Principles

Karel and objectKarel are quite simple and can be used for self-studying. All the text is incorporated in the environment. Furthermore, hands-on activities are incorporated in each learning unit in order to familiarize users with the corresponding concepts before they start implementing them (Xinogalos and Satratzemi, 2005). Finally, the Help module includes everything that an inexperienced user might need to know.

4 Conclusions and Plans for Further Research

The acquisition of problem-solving and programming skills in the era of knowledge society seems to be particularly important. However, teaching and learning problem-solving and programming techniques is widely known to be quite difficult. Karel and objectKarel, which support the imperative/procedural and object-oriented programming techniques respectively, are two environments that can support the teaching and learning process. Their great advantage is that they support the two most popular programming techniques and that they can be used in different learning contexts with various audiences, such as teaching programming concepts to small-aged students or adults, teaching basic problem solving to inexperienced users or advanced problem solving techniques to undergraduate students, and teaching the principles of the two most-used programming techniques.

objectKarel has been used in the classroom with undergraduate students and has been evaluated positively. However, there are many other ways of taking advantage of these environments that have not been applied yet. The most important reason for this, in our opinion, is that teachers – especially in Higher Education - are not appropriately informed regarding the pedagogical use of educational software in general and are not encouraged to utilize such software in the classroom. Initiatives of Ministries of Education, such as the project funded by the Greek Ministry of Education and the European Union mentioned in section 3.1, can have a great impact on the pedagogical utilization of educational software and ICT by teachers.

The aim of this paper was the presentation of the pedagogical benefits of Karel and objectKarel and most importantly their potential uses for teaching and learning programming. The fact that both environments incorporate the necessary didactical material (theory, activities) for supporting the teaching and learning of programming makes their utilization even easier.

Our plans for further research regarding the pedagogical use of the environments for teaching programming include:

- Using Karel for teaching basic programming concepts to High School students.
- Using objectKarel for teaching the main principles of the OOP technique and preparing students of a Technology Management Department for their transition to Java.

References

Bergin, J., Stehlik, M., Roberts, J., Pattis, R.: Karel++ - A Gentle Introduction to the Art of Object-Oriented Programming, 2nd edn. Wiley, New York (1997)

Brusilovsky, P., Calabrese, E., Hvorecky, J., Kouchnirenko, A., Miller, P.: Mini-languages: a way to learn programming principles. Journal of Education and Information Technologies 2, 65–83 (1997)

objectKarel, `http://www.csis.pace.edu/~bergin/temp/findkarel.html`

Pattis, R.E., Roberts, J., Stehlik, M.: Karel - The Robot, A Gentle Introduction to the Art of Programming, 2nd edn. Wiley, New York (1995)

Xinogalos, S., Satratzemi, M., Dagdilelis, V.: An Introduction to object-oriented programming with a didactic microworld: objectKarel. Computers & Education 47(2), 148–171 (2006)

Xinogalos, S., Satratzemi, M., Dagdilelis, V.: Teaching Fundamental Notions of Object Oriented Programming with objectKarel. International Journal of WSEAS Transanctions on Advances in Engineering Education 3(11), 1022–1029 (2006)

Xinogalos, S., Satratzemi, M.: Using Hands-on Activities for Motivating Students with OOP Concepts Before They Are Asked to Implement Them. ACM SIGCSE Bulletin 37(3), 380 (2005)

Xinogalos, S., Satratzemi, M., Dagdilelis, V.: Evaluating objectKarel - an educational programming environment for object oriented programming. In: Mendez-Vilas, A., et al. (eds.) Current Developments in Technology-Assisted Education, vol. 2, pp. 821–825. Formatex press (2006)

Xinogalos, S., Satratzemi, M.: Studying Novice Programmers' Attitudes in Developing and Implementing Algorithms Using an Educational Programming Environment. In: Proceedings of the 10th International Conference on Information Systems Analysis and Synthesis (ISAS 2004) jointly with the International Conference on Cybernetics and Information Technologies, Systems and Applications (CITSA 2004), Orlando, Florida, USA, July 21-25, vol. 1, pp. 198–203 (2004)

Xinogalos, S.: Studying Students' Conceptual Grasp of OOP Concepts in Two Interactive Programming Environments. In: Lytras, et al. (eds.) The Open Knowlege Society: A Computer Science and Information Systems Manifesto, Springer Communications in Computer and Information Science, vol. 19, pp. 578–585 (2008)

An Empirical Study of IT Use in Pakistani Civil Society Organizations

Saqib Saeed, Markus Rohde, and Volker Wulf

Department of Information Systems and New Media, Hölderlin Str. 3, University of Siegen, 57076, Germany

Abstract. As voulantary organizations are differnt from business and governmental organizations in terms of structure, working methodologies and decision making, we are interested in the specific IT requirements and technology use in this sector. In this paper we investigate the Pakistani civil society sector to analyze the involvement of technology in their work settings. The paper also discusses two successful virtual voulantary organizations to highlight the potential of new media. The findings suggest that lack of technological and financial resources hinder them to adopt innovative solutions. The technological use is mostly limited, but the realization of its importance and urge to establish ICT infrastructures exist. So there is need for appropriating technology so that this sector in collaboration with government institutions can serve the public in a better way in new knowledge society.

1 Introduction

The rapid growth of information technology has revolutionized most aspects of human life. This advancement in technology is very helpful for civil society organizations so that they can be better equipped to play their role in knowledge society. Civil society organizations differ from business and government organization in their objectives, organizational structure and decision making. Moreover, lack of funding and permanent employees adds further complexity in establishing IT infrastructures. In order to understand the IT requirements of these organizations, we need to analyze information about NGOs' practice. There has been related work on the use of information technology by civil society organizations. c.f. (Cogburn, 2004; Kavada, 2005; Kavada, 2007; Goatman and Lewis, 2007). These research efforts are carried out in the context of voulantary organizations based in developed countries. We are interested in finding the involvement of IT in work practices of organizations based in technologically backward areas to analyze the effects of digital divide. In order to find empirical data we focused on civil society organizations in Pakistan. Pakistani civil society sector qualifies for an interesting case study due to couple of reasons along with its characteristics of technologically less advanced. The country is confronted by political, social, economic, institutional, and governance problems and there is large presence of civil society organizations. Secondly most NGOs suffer from weak

M.D. Lytras et al. (Eds.): WSKS 2010, Part I, CCIS 111, pp. 521–527, 2010.

management, limited access to resources and problems in their operations. Thus, these NGOs make an interesting case to benefit from information technology potentials (NGORC, 2003).

The history of civil society in Pakistan goes back at the time of its independence in 1947. At that time many voluntary organizations helped refugees by providing humanitarian aid. During the early days of country's existence major focus of voluntary work was on rehabilitation and provision of basic services like health and education. Later in the 1970s military regime, NGOs started emerging to do social work welfare, and in 1980s voulantary organizations focused on local development by the availability of funding from government sources. In the 1990s there was substantial increase in the number of NGOs to take advantage of funding under the Peoples Work Program (ADB, 1999). The actual number of registered organization is estimated to be between 10,000 and 12,000 and the number is estimated to be nearly 60,000 if unregistered groups are also counted - and eight thousand trade unions exist too (Sattar and Baig, 2001). Their size and scope vary from small organizations working at the grassroots level to well-networked organizations working internationally (Mostashari, 2005). They may be dependent on complete voluntary work with small budgets or they may have professional paid staff, whereas the majority lies between the middle. The source of funding for NGOs is distributed between foreign funding structures and indigenous public and private sector (Sattar and Baig, 2001).

2 Empirical Work

In order to get an initial finding what role IT applications play in carrying out work by Pakistani civil society organizations, we established a detailed online questionnaire and targeted only the small voulantary organizations having a small number of permanent employees, because these organizations constitute majority of the Pakistani civil society. We further investigated two virtual organizations to get an insight of their operations by holding telephonic conversations and email questionnaires.

2.1 Online Questionnaire

The online questionnaire was comprised of twenty eight questions about the work practices of civil society organizations. Keeping in mind the low internet speed there were two alternatives of filling the form, either as an online form or by filling it in form of a Microsoft word document. We got response from eighteen differnt organizations, among them eleven were online responses and seven email attachments. After the review of responses three responses were removed based on our eligibility criteria (small local voulantary organization) and completeness.

The geographic location of these organizations was distributed among three provinces of the country. Among them five organizations were from Sindh, three from Punjab, four from Northern Areas, N.W.F.P and Kashmir, whereas three were from the federal capital. The details of permanent staff members, IT staff and available infrastructure are described in table-1.

Table 1. Basic Statistics about the Organizations

S. No	Application area of the organization	Number of permanent Staff	Number of IT staff	Annual IT Budget	Number of available work stations	Internet availability
1	Water and Sanitation	163	2	3000 Dollars(approx)	15-20	Yes
2	Poverty Alleviation	2	2	100 Dollars(approx)	Zero(IT infrastructure in process of setting up)	No
3	Community Development	8	0	500 Dollars(approx)	5	Yes
4	Healthcare	0	0	0	2	No Answer
5	Healthcare	25	1	10%-20%	8	Yes
6	Community Development	11	0	0	6	Yes
7	Social development	12	0	0	4	Yes
8	Community development	35	0	10%	8	Yes
9	Women development	6	0	400 Dollars(approx)	4	Yes
10	Community development	7	2	<10%	3	No Answer
11	Education	17	2	500 Dollars(approx)	10	Yes
12	Capacity building	32	0	20%	9	Yes
13	Education	26	6	30%	12	Yes
14	Community development	23	2	20%	5	Yes
15	Emergency relief	66	0	0	3	Yes

Information technology has introduced new forms of information publishing means to help voulantary organizations to get more visibility. It was observed that among fifteen of these organizations, only six had their own website and from them only one organization was able to update the website regularly. Most of the organizations cited lack of technical knowhow as the major obstacle in updating the website. On the other hand the usage of virtual media to regularly publish online newsletters and reports was also limited. Only eight of the surveyed organizations made some use of ICT applications for the publishing activity and that too was limited to sending emails about organizational activities. The use of blogs and electronic forums was not in practice in any of the organization.

As the volunteers are backbone of most civil society organizations, the mobilization is an important task for them. With the advent of new ICT applications new forms of mobilization like SMS, Emails, online advocacy and online petition campaigns have emerged. In our investigation we found out that none of the organization was maintaining its mailing list through which interested people can be reached.

Among the surveyed organizations only one organization was doing virtual campaigning. Only one of the fifteen organizations was using social networking sites to enhance its public profile, although in a recent social movement in Pakistan use of such technologies was visible (Saeed et al., 2008). There was also a trend of storing the information of volunteers who indulged with the organization's activities in the past. Nine organizations were storing this information manually whereas four organizations were not storing this information. Only one organization was using database systems to store this information while one organization did not answer this question. Ten organizations were using some form of ICT in the hiring process of individuals whereas five organizations were doing the entire process manually.

The collaboration among civil society organizations, donors and government bodies is quite important for the successful completion of goals. Modern communication technologies can improve this entire communication process. In our investigation we found that three organizations were not collaborating with other civil society organizations while the remaining twelve organizations had collaborations with local and foreign organizations. Among them nine organization described that they use email communication. While communicating with donor organizations, ten organizations described that they use email communication. It was also observed that in order to give feedback of projects to donor organization, more complex tools like collaborative authoring; video conferencing etc. were not used. Only one of the fifteen organizations was using this kind of technology to better connect with donor organizations. In order to remain in touch with field activities, multiple communication methods were applied. Twelve of the surveyed organizations used some kind of information technology service like emails and mobile telephone to remain in touch with field activities. The communication with government agencies is also an important task in the collaboration process. Since the government offices in the Pakistan are not much advanced and use of information technology services is scarce, the communication of NGOs and government representatives is mostly based on physical meetings and paper-based communication. Only six of the fifteen organizations described that they use email communication with government official for coordination.

This initial investigation highlighted that the urge for adopting modern technologies is present but shortage of financial and human resources is a big problem. Eight organizations described the shortage of finances as the main difficulty in establishing IT infrastructures. This survey concludes that there is absence of modern sophisticated technology in practice but the email communication seems to be the most used service, as there are variety of free email services available.

2.2 Case Studies

In order to portray the potential of modern technologies for civil society organizations we made two case studies of two virtual voulantary organizations working in Pakistan.

2.2.1 Organization A

This is a small virtual voulantary organization focusing on creating awareness, lobbying and knowledge sharing on drinking water and sanitation. The objective of developing this organization was to provide a platform for the water and sanitation experts in South Asia, focusing Pakistan. This platform helps other people in combating the water and sanitation issues. The start of this virtual organization carried out four years ago as the focal person behind this organization was about to retire from his job and he still wanted to carry on his work in the water and sanitation area. The originator of this organization described his experience as wonderful even though he was not coming up from any IT background. It was also realized that this could have been done better if the IT skills of the involved individuals are improved. The useful information about the water and sanitation issues is available on the website of the organization and the discussion board allows discussing problems related to a specific region and solutions can be discussed by the experts. The group has 1573 members and the monthly email traffic statistics froms the start of the group are as follows.

Table 2. Email traffic Statistics of Organization A

	Jan	Feb	Mar	Apr	May	Jun	Jul	Aug	Sep	Oct	Nov	Dec
2005									65	74	64	15
2006	40	44	19	56	60	23	53	25	28	52	62	81
2007	46	44	77	33	93	89	36	13	25	60	34	31
2008	25	47	33	64	48	37	45	49				

2.2.2 Organization B

The objective of this organization is to promote scientific technological education in the country. It is a totally volunteer-based organization where the people give suggestions and consultations in the matters related to scholarship and higher education opportunities. The evolution of this NGO is also quite interesting as a friend of the founder intended to take higher education in Germany but it was hard to find information as most of the pages were in German. Then the founder helped him to translate available information in English and this triggered to establish a forum where the education opportunities could be advertised. Keeping this in mind, the idea of setting up an education foundation emerged. The lack of financial resources limited it to only a virtual organization but now there are plans to establish a physical office as well. A website and a yahoo group were established in 2002 and recently a Face book group has also been launched. Currently there are around four thousand users of this group and if someone has any question related to educational opportunities in any institution worldwide he can get response over this group. The website was discontinued due to lack of financial resources but is planned to be available again soon. Initially it was only managed by one member but with its popularity people from other countries started managing this group and there are many active moderators who keep on managing the traffic on the group. The traffic statistics of the group are given in the table.3.

Table 3. Email traffic Statistics of Organization-B

	Jan	Feb	Mar	Apr	May	Jun	Jul	Aug	Sep	Oct	Nov	Dec
2008	354	408	461	494	524	439	302	270				
2007	347	289	300	300	416	358	411	343	356	383	334	341
2006	365	254	236	307	356	278	288	313	270	286	278	323
2005	453	329	384	581	588	499	648	569	437	354	352	313
2004	282	216	194	219	296	354	481	441	455	453	441	566
2003	336	266	284	229	331	385	413	326	221	174	146	190
2002				28	22	131	287	195	181	239	273	238

It was also observed that as the volunteers in this organization were more technology literate so they have used the services of this group pages to quite a high level. There have been arranged folders for frequently asked questions for every country and anyone can see those before posting the new question. There is also a maintained database of the users with contact details which helps the users to get in touch with a specific individual.

3 Conclusion

In this paper we investigated the Pakistani civil society sector in an effort to portray the current status of IT use in work settings. As the country is technologically less developed, the findings illustrate some effects of digital divide. The paper also describes two case studies to give an insight on how basic technology can introduce innovative ways of working for civil society organizations. Pakistan is a developing country and has strong presence of cross cultural NGOs who are deprived of modern computing powers so there is more need of collaborative work in Pakistani NGO sector to minimize the effects of digital divide in this sector. Our findings highlight that this sector lacks funding to develop IT infrastructures, thus the open source movement and its technological developments could be part of the solution to the main problem. On the other hand lack of IT skills has been observed also. In this respect wiki-based systems and end user development applications can be developed to help activists in their operations. To cope with the observed problems, participatory development projects could be helpful to develop suitable applications. Furthermore, we see a need for in-depth ethnographic studies for this important sector. The appropriation of technology can help these organizations to serve the humanity in a better way.

As voulantary organizations support the governmental organization in human development so there is requirement for strong active collaboration among them for planning and execution of activities, As voulantary organizations have reach to grass root level they can act as a bridge in governmental policy making and implementation activities. The IT appropriation among voulantary organizations can improve this communication channel so that planning, implementation and evaluation of development activities can be done in time and effectively. On the other hand information and communication technologies can also play its role in providing field information robustly to the government institutions so that the government planning and policies could be based on public's needs. This robust information sharing can lead to proactive responses by government institutions in the emergency situations. The use of new technologies like web 2.0 in the mobilization activities by voulantary organizations increases their reach and this channel can be used to create awareness on governmental initiatives.

References

ADB, A Study of NGOs Pakistan, Asian Development Bank report (1999), http://www.adb.org/NGOs/docs/NGOPakistan.pdf (retrieved September 11, 2008)

Cogburn, D.L.: Diversity Matters, Even at a Distance: Evaluating the Impact of Computer-Mediated Communication on Civil Society Participation in the World Summit on the Information Society. Information Technologies and International Development 1(3-4), 15–40 (2004)

Goatman, A.K., Lewis, B.R.: Charity e-volution? An evaluation of the attitudes of UK charities towards website adoption and use. International Journal of Nonprofit and Voluntary Sector Marketing 12(1), 33–46 (2007)

Kavada, A.: Civil Society Organizations and the Internet: the Case of Amnesty International, Oxfam and the World Development Movement. In: de Jong, W., Shaw, M., Stammers, N. (eds.) Global Activism, Global Media, pp. 208–222. Pluto Press, London, University of Michigan Press, Ann Arbor (2005)

Kavada, A.: The European Social Forum and the Internet: A Case Study of Communication Networks and Collective Action. Ph.D. Thesis University of Westminster, UK (2007)

Mostashari, A.: An Introduction to Non Governmental Organizations Management Iranian Study Group MIT (2005), http://web.mit.edu/isg/NGOManagement.pdf (retrieved September 11, 2008)

NGORC, NGO resource center annual report 2003 (2003), http://www.ngorc.org.pk/downlods/NGORC_Annual_Report_2003.pdf (retrieved October 10, 2007)

Sattar, A., Baig, R.: Civil Society in Pakistan: A Preliminary Report on the CIVICUS Index on Civil Society Project. CIVICUS Index on Civil Society Occasional Paper Series, vol.1(11) (2001)

Saeed, S., Rohde, M., Wulf, V.: ICTs, An alternative sphere for Social Movements in Pakistan: A Research Framework. Paper Presented at IADIS International Conference on E-Society, Algarve, Portugal, April 9-12 (2008)

Towards Understanding IT Needs of Social Activists: The Case of the World Social Forum 2006 Organizing Process

Saqib Saeed, Markus Rohde, and Volker Wulf

Department of Information Systems and New Media, Hölderlin Str. 3, University of Siegen, 57076, Germany

Abstract. Recent literature has highlighted that most civil society organizations lack IT appropriation in their work practices. There is strong need to focus on this application area to empower these organizations by IT capabilities. As there is not much literature about the specific needs assessment of voulantary organizations, there is a need to carry out ethnographic studies to better understand IT requirements of this sector. In this paper we have investigated the organizing process of the World Social Forum 2006 event in Karachi, Pakistan. World Social Forum is an important gathering of social movements and voulantary organizations across the globe, and organizing such an event requires extensive communication and effective planning skills. The objective of this paper is to highlight the need and importance of this research issue. Our intention is to introduce appropriate technology in the organizing process to facilitate social activists.

1 Introduction

Civil society organizations (CSOs) are very diverse in their operations and composition. There are number of factors which make IT usage in this field of application very specific. Most CSOs face significant lack of funding for development, improvement and maintenance of their IT infrastructure. Their activities are mainly run by donations; often it is hard to invest these donations in establishing sustainable IT infrastructure and continuously employing IT professionals. Difference of language, backgrounds, working habits and culture among social activists of organizations, operating in differnt regions adds further complexity in designing an effective IT infrastructure. (Benston, 1990) has described how participatory design methods can be used to help non profit sector organizations. There have been examples of the application of technology in regional non profit organizations by different researchers' cf. (McPhail et al., 1998; Trigg, 2000; Rohde, 2003; Rohde, 2004; Farooq et al., 2005; Farooq et al., 2006). (McIver, 2004) worked with transnational NGOs to develop a multi-lingual collaborative legislative drafting application. Still there has not been much work carried out on typical technological requirements of CSOs.

In order to gain better understanding of issues hindering IT appropriation in civil society organizations, we need empirical evaluation, especially ethnographic studies

M.D. Lytras et al. (Eds.): WSKS 2010, Part I, CCIS 111, pp. 528–536, 2010.

are needed. Keeping this in mind, we turned our focus towards the organizing process of world social forum (WSF). In this paper we investigate the organizational practices in the organizing process of WSF event in Karachi, Pakistan. In 2006 WSF was organized as a poly-centric event and two other locations were Bamako, Mali and Caracas, Venezuela. In the following sections we describe applied research methods, the organizational structure of social forums, the historical background, the organizing process and the use of IT infrastructure of the Karachi event. The paper concludes with a discussion on the activities which provides direction for further information systems development for this community.

2 Research Methods

In order to analyze the WSF event in Karachi, a combination of research methods were used. The initial information was gathered using literature review, and open-ended email questionnaires were sent to the people involved in the organizing process. This information was further refined by reviewing of documents, websites of the event and telephonic follow-up interviews. In order to understand the communication activities, the contents of the emails were analyzed by joining email lists (Yahoo Groups). The interviews and observations at the organizing meeting of European Social Forum in Berlin helped in establishing relationships between the regional and world social forums.

3 Organizational Structure

WSF is a renowned annual event organized by social movement and other civil society networks worldwide. This event initiated as a result of a gathering of community organizers, trade unionists, young people, academics and activists in January 2001 at Porto Alegre, Brazil to rethink and recreate globalization for the advantage of poor and deprived people. The charter of WSF emphasizes that this forum is not a decision making body but an open space for reflective thinking, democratic debate of ideas, formulation of proposals, and exchange of experiences (WSF Charter, 2001). The success of WSF has triggered a number of local, national and regional forums (Kavada, 2006). These forums are related with WSF in the context that they adhere to the charter of the WSF but the organization and management of these forums are independent from each other. The individuals and representatives of CSOs can participate at any level. There exists a weak relationship among participants, who are almost the same who work at smaller level (City, Country, Regional etc). So for every event these volunteers gather in the organizing process and present proposals about the initiatives and program (Juris, 2005). The organizing tasks are divided among the WSF-International Council (IC) and an organizing committee (Kavada, 2007). The organizing committee is responsible for the day to day organizations of event whereas IC is decision making body for WSF.

4 Organizing Process

There were some Pakistani voulantary organizations, who participated in this event from start. So on 5th of July 2005 a provincial consultation in Sindh province was carried out to analyze arrangements for the event. Similar meetings were carried out in other cities like Karachi, Hyderabad, Multan, Lahore, Rawalpindi, Peshawar and Quetta. On 18th October the first country-wide meeting of 86 representatives was held at Karachi to form a National Organizing Committee and different sub-committees. The organizing team consisted of member organizations of the Pakistan Social Forum like community voulantary organizations, labor organizations, boy scouts and girl guides, students, community workers and sports organizations. There was also an office team and a coordination committee with members from all existing groups to take routine immediate actions. There were two joint planning meetings with the Bamako and Caracas chapter but further communication did not take place due to the delay in the Pakistani event. In October 2005 the country was marred by an earthquake and as a result local meetings were held in different cities of Pakistan to discuss delaying the event. After these local meetings a joint meeting of Pakistan Social Forum and the WSF National Organizing Committee on 22nd November decided to postpone the event for two months (Report, 2006).

An Asian meeting of the WSF was held on 16th December 2005 in Hong Kong. The representative of the Pakistani Organizing Committee briefed about the post earthquake situation and the preparation of the event. The financial difficulties were discussed and Indian Organizing Committee assured to take this up with WSF International Council and that a transfer of WSF Mumbai funds to Karachi will also be discussed. The Pakistani Organizing Committee requested other Asian countries to take more responsibilities including fundraising resulting in formation of Asian committee and a South Asian subcommittee. The Asian committee's responsibilities were defined as fundraising, decisions regarding plenaries in Karachi forum, guidance for program and finance committee, identification of speakers and formal approval of decisions of Pakistani organizing committee whereas the South Asian subcommittee would focus on logistical support, increased mobilization in their countries and participation and registration of events at the forum. It was also suggested to have frequent visits of members of the Indian Organizing Committee to Pakistan for help in finalizing arrangements. The meeting approved the 24th -29th March as the revised dates for the Karachi event (Report, 2006).

5 Execution

The forum was held at the KMC Sports Complex, Karachi and it was attended by nearly 40,000 people. The event included a number of activities like conferences, seminars, workshops, demonstrations, processions and cultural events. More than 20, 000 delegates from 58 countries from South Asia, China, Middle East and Europe were present at the Karachi forum (Khaleej Times, 2006). The effective organization of such an event requires a sufficient amount of funding and the Pakistani Organizing Committee had a budget of only 250,000 US Dollars whereas the cost of organizing the WSF event in 2005 was 4 million U.S. dollars, the 2006 event at Caracas had an eight million dollars budget and the Bamako event had 2.5 million dollars (Kirk, 2006). The Karachi event suffered from serious problems in fund raising. There was a big deficit between anticipated and actual funds because many regional organizations were not able to meet their promises (Report, 2006).

The mobilization efforts play an important role in attracting large audience and volunteers for the organizing process. Nearly 1,700 volunteers cooperated with logistics and other groups to make the event a success. The volunteers were mostly students and members of labor, political and women organizations from all over Pakistan. There were 3 volunteers from Germany and Switzerland to show a symbolic international representation. In order to increase local and international participation, a coordinator was designated who maintained the lists of interested foreign participants to facilitate travel and visa arrangements. There were delays at governmental and local levels, several organizations had not done effective mobilization and coordination at their end to increase participation. The communication with local NGOs and general public was mostly offline by arranging meetings and seminars at city levels and by providing supporting published material in form of posters and leaflets. The media can play a vital role in this respect but the coverage of the Indian and other regional media was not as positive, similar to 2004 WSF event in Mumbai. On the contrary, the local print and electronic media covered the event well, along with some foreign media resulting in the awareness of the event. In order to increase the media coverage before and after the event, a media center was established with 150 computers with email and fax facilities for journalists and for the use by delegates (Report, 2006). During the event there were minor administration problems like cancellation of sessions without information, and some venues were impossible to find due to lack of information about them (Chan, 2006).

6 IT Support in the WSF Karachi Event

Once the event was scheduled, the WSF International Council established a website for this poly-centric event which was available in three languages: English, French and Spanish. This website was common for all the three poly-centric events. It was developed by a working group of the Methodology Commission of the International Council using the content management system drupal and mysql as the underlying database. The main objective of this website was to provide a mean for registration of activities for the poly-centric event. Any organization interested to carry out an activity (Workshops, Seminars, etc.) at any of the poly-centric venues needed to register this activity here. The website provided functionality for registration[1] of an individual

[1] The user could be a primary member or an ordinary member. The primary member was the person who is the official administrator of the organizational presentation on the website. The primary member could edit the organizational profile, edit and describe the activities of organizations at any of the three social forums, invite other members of the organization to join that organization' section (ordinary members) and he could join the theme discussion forum for the event. The website also provided the feature of changing the primary member of an organization.

and after registration one could create profile of his organization and describe details of the activity which the organization was going to organize for the WSF. The website also provided the opportunity to search and contact resource persons of the organizations to get information about their planned activities. Furthermore, the web resource offered a database of all activities planned for the event along with relevant information. The website also contained web links of all three events maintained by organizing committees. In order to attract more people, website was advertised in the WSF newsletter and was further replicated by social movements, NGOs, and groups in their own networks throughout the world.

There were a total of 3,089 activities registered online and among them 440 were for the Karachi event. The fields which were present for each activity are described in Table-1. The search facility was also available, based on any of the below mentioned fields. As many social movements do not have internet access, offline registration (fax, personal visit) was also possible. The exact number of activities registered offline could not be gathered.

Table 1. Scheme of the list of Activities

Organization			Activity								
Name	Email	Prime Contact	Title	Location	Type	Scope	Terrain	Transversal Theme	Area1	Area2	Activity Outline

There were a total of 6,177 organizations registered on the website but 11 of them had not filled out their name leaving that field empty. The organizations could be searched based on organizations' name, email, country and contact person. The schema of the organization list is described in Table 2.

Table 2. Scheme of the organization List

Organisation Name	Primary Contact Person	E-mail to Prime Contact	WSF Participation	Members

The hosting Pakistan chapter of the WSF Karachi event was having online representation through a Yahoo group, as this was the free option available to coordinate with other members of civil organizations countrywide. This Yahoo group was working since June 9, 2005. Currently there are 166 members in the group. The group traffic is shown in Table 3. As the traffic indicates, it is a very low communication level in a vibrant country like Pakistan, where the civil society is quite active and nearly 60,000 registered and unregistered groups of NGOs exist (Sattar and Baig, 2001). As the table below shows, the average number of messages for 2005 was 52; in 2006 it exceeded to 60 and reduced to 41 in 2007.

Table 3. Number of Messages received in the group since its existence

	Jan	Feb	Mar	Apr	May	Jun	Jul	Aug	Sep	Oct	Nov	Dec
2007	40	29	67	51	29	22	32	31	44	50	63	34
2006	62	26	74	77	59	78	87	56	42	61	38	58
2005						14	19	59	55	92	57	67

In order to have a platform for publishing additional information about the event, a website was established by Pakistani organizing committe. The website provided information regarding program topics, logistics, accommodation, venues etc. The registration details of delegates were saved for future reference. As there were not any IT people in the organizing team, the work to establish the website and setting up network facilities at the event location were outsourced.

In order to successfully carry out an event of this size, communication with stakeholders plays vital role. The communication with donor agencies and amongst the members of the organizing committee was carried out by using emails and telephone calls. There was also close coordination with other social forum chapters, especially the Indian Social Forum on issues like selection of speakers etc. This communication among organizing members and others was also mostly based on emails and telephone calls followed up by personal meetings. The "Youth and Students" working group also used a Yahoo group to coordinate effectively within volunteers. The objective of this working group was to mobilize young people to contribute to the thematic agenda of the social forum. The group was founded on 15th July 2005 and has 330 members currently. The traffic statistics on this group are shown below in table 4.

Table 4. Number of messages received in the group since its existence

	Jan	Feb	Mar	Apr	May	Jun	Jul	Aug	Sep	Oct	Nov	Dec
2007	31	9	36	15	27	20	29	47	37	25	32	38
2006	110	71	89	53	46	53	46	21	30	31	19	50
2005							26	20	24	87	108	132

7 Lessons Learned

The host chapter, Pakistan Social Forum was not having any presence on the web other than a weak representation in the form of a Yahoo group. A strong online presence could have increased the participation of the new generation, as the intention was to include more youth in the process. The existence of a website of the Pakistan Social Forum could have been a major platform for attracting internet users and along with that the email lists and blogs could have been a major tool to generate debate on the event resulting in enhanced awareness and mobilization. One of the volunteer for IT activities at the social forum described that the lack of resources have hindered them. In our interviews one member of the Karachi organizing committee acknowledged that the Yahoo group was very helpful, since it helped to attract lot of voulanteer to work at the event. In Pakistan the use of social networking sites like Facebook, Orkut etc. is getting increasingly popular (Kirpalani, 2007) and this could have been used as a tool for the enhanced participation of the students' community.

The mobilization for the event mainly took place through seminars and physical meetings at different cities. As these meetings were organized by local member organizations, the direct communication with general public was limited. One participant described that the presence of people who were not directly involved in the organizing process was very poor (Chan, 2006). The organizing committee members were aware of the importance of modern IT infrastructures in the organization of such an event, because they have been part of other events all over the world - but the shortage of technically experienced people hindered them to establish such kind of infrastructure. As it has been observed, there was close cooperation between organizing members belonging to different organizations in the country and with members of the Indian Organizing Committee. Therefore to keep each other updated, it was decided in the December 2005 Asian meeting that all information would be sent on emails and website should be updated frequently - but there were serious problems in this regard, because there were not enough volunteers available who could update the website and there were no specialized mailing lists in place which could help effective communication. The organizers also faced problems in updating the website, because of missing IT competencies and expertise. This resulted in lot of overhead as the information was not available in time and extra queries kept on coming and caused delays in the coordination work. Additionally, the response to email requests from the organizing team members was inefficient and after sending email it was customary to make a follow-up telephone call, resulting in increase in expenditures and time delay. This absence of an effective communication framework also caused more regional and country-wide visits from the members of organizing teams resulting in an increase in expenses. In collaborative work the use of cooperation platforms, in which members can login and contribute, can enhance the productivity, resulting in higher efficiency of activities and smooth communication. The problems of miscommunication resulted in some organizational "hiccups", e.g. one NGO consortium which participated in the Karachi event described that there was lack of coordination between virtual and real world activities: there was no information to the reception desk about which participants had paid online (PNAC, 2006). There were also problems like cancellation of sessions without information, and some venues were impossible to find due to lack of information (Chan, 2006). These types of problems could have been resolved easily by using electronic notice boards/beamers at designated slots displaying important notifications to reduce some organizational shortcomings.

8 Conclusion

There was awareness in the organizing committee that the use of IT could support the organizing process, but the shortage of human and capital resources was a significant limitation. As the organizing process reveals there is extensive collaboration among civil society and government organizations and appropriate information and communication technologies can improve this communication. Secondly if the debates and discussions are stored and analyzed using data management techniques then this could provide an effective input for government policy making and its implementation. A limited amount of ICTs was used in form of email communication and a website. Furthermore, there was a lack of support for the appropriation of technology in CSOs. Our work provides an insight of the work practices of the WSF as one of the most important events for civil society worldwide. According to our findings, some appropriately and needs-oriented designed systems could improve the practice of CSOs and the people participation, especially with respect to the civil society activities in Pakistan. As limited resources and lack of technological skills are major hindrances, open-source-artifacts and end user development could reduce the costs of IT adoption and enhance the usability and learnability of such systems. Thus, there is need for more IT literacy and participatory development efforts, so that this important sector of society can benefit from the advancements of technology and can play its role in knowledge society.

References

Benston, M.: Participatory designs by non-profit groups. Paper Presented at the Participatory Design Conference, Seattle, Washington, March 31-April 1 (1990)

Chan, S.J.: After the big party: how about some action?(March 29, 2006), http://www.ipsterraviva.net/tv/karachi/viewstory.asp?idnews=608 (retrieved September 11, 2008)

Farooq, U., Merkel, C.B., Nash, H., Rosson, M.B., Carroll, J.M., Xiao, L.: Participatory Design as Apprenticeship: Sustainable Watershed Management as a Community Computing Application. Paper Presented at 38th Annual Hawaii International Conference on System Sciences, Big Island, HI, USA, January 3-6 (2005)

Farooq, U., Merkel, C.B., Xiao, L., Nash, H., Rosson, M.B., Carroll, J.M.: Participatory design as a learning process: Enhancing community-based watershed management through technology. In: Depoe, S.P. (ed.) The Environmental Communication Yearbook, vol. 3, pp. 243–267. Erlbaum, Mahweh (2006)

Juris, J.S.: Social Forums and their Margins: Networking Logics and the Cultural Politics of Autonomous Space. Ephemera 5(2), 253–272 (2005)

Kavada, A.: The 'alter-globalization movement' and the Internet: A case study of communication networks and collective action. Paper presented at the Cortona Colloquium 2006: 'Cultural Conflicts, Social Movements and New Rights: A European Challenge, Cortona, Italy, October 20-22 (2006)

Kavada, A.: The European Social Forum and the Internet: A Case Study of Communication Networks and Collective Action. Ph.D Thesis. University of Westminster, UK (2007)

Khaleej Times, World Social Forum concludes in southern Pakistan (March 29, 2006), http://www.khaleejtimes.com/DisplayArticle.asp?xfile=data/subcontinent/2006/March/subcontinent_March1099.xml§ion=subcontinent&col= (retrieved September 11, 2008)

Kirk, A.: The road to Nairobi 2007: What kind of Forum ?(March 28, 2006), http://www.ipsterraviva.net/tv/karachi/viewstory.asp?idnews=603 (retrieved September 11, 2008)

Kirpalani, M.: E-Resistance Blooms in Pakistan, Business Week (November 12, 2007), http://www.spiegel.de/international/business/0,1518,517023,00.html (accessed December 20, 2007)

McIver, W.: Tools for collaboration between tans national NGOs: multilingual, Legislative Drafting. Paper Presented at the International Colloquium on Communication and Democracy: Technology and Citizen Engagement, Fredericton, New Brunswick, Canada, August 4 - 6 (2004)

McPhail, B., Costantino, T., Bruckmann, D., Barclay, R., Clement, A.: CAVEAT Exemplar: Participatory Design in a Non-Profit Volunteer Organisation. Computer Supported Cooperative Work 7(3), 223–241 (1998)

PNAC, Report of PNAC Participation in World Social Forum 2006 Karachi (2006), http://www.pnac.net.pk/Reports/WSF-Report.pdf (retrieved September 11, 2008)

Report, Internal Report on WSF event Karachi (2006)

Rohde, M.: Supporting an Electronic, Community of Practice' of Iranian Civil Society Organizations. IADIS International Journal on WWW/Internet 1(2), 91–106 (2003)

Rohde, M.: Find what binds. Building social capital in an Iranian NGO community system. In: Huysman, M., Wulf, V. (eds.) Social Capital and Information Technology, pp. 75–112. MIT Press, Cambridge (2004)

Sattar, A., Baig, R.: Civil Society in Pakistan: A Preliminary Report on the CIVICUS Index on Civil Society Project CIVICUS. Index on Civil Society Occasional Paper Series, Vol. 1(11) (2001)

Trigg, R.H.: From Sandbox to "Fundbox": Weaving Participatory Design into the Fabric of a Busy Non-profit. Paper Presented at Participatory Design Conference, Seattle, Washington, USA, March 31 - April 1, 1990 (2000)

WSF Charter World Social Forum Charter of Principles (2001), http://www.forumsocialmundial.org.br/main.php?id_menu=4&cd_language=2 (retrieved September 11, 2008)

Assessing the Liquidity of Firms: Robust Neural Network Regression as an Alternative to the Current Ratio

Javier de Andrés, Manuel Landajo, Pedro Lorca, Jose Labra, and Patricia Ordóñez

University of Oviedo, C/Calvo Sotelo, S/N, 33007, Oviedo, Spain
{jdandres,landajo,plorca,labra,patriop}@uniovi.es

Abstract. Artificial neural networks have proven to be useful tools for solving financial analysis problems such as financial distress prediction and audit risk assessment. In this paper we focus on the performance of robust (least absolute deviation-based) neural networks on measuring liquidity of firms. The problem of learning the bivariate relationship between the components (namely, current liabilities and current assets) of the so-called current ratio is analyzed, and the predictive performance of several modelling paradigms (namely, linear and log-linear regressions, classical ratios and neural networks) is compared. An empirical analysis is conducted on a representative data base from the Spanish economy. Results indicate that classical ratio models are largely inadequate as a realistic description of the studied relationship, especially when used for predictive purposes. In a number of cases, especially when the analyzed firms are microenterprises, the linear specification is improved by considering the flexible non-linear structures provided by neural networks.

1 Introduction

Liquidity is the capacity of the firm to pay its short-term debt, and is a key aspect for credit scoring and other financial assessment processes. It is usually measured by using the current assets (CA) to current liabilities (CL) ratio, which is known as the *current ratio*. This quotient is very popular between both academics and analysts. The main reason for using the ratio form is so as to remove the influence of the size of the firm on the numerator variable (e.g., Lev and Sunder, 1979). Such a removal, in principle, would allow comparisons between different firms, or between a firm and the industry norm. However, a number of methodological assumptions---concerning the statistical properties of the components of the ratio---are implied in the use of financial ratios, and when such conditions are not fulfilled, some problems arise. Among these basic assumptions, those that refer to the specific *functional form* of the relationship between numerator and denominator of the ratio are particularly important. The relationship must be *linear* and *strictly proportional.* This has potentially serious consequences, as an incorrectly specified model will tend to make unduly high prediction errors.

An alternative approach is provided by flexible (also called *model-free*, or *nonparametric*) regression techniques, which are capable (when large enough data sets are available) of avoiding the problems posed by incorrect specification of the

M.D. Lytras et al. (Eds.): WSKS 2010, Part I, CCIS 111, pp. 537–544, 2010.

modeled relationships. Model-free regression capabilities have been proved for many modelling paradigms, including kernel regressions (e.g., Pagan and Ullah, 1999), series estimators (e.g., Andrews 1991), and artificial neural networks (ANNs) (e.g., White, 1990). ANNs have been successfully used for the study of a number of relevant topics in accounting and finance research. Examples include financial distress prediction (Altman et al., 1994; Pendharkar and Rodger, 2004), profitability forecasting (De Andrés et al., 2005), and profitability modelling (Landajo et al., 2007, 2008).

In this paper we focus on assessing the suitability of ANN models for the modelling of the statistical relationship between the components of the current ratio. The structure of the paper is as follows: the literature on ratio modelling is briefly reviewed in Section 2. Section 3 outlines methodological issues on ANN-based regressions. A description of the data base and the basic details concerning the implementation of our study appear in Section 4. The results and corresponding analyses are collected in Section 5. The paper ends with a summary of conclusions and implications for government consulting.

2 Review of Literature

The ratio form only is capable of removing the influence of firm size on the numerator variable (Y) when the relationship between numerator and denominator (denoted by X) is linear and strictly proportional. This amounts to assuming that both magnitudes are related by a linear regression model with null intercept term. A number of empirical research works have dealt with the issue of determining the validity of the ratio model and finding a suitable functional form for the relationship between the components of the most popular financial ratios. The samples analyzed by the different authors have varying degrees of firm size and sectoral heterogeneity. Sometimes (e.g., Sudarsanam and Taffler, 1995; Kallunki et al., 1996), the database contains only listed companies, while in other cases (e.g., Lee, 1985; Fieldsend et al., 1987; McLeay and Fieldsend, 1987; Berry and Nix, 1991), the base is made up of the accounts of a wide range of companies. It seems remarkable that (to our best knowledge) no study analyzing small and medium businesses separately has been carried out up to date. As to sectoral homogeneity, some authors (McDonald and Morris, 1985; Berry and Nix, 1991) have conducted tests for companies in a specific branch of activity, while others (e.g., Perttunen and Martikainen, 1989, 1990), studied only an aggregated sample that contains firms from all sectors. Regarding the specific relationship to be analyzed here, possibly because of its extensive use by both academics and practitioners, the current ratio has been the subject of most of the prior studies on the proportionality assumption (i.e., McDonald and Morris, 1985; Lee, 1985; Fieldsend et al., 1987; Perttunen and Martikainen, 1989; Berry and Nix, 1991; Kallunki et al., 1996).

Most of the authors conclude that ratios may be quite unsuitable as a description of many bivariate accounting relationships, but also that simple parametric alternatives such as linear and log-linear structures may be inadequate in a number of cases where these structures provide excessively simplified approximations to the unknown nonlinear regression curves which summarize these specific relationships. In this sense, it is remarkable that non-parametric methods have seldom been tried for the modelling of relationships between accounting variables. Only Trigueiros (1994, 1997) and Trigueiros and Berry (1991) have developed extensions of ratios which incorporate information not contained in linear models.

3 The Models

Our problem may be described as follows: we denote by X the explicative variable (i.e., the denominator in the specific ratio relationship), and Y denotes the variable to forecast (namely, the numerator of the ratio). The models are fitted on the basis of the training set $s^n \equiv \{(x_i, y_i) | i = 1,\ldots,n\}$. Our goal is learning an unknown mapping f^* such that:

$$Y_i = f^*(X_i) + \varepsilon_i; i = 1,\ldots,n \tag{1}$$

with $\{\varepsilon_i\}$ being a random error process. We will consider two alternative situations: Least-squares (LS) regression and Least-absolute deviation (LAD) regression. Estimation, on the basis of data set s^n, of the above regression functions may respectively be carried out by LS and LAD fitting. Since conditional expectations and conditional medians generally differ, LS and LAD estimators will generally converge to different (population) regression lines. In the case of the parametric models, we have considered the following structures: Linear regression models, Log-linear model, and Classical ratio model. For the case of ANN regressions, we have considered a remarkably simple model class, with the following form:

$$N_m(x) = \alpha_0 + \alpha x + \sum_{j=1}^{m} \beta_j F(\gamma_{0j} + \gamma_j x); \quad m = 0,1,\ldots; x \in \mathrm{R} \tag{2}$$

Where $F(z) = (1 + \exp(-z))^{-1}$ (i.e., logistic sigmoids are taken as `hidden units'), and $\alpha, \gamma_j, \alpha_0$ and γ_{0j} are scalars. Theoretical results permit many different model fitting criteria to be used, including several versions of LS and LAD. Here we considered the following variants of the basic neural regression model: ANN for logs, .ANN models fitted by WLS, LAD ANNs, and weighted LAD ANNs.

4 The Database: Basic Design of the Analysis

The information to process was obtained from the annual accounts of commercial and industrial firms located in Spain. We focused on the Small and Medium Enterprises (SME) according to the criteria contained in the European Commision Recommendation of 6 May, 2003. The financial statements analyzed here correspond to years 1998 to 2002. We selected a homogeneous industry. This was the case of the *Manufacture of builders' carpentry and joinery of metal* sector. The following four levels of heterogeneity were settled upon using the NACE classification: (i) all commercial and industrial NACE sectors, (ii) NACE Code D (*Manufacturing*), (iii) NACE Code 28

(*Manufacture of fabricated metal products, except machinery and equipment*) and (iv) NACE Code 2812 (*Manufacture of builders' carpentry and joinery of metal*).

Once the above process was completed, a computational experiment was carried out. The idea is that each specific data set of n cases (i.e., each subsample, from a specific year and sector) is used as a population from which independent (artificial) random sub-samples, both for model fitting and forecasting, are drawn. In particular, for each class of models and each model fitting criterion, we separately applied the following expedient: (1) Set size of the test set to $n_{test} = [n/4]$ (symbol $[\cdot]$ denotes rounding to nearest lower integer), (2) Fix the size of the estimation set ($n - n_{test}$), (3) Randomly extract a test set from the whole data set of n cases, (4) From the rest of the population, draw an estimation set and fit the corresponding model, (5) Evaluate the predictive performance of the model, both on the estimation and the test sets, by using mean absolute error (MAE). For the test set $\{(x_i, y_i) \mid i = 1, \ldots, n_{test}\}$, the expression is as follows:

$$MAE = \frac{1}{n_{test}} \sum_{i=1}^{ntest} \left| y_i - f(x_i, \hat{\theta}) \right| \tag{3}$$

Where f denotes model class (ratio, linear, log-linear, neural) and $\hat{\theta}$ denotes the fitted parameters obtained upon the training sample. The above scheme was repeated 100 times, each with an independently drawn random sample, and at the end we calculated the average of out-of-sample *MAE*s (to be denoted as *AMAE*) over the 100 replications. This expedient was applied independently for each branch, year, model class and model fitting criterion. In total, about 100,000 ANNs had to be fitted, plus all the versions of ratio and linear models (about 45,000 models). All computations were programmed and executed in Matlab 7.2 and run in standard PCs.

5 Results

Table 1 displays, for each year and each sub-sample according to firm size and sectoral heterogeneity, the following items: the best model (in accord with AMAE), its AMAE value and the average number of neurons (for ratio, linear and log-linear models the number of neurons is set to zero).

First of all, the above results indicate a reduced number of non-linearities. A look at Table 1 reveals that whenever the best model is a neural one, the average number of neurons is generally rather small. Neural networks are preferred in 55% of the cases. The various regression-based models account for the remaining 45%.

Another objective of our research was to analyse how the predictive ability (measured by AMAE) of the best models changes as sectoral heterogeneity increases, no matter whether the model is neural or parametric. Apparently, an increase in the prediction error levels occurs when we switch from the most heterogeneous sector (2812 NACE) to the two-digit NACE branch of activity. However, reductions in the error levels are observed when switching from NACE 28 to NACE D, and when switching from NACE D to the subsample that contains firms from all sectors.

Table 1. Average out-of-sample prediction error (AMAE) and network complexity for each level of sectoral heterogeneity, size sub-sample and year

		NACE 2812			NACE 28			NACE D			All sectors		
Size	Year	Mod.	AMAE	Neu.	Mod.	AMAE	Neu.	Mod.	AMAE	Neu.	Mod.	AMAE	Neu.
1	1998	N4	0.0029	0	N4	0.0074	0	N4	0.0057	0	N4	0.0001	0
	1999	R5	0.0027	0	R5	0.0050	0	N4	0.0020	0.28	N4	0.0005	0
	2000	N3	0.0027	0	N4	0.0057	0	N5	0.0020	0	N4	0.0024	0
	2001	N4	0.0043	0	N5	0.0042	0	N4	0.0022	0	R5	0.0038	0
	2002	N4	0.0030	0	N4	0.0026	0.11	N4	0.0020	0	R5	0.0010	0
2	1998	N4	0.0137	0.02	N4	0.0319	0	N5	0.0324	0	R5	0.0007	0
	1999	R5	0.0138	0	N5	0.0226	0	N5	0.0089	0.81	N4	0.0019	0
	2000	N4	0.0138	0	R5	0.0284	0	N4	0.0094	0.81	N5	0.0088	0.11
	2001	N4	0.0217	0	R5	0.0213	0	R5	0.0102	0	N5	0.0161	0
	2002	N5	0.0119	0	N4	0.0090	0	N4	0.0070	0	R5	0.0042	0
3	1998	N5	0.1762	0	N1	0.2522	0.76	R2	0.1217	0	R1	0.0021	0
	1999	R6	0.0971	0	N5	0.1977	0	N3	0.0580	0	N4	0.0407	0.05
	2000	R2	0.1008	0	R5	0.1504	0	N5	0.0640	0	R2	0.0636	0
	2001	R2	0.0972	0	N1	0.1454	0.01	N4	0.0658	0	N2	0.0898	0
	2002	R2	0.0862	0	R2	0.0561	0	R6	0.0915	0	R6	0.0877	0
All	1998	R5	0.0130	0	N4	0.0271	0	R5	0.0237	0	R3	0.0018	0
	1999	R5	0.0120	0	R1	0.0219	0	R2	0.0088	0	R1	0.0024	0
	2000	R5	0.0128	0	N4	0.0240	0.42	R2	0.0086	0	R1	0.0084	0
	2001	R5	0.0156	0	N5	0.0173	0	R5	0.0087	0	R5	0.0135	0
	2002	N5	0.0086	0	R5	0.0067	0	R6	0.0063	0	N5	0.0062	0.02

Size:1. Micro-enterprises **2**. Small enterprises **3**. Medium-size enterprises **A**. Firms of all sizes.
Mod. Model: **R1**. Classical linear regression (OLS) **R2**. Classical log-linear regression (OLS) **R3**. Classical ratio (OLS) **R4**. Classical ratio (Weighted LS) **R5**. Classical linear regression (LAD) **R6**. Classical ratio (LAD) **N1**. ANN (OLS) **N2**. ANN with log x and log y (OLS) **N3**. ANN (Weighted LS) **N4**. ANN (LAD) **N5**. ANN (Weighted LAD).
Neu. Average number of neurons.

Another issue of interest is the analysis of results when we consider different sub-samples according to firm size. The average out-of-sample MAE is very low for the case of micro-enterprise sub-samples and, although it rises for the small firms, it is in the medium-sized enterprises where the highest error levels are observed. When we use the total sample (micro-enterprises, small enterprises and medium-sized enterprises) the error values are lower than in the case of medium-sized and small enterprises, but higher than for micro-enterprises.

Furthermore, another interesting issue emerges: for micro-enterprises, neural networks appear to offer a clear predictive advantage over the ratio, linear and log-linear models. On the other hand, for the samples containing firms of all sizes, regression-based models outperform neural networks. In the case of medium sized-firms there is no clear evidence, at the usual significance levels, of the superiority of any of the models. Another conclusion that follows on from Table 1 is that, for all the modelling paradigms, the robust (LAD) models (both in the naïve and weighted forms) tend to outperform the LS-based estimators in terms of average out-of-sample prediction error. In part this is what we should expect, since predictive error criteria based on absolute errors, instead of quadratic ones, will tend to favor LAD models.

Finally, an additional issue which emerges from Table 1 is that the statistical characteristics of the CA/CL relationship tend to evolve, in the sense that the most suitable structures tend to vary over time. Different model classes tend to be optimal in different periods, although in many cases the best model structure remains the same for two or three consecutive years, so the change is not completely erratic.

6 Concluding Remarks and Implications for Government Consulting

The above results confirm previous evidence in literature that in most cases the basic ratio model, even in LAD versions, is unsuitable as a means of capturing the full structure which appears in accounting data bases, while (LAD) linear regression models and robust neural networks offer much more accurate descriptions. The neural structures used in this paper permit the encompassing of both the ratio and linear forms naturally, providing additional flexibility in order to capture hidden non-linearities.

The evidence from our analysis indicates that robust ANN models may be profitably used in order to extract knowledge in very noisy and heteroskedastic accounting data bases. More specifically, under certain settings (small firms and, especially, microenterprises), where much larger sample sizes are available, neural networks clearly outperformed linear models on modelling firm liquidity.

Our results also indicate that, for the specific case of the relationship between CA and CL (the components of the current ratio), not more than one neuron was needed on average, and very often non-linear terms were rejected by the complexity control criterion. This suggests that much of the variability observed in this statistical relationship should be attributed to inherent randomness, and not to unknown non-linear patterns.

The above results have some implications for government consulting. First, many supervisory and regulatory bodies extensively rely on the use of financial ratios for solvency assessment and financial distress prediction. Among these, we must highlight the case of the banking sector regulation and supervision. Under the Basel II framework, which will be incorporated into the legislation of EU countries, ratios and other financial measurements for managing risks will have an increased importance for risk management. As our results indicate that in some cases the use of ratios may mislead analysts, it could be an advisable politic the inclusion of some of the measures proposed as an alternative to the ratio approach (loglinear regressions, artificial neural networks, etc.) into the set indicators for the assessment of the risk of bank failure.

Second, the assessment of the financial position of firms in certain sectors is frequently used by governments as a criterion for funds granting. To a large extent this analysis, as well as that of banking supervision, relies on financial ratios. The inadequacy of ratios for financial analysis, especially for the case of small businesses and microenterprises, raises some concerns on the efficiency of the procedures used for resources allocation by governments.

Finally, the statistical reports provided by government bodies (i.e. the American Bureau of the Census, the Deutsche Bundesbank in Germany, the Bank of Spain or the BACH project [Bank for the Accounts of Companies Harmonized] for 11 European countries together with the USA and Japan) consist mainly of descriptive statistics of the distribution of financial ratios. These reports are accessible via web on a cost-free basis, and they are widely used by financial analysts and other users of accounting information. As our results suggest that ratios are not an adequate tool for financial analysis, the usefulness of such statistical report can also be questioned.

As to the research lines pointed out by our results, a number of issues stand out. First, our analysis of robust ANNs was limited to the case of the regression line which passes through conditional medians. A straightforward extension would permit the treatment of other (more extreme) percentiles. Quantile regressions are useful in benchmarking analysis, where the analyst is interested in comparing the firm with the best performing companies rather than with the mean or the median of the sector. In Landajo et al. (2008) this idea was implemented by using (fixed-knot) spline-based nonparametric quantile regressions. Neural networks would provide an alternative more flexible implementation.

A further research line is sensitivity measurement. ANNs permit estimation of average derivatives and other sensitivity measures which summarize the effects on the variable to forecast of small variations of the explicative variable. A classical paper by Gallant and White (1992) provides the required theoretical support. Our preliminary results indicate that LAD (linear, neural) estimators provide reasonable estimates for these kinds of indicators. Sensitivity measures would be the most interesting output for an accounting analyst, since they would permit direct interpretation of results provided by complicated functional structures such as ANNs.

References

Altman, E.I., Marco, G., Varetto, F.: Corporate distress diagnosis: comparisons using linear discriminant analysis and neural networks (the Italian experience). Journal of Banking and Finance 18, 505–529 (1994)

Andrews, D.W.K.: Asymptotic normality of series estimators for nonparametric and semiparametric regression models. Econometrica 59(2), 307–345 (1991)

Berry, R.H., Nix, S.: Regression analysis vs. ratios in the cross-section analysis of financial statements. Accounting & Business Research 21(82), 107–115 (1991)

De Andrés, J., Landajo, M., Lorca, P.: Forecasting business profitability by using classification techniques: a comparative analysis based on a Spanish case. European Journal of Operational Research 167(2), 518–542 (2005)

Fieldsend, S., Longford, N., McLeay, S.: Industry effects and the proportionality assumption in ratio analysis: a variance component analysis. Journal of Business Finance & Accounting 14(4), 497–517 (1987)

Gallant, A.R., White, H.: On learning of the derivatives of an unknown mapping with multilayer feedforward networks. Neural Networks 5, 129–138 (1992)

Kallunki, J.H., Martikainen, T., Perttunen, J.: The proportionality of financial ratios: implications for ratio clasifications. Applied Financial Economics 6, 535–541 (1996)

Landajo, M., De Andrés, J., Lorca, P.: Robust neural modeling for the cross-sectional analysis of accounting information. European Journal of Operational Research 177(2), 1232–1252 (2007)

Landajo, M., De Andrés, J., Lorca, P.: Measuring firm performance by using linear and nonparametric quantile regressions. Journal of the Royal Statistical Society, Series C (Applied Statistics) 57(2), 227–250 (2008)

Lee, C.J.: Stochastic properties of cross-sectional financial data. Journal of Accounting Research 23(1), 213–227 (1985)

Lev, B., Sunder, S.: Methodological issues in the use of financial ratios. Journal of Accounting & Economics 1(6), 187–210 (1979)

McDonald, B., Morris, M.H.: The functional specification of financial ratios: an empirical examination. Accounting & Business Research 15(3), 223–228 (1985)

McLeay, S., Fieldsend, S.: Sector and size effects in ratio analysis: an indirect test of ratio proportionality. Accounting & Business Research 17(2), 133–140 (1987)

Pagan, A., Ullah, M.: Nonparametric econometrics. Cambridge University Press, Cambridge (1999)

Pendharkar, P.C., Rodger, J.A.: An empirical study of impact of crossovers operators on the performance of non-binary genetic algorithms based neural approaches for classification. Computers and Operations Research 31, 481–498 (2004)

Perttunen, J., Martikainen, T.: On the proportionality assumption of financial ratios. Finnish Journal of Business Economics 38(4), 343–359 (1989)

Perttunen, J., Martikainen, T.: Distributional characteristics and proportionality of market-based security ratios. Finnish Economic Papers 3(2), 125–133 (1990)

Sudarsanam, P.S., Taffer, R.J.: Financial ratio proportionality and inter-temporal stability: an empirical analysis. Journal of Banking and Finance 19, 45–60 (1995)

Trigueiros, D., Berry, R.: The application of neural network based methods to the extraction of knowledge from accounting reports. Paper Presented at the Twenty-Fourth Annual Hawaii International Conference on System Sciences (1991)

Trigueiros, D.: Incorporating complementary ratios in the analysis of financial statements. Accounting, Management and Information Technologies 4(3), 149–162 (1994)

Trigueiros, D.: Non-proportionality in ratios: an alternative approach. British Accounting Review 29(3), 213–230 (1997)

White, H.: Connectionist nonparametric regression: multilayer feedforward networks can learn arbitrary mappings. Neural Networks 3, 535–549 (1990)

An Innovation Teaching Experience Following Guidelines of European Space of Higher Education in the Interactive Learning

M. Zamorano[1], M.L. Rodríguez[2], A.F. Ramos-Ridao[1], M. Pasadas[2], and I. Priego[3]

[1] Dept. of Civil Engineering, University of Granada, Campus de Fuentenueva s/n, 18071 Granada, Spain

[2] Department of Applied Mathematics, University of Granada, Campus de Fuentenueva s/n, 18071 Granada, Spain

[3] IES José Alcántara, Córdoba, Spain

Abstract. The Area of Environmental Technology in Department of Civil Engineering has developed an innovation education project, entitled *Application of new Information and Communication Technologies in Area of Environmental Technology teaching*, to create a Web site that benefits both parties concerned in teaching-learning process, teachers and students. Here teachers conduct a supervised teaching and students have necessary resources to guide their learning process according to their capacities and possibilities. The project has also included a pilot experience to introduce European Space of Higher Education (ESHE) new teaching concept based on student's work, in one subject of Environmental Science degree, considering interactive learning complementary to presence teaching. The experience has showed strength and weakness of the method and it is the beginning in a gradual process to guide e-learning education in future.

Keywords: E-learning; workload; Moodle; Web site.

1 Introduction

Teaching-learning process consists of two elements: *teaching*, focused on the teacher, and *learning*, focused on the students. Depending on the closeness to one or each element, it is possible to distinguish different teaching-learning models although the best option should consider both elements in a balanced way. The European Union (EU) has defined the new framework of the European Space of Higher Education (ESHE), based on the establishment of the European Credit Transfer and Accumulation System (ECTS) which is defined as a student-centred system based on the required student workload to achieve the objectives of a programme, preferably specified in terms of learning outcomes and competencies to be acquired; the concept of credit should take into account the total workload that a student has to perform to overcome individual subjects and attain the knowledge and skills set out therein, including both the hours of

M.D. Lytras et al. (Eds.): WSKS 2010, Part I, CCIS 111, pp. 545–554, 2010.

attendance, as the effort that the student must devote to study, prepare and conduct examinations (Font 2003).

The adoption of ECTS involves a new approach to teaching methods, forcing a curricula and subjects review (Moon et al. 2007). The Spanish Royal Decree 1125/2003 establishes the European credit system and the system of qualifications in university degrees; as a consequence, the Spanish University System is immersed in a process to reform the organization of the curricula of higher education to adapt it to the new educational models.

Using new Information and Communication Technologies (ICT) in teaching models gives enormous potential to support an advance teaching, learning process and the student experience, both theoretical and practical (Prada 2006),(Löfström et al. 2008), (Moon et al. 2007). The Bologna Declaration marks a turning point in the development of European higher education but it does not mention the importance of virtual dimension (Dumort 2002), (Moon et al. 2007). Late the European Commission became aware of the important current social and educational role of new technologies adopting the first multiannual programme (2004 to 2006) for the effective integration of ICT in education and training systems in Europe (e-Learning Programme) with Decision No 2318/2003/EC of the European Parliament and of the Council. The overall objective of the programme is to support and develop further the effective use of ICT in European education and training systems, as a contribution to a quality education and an essential element of their adaptation to the needs of the knowledge society in a lifelong learning context (European Union, 2003).

The University of Granada (UGR) has developed the Plan of Educational Excellence that includes initiatives in innovation, education, practical support and degrees and services evaluation to improve teaching quality and students training (Andalusian autonomous 2003). In this context, the Area of Environmental Technology, in the Department of Civil Engineering, has developed an innovation educational project entitled *Application of new ICT in the Area of Environmental Technology teaching*, to create a new communication channel that consists on a Web site that benefits both parts concerned in the learning–teaching process, teachers and students. The innovation educational project will recover students' leading role in teaching–learning process and will apply ESHE foundations, although the adaptation of curricula subjects is needed first.

On the other hand, this paper summarizes the adaptation process that has been necessary for the execution of educative reform process in the subject *Solid Waste Treatment, Handling and Recovery* of Environmental Science degree. On the other hand, it also explaining the didactic tools used to implant the new teaching–learning model, describes the website created to support teaching and finally summarizes results and conclusions of this experience.

2 Teaching and Quality Framework at the UGR

Improving the quality of all the areas of university activity is fundamental for training the professionals that society needs. Developing research, preserving and transmitting culture and constituting a critical and scientific presence, based on merit and rigour are also essential as a reference for Spanish society teaching. Within this framework, the UGR maintains a fundamental goal of imparting quality in teaching directed to the full and critical education of students and their preparation for exercising professional activities (European Union 2003).

The first Plan for Educational Excellence of the UGR was approved by the Governing Council of the University. Its goal was to promote a culture of quality and stimulate excellence in teaching; it was conceived as an instrument for developing the UGR institutional policy on evaluation, improvement and innovation. The Plan has coordinated 24 actions, organized into three programs. Four years later, the approval of the UGR's First Plan, the needs derived from new objectives, the laws that regulate university activity, the challenge of European convergence, the expectations generated and the development undergone together with its limitations indicate the importance of bringing the objectives up to date and of revising organization to form a second Plan. As a consequence, the UGR proposes to continue actions of the previous plan and to develop other new ones in the programs reflected in a new plan that coordinates nine programs; the third and fourth programs correspond to a strategic line teaching and innovation model and propose measures for stimulating the connection between research and teaching, for encouraging innovation and for coordinating measures for improvement to respond to the needs proposed in the evaluation processes.

3 Description of the Subject Solid Waste Treatment, Handling and Recovery

3.1 The Subject in Environmental Science Degree

The degree in Environmental Sciences began to be taught at the UGR in 1994, within the range of degrees issued by the Faculty of Science. It responds to the needs of professionals who are trained specifically by and for environment and who are capable to coordinate activities with other multidisciplinary professionals, managers and citizens with more specific activity field.

A pilot project has been conducted for four years to introduce ESHE foundation in this degree. As a result, it has also been needed a restatement of the curricula of subjects and teaching models. The *Solid Waste Treatment, Handling and Recovery* subject has been considered to provide students the necessary skills to know negative impacts as consequence of inadequate waste management and techniques designed to implement actions to minimize these impacts. This is an optional subject with 4 theoretical credits and 2 practical ones. Its characteristics are summarized below.

3.2 Objectives

The overall objective of this subject is the students training in the field of waste management. In order to achieve this overall objective, the following specific targets have been considered: (i) to know basic concepts related to municipal waste impacts and their characteristics, (ii) to apply waste classification and labelling rules, (iii) to know basic principles which should guide waste management actions, (iv) to classify collection and transport waste options and apply design criteria, (v) to know waste reuse, recovery, recycling, valorisation and final disposal in landfills options and apply design criteria to construct an operate treatment plants, (vi) to minimize waste treatment plants negative impacts, (vii) to promote environmental education related to waste management, (viii) to know waste legislative framework and waste management competencies.

3.3 Skills to Be Developed

The skills established to be acquired by the student are as follows: (i) quality of work, (ii) ability to analyse and synthesize, (iii) practical exercises resolution, (iv) organization and planning ability, (v) oral and written communication, (vi) teamwork, (vii) critical reasoning and (viii) decision-making.

3.4 Subject Structure

The subject has been structured into two main parts: theory and practice. The first one consists on theoretical contents that include practical aspects of waste management. Practice sessions were divided into two parts; in the first one, students solved a series of individual exercises in class related to practical contents outlined in previously; in the second part, students grouped in working groups carried out a practical work using theoretical and practical contents and skills learned; they would have to explain to the rest of students the most important aspects of the study

3.5 Applying Tools and Techniques

In order to implement all the techniques and adaptations required to consider ESHE foundations, a subject review which includes contents, working groups and teaching methodology has been necessary. In the case of theoretical lessons only one group was authorized by the university government. In the case of the seminar of problems were four; finally the teacher divided the theoretical group in eight to study development. In any case, the subject planning has been based on the student's personal work as a centre of the learning process. Four tools have been basically used and they are analysed:

1. *Theoretical lessons.* The content has to be modified to consider the new objectives of the subject, as well as the new skills that are expected to be acquired by the students. These lessons are characterized by a lower teacher-student interaction so they are designed primarily as a method of unidirectional transfer of knowledge from teacher to students.

2. *Seminar Problems.* They are lessons of problems with a smaller number of students who work practical contents individually in class: (i) to acquire on scientific and technical knowledge outlined in theoretical lessons, to complete their understanding and deepening, for which several practical activities take place, (ii) to be the natural forum to share students doubts developing practical exercises.
3. *Practical seminars.* They are a natural forum in which each group exposed their work to the rest of students, making a bridge between theory and problem lessons. These seminars seek to promote equal capacity for analysis, synthesis, critical thinking, oral and written expression of foreground, and teamwork.
4. *Environmental Teaching Center Web site.* The subject changes have been carried out based on the student's work, so a virtual platform in the service of the teacher and the student has been developed; it is a bridge of both parts involved in the process of learning and it is a support that provides self-knowledge and independent alternative to the students. In any case this tool will be regarded complementary to traditional method of teaching presence, because the balance in the participation of teacher and student is considered basic if you want proper development of the learning process.

3.6 Evaluation of Students' Knowledge and Skills

The students' evaluation considers the following four marks, affected by different weights in parenthesis. The first one takes into account the results from an individual test which includes theoretical contents and resolution of several exercises (30%); the second one considers individual exercises made in practical seminars (40%); the third mark evaluates work in groups and the oral presentation by each member of the group (20%) and finally the last mark takes into account the individual work of the students, including participation in lessons, use of chats, self-evaluation tests and other resources of Web Site (10%). In order to carry out a continuous evaluation of the knowledge and skills acquired by students in the Web site, self-evaluation test are available to allow the students to know their deficits, as well as the teacher goes exploring the progressive student learning directing the need to clarify the most frequently observed issues.

4 Description of Web Site

Many educational institutions have adopted e-learning system to complement traditional teaching in various disciplines in recent years (Veron et al. 1993), (Jarvela 2002), (Shin et al. 2002), (Lau et al. 2005). In comparison to traditional methods of teaching that emphasize using classroom lectures and demonstration, information technology (IT) can provide an environment that lifts the restrictions of time and space in knowledge delivery and capture. With the advance of computing infrastructure and the Internet, the use of IT for teaching and learning has vastly increased the flexibility and effectiveness of knowledge delivery. In a typical e-learning system, IT components including computer graphics, animations, multimedia effect, databases, and other Internet applications such as e-mail and chat room facilities are incorporated to create a cyberplatform for learning.

Web Site considers teaching methodology based on the e-learning concept, consisting in providing educational programs and learning systems using a computer or other electronic device to provide educational materials. This space can be seen as a Virtual Classroom in which it is organized, emulated and enhanced the learning process that takes place in a traditional classroom.

4.1 Software

Version 1.9 of free software e-learning platform Moodle has been used to create ETC Web site. It is designed to help educators create online courses with opportunities for rich interaction. Its open source license and modular design means that people can develop additional functionality. The decision to choose this software was based on our commitment to provide a reliable system with development possibilities: Moodle is a free, open-source alternative to commercial courseware that is widely used in universities around the world; its large client/developer base, as well as optional commercial development and support, make it the optimal choice; on the other hand Moodle's many features, including forums, quizzes, assignments, and glossaries, will provide Site Generator users a great functionality making easily the use of the e-learning platform by teachers that are not expert on communications and information technologies. Moodle also has import features for use with other specific systems, such as importing quizzes or entire courses from Blackboard or WebCT.

4.2 Web Site Interface Description

Internet direction `http://cem.ugr.es` permits the access to the ETC Web site homepage which has all the subjects in which the area of Environmental Technology has teaching; they are classified by degrees and postgraduate teaching. This page has been designed from a template of Moodle, customizing it for this experience.

4.3 Homepage of the Subject Solid Waste Treatment, Handling and Recovery

In the homepage of this subject customized by the responsible teacher, three main areas are identified:

1. General. It has information about the subject: characteristics, objectives, agenda, consulting books, evaluation criteria, etc. There are too links to subject teachers' personal homepage and a link to a chat to facilitate student-teacher communication to solve and clarify doubts.

2. Main body. This space collects and develops the blocks and thematic structure of the educational program. It contains material to the student for the development and monitoring of the subject. The resources and materials in each block include: notes of theory, practical exercises, Web resources, multimedia resources (including videos and photos), legislation, and other documentation.
3. Workshop. This area annexes documentation from work performed by the students and set out in the workshops.

5 Results in Course 2007/2008

5.1 Resources

Figure 1 shows resources disposal in ETC and the number of times, in percentage, that students have used them. They have used the Web site basically to download class notes and complementary documentation but multimedia sources that include videos or links related to webs have low participation. These results show students have great difficulties to adapt to the learning models based on workload because of the UGR, as in the rest of Spanish universities, teaching-learning models are basically focused on the teacher, as a consequence of a large number of students.

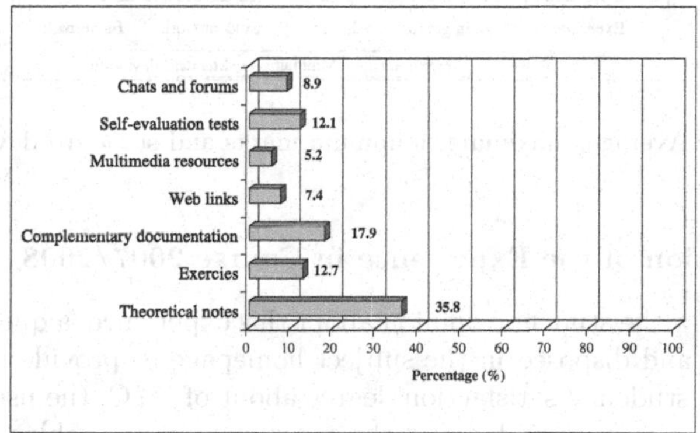

Fig. 1. Resources disposal in ETC and number of times, in percentage, that students have used them

5.2 Evaluation of Students' Knowledge and Skills

At Spanish universities, skills and knowledge acquired by students are evaluated in a range between 0 and 10. In the case values are equal or higher than 9, knowledge and skills acquired by students are classified high; if values are between 7 and 9, the degree of assimilation of knowledge is classified notable and between 5 and 7 low; marks lower than 5 show poor skills and assimilated knowledge so in this case students do not pass the subject. Taking into account these criteria now, the results obtained in the course 2007/2008 are analyzed.

Subject monitoring observed is quite high because only 5.79% of registered students (121) have not followed the subject. Assimilation of knowledge and skills by students are next to an average value that is classified as remarkable, with average marks of 6.66 and 93.39% of students passing the subject. Figure 2 shows the marks of different parts of the subject. As we can see, work and monitoring carried out by students has been quite good, although final marks of individual exam show values quite low if they are compared with the rest of marks; only 25.5 % of students passed the exam. The results of the students evaluation show the great students difficulty to adapt the model teaching based on student workload.

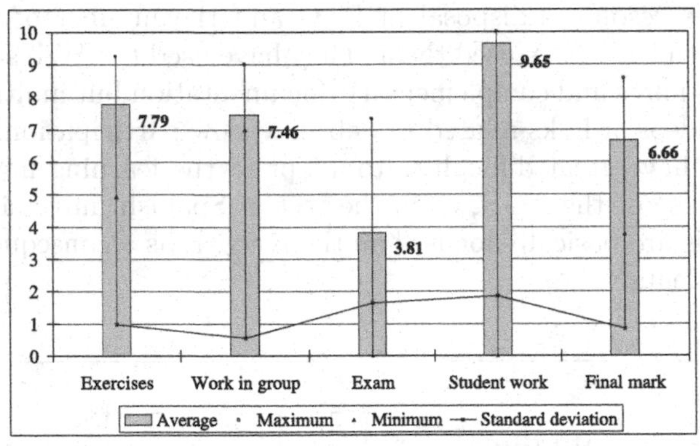

Fig. 2. Average, maximum, minimum marks and standard deviation

5.3 Evaluation of the Experience in Course 2007/2008

In order to know the students' opinion about this experience, a questionnaire has been designed and disposed in the subject homepage to provide information in relation to the students' satisfaction degree about of ETC, the usefulness of the materials and sources provided and the most important problems of teaching-learning model defined. It includes 13 questions rated from 1 to 5 (1 minimum satisfaction degree and 5 maximum satisfaction degree) and classified in 2 blocks, one about the platform in general and the other one to evaluate the subjects. The questionnaire has been available to students for 20 days, at the end of the course, and 52.1% of the student body has participated. Figure 3 shows the average score and standard deviation for each question of the survey, for students of the subject in question, which participated in 24% of the student body; it is possible to conclude that the use of Web site is considered positive, with its design and presentation look worse valued; subject evaluation is fairly good (question 13) with values higher than 3; sources that have been rated worse are the use of chat rooms and forums, self-evaluation and student-teacher communication basically

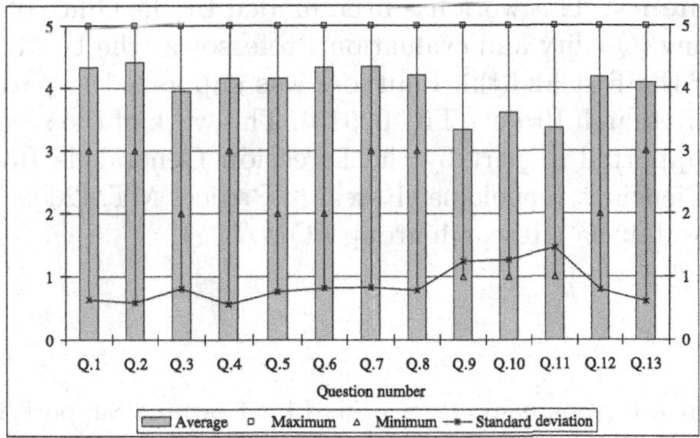

Fig. 3. Results obtained in the survey for assessment of the project

as a consequence of connection problems and the inexperience of teachers in this type of technologies, being necessary to promote the use of chat rooms and forums that make less impersonal monitoring of the subject. Teachers should improve education in ITC to guide students in the use of these technologies and know their advantages and disadvantages so as necessary changes in curricula subjects to implement ESHE principles.

6 Conclusions

The web site developed to be use by all subjects of the Area of Environmental Technology in Civil Engineering Department at the UGR although is a first step the teaching-learning method has been applied to only one subject to identify its strengths and weakness.

The most important strengths detected are: the use of the resources used have opened new possibilities to the students although it is necessary to promote the participation of the students and Moodle's varied features, as forums, quizzes, assignments and glossaries, have provided a great functionality making easier the designer and use of e-learning platform by teachers and students that are not experts on communications and information technologies.

Some weaknesses have been detected. In the first place, the need for modifying students learning process to assimilate theoretical contents and develop practical skills too, including the capacities to analyze, discriminate, classify and synthesize; secondly improving technical medium are needed to avoid that computer capacity could be got carried away; and finally, improving communication tools in the Web site, forums and chats are necessary.

It is possible to conclude that results of this experience could contribute to guide teacher from Spanish Universities to reform the organization of the curricula of higher education and to adapt it to the new educational models established by Spanish Government in Royal Decree 1125/2003, on the European credit system.

Acknowledgments. This work has been funded by the Office of the Vice President of Planning, Quality and evaluation Professor at the UGR.

The work of the first and third authors was supported in part by the Junta de Andalucía (Research Project TIC-02913). The work of the second and fourth authors was supported in part by the Dirección General de Investigación del Ministerio de Ciencia y Tecnología (Research Project MTM2005–01403) and by the Junta de Andalucía (Research group FQM/191).

References

Contero, M., Naya, F., Company, P., Saorín, J.L.: Learning Support Tools for Developing Spatial Abilities in Engn. Design. J. Eng. Educ. 22, 470–477 (2006)

Dumort, A.: Guiding Principles of The Virtual European Space of Higher Education. Revista Electrónica Teoría de la Educación 7, 185–197 (2002) (in Spanish)

Font, A.: European Space of Higher Education (ESHE). In: 9th Conference of Law Faculties Deans in the Spanish Universities (2003)

Jarvela, S., Hakkinen, P.: Web-based cases in teaching and learning-the quality of discussions and a stage of perspective taking in asynchronous communication. International Journal of Interactive Learning Environments 10, 1–22 (2002)

Lau, H.Y.K., Mak, K.L.: A Configurable E-Learning System for Industrial Engineering. Int. Engng. Ed. 21, 262–276 (2005)

Löfström, E., Nevgi, A.: University teaching staffs' pedagogical awareness displayed through ICT-facilitated teaching. Interactive Learning Env. 16, 101–116 (2008)

Moon, Y., Sánchez, T., Durán, A.: Teaching Professional Skills to Engineering Students with Enterprise Resource Planning (ERP): an International Project. Int. Engng. Ed. 23, 759–771 (2007)

Official Journal of the Spanish State: Royal Decree 1125 establishing the European credit system and the system of qualifications in university degrees. N. 224, 34355-34356 (2003) (in Spanish)

Official Journal of the European Union: Decision No 2318 of the European Parliament and of the Council of 5 December 2003 adopting a multiannual programme (2004 to 2006) for the effective integration of information and communication technologies (ICT) in education and training systems in Europe (eLearning Programme). No. 327, 45–68 (2003)

Official Journal of the Spanish State: Law 6 stablishing University Spanish System. No. 307, 49400–49425 (2001) (in Spanish)

Official Journal of Andalusian autonomous region Goverment: Decree 325 approving Statutes of the University of Granada. No. 236, 25745–25776 (2003) (in Spanish)

de Prada, E.: Adapting to ECTS through the creation and use of a web page. RELATEC 5, 235–249 (2006)

Shin, D., Yoon, E.S., Park, S.J., Lee, E.S.: Web-based interactive virtual laboratory system for unit operations and process systems engineering education. Computer and Chemical Engineering 24, 381–385 (2002)

Veron, D.T., Blake, R.L.: Does problem-based learning work? A meta-analysis of evaluative Research. Acad. Med. 68, 550–563 (1993)

An Ontology-Based Framework for Web Service Integration and Delivery to Mobility Impaired Users

Dionysios D. Kehagias and Dimitrios Tzovaras

Informatics and Telematics Institute, Centre for Research and Technology Hellas, Thessaloniki, Greece
diok@iti.gr,
Dimitrios.Tzovaras@iti.gr

Abstract. This paper describes an ontology-based framework whose purpose is to collect content from various existing Web services in order to fulfill the information needs of mobility impaired users, while they are planning a trip, moving from a city to another, or performing home control activities during the trip. In order to access the user-requested content the tool is equipped with semantic Web service search and discovery mechanisms. The service alignment tool, which is part of the presented framework, enables different service providers to map their Web services against a set of ontologies in order to support the discovery and invocation of services.

1 Introduction

Nowadays a large amount of content about tourism, leisure and transport services is available on the Web. Users who plan a new trip typically need to get access to several information resources. In most common use cases, travelers access the content they desire by manually searching via a typical Web browser. However, when it comes to exploit available information during the trip, a more sophisticated and automatic way of information and service discovery is required.

Web services (WSs), which are increasingly becoming the de facto middleware standard for distributed Web-based applications are appropriate for this purpose. WS technology allows online access to desired content through suitable software interfaces, thus solving interoperability problems between heterogeneous and distributed Internet-based applications. Today, searching for WSs involves keyword search in UDDI[1] registries. This practice is inefficient and unreliable because it does not support service discovery based on service capabilities and special user needs. In this paper we present a software infrastructure and supporting tools to enable:

- Ontology-based WS discovery
- Retrieval of content which becomes available through the discovered WS
- Delivery of the retrieved content to the end-users via a wide range of client applications

[1] Universal Description, Discovery, and Integration (UDDI), http://uddi.org/

M.D. Lytras et al. (Eds.): WSKS 2010, Part I, CCIS 111, pp. 555–563, 2010.

Work presented in this paper has been developed in the context of an integrated European project called ASK-IT[2], whose goal is to develop an ambient intelligence framework that supports the needs of mobility impaired (MI) users as they move from one location to another. The ASK-IT framework consists of an ontology that describes the MI user needs and defines relevant services, as well as a tool that facilitates the integration of existing services in a common ontological framework. By this tool, existing service providers (SPs) become capable of registering their services in the ontological framework thus allowing ontological descriptions of services that facilitate their discovery by the use of semantic queries.

Two important initiatives have emerged with respect to ontological descriptions of WSs: OWL-S and WSMO. OWL-S defines an upper ontology in the form of a generic Service concept. In order to make use of OWL-S upper ontology, the lower ontological levels must be defined. WSMO seeks to create ontologies for describing various aspects related to Semantic Web services, aiming at solving the integration problem (Roman et al. 2005). WSMO takes the Web Service Modeling Framework (WSMF) (Fensel et al. 2002) as starting point and further refines and extends its concepts. WSMX is an execution environment for dynamic discovery, selection, mediation and invocation of WSs based on WSMO (Haller et al. 2005).

In most cases, ontological descriptions for WSs are used to support WS discovery. For instance, in (Ramachandran et al. 2006) an inference engine is used to submit queries to an ontology about atmospheric data. An alternative method in (Hübner et al. 2004) uses a Semantic Web enabled search engine in order to perform discovery of interconnected and semantically unified geographic information resources. Sriharee (Sriharee 2006) develops ontologies to describe a rating model that is used for more accurate WS discovery results. In (Zhang 2005) an ontology-based knowledge base about WSs is constructed in order to facilitate the discovery of WSs.

Many tools have been also developed to facilitate the description of WSs in ontological terms. Such a tool, called WSDL2OWL-S (Paolucci et al. 2003), converts WSs descriptions from WSDL to OWL-S. This allows the automatic provision of ontological descriptions for already existing services. Although promising, this tool as well as its supporting transformation process from WSDL to OWL-S is still in its infancy and requires manual intervention on a practical level. This is mainly due to the fact that OWL-S is richer than WSDL in semantics. Thus the transformation from WSDL to OWL-S is a semantics-loss process.

In order to overcome the lack of semantics in WSDL a proposal was submitted, available as a W3C recommendation (Akkiraju et al. 2005) that introduces WSDL-S, an effort to enhance WSDL expressiveness by adding semantics in it. Although promising, this effort suffers from limited support by existing tools.

Many tools have been developed that support the automatic synthesis and invocation of Web services. The majority of them provide adequate user interfaces for semi-automatic and automatic Web service composition. Such a tool is the Web Service Composer that allows the user to compose a sequence of Web Service workflows and invoke Web services annotated in DAML-S (Sirin et al. 2003).

None of the aforementioned systems use any tool to facilitate the integration of existing WSs by the corresponding SPs in the way it is supported in our framework. As

[2] ASK-IT project homepage: `http://www.ask-it.org/`

opposed to these systems, our framework provides a service alignment tool that allows SPs to register their services within the context of a set of domain ontologies.

This paper is structured as follows. Next section presents an overview of the structure of the ontological framework which provides the required ontologies on which the service discovery and invocation processes are relied. Section 3 describes the service alignment process and explains how this is performed by the registered service providers, by the use of a specifically developed tool (Service Alignment Tool). An application scenario, which is realized via the proposed infrastructure is described in Section 4, while Section 5 concludes the paper and outlines future work.

2 The Ontologies

The development of the ontologies[3] was originally motivated by the need for providing elderly and disabled users with accurate information that describes the specificities of their various impairment types.

For the development of the ontology several existing ontologies and tools related to MI users were investigated. For instance, in (Yesilada et al. 2004) authors introduce a semi-automated tool that supports travel and mobility of visually impaired users. This tool transforms existing web pages, by using a travel ontology, in order to extract information that may be relevant to the user. Thus, it enhances navigation capabilities on behalf of visually impaired users.

The work described in (Karim et al. 2006) provides an ontology that enables mappings amongst various impairments and attributes of user interfaces. This enables to improve access to personal information systems by making it possible for user interface developers to adapt them to the user needs. The ontology covers many MI user attributes following a similar approach to the one adopted by the ASK-IT project. Although many advanced use cases, such as trip planning, can be realized, the main focus remains on the UI customization according to user impairments.

Together with the aforementioned approaches, which focus on the attributes of MI users, additional efforts were also considered, including more generic ontologies that have been applied in similar application domains, such as travelling and accessing tourism and leisure information. These ontologies, however, fail to address those specificities of MI users. A typical example of such an ontology is a common travel ontology (Choi et al. 2006).

The ASK-IT ontologies are classified according to the following domains.

- *Service ontology*. This ontology includes skeleton descriptions about the supported services. The main purpose of this domain is to enable efficient search and retrieval of WSs, through appropriate interfaces, when the requesting party is aware of the use case in which the user is acting. It provides interrelationships between the user groups, use cases categories and existing service types. A fragment of this ontology is illustrated in Figure 1.
- *Transportation ontology*. This ontology includes transport-related information and data types, which can be filled in by content providers and serve a variety of MI people levels of accessibility.

[3] The ASK-IT ontologies are available at: `http://askit.iti.gr/ontology/`

- *Tourism and Leisure ontology*. Tourism-related content is defined as anything that would interest a tourist who visits an area or city. This include, among others, useful content about hotels, museums, interesting places, as well as information about tourism offices, embassies, airlines, useful telephone numbers and addresses and so on.

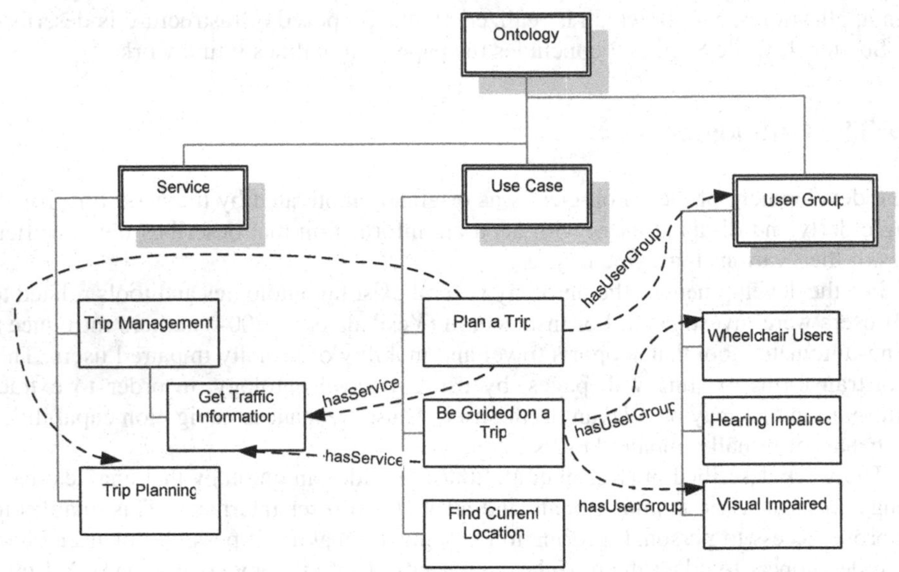

Fig. 1. An indicative part of the ASK-IT service ontology in tree-like form

- *Personal Support Services ontology*. This ontology includes information about travel companion, specific care at the hotel, eating, paramedical support, etc. These services will be used by MI people who seek to hire local assistance that matches their needs (including language, expertise, specific preferences).
- *e-Learning and e-Working ontology*. It includes concepts based on services for work and education on a long-distance basis with special considerations for MI user groups.
- *Social Relations and Community Building ontology*. This ontology contains information about social relations, registration to communities and social events. It mainly includes specific aspects of assisting devices which play a significant role to the establishment of social relations between users. In addition, the ontology contains concepts related to potential meeting places, as well as community registration procedures for all supported user groups.

The aforementioned ontologies have been authored using the Protégé tool (Noy et al. 2004) and they are stored in OWL-DL, because the latter is widely supported by the most common tools and represents the most stable standard among the ontology description languages available today. All ontologies include more than 1400 concepts and 1100 relationships.

3 Service Alignment

Service alignment is the process of registering an existing Web service into the back-end subsystem of the ASK-IT framework so that it adheres to the ontological definitions of services. This process is performed by any SP who is interested to provide one or more services that deliver content in the one of the application domains and for those user groups that are defined in the context of the ASK-IT project. Service alignment is facilitated by the *Service Alignment Tool* (SAT), which is equipped with a Web-based user-friendly interface, shown in Figure 2. The aforementioned process results into the completion of service integration whose purpose is to enable the efficient invocation of services whenever it is requested by any of the integrated client applications.

3.1 Service Integration

SPs participate in the service alignment process by being able to establish relationships between the services and the ontologies. WSs are described in the Service ontology by the Service model that defines the operations and the structure that should characterize any registered WS.

Before the alignment takes place, SAT collects information about the SPs. Any registered provider has the ability to navigate through the supported models as these are defined in the service ontology. SPs co-relate their WSs with the ontologies. By doing so WSs are consistently annotated. The alignment mechanism facilitates a flexible standardization process. In this context, "similarity" between the ontology and the WS is established when the following criteria are satisfied:

- The inputs of the supported WS operations are identical to the inputs provided by the service model's operations.
- The outputs of the real WS operations are described by the outputs provided by the service model in the ontology.

The SAT allows an SP to see the defined operations in the ontology, which are defined in an analogous manner to those in a WSDL file. Furthermore, by clicking on the operation models, SPs can get information about the inputs and outputs that their services must have in order to comply with the model.

After the identification of the appropriate model, the providers should select from a drop-down list the operation that complies with the service they want to register. Thus, they provide the URL of the WSDL file that describes the service. At this point, the tool automatically parses the WSDL file and extracts the required information. In this context, any service can be described by the triplet:

$$\mathbf{S} = <P\_id, wsdl, op[\ ]>,$$

where *P_id* is the provider's identifier, *wsdl* is the URL to the WSDL service description and, *op*[ ] is a list of defined operations. Each operation is defined as:

$$op = <name, i_1, \ldots i_n, o>,$$

where *name* is the name of the operation, $i_1, \ldots i_n$ its inputs and o its output.

Let us assume that service **S** is described in the ontology by the service model $\mathbf{S}_m$. Two arbitrary operations *op* **S** and op_n $\mathbf{S}_n$ have a degree of similarity equal to 1, when they have equal number of inputs and also:

$$i_k \equiv im_k \text{ and } o \equiv om,\ \forall i_k, o \in op \text{ and } im_k,\ om \in op_n, \textit{ where } k = 1 \ldots n.$$

The alignment process which is performed by the provider is initiated by the determination of the degree of similarity between the operation defined in the ontology and the one that has been selected to be included as part of a registered service. It is up to the service provider to verify the accuracy of the alignment operation and select the service to be aligned.

The last step of the service alignment procedure involves mapping of inputs and outputs between the service to be aligned and the ASK-IT ontological service model. This process, which is supported by drag and drop operations on the GUI is illustrated in the snapshot of Figure 2. Once this final step is completed, the information of the alignment operation is stored in a registry of services, known as Service Repository (SR). In this way the invocation of services is enabled through the back-end system. The invocation mechanism handles incoming requests for specific content by the client applications and launches the appropriate services in order to receive the required content.

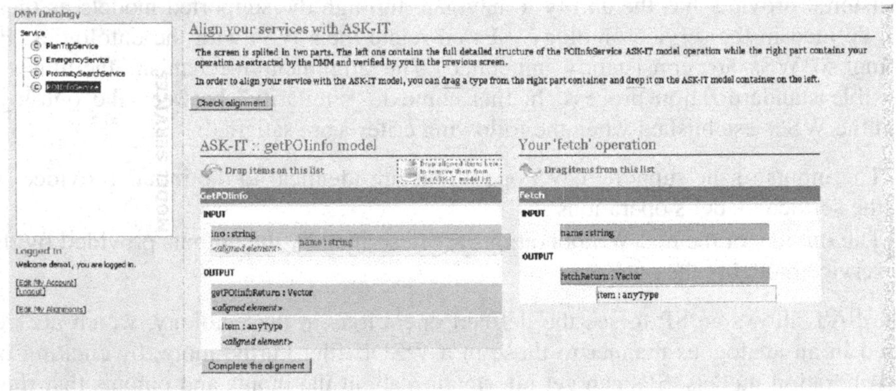

Fig. 2. A snapshot of the service alignment tool user interface. Service providers may exploit drag-and-drop functionality in order to provide mappings of data types and operations defined in their services to the corresponding fields defined in ASK-IT ontology services.

3.2 Service Invocation

As soon as a service alignment process is completed, the newly aligned service is integrated within the system's back-end and at the same time a new entry is added in the SR. Actual service integration involves manual generation and compilation of the required source code of the wrapper that corresponds to the newly aligned service. This wrapper provides the necessary mappings and transformations between SP's native data type formats and the ASK-IT ontological description of data types and services.

After the completion of the alignment process the invocation of the real Web services is then performed based on the SOAP protocol. Each WS is described by a WSDL file which contains a complete description of the WS that facilitates the invocation process.

This software, often referred to as the Web service client stub is a Web service client. Thus, in order for the DMM to be able to access a Web service, it should have the client stub code of the integrated service, which provides the ability to call the service each time this is requested by the user interface. It is requested, specifically to call the aligned service when a request for the corresponding service model arrives.

4 An Indicative Scenario

The ASK-IT framework supports a wide range of use cases that are enabled after the integration of WSs via the SAT. Figure 3 illustrates various snapshots of the PDA version of the end-user application for different use cases. The user localization module of ASK-IT (Figure 3.1, 3.2) shows a map that displays user location based on GPS information. Seamless indoor to outdoor localization is also supported. If the user starts from an indoor area (Figure 3.1) and an appropriate network of indoor location-aware sensors is installed (Zigbee devices in our case), an indoor map displays the user position. While the user goes outdoors, the map automatically changes and now displays the user's location in the outdoor area (Figure 3.2). The reverse action is also supported as the user goes from outdoors to indoors.

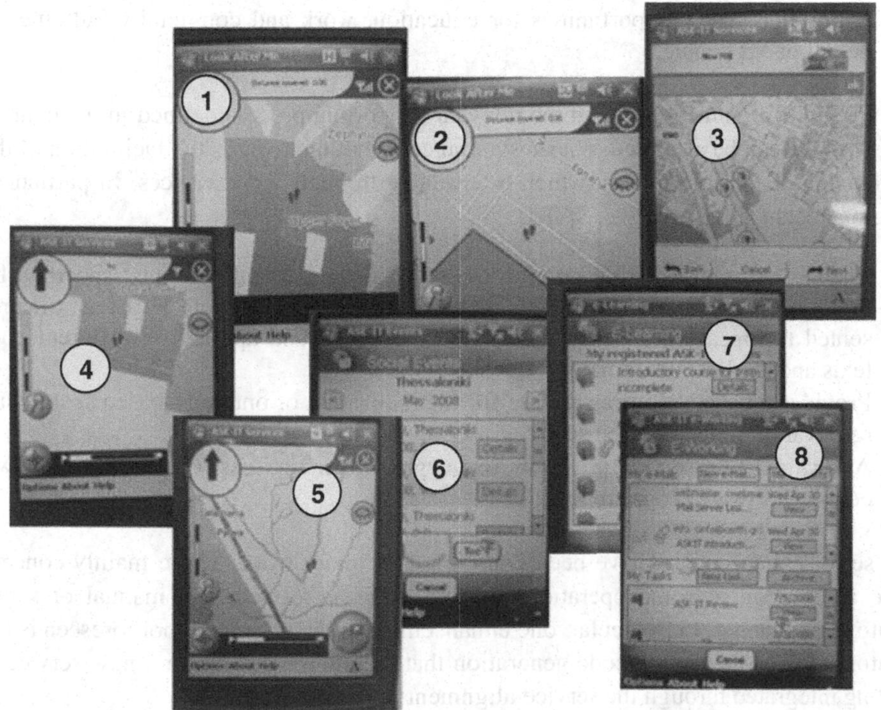

Fig. 3. Snapshots of the ASK-IT PDA end-user application

5 Implications and Future Work

ASK-IT project was developed in order to facilitate mobility of MI users. Until today the overall framework - composed of the back-end subsystem presented in this paper and a number of client applications (one small sample of which was demonstrated in Section 4) - has been successfully tested at 7 pilot sites, hosted by an equal number of European cities. Specifically, the pilot sites were Newcastle (UK), Nuremberg (Germany), Genoa (Italy), Helsinki (Finland), Bucharest (Romania), Athens and Thessaloniki (Greece). For the purpose of running successsful demo applications, local SPs and stakeholders from various municipal or national organizations for each one of the aforementioned cities prepared one or two-days events to demonstrate the client applications and how content is retrieved from real WS. The basic requirement for the operation of the framework on a municipality level is the availability of a set of local SPs to provide localized services and the integration of these services into the ASK-IT framework.

Based on experience from the pilot demonstrators, the social impact of ASK-IT may be outlined as follows:

- ASK-IT facilitates the provision of information and services to the user groups of MI and disabled people, thus reducing social isolation and enabling the exploitation of IT on behalf of these people.
- It introduces new opportunities for education, work and community building on behalf of MI people,

The service alignment tool and the relevant supporting process defined in the context of ASK-IT can be also seen as a substantial contribution towards the facilitation of the provision of the information which is available through Web services. In particular, from a technical perspective, SAT:

- Enables an ontological description of services in a particular context specified by the information needs of MI users. Even though ASK-IT targets MI users, the presented technical infrastructure may be generalized and applied on different contexts and application domains.
- Provides a technical infrastructure for the realization of ontology-based search and retrieval of Semantic Web services
- Allows existing service providers to integrate their services without prior knowledge of software programming.

A set of enhancements have been considered as future work. These mainly concern the automation of some operations that are now performed in a manual or semi-automatic manner. In particular, one enhancement of the presented tool foreseen is the automation of the source code generation that is required each time a new service is being integrated through the service alignment process.

References

Akkiraju, R., Farrell, J., Miller, J., Nagarajan, M., Schmidt, M., Sheth, A., Verma, K.: Web Service Semantics – WSDL-S. Technical report. W3C Member Submission (2005) `http://www.w3.org/Submission/WSDL-S/` (retrieved October 6, 2008)

Choi, C., Cho, M., Kang Young, E., Kim, P.: Travel ontology for recommendation system based on semantic web. In: The 8th International Conference on Advanced Communication Technology (ICACT 2006), pp. 624–627. IEEE Press, Los Alamitos (2006)

Fensel, D., Bussler, C.: The Web service Modelling Framework WSMF. Electronic Commerce Research and Applications 1(2), 113–137 (2002)

Haller, A., Cimpian, E., Mocan, A., Oren, E., Bussler, C.: WSMX - a semantic service-oriented architecture. In: Proceedings of the 1st International Conference on Web Services, pp. 321–328. IEEE Press, Los Alamitos (2005)

Hübner, S., Spittel, R., Visser, U., Vögele, T.J.: Ontology-Based Search for Interactive Digital Maps. IEEE Intelligent Systems 19(3), 80–86 (2004)

Karim, S., Tjoa, A.M.: Towards the Use of Ontologies for Improving User Interaction for People with Special Needs. In: Miesenberger, K., et al. (eds.) ICCHP 2006. LNCS, vol. 4061, pp. 77–84. Springer, Heidelberg (2006)

Noy, N.F., Sintek, M., Decker, S., Crubezy, M., Fergerson, R.W., Musen, M.A.: Creating Semantic Web Contents with Protege-2000. IEEE Intelligent Systems 16(2), 60–71 (2004)

Paolucci, M., Srinivasan, N., Sycara, K., Nishimura, T.: Towards a semantic choreography of web services: From WSDL to DAML-S. In: Proc. 2003 International Conference for Web Services, pp. 22–26. IEEE Press, Los Alamitos (2003)

Ramachandran, R., Movva, S., Graves, S., Tanner, S.: Ontology-based Semantic Search Tool for Atmospheric Science. In: 22nd International Conference on Interactive Information Processing Systems (IIPS) (2006) (preprints)

Roman, D., Keller, U., Lausen, H., De Bruijn, J., Lara, R., Stollberg, M., Polleres, A., Feier, C., Bussler, C., Fensel, D.: Web Service Modeling Ontology. Applied Ontology 1(1), 77–106 (2005)

Sirin, E., Hendler, J.A., Parsia, B.: Semi-automatic composition of web services using semantic descriptions. In: Proc. Workshop on Web Services: Modeling, Architecture and Infrastructure (WSMAI), pp. 17–24. ICEIS Press (2003)

Sriharee, N.: Semantic Web Services Discovery Using Ontology-based Rating Model. In: Proceedings of the 2006 IEEE/WIC/ACM International Conference on Web Intelligence, pp. 608–616. IEEE Press, Los Alamitos (2006)

Yesilada, Y., Harper, S., Goble, C., Stevens, R.: Screen readers cannot see (ontology based semantic annotation for visually impaired web travellers). In: Koch, N., Fraternali, P., Wirsing, M. (eds.) ICWE 2004. LNCS, vol. 3140, pp. 445–458. Springer, Heidelberg (2004)

Zhang, P., Li, J.: Ontology Assisted Web Services Discovery. In: Proceedings of the 2005 IEEE International Workshop on Service-Oriented System Engineering, pp. 45–50. IEEE Press, Los Alamitos (2005)

Knowledge Management through the Equilibrium Pattern Model for Learning

Akila Sarirete[1], Elizabeth Noble[1], and Azeddine Chikh[2]

[1] Effat College, PO Box 34689, Jeddah 21478, Saudi Arabia
asarirete@effatcollege.edu.sa,
enoble@effatcollege.edu.sa

[2] Information Systems Department, College of Computer & Information Sciences, King Saud University
az_chikh@ccis.ksu.edu.sa

Abstract. Contemporary students are characterized by having very applied learning styles and methods of acquiring knowledge. This behavior is consistent with the constructivist models where students are co-partners in the learning process. In the present work the authors developed a new model of learning based on the constructivist theory coupled with the cognitive development theory of Piaget. The model considers the level of learning based on several stages and the move from one stage to another requires learners' challenge. At each time a new concept is introduced creates a disequilibrium that needs to be worked out to return back to its equilibrium stage. This process of "disequilibrium/equilibrium" has been analyzed and validated using a course in computer networking as part of Cisco Networking Academy Program at Effat College, a women college in Saudi Arabia. The model provides a theoretical foundation for teaching especially in a complex knowledge domain such as engineering and can be used in a knowledge economy.

1 Introduction

In a traditional transfer learning model the teacher serves as the repository and transmitter of knowledge. Learning often takes place in classrooms, with teachers that instruct courses containing learning objects that can be put together or organized (Downes, 2005). Learning initiatives are working with the basic assumption of learning as an individual. However, educators realized that this might not be the best approach for learning and gradually we are witnessing a movement towards more practice-based, life-long learning initiatives. This type of learning makes the central starting point to the social learning theory of Wenger (1998).

To understand more this theory of social learning, three types of learning initiatives are analyzed: *behaviorist, cognitive and constructivist*. Contemporary students are characterized by having very applied learning styles and methods of acquiring knowledge. This behavior is consistent with the constructivist models. In these models the students are co-partners in the learning process. This approach towards learning is a different phenomenon which offers opportunities to learning and teaching. The cognitive theorists suggest that learning is a staged process which requires active engagement of both

M.D. Lytras et al. (Eds.): WSKS 2010, Part I, CCIS 111, pp. 564–572, 2010.

student and teacher. The stages of cognitive development are enablers of the ability to think, to be a problem solver, and to be creative.

2 Learning Theories

The following sections discuss these theories which have influenced educational curriculums, relationships of teacher and students, and the developed methodologies which have been employed in educational practice. These theories have been based on assumptions of students, the needs of students, and desired educational outcomes. Contextual analyses of students today suggest that the students have needs to learn through application, and through relational peer to peer interactions.

2.1 Behaviorist Learning Theory

This theory is based on the stimulus response principle and selective reinforcement. This approach highlights the performance rather than the reasons why a methodology has been adopted by the learner. Learning is considered as the result of encouragement and responses through the use of rewards. A content area is broken into component sub-skills which are sequenced and then transmitted to the learner, often by direct instruction. After absorbing the specific parts of a content area, the learner is able to put them together as a whole and apply them when needed. This theory sees the learner as a passive learner who needs external motivation and who is affected by reinforcement (von Glasersfeld, 1996; Chen, 2003).

2.2 Cognitive Learning Theory

The cognitive theory is influenced by the cognitive psychology and focuses directly on the structure and operation of the human mind. This theory is based on the information processing approach, which deal with the way people collect, store, modify, and interpret information from their environment, how the information is retrieved and stored, and how people use this knowledge and information in their activities (Chen, 2003). This theory, focuses on internal cognitive structures, and learning is viewed as transformations in these cognitive structures (Wenger, 1998; Hoadley and Kilner, 2005).

2.3 Constructivist Learning Theory

The constructivist theory builds on the cognitive approach and views learning as a process of knowledge construction, with concept development and comprehensive understanding as the main objectives. The learner is considered as a designer of learning by actively construing and modifying his knowledge. It's not an accumulative process but rather an ongoing, recursive, elaborative process as stated by Proulx (2006). Formalization of the theory of constructivism is generally attributed to Jean Piaget (Wankat and Oreovicz, 1993). He suggested that through processes of accommodation and assimilation, individuals construct new knowledge from their experiences. When individuals assimilate, they incorporate the new experience into an already existing framework without changing that framework. According to von Glasersfeld (1996) and Chen (2003) constructivism is described in two parts. First, learning is a process of knowledge construction instead of absorption and not seen as a passive one. Because knowledge is constructed based on one's own perceptions and conceptions of the world, everyone constructs a different meaning or concept. This implies that learning takes place when learners are actively involved in the process. Second, knowledge is considered highly related to the environment in which learning is experienced and knowledge is constructed. This implies that learning should be task-oriented and focused on the practices of the communities (Wenger, 1998).

2.4 Social Learning Theory

The constructivism approach of learning focuses on the individual construal of knowledge and does not reject the importance of the social in this individual construal of knowledge. The social learning theory of Wenger (1998) further elaborates on this constructivist theory and places learning in the context of our lived experience of social participation in the world. Learning is considered as part of human nature and is life sustaining and inevitable. Participation is essential for learning and implies that learning is a matter of engaging and contributing to the practices in which they are involved. Engagement in social practice is the fundamental process by which we learn and so become who we are. According to social learning theory, learning is situated in practice and the social groups in which learning takes place are defined as communities of practice (CoPs). This concept of learning in a group is known as "social learning" as opposed to "individual learning".

2.5 Learning and Practice

The four learning models described in the previous sections overlap in many cases, and depend most of the time on the definition of learning (learning as changed behavior, learning as developmental changes, learning as changed mental representations, and learning as changed social practices.). Hoadley and Kilner (2005) argue that the CoPs could be a setting for learning regardless of the learning theory to which the designer assigns. According to a recent research by Wenger (2007), learning is traditionally viewed as a vertical process that involves a producer giving knowledge to a recipient. From this "vertical" perspective, theory is often considered a superior mode of learning. Practice is seen as an application of the theory that follows learning. However, practice is beginning to be considered as an equal partner. A more horizontal view emerged from this vertical view which is a process involving negotiation among learning partners through an application of CoPs. By definition, CoPs are structures that enable peer-to-peer learning among practitioners. They are horizontal structures where the responsibility for managing knowledge is in the hands of practitioners. The central point as stated by Wenger (2007) is the *negotiation of mutual relevance* of different forms of knowledgeability as key to the production and transfer of effective knowledge.

3 Equilibrium Concept in Learning

Stressing on the horizontal view of learning or the peer-to-peer learning, we notice that learning happens when people work as partners and share their knowledge together.

These learners can be a teacher and students' partners, or people in a community who want to learn from each other for a purpose of long life learning. One of the concepts introduced by Piaget in his theory of learning about constructivism is the concept of "equilibrium" (Piaget 1965; Wankat and Oreovicz, 1993). Equilibrium means that at any time a person in a learning situation has to accommodate her mental development to reach a stable mental state. Mental development occurs because the organism has a natural desire to operate in a state of equilibrium. "When information is received from the outside world which is too far from the mental structure to be accommodated but makes enough sense that rejecting it is difficult, then the person is in a state of *disequilibrium"* (Wankat and Oreovicz, 1993). The desire for equilibration is a very strong motivator to either change the structure or reject the data. The more often the person receives input which requires some formal logic, the more likely she has to accommodate to the new situation. As stated by Ackermann (2001), Piaget describes the genesis of internal mental stability in terms of successive plateaus of equilibrium. This concept of equilibrium stresses the shift from a knowledge-push to a knowledge-pull model (Naeve, 2005). In the knowledge-pull case, people create an environment where they can pull content that meets their particular needs from a wide selection of high-value but less structured resources (such as information repositories, communities and experts, which helps create flexible, real time learning (Chatti et al., 2007).

3.1 Disequilibrium/Equilibrium Formulation

We propose in this present paper to generalize the concept of equilibrium to a group of learners (in a classroom or a community setting). We consider a group of learners $L_1, L_2, \ldots, L_n$, each one having some knowledge K_i ($i = 1, 2, \ldots, n$) about some topic they want to learn. Initially, one of the learners (let's say L1) introduces some new situation of learning where the new knowledge is $K = K_1 + \Delta K$, where ΔK is the partial knowledge that is not known by others. This introduces some disequilibrium in the group. Therefore, everyone in the group needs to adjust his/her mental state to the new situation. Adjusting the knowledge means sharing what they already know and seek what is unknown. We formalize this as follows. L_i has knowledge K_i as stated by equation (1).

$$K_i = K_1 + \Delta K_i\ ,\ i = 2, \ldots, n \qquad (1)$$

L_i has the same initial knowledge K_1 as learner L_1 and some other knowledge about the new situation ΔK_i. To create equilibrium, all learners share their partial knowledge about the learning situation, the new knowledge can be formulated as the sum of individuals knowledge and can be written as $\sum \Delta K_i$ ($i = 2, \ldots, n$).
If $\Delta K = \sum \Delta K_i$ ($i = 2, \ldots, n$) then the equilibrium is established; If $\Delta K \neq \sum \Delta K_i$ a new process Ω of learning should be triggered to establish equilibrium thus equation (2) should be verified. This process should challenge learners and create new knowledge ($\Omega(K)$).

$$\Delta K = \Omega(K) + \sum \Delta K_i \ \ (i = 2, \ldots, n) \qquad (2)$$

An example of process can be information gathering, problem solving, dialogue, information analysis, experiences, best practices, etc. This leads the learners to be involved in a cycle of learning where they need to establish equilibrium among themselves. The equilibrium is established when the new knowledge is assessed and learners show that they have enough knowledge to move a step forward. If after assessment, learners do not fulfill the criteria of equality, they are challenged by a new process of learning (Ω) until equilibrium is established. Figure 1 shows a schematic representation of the model where the learners are considered as actors with some initial knowledge about a situation. The assessment is a part of the teaching and learning process, it is introduced at the disequilibrium stage. Testing is required to confirm the equilibrium state. The assessment provides a guide to what subjects need to be taught; what skills need to be acquired and what attitudes need to be modeled. In a course setting, this teaching process is reiterated over the syllabus or course report to accomplish the course goals and objectives. The use of external standardized testing is employed as confirmatory to the process. The external testing offers a confirmation of the course and the teaching.

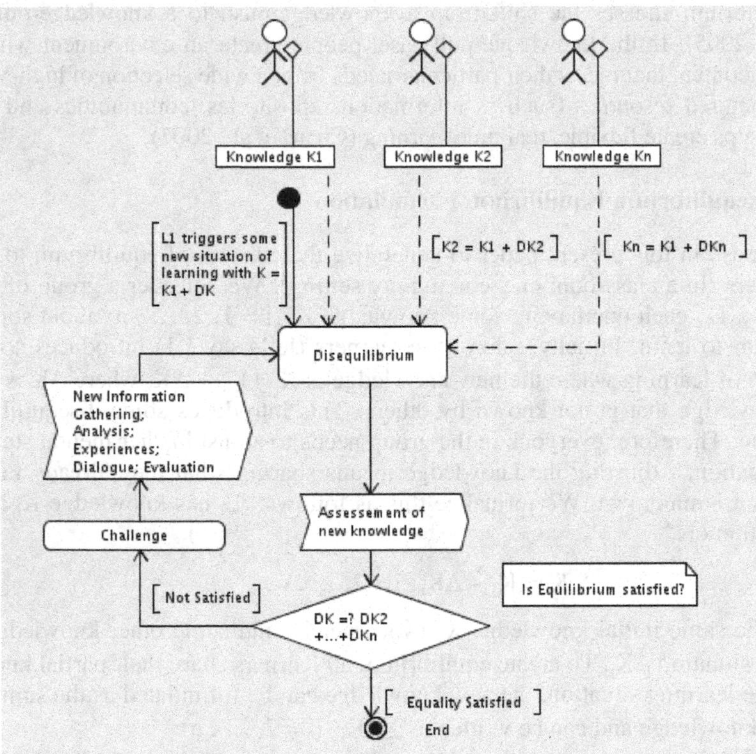

Fig. 1. Schematic representation of the model within a learning situation

4 Application of the Equilibrium Pattern Model for an Effective Learning

The cognitive and moral development of students as modeled in the various Student Development theories suggest that most campus life is inclusive of formal and informal learning in the area of moral development and character education (Noble and Jamal Al-Lail, 2008). Academics and ethical learning represent a holistic approach to education. The growth in cognitive and moral development that students experience follow several stages of development as summarized in table 1 below. The equilibrium model as described in the previous section advances the students from one stage to another.

Table 1. Student Character Development

Cognitive Development	Moral Development	Ages for Growth
Piaget Stages (Wankat and Oreovicz, 1993)	**Kohlberg Stages (Kohlberg, and Turiel, 1971)**	**Ages**
Stage 1 Pre-conventional	0 Ego centric	0-2
	1 The punishment and obedience orientation	2-7
	2 Fairness and Equal sharing	2-11
Stage 2 Conventional	3 Good Boy Good Girl conformity to stereotypes	11-16
	4 Law and Order obey all rules and enforce social order	11-20
Stage 3 Post Conventional Principled Autonomous	5 Social Contract	College-Adult
	6 Social Justice	College-Adult

Chickering's Psychosocial Theory of Student Development

The Arthur Chickering's psychosocial model is one of the most widely cited theories of student development (University of Dallas, 2008). The proposed model is articulated around seven vectors along which traditionally aged college students develop. Table 2 shows the seven vectors of development which are general tasks of identity resolution. Using the equilibrium model student progress from one stage to another, until maturation, at different rates and may recycle through some vectors. As stated in Arthur Chickering's model, development is not simply a maturation process, but requires stimulation through challenge and support.

Table 2. Student Development Theme (Chickering Model)

Student Development Theme	College Year
Developing Confidence	1,2
Managing Emotions	1,2
Moving Through Autonomy Toward Interdependence	1,2
Developing Mature Interpersonal Relationships	1,2
Establishing Identity: based on feedback from significant others, developing comfort with self	3
Developing Purpose: developing clear life goals and committing to personal interests and activities	3
Developing Integrity: moving from moralistic thinking to acknowledging and accepting the beliefs of others.	3,4

5 Case Study: Qualitative Evaluation of the Equilibrium Model

The following sections discuss these theories which have influenced educational curriculums. The research methods of this study require a qualitative approach to describe and to define the learning theory relevance and application. Qualitative methods afford the opportunity to engage in an in-depth review of data, and an analysis which is both contextual, and comparative. Case study methods were chosen to provide an in-depth analysis.

The case study is conducted at Effat College, a Women College in Saudi Arabia. The case study applies and validates the equilibrium model proposed in the previous sections using a course in Computer Networking as part of Cisco Networking Academy Program at the college. The model was applied to several groups of students from year 2004 till year 2008. The students were mainly professionals working in Information Technology sectors, IT support, and graduate students seeking jobs in the networking field. The course is divided into four levels and spans for a period of six to eight months. The learning environment uses in addition of the teacher, and the student knowledge in the field the Cisco Online Curriculum (http://cisco.netacad.net) and the internet resources. Hands-on labs and lab material are important resources for students. The teacher's role is to support the students in their learning process and to challenge them with new knowledge to acquire. To apply the equilibrium model, students already have some knowledge about the topic that will be discussed during the class. The teacher then introduces during a one class–period the new concept (disequilibrium stage) and encourages students to discuss, brainstorm, and show what they know and then share it with the rest of the group. To reach the equilibrium stage students are assessed on their knowledge by standardized test exams or hands-on activities. If they are still in disequilibrium stage (confused with one topic or concept) they are challenged with some new activities such as simulation exercises using Packet Tracer tool provided by Cisco Networking Academy which simulates the networking process and/or apply what they know using the lab material consisting of real networking devices. This assessed process ensures that the students will reach the equilibrium stage after some activities. From the teacher experience, students who took the course returned to class and shared their hands-on experience and shared the peer-to-peer experience as developing the ability to acquire more knowledge in the field and seek for more. The model as detailed here provides that students are allowed to redo assessment exams. This process helps them review the missing concepts and come back with a better knowledge. The key benefit for students to acquire knowledge in this way is to increase their chances of employability, to acquire additional skills and practice and to be awarded with industry certification that can help them grow in their careers.

6 Impact of the Equilibrium Model on Government Initiatives

The educational sector needs, related to developing policy to transform the economy from a consumer economy to a Knowledge Economy, are to design an educational system which meets the needs of all students to achieve their potential. The use of learning theory as a component of the knowledge management in classroom and in learning technologies is an emphasis. This paper is a step toward developing a discussion which addresses the more systematic synthesis of possible options. The critical need in this effort is to devise education institutions which can provide reliable results for students and for educators in an efficient educational program. This approach in this paper is evaluable and offers assessments which can be student centered.

7 Conclusions

The use of learning theories to consider educational practice affords an opportunity to review the student needs, the teacher student relationship, the curriculum and the methods of instruction.

A learning model based on the constructivist theory coupled with the cognitive development theory of Piaget has been developed. The process of "disequilibrium/equilibrium" has been analyzed and validated using a course in Computer Networking as part of Cisco Networking Academy Program at Effat College, a women college in Saudi Arabia. The model provides a theoretical foundation in managing knowledge for teaching especially in the complex knowledge and skill domains such as engineering. The learning model sees the level of learning first based on the cognitive stages, the learning is stimulated by challenge which results in increased cognitive development; and in a move from one stage to another. The learners need to be challenged to produce the stage advancement. At each time a new concept is introduced into the community of learners; disequilibrium is introduced and the process to move toward equilibrium is reasserted. The authors believe that this model provide a key to the theoretical foundation for teaching, especially in a complex knowledge domain such as engineering.

Additional studies to confirm the results might include more study on the use of assessments in the learning process, and the use of learning probes as challenge, are the appropriate modalities for engineering students. The hypothesis of interest is the statement of Perry that engineering students need to be at the highest cognitive development level to be competent and qualified engineers. Perry suggests that the engineering needs to have all the ability of the abstract reason as described by Piaget.

References

Ackermann, E.: Piaget's Constructivism, Papert's Constructionism: What's the difference ? (2001), http://learning.media.mit.edu/content/publications/EA.Piaget%20_%20Papert.pdf (retrieved July 22, 2008)

Chatti, M.A., Jarke, M., Frosch-Wilke, D.: The future of e-learning: a shift to knowledge networking and social software. Int. J. Knowledge and Learning 3(4/5), 404–420 (2007)

Chen, C.: A constructivist approach to teaching: Implications in teaching computer networking. Information Technology, Learning, and Performance Journal 21(2), 17–27 (2003), http://www.osra.org/itlpj/chenfall2003.pdf

Downes, S.: Feature: e-learning 2.0. eLearn Magazine, vol. 10, pp. 1–6 (October 2005), http://www.elearnmag.org/subpage.cfm?section=articles&article=29-1

Hoadley, C.M., Kilner, P.G.: Using Technology to Transform Communities of Practice into Knowledge-building communities. SIGGROUP Bulletin 25(1), 31–39 (2005)

Kohlberg, L., Turiel, E.: Moral development and moral education. In: Lesser, G. (ed.) Psychology and Educational Practice. Scott Foresman (1971)

Naeve, A.: The human semantic web – shifting from knowledge push to knowledge pull. International Journal of Semantic Web and Information Systems (IJSWIS) 1(3), 1–30 (2005)

Noble, E., Jamal Al-Lail, H.: Effat Learning Model. Presentation Submission to American Association for Colleges and Universities (January 2009) (submitted July 25, 2008) (to be published in Conference Proceeding 2009)

Piaget, J.: The moral judgment of the child. The Free Press, New York (1965)

Proulx, J.: Constructivism: A re-equilibration and clarification of the concepts, and some potential implications for teaching and pedagogy. Radical Pedagogy. Department of Secondary Education, University of Alberta (2006), http://radicalpedagogy.icaap.org/content/issue8_1/proulx.html (retrieved May 6, 2007)

University of Texas, Dallas, Student Development Theories (2008), http://www.utdallas.edu/dept/ugraddean/theory.htm (retrieved August 5, 2008)

von Glasersfeld, E.: Introduction: Aspects of constructivism. In: Fosnot, C.T. (ed.) Constructivism: Theory, Perspectives, and Practice, pp. 3–7. Teacher College Press, New York (1996)

Wankat, P.C., Oreovicz, F.S.: Models of cognitive development: Piaget and Perry. Teaching Engineering, ch. 14 (1993), http://ntsat.oulu.fi/ook/te/Chapter14.pdf (retrieved July 21, 2008)

Wenger, E.: Communities of Practice: Learning, Meaning and Identity. Cambridge University Press, New York (1998)

Wenger, E.: Learning is a Small Planet, project on learning initiative (2007), http://www.ewenger.com/research/index.htm (retrieved May 7, 2007)

Accelerated Modular Multiplication Algorithm of Large Word Length Numbers with a Fixed Module

N.G. Bardis[1,2], A. Drigas[1], A.P. Markovskyy[3], and I. Vrettaros[1]

[1] National Centre for Scientific Research "Demokritos", Institute of Informatics & Telecommunications - Net Media Lab, Terma Patriarchou Grigoriou & Neapoleos 27, Ag.Paraskevi - Athens, 15310, Greece
bardis@ieee.org,
dr@imm.demokritos.gr,
jvr@imm.demokritos.gr
[2] Hellenic Army Academy, Department of Mathematics and Engineering Science, Hellenic Army Academy, Vari, Greece
[3] National Technical University of Ukraine, Department of Computer Engineering, 37, Peremohy, pr. Kiev 252056, KPI 2003, Ukraine
markovskyy@mail.ru

Abstract. A new algorithm is proposed for the software implementation of modular multiplication, which uses pre-computations with a constant module. The developed modular multiplication algorithm provides high performance in comparison with the already known algorithms, and is oriented at the variable value of the module, especially with the software implementation on micro controllers and smart cards with a small number of bits.

1 Introduction

The operations of modular multiplication and modular exponentiation are the computational basis of an important category of the contemporary information security algorithms, which are based on the number theory [Cohen, 1995]. In particular, the computational implementation of such important operations for the contemporary technologies where information security mechanisms are provided (Public Key Algorithms for encryption (RSA, ECC), Diffie-Hellman key exchange algorithm, Digital Signature Algorithms and Digital Signature Standard), are based on the operations of modular involution and modular multiplication. In order to provide the acceptable security level concerning attacks, the aforementioned algorithms utilize numbers with word lengths of thousands of bits. Thus, for the majority of applications, information security under contemporary conditions requires that the length of the numbers utilized in the algorithms (based on elliptical curves (ECC)), should range from 128 to 256 bits, while the length of the numbers utilized in the algorithms (based on exponential transformation) should range from 1024 to 2048 bits [Menezer et all, 1997].

M.D. Lytras et al. (Eds.): WSKS 2010, Part I, CCIS 111, pp. 573–581, 2010.

Software implementation of modular multiplication for such long bit numbers on general-purpose processors or micro-controllers with a fixed number of bits (from 8 to 64) is very time consuming. Accordingly, the software implementation of information security, which is based on public key algorithms, on the universal processors, is carried out several orders slower in comparison with the symmetric algorithms (such as DES or AES), with the condition of ensuring adjacent levels of security attacks. The problem of the speed performance of the modular arithmetic operations of large numbers during the cryptographic algorithms implementation, is especially grave for low-length bit micro-controllers [Dhem J.-F., Quisquater J.-J. , 2000].

The basic operation of the modular arithmetic utilized in algorithms of that class, is the modular involution, i.e., the calculation $A^K \, mod \, M$. In this case, the majority of the cases of modular involution are carried out by the method of "squaring and multiplications" [Bosselaers et al., 1993], which uses a number of multiplications close to the theoretical minimum. Based on this, in order to increase the performance of the algorithms implementation by software, it is important to decrease the time needed for the modular multiplication.

Consequently, searching for possibilities to increase the performance of modular multiplications with the use of software implementation on the general purpose processors and micro-controllers, is important and vital.

2 Principal Notations and Effectiveness Estimation Model of the Modular Multiplication Algorithms

The basic operation of the modular arithmetic, utilized in the information security algorithms is modular multiplication, i.e., the calculation $R=A \cdot B \, mod \, M$.

It is assumed that the result R, coefficient A, multiplicand B and module M are n-bits binary numbers, and that the high-order bit of the module is equal to one: $2^{n-1} \leq M$ 2^n, and that the co-factors are lower than the module: $A<M$, $B<M$.

It is also assumed that the operation of modular multiplication is performed on the k- bits general purpose processors, microprocessors or micro-controllers.

Accordingly, each of the numbers, which participate in the operation of modular multiplication can be represented in the form of s = n/k - bits words:

$$A = \sum_{j=0}^{s-1} a_j \cdot 2^{j \cdot k}, B = \sum_{j=0}^{s-1} b_j \cdot 2^{j \cdot k}, M = \sum_{j=0}^{s-1} m_j \cdot 2^{j \cdot k} \quad (1)$$

where a_j, b_j, m_j – k-bits word, $j \in \{0,\ldots,s-1\}$.

In contrast to the classical modular multiplication algorithm [Bosselaers et al., 1993], contemporary algorithms [Laszlo Hars, 2004],[Montgommery, 1985], do not use the operation of division, which is ineffectively realized on the general purpose processors. Based on this, as a criterion of the productivity evaluation of the software implementation of modular multiplication algorithms, the total operation time of multiplication and addition, which are the basic operations of the contemporary algorithms of modular multiplication, is usually examined [Menezer et all, 1997].

It is assumed that the result of the multiplication command of two k- bits numbers is a 2k - bits representation. By denoting:

q_m – as the number of the required multiplication commands
t_m – as the execution time needed for each command
q_a – as the number of additional commands
t_a - as the execution time of each additional command

the estimation time of modular multiplication calculation of n- bits numbers, which is acceptable for the comparative accuracy analysis is: $q_m \cdot t_m + q_a \cdot t_a$

If the execution time of the multiplication and addition commands on the processor is $w = t_{mul}/t_a$,, then the execution time of the modular multiplication can be represented as $t_a \cdot (w \cdot q_m + q_a)$.

3 Brief Analysis of the Contemporary State of the Acceleration Problem: The Software Implementation of the Modular Multiplication

The classical algorithm for the modular multiplication software implementation [Bosselaers et all, 1993] without detailing the method of the Reduce(X) procedure execution (which returns the modular reduction of X), is described as follows in the C++ language, in Algorithm 1.

Algorithm 1. Classical scheme of word-by-word Modular Multiplication

```
R=0;
for(i=0; i<s; i++)
{
  Y=0;
  for (j=0; j<s; j++)
  Y+= (a_i*b_j)<<(j*k);
  R += Reduce(Y);
  if (i<s–1)
  {
   B<<=k;
   Reduce(B);
  }
}
Reduce(R);
```

The operation of multiplication is performed word-by-word: each j -th (j=0,…, s-1) the k- bits word of coefficient a_j is multiplied by shifting each of s words of multiplicand in B. The obtained product 2k- bits are added, forming (n+k) - bits, which is a partial representation of the product:

$$a_j \cdot B = \sum_{i=0}^{s-1} a_j \cdot b_i \cdot 2^{i \cdot k} \qquad (2)$$

Following this, the modular reduction of the partial expression is carried out, obtaining j-th partial residual $R_j = a_j{\cdot}B \ mod \ M$. The result of the modular multiplication $R{=}A{\cdot}B \ mod \ M$ is formed as the sum of the modular reductions of the partial expression of the product: $R{=}(R_0{+}R_1{+}\ldots{+}R_{s\text{-}1})mod \ M$.

The classical modular reduction algorithm is achieved with the use of the operation of the integer division of 2k bits divisible to the k- bits divider, obtaining a quotient and a residual. Since the division of the n- bits numbers on the k- bits processor (n>>k) is carried out very ineffectively, the calculation of the reduction in the classical algorithm requires s(s+2.5) operations of multiplication and s operations of the integer division [Laszlo Hars, 2004].

At present, various algorithms are proposed [Dhem J.-F., Quisquater J.-J. 2000], [Laszlo Hars, 2004], [Menezer et all, 1997], which increase the performance of the software implementation of the modular multiplication operation. The largest part of the aforementioned algorithms realize the increase in the performance of modular multiplication due to the acceleration of modular reduction by the exception of the operation of integer division, which is used in the classical algorithm [Bosselaers, et all, 1993]. Nowadays, the most effective method of modular multiplication is the Montgomery algorithm [Montgommery, 1985], which is well adjusted to the architecture of universal processors. The Montgomery algorithm substitutes the operation of division into the random module M by the divisions into power of 2, which effectively are realized by SHIFTS. The operation of modular reduction in Montgomery's algorithm requires s(s+1) operations of multiplication.

The general computational complexity of the implementation of the Montgomery modular multiplication algorithm on a k - bits processor is determined by $2s^2{+}s$ operations of multiplication and by $4s^2{+}4s{+}2$ additions. Accordingly, the calculation time T_M of Montgomery's algorithm on the k- bits processor can be calculated approximately as follows:

$$T_M = (2 \cdot s^2 + s) \cdot t_m + (4 \cdot s^2 + 4 \cdot s + 2) \cdot t_a = t_a \cdot (s^2 \cdot (2 \cdot w + 4) + s \cdot (w + 4) + 2) \qquad (3)$$

Known algorithms assume that each calculation of modular multiplication is produced with the new values of co-factors A, B and of the module M. However, the analysis of the practical application of information security algorithms, which use modular multiplication, shows that both their keys, and respectively the module change relatively rarely. This offers the potential possibilities of further decrease of the computational complexity of modular multiplication by simplification in the reduction. The practical implementation of such possibilities requires special research and development. On this basis new modular multiplication algorithms should be developed, which will contain a constant module.

The purpose of this work is the development of an effective modular multiplication algorithm of large numbers on general purpose processors with a constant module.

4 Analysis of the Possibilities of Accelerating the Modular Multiplication in the Information Security Systems

The information security algorithms are based on cryptographic properties. This particular cryptographic property has to do with the non solution using an analytical method of "number theory" tasks. These algorithms require the special complex procedures of the generation of keys.

In particular, the widely used (in practice) algorithm RSA [Menezer et all, 1997] uses a complex procedure to obtain the three numbers d, e and M, of length n from 1024 to 2048 bits, which satisfy the identity $A^{de} \equiv A$. The process of the coding of the block A of a certain message consists of the calculation of $C=A^e \bmod M$, and the decoding of block A is realized with the calculation of $A=C^d \bmod M$. The pair of numbers $<d,M>$ composes the public key, while the pair $<e,M>$ composes the private key.

One of the aforementioned keys depending on the protocol that the RSA uses is public, while the other is private. The analysis of the practical use of an RSA algorithm shows that the keys change relatively rarely so that with the use of the same key, tens of thousands of information blocks are processed. This makes it possible to consider that in the process of computational implementation, the RSA key and consequently the module are both in effect constant. Analogous reasonings can also be applied to a number of other, standardized and widely utilized in practice information security algorithms and in particular to the Digital Signature Standard algorithm [Menezer et all, 1997].

The constancy of the module M makes it possible to simplify the calculation of modular reduction in the multiplication process due to the use of precomputational results. Such pre-computations depend only on the value of the module M and therefore, they are carried out once with a change in the module. The results of the pre-computations remain in the tabular memory and are used repeatedly with each modular multiplication calculation.

In the modular multiplication implementation, the part of the computational resources is strictly used for the calculation of multiplication and the other part for the modular reduction implementation.

In different modular multiplication algorithms [Montgommery, 1985], [Barrett, 1987] the specific weight of expenditures for these two procedures varies. Table 1 gives the quantity of the multiplication operations and the word divisions, which are utilized in the most known modular multiplication algorithms for the calculation of the product A·B and the modular reduction implementation [Laszlo Hars, 2004], [Hong S.M., Oh S.Y., Yoon H,1996.

It is obvious that the possibilities of decreasing the number of operations for the calculation of the product A·B due to the pre-computations with a constant module, are completely limited, since the module itself is not used directly in such calculations.

Table 1. Quantity of operations of multiplication

Algorithm	Quantity multiplications k–bits word for calculation A·B	Quantity multiplications k–bits word for modular reduction	Quantity divisions word for modular reduction
Classical	s^2	$s^2+2.5\cdot s$	s
Barrett	s^2	$s^2+4\cdot s$	0
Montgomery	s^2	s^2+s	0

Therefore, the basic reserve for increasing the speed of the software implementation of modular multiplication, is the use of pre-computations for decreasing the computational complexity of modular reduction. Data analysis, given in Table I shows that with the use of pre-computations, the greatest effect of the decrease in the implementation time of modular multiplication, is achieved. This takes place due to the reduction of the time expenditures for the modular reduction.

5 Modular Multiplication Organization Based on Pre-computations with the Fixed Module

In the classical algorithm (Algorithm 1) the modular reduction procedure, Reduce(X), is carried out from the partial products $a_j{\cdot}B$ and by shifting the code of multiplicand B by k bits to the left. In both cases, the length of the reduced number X is not more than *(s+1) k-* - bits words or more than $(s+1){\cdot}k=(n+k)$ bits $x_0, x_1, x_2,\ldots,x_{n+k-1}$:

$$X = \sum_{j=0}^{n+k-1} x_j \cdot 2^j , x_j \in \{0,1\} \tag{4}$$

The number X can be represented in the form of the sum of two components: (n–1)-bits number X'', which coincides with (n–1) low-order digits X and (n+k)- bits number X′, which consists of (k+1) high-order digits, coinciding with the similar bits of X and (n–1) low-order digits, equal to zero:

$$X = \sum_{j=0}^{n+k-1} x_j \cdot 2^j = X'+X'', X' = \sum_{j=n-1}^{n+k-1} x_j \cdot 2^j , X'' = \sum_{i=0}^{n-2} x_i \cdot 2^i \tag{5}$$

In accordance with the property of congruence for the modular reduction, the residual *X mod M* can be represented in the form of the modular reduction as the sum of the residuals of the components X composing X' and X'':

$$X \bmod M = (\sum_{j=0}^{n+k-1} x_j \cdot 2^j) \bmod M = (X'+X'') \bmod M = \tag{6}$$

$$= (X' \bmod M + X'' \bmod M) \bmod M$$

Since the high order digits, (n–1)- bits of module M are equal to one, and the X'' is equal to (n–1)- bits number, then X''<M and, accordingly X''mod M = X''. Number X'contains only k+1 significant digits. The rest n–1 low-order digits are equal to zero. Consequently, X' and accordingly X' mod M assume only 2^{k+1} different values. All possible n- bits values of X'mod M for the appropriate X', can be pre-computed and stored in the memory as tables. If we designate through Z the binary code, which consists of (k+1) high order significant digits X':

$$Z = \sum_{j=n-1}^{n+k-1} x_j \cdot 2^{j-n+1}$$

and with T(Z) – n- bits code of the tabular value T(Z) = X0modM, then the modular reduction procedure Reduce(X) is realized in accordance with the following expression:

$$\mathrm{Re}duce(X) = X \bmod M = (T(Z) + X'') \bmod M \tag{7}$$

In this case, the computational complexity of the modular reduction implementation is determined by maximum two operations of addition between (n+k)- bits numbers: the first for the calculation of $T(Z)+X''$ and the second for executing the subtraction $(T(Z)+X'')-M$, if $T(Z)+X''\geq M$.

Since $0\leq T(Z)+X''<2\cdot M$, for the modular reduction $(T(Z)+X'') \bmod M$ not more than one subtraction of n- bits numbers, is required. Therefore, the execution time of the procedure will not exceed $2\cdot(s+1)\cdot t_a$, with the average value of $1.5\cdot s\cdot t_a$. The storage memory, which is required for storing all the pre-computed possible values of T(Z) comprises $2^{k+1}\cdot$n bits or $2^{k+1}\cdot$s of k- bits words.

The proposed approach is especially effective in the implementation of modular multiplication on the low-bits microprocessors, micro-controllers and smart cards. In this case, the memory size for storing the results of pre-computations with a constant module, proves to be completely acceptable for the majority of applications. For example, for the accelerated multiplication implementation of the 1024- bits numbers on the 8- bits micro-controller, the capacity of the required storage memory will compose of $(2^9\cdot 128)=2^{16}$ of bytes (64 Kbyte). For the accelerated modular multiplication implementation on the 16-bits processor r, the above capacity requires storage memory, which substantially grows and therefore decreases the effectiveness of the application of pre-computations.

In order to decrease the capacity of the memory required for storing the results of pre-computations T(Z), its multi-section organization, is proposed.

The essence of the proposed tables organization of pre-computations lies in the fact that the value $X'$is divided into q components:

$$X' = X_1' + X_2' + \ldots + X_q'$$

with lengths $n+r_1$, $n+r_1+r_2$, …, $n+r_1+\ldots+r_q$, since $r_1+r_2+\ldots+r_q=k+1$.

Each i- th constituting X_i' $(i=1,\ldots,q)$ contains ri high order significant digits, which coincide with the digits $x_{n+h}, x_{n+h+1}, \ldots, x_{n+h+ri}$ of number X (h=0 for i=1 and h $=r_1 + \ldots + r_{i-1}$ for i>1), and the rest of the low-order digits are equal to zero:

$$X'_i = \sum_{h=g_i}^{g_i+r_i} x_{n+h} \cdot 2^{n+h}, g_i = \sum_{t=1}^{i-1} r_t, \forall i \in \{2,\ldots,q\}, g_1 = 0 \tag{8}$$

Following this, in accordance with the property of congruence the modular reduction X mod M can be represented in the form:

$$X \bmod M = (X'_1 \bmod M + X'_2 \bmod M + ... + X'_q \bmod M + X'') \bmod M$$

In order to determine each of the values of X'_i *mod M*, the use of the precomputations results is proposed, where the results are previously calculated for all possible codes X'_i. Since a quantity of significant (non zero) bits in code X'_i is equal to r_i , then the number of different values X'_i will comprise 2^{r_i} , and the memory capacity for storing all possible values of X'_i *mod M* respectively will be $2^{r_i} \cdot n$ bit.

If we denote through Z_i the binary r_i - bits code, which contains only r_i high order significant digits X'_i, then,

$$Z_i = \sum_{h=g_i}^{g_i+r_i} x_{n+h} \cdot 2^{h-g_i}, g_i = \sum_{t=1}^{i-1} r_t, \forall i \in \{2,...,q\}, g_1 = 0 \tag{9}$$

If we denote through $T_i(Z_i)$ – n bits code of the tabular value $T_i(Z_i) = X'_i$ *mod M*, then the modular reduction procedure is realized in accordance with the following expression:

$$X \bmod M = (\sum_{i=1}^{q} T_i(Z_i) + X'') \bmod M \tag{10}$$

The total volume of the tabular memory for storing $T_1(Z_1), T_2(Z_2),\ldots,T_q(Z_q)$) comprises $n \cdot \sum_{i=1}^{q} 2^{r_i}$ bits. The aforementioned example of storing T(Z) in one table, can be examined as a special case of the results organization within subdivided tables, with pre-computations for q=1. The use of multi-section tables makes it possible to substantially decrease the memory capacity of their storage. For example, under the conditions of the example given above, for the accelerated multiplication implementation of 1024- bits numbers on the 8- bits micro-controller with the two-section memory (q=2, r_1 =5, r_2=4=2), the required memory capacity will compose of $1024\cdot(2^5+2^4)$ = $10^{10}\cdot 48$ bits or 6144 bytes or 10.67 times less than during the single-section organization of tabular memory.

From another point of view, the use of multi-section organization of the tabular memory is combined with the increase of the execution time of the modular reduction. The calculation of the sum of expression (10) requires q(s+1) operations of summing up k- bits words. The number of significant digits of the sum code will not exceed in this case n+q, so that, if $r_1 \geq q+1$, then for executing the modular reduction of sum with the use of the first table $T_1(Z_1)$, 1.5(s+1) addition operations are required, on average. The total number of the additional operations is: $(q+1.5)\cdot(s+1)$.

6 Conclusions

The problem of increasing the performance of the modular multiplication software implementation, which is the basic computational operation used in a wide circle of information security algorithms was researched. It is shown that during the practical application of information security algorithms, based on the analytically insoluble tasks of the "number theory", the keys and consequently the module, change relatively rarely. Based on the conducted research, a new algorithm was proposed for the modular multiplication that differs from the classical organization of the modular reduction execution. Reduction in the computational complexity of the software implementation is achieved by the use of pre-computations results, which depend only on the module and which are stored in the tabular memory. The performance estimation of the proposed algorithm and memory use for storing the pre-computations tables are theoretically substantiated.

The executed analysis showed that the speed of the software implementation of modular multiplication on the micro-controllers with the use of the proposed algorithm grows 1.5-2, in comparison with the most effective algorithm today, the Montgomery algorithm.

References

Bosselaers, A., Govaerts, R., Vandewalle, J.: Comparison of three modular reduction functions. In: Stinson, D.R. (ed.) CRYPTO 1993. LNCS, vol. 773, pp. 175–186. Springer, Heidelberg (1993)

Dhem, J.-F., Quisquater, J.-J.: Resent results on modular multiplications for smart cards. In: Schneier, B., Quisquater, J.-J. (eds.) CARDIS 1998. LNCS, vol. 1820, pp. 350–366. Springer, Heidelberg (2000)

Hars, L.: Long Modular multiplication for Cryptographic Applications. In: Joye, M., Quisquater, J.-J. (eds.) CHES 2004. LNCS, vol. 3156, pp. 45–61. Springer, Heidelberg (2004)

Hong, S.M., Oh, S.Y., Yoon, H.: New modular multiplication algorithms for fast modular exponentiation. In: Maurer, U.M. (ed.) EUROCRYPT 1996. LNCS, vol. 1070, pp. 166–177. Springer, Heidelberg (1996)

Menezer, A.J., Van Oorschot, P.C., Vanstone, S.A.: Handbook of Applied Cryptography. CRC Press, Boca Raton (1997)

Montgommery, P.L.: Modular multiplication without trial division. Mathematics of Computation 44, 519–521 (1985)

Barrett, P.: Implementing the River Shamir and Adleman public key encryption algorithm on a standard digital signal processor. In: Odlyzko, A.M. (ed.) CRYPTO 1986. LNCS, vol. 263, pp. 311–323. Springer, Heidelberg (1987)

Cohen, H.: A Course in Computational Algebraic Number Theory, 2nd edn. Graduate Texts in Mathematics. Springer, Heidelberg (1995)

Check Sum Optimization for Transmission and Storage of Digital Information

N.G. Bardis[1,2], A. Drigas[1], A.P. Markovskyy[3], and I. Vrettaros[1]

[1] National Centre for Scientific Research "Demokritos", Institute of Informatics & Telecommunications - Net Media Lab, Terma Patriarchou Grigoriou & Neapoleos 27, Ag.Paraskevi - Athens, 15310, Greece
bardis@ieee.org,
dr@imm.demokritos.gr,
jvr@imm.demokritos.gr

[2] Hellenic Army Academy, Department of Mathematics and Engineering Science, Hellenic Army Academy, Vari, Greece

[3] National Technical University of Ukraine, Department of Computer Engineering, 37, Peremohy, pr. Kiev 252056, KPI 2003, Ukraine
markovskyy@mail.ru

Abstract. In this paper a new approach to increase the effectiveness of the errors detection using check sum during the data transmission based on the optimization of coding with special differential Boolean transformations is proposed. A method for obtaining such transformations are developed and examples of coding for check sum functions is given.

1 Introduction

The present level of computer networks and telecommunication systems development is inseparably connected with the problem information integrity, which includes: the ensuring of high reliability during information transmission and the information storage in memories. The dynamic expansion of using the communication channels which undergo potentially interferences and the complex methods of packing the transferred information are combined with the increase of appearing errors during the data transmission. A similar situation occurs also during the storage of data on magnetic means: a constant increase in the longitudinal and transverse density of information storage on such means is also combined with an increase of appearing errors [Klove 2007].

At the same time, the extensive usage of information technologies in all human activities, including in these IT's and the technogenic risks, requires the increasing in the reliability of all components of the computer systems, including the reliability during the transmission and the storage of information [Saxena et all, 1987]. A continuous increase in the speeds of data transmission in the telecommunications network systems dictates the stringent requirements for the effectiveness of the means of error

M.D. Lytras et al. (Eds.): WSKS 2010, Part I, CCIS 111, pp. 582–590, 2010.

control. This effectiveness must be commensurate with the channel characteristics as the bandwidth and the rate of transmitted data. This condition determines the needs for a radical increase of the error control reliability of the means of error control. These means should have an increased speed and allow the parallel processing in hardware implementation.

Thus, these characteristics specify the urgency and practical importance of the new development and the improvement of the known means for the increase of reliability during the data transmission and data storage in the computer systems and telecommunications networks.

2 Analysis of the Error Detection Problems during the Transmission and Storage of the Digital Information

The present level of computer networks and telecommunication systems development is inseparably connected with the problem information integrity, which includes: the ensuring of high reliability during information transmission and the information storage in memories. The dynamic expansion of using the communication channels which undergo potentially interferences and the complex methods of packing the transferred information are combined with the increase of appearing errors during the data transmission. A similar situation occurs also during the storage of data on magnetic means: a constant increase in the longitudinal and transverse density of information storage on such means is also combined with an increase of appearing errors [Klove 2007].

At the same time, the extensive usage of information technologies in all human activities, including in these IT's and the technogenic risks, requires the increasing in the reliability of all components of the computer systems, including the reliability during the transmission and the storage of information [Saxena et all, 1987]. A continuous increase in the speeds of data transmission in the telecommunications network systems dictates the stringent requirements for the effectiveness of the means of error control. This effectiveness must be commensurate with the channel characteristics as the bandwidth and the rate of transmitted data. This condition determines the needs for a radical increase of the error control reliability of the means of error control. These means should have an increased speed and allow the parallel processing in hardware implementation.

Thus, these characteristics specify the urgency and practical importance of the new development and the improvement of the known means for the increase of reliability during the data transmission and data storage in the computer systems and telecommunications networks.

For guaranteeing the reliable data transmission in communication channels of computer networks a large number of means is used, of which important place occupies the coding of the transmitted information. In the majority of systems the transmission and the storage of information are carried out by blocks and respectively the integrity data transmission or data storage of each block is controlled separately.

With the use of special coding it is possible to distinguish two approaches for the correction of the appearing errors:

- the error detection by special codes and their correction by retransmitting the block upon request during the error detection (ARQ-Automatic Repeat Request);

- the correction of the appearing errors due to applications of correcting codes without the repeated transmission (FEC-Forward Error Correction).

It is obvious that the first of the mentioned approaches is not applied for the error correction during data storage. The main advantage of ARQ besides the diagrams of the FEC lies in the fact that the error detection requires simpler decoding hardware and smaller redundancy than the error correction method. The implementation of error detection has substantial smaller computational complexity which makes it possible to calculate the error control functions considerably faster. Furthermore, the effectiveness of ARQ is less and depends on the multiplicity of the appearing errors [Shu Lin et all, 1983].

The choice between the two approaches for the elimination of the appearing errors depends on intensity and the nature of the appearing errors. The basic sources of errors in digital data channels are the inter bit interferences, the externally produced noise and the thermal noise of transmission means [Klove 2007].

The nature of the appearing errors depends not only on their source, but also on the type of transmission means and on modulation of signals method. Thus, in the ether communication channels the prevailing source of the transmitted errors is the externally produced noise and in this case the intensity of the appearing errors is sufficiently high so that the application of FEC technologies proves to be more preferable. In the wire systems of digital data transmission, in which the intensity of errors is several orders lower in comparison with the wireless channels, the use of ARQ is considered to be more effective [Fletcher, 1983].

In the cable channels with the sequential data transmission without modulation, the transmitted error has the same nature, and the channels themselves correspond to the binary symmetrical channel model. This model assumes the appearance of erroneous transmission of zero or one with equal probabilities, since the probability pj that j errors occur during the transmission of the n-bit code is determined for the binary symmetrical channel by the expression:

$$p_m = \binom{n}{j} \cdot p^j \cdot (1-p)^{n-j} \tag{1}$$

where p is the probability of the erroneous transmission of one bit.

For errors detection by the per block data transmission the CRC codes and the CS are used more often [Klove 2007]. The CS method in comparison with CRC is substantially simpler and ensures the maximum rate of the error control and it is an influential factor on a constant increase in the channel capacity of data transmission.

In contrast to CRC, the structure of the operations which are performed with the check sum calculation, it allows the parallel process which makes it possible to implement effectively this control by hardware, so that the time for the calculation of error control practically will not affect the performance of the data transmission.

Let us denote by $D_1,D_2,\ldots,D_k$ the k codes with n-bit size, which compose the transmission block, and by $D_1',D_2',\ldots,D_k'$ we denote the blocks on the receiver end. The CS's on the receiver and the sender are calculated with the same way: $S_S = D_1 \oplus D_2 \oplus \ldots \oplus D_k$ and $S_R = D_1' \oplus D_2' \oplus \ldots \oplus D_k'$.

The usual check sum assumes that the data transmission is carried out as a block and organized as k codes $D_1, D_2, \ldots, D_k$ with length n bits. In this case the length n of the code is determined by the architecture of the control organization and its value can coincide with the number of simultaneously transferred bits, and it can differ from it. At the end of the transmission of the data block, the transmitter sends to the receiver the check sum S_S, which is XORed with the check sum that is calculated on the receiver S_R and obtains the differential code $\Delta = S_S \oplus S_R$ of size n. If $\Delta = 0$ then we consider that no errors have arisen. For the symmetrical binary channel and, taking into account that in practice the relation $k >> n$ holds, then we can consider that during the transmission of one code only one error can arise. The low reliability of the error detection of the even error multiplicity is the main disadvantage of the check sum. Actually, the most probable occurrence between them is the two-fold error (situation of appearance of single errors in two from k transmitted codes) and the code Δ can attain only n^2 different values of all the 2^n possible. It is means that for the studied model the usual check sum is ineffectively coding of two-fold error. Because of this the probability P_2 of the nondetection of the two-fold error is reasonable high and determined by formula:

$$P_2 = \frac{1}{n} \tag{2}$$

Thus, the reliability level of the error detection when using the check sum can increase due to the coding optimization, i.e., the calculation of check sums on the transmitter and the receiver in the form: $S_S = F(D_1) \oplus F(D_2) \oplus \ldots \oplus F(D_k)$ and $S_R = F(D_1') \oplus F(D_2') \oplus \ldots \oplus F(D_k')$, where F is the function of coding, defined by the system of Boolean functions.

In the paper [Bardis, 2004] an orthogonal system of Boolean functions that satisfy the SAC criterion is used as coding function. In this case, with the appearance of the two-fold error the code Δ has $n!/((n/2)!)^2$ different values and correspondingly the probability of the non detection of the two-fold error substantially decreases in comparison with the usual check sum. Usually these types of Boolean transformations are used in cryptographic algorithms and their design methods have been developed in [Klove 2007]. A Boolean function $f(x_1, \ldots, x_n)$ defined on a set Z of all possible 2^n n-tuples of n variables, satisfies the SAC, if a complement of a single incoming n-tuple data bit changes the output of the Boolean function with probability 50%:

$$\forall j \in \{1, \ldots, n\}: \quad \sum_{x_1, \ldots, x_n \in Z} \left(f(x_1, \ldots, x_j, \ldots, x_n) \oplus f(x_1, \ldots, \overline{x_j}, \ldots, x_n) \right) = 2^{n-1} \tag{3}$$

If one of the n inputs of the avalanche transformation is changed then half of its outputs will be changed. This means, that there is an "avalanche amplifier" which by changing one of the n-tuple incoming data bit transforms half of the outputs. Because every function of this system satisfies the Avalanche Criterion, these transformations are called "avalanche".

Let's denote with $F(D)$, the Boolean orthogonal avalanche transformation on the n-bits code D. So transformation $F(D)$ consist of orthogonal Boolean functions

$f_1(D), f_2(D), \ldots, f_n(D)$, every of which satisfies the Avalanche Criterion. The length of the transformed code $R=F(D)$ is n bits long, as well. The orthogonality of the $F(D)$ transformation indicates the one-to-one correspondence of codes D and R. The avalanche properties of the $F(D)$ transformation indicate that if one bit of the input code D is changed then, on average, $n/2$ bits of the output code $R=F(D)$ will be changed also.

Example of the Boolean orthogonal avalanche transformation $F(D)$ on the 8-bits code D (n=8) is given from [Bardis N.G, Markovskyy, 2004].

Thus, if a single error appears, then $n/2$ bits of the modified checksum will change. If a second error appears then another $n/2$ bits of the modified checksum will change. It is clear that the probability of the masking interaction of $n/2$ erroneous bit pairs is less than the probability of the masking interaction of a single bit pair.

It has been shown that the probability P_{2f} that the dual bit erors will not be detected in case orthogonal avalanche transformation $F(D)$ using is determined as follows:

$$P_{2f} = \frac{1}{\binom{n}{n/2}} = \frac{((n/2)!)^2}{n!} = \prod_{j=0}^{n/2-1} \frac{j+1}{(n-j)} \tag{4}$$

Thus, the probability of detecting dual errors during block transmission using the checksum control shceme orthogonal avalanche transformation $F(D)$, increases by t_2 times in comparion to the ordinary checksum scheme. The numerical value of the t_2 increase is determined by the formula:

$$t_2 = \prod_{j=1}^{n/2-1} \frac{n-j}{j+1} \tag{5}$$

For example, for n=8, the probability that the dual errors will not be detected is decreased by 8.7 times in comparison to the traditional checksum.

In case orthogonal avalanche transformation $F(D)$ using, with the appearance of the two-fold error the code Δ has $n!/((n/2)!)^2$ different values and correspondingly the probability of the non detection of the two-fold error substantially decreases in comparison with the usual check sum.

However in this case the $n!/((n/2)!)^2$ coding variants of the two-fold error are substantially less than the total number of all possible codes $\Delta - 2^n$ and therefore in this case the optimization of coding is not achieved. Consequently, an increase in the reliability of detection of prevailing type errors by check sum can be achieved due to further optimization of its coding via the selection of corresponding functional transformation.

The purpose of this approach is to increase the reliability of error control by using check sum due to development of the functional transformations which optimize its coding for the prevailing forms of errors in the binary symmetrical channel.

3 Optimization of the Check Sum Coding

For the practical implementation of error detection based on coding check sum optimization for detecting the appearing errors a calculation method of the modified check sum is proposed, similarly as in work [Bardis and Markovskyy, 2004]. In this proposed method as terms are used codes which are obtained from Boolean transformations over the controlled codes. These Boolean transformations consist of a system of m Boolean functions with n variables:

$$F(D) = \{f_1(D), f_2(D), \ldots, f_m(D)\} \tag{6}$$

where D is an n-bit code: D={d1,d2,…,dn}, ∀j∈{1,…,n}: dj∈{0,1}.

With the appearance of a single error in the jth bit of the code Di it is transformed into Di′={d1,…,dj⊕1,…,dn} and the differential Δ of the check sum can be represented in the form of the differentials values of the functions f1,f2,…,fm with the variable dj on the binary tuples {d1,d2,…,dj-1,dj+1,…,dn}:

$$\begin{aligned} &\Delta = F(D_i) \oplus F(D_i') = \\ &\{f_1(D_i) \oplus f_1(D_i'), \ldots, f_m(D_i) \oplus f_m(D_i')\} = \\ &= \{\frac{\partial f_1}{\partial d_j}, \frac{\partial f_2}{\partial d_j}, \ldots, \frac{\partial f_m}{\partial d_j}\} \end{aligned} \tag{7}$$

The optimization of single error coding in the modified *m* bits check sum can be achieved, if the number of possible values of the code of *Δ* equals 2^m. Since the number of versions of the single error localization in the code *D* is equal to *n*, so that the single error could be one way coded by check sum it is enough that $m = \lceil \log_2 n \rceil$ holds. In this case the binary code formed by a change in the functions with the appearance of error in the jth bit of the code *D*, i.e., with a change in the variable d_j , is equal to j-1:

$$\forall j \in \{1, \ldots, n\}: \sum_{t=0}^{\lceil \log_2 n \rceil - 1} \frac{\partial f_t}{\partial d_j} \cdot 2^t = j - 1 \tag{8}$$

It is obvious that the condition (8) is satisfied if each of the functions $f_1, f_2, \ldots, f_m$ is linear, and the *q* function f_q includes the variable d_j (i.e., the value of the q bit of the binary number j-1 is equal to one). For example, if *n=8*, then *m=3* and the system of functions which satisfy (8) can be as follows:

$$\begin{aligned} f_1 &= d_2 \oplus d_4 \oplus d_6 \oplus d_8 \\ f_2 &= d_3 \oplus d_4 \oplus d_7 \oplus d_8 \\ f_3 &= d_5 \oplus d_6 \oplus d_7 \oplus d_8 \end{aligned} \tag{9}$$

In this case, the length size of check sum of its coding is substantially lower than the code length size of *Δ*: *m<n*, however, the probability that the error of any multiplicity larger than one (single errors they are detected always) corresponds to expression (2). For example, the two-fold error is not detected only when both errors occurred in one and the same bit.

In order to decrease the probability of not detecting the multiplicity errors, it is necessary in addition of the Boolean system (8) which forms the set Ξ_1, to use a system of u functions which compose the set Ξ_2 so that $F=\{\Xi_1, \Xi_2\}$.

In order to detect the two-fold error with high reliability it is necessary that a number of conditions are fulfilled. Since two errors, localized in different bits of the transferred codes are always detected using the functions of the set Ξ_1, and so for detecting the errors which appear in the same bit on different codes of block it is necessary that the probability of the values agreeing of the differentials functions of the set Ξ_2 with the change of one variable, should be as small as possible or near to zero. Therefore the functions differentials of this set must not be constant, i.e., the functions must be nonlinear, moreover the functions differentials $f_{m+1}, f_{m+2}, \ldots, f_{m+u}$, on any of the variables must constitute an orthogonal system of functions.

For the realization of this condition two methods for the functions synthesis of the set of Ξ_2 are proposed. According to the first method the functions of $f_{m+1}, f_{m+2}, \ldots, f_{m+u}$ are defined on a set with n variables, which coincide with the values of the bits of the transferred codes and the set of their possible values forms the set Z. In this case the number of functions of the set Ξ_2 is equal to n-1, i.e., $u=n-1$, and the functions $f_{m+1}, f_{m+2}, \ldots, f_{m+u}$ must satisfy the condition:

$$\forall j \in \{1,\ldots, n\},\ a_t \in \{0,1\}: \qquad \sum_{D\in Z} \bigoplus_{t=1}^{u} a_t \cdot \frac{\partial f_{m+t}}{\partial d_j} = 2^{u-1} \tag{10}$$

Below is given an example of a system of 7 Boolean functions with eight variables (n=8), which compose the set Ξ_2 and satisfy the condition (10):

$$\begin{aligned}
f_4 &= d_1\cdot d_2 \oplus d_3\cdot d_4 \oplus d_5\cdot d_7 \oplus d_6\cdot d_8\\
f_5 &= d_1\cdot d_3 \oplus d_2\cdot d_4 \oplus d_5\cdot d_8 \oplus d_6\cdot d_7\\
f_6 &= d_1\cdot d_4 \oplus d_2\cdot d_5 \oplus d_3\cdot d_6 \oplus d_7\cdot d_8\\
f_7 &= d_1\cdot d_5 \oplus d_2\cdot d_6 \oplus d_3\cdot d_7 \oplus d_4\cdot d_8\\
f_8 &= d_1\cdot d_6 \oplus d_2\cdot d_7 \oplus d_3\cdot d_8 \oplus d_4\cdot d_5\\
f_9 &= d_1\cdot d_7 \oplus d_2\cdot d_8 \oplus d_3\cdot d_5 \oplus d_4\cdot d_6\\
f_{10} &= d_1\cdot d_8 \oplus d_2\cdot d_3 \oplus d_4\cdot d_7 \oplus d_5\cdot d_6
\end{aligned} \tag{11}$$

The differentials on any of the 8 variables in the 7 functions, which compose the set Ξ_2, form the system of orthogonal Boolean functions. For example, the differentials of the 4th variable $d4$ form the system of linear functions, the orthogonality property of which is obvious:

$$\frac{\partial f_4}{\partial d_4} = d_3;\ \frac{\partial f_5}{\partial d_4} = d_2;\ \frac{\partial f_6}{\partial d_4} = d_1;\ \frac{\partial f_7}{\partial d_4} = d_8;$$
$$\frac{\partial f_8}{\partial d_4} = d_5;\ \frac{\partial f_9}{\partial d_4} = d_6;\ \frac{\partial f_{10}}{\partial d_4} = d_7$$

The differentials of functions f_1, f_2, f_3 in terms of the variable $d4$ are equal and they correspond to the number of the variable x_4:j-$1=011_2=3$.

The validity of the conditions (10) ensures the two errors detection, if they occur in the same bits of different codes. This means that the two-fold error will not be detected only when both errors will occur in one and the same bit *j* during the transmission of the two codes D_i and D_e, i.e., $i,e \in \{1,\ldots,k\}$, which either are equal or they are different only on the jth bit. This probability is determined by the formula:

$$p_2 = \frac{1}{2^{n-1} \cdot n} \tag{12}$$

It is obvious that formula (12) determines the probability of the non detection not only of two-fold, but also of errors of any multiplicity larger than one. Comparison with the expression (2) shows that the reliability of the two-fold error detection is substantially increased in comparison with the usual check sum. Thus, the essence of the first of the proposed methods for the coding optimization of the check sum lies in the fact that the transformation function of the total components of the set Ξ_2 is selected in such a way that their differentials on any of the variables will depend on the code *D*. The two-fold error will not be detected only when both errors will occur in one and the same bit of the pair of the same codes, or the pair of the codes is different only in this bit.

If we consider that the appearance of each of the *n*-bit codes in the block is equally probable, then the probability of the two-fold error which satisfied these conditions is determined by the formula (12). However, in practice very frequent is the situation, when some codes in the block are repeated sufficiently frequently. This situation is characteristic for the text documents and for the images. Hence, in this case, the effectiveness of the proposed method of coding the components of check sum decreases. .

4 Conclusions

The proposed method is based on the coding optimization to increase the effectiveness of the error detection during data transmission and data storage using the check sums. This makes it possible to significantly decrease the probability of the mutual masking of even multiplicity errors both in comparison with the usual check sum and the use of SAC transformations for coding of its components.

A method for obtaining special differential Boolean functional transformations which optimize the check sum coding of the codes in block are developed. This method are developed from the point of view of the criterion of error detection which appears in the binary symmetrical channel. Example of the transformations which optimize coding check sum for both the proposed methods are given.

The estimations of the probability of error detecting of different multiplicity are theoretically substantiated. It is proven that during coding of the check sum components using functions which depend both on the transmitted codes and on the number of the code in the block, all errors of multiplicity less than 3 will be detected.

The analysis carried out showed that using the proposed method makes it possible to decrease in several orders the probability of the non detection of multiply errors in comparison with the known schemes of the check sum calculation.

The structure of the functional transformation is considerably simpler in comparison with the transformations of the CRC method and allows multilevel parallel process on hardware implementation which makes it possible to ensure the high performance of the error control without delays in the process of data transmission.

The developed method can be used for the effective errors control realization in the promising high-speed transmission channels of the digital information of computer networks.

References

Bardis, N.G., Markovskyy, A.P.: Utilization of of Avalanche Transformation for Increasing of Echoplex and Checksum Data Transmission Control Reliability. In: 2004 International Symposium on Information Theory and its Applications (ISITA 2004), Parma, Italy, Okt 10-13, pp. 656–660 (2004)

Torleiv, K.: Codes for Error Detection, Serial on Coding Theory and Cryptography, vol. 2, p. 201. World Scientific, Singapore (2007)

Saxena, N.R., McCluskey, E.J.: Extended precision checksums. In: Proc.17-th Intern. Symp. Fault-Tolerant Comput.: FCTS-17, Pittsburgrh, USA, pp. 142–147 (1987)

Fletcher, J.: An Arithmetic Checksum for Serial Transmissions. IEEE Transaction on Communication 30(1), 76–85 (1983)

Lin, S., Costello Jr., D.J.: Error Control Coding, p. 603. Prentice-Hall, Inc., Englewood Cliffs (1983) ISBN 0-13-283796-X

A Web-Based Learning Information System Resource and Knowledge Management

Hugo Rego, Tiago Moreira, and Francisco José Garcia

Department Of Computer Sciences, University of Salamanca Spain

Abstract. AHKME e-learning system main aim is to provide a modular and extensible system with adaptive and knowledge management abilities for students and teachers. This system is based on the IMS specifications representing information through metadata, granting semantics to all contents in it, giving them meaning. Metadata is used to satisfy requirements like reusability, interoperability and multipurpose. The system provides authoring tools to define learning methods with adaptive characteristics, and tools to create courses allowing users with different roles, promoting several types of collaborative and group learning. It is also endowed with tools to retrieve, import and evaluate learning objects based on metadata, where students can use quality educational contents fitting their characteristics, and teachers have the possibility of using quality educational contents to structure courses. The metadata management and evaluation play an important role in order to get the best results in the teaching/learning process.

1 Introduction

In learning environments, information has to be perceived and processed into knowledge, so the question emerged: how do we represent knowledge?. Regarding this issue there have been the development of several standards and specifications providing a semantic representation of knowledge through ontologies in which concepts are clearly and unambiguously identified, providing a set of semantic relation types which allow representing meaning by linking concepts together (Mendes et al., 2001) (Berners-Lee et al., 2001).

Here we present AKHME a system that supports both knowledge representation (KR) and management (KM) based on metadata described by the IMS specifications, which goals and main contributions are: the learning object (LO) management and quality evaluation, where we tried to introduce some intelligence to these processes through intelligent agents; the usage of the IMS specifications to standardize all the resources of the platform; and the interaction of all subsystems through the feedback between them allowing the system to adapt to students/teachers characteristics and to new contexts. As we know, the timely and correct management of knowledge became a sustainable source of competitive advantage, as well as a way to connect people to quality knowledge as well as people to people in order to peak performance. In the educational field KM and advanced systems can be used to explore how technologies can leverage knowledge sharing and learning and enhance performance (Chatti et al., 2001)(Grace et al., 2005). We are trying to implement a system that adapts to students

M.D. Lytras et al. (Eds.): WSKS 2010, Part I, CCIS 111, pp. 591–599, 2010.

and teachers characteristics and to new contexts, using KR and KM, by capturing users' behavior and interaction, allowing decision makers to check which resources, course formats and learning strategies have best or worst results in determined contexts, helping them to define strategies on how to address certain types of students and contexts.

2 Standards and Specifications Comparative Analysis

To structure content and information using nowadays pedagogical models there has been the development of several standards and specifications like Sharable Content Object Reference Model (SCORM)(ADL, 2006), a project from Advanced Distributed Learning (ADL), which is a kind of a standard integrator, making it dependent of the standards it integrates, and the IMS specifications (IMS, 2002) developed by the IMS consortium, that allows for example to structure the learning process, describe LOs through metadata, design learning units and courses, evaluate and characterize users. The use of standards help to achieve more stable systems, reducing development and maintenance time, allowing backward compatibility and validation, increasing search engine success, making everything cross systems, among many other advantages (Totkov et al., 2004).

In order to choose the specifications that would best fit our needs we started to analyze the support of several features, like described on table 1 where we have analyzed the IMS Specifications, AICC, SCORM and Dublin Core (Dublin Core, 2005), from which we have chosen the IMS specifications, since they allow most of the aspects we've analyzed and that we considered important to reach our goals.

Table 1. Standards and specifications comparative analysis

Features		IMS	AICC	SCORM	Dublin Core
Metadata		✓		✓	✓
Learner Profile		✓			
Content Packaging		✓	✓	✓	
Q&T Interoperability		✓			
DR Interoperability		✓			✓
Content structure		✓	✓	✓	
Content Communication			✓	✓	
Learning Design		✓			
Simple Sequencing		✓		✓	
Accessibility		✓			
Bindings	XML	✓		✓	✓
	RDF	✓			✓
Learner registration		✓			

3 AHKME Description

AHKME is an e-learning system that is divided in four different subsystems: Learning Object Manager and Learning Design subsystem, Knowledge Management subsystem, Adaptive subsystem and Visualization and Presentation subsystem, as seen on figure 1.

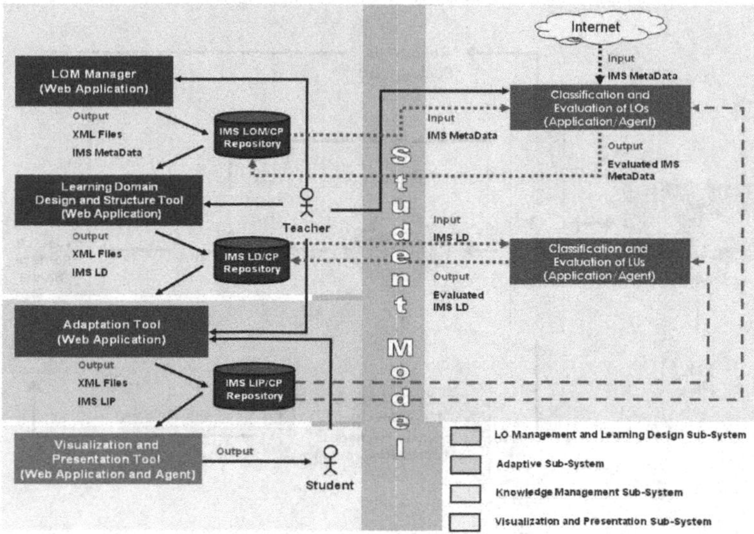

Fig. 1. AHKME's structure

These subsystems were structured taking into account a line of reasoning, where first we have the LOs creation and management process, which is followed by the course creation process through learning design (LD). In parallel with these two processes the KM subsystem evaluates the quality LOs and courses. Then they pass through an adaptive process based on the students' characteristics to be presented to them.

We will now present the different subsystems that compose this system giving more focus on the components of the system that provide the management and evaluation of resources through their metadata, the Learning Object Manager and Learning Design subsystem and the Knowledge Management subsystem.

3.1 Learning Objects Manager and Learning Design Subsystem

This subsystem is mainly divided in two tools, the one that deals with LOs and the other that deals with the courses.

The Learning Objects Manager tool allows teachers to define/create metadata to describe LOs. It uses the IMS Learning Resource Metadata (IMSLRM) specification (Barker et al., 2006) that is based on the IEEE LOM standard that allows the KR/KM through LOs (IEEE, 2002).

This tool allows the user to edit LOs and associate descriptive metadata to them. It passes the information into a XML manifest, that gathers all the XML files with their metadata and all the resources used by a LO. Besides it has an information packaging feature that gathers their manifests with the LOs and stores them in a MySQL database, what enables the management of these packages that will be used in courses' design. The tool's architecture is described on figure 2.

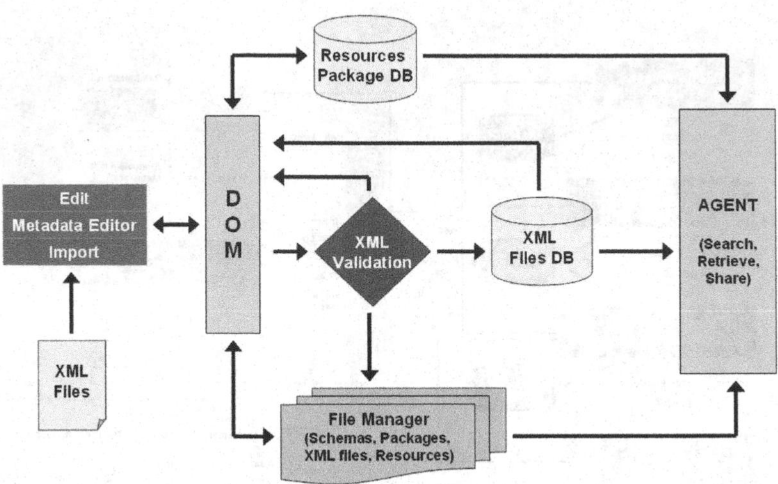

Fig. 2. LO Manager Architecture

The information packaging enables the creation of packages of LOs and courses with their metadata, so they can be easily transported and reused in other systems, going towards reusability and interoperability, using the IMS CP specification (IMS, 2002). All these information pass through a validation process to check if it is in conformance with the IMS specifications, and all the communication between tools and databases is done through XML Document Object Model.

The LOs are in constant evaluation made by the KM that has tools that communicate with the LO Manager through the usage of the IMS specifications for LOs, which main advantage is that through the association of descriptive tags, we can better index them, find them, use and reuse them.

In order to facilitate the insertion of metadata we provide an automation of this process, advising the most commonly used values for the elements on the LO cataloging in order to describe the LO's through the most adequate metadata elements.

In order to better search and retrieve LO's this subsystem is endowed with a search engine. The search of LOs is a very important task in order to reach reusability. The descriptive metadata associated to LOs becomes now more important than ever. The search engine is based on an intelligent agent that receives as inputs the metadata elements from IMSLRM (Barker et al., 2006) for their search and retrieval.

When the teacher accesses the LO search engine, he can choose from two different types of search – simple or advanced. If the teacher chooses a simple search the agent automatically presents the metadata elements mostly used in searches for him to fill. This metadata fields may vary depending on the frequency in which they are used. Otherwise, if the teacher chooses an advanced search, he may choose whatever elements he wants to search for. Finally, the search engine, presents the LOs according to the teacher's search query with the respective quality evaluation allowing him to choose the LOs with more quality to integrate the courses he is creating.

The part of the subsystem referring to the Learning Design provides a tool where teachers can define learning design components, create and structure courses using level A of the IMS LD specification to define activities, sequence and users' roles, and to define metadata to describe the courses, making possible the KR of the courses.

In the process of course creation an XML manifest is generated gathering all the XML files associated with the course, as well as all the LOs, metadata and resource files needed for the course.

The platform, through this tool, allows the design of learning units where the participants can assume different roles. These roles can be student or staff, what makes possible collaborative and group learning, which importance is recognized at the training and educational levels (Graf et al., 2005).

The use of the IMS LD allows the users to structure courses with metadata in XML files that can be reused in the construction of other courses making easier the portability of learning information to interact with *Learning Management Systems* (LMS).

This tool also provides the creation of packages with the courses that are also stored in a data repository, to reach a more efficient management and communicates with the knowledge management subsystem in order to evaluate the courses. After the evaluation this tool allows the restructuring of courses allowing the user to interact with the LD process.

3.2 Knowledge Management Subsystem

Knowledge management and e-learning are two concepts that are strictly related, as e-learning needs an adequate management of educational resources to promote quality learning, to allow students to develop in an active and efficient way, needing to make content quality evaluation systematic evaluation a valued practice if the promise of ubiquitous, high quality Web-based education is to become a reality (Vargo et al., 2003). Taking this into account we have decide to create a subsystem which main objective is to assure quality to the information in the platform through the evaluation of LOs and courses.

3.2.1 LO Evaluation

To archive a LOs' optimal evaluation, it is necessary to consider quality criteria, for this reason the weighted criteria presented in Table 2 were proposed (Morales et al, 2004) where the final evaluation value is the sum of all the classifications of each category multiplied by their weight and has the following rating scale:0=not present;1=Very low; 2=Low;3=Medium;4=High;5=Very High. To use these criteria we have made a match between the IMSLRM educational category elements and the categories described on Table 2.

For now we have just considered the educational category because it has most of the LOs' technical and educational aspects we found important to evaluate.

With these quality evaluation criteria defined we are developing two different tools to evaluate the quality of LOs. One of the tools allows teachers and experts to import, analyze, change, classify and evaluate LOs through a Web application based on the criteria presented before. This tool is an evaluation collaborative system in which

Table 2. Evaluation criteria categories and matching with the IMSLRM educational category

Eval. criteria categories	Weight	IMSLRM Ed. elements	Description
Psychopedagogical	30%	intended end user role; typical age range; difficulty	Criteria that can evaluate, for example, if the LO has the capacity to motivate the student for learning;
Didactic-curricular	30%	learning-resource type; context; typical learning time; description	Criteria to evaluate if the LO helps to archive the unit of learning objectives, etc;
Technical-aesthetic	20%	semantic density; language	Criteria to evaluate the legibility of the LO, the colors used, etc;
Functional	20%	interactivity type; interactivity level	Criteria to evaluate LOs accessibility among other aspects to guarantee that it doesn't obstruct the learning process;

experts and teachers analyze LOs and give them an individual evaluation. After this individual evaluation, all the persons that evaluated the LO gather in a sort of forum to reach to its final evaluation.

The other tool is an intelligent agent that automatically evaluates LOs basing its final evaluation on previous evaluations. A schematic representation of the agent is presented on figure 3.

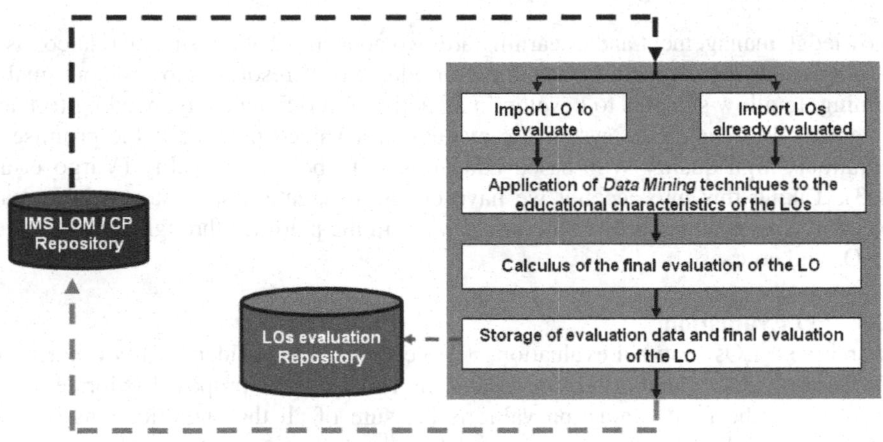

Fig. 3. Schematic representation of the agent

In order to do the evaluation, the agent starts to import the LO to evaluate and others already evaluated and applies data mining techniques (decision trees) to the educational characteristics defined in the IMSLRM specification.

After the calculus of the final evaluation of the LO, the agent stores this information in an auxiliary database made for this purpose and also inserts it in the annotation element described by the IMS LRM specification.

With these two tool LOs are constantly being availed of their quality, playing an important role in the reusability of the LOs for different contexts. Meanwhile we are testing these tools in order to verify their reliability. We will also try to include the feedback from the adaptive subsystem in the evaluation process, as well as the results that derive from the usage of the LO's/courses from students and teachers.

3.3 Adaptive Subsystem

The objective of this subsystem is to determine the most adequate learning method according to students' characteristics, the learning design and the interaction with the student. It establishes the best adaptive characteristics taking into account a specific learning method of the student, resources and assessments. This subsystem, for each student, stores his learning style, his characteristics, previous and actual knowledge.

The tool provided by this subsystem allows the user to fill inquiries, based on data and metadata about the student, defined by the IMS *Learning Information Package* (LIP) specification. This specification is based in a data model to represent knowledge that describes the characteristics (language, previous and actual knowledge about a certain matter, etc) of the students, necessary for general management and storage of historical data about learning, objectives and works developed (Smythe et al., 2001)(Smythe, 2005). Based on the results of the inquiries an agent automatically generates adaptive rules, through the use of fuzzy logic, to generate models of adaptation that will reflect on the presentation of the courses. This information is stored in XML files and this subsystem allows the creation of packages with this information, which is stored in a data repository to facilitate its management (Brusilovsky et al., 2004).

3.4 Visualization and Presentation Subsystem

This subsystem presents the educational contents to the students taking into account the adaptive meta-model generated for each student.

This subsystem is where is defined the integration with LMSs, front-end to the students. The objective for this integration is to give an opportunity for LMSs to benefit from AHKMEs' functionalities, as well as to give a front-end to AHKME system.

This integration can be done in different ways: In case of Moodle being developed in PHP and with a MySQL database, it can be directly integrated into the LMS; In other cases it can be done through a specific profile in the LMS that gives access to this Back-Office to a Course Instructor and Designer; If we want to integrate with some commercial platform like Blackboard ou WebCT (currently Blackboard Learning System), it can be done, through a plug-in like a Powerlink (WebCT) or a building block (Bb); It always gives the possibility of integrating the courses by importing it to the LMS that supports the IMS specifications.

An agent can be developed in order to register the feedback of students and teachers regarding course usage, using the IMS LIP specification, so this information feeds the adaptive subsystem in order to be considered on the LD process in similar contexts.

This subsystem also gives a front-end to our system, combining tools from different platforms, collaborative, interactive, communication and community tools.

4 Conclusions

In this article we've presented AHKME system and how it uses metadata annotation for learning resource management and evaluation.

The IMS specifications, which use the combination of metadata and XML potentialities, are excellent to represent knowledge, dividing information in several meaningful chunks (LOs) providing their description through metadata and storage in XML files, therefore permitting their cataloguing, localization, indexation, reusability and interoperability, through the creation of information packages. These specifications grant the capacity to design learning units that simultaneously allow users with different roles promoting several types of both collaborative and group learning.

Through knowledge management we have a continuous evaluation of contents, granting quality to all the resources in the platform for teachers and students to use.

AHKME's main contributions are: the LO management and quality evaluation; the usage of the IMS specifications to standardize all the resources it tries to reach interoperability and compatibility of its learning components, and the interaction of all subsystems through the feedback between them allowing the platform to adapt to the students and teachers characteristics and to new contexts, using knowledge representation and management to grant success to the teaching/learning process.

Thus, it's very important to have the resources well catalogued, available and with quality to create quality courses, but quality courses don't just depend on quality resources, but also in the design of activities to reach learning objectives.

Being a multipurpose platform it can be applied to several kinds of matters, students, and learning strategies, in both training and educational environments being able to be fully integrated with other systems.

In terms of future work, we will add the level B of the IMS LD specification in the learning design tool, to include properties and generic conditions. In the adaptive subsystem we will add some functionality according to the IMS Question and Test Interoperability and Enterprise specification. In the KM subsystem we will add the feature of course quality evaluation through the development of some tools.

Acknowledgments

This work has been partly financed by Ministry of Education and Science as well as FEDER KEOPS project (TSI2005-00960). We would like to thank the GRIAL Research Group.

References

ADL, ADL: Sharable Content Object Reference Model (SCORM 2004), 3rd edn. - Overview Version 1.0 (2006)

Berners-Lee, T., Hendler, J., Lassila, O.: The Semantic Web. Scientific American 284(5), 34–43 (2001)

Chatti, M.A., Jarke, M., Frosch-Wilke, D.: The future of e-learning: a shift to knowledge networking and social software. Int. J. Knowledge and Learning 3(4/5), 404–420 (2007)

Core, D.: Dublin Core Metadata Initiative (2005) ,http://dublincore.org

Grace, A., Butler, T.: Learning management systems: a new beginning in the management of learning and knowledge. Int. J. Knowledge and Learning 1(1/2), 12–24 (2005)

IEEE: IEEE LTSC Working Group 12: Draft Standard for Learning Object Metadata. Institute of Electrical and Electronics Engineers, Inc. (2002)

IMS.: IMS Specifications, IMS Global Learning Consortium, Inc. (2004), http://www.imsglobal.org

Mendes, M.E.S., Sacks, L.: Dynamic Knowledge Representation for e-Learning Applications. In: Proceedings of the 2001 BISC International Workshop on Fuzzy Logic and the Internet, FLINT 2001, Memorandum No. UCB/ERL M01/28, pp. 176–181. University of California, Berkeley (August 2001)

Morales, E., García, F.J., Moreira, T., Rego, H., Berlanga, A.: Units of Learning Quality Evaluation. In: Proceedings SPDECE 2004 Design. CEUR Workshop, Guadalajara, Spain, vol. 117 (2004) ISSN 1613-0073,http://ceur-ws.org/Vol-117

Totkov, G., Krusteva, C., Baltadzhiev, N.: About the Standardization and the Interoperability of E-Learning Resources. In: CompSysTech 2004 - International Conference on Computer Systems and Technologies, Bulgaria (2004)

Graf, S., List, B.: An Evaluation of Open Source E-Learning Platforms Stressing Adaptation Issues. In: ICALT 2005 - The 5th IEEE International Conference on Advanced Learning Technologies (2005)

Barker, P., Campbell, L.M., Roberts, A., Smythe, C.: IMS Meta-data Best Practice Guide for IEEE 1484.12.1-2002 Standard for Learning Object Metadata - Version 1.3 Final Specification. IMS Global Learning Consortium, Inc. (2006)

Smythe, C., Tansey, F., Robson, R.: IMS Learner Information Packaging Information Model Specification - Final Specification Version 1.0. IMS Global Learning Consortium, Inc. (2001)

Smythe, C.: IMS Learner Information Package Summary of Changes - Version 1.0.1 Final Specification. IMS Global Learning Consortium, Inc. (2005)

Brusilovsky, P., Nejdl, W.: Adaptive Hypermedia and Adaptive Web. In: M. P. Practical Handbook of Internet Computing. Chapman & Hall/ CRC Press, Baton Rouge, USA (2004)

Vargo, J., Nesbit, J.C., Belfer, K., Archambault, A.: Learning object evaluation: computer-mediated collaboration and inter-rater reliability. International Journal of Computers and Applications 25(3) (2003)

Retraction Note to: Application of Scientific Approaches for Evaluation of Quality of Learning Objects in eQNet Project

Eugenijus Kurilovas[1,2,3] and Silvija Serikoviene[1]

[1] Institute of Mathematics and Informatics, Akademijos str. 4, 08663 Vilnius, Lithuania
[2] Vilnius Gediminas Technical University, Sauletekio al. 11, 10223 Vilnius, Lithuania
[3] Centre of Information Technologies in Education, Suvalku str. 1, 03106 Vilnius, Lithuania
eugenijus.kurilovas@itc.smm.lt, silvija.serikoviene@gmail.com

M.D. Lytras et al. (Eds.): WSKS 2010, Part I, CCIS 111, pp. 437–443, 2010.

DOI 10.1007/978-3-642-16318-0_76

The paper starting on page 437 of this volume has been retracted as it is a duplicate of the paper starting on page 329 of the same volume.

The original online version for this chapter can be found at
http://dx.doi.org/10.1007/978-3-642-16318-0_54

Author Index

Printed in the United States
By Bookmasters